Study Guide
to Accompany
McConnell and Brue
Microeconomics

Study Guide
to Accompany
McConnell and Brue

Micro-
Economics
TWELFTH EDITION

William B. Walstad
Professor of Economics
University of Nebraska—Lincoln

Robert C. Bingham
Late Professor of Economics
Kent State University

McGraw-Hill, Inc.

New York   St. Louis   San Francisco   Auckland   Bogotá
Caracas   Lisbon   London   Madrid   Mexico   Milan   Montreal   New Delhi
Paris   San Juan   Singapore   Sydney   Tokyo   Toronto

Study Guide to Accompany McConnell and Brue: Microeconomics

1 2 3 4 5 6 7 8 9 0   **SEM SEM**   9 0 9 8 7 6 5 4 3 2

ISBN 0-07-045619-4

This book was set in Helvetica by Waldman Graphics, Inc.
The editors were Michael R. Elia, Scott D. Stratford, and Edwin Hanson;
the production supervisor was Annette Mayeski.
The cover was designed by Joseph A. Piliero.
Semline Inc., was printer and binder.

About the Authors

William B. Walstad is a professor of economics at the University of Nebraska—Lincoln where he directs the Center for Economic Education and the National Center for Research in Economic Education. He received his Ph.D. degree from the University of Minnesota and taught at the University of Missouri—St. Louis before moving to Nebraska. Professor Walstad has been honored by the College of Business Administration at Nebraska with a Distinguished Teaching Award. He also received the Henry H. Villard Research Award for his published research in economic education. He co-edited *The Principles of Economics Course: A Handbook for Instructors* (McGraw-Hill) and developed three national tests on economics for the Joint Council on Economic Education. He enjoys being with his family and likes to travel.

Robert C. Bingham was an undergraduate student at DePauw University and obtained M.A. and Ph.D. degrees from Northwestern University. He taught at the University of Nebraska—Lincoln where he was a colleague of Professor McConnell before coming to Kent State University from which he retired in 1985. He was the author of several other study guides and supplements for the principles of economics courses.

To
Karen, Laura, and Kristin

Contents

How to Use the Study Guide to Learn Microeconomics

This **Study Guide** is designed to help you read and understand Campbell R. McConnell and Stanley L. Brue's textbook, **Microeconomics**, Twelfth Edition. If used properly, a guide can be a great aid to you in what is probably your first course in economics.

No one pretends that the study of economics is easy, but it can be made easier. Of course a study guide will not do your work for you, and its use is no substitute for reading the text. You must be willing to read the text, spend time on the subject, and work at learning if you wish to understand economics.

Many students do read their text and work hard on their economics course and still fail to learn the subject. This is because principles of economics is a new subject for them, and they have had no previous experience in learning economics. They want to learn but do not know just how to go about it. Here is where the **Study Guide** can help. Let us first see what the **Study Guide** contains and then how to use it.

■ WHAT THE STUDY GUIDE IS

The **Study Guide** contains twenty-six chapters—one for each chapter in the text and a **glossary**. Each **Study Guide** chapter has ten parts.

1. An **introduction** explains what is in the chapter of the text and how it is related to material in earlier and later chapters. It points out topics to which you should give special attention, and reemphasizes difficult or important principles and facts.
2. A **checklist** tells you the things you should be able to do when you have finished the chapter.
3. A **chapter outline** shows how the chapter is organized and summarizes briefly the essential points made in the chapter.
4. A list of the **important terms** found in the chapter points out what you must be able to define in order to understand the material in the chapter. A definition of each of these terms will be found in the glossary at the end of the **Study Guide**.
5. **Fill-in questions** (short-answer and list questions) help you to learn and remember the important generalizations and facts in the chapter.

6. **Problems and projects** assist you in learning and understanding economic relationships and get you to think about certain economic problems.
7. **True-false questions** can be used to test your understanding of the material in the chapter.
8. **Multiple-choice questions** also give you a chance to check your knowledge of the chapter content and to prepare for this type of course examination.
9. **Discussion questions** can be used to test yourself, to identify important questions in the chapter, and to prepare for examinations.
10. **Answers** to fill-in questions, to the problems and projects, to true-false questions, and to the multiple-choice questions are found at the end of each chapter. You are also given the references to the specific pages in the textbook for each true-false, multiple choice, and discussion question.

■ HOW TO STUDY AND LEARN
WITH THE HELP OF THE STUDY GUIDE

1. **Read and outline.** For best results, quickly read the introduction, outline, list of terms, and checklist in the **Study Guide** before you read the chapter in the text. Then read the chapter in the text slowly and keep one eye on the **Study Guide** outline and the list of terms. The outline contains only the major points in the chapter. Highlight the chapter as you read it by identifying the major **and the minor** points and by placing outline numbers or letters (such as I or A or 1 or a) in the margins. Circle the important terms. When you have completed the chapter, you will have the chapter outlined and it will give you a set of notes on the chapter. Be careful to highlight or underline only the really important or summary statements.
2. **Review and reread.** After you have read the chapter in the text once, return to the introduction, outline, and list of terms in the **Study Guide**. Reread the introduction and outline. Does everything there make sense? If not, go to the text and reread the topics that you do not remember well or that still confuse you. Look at the outline. Try to recall each of the minor topics or points that were contained in the text under each of the major points in the outline. When you come to the list of terms go over them

one by one. Define or explain each to yourself and then look for the definition of the term either in the text chapter or in the glossary. Compare your own definition or explanation with that in the text or glossary. The quick way to find the definition of a term in the text is to look in the index of the text for the page or pages on which that term or concept is mentioned. Make any correction or change in your own definition or explanation that is necessary.

3. *Test and check answers.* When you have done all this, you will have a pretty fair general idea of what is in the text chapter. Now take a look at the fill-in questions, the problems and projects, and the self-test questions. Tackle each of these three sections one at a time, using the following procedure. (1) Answer as many questions as you can without looking in the text or in the answer section. (2) Check the text for whatever help you need. It is a good idea to do more than merely look for answers in the text. Reread any section for which you were not able to answer questions. (3) Then consult the answer section at the end of the chapter for the correct answers and reread any section of the text for which you missed questions. (See the text page references that are given with the answer to each true-false or multiple choice question.)

The questions in these three sections are not all of equal difficulty. Do not expect to get them all right the first time. Some are designed to pinpoint things of importance which you will probably miss the first time you read the text and to get you to read about them again. None of the questions is unimportant. Even those that have no definite answers will bring you to grips with many important economic questions and increase your understanding of economic principles and problems.

For the discussion questions, it is not necessary to write out answers. All you need to do is mentally outline your answer. For the more difficult questions you may want to write out a brief outline of the answer or a full answer. Do not avoid the difficult questions just because they are more work. Answering these questions is often the most valuable work a student can do toward acquiring an understanding of economic relationships and principles. Although no answers are given in the ***Study Guide*** to the discussion questions, the answer section does list page references in the text for each question. You are ***strongly*** encouraged to read those text pages for an explanation to the question or for better insight into the question content.

4. *Double check.* Before you turn to the next chapter in the text and ***Study Guide***, return to the checklist. If you cannot honestly check off each of the items in the list, you have not learned what the author of the text and of this ***Study Guide*** hoped you would learn.

■ **SOME FINAL WORDS**

Perhaps the method of using the ***Study Guide*** outlined above seems like a lot of work. It is! Study and learning necessarily entail work on your part. This is a fact you must accept if you are to learn economics.

After you have used the ***Study Guide*** to study three or four chapters, you will find that some sections are of more value to you than others. Let your own experience determine how you will use it. But do not discontinue use of the ***Study Guide*** after three or four chapters merely because you are not sure whether it is helping you. ***Stick with it.***

In addition to the material in the ***Study Guide***, there are questions at the end of each chapter in the text. Some of these questions are similar to questions in the ***Study Guide***, but none is identical. It will be worthwhile for you to examine all the questions at the end of each chapter and to work out or outline answers for them. Students who have trouble with the problems in the ***Study Guide*** will find the end-of-chapter problems useful in determining whether they have actually mastered their difficulties.

For those of you who either have trouble with or wish to learn more rapidly the sections of the text containing explanations of economic theory (or principles), let me recommend ***Economic Concepts: A Programmed Approach***, by Professor Robert Bingham as revised by Professor Henry Pope. A programmed book is a learning device which speeds and increases comprehension. Its use will greatly expand your understanding of economics.

■ **ACKNOWLEDGMENTS**

The ***Study Guide to accompany Microeconomics*** is based on the late Professor Robert Bingham's study guide for the previous editions of Professor McConnell's ***Economics***. He worked with great care and wanted the ***Study Guide*** to be a valuable aid for students. Many past users of the ***Study Guide*** will attest to his success. Although Professor Bingham did not participate directly in this revision, his work remains a major contribution to this edition.

I also wish to acknowledge other help I received. Campbell McConnell and Stanley Brue offered many helpful comments for the revision. Professor Thomas Phelps of Pierce College and Professor Janet West of the University of Nebraska–Omaha provided many good suggestions in their reviews of the ***Study Guide***. Bart Nemmers, a graduate student at the University of Nebraska–Lincoln, helped me check the self-test questions and identify the textbook pages given with the answers. Students in my principles of economics classes also helped me with their comments and questions about material. Finally, the team at McGraw-Hill, especially Scott Stratford, Michael Elia, and Edwin Hanson, gave me great assistance with the editorial and production work. Despite the many contributions from others, all responsibility for errors and omissions are mine.

William B. Walstad

CHAPTER 1

The Nature and Method of Economics

Chapter 1 introduces you to economics—the study of how people decide how to use scarce productive resources to satisfy material wants. Knowledge of economics is important because it is essential for well-informed citizenship and it has many practical applications to personal decisions. The purpose of this chapter is to explain the nature of the subject and to describe the methods that economists use to study economic questions.

Economists use three different approaches to examine economic topics. The gathering of relevant facts about an economic problem is called **descriptive economics**. **Economic theory** or economic analysis involves the derivation of principles using inductive or deductive methods. **Policy economics** entails the formulation of policies or recommended solutions to economic problems.

The heart of the chapter is the discussion of economic principles in the economic theory section. Economic principles are generalizations. Because the economist cannot employ laboratory experiments to test the generalizations, these principles are always imprecise and subject to exceptions. Economics is a science but it is not an exact science. Economic principles are also simplifications—approximations of a complex world—and both the formulation and application of these principles present many opportunities for making serious mistakes. Economic principles are not the answers to economic questions but are tools—intellectual tools—for analyzing economic problems and for finding policies to solve these problems.

The selection of economic policies to follow depends not only on economic principles but also on the value judgments and the weight given to particular economic goals. Here we move from economic theory and positive economics, which investigates **what is**, to normative economics, which incorporates subjective or value-laden views of **what ought to be**. Many of the apparent disagreements among economists are over normative policy issues and involve deciding which economic goals for our economy are most important in making the case for a policy solution.

Clear thinking about economic questions requires that the beginning student avoid many pitfalls. Errors of commission and omission can occur from bias, loaded terminology, imprecise definitions, fallacies of composition, and confusing correlation with causation. If you can guard against these potential hazards, you can use the economic perspective to improve your understanding of actions and events at the macroeconomic or the microeconomic level.

■ CHECKLIST

When you have studied this chapter you should be able to:

☐ Write a formal definition of economics.
☐ Give two good reasons for studying economics.
☐ Define descriptive economics, economic theory, and policy economics.
☐ Distinguish between induction and deduction in economic reasoning.
☐ Explain what an economic principle is and how economic principles are obtained.
☐ Discuss how economic principles are generalizations and abstractions.
☐ Explain what the "other things equal" (**ceteris paribus**) assumption is and why this assumption is employed in economics.
☐ Discuss the distinction between macroeconomics and microeconomics.
☐ Give examples of positive and normative economics.
☐ Identify the eight economic goals.
☐ State four significant points about economic goals.
☐ Recognize the "pitfalls to straight thinking" when confronted with examples of them.
☐ Describe the economic perspective and give an example of its application.

■ CHAPTER OUTLINE

1. Economics is concerned with the efficient use of limited productive resources to achieve the maximum satisfaction of human material wants.

2. Citizens in a democracy must understand elementary economics to comprehend the present-day problems of their society and to make intelligent decisions when they vote. Economics is an academic rather than a vocational subject, but a knowledge of it is valuable to business executives, consumers, and workers.

3. Economists gather relevant facts to obtain economic principles that may be used to formulate policies which will solve economic problems.

a. Descriptive economics is the gathering of relevant facts about the production. exchange, and consumption of goods and services.

b. Economic theory is the analysis of the facts and the derivation of economic principles.

(1) To obtain and test their principles economists use both the inductive and the deductive methods.

(2) Economic principles are also called laws, theories, and models.

(3) Each of these principles is a generalization.

(4) Economists employ the *ceteris paribus* (or "other things equal") assumption to obtain these generalizations.

(5) These principles are also abstractions from reality.

(6) Economists can derive principles about economic behavior at the macroeconomic or the microeconomic level of analysis.

c. Policy economics is the combination of economic principles and economic values (or goals) to control economic events.

(1) Values are the judgments people make about what is desirable (good, just) and what is undesirable (bad, unjust).

(2) Positive economics concerns **what is**, or the scientific analysis of economic behavior; normative economics suggests **what ought to be** in offering answers to policy questions.

(3) There are eight major economic goals that are often important to consider—economic growth, full employment, economic efficiency, price level stability, economic freedom, equitable distribution of income, economic security, and a balance of trade.

(4) Economic goals can be complementary or conflicting; issues related to goal interpretation or setting priorities can cause problems.

(5) The three steps in creating an economic policy designed to achieve an economic goal involve defining the goal, identifying the effects of alternative policies, and evaluating the results.

4. Straight thinking in the study and use of economic principles requires strict application of the rules of logic in which personal emotions are irrelevant, if not detrimental. The pitfalls encountered by beginning students in studying and applying economic principles include:

a. bias or preconceived beliefs not warranted by facts;

b. loaded terminology or the use of terms in a way which appeals to emotion and leads to a nonobjective analysis of the issues;

c. the definition by economists of terms in ways which may not be the same as the ways in which these terms are more commonly used;

d. the fallacy of composition or the assumption that what is true of the part is necessarily true of the whole;

e. and the **post hoc fallacy** or the mistaken belief that when one event precedes another the first event is the cause of the second.

5. The economic perspective is a cost-benefit perspective. People, either as individuals or in groups, make economic choices by evaluating the costs and benefits of decisions.

■ **IMPORTANT TERMS**

Economics	Microeconomics
Descriptive economics	Positive and normative statements
Economic theory (analysis)	Economic goals
Policy economics	Value judgment
Economic principles (law)	Conflicting or complementary goals
Induction	Loaded terminology
Deduction	Fallacy of composition
Generalization	*Post hoc, erto propter hoc fallacy*
Economic model	
Abstraction	Correlation
"Other things equal" (*ceteris paribus*) assumption	Causation
	Economic perspective
Macroeconomics	

■ **FILL-IN QUESTIONS**

1. Economics as a subject:
   a. Is, first of all, the study of the

   _____,

   _____,

   and _____
   of the material goods and services that satisfy human wants.

   b. But, more formally, it is concerned with the efficient

   use of _____ productive resources to

   achieve the _____ satisfaction of these wants.

2. An understanding of economics is essential if we are

   to be well-informed _____ and it has many
   personal applications even though it is an academic and

   not a _____ subject.

3. Economics, like other sciences, begins with the facts found in the world around us.

a. The gathering of relevant facts is the part of the economics called _____ economics.

b. Economic _____ involves deriving general principles about the economic behavior of people and institutions. When economists develop economic principles from studying facts, they are using the _____ method; whereas the _____ method uses facts to test the validity of hypotheses or economic theories.

c. The formulation of recommended solutions or remedies for economic problems is referred to as _____ economics.

4. Economic principles are also called _____.

These principles are _____ about people's economic behavior and as such necessarily involve _____ from reality.

5. Economists know that the amount consumers spend for goods and services in any year depends upon their after-tax income in that year and several factors other than their income. To look at the relationship between the spending and income of consumers, economists often assume that these other factors are constant and do not change; and when economists do this they make the _____ assumption.

6. Macroeconomics is concerned with the _____ output of the economy and the _____ level of prices, while microeconomics is concerned with output in a(n) _____

_____

and the price of a(n) _____

_____

7. There are two different types of statements that can be made about economic topics. A (positive, normative) _____ statement explains **what is** by offering a scientific proposition about economic behavior that is based on economic theory and facts. A _____ statement includes a value judgment about an economic policy or the economy that suggests **what ought to be**. Many of the reported disagreements among economists usually involve _____ statements.

8. Eight widely accepted economic goals in the United States are the following:

a. _____
b. _____
c. _____

d. _____
e. _____
f. _____
g. _____
h. _____

9. Increases in economic growth that promote full employment would be an example of a set of (conflicting, complementary) _____ economic goals. Efforts to achieve an equitable distribution of income that reduce economic efficiency and growth would be an example of a set of _____ economic goals.

10. The three steps involved in the formulation of economic policy are:

a. _____
b. _____
c. _____

11. There are many pitfalls to straight thinking in economics. For example, the statement that "what is good for the individual is also good for the group" may not be correct because of the fallacy of _____. The person who believes that "washing a car will cause it to rain tomorrow" is expressing a _____ fallacy.

12. The economic perspective is a _____ perspective. People and institutions are assumed to make (rational, irrational) _____ decisions by weighing the _____ and _____ of economic actions.

■ **PROBLEMS AND PROJECTS**

1. **News report:** "The Russian demand for wheat in the United States increased and caused the price of wheat in the United States to rise." This is a **specific** instance of a more **general** economic principle. Of which economic **generalization** is this a particular example? _____

_____

2. Below are four statements. Each of them is an example of one of the pitfalls frequently encountered in the study of economics. Indicate in the space following each statement the type of pitfall involved.

a. "Investment in stocks and bonds is the only way to build real capital assets." _____

b. "An unemployed worker can find a job if he looks diligently and conscientiously for employment; therefore, all unemployed workers can find employment if they are diligent and conscientious in looking for a job."

_____

c. *Walstad:* "Regulation of public utilities in the United States is an immoral and unconscionable interference with the God-given right of private property and, as you know, old chum, there is no private property in the communist nations." *McConnell:* "It is far from that, my boy. You know perfectly well that it is an attempt to limit the unmitigated avarice of mammoth corporations in order, as the Constitution commands, to promote the general welfare of a democratic America." _____

_____

d. "The stock market crash of 1929 was followed by and resulted in 10 years of Depression." _____

_____

3. Below is a list of economic statements. Indicate in the space to the right of each whether they are positive (P) or normative (N). Then in the last four lines below, write two of your own examples of positive statements and two examples of normative economic statements.

a. New York City should control the rental price of apartments. _____

b. Consumer prices rose at an annual rate of 5% last year. _____

c. Most people who are unemployed are just too lazy to work. _____

d. Generally speaking, if you lower the price of a product, people will buy more of that product. _____

e. The profits of drug companies are too large and ought to be used to conduct research on new medicines. _____

f. Government should do more to help the poor.

_____

g. _____ P _____

h. _____ P _____

i. _____ N _____

j. _____ N _____

Circle the T if the statement is true; the F if it is false.

1. Economics deals with the activities by which humans can earn a living and improve their standard of living.
   T   F

2. Economics is academic and of little value because it does not teach the student how to earn a living.   T   F

3. Gathering the relevant economic facts from which economic principles are derived is called economic analysis.   T   F

4. In economics the terms "law," "principle," "theory," and "model" mean essentially the same thing.   T   F

5. The "other things equal" or *ceteris paribus* assumption is made in order to simplify the reasoning process.
   T   F

6. The deductive method is the scientific method and the method used to derive economic principles from economic facts.   T   F

7. Economic principles enable us to predict the economic consequences of many human actions.   T   F

8. One of the widely (though not universally) accepted economic goals of Americans is an equal distribution of income.   T   F

9. The first step in the formulation of an economic policy, the statement of goals, may be an occasion for disagreement because different people may have different and conflicting goals to be achieved.   T   F

10. Once a single goal or end has been determined as the sole objective of economic policy, there is seldom any question of which policy to adopt to achieve that goal.
    T   F

11. If you speak of "capital" to most people, they understand you to be referring to money. The economist, therefore, is obligated to use the term "capital" to mean money.   T   F

12. When value judgments are made about the economy or economic policy, this is referred to as positive economics.   T   F

13. Microeconomic analysis is concerned with the performance of the economy as a whole or its major aggregates.   T   F

14. The economic perspective views individuals or institutions as making rational choices based on the analysis of the costs and benefits of decisions.   T   F

15. The statement that "the legal minimum wage should be raised to give working people a decent income" is an example of a normative statement.   T   F

Circle the letter that corresponds to the best answer.

1. Which statement would be the best one to use to complete a short definition of economics? "Economics is the study of:
  (a) how business produces goods and services."
  (b) the efficient use of scarce productive resources."
  (c) the equitable distribution of society's income and wealth."
  (d) the printing and circulation of money in the economy."

2. Which of the following terms is *not* found in a sophisticated definition of economics?
  (a) efficient use
  (b) unlimited productive resources
  (c) maximum satisfaction
  (d) human and material wants

3. Economics is a practical field of study in several ways. Which one of the following is *not* an element of its practicality?
  (a) every person affects and is affected by the operation of the economy
  (b) every person has to earn a living in some manner, and economics develops skills and trains the student in the art of making a living
  (c) every person in a democracy is confronted with its political problems, many of which are economic in nature
  (d) every person who understands the overall operation of the economy is in a better position to solve personal economic problems

4. One economic principle states that the lower the price of a commodity, the greater will be the quantity of the commodity which consumers will wish to purchase. On the basis of this principle *alone*, it can be concluded that:
  (a) if the price of mink coats falls, more mink coats will be purchased by consumers
  (b) if the price of mink coats falls, Mrs. James will purchase two instead of one
  (c) if the price of mink coats falls and there are no important changes in the other factors affecting their demand, the public will probably purchase a greater quantity of mink coats than it did at the higher price
  (d) if more mink coats are purchased this month than last month, it is because the price of mink coats has fallen

5. An economic model is *not*:
  (a) an ideal type of economy or an economic policy for which we ought to strive to achieve
  (b) a tool which the economist employs in order to predict
  (c) one or a collection of economic principles
  (d) an explanation of how the economy or a part of the economy functions in its essential details

6. When economic principles or theories are developed from factual evidence, this method of economic reasoning is called:
  (a) descriptive economics
  (b) hypothesis testing
  (c) deduction
  (d) induction

7. Knowing that as the price of a commodity rises the quantity of the commodity sold decreases and that the imposition of a higher tax on a commodity increases its price, the economist concludes that if a government increases the tax on gasoline, less gasoline will be sold. This is an example of:
  (a) prediction
  (b) control
  (c) policy
  (d) the fallacy of composition

8. Which of the following economic goals is subject to reasonably accurate measurement?
  (a) economic security
  (b) full employment
  (c) economic freedom
  (d) an equitable distribution of income

9. To say that two economic goals are conflicting or mutually exclusive means that:
  (a) it is not possible to achieve both goals
  (b) these goals are not accepted as goals
  (c) the achievement of one of the goals results in the achievement of the other
  (d) it is possible to quantify both goals

10. Which of the following would be studied in *microeconomics*?
  (a) the output of the entire economy
  (b) the total number of workers employed in the United States
  (c) the general level of prices in the American economy
  (d) the output and price of wheat in the United States

11. Sandra states that "there is a high correlation between consumption and income." Arthur replies that it occurs because "people consume too much of their income and don't save enough."
  (a) both Sandra's and Arthur's statements are positive
  (b) both Sandra's and Arthur's statements are normative
  (c) Sandra's statement is positive and Arthur's statement is normative
  (d) Sandra's statement is normative and Arthur's statement is positive

12. During World War II the United States employed price control to prevent inflation; this was referred to as "a fascist and arbitrary restriction of economic freedom" by some and as "a necessary and democratic means of pre-

venting ruinous inflation" by others. Both labels are examples of:
- **(a)** economic bias
- **(b)** the fallacy of composition
- **(c)** the misuse of commonsense definitions
- **(d)** loaded terminology

13. If an individual determines to save a larger percentage of his/her income he/she will no doubt be able to save more. To reason, therefore, that if all individuals determine to save a larger percentage of their incomes they will be able to save more is an example of:
- **(a)** the *post hoc, ergo propter hoc* fallacy
- **(b)** the fallacy of composition
- **(c)** economic bias
- **(d)** using loaded terminology

14. The government increases its expenditures for road-construction equipment and later the average price of this equipment falls. The reason that the lower price was due to the increase in government expenditures may be an example of:
- **(a)** the *post hoc, ergo propter hoc* fallacy
- **(b)** the fallacy of composition
- **(c)** imprecise definition
- **(d)** using loaded terminology

15. Which one of the following is a normative economic statement?
- **(a)** the consumer price index rose 5.6% last month
- **(b)** the unemployment rate of 6.8% is too high
- **(c)** the average rate of interest on loan is 8.6%
- **(d)** the economy grew at an annual rate of 2.6%

16. The economist sometimes assumes that "other things are held constant" when studying an economic problem. This statement would best be an example of:
- **(a)** the *post hoc, ergo propter hoc* fallacy
- **(b)** the fallacy of composition
- **(c)** deductive reasoning
- **(d)** *ceteris paribus*

17. The development of an economic theory and the testing of this theory by an appeal to facts is:
- **(a)** induction
- **(b)** deduction
- **(c)** policy economics
- **(d)** normative economics

18. Which economic goal is associated with the idea that we want to get the maximum benefits at the minimum cost from the limited productive resources which are available?
- **(a)** full employment
- **(b)** economic growth
- **(c)** economic security
- **(d)** economic efficiency

19. If economic growth tends to produce a more equitable distribution of income among people in a nation, then this relationship between the two economic goals appears to be:
- **(a)** deductive
- **(b)** conflicting
- **(c)** complementary
- **(d)** mutually exclusive

20. When we look at the whole economy or its major aggregates, our analysis would be at the level of:
- **(a)** microeconomics
- **(b)** macroeconomics
- **(c)** positive economics
- **(d)** normative economics

■ **DISCUSSION QUESTIONS**

1. Define economics in both a less and a more sophisticated way. In your latter definition, explain the meaning of "resources" and "wants."

2. What are the principal reasons for studying economics?

3. What is the relationship between facts and theory?

4. Define and explain the relationships between descriptive economics, economic theory, and applied economics.

5. What is a "laboratory experiment under controlled conditions"? Does the science of economics have any kind of laboratory? Why do economists employ the "other things equal" assumption?

6. Why are economic principles and models necessarily generalizations and abstract?

7. Why do economists disagree?

8. What does it mean to say that economic principles can be used for prediction?

9. Of the eight economic goals listed in the text, which one would you *rank* first, second, third, etc.? Would you add any other goals to this list? If economic goals 2 and 4 were conflicting, which goal would you prefer? Why? If goals 1 and 5 were conflicting, which would you prefer? Why?

10. What procedure should be followed in formulating sound economic policies?

11. Explain each of the following:
- **(a)** fallacy of composition;
- **(b)** loaded terminology;
- **(c)** the *post hoc, ergo propter hoc* fallacy.

12. Explain briefly the difference between
- **(a)** macroeconomics and microeconomics;
- **(b)** deduction and induction; and
- **(c)** correlation and causation.

13. What are some current examples of positive economic statements and normative economic statements?

14. Describe the economic perspective and give an example of its application.

■ **ANSWERS**

Chapter 1 The Nature and Method of Economics

FILL-IN QUESTIONS

1. *a.* production, distribution, consumption; *b.* limited (scarce), maximum

2. citizens, vocational

3. *a.* descriptive; *b.* theory, inductive, deductive; *c.* policy

4. laws (or theories or models), generalizations, abstractions

5. "other things equal" (***ceteris paribus***)

6. total, general, individual industry, particular product

7. positive, normative, normative

8. *a.* economic growth; *b.* full employment; *c.* economic efficiency; *d.* price stability; *e.* economic freedom; *f.* equitable distribution of income; *g.* economic security; *h.* balance of trade

9. complementary, conflicting

10. *a.* a clear statement of the objectives and goals; *b.* an analysis of all possible solutions; *c.* an evaluation of the results

11. composition; ***post hoc, ergo propter hoc***

12. cost-benefit, rational, costs, benefits (either order for last two)

PROBLEMS AND PROJECTS

1. An increase in the demand for an economic good will cause the price of that good to rise.

2. *a.* definitions; *b.* the fallacy of composition; *c.* loaded terminology; *d.* the ***post hoc, ergo propter hoc*** fallacy.

3. *a.* N; *b.* P; *c.* N; *d.* P; *e.* N; *f.* N

SELF-TEST*

1. T, p. 1	**5.** T, p. 5	**9.** T, pp. 7–8	**13.** F, p. 5
2. F, pp. 2–3	**6.** F, pp. 3–4	**10.** F, pp. 7–8	**14.** T, pp. 9–10
3. F, p. 3	**7.** T, pp. 3–4	**11.** F, p. 8	**15.** T, p. 6
4. T, p. 4	**8.** F, p. 7	**12.** F, p. 6	

1. *b*, pp. 1–2	**6.** *d*, pp. 3–4	**11.** *c*, p. 6	**16.** *d*, p. 5
2. *b*, p. 1	**7.** *a*, p. 5	**12.** *d*, p. 8	**17.** *b*, pp. 3–4
3. *b*, pp. 2–3	**8.** *b*, p. 7	**13.** *b*, pp. 8–9	**18.** *d*, pp. 6–7
4. *c*, pp. 4–5	**9.** *a*, p. 7	**14.** *a*, pp. 8–9	**19.** *c*, p. 7
5. *a*, p. 4	**10.** *d*, p. 5	**15.** *b*, p. 6	**20.** *b*, p. 5

Page references are for the textbook.

1. p. 1	**5.** pp. 4–5	**9.** pp. 6–8	**12.** pp. 3–4; 5; 9
2. pp. 2–3	**6.** pp. 4–5	**10.** pp. 7–8	**13.** p. 6
3. pp. 3–4	**7.** p. 6	**11.** pp. 8–9	**14.** pp. 9–11
4. p. 4	**8.** p. 6		

Appendix to Chapter 1 Graphs and Their Meaning

This appendix provides an introduction to graphing in economics. Graphs help illustrate and simplify the economic theories and models that will be presented throughout this book. The old saying that "a picture is worth a thousand words" applies to economics; graphs are the way that economists "picture" relationships between economic variables.

You will need to master the basics of graphing if these "pictures" are to be of any help to you. The appendix explains how to achieve that mastery. It begins by showing you how to construct a graph from a table of data on two variables, such as income and consumption. Economists usually, but not always, place the independent variable (income) on the horizontal axis and the dependent variable (consumption) on the vertical axis of the graph. Once the data points are plotted and a line drawn to connect the plotted points, you can determine whether there is a direct or an inverse relationship between the variables. Identifying a direct and an inverse relationship between variables is an essential skill that will be used repeatedly in this book.

Information from data in graphs and tables can be written in an equation. This work involves determining the slope and intercept from a straight line in a graph or data in a table. Using values for the slope and intercept, you can write a linear equation that will enable you to calculate what the dependent variable would be for a given level of the independent variable.

Some graphs used in the book are nonlinear. With nonlinear curves, the slope of the line is no longer constant throughout but varies as one moves along the curve. This slope can be estimated at a point by determining the slope of a straight line that is drawn tangent to the curve at that point. Similar calculations can be made for other points to see how the slope changes along the curve.

■ **APPENDIX CHECKLIST**

When you have studied this appendix you should be able to:

☐ Explain why economists use graphs.
☐ Construct a graph of two variables using the numerical data from a table.
☐ Make a table with two variables from data on a graph.
☐ Distinguish between a direct and an inverse relationship when given data on two variables.

☐ Identify dependent and independent variables in economic examples and graphs.
☐ Calculate the slope of a straight line between two points and determine the vertical intercept for the line.
☐ Write a linear equation using the slope of a line and the vertical intercept; when given values for the independent variable, determine values for the independent variable.
☐ Estimate the slope of a nonlinear curve at a point using a line that is tangent to the curve at that point.

■ **APPENDIX OUTLINE**

1. Graphs illustrate the relationship between variables to give economists and students another means, in addition to verbal explanation, of understanding economic phenomena. Graphs serve as an aid in describing economic theories and models.

2. The construction of a simple graph involves the plotting of numerical data about two variables from a table.
   a. Each graph has a horizontal and a vertical axis that can be labeled for each variable and then scaled for the range of the data point that will be measured on the axis.
   b. Data points are plotted on the graph by drawing perpendiculars from the scaled points on the two axes to the place on the graph where the perpendiculars intersect.
   c. A line or curve can then be drawn to connect the points plotted on the graph.

3. A graph provides information about relationships between variables.
   a. A line that is upward sloping to the right on a graph indicates that there is a positive or *direct* relationship between two variables: an increase in one is associated with an increase in the other; a decrease in one is associated with a decrease in the other.
   b. A line that is downward sloping to the right means that there is a negative or *inverse* relationship between the two variables because the variables are changing in opposite directions: an increase in one is associated with a decrease in the other; a decrease in one is associated with an increase in the other.

4. Economists are often concerned with determining cause and effect in economic events.
   a. A dependent variable changes (increases or decreases) because of a change in another variable.
   b. An independent variable produces or "causes" the change in the dependent variable.
   c. In a graph, mathematicians place an independent variable on the horizontal axis and a dependent variable on the vertical axis; economists are more arbitrary about which variable is placed on an axis.

5. Economic graphs are simplifications of economic relationships. When graphs are plotted, there is usually an implicit assumption made that all other factors are being held constant. This "other things equal" or *ceteris paribus* assumption is used to simplify the analysis so the study can focus on the two variables of interest.

6. A slope and intercept can be calculated for a straight line and written in the form of a linear equation.
   a. The slope of a straight line is the ratio of the vertical change to the horizontal change between two points. A positive slope indicates that the relationship between two variables is direct; a negative slope means there is an inverse relationship between the variables.
   b. Where the line intersects the vertical axis of the graph is the vertical intercept.
   c. A linear equation is written as $y = a + bx$. Once the values for the intercept (a) and the slope (b) are calculated, then given any value of the independent variable (x), the value of the dependent variable (y) can be determined.

7. The slope of a straight line is constant, but the slope of a nonlinear curve changes throughout. To estimate the slope of a nonlinear curve at a point, the slope of a line tangent to the curve at that point is calculated.

■ **IMPORTANT TERMS**

Vertical and horizontal axes
Direct (positive) and inverse (negative) relationships
Dependent and independent variables
Slope of a line
Vertical intercept
Linear equation
Nonlinear curve
Tangent

■ **FILL-IN QUESTIONS**

1. The relationship between two economic variables can be visualized with the aid of a two-dimensional graph.
   a. Customarily, the (dependent, independent) _____ _____ variable is placed on the horizontal axis and the _____ variable is placed on the vertical axis. The _____ variable is said to change because of a change in the _____ variable.
   b. The vertical and horizontal (scales, ranges) _____ on the graph are calibrated to reflect the _____ of values in a table of data points on which the graph is based.
   c. Other variables, beyond the two in the graph, that might affect the economic relationship are assumed to be (changing, held constant) _____.

Ceteris paribus also means that other variables are

_____

2. The graph of a straight line that slopes downward to the right indicates that there is (a direct, an inverse)

_____ relationship between the two variables. A graph of a straight line that slopes upward to the right tells us that the relationship is (direct, inverse)

_____. When the value of one variable increases and the value of the other variable increases, then

the relationship is _____; when the value of one increases, while the other decreases, the relationship is

_____

3. The slope of a straight line between two points is defined as the ratio of the (vertical, horizontal)

_____ change to the _____ change. When two variables move in the same direction,

the slope will be (negative, positive) _____; when the variables move in opposite directions the slope

will be _____. The point at which the line

meets the vertical axis is called the _____

4. We can express the graph of a straight line with a linear equation that can be written as $y = a + bx$.

   a. *a* is the (slope, intercept) _____ and *b* is

   the _____

   b. *y* is the (dependent, independent) _____

   variable and *x* is the _____
   variable.

   c. If *a* was 2, *b* was 4, and *x* was 5, then *y* would be

   _____ . If the value of *x* changed to 7, then

   y would be _____. If the value of *x* changed

   to 3, then *y* would be _____

5. The slope of a (straight line, nonlinear curve)

_____ is constant throughout; the slope of a

_____ varies from point to point. An estimate of the slope of a nonlinear curve at a point can be made by calculating the slope of a straight line that is

_____ to the point on the curve.

■ PROBLEMS AND PROJECTS

1. Next are three exercises in making graphs. On the graphs plot the economic relationships contained in each exercise. Be sure to label each axis of the graph and to indicate the unit of measurement and scale used on each axis.

   a. Graph national income on the horizontal axis and consumption expenditures on the veritcal axis; connect the seven points and label the curve "Consumption Schedule." The relationship between national income and consumption expenditures is a(n) (direct, inverse)

_____ one and the Consumption Schedule

a(n) (up-, down-) _____ sloping curve.

National income, billions of dollars	Consumption expenditures, billions of dollars
$ 600	$ 600
700	640
800	780
900	870
1000	960
1100	1050
1200	1140

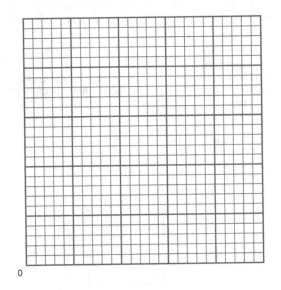

0

   b. Graph investment expenditures on the horizontal axis and the rate of interest on the vertical axis; connect the seven points and label the curve "Investment Schedule." The relationship between the rate of interest and investment expenditures is a(n) (direct, inverse)

_____ one and the Investment Schedule a(n)

(up-, down-) _____ sloping curve.

Rate of interest, %	Investment expenditures, billions of dollars
8	$220
7	280
6	330
5	370
4	400
3	420
2	430

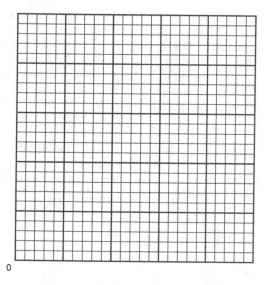

0

c. Graph average salary on the horizontal axis and wine consumption on the vertical axis; connect the seven points.

Average salary, American college professors	Annual per capita wine consumption in liters
$52,000	11.5
53,000	11.6
54,000	11.7
55,000	11.8
56,000	11.9
57,000	22.0
58,000	22.1

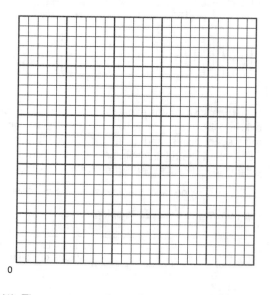

0

(1) The average salary of a college professor and wine consumption (are, are not) _____ **correlated**. The higher average salary (is, is not)

_____ the **cause** of the greater consumption of wine.

(2) The relationship between the two variables may be purely _____ ; or, as is more likely, both the higher salaries and the greater consumption of wine may be the result of the higher _____ in the American economy.

2. This question is based on the graph below.

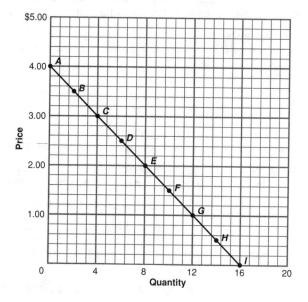

a. Construct a table for points **A–I** from the data shown in the graph.

b. According to economists, price is the (independent, dependent) _____ variable and quantity is the _____ variable.

c. Write a linear equation that summarizes the data.

3. The following three sets of data each show the relationship between an independent variable and a dependent variable. For each set, the independent variable is in the left column and the dependent variable is in the right column.

(1)		(2)		(3)	
A	B	C	D	E	F
0	10	0	100	0	20
10	30	10	75	50	40
20	50	20	50	100	60
30	70	30	25	150	80
40	90	40	0	200	100

a. Write an equation that summarizes the data for each set: (1), (2), and (3).
b. State whether each data set shows a positive or inverse relationship between the two variables.

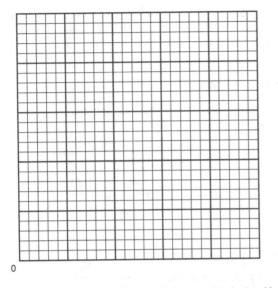

0

c. Graph data sets 1 and 2 on the graph above. Use the same horizontal scale for both sets of independent variables and the same vertical scale for both sets of dependent variables.

4. This problem is based on the following graph.

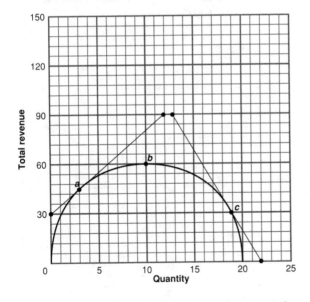

a. The slope of the straight line through point **a** is?
b. The slope of the straight line through point **b** is?
c. The slope of the straight line through point **c** is?

■ **SELF-TEST**

Circle the T if the statement is true; the F if it is false.

1. Graphs are designed by economists to confuse students and the public.   **T F**

2. If the straight line on a two-variable graph is downward sloping to the right, then there is a positive relationship between the two variables.   **T F**

3. A variable that changes as a consequence of a change in another variable is considered to be a dependent variable.   **T F**

4. Economists always put the independent variable on the horizontal axis and the dependent variable on the vertical axis of a two-variable graph.   **T F**

5. *Ceteris paribus* means that other variables are changing at the same time.   **T F**

6. In the ratio for the calculation of the slope of a straight line, the vertical change is in the numerator and the horizontal change is in the denominator.   **T F**

7. If the slope of the linear relationship between consumption and income was .90, then it tells us that for every $1 increase in income there will be a $.90 increase in consumption.   **T F**

8. If a linear equation was $y = 10 + 5x$, the vertical intercept is 5.   **T F**

9. When a line is tangent to a nonlinear curve, then it intersects the curve at a particular point.   **T F**

10. If the slope of a straight line on a two-variable (x, y) graph was .5 and the vertical intercept was 5, then a value of 10 for x means y is also 10.   **T F**

11. A slope of -4 for a straight line in a two-variable graph indicates that there is an inverse relationship between the two variables.   **T F**

12. If x is an independent variable and y is a dependent variable, then a change in y results in a change in x.   **T F**

13. An upward slope for a straight line that is tangent to a nonlinear curve would indicate that the slope of the line is positive.   **T F**

14. If one pair of x, y points was (13, 10) and the other was (8, 20), then the slope of the straight line between the two sets of points in the two-variable graph, with x on the horizontal axis and y on the vertical axis, would be 2.   **T F**

15. When the value of x is 2, a value of 10 for y would be calculated from a linear equation of $y = -2 + 6x$. **T F**

Circle the letter that corresponds to the best answer.

1. If an increase in one variable is associated with a decrease in another variable, then we can conclude that the variables are:
(a) nonlinear
(b) directly related
(c) inversely related
(d) positively related

2. The ratio of the absolute vertical change to the absolute horizontal change between two points of a straight line is the:
- **(a)** slope
- **(b)** vertical intercept
- **(c)** horizontal intercept
- **(d)** point of tangency

3. There are two sets of *x, y* points on a straight line in a two-variable graph with *y* on the vertical axis and *x* on the horizontal axis. If one set of points was (0, 5) and the other set (5, 20), the linear equation for the line would be:
- **(a)** $y = 5x$
- **(b)** $y = 5 + 3x$
- **(c)** $y = 5 + 15x$
- **(d)** $y = 5 + .33x$

4. In a two-variable graph of data on the price and quantity of a product, economists place:
- **(a)** price on the horizontal axis because it is the independent variable and quantity on the vertical axis because it is the dependent variable
- **(b)** price on the vertical axis because it is the dependent variable and quantity on the horizontal because it is the independent variable
- **(c)** price on the vertical axis even though it is the independent variable and quantity on the horizontal axis even though it is the dependent variable
- **(d)** price on the horizontal axis even though it is the dependent variable and quantity on the vertical axis even though it is the independent variable

5. In a two-dimensional graph of the relationship between two economic variables, an assumption is usually made that:
- **(a)** both variables are linear
- **(b)** both variables are nonlinear
- **(c)** other variables are held constant
- **(d)** other variables are permitted to change

6. When the slope of a straight line to a point tangent to a nonlinear curve is zero, then the straight line is:
- **(a)** vertical
- **(b)** horizontal
- **(c)** upward sloping
- **(d)** downward sloping

The next four questions (7, 8, 9, and 10) are based on the following four data sets. In each set, the independent variable is in the left column and the dependent variable is in the right column.

(1)		(2)		(3)		(4)	
A	B	C	D	E	F	G	H
0	1	0	12	4	5	0	4
3	2	5	8	6	10	1	3
6	3	10	4	8	15	2	2
9	4	15	0	10	20	3	1

7. There is an inverse relationship between the independent and dependent variable in data sets:
- **(a)** 1 and 4
- **(b)** 2 and 3
- **(c)** 1 and 3
- **(d)** 2 and 4

8. The vertical intercept is 4 in data set:
- **(a)** 1
- **(b)** 2
- **(c)** 3
- **(d)** 4

9. The linear equation for data set 1 is:
- **(a)** $B = 3A$
- **(b)** $B = 1 + 3A$
- **(c)** $B = 1 + .33A$
- **(d)** $A = 1 + .33B$

10. The linear equation for data set 2 is:
- **(a)** $C = 12 - 1.25D$
- **(b)** $D = 12 + 1.25C$
- **(c)** $D = 12 - .80C$
- **(d)** $C = 12 - .80D$

Answer the next four questions (11, 12, 13, and 14) on the basis of the following diagram.

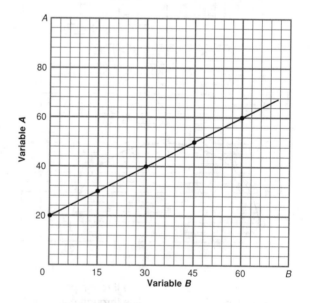

11. The variables *A* and *B* are:
- **(a)** positively related
- **(b)** negatively related
- **(c)** indirectly related
- **(d)** nonlinear

12. The slope of the line is:
- **(a)** .33
- **(b)** .67

(c) 1.50
(d) 3.00

13. The vertical intercept is:
  (a) 80
  (b) 60
  (c) 40
  (d) 20

14. The linear equation for the slope of the line is:
  (a) $A = 20 + .33B$
  (b) $B = 20 + .33A$
  (c) $A = 20 + .67B$
  (d) $B = 20 + .67A$

Answer the next two questions (15 and 16) on the basis of the following diagram.

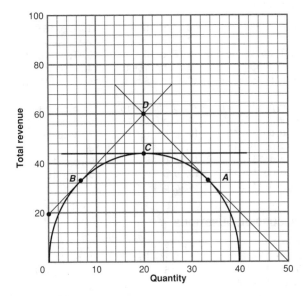

15. The slope of the line tangent to the curve at point **A** is:
  (a)   2
  (b) − 2
  (c) − 1.5
  (d) − 0.5

16. The slope of the line tangent to the curve at point **B** is:
  (a) − 2
  (b)   2
  (c)   3
  (d)   0.5

17. The slope of the line tangent to the curve at point **C** is:
  (a) − 1
  (b)   1
  (c)   0
  (d)   undefined

18. Assume that the relationship between concert ticket prices and attendance is expressed in the equation $P = 25 - 1.25Q$, where P equals ticket price and Q equals concert attendance in thousands of people. On the basis of this equation, it can be said that:
  (a) more people will attend the concert when the price is high compared to when the price is low
  (b) if 12,000 people attended the concert, then the ticket price was $10
  (c) if 18,000 people attend the concert, then entry into the concert was free
  (d) an increase in ticket price by $5 reduces concert attendance by 1,000 people

19. If you know that the equation relating consumption (C) to income (Y) is $C = \$7,500 + .2Y$, then:
  (a) consumption is inversely related to income
  (b) consumption is the independent variable and income is the dependent variable
  (c) if income is $15,000, then consumption is $10,500
  (d) if consumption is $30,000, then income is $10,000

20. If the dependent variable changes by 22 units when the independent variable changes by 12 units, then the slope of the line is:
  (a) 0.56
  (b) 1.83
  (c) 2.00
  (d) 3.27

■ **DISCUSSION QUESTIONS**

1. Why do economists use graphs in their work? Give two examples of a graph that illustrates the relationship between two economic variables.

2. What does the slope tell you about a straight line? How would you interpret a slope of 4? A slope of − 2? A slope of .5? A slope of − .25?

3. If the vertical intercept increases in value but the slope of a straight line stays the same, what happens to the graph of the line? If the vertical intercept decreases in value, what will happen to the line?

4. How do you interpret a vertical line on a two-variable graph? How do you interpret a horizontal line?

5. When you know that the price and quantity of a product are inversely related, what does this tell you about the slope of a line? What do you know about the slope when the two variables are positively related?

6. Which variable is the dependent and which is the independent in the following economic statement: "A decrease in business taxes had a positive effect on investment spending." How do you tell the difference between a dependent and independent variable when examining economic relationships?

7. Why is an assumption made that all other variables are held constant when we construct a two-variable graph of the price and quantity of a product?

8. How do mathematicians and economists differ at times in the way that they construct two-dimensional graphs? Give an example.

9. If you know that the equation relating consumption (**C**) to income (**Y**) is **C** = 10,000 + 5**Y**, then what would consumption be when income is $5,000? Construct an income-consumption table for five different levels of income.

10. How do the slopes of a straight line and a nonlinear curve differ? How do you estimate the slope of a nonlinear curve?

Point	Price	Quantity
A	$4.00	0
B	3.50	2
C	3.00	4
D	2.50	6
E	2.00	8
F	1.50	10
G	1.00	12
H	.50	14
I	.00	16

b. independent, dependent; *c.* **P** = 4.00 − .25**Q**

3. *a.* (1) **B** = 10 + 2**A**; (2) **D** = 100 − 2.5**C**; (3) **F** = 20 + .4**E**; *b.* (1) positive; (2) inverse; (3) positive

4. *a.* 5; *b.* 0; *c.* − 10

■ **ANSWERS**

Appendix to Chapter 1 Graphs and Their Meaning

FILL-IN QUESTIONS

1. *a.* independent, dependent, dependent, independent; *b.* scales, ranges; *c.* held constant, held constant

2. inverse, direct, direct, inverse

3. vertical, horizontal, positive, negative, vertical intercept

4. *a.* intercept, slope; *b.* dependent, independent; *c.* 22, 30, 14

5. straight line, nonlinear curve, tangent

PROBLEMS AND PROJECTS

1. *a.* direct, up-; *b.* inverse, down-; *c.* (1) are, is not; (2) coincidental, incomes (standard of living, or some other such answer)

2. *a.*

SELF-TEST

1. F, p. 13	**6.** T, p. 15	**11.** T, p. 15
2. F, p. 14	**7.** T, pp. 15−16	**12.** F, pp. 14−15
3. T, pp. 14−15	**8.** F, p. 16	**13.** T, pp. 16−17
4. F, p. 15	**9.** F, pp. 16−17	**14.** F, pp. 15−16
5. F, p. 15	**10.** T, p. 16	**15.** T, pp. 15−16

1. *c*, p. 14	**8.** *d*, pp. 15−16	**15.** *b*, pp. 16−17
2. *a*, p. 15	**9.** *c*, pp. 15−16	**16.** *b*, pp. 16−17
3. *b*, pp. 15−16	**10.** *c*, pp. 15−16	**17.** *c*, pp. 16−17
4. *c*, pp. 14−15	**11.** *a*, p. 14	**18.** *b*, p. 16
5. *c*, p. 15	**12.** *b*, p. 15	**19.** *c*, p. 15
6. *b*, pp. 16−17	**13.** *d*, p. 16	**20.** *b*, p. 15
7. *d*, p. 14	**14.** *c*, p. 16	

DISCUSSION QUESTIONS

1. p. 13	**5.** p. 14	**8.** p. 15
2. pp. 15−16	**6.** pp. 14−15	**9.** p. 16
3. pp. 15−16	**7.** p. 15	**10.** pp. 16−17
4. pp. 13−14		

CHAPTER 2

The Economizing Problem

The aim of Chapter 2 is to explain the central problem of economics. The problem is that resources—the ultimate means of satisfying material wants—are scarce *relative* to the insatiable wants of society. Economics as a science is the study of the various aspects of the behavior of society in its effort to allocate the scarce resources—land, labor, capital, and entrepreneurial ability—in order to satisfy as best it can its unlimited desire for consumption.

The production possibilities table and curve are used in this chapter to illustrate the meaning of the scarcity of resources and increasing opportunity costs. It is both an illustrative device that will help you to understand several economic concepts and problems and a tool that has many applications in the real world.

Every economy is faced with the problem of scarce resources and has to find ways to respond to the economic problem. No economy answers the problem in the same way that another economy does. Between the extremes of pure (or laissez faire) capitalism and the command economy (communism) are various economic systems; all these systems are different devices—different methods of organization—for finding an answer to the economic problem of relative scarcity. Chapters 3 through 6 will explain in greater detail how the United States economy is organized and operates to address the economizing problem.

In Chapter 2 of the textbook are a number of economic definitions and classifications. It would be worthwhile for you to learn these definitions *now.* They will be used later on and it will be necessary for you to know them if you are to understand what follows.

■ CHECKLIST

When you have studied this chapter you should be able to:

☐ Write a definition of economics that incorporates the relationship between resources and wants.
☐ Identify the four economic resources and the type of income associated with each.
☐ Explain why full employment and full production are necessary for the efficient use of resources.

☐ Distinguish between allocative efficiency and productive efficiency.
☐ State the four assumptions made when a production possibilities table or curve is constructed.
☐ Construct a production possibilities curve when you are given the appropriate data.
☐ Define opportunity cost and utilize a production possibilities curve to explain the concept.
☐ State the law of increasing opportunity costs and, in as few words as possible, present the economic rationale for this law.
☐ Use a production possibilities curve to illustrate economic growth, underemployment of resources, and increasing opportunity costs.
☐ Give real-world applications of the production possibilities curve.
☐ List the two major characteristics of pure capitalism and the command economy.

■ CHAPTER OUTLINE

1. The bases upon which the study of economics rests are two facts.
   a. Society's material wants are unlimited.
   b. The economic resources which are the ultimate means of satisfying these wants are scarce in relation to the wants.
   (1) Economic resources are classified as land, capital, labor, and entrepreneurial ability.
   (2) The payments received by those who provide the economy with these four resources are rental income, interest income, wages, and profits, respectively.
   (3) Because these resources are scarce (or limited) the output that the economy is able to produce is also limited.

2. Economics, then, is the study of how society's scarce resources are used (administered) to obtain the greatest satisfaction of its material wants.
   a. To be efficient in the use of its resources an economy must achieve both full employment and full production. Full production implies that there are

(1) allocative efficiency, which means that resources are devoted to those goods most wanted by society; and

(2) productive efficiency, which means that goods and services are being produced in the least-cost way.

b. The production possibilities table indicates the alternative combinations of goods and services an economy is capable of producing when it has achieved full employment and full production.

(1) The four assumptions that are usually made when a production possibilities table is constructed is that there are economic efficiency, fixed resources, fixed technology, and two products being considered.

(2) The table illustrates the fundamental choice every society must make: what quantity of each product it wants produced.

c. The data contained in the production possibilities table can be plotted on a graph to obtain a production possibilities curve.

d. Which of these alternative combinations society chooses—which product-mix it selects—depends upon the preferences of that society; and preferences are subjective and nonscientific.

e. The opportunity cost of producing an additional unit of one product is the amounts of other products that are sacrificed; and the law of increasing opportunity costs is that the opportunity cost of producing additional units of a product increases as more of that product is produced.

(1) The law of increasing opportunity cost results in a production possibilities curve that is concave (from the origin).

(2) The opportunity cost of producing additional units of a product increases as more of the product is produced because resources are not completely adaptable to alternative uses.

(3) The production possibilities curve illustrates the concepts of scarcity, choice, opportunity cost, and increasing opportunity costs.

3. The following modifications make the production possibilities concept more realistic.

a. The failure to achieve full employment or full production reduces the output of the economy.

b. Improvements in technology and increased amounts of resources expand the output the economy is capable of producing.

c. The combination of goods and services an economy chooses to produce today helps to determine its production possibilities in the future.

d. There are many real-world applications of the production possibilities curve and table.

4. Different economic systems differ in the way they respond to the economizing problem.

a. At one extreme is pure capitalism, which relies upon

the private ownership of its economic resources and the market system.

b. At the other extreme, the command economy uses the public ownership of its resources and central planning.

c. Economies in the real world lie between these two extremes and are hybrid systems.

d. Some underdeveloped nations have traditional (or customary) economies which are shaped by the customs and traditions of the society.

■ **IMPORTANT TERMS**

The economizing problem

Unlimited wants

Scarce resources

Land, capital, labor, and entrepreneurial ability

Factors of production

Investment

Consumer goods

Capital goods

Real capital

Money (financial) capital

Rental income, interest income, wages, and profit

Utility

Economics

Economic efficiency

Full employment

Full production

Allocative efficiency

Productive efficiency

Production possibilities table

Production possibilities curve

Optimal product mix

Opportunity cost

Law of increasing opportunity costs

Unemployment

Underemployment

Economic growth

Pure (laissez-faire) capitalism

Command economy (communism)

Authoritarian capitalism

Market socialism

Traditional (customary) economies

■ **FILL-IN QUESTIONS**

1. The two fundamental facts that provide the foundation of economics are:

a. _____

b. _____

2. Complete the following classification of resources:

a. _____

(1) _____

_____

(2) _____

b. _____

(1) _____

(2) _____

3. Both consumer goods and capital goods satisfy human wants. The consumer goods satisfy these wants (directly, indirectly) _____ and the capital goods satisfy them _____

4. The incomes of individuals are received from supplying resources. Four types of incomes are _____, _____, _____, and _____

5. Economics can be defined as _____
_____
_____
_____

6. Economic efficiency requires that there be both full (employment, production) _____ of resources, and full _____ so as to make the most valued contributions to national output. Full _____ implies that there is both (allocative, productive) _____ efficiency, which means that resources are devoted to those goods most wanted by society, and that there is _____ efficiency, which means that goods and services are being produced in the least-cost way.

7. When a production possibilities table or curve is constructed, four assumptions are made. These assumptions are:

a. _____

b. _____

c. _____

d. _____

8. In the next column is a production possibilities curve for tractors and suits of clothing.
a. If the economy moves from point **A** to point **B** it will produce (more, fewer) _____ tractors and (more, fewer) _____ suits of clothing.
b. If the economy is producing at point **X,** some of the resources of the economy are either _____ or _____

Tractors / Suits of clothing

c. If the economy moves from point **X** to point **B** (more, fewer) _____ tractors and (more, fewer) _____ suits will be produced.
d. If the economy is to produce at point **Y,** it must either _____ or _____

9. All the combinations of products shown in the production possibilities table (or on the curve) can be achieved only if there are full employment and full production in the economy; the best combination of products depends upon the (values, resources, technology) _____ of that society and is a (scientific, nonscientific) _____ matter.

10. The quantity of other goods and services an economy must go without in order to produce more low-cost housing is the _____ of producing the additional low-cost housing.

11. The cost of producing a commodity tends to increase as more of the commodity is produced because _____
_____
_____

12. The more an economy consumes of its current production, the (more, less) _____ it will be capable of producing in future years if other things are equal.

13. In:
a. pure capitalism property resources are (publicly, privately) _____ owned and the means employed to direct and coordinate economic activity is the _____ system.
b. a command economy the property resources are (publicly, privately) _____ owned and the coordinating device is central _____

■ PROBLEMS AND PROJECTS

1. Below is a list of resources. Indicate in the space to the right of each whether the resource is land, capital (C), labor, entrepreneurial ability (EA), or some combinations of these.

a. Fishing grounds in the North Atlantic _____

b. A cash register in a retail store _____

c. Uranium deposits in Canada _____

d. An irrigation ditch in Nebraska _____

e. The work performed by the late Henry Ford _____

f. The oxygen breathed by human beings _____

g. An IBM plant in Rochester, Minnesota _____

h. The food on the shelf of a grocery store _____

i. The work done by a robot at an auto plant _____

j. The tasks accomplished in perfecting a

   new computer for commercial sales _____

k. A carpenter building a house _____

2. A production possibilities table for two commodities, wheat and automobiles, is found below. The table is constructed employing the usual assumptions. Wheat is measured in units of 100,000 bushels and automobiles in units of 100,000.

Combination	Wheat	Automobiles
A	0	7
B	7	6
C	13	5
D	18	4
E	22	3
F	25	2
G	27	1
H	28	0

a. Follow the general rules for making graphs (see Chapter 1); plot the data from the table on the graph below to obtain a production possibilities curve. Place wheat on the vertical axis and automobiles on the horizontal axis.

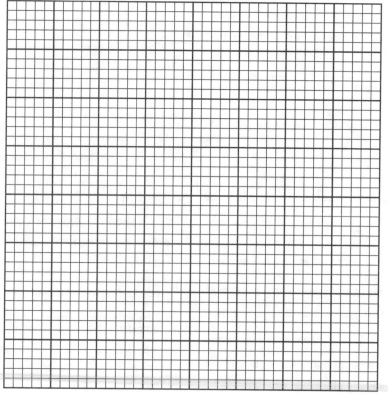

0

b. Fill in the table below showing the opportunity cost per unit of producing the 1st through the 7th automobile.

Automobiles	Cost of production
1st	——
2d	——
3d	——
4th	——
5th	——
6th	——
7th	——

3. Below is a production possibilities curve.

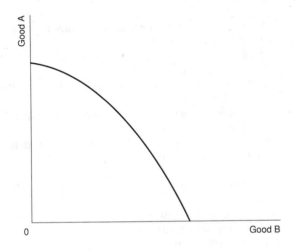

Draw on this graph:
  a. A production possibilities curve which indicates greater efficiency in the production of good A.
  b. A production possibilities curve which indicates greater efficiency in the production of good B.
  c. A production possibilities curve which indicates an increase in the resources available to the economy.

4. Below is a list of economic goods. Indicate in the space to the right of each whether the good is a consumer good (CON), a capital good (CAP), or that it depends (DEP) upon who is using it and for what purpose.

  a. An automobile _____

  b. A tractor _____

  c. A taxicab _____

  d. A house _____

  e. A factory building _____

  f. An office building _____

  g. An ironing board _____

  h. A refrigerator _____

  i. A telephone _____

  j. A quart of a soft drink _____

  k. A cash register _____

  l. A screwdriver _____

■ **SELF-TEST**

Circle the T if the statement is true; the F if it is false.

1. The wants with which economics is concerned include only those wants which can be satisfied by goods and services.   T F

2. Money is a resource and is classified as "capital."   T F

3. Profit is the reward paid to those who provide the economy with capital.   T F

4. Resources are scarce because society's material wants are unlimited and productive resources are limited.   T F

5. Economic efficiency requires that there be both full employment of resources and full production.   T F

6. Allocative efficiency means that goods and services are being produced by society in the least-cost way.   T F

7. Only allocative efficiency is necessary for there to be full production.   T F

8. The opportunity cost of producing antipollution devices is the other goods and services the economy is unable to produce because it has decided to produce these devices.   T F

9. The opportunity cost of producing a good tends to increase as more of it is produced because resources less suitable to its production must be employed.   T F

10. Drawing a production possibilities curve concave to the origin is the geometric way of stating the law of increasing opportunity costs.   T F

11. Given full employment and full production, it is not possible for an economy capable of producing just two goods to increase its production of both.   T F

12. Economic growth means an increase in the ability of an economy to produce goods and services; and it is shown by a movement of the production possibilities to the right.   T F

13. The more capital goods an economy produces today, the greater will be the total output of all goods it can produce in the future, other things being equal.   T F

14. It is economically desirable for a nation to have unemployed resources at the outset of a war because it can increase its production of military goods without having to decrease its production of civilian goods.   **T   F**

15. In the economic system called authoritarian capitalism most property is publicly owned but the market system is used to coordinate economic activity.   **T   F**

Circle the letter that corresponds to the best answer.

1. An "innovator" is defined as an entrepreneur who:
   (a) makes basic policy decisions in a business firm
   (b) combines factors of production to produce a good or service
   (c) invents a new product or process for producing a product
   (d) introduces new products on the market or employs a new method to produce a product

2. An economy is efficient when it has achieved:
   (a) full employment
   (b) full production
   (c) either full employment or full production
   (d) both full employment and full production

3. When a production possibilities schedule is written (or a production possibilities curve is drawn) four assumptions are made. Which of the following is *not* one of those assumptions?
   (a) only two products are produced
   (b) the nation is not at war
   (c) the economy has both full employment and full production
   (d) the quantities of all resources available to the economy are fixed

4. At point *A* on the production possibilities curve in the following illustration:

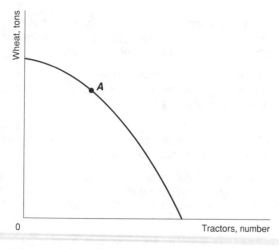

   (a) more wheat than tractors is being produced

   (b) more tractors than wheat are being produced
   (c) the economy is employing all its resources
   (d) the economy is not employing all its resources

5. The combinations of products in a society's production possibilities table which is its optimal product-mix depends upon that society's:
   (a) resources
   (b) technology
   (c) level of employment
   (d) values

6. The production possibilities curve is:
   (a) concave
   (b) convex
   (c) linear
   (d) positive

7. What is the economic rationale for the law of increasing opportunity cost?
   (a) full production and full employment of resources has not been achieved
   (b) economic resources are not completely adaptable to alternative uses
   (c) economic growth is being limited by the pace of technological advancement
   (d) an economy's present choice of output is determined by fixed technology and fixed resources

8. A farmer who produces his crops by inefficient methods is:
   (a) an unemployed worker
   (b) an underemployed worker
   (c) a fully employed worker
   (d) an apparently unemployed worker

9. If there is an increase in the resources available within the economy:
   (a) more goods and services will be produced in the economy
   (b) the economy will be capable of producing more goods and services
   (c) the standard of living in the economy will rise
   (d) the technological efficiency of the economy will improve

10. If the production possibilities curve on the next page moves from position *A* to position *B,* then:
   (a) the economy has increased the efficiency with which it produces wheat
   (b) the economy has increased the efficiency with which it produces tractors
   (c) the economy has put previously idle resources to work
   (d) the economy has gone from full employment to less-than-full employment

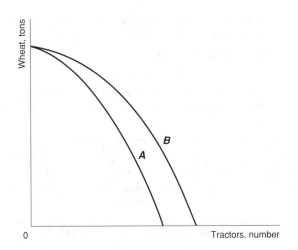

11. Which would be the best example of allocative efficiency? When society devoted resources to the production of:
- **(a)** slide rules instead of hand-held calculators
- **(b)** horse-drawn carriages instead of automobiles
- **(c)** word processors instead of manual typewriters
- **(d)** long-play records instead of compact discs or cassettes

12. Which situation would most likely shift the production possibilities curve for a nation in an outward direction?
- **(a)** deterioration in product quality
- **(b)** reductions in the supply of resources
- **(c)** increases in technological advances
- **(d)** rising levels of discrimination

13. The opportunity cost of a new public stadium is the:
- **(a)** money cost of hiring guards and staff for the new stadium
- **(b)** cost of constructing the new stadium in a future year
- **(c)** change in the real estate tax rate to pay off the new stadium
- **(d)** other goods and services that must be sacrificed to construct the new stadium

14. The public ownership of property resources and the use of a market system to direct and coordinate economic activity is characteristic of:
- **(a)** pure capitalism
- **(b)** the command economy
- **(c)** market socialism
- **(d)** authoritarian capitalism

Answer the next three questions (15, 16, and 17) on the basis of the data given in the following production possibilities table.

	Production possibilities (alternatives)					
	A	B	C	D	E	F
Capital goods	100	95	85	70	50	0
Consumer goods	0	100	180	240	280	300

15. The choice of alternative B compared with alternative D would tend to promote:
- **(a)** a slower rate of economic growth
- **(b)** a faster rate of economic growth
- **(c)** increased consumption in the present
- **(d)** central economic planning

16. If the economy is producing at production alternative D, the opportunity cost of 40 more units of consumer goods is about:
- **(a)** 5 units of capital goods
- **(b)** 10 units of capital goods
- **(c)** 15 units of capital goods
- **(d)** 20 units of capital goods

17. In the table, the law of increasing opportunity costs is suggested by the fact that:
- **(a)** greater and greater quantities of consumer goods must be given up to get more capital goods
- **(b)** smaller and smaller quantities of consumer goods must be given up to get more capital goods
- **(c)** capital goods are relatively more scarce than consumer goods
- **(d)** the production possibilities curve will eventually shift outward as the economy expands

18. Productive efficiency means that:
- **(a)** the law of increasing opportunity cost has reached a maximum
- **(b)** the least-costly methods are being used to produce a product
- **(c)** resources are being devoted to the production of products most desired by society
- **(d)** the amount of other products which must be sacrificed to obtain production of a given product is at a minimum

19. Which situation would most likely cause a nation's production possibilities curve to shift inward?
- **(a)** investing more resources in new plants and equipment
- **(b)** eliminating discrimination based on race and ethnic background
- **(c)** increasing international trade or incurring a trade deficit
- **(d)** going to war with another nation and suffering a major defeat

20. The private ownership of property resources and use of the market system to direct and coordinate economic activity is characteristic of:
   (a) pure capitalism
   (b) the command economy
   (c) market socialism
   (d) the traditional economy

■ **DISCUSSION QUESTIONS**

1. Explain what is meant by the "economizing problem." Why are resources scarce?

2. In what sense are wants satiable and in what sense are they insatiable?

3. What are the four economic resources? How is each of these resources defined? What is the income earned by each of them called?

4. When is a society economically efficient? What is meant by "full production" and how does it differ from "full employment"? Explain why full production implies both allocative and productive efficiency.

5. What four assumptions are made in drawing a production possibilities curve or schedule? How do technological advance and an increased supply of resources in the economy affect the curve or schedule?

6. Why cannot an economist determine which of the combinations in the production possibilities table is "best"? What determines the optimal product-mix?

7. What is opportunity cost? What is the law of increasing opportunity cost? Why do costs increase?

8. What is the important relationship between the **composition** of the economy's current output and the **location** of future production possibilities curves?

9. Describe some real-world applications of the production possibilities curve.

10. Pure capitalism and the command economy differ in two important ways. Compare these two economic systems with each other and with authoritarian capitalism and market socialism.

■ **ANSWERS**

Chapter 2 The Economizing Problem

FILL-IN QUESTIONS

1. *a.* society's material wants are unlimited; *b.* economic resources, which are the ultimate means of satisfying these wants, are scarce in relation to these wants

2. *a.* property resources; (1) land or raw materials, (2) capital; *b.* human resources; (1) labor, (2) entrepreneurial ability

3. directly, indirectly

4. rental income, interest income, wages profits

5. the social science concerned with the problem of using or administering scarce resources to attain maximum fulfillment of unlimited wants

6. employment, production, production, allocative, productive

7. *a.* the economy is operating at full employment and full production; *b.* the available supplies of the factors of production are fixed; *c.* technology does not change during the course of the analysis; *d.* the economy produces only two products

8. *a.* fewer, more; *b.* unemployed, underemployed; *c.* more, more; *d.* increase resource supplies, improve its technology

9. values, nonscientific

10. opportunity cost

11. economic resources are not completely adaptable among alternate uses

12. less

13. *a.* privately, market; *b.* publicly, planning

PROBLEMS AND PROJECTS

1. *a.* land; *b.* C; *c.* land; *d.* C; *e.* EA; *f.* land; *g.* C; *h.* C; *i.* C; *j.* EA; *k.* labor

2. *b.* 1, 2, 3, 4, 5, 6, 7 units of wheat

4. *a.* DEP; *b.* CAP; *c.* CAP; *d.* CAP; *e.* CAP; *f.* CAP; *g.* DEP; *h.* DEP; *i.* DEP; *j.* DEP; *k.* CAP; *l.* DEP

SELF-TEST

1. T, pp. 19–20	**6.** F, p. 22	**11.** T, pp. 23–24
2. F, pp. 20–21	**7.** F, p. 22	**12.** T, p 26
3. F, p. 21	**8.** T, p. 23	**13.** T, pp. 27–28
4. T, pp. 20–21	**9.** T, pp. 23–24	**14.** F, p. 29
5. T, p. 22	**10.** T, p. 25	**15.** F, p. 31

1. *d*, p. 21	**8.** *b*, p. 22	**15.** *b*, pp. 27–28
2. *d*, p. 22	**9.** *b*, p. 26	**16.** *d*, pp. 27–28
3. *b*, p. 23	**10.** *b*, p. 27	**17.** *a*, p. 25
4. *c*, p. 24	**11.** *c*, p. 22	**18.** *b*, p. 22
5. *d*, pp. 24–25	**12.** *c*, pp. 26–27	**19.** *d*, pp. 28–29
6. *a*, p. 25	**13.** *d*, p. 25	**20.** *a*, p. 30
7. *b*, p. 25	**14.** *c*, p. 30	

DISCUSSION QUESTIONS

1. pp. 19–20	**5.** pp. 23–25	**8.** p. 25
2. pp. 20–21	**6.** p. 24	**9.** pp. 27–28
3. pp. 20–21	**7.** p. 24	**10.** pp. 30–31
4. p. 22		

CHAPTER 3

Pure Capitalism and the Circular Flow

Chapter 3 has three principal aims: to outline six ideological and institutional characteristics of pure capitalism, to explain three practices found in all modern economies, and to sketch in extremely simple terms the fundamental operation of a capitalistic economy. A more detailed explanation of the institutions, practices, and behavior of the United States economy—which is not *purely* capitalistic—is found in the chapters that follow. If the aims of this chapter are accomplished, you can begin to understand the system and methods employed by our economy to solve the economizing problem presented in Chapter 2 and to find answers to the Five Fundamental Questions that will be discussed later in Chapter 5.

The resources of the American economy are owned by its citizens, who are free to use them as they wish in their own self-interest; prices and markets serve to express the self-interests of resource owners, consumers, and business firms; and competition serves to regulate self-interest—to prevent the self-interest of any person or any group from working to the disadvantage of the economy as a whole and to make self-interest work for the benefit of the entire economy.

The three practices of all modern economies are the employment of large amounts of capital, extensive specialization, and the use of money. Economies use capital and engage in specialization because it is a more efficient use of their resources; it results in larger total output and the greater satisfaction of wants. But when workers, business firms, and regions within an economy specialize they become dependent on each other for the goods and services they do not produce for themselves. To obtain these goods and services they must engage in trade. Trade is made more convenient by using money as a medium of exchange.

The principle of comparative advantage is the basis for all trade between individuals, firms, regions, and nations. You ought to be sure that you understand what is meant by comparative advantage, and how specialization is determined by comparative advantage. You should also know why specialization and trade tend to increase the production possibilities in an economy and the interdependence among the members of an economy.

The circular-flow-of-income model (or diagram) is a device which illustrates for a capitalistic economy the relation between households and businesses, the flow of money and economic goods and services between households and businesses, their dual role as buyers and sellers, and the two basic types of markets essential to the capitalistic process.

Understand these essentials of the economic skeleton first; then a little flesh—a little more reality, a little more detail—can be added to the bones. Understanding the skeleton makes it much easier to understand the whole body and its functioning.

■ CHECKLIST

When you have studied this chapter you should be able to:

☐ Identify and explain the six important institutional characteristics of capitalism.
☐ Name and explain the three characteristics of all modern economies.
☐ Compute the comparative costs of production from production possibilities data.
☐ Determine which of two economic units has a comparative advantage and show the gains from trade when you are given cost data for the two units.
☐ Indicate the range in which the terms of trade will be found.
☐ Draw the circular flow diagram; and correctly label the real and money flows and the two major types of markets.

■ CHAPTER OUTLINE

1. The United States economy is not pure capitalism, but it is a close approximation of pure capitalism. Pure capitalism has the following six peculiarities that distinguish it from other economic systems.

   a. Private individuals and organizations own and control its property resources by means of the institution of private property.

b. These individuals and organizations possess both the freedom of enterprise and the freedom of choice.

c. Each of them is motivated largely by self-interest.

d. Competition prevents them as buyers and sellers from exploiting others.

e. Markets and prices (the market system) are used to communicate and coordinate the decisions of buyers and sellers.

f. And the role of government is limited in a competitive and capitalistic economy.

2. In common with other advanced economies of the world, the American economy has three major characteristics.

a. It employs complicated and advanced methods of production and large amounts of capital equipment to produce goods and services efficiently.

b. It is a highly specialized economy; and this specialization increases the productive efficiency of the economy.

c. It also uses money extensively to facilitate trade and specialization.

3. Specialization and trade among economic units (individuals, firms, states, regions, or nations) are based on the principle of comparative advantage. This concept can be illustrated with a hypothetical example of trade between two states that produce two products.

a. Suppose the production possibilities curve for each state is a straight line (there is a constant cost ratio), and the slope of each line is different for each state.

b. Each state will find it profitable to trade because there will be a comparative (cost) advantage in the production of one of the two products; each state can produce one of the products at a lower opportunity cost than the other state.

c. The terms of trade—the ratio at which one product is traded for another—lies between the cost ratios for the two states.

d. Each state gains from this trade because specialization allows more total production from the same resources and permits a better allocation of resources; specialization and trade have the effect of easing the fixed constraints of the production possibilities curve for each state.

e. Specialization can have three potential drawbacks: more monotonous work; more dependence on the production of others; and more conflict over the exchange of the increased output.

4. The circular flow model is a device used to clarify the relationships between households and business firms in a purely capitalistic economy.

a. In resource markets households supply and firms demand resources and in product markets the firms supply and households demand products. Households use the incomes they obtain from supplying resources

to purchase the goods and services produced by the firms; and in the economy there is a real flow of resources and products and a money flow of incomes and expenditures.

b. The circular flow model has several limitations.

■ **IMPORTANT TERMS**

Private property	Terms of trade
Self-interest	Money
Competition	Medium of exchange
Market	Barter
Freedom of choice	Coincidence of wants
Freedom of enterprise	Circular flow model
Roundabout production	Households
Specialization	Resource market
Division of labor	Product market
Comparative advantage	

■ **FILL-IN QUESTIONS**

1. The ownership of property resources by private individuals and organizations is the institution of _____ _____

2. Two basic freedoms encountered in a capitalistic economy are the freedoms of _____ and _____

3. Self-interest means that each economic unit attempts to _____; this self-interest might work to the disadvantage of the economy as a whole if it were not regulated and constrained by _____

4. According to the economist, competition is present if two conditions prevail; these two conditions are:

a. _____

b. _____

5. If the number of buyers and sellers in a market is large, no single buyer or seller is able to _____ the price of the commodity bought and sold in that market.

6. In a capitalistic economy individual buyers communicate their demands and individual sellers communicate their supplies in the _____ of the economy; and their decisions are coordinated by the _____ determined there by demand and supply.

7. In the ideology of pure capitalism government is assigned (no, a limited, an extensive) ————— role.

8. The three practices or institutions common to all modern economies are ——————————————————,

—————————————————————,

and ———————————————————

9. Modern economies make extensive use of capital goods and engage in roundabout production because it is more ————— than direct production.

10. If an economy engages in extensive specialization the individuals living in the economy are extremely —————————; and if these individuals are to enjoy the benefits of specialization there must be ————— among them.

11. Modern economies practice specialization and the division of labor because the self-sufficient producer or worker tends to be a(n) ————— one.

12. When one state or nation has a lower opportunity cost of producing a product relative to another state or nation it has a —————————; the amount of one product that must be given up to obtain one unit of another product is the —————————

13. In modern economies money functions chiefly as a(n) ——————————————————

14. Barter between two individuals will take place only if there is a(n) ————————————————

15. For an item to be "money," it must be ————— ——————————————————

16. In the circular flow model:
   a. Households are demanders and businesses are suppliers in the ————— markets; and businesses are demanders and households are suppliers of the ————— markets of the economy.

   b. The two flows are called the ————— flow and the ————— flow.

   c. The expenditures made by businesses are a ————— to them and become the ————— of households.

■ **PROBLEMS AND PROJECTS**

1. The countries of Lilliput and Brobdingnag have the production possibilities tables for apples and bananas shown below.
   Note that the costs of producing apples and bananas are constant in both countries.

LILLIPUT PRODUCTION POSSIBILITIES TABLE

Product	Production alternatives					
(lbs.)	A	B	C	D	E	F
Apples	40	32	24	16	8	0
Bananas	0	4	8	12	16	20

BROBDINGNAG PRODUCTION POSSIBILITIES TABLE

Product	Production alternatives					
(lbs.)	A	B	C	D	E	F
Apples	75	60	45	30	15	0
Bananas	0	5	10	15	20	25

   a. In Lilliput the cost of producing:

   (1) 8 apples is ————— bananas

   (2) 1 apple is ————— bananas
   b. In Brobdingnag the cost of producing:

   (1) 15 apples is ————— bananas

   (2) 1 apple is ————— bananas
   c. In Lilliput the cost of producing:

   (1) 4 bananas is ————— apples

   (2) 1 banana is ————— apples
   d. In Brobdingnag the cost of producing:

   (1) 5 bananas is ————— apples

   (2) 1 banana is ————— apples
   e. The cost of producing 1 apple is lower in the country of ————————————————— and the cost of producing 1 banana is lower in the country of —————————————————
   f. Lilliput has a comparative advantage in the production of ————————————————— and Brobdingnag has a comparative advantage in the production of —————————————————
   g. The information in this problem is not sufficient to determine the exact terms of trade; but the terms of trade will be *greater* than ————— apples for 1 banana and *less* than ————— apples for 1 banana. Put another way, the terms of trade will be between ————— bananas for 1 apple and ————— bananas for 1 apple.

h. If neither nation could specialize, each would produce production alternative C. The combined production of apples in the two countries would be _____ apples and the combined production of bananas would be _____ bananas.

(1) If each nation specializes in producing the fruit for which it has a comparative advantage, their combined production will be _____ apples and _____ bananas.

(2) Their gain from specialization will be _____ apples and _____ bananas.

2. Here is another problem to help you understand the principle of comparative advantage and the benefits of specialization. A tailor named Hart has the production possibilities table for trousers and jackets given below. He chooses production alternative D.

HART'S PRODUCTION POSSIBILITIES TABLE

Product	Production alternatives					
	A	B	C	D	E	F
Trousers	75	60	45	30	15	0
Jackets	0	10	20	30	40	50

Another tailor, Schaffner, has the production possibilities table below and produces production alternative E.

SCHAFFNER'S PRODUCTION POSSIBILITIES TABLE

Product	Production alternatives						
	A	B	C	D	E	F	G
Trousers	60	50	40	30	20	10	0
Jackets	0	5	10	15	20	25	30

a. To Hart

(1) the cost of one pair of trousers is _____ jackets

(2) the cost of one jacket is _____ pairs of trousers
b. To Schaffner

(1) the cost of one pair of trousers is _____ jackets

(2) the cost of one jacket is _____ pairs of trousers
c. If Hart and Schaffner were to form a partnership to make suits

(1) _____ should specialize in the making of trousers because he can make a pair of trousers at the cost of _____ of a jacket while it costs his partner _____ of a jacket to make a pair of trousers.

(2) _____ should specialize in the making of jackets because he can make a jacket at the cost of _____ pairs of trousers while it costs his partner _____ pairs of trousers to make a jacket.

d. Without specialization and between them Hart and Schaffner were able to make 50 pairs of trousers and 50 jackets. If each specializes completely in the item in the production of which he has a comparative advantage, their combined production will be _____ pairs of trousers and _____ jackets. Thus the gain from specialization is _____

_____

e. When Hart and Schaffner come to divide the income of the partnership between them, the manufacture of a pair of trousers should be treated as the equivalent of from _____ to _____ jackets (or a jacket should be treated as the equivalant of from _____ to _____ pairs of trousers).

3. In the circular flow diagram below, the upper pair of flows (*a* and *b*) represent the product market and the lower pair (*c* and *d*) the resource market.

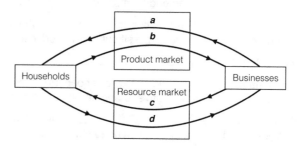
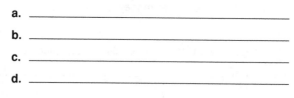

Supply labels or explanations for each of the four flows:

a. _____

b. _____

c. _____

d. _____

■ **SELF-TEST**

Circle the T if the statement is true; the F if it is false.

1. The United States economy can correctly be called "pure capitalism."   **T   F**

2. There are in the United States legal limits to the right of private property.   **T   F**

3. The freedom of business firms to produce a particular consumer good is always limited by the desires of consumers for that good.   **T   F**

4. When a market is competitive the individual sellers of the commodity are unable to reduce the supply of the commodity enough to drive its price upward.   **T   F**

5. In a purely capitalistic economy it is consumers who ultimately decide what goods and services the economy will produce. T F

6. The market system is not employed in communistic and socialistic economies. T F

7. The employment of capital to produce goods and services requires that there be "roundabout production" but it is more efficient than "direct" production. T F

8. Increasing the amount of specialization in an economy generally leads to the more efficient use of its resources. T F

9. Money is a device for facilitating the exchange of goods and services. T F

10. "Coincidence of wants" means that two persons desire to acquire the same good or service. T F

11. Cigarettes may serve as money if sellers are generally willing to accept them as money. T F

12. In the circular flow model, the household functions on the demand side of the resource and product markets. T F

13. The pursuit of economic self-interest is the same thing as selfishness. T F

14. A gas station is an example of a market. T F

15. Human and geographic specialization are both essential in achieving efficiency in the use of resources. T F

16. If a person, firm, or region has a comparative advantage in the production of a particular commodity, it should specialize in the production of that commodity. T F

17. One way that human specialization can be achieved is through a division of labor in productive activity. T F

18. If one nation has a better comparative advantage in the production of a commodity than another nation, then it has a higher opportunity cost of production than the other nation. T F

19. The economic effects of specialization and trade between nations are similar to increasing the quantity of resources or to achieving technological progress. T F

20. One of the limitations of the simple model of the circular flow is that flows of output and income are constant. T F

Circle the letter that corresponds to the best answer.

1. Which of the following is **not** one of the six characteristics of capitalism?
(a) competition
(b) central economic planning
(c) private property
(d) freedom of enterprise and choice

2. Maximization of profits appears to be in the self-interest of:
(a) business firms
(b) landowners
(c) workers
(d) consumers

3. To decide how to use its scarce resources to satisfy human wants pure capitalism relies on:
(a) central planning
(b) roundabout production
(c) a price system
(d) the coincidence of wants

4. In pure capitalism the role of government is best described as:
(a) nonexistent
(b) limited
(c) significant
(d) extensive

5. Which of the following is **not** a necessary consequence of specialization?
(a) people will use money
(b) people will engage in trade
(c) people will be dependent upon each other
(d) people will produce more of some things than they would produce in the absence of specialization

6. In an economy in which there are full employment and full production, constant amounts of resources, and unchanging technology:
(a) to increase the production of capital goods requires an increase in the production of consumer goods
(b) to decrease the production of capital goods necessitates a decrease in the production of consumer goods
(c) to increase the production of capital goods is impossible
(d) to increase the production of capital goods requires a decrease in the production of consumer goods

7. Which of the following is **not** a characteristic of competition as the economist sees it?
(a) the widespread diffusion of economic power
(b) a large number of buyers in product markets
(c) several sellers of all products
(d) the relatively easy entry into and exit of producers from industries

Answer the next four questions (8, 9, 10, and 11) on the basis of the data given for two regions, Slobovia and Utopia, which have the production possibilities tables below.

SLOBOVIA PRODUCTION POSSIBILITIES TABLE

	Production alternatives					
Product	A	B	C	D	E	F
Cams	1,500	1,200	900	600	300	0
Widgets	0	100	200	300	400	500

UTOPIA PRODUCTION POSSIBILITIES TABLE

	Production alternatives				
Product	A	B	C	D	E
Cams	4,000	3,000	2,000	1,000	0
Widgets	0	200	400	600	800

8. In Slobovia, the comparative cost of:
(a) 1 cam 3 widgets
(b) 1 widget is ⅓ cam
(c) 1 cam is ⅓ widget
(d) 3 widgets is 1 cam

9. Which of the following statements is *not* true?
(a) Slobovia should specialize in the production of widgets
(b) Slobovia has a comparative advantage in the production of widgets
(c) Utopia should specialize in the production of widgets
(d) Utopia has a comparative advantage in the production of cams

10. The terms of trade will be:
(a) greater than 7 cams for 1 widget
(b) between 7 cams for 1 widget and 5 cams for 1 widget
(c) between 5 cams for 1 widget and 3 cams for 1 widget
(d) less than 3 cams for 1 widget

11. Assume that if Slobovia did not specialize it would produce alternative C and that if Utopia did not specialize it would select alternative B. The gains from specialization are:
(a) 100 cams and 100 widgets
(b) 200 cams and 200 widgets
(c) 400 cams and 500 widgets
(d) 500 cams and 400 widgets

12. When workers specialize in various tasks to produce a commodity, the situation is referred to as:
(a) double coincidence of wants
(b) roundabout production
(c) division of labor
(d) terms of trade

13. The two kinds of market found in the circular flow model are:
(a) the real and the money markets
(b) the real and the product markets
(c) the money and the resource markets
(d) the product and the resource markets

14. In the circular flow model businesses:
(a) demand both products and resources
(b) supply both products and resources
(c) demand products and supply resources
(d) supply products and demand resources

15. One of the limitations of the circular flow model found in this chapter is that:
(a) no mention is made of the role of government
(b) it is assumed households save some of their income
(c) too much attention is paid to how resource and produce prices are determined
(d) it "ensnares the viewer in a maze of detail"

■ **DISCUSSION QUESTIONS**

1. Explain the several elements—institutions and assumptions—embodied in pure capitalism.

2. What do each of the following seek if they pursue their own self-interest? Consumers, resource owners, and business firms.

3. Explain what economists mean by competition. Why is it important to have competition in an economy whose members are motivated by self-interest?

4. What are the advantages of "indirect" or "roundabout" production?

5. How does an economy benefit from specialization and the division of labor?

6. What disadvantages are there to specialization and the division of labor?

7. Explain what is meant by comparative cost and comparative advantage. What determines the terms of trade? What is the gain that results from specialization in the products in the production of which there is a comparative advantage?

8. What are the principal disadvantages of barter?

9. What is money? What important function does it perform? Explain how money performs this function and how it overcomes the disadvantages associated with barter. Why are people willing to accept paper money in exchange for the goods and services which they sell?

10. In the circular-flow-of-income model:
(a) What two markets are involved?
(b) What roles do households play in each of these markets?
(c) What roles do businesses play in each of these markets?
(d) What two income flows are pictured in money terms? In real terms?
(e) What two expenditure flows are pictured in money terms? In real terms?

11. What are the shortcomings of the circular-flow-of-income model?

12. Give several international examples of specialization and efficiency.

■ **ANSWERS**

Chapter 3 Pure Capitalism and the Circular Flow

FILL-IN QUESTIONS

1. private property

2. enterprise, choice

3. do what is best for itself, competition

4. *a.* large numbers of independently acting buyers and sellers operating in the markets; *b.* freedom of buyers and sellers to enter or leave these markets

5. control (rig, affect)

6. markets, prices

7. a limited

8. the extensive use of capital, specialization, the use of money

9. efficient

10. interdependent, exchange (trade)

11. inefficient

12. comparative advantage; terms of trade

13. medium of exchange

14. coincidence of wants

15. generally acceptable by sellers in exchange

16. *a.* product, resource; *b.* real, money (either order); *c.* cost, income

PROBLEMS AND PROJECTS

1. *a.* (1) 4, (2) ½; *b.* (1) 5, (2) ⅓; *c.* (1) 8, (2) 2; *d.* (1) 15, (2) 3; *e.* Brobdingnag, Lilliput; *f.* bananas, apples; *g.* 2, 3, ⅓, ½; *h.* 69, 18, (1) 75, 20, (2) 6, 2

2. *a.* (1) ⅔, (2) 1½; *b.* (1) ½, (2) 2; *c.* (1) Schaffner, ½, ⅔; (2) Hart, 1½, 2; *d.* 60, 50, 10 pairs of trousers; *e.* ½, ⅔, 1½, 2

3. *a.* goods and services; *b.* expenditures for goods and services; *c.* money income payments (wages, rent, interest, and profit); *d.* services or resources (land, labor, capital, and entrepreneurial ability)

SELF-TEST

1. F, p. 35	11. T, p. 42
2. T, p. 36	12. F, p. 44
3. T, p. 36	13. F, p. 36
4. T, pp. 36–37	14. T, p. 37
5. T, p. 36	15. T, p. 39
6. F, p. 38	16. T, pp. 39–40
7. T, p. 38	17. T, p. 39
8. T, p. 39	18. F, pp. 39–40
9. T, p. 42	19. T, pp. 40–41
10. F, pp. 41–42	20. F, p. 45

1. *b*, pp. 36–37	9. *c*, pp. 39–40
2. *a*, p. 36	10. *c*, p. 40
3. *c*, p. 36	11. *a*, pp. 39–40
4. *b*, p. 38	12. *c*, p. 39
5. *a*, pp. 40–41	13. *d*, pp. 43–44
6. *d*, p. 39	14. *d*, pp. 44–45
7. *c*, pp. 36–37	15. *a*, p. 45
8. *c*, pp. 39–40	

DISCUSSION QUESTIONS

1. pp. 35–36	7. pp. 39–41
2. p. 36	8. pp. 41–42
3. pp. 36–37	9. pp. 41–42
4. pp. 38–39	10. pp. 43–45
5. p. 39	11. p. 45
6. p. 41	12. p. 39

Understanding Individual Markets: Demand and Supply

Chapter 4 is an introduction to the most fundamental tools of economic analysis: demand and supply. If you are to progress successfully into the later chapters it is essential that you understand what is meant by demand and supply and how to use these powerful tools.

Demand and supply are simply "boxes" or categories into which all the forces and factors that affect the price and the quantity of a good bought and sold in a competitive market can conveniently be placed. Demand and supply determine price and quantity exchange and it is necessary to see *why* and *how* they do this.

Many students never do understand demand and supply because they never learn to *define* demand and supply *exactly* and because they never learn (1) what is meant by an increase or decrease in demand or supply, (2) the important distinctions between "demand" and "quantity demanded" and between "supply" and "quantity supplied," (3) the equally important distinctions between an increase (or decrease) in demand and an increase (or decrease) in quantity demanded and between an increase (or decrease) in supply and an increase (or decrease) in quantity supplied.

Having learned these, however, it is no great trick to comprehend the so-called "law of supply and demand." The equilibrium price—that is, the price which will tend to prevail in the market as long as demand and supply do not change—is simply the price at which *quantity demanded* and *quantity supplied* are equal. The quantity bought and sold in the market (the equilibrium quantity) is the quantity demanded and supplied at the equilibrium price. If you can determine the equilibrium price and quantity under one set of demand and supply conditions, you can determine them under any other set and so will be able to analyze for yourself the effects of changes in demand and supply upon equilibrium price and quantity.

The chapter includes a brief examination of the factors that determine demand and supply and of the ways in which changes in these determinants will affect and cause changes in demand and supply. A graphic method is employed in this analysis in order to facilitate an understanding of demand and supply, equilibrium price and quantity, changes in demand and supply, and the resulting changes

in equilibrium price and quantity. In addition to understanding the *specific* definitions of demand and supply, it is necessary to understand the two counterparts of demand and supply: the demand *curve* and the supply *curve*. These are simply graphic (or geometric) representations of the same data contained in the schedules of demand and supply.

If you wonder why an entire chapter has been devoted to demand and supply you will find the answer in the last major section of the chapter. Demand and supply have so many applications that they are the most important single tool in economics. The example given in the last section is the application of supply and demand to the foreign exchange market.

You will use supply and demand over and over again. It will turn out to be as important to you in economics as jet propulsion is to the pilot of a Boeing 767. You can't get off the ground without it.

■ CHECKLIST

When you have studied this chapter you should be able to:

☐ Define a market.
☐ Define demand and state the law of demand.
☐ Graph the demand curve when you are given a demand schedule.
☐ Explain the difference between individual and market demand.
☐ List the major nonprice determinants of demand and explain how each one shifts the demand curve.
☐ Distinguish between a change in demand and a change in the quantity demanded.
☐ Define supply and state the law of supply.
☐ Graph the supply curve when you are given a supply schedule.
☐ List the major nonprice determinants of supply and explain how each shifts the supply curve.
☐ Distinguish between a change in supply and a change in the quantity supplied.

☐ Determine when you are given the demand for and the supply of a good what the equilibrium price and the equilibrium quantity will be.

☐ Explain why the price of a good and the amount of the good bought and sold in a competitive market will be the equilibrium price and the equilibrium quantity, respectively.

☐ Predict the effects of changes in demand and supply on equilibrium price and equilibrium quantity; and on the prices of substitute and complementary goods.

☐ Explain the meaning of the rationing function of prices.

☐ Explain why violations of the "other things equal" assumption may cause confusion about the validity of the laws of demand and supply.

☐ Define the characteristics of the foreign exchange market.

☐ Demonstrate how supply and demand analysis applies to the foreign exchange market.

■ CHAPTER OUTLINE

1. A market is any institution or mechanism that brings together the buyers and the sellers of a particular good or service; and in this chapter it is assumed that markets are purely competitive.

2. Demand is a schedule of prices and the quantities which buyers would purchase at each of these prices during some period of time.

    a. As price rises, other things being equal, buyers will purchase smaller quantities, and as price falls they will purchase larger quantities; this is the law of demand.

    b. The demand curve is a graphic representation of demand and the law of demand.

    c. Market (or total) demand for a good is a summation of the demands of all individuals in the market for that good.

    d. The demand for a good depends upon the tastes, income, and expectations of buyers; the number of buyers in the market; and the prices of related goods.

    e. A change (either an increase or a decrease) in demand is caused by a change in any of the factors (in **d**) which determine demand, and means that the demand schedule and demand curve have changed.

    f. A change in demand and a change in the quantity demanded are **not** the same thing.

3. Supply is a schedule of prices and the quantities which sellers will offer to sell at each of these prices during some period of time.

    a. The law of supply means, other things being equal, that as the price of the good rises larger quantities will be offered for sale, and that as the price of the good falls smaller quantities will be offered for sale.

    b. The supply curve is a graphic representation of supply and the law of supply; the market supply of a good is the sum of the supplies of all sellers of the good.

    c. The supply of a good depends upon the techniques used to produce it, the prices of the resources employed in its production, the extent to which it is taxed or subsidized, the prices of other goods which might be produced, the price expectations of sellers, and the number of sellers of the product.

    d. Supply will change when any of these determinants of supply changes; a change in supply is a change in the entire supply schedule or curve.

    e. A change in supply must be distinguished from a change in quantity supplied.

4. The market or equilibrium price of a commodity is that price at which quantity demanded and quantity supplied are equal; and the quantity exchanged in the market (the equilibrium quantity) is equal to the quantity demanded and supplied at the equilibrium price.

    a. The rationing function of price is the elimination of shortages and surpluses of the commodity.

    b. A change in demand, supply, or both changes both the equilibrium price and the equilibrium quantity in specific ways.

    c. In resource markets suppliers are households and demanders are business firms, and in product markets suppliers are business firms and demanders are householders; and supply and demand are useful in the analysis of prices and quantities exchanged in both types of markets.

    d. When demand and supply schedules (or curves) are drawn up it is assumed that all the nonprice determinants of demand and supply remain unchanged.

5. Understanding how demand and supply determine price and quantity in a competitive market is a powerful tool which has a large number of applications; for example, supply and demand can be used to explain the market for foreign exchange.

    a. National currencies are traded in the *foreign exchange market* where exchange rates are established; the *exchange rate* is the price paid in one nation's currency to buy 1 unit of another nation's currency ($0.01 U.S. = 1 Japanese yen).

    b. The exchange rate for a nation's currency is determined by the supply of that currency and the demand for that currency; when the supply or demand for this currency changes, then the exchange rate of this currency will change (move from $0.01 = 1 yen to $0.02 = 1 yen).

    c. Increases in exchange rate or price of a unit of foreign currency (the dollar price of a yen increases) means that there has been a *depreciation* in the value of one currency (the dollar) relative to the foreign currency (the yen); conversely, decreases in the exchange rate for a foreign currency (a decrease in the dollar price of the yen) means that there has been an *appreciation* in the value of one currency (the dollar) relative to the foreign currency (the yen).

■ IMPORTANT TERMS

Market	Independent goods
Demand schedule	Supply schedule
Law of demand	Quantity supplied
Diminishing marginal utility	Law of supply
Quantity demanded	Supply curve
Income effect	Nonprice determinant of supply
Substitution effect	Increase (or decrease) in supply
Demand curve	Equilibrium price
Individual demand	Equilibrium quantity
Total or market demand	Rationing function of prices
Nonprice determinant of demand	Price-increasing (-decreasing) effect
Increase (or decrease) in demand	Quantity-increasing (-decreasing) effect
Normal (superior) good	Foreign exchange market
Inferior good	Depreciation and appreciation of the dollar
Substitute (competing) goods	
Complementary goods	

■ FILL-IN QUESTIONS

1. A market is the institution or mechanism that brings together the _____ and the _____ of a particular good or service.

a. In resource markets prices are determined by the demand decisions of (business firms, households) _____ and the supply decisions of _____

b. In product markets prices are determined by demand decisions of _____ and the supply decisions of _____

2. The relationship between price and quantity in the demand schedule is a(n) (direct, inverse) _____ _____ relationship; in the supply schedule the relationship is a(n) _____ one.

3. The added satisfaction or pleasure obtained by a consumer from additional units of a product decreases as her or his consumption of the product increases. This phenomenon is called _____

4. A consumer tends to buy more of a product as its price falls because:

a. The purchasing power of the consumer is increased and the consumer tends to buy more of this product (and of other products); this is called the (income, substitution) _____ effect;

b. The product becomes less expensive relative to similar products and the consumer tends to buy more of this and less of the similar products; and this is called the _____ effect.

5. When demand or supply is graphed, price is placed on the (horizontal, vertical) _____ axis and quantity on the _____ axis.

6. When a consumer demand schedule or curve is drawn up, it is assumed that five factors that determine demand are fixed and constant. These five determinants of consumer demand are:

a. _____
b. _____
c. _____
d. _____
e. _____

7. A decrease in demand means that consumers will buy (larger, smaller) _____ quantities at every price or will pay (more, less) _____ for the same quantities.

8. A change in income or in the price of another product will result in a change in the (demand for, quantity demanded of) _____ the given product, while a change in the price of the given product will result in _____

9. The fundamental factors which determine the supply of any commodity in the product market are:

a. _____
b. _____
c. _____
d. _____
e. _____
f. _____

10. The equilibrium price of a commodity is the price at which _____

11. If quantity demanded exceeds quantity supplied, price is (above, below) _____ the equilibrium price; and the (shortage, surplus) _____ will cause the price to (rise, fall) _____

12. In the spaces below each of the following, indicate the effect [*increase* ($+$), *decrease* ($-$), or *indeterminate* (?)] upon equilibrium price (**P**) and equilibrium quantity (**Q**) of each of these changes in demand and/or supply.

	P	**Q**
a. Increase in demand, supply constant	___	___
b. Increase in supply, demand constant	___	___
c. Decrease in demand, supply constant	___	___
d. Decrease in supply, demand constant	___	___
e. Increase in demand, increase in supply	___	___
f. Increase in demand, decrease in supply	___	___
g. Decrease in demand, decrease in supply	___	___
h. Decrease in demand, increase in supply	___	___

13. If supply and demand establish a price for a good such that there is no shortage or surplus of the good, then price is successfully performing its _____

14. To assume that all the nonprice determinants of demand and supply do not change is to employ the _____ assumption.

15. When the dollar price of foreign currency increases, there has been a(n) (appreciation, depreciation) _____ in value of the dollar. When the dollar price of foreign currency decreases, there has been a(n) _____ in the value of the dollar; for example, if the dollar price of a German mark (DM) decreases from $0.60 = 1 DM to $0.50 = 1 DM, then it means that there has been a(n) _____ in the value of the dollar; but if the dollar price of a German mark increases from $0.40 = 1 DM to $0.55 = 1 DM, then it means that there has been a(n) _____ in the value of the dollar.

16. In the market for Japanese yen, an increase in the (demand for, supply of) _____ yen will decrease the dollar price of yen, while an increase in the _____ yen will increase the dollar price of yen.

If the dollar price of the yen increases, then Japanese goods imported into the United States will be (more, less) _____ expensive to American consumers, while American goods exported to Japan will be _____ expensive for Japanese consumers.

■ **PROBLEMS AND PROJECTS**

1. Using the demand schedule below, plot the demand curve on the graph on the next page. Label the axes and indicate for each axis the units being used to measure price and quantity.

Price	Quantity demanded, 1,000 bushels of soybeans
$7.20	10
7.00	15
6.80	20
6.60	25
6.40	30
6.20	35

a. Plot the supply schedule which follows on the same graph.

Price	Quantity supplied, 1,000 bushels of soybeans
$7.20	40
7.00	35
6.80	30
6.60	25
6.40	20
6.20	15

b. The equilibrium price of soybeans will be $_____

c. How many thousand bushels of soybeans will be exchanged at this price? _____

d. Indicate clearly on the graph the equilibrium price and quantity by drawing lines from the intersection of the supply and demand curves to the price and quantity axes.

e. If the Federal government supported a price of $7.00 per bushel there would be a (shortage, surplus) _____ of _____ bushels of soybeans.

2. The demand schedules of three individuals (Robert, Charles, and Lynn) for loaves of bread are shown on the next page. Assuming there are only three buyers of bread, draw up the total or market demand schedule for bread.

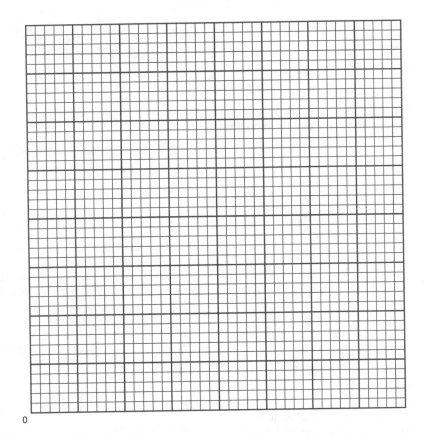

0

	Quantity demanded, loaves of bread			
Price	Robert	Charles	Lynn	Total
$.40	1	4	0	_____
.36	3	5	1	_____
.32	6	6	5	_____
.28	10	7	10	_____
.24	15	8	16	_____

3. Below is a demand schedule for bushels of apples. In columns 3 and 4 insert **any** new figures for quantity which represent in column 3 an increase in demand and in column 4 a decrease in demand.

(1)	(2)	(3)	(4)
Price	Quantity demanded	Demand increases	Demand decreases
$6.00	400	_____	_____
5.90	500	_____	_____
5.80	600	_____	_____
5.70	700	_____	_____
5.60	800	_____	_____
5.50	900	_____	_____

4. Assume that O'Rourke has, when his income is $100 per week, the demand schedule for good A shown in columns 1 and 2 of the table below and the demand schedule for good B shown in columns 4 and 5. Assume that the prices of A and B are $.80 and $5, respectively.

Demand for A (per week)			Demand for B (per week)		
(1)	(2)	(3)	(4)	(5)	(6)
Price	Quantity demanded	Quantity demanded	Price	Quantity demanded	Quantity demanded
$.90	10	0	$5.00	4	7
.85	20	10	4.50	5	8
.80	30	20	4.00	6	9
.75	40	30	3.50	7	10
.70	50	40	3.00	8	11
.65	60	50	2.50	9	12
.60	70	60	2.00	10	13

a. How much A will O'Rourke buy? _____

How much B? _____

b. Suppose that, as a consequence of a $10 increase in O'Rourke's weekly income, the quantities demanded of A become those shown in column 3 and the quantities demanded of B become those shown in column 6.

(1) How much A will he now buy? _____

How much B? _____

(2) Good A is (normal, inferior) _____

(3) Good B is _____

5. The market demand for good X is shown in columns 1 and 2 of the table below. Assume the price of X to be $2 and constant.

(1) Price	(2) Quantity demanded	(3) Quantity demanded	(4) Quantity demanded
$2.40	1,600	1,500	1,700
2.30	1,650	1,550	1,750
2.20	1,750	1,650	1,850
2.10	1,900	1,800	2,000
2.00	2,100	2,000	2,200
1.90	2,350	2,250	2,450
1.80	2,650	2,550	2,750

a. If as the price of good Y rises from $1.25 to $1.35 the quantities demanded of good X become those shown in column 3, it can be concluded that X and Y are (substitute, complementary) _____ goods.

b. If as the price of good Y rises from $1.25 to $1.35 the quantities of good X become those shown in column 4, it can be concluded that X and Y are

_____ goods.

6. In a local market for hamburger on a given date, each of 300 sellers of hamburger has the following supply schedule.

(1) Price	(2) Quantity supplied— one seller, lb.	(3) Quantity supplied— all sellers, lb.
$2.05	150	_____
2.00	110	_____
1.95	75	_____
1.90	45	_____
1.85	20	_____
1.80	0	_____

a. In column 3 construct the market supply schedule for hamburger.

b. At the top of the next column is the market demand schedule for hamburger on the same date and in the same local market as that given above.

Price	Quantity demanded, lb.
$2.05	28,000
2.00	31,000
1.95	36,000
1.90	42,000
1.85	49,000
1.80	57,000

If the Federal government sets a price on hamburger at $1.90 a pound the result would be a (shortage, surplus)

_____

of _____ pounds of hamburger in this market.

7. Each of the following events would tend to increase or decrease either the demand for or the supply of computer games and, as a result, increase or decrease the price of these games. In the first blank indicate the effect upon demand or supply (increase, decrease); and in the second indicate the effect on price (increase, decrease).

a. It becomes known that a local department store is going to have a sale on these games three months from

now. _____ ;

b. The workers who produce the games go on strike for over two months. _____ ;

c. The workers in the industry receive a 90-cent-an-hour wage increase. _____ ;

d. The average price of movie tickets increases.

_____ ; _____

e. The firms producing the games undertake to produce a large volume of missile components for the Defense Department. _____ ;

f. It is announced by a private research institute that children who have taken to playing computer games also improve their grades in school. _____ ;

g. Because of the use of mass-production techniques, the amount of labor necessary to produce a game decreases. _____ ;

h. The price of computers increases _____ ;

i. The average consumer believes that a shortage of games is developing in the economy. ⎯⎯⎯⎯⎯⎯⎯;

⎯⎯⎯⎯⎯⎯⎯⎯⎯⎯⎯⎯⎯⎯⎯⎯⎯⎯⎯⎯⎯⎯⎯⎯⎯

j. The Federal government imposes a $5 per game tax upon the manufacturers of computer games. ⎯⎯⎯⎯

⎯⎯⎯⎯⎯⎯⎯⎯⎯⎯; ⎯⎯⎯⎯⎯⎯⎯⎯⎯⎯⎯

■ SELF-TEST

Circle the T if the statement is true; the F if it is false.

1. A market is any arrangement that brings the buyers and sellers of a particular good or service together. **T F**

2. Demand is the amount of a commodity or service which a buyer will purchase at a particular price. **T F**

3. The law of demand states that as price increases, other things being equal, the quantity of the product demanded increases. **T F**

4. In graphing supply and demand schedules, supply is put on the horizontal axis and demand on the vertical axis. **T F**

5. If price falls, there will be an increase in demand. **T F**

6. If the demand curve moves from D_1 to D_2 in the graph shown below, demand has increased. **T F**

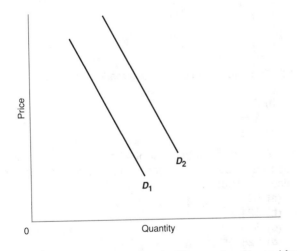
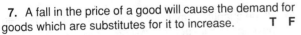

7. A fall in the price of a good will cause the demand for goods which are substitutes for it to increase. **T F**

8. If two goods are complementary, an increase in the price of one will cause the demand for the other to increase. **T F**

9. If the market price of a commodity is for a time below its equilibrium price, the market price will tend to rise because demand will decrease and supply will increase. **T F**

10. The equilibrium price of a good is the price at which the demand and the supply of the good are equal. **T F**

11. The rationing function of prices is the elimination of shortages and surpluses. **T F**

12. The interaction of the demand for, and supply of, Japanese yen will establish the dollar price of Japanese yen. **T F**

13. An increase in incomes in the United States would tend to cause the dollar price of the Japanese yen to fall. **T F**

14. When the dollar price of another nation's currency increases, there has been an appreciation in the value of the dollar. **T F**

15. When the dollar depreciates relative to the value of the currencies of the trading partners of the United States, then goods imported into the United States will tend to become more expensive. **T F**

Circle the letter that corresponds to the best answer.

1. The markets examined in this chapter are:
(a) purely competitive markets
(b) markets for goods and services
(c) markets for products and resources
(d) all of the above

2. Which of the following could cause a decrease in consumer demand for product X?
(a) a decrease in consumer income
(b) an increase in the prices of goods which are good substitutes for product X
(c) an increase in the price which consumers expect will prevail for product X in the future
(d) a decrease in the supply of product X

3. If two goods are substitutes for each other, an increase in the price of one will necessarily:
(a) decrease the demand for the other
(b) increase the demand for the other
(c) decrease the quantity demanded of the other
(d) increase the quantity demanded of the other

4. The income of a consumer decreases and his/her demand for a particular good increases. It can be concluded that the good is:
(a) normal
(b) inferior
(c) a substitute
(d) a complement

5. If the supply curve moves from S_1 to S_2 on the graph below, there has been:
(a) an increase in supply
(b) a decrease in supply
(c) an increase in quantity supplied
(d) a decrease in quantity supplied

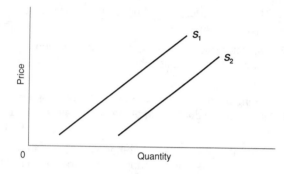

6. An increase in demand and a decrease in supply will:
(a) increase price and increase the quantity exchanged
(b) decrease price and decrease the quantity exchanged
(c) increase price and the effect upon quantity exchanged will be indeterminate
(d) decrease price and the effect upon quantity exchanged will be indeterminate

7. An increase in supply and an increase in demand will:
(a) increase price and increase the quantity exchanged
(b) decrease price and increase the quantity exchanged
(c) affect price in an indeterminate way and decrease the quantity exchanged
(d) affect price in an indeterminate way and increase the quantity exchanged

8. Which of the following could *not* cause an increase in the supply of cotton?
(a) an increase in the price of cotton
(b) improvements in the art of producing cotton
(c) a decrease in the price of the machinery and tools employed in cotton production
(d) a decrease in the price of corn

9. The law of supply states that, other things being constant, as price increases:
(a) supply increases
(b) supply decreases
(c) quantity supplied increases
(d) quantity supplied decreases

10. Demand and supply may be employed to explain how price is determined in:
(a) product markets
(b) resource markets
(c) markets for foreign currency
(d) all of the above markets

11. When government sets the price of a good and that price is below the equilibrium price the result will be:
(a) a surplus of the good
(b) a shortage of the good
(c) an increase in the demand for the good
(d) a decrease in the supply of the good

12. A decrease in supply and a decrease in demand will:
(a) increase price and decrease the quantity exchanged
(b) decrease price and increase the quantity exchanged
(c) increase price and affect the quantity exchanged in an indeterminate way
(d) affect price in an indeterminate way and decrease the quantity exchanged

13. A decrease in the price of a product would most likely be caused by:
(a) an increase in business taxes
(b) an increase in consumer incomes
(c) a decrease in resource costs for production
(d) a decrease in the price of a complementary good

*The next three questions (**14, 15,** and **16**) refer to the following table. Consider the following supply and demand schedules for corn.*

Price	Quantity demanded	Quantity supplied
$20	395	200
22	375	250
24	350	290
26	320	320
28	280	345
30	235	365

14. The equilibrium price in this market is:
(a) $22
(b) $24
(c) $26
(d) $28

15. An increase in the cost of labor lowers the quantity supplied by 65 units at each price. The new equilibrium price would be:
(a) $22
(b) $24
(c) $26
(d) $28

16. If the quantity demanded increases by 130 units, then the new equilibrium quantity will be:
(a) 290
(b) 320
(c) 345
(d) 365

17. Assume that in a competitive market video tape players (VCRs) double in price. What will most likely happen in that market to the equilibrium price and quantity of video tapes?
(a) price will increase; quantity will decrease
(b) price will decrease; quantity will increase
(c) price will decrease; quantity will decrease
(d) price will increase; quantity will increase

18. If the equilibrium exchange rate changes so that the dollar price of Japanese yen increases:
(a) the dollar has appreciated in value
(b) the dollar has depreciated in value
(c) Americans will be able to buy more Japanese goods
(d) Japanese will be able to buy fewer U.S. goods

19. A decrease in the United States demand for Japanese goods will:
(a) increase the demand for Japanese yen and increase the dollar price of yen
(b) increase the demand for Japanese yen but decrease the dollar price of yen
(c) decrease the demand for Japanese yen and decrease the dollar price of yen
(d) decrease the demand for Japanese yen but increase the dollar price of yen

20. If the exchange rate for one United States dollar changes from 1.4 German marks to 1.7 German marks, then there has been:
(a) an appreciation in the value of the mark
(b) a depreciation in the value of the dollar
(c) a depreciation in the value of the mark
(d) an increase in the price of the mark

■ DISCUSSION QUESTIONS

1. How is a market defined?

2. Carefully define demand and state the law of demand. Now define supply and state the law of supply.

3. Two decades ago the price of coffee in the United States rose as a result of bad weather in coffee-producing regions. Employ the income-effect and the substitution effect concepts to explain why the quantity of coffee demanded in the U.S. declined dramatically. A few years later when the weather became normal the price of coffee fell. Use the diminishing-marginal-utility notion to explain why the quantity of coffee demanded rose.

4. Explain the difference between an increase in demand and an increase in quantity demanded, and between a decrease in supply and a decrease in quantity supplied.

5. Neither demand nor supply remains constant for long because the factors which determine demand and supply

do not long remain constant. What are these factors? How do changes in them affect demand and supply?

6. How are normal, inferior, substitute, complementary, and independent goods defined, and how can these concepts be used to predict the way in which a change in income or in the price of another good will affect the demand for a given good?

7. Given the demand for and the supply of a commodity, what price will be the equilibrium price of this commodity? Explain why this price will tend to prevail in the market and why higher (lower) prices, if they do exist temporarily, will tend to fall (rise).

8. Analyze the following quotation and explain the fallacies contained in it: "An increase in demand will cause price to rise; with a rise in price, supply will increase and the increase in supply will push price down. Therefore, an increase in demand results in little change in price because supply will increase also."

9. What is meant by the "rationing function of prices"?

10. What is the difference between individual and market demand; and what is the relationship between these two types of demand? Does this distinction and relationship also apply to individual and market supply?

11. Why might an appreciation of the value of the United States dollar relative to the Japanese yen depress the American economy and stimulate the Japanese economy? Why might a government intervene in the foreign exchange market and try to increase or decrease the value of its currency?

■ ANSWERS

Chapter 4 Understanding Individual Markets: Demand and Supply

FILL-IN QUESTIONS

1. buyers (demanders), sellers (suppliers) (either order); *a.* business firms, households; *b.* households, business firms

2. inverse, direct

3. diminishing marginal utility

4. *a.* income; *b.* substitution

5. vertical, horizontal

6. *a.* the tastes or preferences of consumers; *b.* the number of consumers in the market; *c.* the money income of consumers; *d.* the prices of related goods; *e.* consumer expectations with respect to future prices and incomes

7. smaller, less

8. demand for, a change in the quantity demanded of the product

9. *a.* the technique of production; *b.* resource prices; *c.* taxes and subsidies; *d.* prices of other goods; *e.* price expectations; *f.* the number of sellers in the market

10. quantity demanded and quantity supplied are equal

11. below, shortage, rise

12. *a.* +, +; *b.* −, +; *c.* −, −; *d.* +, −; *e.* ?, +; *f.* +, ?; *g.* ?, −; *h.* −, ?

13. rationing function

14. other things being equal

15. depreciation, appreciation, appreciation, depreciation

16. supply of, demand for, more, less

PROBLEMS AND PROJECTS

1. *b.* 6.60; *c.* 25,000; *e.* surplus, 20,000

2. Total: 5, 9, 17, 27, 39

3. Each quantity in column 3 is greater than in column 2, and each quantity in column 4 is less than in column 2.

4. *a.* 30, 4; *b.* (1) 20, 7; (2) inferior; (3) normal (superior)

5. *a.* complementary; *b.* substitute

6. *a.* 45,000; 33,000; 22,500; 13,500; 6,000; 0 *b.* shortage, 28,500

7. *a.* decrease demand, decrease price; *b.* decrease supply, increase price; *c.* decrease supply, increase price; *d.* increase demand, increase price; *e.* decrease supply, increase price; *f.* increase demand, increase price; *g.* increase supply, decrease price; *h.* decrease demand, decrease price, *i.* increase demand, increase price; *j.* decrease supply, increase price

SELF-TEST

1. T, p. 47
2. F, p. 48
3. F, p. 48
4. F, pp. 49−50
5. F, pp. 49−50
6. T, pp. 51−52
7. F, p. 52
8. F, p. 52
9. F, p. 57
10. F, p. 57
11. T, p. 58
12. T, pp. 62−63
13. F, pp. 63−64
14. F, pp. 63−64
15. T, p. 64

1. *d,* p. 47
2. *a,* pp. 50−51
3. *b,* p. 49
4. *b,* p. 52
5. *a,* pp. 55−56
6. *c,* pp. 60−61
7. *d,* p. 61
8. *a,* pp. 55−56
9. *c,* p. 54
10. *d,* p. 61
11. *b,* pp. 57−58
12. *d,* pp. 60−61
13. *c,* pp. 59−60
14. *c,* pp. 57−58
15. *d,* pp. 55−57
16. *d,* pp. 51, 59
17. *c,* p. 52
18. *b,* pp. 63−64
19. *c,* p. 64
20. *c,* pp. 63−64

DISCUSSION QUESTIONS

1. p. 47
2. pp. 48−49, 54
3. pp. 48−49
4. pp. 51−53; 55−56
5. pp. 50−53; 55−56
6. p. 52
7. pp. 57−58
8. pp. 58−61
9. p. 58
10. pp. 50, 54
11. pp. 63−64

CHAPTER 5

The Private Sectors and the Market System

In the American economy, there are private sectors and a public sector. Chapter 5 discusses the private sectors: the 94 million households, the roughly 18 million business firms in the country, and our trade with other nations in the foreign sector. Chapter 6 deals with the public sector of the economy: the Federal, state, and local governments found in the United States. These two chapters will acquaint you with a few of the facts relevant to an understanding of our economy.

Also, in Chapters 2, 3, and 4 you examined the institutions and characteristics of pure capitalism and saw how supply and demand determine equilibrium prices and equilibrium quantities in resource and product markets. The second part of Chapter 5 draws these elements together into an explanation of the ways in which the market system finds answers to basic economic questions.

Chapter 5 begins with an examination of the households of the economy, the distribution of income in the United States, and the uses to which the households put their incomes. Two different distributions of income are examined. American households earn five kinds of income and receive transfer payments. The way in which the total personal income received by all American households is divided among the five types of earned income and transfer payments is called the *functional distribution.* The way in which the total personal income received by all households is distributed among the various income classes is called the *personal* distribution of income. Attention should be concentrated on the *general* facts of income distribution (not the exact figures), the conclusions which are drawn from these general facts, and the definitions of the new terms employed. In the examination of the different uses households make of their incomes, several new terms and concepts are introduced; and figures are employed in the discussion. Again, attention should be paid to the generalizations and to the new terms.

Business firms of the United States are the next focus of the chapter. It is apparent that what most characterizes American business is the differences among firms insofar as their size and legal form are concerned, as well as in the products they produce. You should note the distinc-

tions between a proprietorship, a partnership, and a corporation and the advantages and disadvantages of each.

You will also find that the American economy can be divided into ten sectors or industry classes. The privately owned business firms are found in eight of these industry classes. These eight sectors are not equal in terms of the number of firms in the class, the contribution to the national income made by the industry class, and the number of full-time workers employed by the sector. These facts serve as an introduction to two major observations. In the economy as a whole and in the manufacturing sector a relatively few firms produce a relatively large part of the output of that sector.

These two observations indicate that big business is an important characteristic of the American economy. The corollary of these observations is that the American economy also has a large number of small business firms. But the problems created by big business and the ways in which government deals with these problems are topics examined later in the text.

The discussion of the private sectors concludes with a look at the foreign sector of the economy of the United States. The volume, patterns, and linkages of our trade with the rest of the world are described. In addition, our growing international trade has economic implications for our: (1) living standards; (2) ability to compete in a world economy; (3) banking and finance; and (4) macroeconomic instability and policy.

The latter part of Chapter 5 describes the operation of the competitive market system. There are Five Fundamental Questions that any economic system must answer in attempting to use its scarce resources to satisfy its material wants. The five questions or problems are: (1) How much output is to be produced? (2) What is to be produced? (3) How is the output to be produced? (4) Who is to receive the output? (5) Can the economic system adapt to change? Only the last four questions will be discussed in this chapter. Answers to the first question will await the presentation of material on macroeconomics.

The explanation of how the market system finds answers to the last four of the Five Fundamental Questions is only an approximation—a simplified version or a model—of the methods actually employed by the American economy. Yet this simple model, like all good models, contains enough realism to be truthful and is general enough to be understandable.

The "Operation of the Market System" is both the most important part of this chapter and the part you will find most difficult. If you will try to understand how the American system of prices and markets finds answers for each of the four basic questions by examining them *individually* and in the order in which they are presented, you will more easily understand how the market system as a whole operates. Actually the market system finds answers for all these questions simultaneously, but it is much simpler to consider them as if they were separate questions.

A few final words of advice to you. Be sure to understand the *importance* and *role* of each of the following in the operation of the market system: (1) the rationing and directing functions of prices, (2) the profit motive of business firms, (3) the entry into and exodus of firms from industries, (4) competition, and (5) consumer sovereignty.

□ Explain how a competitive market system determines what will be produced.
□ Distinguish between normal profit and economic profit.
□ Predict what will happen to the price charged by and the output of a prosperous and an unprosperous industry; and explain why these events will occur.
□ Explain how production is organized in a competitive market system.
□ Find the least-cost combination of resources when you are given the technological data and the prices of the resources.
□ Explain how a competitive market system determines the distribution of total output.
□ Describe the guiding function of prices to accommodate change in the competitive market system.
□ Explain how the competitive market system initiates change by fostering technological advances and capital accumulation.
□ State how the "invisible hand" in the competitive market system tends to promote public or social interests.
□ Present the case for the competitive market system.

■ **CHECKLIST**

When you have studied this chapter you should be able to:

□ Define and distinguish between a functional and a personal distribution of income.
□ State the relative size of the five sources of personal income in the functional distribution.
□ List the three uses to which households put their personal incomes and state the relative size of each.
□ Distinguish among durable goods, nondurable goods, and services.
□ Explain the difference among a plant, a firm, and an industry; and between limited and unlimited liability.
□ State the advantages and disadvantages of the three legal forms of business enterprise.
□ Report the relative importance of each of the legal forms of business enterprise in the American economy.
□ State which two industry classes contain the largest and the smallest number of privately owned business firms, produce the largest and the smallest percentages of the national income, and employ the greatest and the smallest number of full-time workers.
□ Cite evidence to indicate that large corporations dominate the economy and some major American industries; and indicate in which industry classes big business is and is not a dominant force.
□ Describe the main characteristics of our volume and pattern of trade with other nations.
□ Explain four economic implications of our growing international trade.
□ Identify the Five Fundamental Questions.

■ **CHAPTER OUTLINE**

1. Households play a dual role in the economy. They supply the economy with resources, and they purchase the greatest share of the goods and services produced by the economy. They obtain their personal incomes in exchange for the resources they furnish the economy and from the transfer payments they receive from government.

   a. The functional distribution of income indicates the way in which total personal income is divided among the five sources of earned income (wages and salaries, proprietors' income, corporate profits, interest, and rents) and transfer payments.

   b. The personal distribution of income indicates the way in which total personal income is divided among households in different income classes.

2. Households use their incomes to purchase consumer goods, to pay taxes, and to accumulate savings.

   a. Personal taxes constitute a deduction from a household's personal income; what remains after taxes can be either saved or spent.

   b. Saving is what a household does not spend of its after-tax income.

   c. Households spend for durable goods, nondurable goods, and services.

3. The business population of the American economy consists of many imperfectly defined and overlapping industries; business firms which operate one or more plants and produce one or more products are the components of these industries.

4. The three principal legal forms of organization of firms are the proprietorship, the partnership, and the corporation; each form has special characteristics, advantages, and disadvantages. The form of organization which any business firm should adopt depends primarily upon the amount of money capital it will require to carry on its business. Although the proprietorship is numerically dominant in the United States, the corporation accounts for the major portion of the economy's output.

5. An examination of the ten industry classes found in the American economy reveals at least four important facts and leads to the conclusion that large firms are a characteristic of the American economy and that many of its industries are dominated by big businesses.

6. The merchandise trade of the United States with other nations has increased in absolute terms and as a percentage of our national output. Our major trading partner is Canada, not Japan. In recent years, the United States has had trade deficits because our economy has imported more goods and services than it has exported to other nations. These large trade deficits are financed by borrowing from other nations.

7. International trade produces sizable economic benefits because there is more efficient use of world resources and it strengthens competition. The dramatic improvements in communications also mean that the banking industry and financial markets operate on a global basis. The one potential drawback of the increased trade is that the domestic economy is more vulnerable to influence from changes in the world economy. The involvement in a world economy becomes a potential source of macroeconomic instability in the domestic economy and can present new problems for economic policymakers.

8. There are Five Fundamental Questions which must be answered by every economic system:
   (1) How much output is to be produced?
   (2) What is to be produced?
   (3) How is output to be produced?
   (4) Who is to receive the output?
   (5) Can the economic system adapt to change?

9. The system of prices and markets and the choices of households and business firms furnish the economy with answers to the last four Fundamental Questions.
   a. The demands of consumers for products and the desires of business firms to maximize their profits determine what and how much of each product is produced (and its price).
   b. The desires of business firms to maximize profits by keeping their costs of production as low as possible guide them to employ the most efficient techniques of production and determine their demands for and prices of the various resources; competition forces them to use the most efficient techniques and ensures that only the most efficient will be able to stay in business.

   c. With resource prices determined, the money income of each household is determined; and with product prices determined, the quantity of goods and services which these money incomes will buy is determined.
   d. The market system is able to accommodate itself to changes in consumer tastes, technology, and resource supplies.
   (1) The desires of business firms for maximum profits and competition lead the economy to make the appropriate adjustments in the way it uses its resources.
   (2) Competition and the desire to increase profits promote both better techniques of production and capital accumulation.
   e. Competition in the economy compels firms seeking to promote their own interests to promote (as though led by an "invisible hand") the best interest of society as a whole: an allocation of resources appropriate to consumer wants, production by the most efficient means, and the lowest possible prices.

10. The market system has been praised for its merits. The two major merits of the system are that it efficiently allocates scarce resources and allows individuals large amounts of personal freedom.

■ IMPORTANT TERMS

Private sectors	Limited liability
Functional distribution of income	Double taxation
Personal distribution of income	Separation of ownership and control
Personal consumption expenditures	Five Fundamental Questions
Durable good	Normal profit
Nondurable good	Economic cost
Services	Economic profit
Personal taxes	Expanding (prosperous) industry
Personal saving	Declining (unprosperous) industry
Plant	
Firm	Dollar votes
Industry	Consumer sovereignty
Horizontal combination	Derived demand
Vertical combination	Guiding function of prices
Conglomerate combination	Self-limiting adjustment
Sole proprietorship	Technological advance
Partnership	Capital accumulation
Corporation	Invisible hand
Unlimited liability	Allocative efficiency

■ **FILL-IN QUESTIONS**

1. The approximately _____ million house-holds in the United States play a dual role in the economy because they _____

and _____

_____

2. The largest single source of income in the United States is _____ and is equal to about _____% of total income.

3. In the United States the poorest 20% of all American families receive about _____% of total personal income and the richest 20% of these families receive about _____% of total personal income.

4. The total income of households is disposed of in three ways: _____ ,

_____ ,

and _____

5. Households use about _____% of their total income to pay personal taxes; and the greatest part of their personal taxes are the personal _____ taxes which they pay to the (Federal, state, local) _____ government.

6. Households save primarily in order to obtain _____ and for purposes of _____

7. Based on their durability, consumer spending is classified as spending for _____ ,

_____ ,

and _____

8. There are today about _____ business firms in the United States. The legal form of the great majority of these firms is the _____; but the legal form that produces over one-half the output of the American economy is the _____

9. The liabilities of a sole proprietor and of partners are _____ but the liabilities of stockholders in a corporation are _____

10. Indicate in the spaces to the right of each of the following whether these business characteristics are associated with the proprietorship (PRO), partnership (PART),

corporation (CORP), two of these, or all three of these legal forms.

a. Much red tape and legal expense in beginning the firm _____

b. Unlimited liability _____

c. No specialized management _____

d. Has a life independent of its owner(s) _____

e. Double taxation of income _____

f. Greatest ability to acquire funds for the expansion of the firm _____

g. Permits some but not a great degree of specialized management _____

h. Possibility of an unresolved disagreement among owners over courses of action _____

i. The potential for the separation of ownership and control of the business _____

11. Of the eight industry classes in which privately owned business firms are found:

a. The two which contain the greatest number of firms are _____ and _____

b. The two which make the largest contribution to the national income and employ the most full-time workers are _____ and _____ trade.

12. The public sector produces roughly one-_____-th of all the goods and services produced in the American economy.

13. The United States is often called a big business economy because a relatively _____ firms produce a relatively _____ part of the output of the economy and of some industries.

14. The imports and exports of the United States are about _____% of the domestic output.

15. Our major trading partner is _____

16. The United States incurred a $_____ billion trade (surplus, deficit) _____ in 1990.

17. List four economic implications of growing international trade and finance:

a. _____

b. _____

c. _____

d. _____

18. List the Five Fundamental Questions which every economy must answer.

a. _____

b. _____

c. _____

d. _____

e. _____

19. The competitive market system is a mechanism for both _____ the decisions of producers and households and _____ these decisions.

20. A *normal* profit (is, is not) _____ an economic cost because it is a payment that (must, need not) _____ be paid to (workers, landowners, suppliers of capital goods, entrepreneurs) _____ but a *pure* (or *economic*) profit (is, is not) _____ an economic cost because it (must, need not) _____ be paid to them to obtain and retain the services they provide to the firm.

21. Pure or economic profits are equal to the total _____ of a firm less its total _____

22. Business firms tend to produce those products from which they can obtain:

a. at least a (pure, normal) _____ profit; and

b. the maximum _____ profit.

23. If firms in an industry are obtaining economic profits, firms will (enter, leave) _____ the industry, the price of the industry's product will (rise, fall) _____, the industry will employ (more, fewer) _____ resources, produce a (larger, smaller) _____ output, and the industry's economic profits will (increase, decrease) _____ until they are equal to _____

24. Consumers:

a. vote with their _____ for the production of a good or service when they buy that good or service;

b. are said, because firms are motivated by their desire for profits to produce the goods and services consumers vote for in this way, to be (dependent, sovereign) _____

c. (restrict, expand) _____ the freedom of firms and resource suppliers.

25. Because firms are interested in obtaining the largest economic profits possible the technique they select to produce a product is the one that enables them to produce that product in the least _____ly way.

26. In determining how the total output of the economy will be divided among its households the market system is involved in two ways:

a. it determines the money _____ each of the households receives; and

b. it determines the _____ they have to pay for each of the goods and services produced.

27. In industrial economies:

a. the changes which occur almost continuously are changes in consumer _____, in _____, and in the supplies of _____;

b. to make the adjustments in the way it uses its resources that are appropriate to these changes a market economy allows price to perform its _____ function.

28. The competitive market system tends to foster technological change.

a. The incentive for a firm to be the first to employ a new and improved technique of production or to produce a new and better product is a greater economic _____;

b. and the incentive for other firms to follow its lead is the avoidance of _____

29. The entrepreneur uses money which is obtained either from _____ or from _____ to acquire capital goods.

30. If the market system is competitive, there is an identity of _____ interests and the _____ interest: firms seem to be guided by an _____ to allocate the economy's resources efficiently.

31. The chief economic advantage of the market system is that _____ and its chief noneconomic advantage is that _____ _____ _____

■ **PROBLEMS AND PROJECTS**

1. The table below shows the functional distribution of total income in the United States in 1990.

	Billions of dollars
Wages and salaries	$2,905
Proprietors' income	325
Corporate profits	324
Interest	392
Rents	19
Total earnings	3,964

Of the total earnings about _____% were wages and salaries, and about _____% were corporate profits.

2. Below are six numbers and each of them is a percentage. Match these six numbers with the six phrases that follow:

82	12
35	11
56	9

A. Percentage of U.S. merchandise exports going to developing countries. _____

B. Percentage of the domestic output which is contributed by the government sector of the economy. _____

C. Percentage of the privately owned business firms in the United States which are in the agriculture, forestry, and fishing sector of the economy. _____

D. Percentage of business firms in the United States which are partnerships. _____

E. Percentage of personal consumption expenditures which are for services. _____

F. Percentage of the income of consumers which is used for personal consumption expenditures. _____

3. Indicate to the best of your ability in which industry *class* you would put each of these firms.
  a. Sears, Roebuck and Company
  b. The General Electric Company
  c. A used-car dealer in your town
  d. Macy department stores
  e. Your local electric company
  f. A new-car dealer
  g. The Mars Candy Company
  h. The Aluminum Company of America
  i. The Revere Copper and Brass Company
  j. General Mills

4. Assume that a firm can produce *either* product A, product B, or product C with the resources it currently employs.

These resources cost the firm a total of $50 per week. Assume, for the purposes of the problem, that the firm's employment of resources cannot be changed. The market prices of and the quantities of A, B, and C these resources will produce per week are given below. Compute the firm's profit when it produces A, B, or C; and enter these profits in the table below.

Product	Market price	Output	Economic profit
A	$7.00	8	$_____
B	4.50	10	_____
C	.25	240	_____

a. Which product will the firm produce? _____

b. If the price of A rose to $8, the firm would _____

_____

(Hint: You will have to recompute the firm's profit from the production of A.)

c. If the firm were producing A and selling it at a price of $8, what would tend to happen to the number of firms producing A?

_____

5. Suppose that a firm can produce 100 units of product X by combining labor, land, capital, and entrepreneurial ability in three different ways. If it can hire labor at $2 per unit, land at $3 per unit, capital at $5 per unit, and entrepreneurship at $10 per unit; and if the amounts of the resources required by the three methods of producing 100 units of product X are indicated in the table, answer the questions below it.

	Method		
Resource	1	2	3
Labor	8	13	10
Land	4	3	3
Capital	4	2	4
Entrepreneurship	1	1	1

a. Which method is the least expensive way of producing 100 units of X? _____

b. If X sells for 70 cents per unit, what is the economic profit of the firm? $_____

c. If the price of labor should rise from $2 to $3 per unit and if the price of X is 70 cents,
(1) the firm's use of:

Labor would change from _____ to _____

Land would change from _____ to _____

Capital would change from _____ to _____

Entrepreneurship would not change.

(2) The firm's economic profit would change from
$_____ to $_____

■ **SELF-TEST**

Circle the T if the statement is true; the F if it is false.

1. The personal distribution of income describes the manner in which society's total personal income is divided among wages and salaries, corporate profits, proprietors' income, interest, and rents.   **T   F**

2. Limited liability refers to the fact that all members of a partnership are liable for the debts incurred by one another.   **T   F**

3. In both relative and absolute terms, personal taxes have exceeded personal saving in recent years.   **T   F**

4. Most of the personal saving in the American economy is done by those households in the top 10% of its income receivers.   **T   F**

5. *Dissaving* means that personal consumption expenditures exceed after-tax income.   **T   F**

6. A "durable good" is defined as a good which has an expected life of one year or more.   **T   F**

7. A plant is defined as a group of firms under a single management.   **T   F**

8. An industry is a group of firms that produce the same or nearly the same products.   **T   F**

9. The corporate form of organization is the least used by firms in the United States.   **T   F**

10. The corporation in the United States today always has a tax advantage over other legal forms of business organization.   **T   F**

11. Whether a business firm should incorporate or not depends chiefly upon the amount of money capital it must have to finance the enterprise.   **T   F**

12. The wholesale and retail trade and the service industries contain a relatively large number of firms but are not important sources of income and employment in the American economy.   **T   F**

13. Corporations produce over one-half the total output produced by privately owned business firms in the United States.   **T   F**

14. Increased international trade creates more macroeconomic stability for the United States.   **T   F**

15. Foreign competition gives consumers a greater variety of goods and services and forces domestic producers to be more efficient.   **T   F**

16. Business firms try to maximize their normal profits.   **T   F**

17. Industries in which economic profits are earned by the firms in the industry will attract the entry of new firms into the industry.   **T   F**

18. If firms have sufficient time to enter industries, the economic profits of an industry will tend to disappear.   **T   F**

19. Business firms are really only free to produce whatever they want in any way they wish if they do not want to maximize profits or to minimize losses.   **T   F**

20. To say that the demand for a resource is a derived demand means that it depends upon the demands for the products the resource is used to produce.   **T   F**

21. Resources will tend to be used in those industries capable of earning normal or economic profits.   **T   F**

22. Economic efficiency requires that a given output of a good or service be produced in the least costly way.   **T   F**

23. If the market price of resource A decreases, firms will tend to employ smaller quantities of resource A.   **T   F**

24. Changes in the tastes of consumers are reflected in changes in consumer demand for products.   **T   F**

25. The incentive which the market system provides to induce technological improvement is the opportunity for economic profits.   **T   F**

26. In a capitalistic economy it is from the entrepreneur that the demand for capital goods arises.   **T   F**

27. The tendency for individuals pursuing their own self-interests to bring about results which are in the best interest of society as a whole is often called the "invisible hand."   **T   F**

28. The basic economic argument for the market system is that it promotes an efficient allocation of resources.   **T   F**

29. One of the Five Fundamental Questions is who will control the output.   **T   F**

Circle the letter that corresponds to the best answer.

1. The functional distribution for the United States shows that the largest part of the personal income is:
   (a) wages and salaries
   (b) proprietors' income
   (c) corporate profits
   (d) interest and rents

2. The part of after-tax income which is not consumed is defined as:
 (a) saving
 (b) capital investment
 (c) wages and salaries
 (d) nondurable goods expenditure

3. If in an economy personal consumption expenditures were 80% of income and personal taxes were 8% of income, then personal savings would be:
 (a) 8% of income
 (b) 10% of income
 (c) 12% of income
 (d) 88% of income

4. Expenditures for *nondurable* goods in recent years have amounted to approximately what percentage of personal consumption expenditures?
 (a) 32%
 (b) 42%
 (c) 50%
 (d) 65%

5. Which of the following is a true statement?
 (a) the durable goods and service parts of personal consumption expenditures vary more over time than do the expenditures for nondurables
 (b) expenditures for nondurables vary more than do the expenditures for durable goods and services
 (c) expenditures for nondurables vary more than the expenditures for services and less than the expenditures for durables
 (d) expenditures for nondurables vary more than the expenditures for durables and less than the expenditures for services

6. In recent years personal taxes have been approximately what percentage of total income?
 (a) 13%
 (b) 22%
 (c) 24%
 (d) 80%

7. Approximately how many million business firms are there in the United States?
 (a) 5
 (b) 8
 (c) 18
 (d) 28

8. A group of three plants which is owned and operated by a single firm and which consists of a farm growing wheat, a flour milling plant, and a plant which bakes and sells bakery products is an example of:
 (a) a horizontal combination
 (b) a vertical combination
 (c) a conglomerate combination
 (d) a corporation

9. Limited liability is associated with:
 (a) only proprietorships
 (b) only partnerships
 (c) both proprietorships and partnerships
 (d) only corporations

10. Which of the following forms of business organization can most effectively raise money capital?
 (a) corporation
 (b) partnership
 (c) proprietorship
 (d) vertical combination

11. Which of the following industry classes has the largest number of firms?
 (a) agriculture, forestry, and fishing
 (b) manufacturing
 (c) wholesale and retail trade
 (d) mining

12. About what percentage of the domestic output of the United States is produced by government?
 (a) 3%
 (b) 5%
 (c) 10%
 (d) 12%

13. A deficit in merchandise trade with other nations is produced when a nation's:
 (a) exports are greater than imports
 (b) imports are greater than exports
 (c) imports are greater than currency appreciation
 (d) exports are greater than currency appreciation

14. One of the major benefits of international trade and finance for the United States is:
 (a) lower living standards
 (b) less efficient use of world resources
 (c) greater competition among businesses
 (d) greater economic security for domestic banks and financial markets

15. If incomes increased significantly in the major industrial countries that trade with the United States, this development would most likely:
 (a) increase United States exports
 (b) decrease United States exports
 (c) decrease United States imports of oil
 (d) have no significant effect on the imports or exports of the United States

16. The competitive market system is a method of:
 (a) communicating and synchronizing the decisions of consumers, producers, and resource suppliers
 (b) centrally planning economic decisions
 (c) promoting productive efficiency, but not allocative efficiency
 (d) promoting allocative efficiency, but not productive efficiency

17. Which of the following best defines economic costs?
(a) total payments made to workers, landowners, suppliers of capital, and entrepreneurs
(b) only total payments made to workers, landowners, suppliers of capital, and entrepreneurs which must be paid to obtain the services of their resources
(c) total payments made to workers, landowners, suppliers of capital, and entrepreneurs less normal profits
(d) total payments made to workers, landowners, suppliers of capital, and entrepreneurs plus normal profits

18. If less-than-normal profits are being earned by the firms in an industry, the consequences will be that:
(a) lower-priced resources will be drawn into the industry
(b) firms will leave the industry, causing the price of the industry's product to fall
(c) firms will leave the industry, causing the price of the industry's product to rise
(d) the price of the industry's product will fall and thereby cause the demand for the product to increase

19. Which of the following would *not* necessarily result, sooner or later, from a decrease in consumer demand for a product?
(a) a decrease in the profits of the industry producing the product
(b) a decrease in the output of the industry
(c) a decrease in the supply of the product
(d) an increase in the prices of resources employed by the firms in the industry

20. If firm A does not employ the most "efficient" or least costly method of production, which of the following will *not* be a consequence?
(a) firm A will fail to earn the greatest profit possible
(b) other firms in the industry will be able to sell the product at lower prices
(c) new firms will enter the industry and sell the product at a lower price than that at which firm A now sells it
(d) firm A will be spending less on resources and hiring fewer resources than it otherwise would

21. Which of the following is *not* a factor in determining the share of the total output of the economy received by any household?
(a) the price at which the household sells its resources
(b) the quantities of resources which the household sells
(c) the tastes of the household
(d) the prices which the household must pay to buy products

22. If an increase in the demand for a product and the resulting rise in the price of the product cause the supply of the product, the size of the industry producing the prod-

uct, and the amounts of resources devoted to its production to expand, price is successfully performing its:
(a) guiding function
(b) rationing function
(c) medium-of-exchange function
(d) standard-of-value function

23. In a capitalistic economy characterized by competition, if one firm introduces a new and better method of production, other firms will be forced to adopt the improved technique:
(a) to avoid less-than-normal profits
(b) to obtain economic profits
(c) to prevent the price of the product from falling
(d) to prevent the price of the product from rising

24. Which of the following would be an indication that competition does not exist in an industry?
(a) less-than-normal profits in the industry
(b) inability of the firms in the industry to expand
(c) inability of firms to enter the industry
(d) wages lower than the average wage in the economy paid to workers in the industry

25. The chief economic virtue of the competitive market system remains that of:
(a) allowing extensive personal freedom
(b) efficiently allocating resources
(c) providing an equitable distribution of income
(d) eliminating the need for decision making

*Answer the next two questions (**26** and **27**) on the basis of the following information.*

Suppose 50 units of product X can be produced by employing just labor and capital in the four ways shown below. Assume the prices of labor and capital are $5 and $4, respectively.

	A	B	C	D
Labor	1	2	3	4
Capital	5	3	2	1

26. Which technique is economically most efficient in producing product X?
(a) A
(b) B
(c) C
(d) D

27. If the price of product X is $1.00, then the firm will realize:
(a) an economic profit of $28
(b) an economic profit of $27
(c) an economic profit of $26
(d) an economic profit of $25

■ DISCUSSION QUESTIONS

1. Explain the difference between a functional and a personal distribution of income. Rank the five types of earned income in the order of their size.

2. Which would result in greater total saving and less consumption spending out of a national income of a given size: a more or less nearly equal distribution of income?

3. The purchase of what type of consumer goods is largely postponable? Why is this? How is it possible for a family's personal consumption expenditures to exceed its after-tax income?

4. What is the difference between a plant and a firm? Between a firm and an industry? Which of these three concepts is the most difficult to apply in practice? Why? Distinguish between a horizontal, a vertical, and a conglomerate combination.

5. What are the principal advantages and disadvantages of each type of the three legal forms of business organization? Which of the disadvantages of the proprietorship and partnership accounts for the employment of the corporate form among the big businesses of the American economy?

6. Explain what "separation of ownership and control" of the modern corporation means. What problems does this separation create for stockholders and the economy?

7. What figures can you cite to show that the typical firm engaged in agriculture is relatively small and that the average firm engaged in manufacturing is relatively large? Are firms engaged in wholesaling and retailing; mining; finance, insurance, and real estate; and services relatively large or relatively small?

8. Is the American economy and manufacturing in the United States dominated by big business? What evidence do you use to reach this conclusion?

9. Describe the merchandise trade import and export patterns for the United States. What percentage of our exports and imports are with
  (a) industrial countries;
  (b) OPEC countries; and
  (c) developing countries other than OPEC

10. Explain how increasing international trade for the United States affects
  (a) living standards;
  (b) competition;
  (c) banking and finance; and
  (d) macroeconomic stability and policy.

11. What are the Five Fundamental Questions?

12. In what way do the desires of entrepreneurs to obtain economic profits and to avoid losses make consumer sovereignty effective?

13. Why is the ability of firms to enter industries which are prosperous important to the effective functioning of competition?

14. Explain *in detail* how an increase in the consumer demand for a product will result in more of the product being produced and in more resources being allocated to its production.

15. To what extent are firms "free" to produce what they wish by methods which they choose? Do resource owners have freedom to use their resources as they wish?

16. What is meant when it is said that competition is the mechanism which "controls" the market system? How does competition do this? What do critics of the price system argue tends to happen to this controlling mechanism as time passes, and why do they so argue?

17. What are the two important functions of prices? Explain the difference between these two functions.

18. "An invisible hand operates to identify private and public interests." What are private interests and what is the public interest? What is it that leads the economy to operate as if it were directed by an invisible hand?

19. If the basic economic decisions are not made in a capitalistic economy by a central authority, how are they made?

20. Households use the dollars obtained by selling resource services to "vote" for the production of consumer goods and services. Who "votes" for the production of capital goods, why do they "vote" for capital-goods production, and where do they obtain the dollars needed to cast these "votes"?

■ ANSWERS

Chapter 5 The Private Sectors and the Market System

FILL-IN QUESTIONS

1. 94, furnish resources, buy the bulk of the total output of the economy

2. wages and salaries, 73

3. 5, 44

4. personal consumption, personal saving, personal taxes

5. 13, income, federal

6. security, speculation

7. services, nondurable goods, durable goods (any order)

8. 18 million, sole proprietorship, corporation

9. unlimited, limited

10. *a.* CORP; *b.* PRO and PART; *c.* PRO; *d.* CORP; *e.* CORP; *f.* CORP; *g.* PART; *h.* PART; *i.* CORP

11. *a.* agriculture, forestry, and fishing; services; *b.* services, wholesale and retail

12. eight

13. few, large

14. 7–9

15. Canada

16. 108, deficit

17. *a.* increased productive efficiency and living standards; *b.* increased worldwide competition; *c.* financial markets and banking industries operate globally; and *d.* more macroeconomic instability and possibly less effective domestic policy

18. *a.* at what level to utilize resources in the productive process; *b.* what collection of goods and services best satisfies its wants; *c.* how to produce this total output; *d.* how to divide this output among the various economic units of the economy; *e.* how to make the responses required to remain efficient over time

19. communicating, synchronizing (coordinating)

20. is, must, entrepreneurs, is not, need not

21. revenues, costs

22. *a.* normal; *b.* pure (economic)

23. enter, fall, more, larger, decrease, zero

24. *a.* dollars; *b.* sovereign; *c.* restrict

25. cost

26. *a.* income; *b.* prices

27. *a.* preferences (tastes), technology, resources; *b.* guiding

28. *a.* profit; *b.* losses (bankruptcy)

29. profits, borrowed funds

30. private, public (social), invisible hand

31. it efficiently allocates resources, it emphasizes personal freedom

PROBLEMS AND PROJECTS

1. 13, 8

2. A. 35; B. 12; C. 11; D. 9; E. 56; F. 82

3. Firms **a, c, d**, and **f** are in wholesale and retail trade; firms **b, g, h, i**, and **j** are in manufacturing; firms **h** and **i** are also in mining; firm **e** is in transportation, communications, and public utilities

4. $6, −$5, $10; *a.* C; *b.* produce A and have an economic profit of $14; *c.* it would increase

5. *a.* method 2; *b.* 15; *c.* (1) 13, 8; 3, 4; 2, 4; (2) 15, 4

SELF-TEST

1. F, p. 68	**17.** T, p. 79
2. T, p. 73	**18.** T, p. 79
3. T, pp. 68–69	**19.** T, p. 80
4. T, p. 69	**20.** T, p. 80
5. T, p. 69	**21.** T, pp. 80–81
6. T, p. 70	**22.** T, p. 81
7. F, p. 71	**23.** F, p. 81
8. T, p. 71	**24.** T, p. 82
9. F, p. 72	**25.** T, p. 83
10. F, pp. 73–74	**26.** T, p. 83
11. T, p. 74	**27.** T, p. 83
12. F, p. 75	**28.** T, p. 85
13. T, pp. 75–76	**29.** F, pp. 78, 85
14. F, p. 77	
15. T, p. 77	
16. F, p. 79	

1. *a,* p. 67	**15.** *a,* p. 77
2. *a,* p. 69	**16.** *a,* p. 78
3. *c,* pp. 68–69	**17.** *b,* p. 79
4. *a,* p. 70	**18.** *c,* p. 79
5. *a,* p. 70	**19.** *d,* pp. 79–80
6. *a,* p. 69	**20.** *d,* p. 81
7. *c,* p. 72	**21.** *c,* pp. 81–82
8. *b,* p. 71	**22.** *a,* p. 82
9. *d,* p. 73	**23.** *a,* p. 83
10. *a,* p. 73	**24.** *c,* pp. 83–84
11. *c,* p. 75	**25.** *b,* p. 85
12. *d,* p. 75	**26.** *b,* p. 81
13. *b,* p. 77	**27.** *a,* pp. 79, 81
14. *c,* p. 77	

DISCUSSION QUESTIONS

1. pp. 67–68	**11.** p. 78
2. pp. 68–69	**12.** p. 80
3. pp. 69–70	**13.** p. 79
4. p. 71	**14.** p. 80
5. pp. 72–74	**15.** p. 80
6. p. 74	**16.** pp. 83–85
7. p. 75	**17.** pp. 82–83
8. pp. 75–76	**18.** pp. 83–84
9. pp. 76–77	**19.** p. 85
10. p. 77	**20.** p. 83

The Public Sector

Chapter 6 introduces you to the five basic functions performed by the Federal, state, and local governments in America's mixed capitalistic economy. This is an examination of the role of government (the public sector) in an economy which is neither a purely planned nor a purely market-type economy. The discussion points out the degree and the ways in which government causes the American economy to differ from pure capitalism. The chapter does not attempt to list all the *specific* ways in which government affects the behavior of the economy. Instead it provides a *general* classification of the tasks performed by government.

The chapter begins by discussing the two major functions of government. First, the legal and social framework for the operation of the market system is provided by government. Second, government actions can be taken to maintain competition in the economy. In addition, the chapter explains how government influences the market system in three other ways: by redistributing wealth and income; altering domestic output; and stabilizing the economy.

The chapter also returns to the circular flow model that was first presented in Chapter 3. The model has now been modified to include government along with businesses and households. The addition of government changes the real and monetary flows in the model. The twelve linkages among the household, business, and government sectors in the model are described in detail.

The facts of public-sector or government finance in the United States presented in the second half of Chapter 6 center on two questions: Where do governments get their incomes? On what do they spend these incomes?

The organization of the government finance discussion is relatively simple. First, the trends which taxes collected and expenditures made by all levels of government—Federal, state, and local—have taken since 1929 and the causes of the increases in expenditures and taxes are examined briefly. Second, a closer look is taken at the major items upon which the Federal government spends its income, the principal taxes it levies to obtain its income, and the relative importance of these taxes. Third, the chapter looks at the major expenditures of and the major taxes of

the state and the local governments, and at fiscal federalism.

What should you get out of this discussion of government finance? There are at least two important sets of facts: (1) the trends which taxes and government expenditures have taken in recent years and why; and (2) the relative importance of the principal taxes and the relative importance of the various expenditure items in the budgets of the three levels of government. Also, remember to avoid memorizing statistics. You should look instead for the trends and generalizations which these statistics illuminate.

■ CHECKLIST

When you have studied this chapter you should be able to:

☐ Explain in one or two sentences why the American economy is *mixed* rather than *pure* capitalism.

☐ Enumerate the five economic functions of government in the United States and explain the difference between the purpose of the first two and the purpose of the last three functions.

☐ Define monopoly and explain why government wishes to prevent monopoly and to preserve competition in the economy.

☐ Explain why government feels it should redistribute income and list the three principal policies it employs for this purpose.

☐ Define a spillover cost and a spillover benefit; explain why a competitive market fails to allocate resources efficiently when there are spillovers; and list the things government may do to reduce spillovers and improve the allocation of resources.

☐ Define a public good and a private good and explain how government goes about reallocating resources from the production of private to the production of public goods.

☐ Draw a circular flow diagram that includes businesses, households, and government; label all the flows in the diagram; and use the diagram to explain how government alters the distribution of income, the allocation of resources, and the level of activity in the economy.

☐ List the five causes of the historical expansion and the present size of government tax revenues and expenditures.

☐ Explain the differences between government purchases and transfer payments and the effect of each of these two kinds of expenditures on the composition of the national output.

☐ Describe the three largest categories of expenditures and the two greatest sources of revenue of the Federal government.

☐ Define and explain the difference between the marginal and the average tax rate.

☐ Describe the progressivity of the Federal personal income tax.

☐ List the two largest sources of tax revenue and the four largest types of expenditures of state governments; also list the largest single source of tax revenue and the largest category of expenditures of local governments.

■ CHAPTER OUTLINE

1. The American economy is neither a pure market economy nor a purely planned economy. It is an example of mixed capitalism in which government affects the operation of the economy in important ways.

2. Government in the American economy performs five economic functions. The first two of these functions are designed to enable the market system to operate more effectively; and the other three functions are designed to eliminate the major shortcomings of a purely market-type economy.

3. The first of these functions is to provide the legal and social framework that makes the effective operation of the market system possible.

4. The second function is the maintenance of competition and the regulation of monopoly.

5. Government performs its third function when it redistributes income to reduce income inequality.

6. When government reallocates resources it performs its fourth function.
   a. It reallocates resources to take account of spillover costs and benefits.
   b. It also reallocates resources to provide society with public (social) goods and services.
   c. It levies taxes and uses the tax revenues to purchase or produce the public goods.

7. Its fifth function is stabilization of the price level and the maintenance of full employment.

8. A circular-flow diagram that includes the public sector as well as business firms and households in the private sector of the economy reveals that government purchases public goods from private businesses, collects taxes from and makes transfer payments to these firms, purchases labor services from households, and collects taxes from and makes transfer payments to these households; and government can alter the distribution of income, reallocate resources, and change the level of economic activity by affecting the real and monetary flows in the diagram.

9. Government's functions in the economy are felt most directly when it collects revenue by taxation and expends this revenue for goods and services; but there is an important difference between the voluntary transactions in the private and the compulsory transactions in the public sector of the economy.

10. In both absolute and relative terms, government tax collections and spending have increased during the past sixty or so years.
   a. The increased tax collections and spending are the result of hot and cold wars, population increases, urbanization and the greater demand for social goods, pollution of the environment, egalitarianism, and inflation.
   b. Government spending consists of purchases of goods and services and of transfer payments; but these two types of spending have different effects on domestic output.

11. At the Federal level of government about:
   a. 39% of the total expenditure is for income security, about 24% is for national defense, and some 15% is for interest on the national debt; and
   b. the major sources of revenue are personal income, payroll, and corporate income taxes.

12. At the other two levels of government:
   a. state governments depend largely on sales and excise taxes and personal income taxes, and use a large part of their revenues for education and public welfare;
   b. local governments rely heavily upon property taxes and spend the greatest part of their revenues for education;
   c. tax revenues are less than expenditures and the Federal government shares some of its revenues with these governments by making grants to them.

■ IMPORTANT TERMS

Market economy	Spillover benefit
Mixed capitalism	Subsidy
Monopoly	Public (social) good
Spillover (externality)	Private good
Spillover cost	Exclusion principle

Quasi-public good
Free-rider problem
Government purchase
Government transfer payment
Personal income tax
Marginal tax rate
Average tax rate

Progressive tax
Payroll tax
Corporate income tax
Sales tax
Excise tax
Property tax
Fiscal federalism

■ FILL-IN QUESTIONS

1. All actual economies are "mixed" because they combine elements of a _____ economy and a role for _____.

2. List the five economic functions of government.

a. _____

b. _____

c. _____

d. _____

e. _____

3. To control monopoly in the United States government has:

a. created commissions to _____ the prices and the services of the _____ monopolies; and taken over at the local level the _____ of electric and water companies;

b. enacted _____ laws to maintain competition.

4. The market system, because it is an impersonal mechanism, results in an (equal, unequal) _____ distribution of income. To redistribute income from the upper- to the lower-income groups the Federal government has:

a. provided _____ payments;

b. engaged in _____ intervention;

c. used the _____ tax to raise much of its revenues.

5. Government frequently reallocates resources when it finds instances of _____ failure; and the two major cases of such failure occur when the competitive market system either

a. _____

b. or _____

6. Competitive markets bring about an optimum allocation of resources only if there are no _____ costs or benefits in the consumption and production of the good or service.

7. There is a spillover whenever some of the costs of producing a product or some of the benefits from consuming it accrue to _____

8. Whenever in a competitive market there are:
a. spillover costs the result is an (over-, under-) _____ allocation of resources to the production of the good or service;

b. spillover benefits the result is an _____ allocation of resources to the production of the good or service.

9. What two things can government do to:
a. Make the market reflect spillover costs?

(1) _____

(2) _____

b. Make the market reflect spillover benefits?

(1) _____

(2) _____

10. Public (social) goods tend to be goods which are not subject to the _____ principle and which are (divisible, indivisible) _____. Quasi-public goods are goods which could be subjected to the exclusion principle but which are provided by government because they have large spillover _____

11. To reallocate resources from the production of private to the production of public goods government reduces the demand for private goods by _____ consumers and firms and then _____ public goods.

12. To stabilize the economy, government:
a. when there is less than full employment (increases, decreases) _____ aggregate demand by (increasing, decreasing) _____ its expenditures for public goods and services and by (increasing, decreasing) _____ taxes.

b. where there are inflationary pressures _____ _____ aggregate demand by _____ its expenditures for public goods and services and by _____ taxes.

13. Throughout most of its history government in the United States has performed in some degree each of the five functions except that of _____

_____

14. The functions of government are most directly felt by the economy through the _____ it makes and the _____ it collects.

15. An examination of the public sector of the American economy reveals that:
   a. between 1929 and 1991 government **purchases** of goods and services as a percentage of domestic output have tended to (increase, decrease, remain constant) _____ and since the early 1950s have been about (10, 20, 30) _____% of the domestic output;
   b. but government **transfer payments** as a percentage of domestic output during the past 20 or so years have (increased, decreased, remained constant) _____;
   c. and the tax revenues required to finance both government expenditures and transfer payments are today about (10, 20, 30) _____% of domestic output.

16. Government transfer payments are defined as _____ and are (exhaustive, nonexhaustive) _____

17. When government raises $20 billion by taxation and uses it to purchase goods it shifts resources from the production of (private, public) _____ goods to the production of _____ goods; but these expenditures are (exhaustive, nonexhaustive) _____ because they absorb resources and are part of current production.

18. The most important source of revenue for the Federal government is the _____ tax; next in importance are the _____ taxes. The three largest categories of Federal expenditures are for _____, for _____, and for interest on the _____

19. The Federal government uses the personal income tax to obtain most of the _____ it requires to finance its expenditures. In fact, the personal income

tax accounts for _____% of Federal tax revenues. The Federal government also receives _____% from payroll taxes and _____% from corporate income taxes.

20. The state governments rely primarily upon _____ and _____ taxes for their incomes which they spend mostly on _____ and _____

21. At local levels of government the single most important source of revenue is the _____ tax and the single most important expenditure is for _____

22. The amount by which the expenditures of state and local governments exceed their tax revenues is largely filled by grants from the _____ government; these grants account for _____% to _____% of all revenue received by state and local governments.

■ **PROBLEMS AND PROJECTS**

1. Below is a list of various government activities. Indicate in the space to the right of each into which of the five classes of government functions the activity falls. If it falls under more than one of the functions, indicate this.

   a. Maintaining an army _____
   b. Providing for a system of unemployment compensation _____
   c. Establishment of the Federal Reserve Banks _____

_____
   d. Insuring employees of business firms against industrial accidents _____
   e. Establishment of an Antitrust Division in the Department of Justice _____
   f. Making it a crime to sell stocks and bonds under false pretenses _____
   g. Providing low-cost lunches to school children _____

_____
   h. Taxation of whisky and other spirits _____

_____
   i. Regulation of organized stock, bond, and commodity markets _____
   j. Setting tax **rates** higher for larger incomes than for smaller ones _____

2. The circular flow diagram below includes business firms, households, and government (the public sector). Also shown are the product and resource markets.

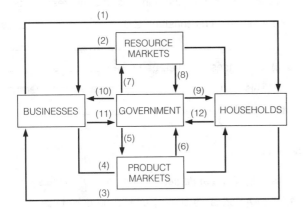

a. Supply a label or an explanation for each of the twelve flows in the model:

(1) _____

(2) _____

(3) _____

(4) _____

(5) _____

(6) _____

(7) _____

(8) _____

(9) _____

(10) _____

(11) _____

(12) _____

b. If government wished to

(1) expand output and employment in the economy it would increase expenditure flows _____ or

_____ , decrease net tax flows

_____ or _____ , or do both;

(2) increase the production of public (social) goods and decrease the production of private goods in the

economy it would increase flows _____

and _____ or _____ ;

(3) redistribute income from high-income to low-income households it would (increase, decrease)

_____ the net taxes (taxes minus transfers)

paid by the former and _____ the net taxes

paid by the latter in flow _____

3. On the following graph are the demand and supply curves for a product bought and sold in a competitive market. Assume that there are no spillover benefits or costs.

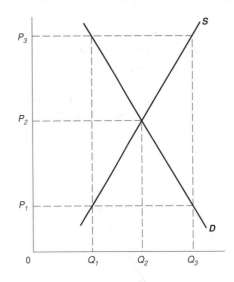

a. Were this market to produce an output of Q_1 there

would be an (optimal, under-, over-) _____
allocation of resources to the production of this product.
b. Were this market to produce Q_3 there would be an

_____ allocation of resources to this
product.
c. The equilibrium output is _____

and at this output there is an _____
allocation of resources.

4. On two graphs that follow are product demand and supply curves that do **not** reflect either the spillover costs of producing the product or the spillover benefits obtained from its consumption.

a. On the first graph draw in another curve that reflects the inclusion of spillover costs.

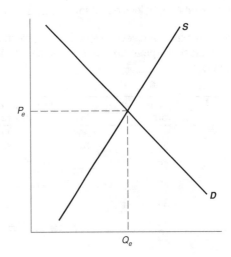

(1) Government might force the (demand for, supply of) _____ the product to reflect the spillover costs of producing it by (taxing, subsidizing) _____ the producers.

(2) The inclusion of spillover costs in the total cost of producing the product (increases, decreases) _____ the output of the product and _____ its price.

b. On the next graph draw in a supply curve that reflects the inclusion of spillover **benefits.**

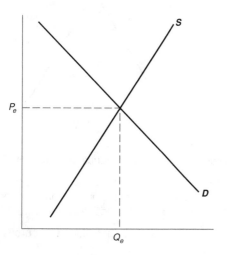

(1) Indicate on the graph the output that is optimal when spillover benefits are included.

(2) To bring about the production of this optimal output government might (tax, subsidize) _____ the producers of this product, and this would (increase, decrease) _____ the supply of the product.

(3) This optimal output is (greater than, less than, equal to) _____ Q_e; and the price of the product is (above, below, equal to) _____ P_e.

5. In the table below are several levels of taxable income and hypothetical marginal tax rates for each $1000 increase in income.

Taxable income	Marginal tax rate, %	Tax	Average tax rate, %
$1500		$300	20
2500	22	520	20.8
3500	25	_____	_____
4500	29	_____	_____
5500	34	_____	_____
6500	40	_____	_____

a. At the four income levels compute the tax and the average tax rate.

b. As the marginal tax rate:

(1) increases the average tax rate (increases, decreases, remains constant) _____

_____

(2) decreases the average tax rate _____

c. This tax is _____ because the average tax rate increases as income _____

Circle the T if the statement is true; the F if it is false.

1. The American economy cannot be called "capitalistic" because its operation involves some "planning by government." **T F**

2. When the Federal government provides for a monetary system, it is functioning to provide the economy with public goods and services. **T F**

3. An economy in which strong and effective competition is maintained will find no need for programs designed to redistribute income. **T F**

4. Competitive product markets ensure an optimal allocation of an economy's resources. **T F**

5. In a competitive product market and in the absence of spillover costs, the supply curve or schedule reflects the costs of producing the product. **T F**

6. If demand and supply reflected all the benefits and costs of a product, the equilibrium output of a competitive market would be identical with its optimal output. **T F**

The following graph should be used to answer true-false question 7 and multiple-choice question 3.

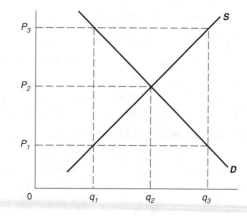

7. Assuming there are no spillover costs or benefits, the production of q_1 units of this product would result in an overallocation of resources to the production of the product. **T F**

8. The inclusion of the spillover benefits would increase the demand for a product. **T F**

9. When there are spillover costs involved in the production of a product, more resources are allocated to the production of that product and more of the product is produced than is optimal or most efficient. **T F**

10. Subsidizing the firms producing goods which provide spillover benefits will usually result in a better allocation of resources. **T F**

11. Governments have undertaken to provide lighthouse services because these services have social benefits and private producers of such services encounter the free-rider problem. **T F**

12. In performing its stabilization function when there is widespread unemployment and no inflation in the economy, government should decrease its spending for public goods and services and increase taxes. **T F**

13. Net taxes for businesses are taxes paid by business less a depreciation allowance. **T F**

14. Flood control projects are usually undertaken by government because of the free-rider problem. **T F**

15. When the Federal government takes actions to control unemployment or inflation it is performing the allocative function of government. **T F**

16. Government purchases of goods and services are called **nonexhaustive** and government transfer payments are called **exhaustive** expenditures. **T F**

17. When a government levies taxes and uses the tax revenue to make transfer payments it shifts resources from the production of private goods to the production of public goods. **T F**

18. The level of Federal expenditures in 1990 was about $1,031 billion. **T F**

19. The chief source of revenue for the Federal government is the corporate income tax. **T F**

20. The Federal government levies sales taxes on tobacco and gasoline. **T F**

21. Total taxes collected by the Federal government are approximately equal to the amount of taxes collected by all state and local governments. **T F**

22. If the marginal tax rate is higher than the average tax rate, the average tax rate will fall. **T F**

23. Property taxes are the largest percentage of the total budget of local governments. **T F**

24. The largest expenditure by state governments is for highways. **T F**

25. Fiscal federalism involves the sharing of sales tax receipts among local, state, and Federal governments. **T F**

Circle the letter that corresponds to the best answer.

1. Which of the following is **not** one of the methods utilized by government to control monopoly?
(a) the imposition of special taxes on monopolists
(b) government ownership of monopolies
(c) government regulation of monopolies
(d) antitrust laws

2. One of the following is **not** employed by government to redistribute income. Which one?
(a) the negative income tax
(b) direct market intervention
(c) income taxes which take a larger part of the incomes of the rich than the poor
(d) public assistance programs

Use the graph on page 58 to answer the following question.

3. If there are neither spillover costs nor spillover benefits, the output which results in the optimal allocation of resources to the production of this product is:
(a) q_1
(b) q_2
(c) q_3
(d) none of these outputs

4. When the production and consumption of a product entail spillover costs, a competitive product market results in an:
(a) underallocation of resources to the product
(b) overallocation of resources to the product
(c) optimal allocation of resources to the product
(d) a higher price for the product

5. Which of the following is the best example of a good or service providing the economy with spillover benefits?
(a) an automobile
(b) a drill press
(c) a high school education
(d) an operation for appendicitis

6. In the American economy the reallocation of resources needed to provide for the production of public goods is:
(a) government subsidies to the producers of social goods
(b) government purchases of social goods from producers
(c) direct control of producers of both private and social goods
(d) direct control of producers of social goods only

7. Which of the following is characteristic of public goods?
   (a) they are indivisible
   (b) they are sold in competitive markets
   (c) they are subject to the exclusion principle
   (d) they can be produced only if large spillover costs are incurred

8. Quasi-public goods are goods and services:
   (a) to which the exclusion principle could not be applied
   (b) which have large spillover benefits
   (c) which would not be produced by private producers through the market system
   (d) which are indivisible

9. To redistribute income from high-income to low-income households government might:
   (a) increase transfer payments to high-income and decrease transfer payments to low-income households
   (b) increase the taxes paid by high-income and increase the transfer payments to low-income households
   (c) increase the taxes paid by low-income and decrease the taxes paid by high-income households
   (d) decrease the taxes paid by high-income and decrease the transfer payments to low-income households

10. To reallocate resources from the private to the public sector of the economy government should:
   (a) increase its expenditures for the goods it purchases from business firms
   (b) increase the transfer payments it makes to households
   (c) increase its expenditures for the labor services it purchases from households
   (d) do either or both *a* and *c*

11. To prevent or slow inflation in the economy government would most likely:
   (a) increase its expenditures for the goods and services it purchases from business firms and households
   (b) increase the transfer payments it makes to business firms and the public
   (c) increase the taxes it collects from business firms and the public
   (d) do either or both *a* and *c*

12. Which of the following is the best example of a good or service providing the economy with a spillover cost?
   (a) a textbook
   (b) an automobile
   (c) a business suit
   (d) an audit of a business firm's books

13. There is a "free-rider" problem when people:
   (a) are willing to pay for what they want
   (b) are not willing to pay for what they want
   (c) benefit from a good without paying for its cost
   (d) want to buy more than is available for purchase in the market

14. In the circular flow model, net taxes are:
   (a) taxes minus depreciation
   (b) taxes minus transfer payments
   (c) subsidies minus transfer payments
   (d) business receipts minus household expenditures

15. In the circular flow model, government provides goods and services and receives net taxes from:
   (a) colleges and universities
   (b) businesses and households
   (c) resource and product markets
   (d) foreign nations and corporations

16. Today all government expenditures (purchases plus transfer payments) equal approximately what percentage of the American economy's total output?
   (a) 10%
   (b) 18%
   (c) 23%
   (d) 30%

17. Which of the following is *not* one of the causes of the present size of government expenditures in the United States?
   (a) national defense
   (b) property taxes
   (c) population growth
   (d) egalitarianism

18. Which of the following would *not* be a government transfer expenditure?
   (a) salaries and benefits for military personnel
   (b) social security payments to the aged
   (c) unemployment compensation benefits
   (d) payments to the widows of war veterans

19. Which of the following accounts for the largest percentage of all Federal expenditures?
   (a) income security
   (b) national defense
   (c) interest on the public debt
   (d) veterans' services

20. Which of the following is the largest source of the tax revenues of the Federal government?
   (a) sales and excise taxes
   (b) property taxes
   (c) payroll taxes
   (d) personal income taxes

21. A tax that would most likely alter consumer expenditures on a product would be:
   (a) an excise tax
   (b) a general sales tax
   (c) a personal income tax
   (d) a corporate income tax

22. Which of the following pairs represents the chief source of income and the most important type of expenditure of state governments?
  (a) personal income tax and expenditures for education
  (b) personal income tax and expenditures for highways
  (c) sales and excise taxes and expenditures for highways
  (d) sales and excise taxes and expenditures for public welfare

23. Which of the following pairs represents the chief source of income and the most important type of expenditure of *local* governments?
  (a) property tax and expenditures for highways
  (b) property tax and expenditures for education
  (c) sales and excise taxes and expenditures for public welfare
  (d) sales and excise taxes and expenditures for police, fire, and general government

The next two questions (24 and 25) are based on the portion of the tax table given below.

Taxable income	Total tax
$ 0	$ 0
30,000	5,000
70,000	15,000
150,000	42,000

24. The marginal tax rate at the $70,000 level of taxable income is:
  (a) 16.6
  (b) 21.4
  (c) 25.0
  (d) 28.0

25. The average tax rate at the $150,000 level of taxable income is:
  (a) 21.4
  (b) 28.0
  (c) 31.5
  (d) 33.8

■ DISCUSSION QUESTIONS

1. Why is it proper to refer to the United States economy as "mixed capitalism"?

2. What are the five economic functions of government in America's mixed capitalistic economy? Explain what the performance of each of these functions requires government to do.

3. Would you like to live in an economy in which government undertook only the first two functions listed in the text? What would be the advantages and disadvantages of living in such an economy?

4. Why does the market system provide some people with lower income than it provides others?

5. What is "market failure" and what are the two major kinds of such failures?

6. What is meant by a spillover in general and by spillover cost and spillover benefit in particular? How does the existence of such costs and benefits affect the allocation of resources and the prices of products? If a market could be required to take these costs and benefits into account, how would the allocation of resources and the price of the product bought and sold in that market be changed?

7. What methods do government employ to:
  (a) redistribute income;
  (b) reallocate resources to take account of spillover costs;
  (c) reallocate resources to take account of spillover benefits?

8. Distinguish between a private and a public good. Include in your answer an explanation of the "exclusion principle" and the distinction between divisible and indivisible goods.

9. What basic method does government employ in the United States to reallocate resources away from the production of private goods and toward the production of social goods?

10. In a circular flow diagram that includes not only business firms and households but also government (or the public sector), what are the four flows of money into or out of the government sector of the economy? Using this diagram, explain how government redistributes income, reallocates resources from the private to the public sector, and stabilizes the economy.

11. What are the causes of the historical growth and the present size of government spending and taxes in the American economy?

12. Government expenditures fall into two broad classes: expenditures for goods and services, and transfer payments. Explain the difference between these and give examples of expenditures which fall into each of the two classes.

13. Explain the difference between exhaustive and nonexhaustive government spending.

14. When government collects taxes and spends the tax revenues it affects the composition of the total output of the economy. What is the effect on total output if government uses the tax revenues to purchase goods and services? What is the effect if it uses them to make transfer payments?

15. Explain precisely the difference between the marginal tax rate and the average tax rate.

16. Explain how the Federal personal income tax enables the Federal government to perform three (of the five) economic functions.

17. Explain in detail the differences that exist among Federal, state, and local governments in the taxes upon which they primarily rely for their revenues and the major purposes for which they use these revenues.

18. Why does the Federal government share its tax revenues with state and local governments? How has this fiscal federalism changed in recent years?

■ **ANSWERS**

Chapter 6 The Public Sector

FILL-IN QUESTIONS

1. market, government

2. *a.* provide legal foundation and social environment; *b.* maintain competition; *c.* redistribute income and wealth; *d.* reallocate resources; *e.* stabilize the economy

3. *a.* regulate, natural, ownership; *b.* antitrust (antimonopoly)

4. unequal; *a.* transfer; *b.* market; *c.* income

5. market; *a.* produces the "wrong" amounts of certain goods and services; *b.* fails to allocate any resources to the production of certain goods and services whose production is economically justified

6. spillover

7. people other than the buyers and sellers (third parties)

8. *a.* over; *b.* under

9. *a.* (1) enact legislation, (2) pass special taxes; *b.* (1) subsidize production, (2) finance or take over the production of the product

10. exclusion, indivisible, benefits

11. taxing, spends the revenue to buy

12. *a.* increases, increasing, decreasing; *b.* decreases, decreasing, increasing

13. stabilizing the economy

14. expenditures, taxes

15. *a.* increase, 20; *b.* increased; *c.* 30

16. expenditures for which government currently receives no good or service in return, nonexhaustive

17. exhaustive

18. personal income, payroll, income security, national defense, public debt

19. revenue, 45, 37, 9

20. sales and excise, personal income, public welfare, education

21. property, education

22. federal, 15, 20

PROBLEMS AND PROJECTS

1. *a.* reallocates resources; *b.* redistributes income; *c.* provides a legal foundation and social environment *and* stabilizes the economy; *d.* reallocates resources; *e.* maintains competition; *f.* provides a legal foundation and social environment *and* maintains competition; *g.* redistributes income; *h.* reallocates resources; *i.* provides a legal foundation and social environment; *j.* redistributes income

2. *a.* (1) business pay costs for resources that becomes money income for households; (2) households provide resources to businesses; (3) household expenditures become receipts for businesses; (4) business provide goods and services to households; (5) government spends money in product market; (6) government receives goods and services from product market; (7) government spends money in resource market; (8) government receives resources from resource market; (9) government provides goods and services to households; (10) government provides goods and services to businesses; (11) business pays net taxes to government; (12) households pay net taxes to government; *b.* (1) 5, 7 (either order), 11, 12 (either order); (2) 9, 10, 11 (either order); (3) increase, decrease, 12

3. *a.* under; *b.* over; *c.* Q_2, optimal

4. *a.* (1) supply of, taxing, (2) decreases, increases; *b.* (2) subsidize, increase, (3) greater than, below

5. *a.* tax: $770, 1,060, 1,400, 1,800; average tax rate: 22%, 23.6%, 25.5%, 27.7%; *b.* (1) increases, (2) decreases; *c.* progressive, increases

SELF-TEST

1. F, p. 88	**8.** T, p. 92	**14.** T, pp. 93–94	**20.** F, p. 99
2. F, p. 89	**9.** T, p. 91	**15.** F, p. 94	**21.** F, pp. 98, 100
3. F, p. 90	**10.** T, pp. 92–93	**16.** F, p. 96	**22.** F, p. 99
4. F, pp. 90–91	**11.** T, p. 93	**17.** F, pp. 96–97	**23.** T, p. 100
5. T, p. 91	**12.** F, p. 94	**18.** T, p. 98	**24.** F, p. 100
6. T, p. 90	**13.** F, p. 96	**19.** F, p. 98	**25.** F, p. 102
7. F, p. 91			

1. *a*, p. 90	**8.** *b*, pp. 93–94	**14.** *b*, p. 96	**20.** *d*, p. 98
2. *a*, p. 90	**9.** *b*, p. 90	**15.** *b*, p. 96	**21.** *a*, p. 99
3. *b*, p. 92	**10.** *d*, p. 94	**16.** *d*, p. 97	**22.** *d*, p. 100
4. *d*, p. 91	**11.** *c*, p. 94	**17.** *b*, pp. 97–98	**23.** *b*, p. 100
5. *c*, p. 92	**12.** *b*, pp. 90–91	**18.** *a*, pp. 97–98	**24.** *c*, p. 99
6. *b*, p. 94	**13.** *c*, p. 93	**19.** *a*, p. 98	**25.** *b*, p. 99
7. *a*, pp. 93–94			

DISCUSSION QUESTIONS

1. p. 88	**6.** pp. 90–93	**11.** pp. 97–98	**15.** p. 99
2. pp. 88–89	**7.** pp. 90–93	**12.** pp. 96–97	**16.** pp. 98–99
3. pp. 88–94	**8.** p. 93	**13.** pp. 96–97	**17.** pp. 98–101
4. p. 90	**9.** p. 94	**14.** p. 96	**18.** p. 102
5. p. 90	**10.** pp. 94–96		

CHAPTER 7

Demand and Supply: Elasticities and Applications

In this chapter, the text begins the intensive study of *microeconomics*. This study will examine the economic decision-making of individual units in the economy, such as households, business, and government agencies, and it will discuss the markets and prices for specific goods and services. The central questions to be answered in this in-depth study of microeconomics are what goods and services are to be produced, how are the goods and services to be produced, who is to receive income generated by production, and how can the economy adapt to change. You learned in Chapter 5 that it is the market system in the American economy that answers these four fundamental questions. You should also remember from Chapter 4 that supply and demand determine the price and quantity of a good or service that is bought and sold in a competitive market.

Chapter 7 is basically a continuation of Chapter 4, as you might have guessed from the chapter title. In the earlier part of the book, it was necessary only for you to have an elementary knowledge of supply and demand. Now the economic principles, problems, and policies to be studied require a more detailed examination and analysis of supply and demand. Therefore, before you start to read Chapter 7 you are urged—you would be commanded if this were possible—to read and study Chapter 4 again. It is absolutely essential that you master Chapter 4 if the new material in this chapter is to be understood.

The concept of price elasticity of demand, to which the major portion of Chapter 7 is devoted, is of great importance for studying material found in the remainder of the text. It is essential that you understand (1) what price elasticity measures; (2) how the price-elasticity formula is applied to measure the price elasticity of demand; (3) the difference between price elastic, price inelastic, and unitary price elastic demand; (4) how total revenue varies by the type of price elasticity of demand; (5) the meaning of perfect price elasticity and perfect price inelasticity of demand; (6) the four major determinants of price elasticity of demand; and (7) the practical application of the concept to many economic issues.

When you have become thoroughly acquainted with the price elasticity of demand concept, you will find that you have very little trouble understanding the elasticity of *supply*. The transition requires no more than the substitution of the words "quantity supplied" for the words "quantity demanded." Here attention should be concentrated on the meaning of price elasticity of supply and the effect of time on it.

The chapter also introduces you to two other elasticity concepts. The *cross elasticity of demand* measures the sensitivity of a change in the quantity demanded for one product due to a change in the price of another product. This concept is especially important to identifying substitute, complementary, or independent goods. The *income elasticity of demand* assesses the change in the quantity demanded of a product resulting from a change in consumer incomes. It is useful for categorizing products as superior, normal, or inferior.

The final section of the chapter discusses *price ceilings* and *price floors* that are created when legal prices are imposed on the competitive market by government. You should note that these ceilings and floors prevent supply and demand from determining the equilibrium price and quantity of a commodity in the market. The economic consequence of this interference in the market will be shortages of surpluses of the commodity. Among the applications presented in this section to illustrate the economic effects of price ceilings or price floors are: (1) price controls during World War II; (2) rent controls; (3) limits on interest rates for credit cards; and (4) price supports for agricultural products.

The concepts of demand and supply, which have been expanded in Chapter 7 to include discussion of elasticity and price ceilings and price floors, are the foundations of the next ten chapters in the text. If you master the topics in Chapter 7, you will be prepared to understand the material in these chapters.

■ **CHECKLIST**

When you have studied this chapter you should be able to:

☐ Define price elasticity of demand and compute the coefficient for it when you are given the demand data.
☐ State two reasons why the formula for price elasticity of demand uses percentages rather than absolute amounts in measuring consumer responsiveness.
☐ Explain the meaning of elastic, inelastic, and unitary price elasticity of demand.
☐ Define and illustrate graphically the concepts of perfectly price elastic and perfectly price inelastic demand.
☐ State the midpoint formula for price elasticity of demand and explain how it refines the original formula for price elasticity.
☐ Describe the relationship between price elasticity of demand and the price range for most demand curves.
☐ Explain why the slope of the demand curve is *not* a sound basis for judging price elasticity.
☐ Apply the total-revenue test to determine whether demand is elastic, inelastic, or unitary elastic.
☐ Illustrate graphically the relationship between price elasticity of demand and total revenue.
☐ List the four major determinants of the price elasticity of demand; and explain how each determinant affects price elasticity.
☐ Describe seven practical applications of the concept of price elasticity of demand.
☐ Define the price elasticity of supply and compute the coefficient for it when given the relevant data.
☐ Explain the effect of time on price elasticity of supply.
☐ Define cross elasticity of demand and compute the coefficient for it when given relevant data.
☐ Define income elasticity of demand and compute the coefficient for it when given relevant data.
☐ Explain the economic consequences of price ceilings and give four examples of the use of price ceilings.
☐ Describe how price floors affect the price and quantity of a product in a market.

■ **CHAPTER OUTLINE**

1. It is necessary to review the analysis of supply and demand and the concepts found in Chapter 4 before studying this chapter.

2. Price elasticity of demand is a measure of the sensitivity of quantity demanded to changes in the price of a product; and when quantity demanded is relatively sensitive (insensitive) to a price change demand is said to be elastic (inelastic).

a. The exact degree of elasticity can be measured by using a formula to compute the elasticity coefficient.
(1) The changes in quantity demanded and in price are comparisons of consumer responsiveness to price changes of different products.
(2) Because price and quantity demanded are inversely related to each other the price elasticity of demand coefficient is a negative number; but economists ignore the minus sign in front of the coefficient and focus their attention on its absolute value.
(3) Demand is elastic (inelastic, unit elastic) when the percentage change in quantity is greater than (less than, equal to) the percentage change in price and the elasticity coefficient is greater than (less than, equal to) 1.
(4) Perfectly inelastic demand means that a change in price results in no change in quantity demanded of a product, whereas perfectly elastic demand means that a small change in price causes buyers to purchase all they desire of a product.
b. In measuring the percentage changes in quantity and in price the average of the two quantities and the average of the two prices are used as the reference points. It is important to note that graphically the elasticity of demand:
(1) is not the same at all prices and that demand is typically elastic at higher and inelastic at lower prices;
(2) cannot be judged from the slope of the demand curve.
c. The way in which total revenue changes (increases, decreases, or remains constant) when price changes is a test of the elasticity of demand for a product.
(1) When demand is *elastic*, a decrease in price will increase total revenue, and a decrease in price will increase total revenue.
(2) When demand is *inelastic*, a decrease in price will decrease total revenue, and an increase in price with increase total revenue.
(3) When demand is *unit elastic*, an increase or decrease in price will not affect total revenue.
d. The price elasticity of demand for a product depends upon the number of good substitutes for the product, its relative importance in the consumer's budget, whether it is a necessity or a luxury, and the period of time under consideration.
e. Price elasticity of demand is of practical importance in matters of public policy and in the setting of prices by the individual business firm. The concept is relevant to wage bargaining, bumper crops in agriculture, automation, airline deregulation, excise taxes, heroin and street crime, and minimum wage laws.

3. Price elasticity of supply is a measure of the sensitivity of quantity supplied to changes in the price of a product.
a. There is both a general formula and a midpoint for-

mula that is similar to those for the price elasticity of demand, but "quantity supplied" replaces "quantity demanded."

b. The price elasticity of supply depends primarily on the amount of time sellers have to adjust to a price change; supply will tend to be more price inelastic in the short run than in the long run.

c. There is no total-revenue test for price elasticity of supply because price and total revenue move in the same direction regardless of the degree of price elasticity of supply.

4. There are two other elasticity concepts of importance.

a. The cross elasticity of demand measures the degree to which the quantity demanded of one product is affected by a change in the price of another product; cross elasticities of demand are positive for substitute goods, negative for complementary goods, and essentially zero for independent goods.

b. The income elasticity of demand measures the effect of a change in income on the quantity demanded of a product; income elasticities of demand are positive for normal or superior goods, and negative for inferior goods.

5. Supply and demand analysis and the elasticity concepts have many important applications.

a. Legal price ceilings and price floors prevent price from performing its rationing function.

(1) A price ceiling results in a shortage of the commodity; may bring about formal rationing by government and a black market; and causes a misallocation of resources.

(2) A price floor creates a surplus of the commodity; and may induce government to undertake measures either to increase the demand for or to decrease the supply of the commodity.

b. There are many examples of price ceilings and shortages created by legal prices:

(1) Price controls were imposed on many commodities during World War II;

(2) Rent controls have been established by cities in an attempt to restrain rent increases in housing markets; and

(3) Bills have been introduced in Congress to restrict the interest rate that can be charged to holders of credit cards.

c. Pricing below the equilibrium price is not just practiced by government. Businesses may price a product below the market-clearing price to generate excess demand. For example, rock stars may price concert tickets below the market-clearing price to generate publicity and enthusiasm for the concert.

d. There are also illustrations of price floors resulting from legal prices set by government to support the price of some agricultural products.

■ **IMPORTANT TERMS**

Price elasticity of demand
Elastic demand
Inelastic demand
Unit elasticity
Perfect inelasticity of demand
Perfect elasticity of demand
Total-revenue test
Price elasticity of supply
Elastic supply

Inelastic supply
Market period
Short run
Long run
Increasing-cost industry
Constant-cost industry
Cross elasticity of demand
Income elasticity of demand
Price ceiling
Price floor

Note: Before answering the Fill-in, Self-test, and Discussion questions and working out the Problems and Projects, you should return to Chapter 4 in this study guide and review the important terms, answer the questions, and rework the problems.

■ **FILL-IN QUESTIONS**

1. The efficient use of an economy's available resources requires that these resources be _____ employed and that they be _____ among alternative uses in an efficient way.

a. The present chapter begins the study of the (latter, former) _____ aspect of the efficient use of resources and the study of (macro-, micro-) _____ economics.

b. This requires an analysis of the _____ system and how individual _____ are determined in various kinds of markets in the economy.

2. If a relatively large change in price results in a relatively small change in quantity demanded, demand is _____; if a relatively small change in price results in a relatively large change in quantity demanded, demand is _____

3. The price elasticity formula is based on _____ rather than absolute amounts because it avoids the problems caused by the arbitrary choice of units, and because it permits a meaningful _____ of consumer responsiveness to changes in the prices of different products.

4. If a change in price causes no change in quantity demanded, demand is perfectly (elastic, inelastic)

_____ and the demand curve is (horizontal, vertical) _____; if an extremely small change in price results in an extremely large change in quantity demanded, demand is _____ and the demand curve is _____

5. The midpoints formula for the price elasticity of demand uses the _____ of the two quantities as a reference point in calculating the percentage change in quantity and the _____ of the two prices as a reference point in calculations of the percentage change in price.

6. Two characteristics of the price elasticity of a linear demand curve are that elasticity (is constant, varies) _____ over the different price ranges, and the slope is a(n) (sound, unsound) _____ basis for judging its elasticity.

7. If the price of a commodity declines,
   a. When demand is inelastic the loss of revenue due to the lower price is _____ the gain in revenue due to the greater quantity demanded.
   b. When demand is elastic the loss of revenue due to the lower price is _____ the gain in revenue due to the greater quantity demanded.
   c. When demand is of unitary elasticity the loss of revenue due to the lower price is _____ the gain in revenue due to the greater quantity demanded.

8. If demand is elastic, price and total revenue are (directly, inversely) _____ related; if demand is inelastic, they are _____ related.

9. Complete the summary table below.

If demand is	The elasticity coefficient is	If price rises, total revenue will	If price falls, total revenue will
Elastic	_____	_____	_____
Inelastic	_____	_____	_____
Of unitary elasticity	_____	_____	_____

10. List four determinants of the price elasticity of demand:
   a. _____
   b. _____

   c. _____
   d. _____

11. The price elasticity of supply measures the percentage change in (price, quantity supplied) _____ divided by the percentage change in _____

12. The most important factor affecting the price elasticity of supply is _____.
Typically, the price elasticity of supply is (more, less) _____ elastic in the short run than in the long run.

13. The measure of the sensitivity of the consumption of one product given a change in the price of another product is the _____ elasticity of demand. The measure of the responsiveness of consumer purchases to changes in income is the _____ elasticity of demand.

14. When the cross elasticity of demand is positive, two products are (complements, substitutes, independent) _____, but when the cross elasticity of demand is negative, they are _____. A zero cross elasticity suggest that two products are _____

15. If consumers increase purchases of a product as consumer incomes increase, then a good is classified as (inferior, normal, or superior) _____; if consumers decrease purchases of a product as consumer incomes increase, then a good is classified as _____

16. If the demand and supply schedules for a certain product are those given in the table, answer the following questions.

Quantity demanded	Price	Quantity supplied
12,000	$10	18,000
13,000	9	17,000
14,000	8	16,000
15,000	7	15,000
16,000	6	14,000
17,000	5	13,000
18,000	4	12,000

   a. The equilibrium price of the product is $_____ and the equilibrium quantity is _____
   b. If the government imposes a price ceiling of $5 on this product, there would be a (shortage, surplus) _____ of _____ units.
   c. If the government supports a price of $8, there would be a _____ of _____ units.

17. Price ceilings imposed by the United States government have usually occurred during _____ periods, result in _____ of the commodities, and require that the government institute _____

18. The two most common examples of government imposed minimum prices are _____

_____

and _____

19. A minimum price imposed by the government on a commodity causes a _____ of the commodity and requires that the government either _____

_____

or _____ to eliminate this.

20. Price ceilings and price floors prevent prices from performing their _____ function.

■ **PROBLEMS AND PROJECTS**

1. In the following table, using the demand data given, complete the table by computing total revenue at each of the seven prices and the six price elasticity coefficients between each of the seven prices, and indicate whether demand is elastic, inelastic, or of unitary elasticity between each of the seven prices.

Price	Quantity demanded	Total revenue	Elasticity coefficient	Character of demand
$1.00	300	$_____		
.90	400	_____	_____	_____
.80	500	_____	_____	_____
.70	600	_____	_____	_____
.60	700	_____	_____	_____
.50	800	_____	_____	_____
.40	900	_____	_____	_____

2. Use the data from the table above for this problem. On the first graph in the next column, plot the demand curve (price and quantity demanded) and indicate the elastic, unitary, and inelastic portions of the demand curve. On the second graph in the next column, plot the total revenue on the vertical axis and the quantity demanded on the horizontal axis. (**Note:** The scale for quantity demanded that you plot on horizontal axis of each graph should be the same on both graphs.)

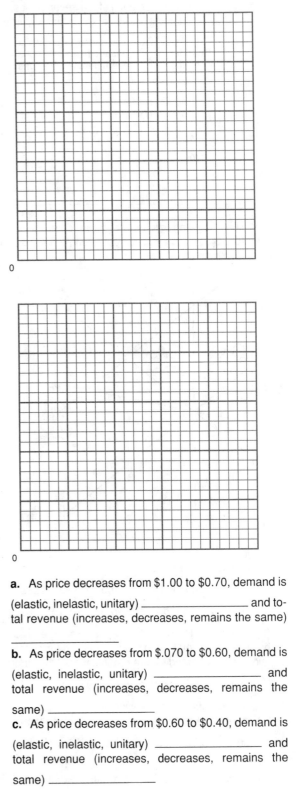

0

0

a. As price decreases from $1.00 to $0.70, demand is (elastic, inelastic, unitary) _____ and total revenue (increases, decreases, remains the same) _____

b. As price decreases from $.070 to $0.60, demand is (elastic, inelastic, unitary) _____ and total revenue (increases, decreases, remains the same) _____

c. As price decreases from $0.60 to $0.40, demand is (elastic, inelastic, unitary) _____ and total revenue (increases, decreases, remains the same) _____

3. Using the supply data in the schedule shown below, complete the table by computing the six price elasticity of supply coefficients between each of the seven prices, and indicate whether supply is elastic or of unitary elasticity.

Price	Quantity supplied	Elasticity coefficient	Character of supply
$1.00	800		
.90	700	———	———
.80	600	———	———
.70	500	———	———
.60	400	———	———
.50	300	———	———
.40	200	———	———

4. On the following graph are three different supply curves (S_1, S_2, and S_3) for a product bought and sold in a competitive market.

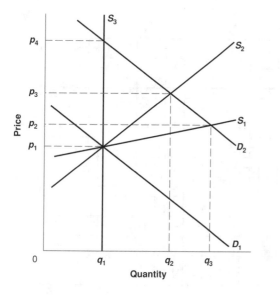

a. The supply curve for the:

(1) market period is the one labeled _____

(2) short run is the one labeled _____

(3) long run is the one labeled _____

b. No matter what the period of time under consideration, if the demand for the product were D_1, the equilibrium price of the product would be _____

and the equilibrium quantity would be _____

(1) in the market period the equilibrium price would increase to _____ and the equilibrium

quantity would _____

(2) in the short run the price of the product would in-

crease to _____ and the quantity would

increase to _____

(3) in the long run the price of the product would be

_____ and the quantity would be

_____

d. The longer the period of time allowed to sellers to adjust their outputs the (more, less) _____ elastic is the supply of the product.

e. The more elastic the supply of a product, the

(greater, less) _____ is the effect on

equilibrium price and the _____ is the effect on equilibrium quantity of an increase in demand.

5. For the following three cases, use a midpoints formula to calculate the coefficient for the cross elasticity of demand and identify the relationship between the two goods (complement, substitute, or independent).

a. The quantity demanded for good A increases from 300 to 400 as the price of good B increases from $1.00

to $2.00. Coefficient: _____ Relationship: _____

b. The quantity demanded for good J decreases from 2000 to 1500 as the price of good K increases from $10

to $15. Coefficient: _____ Relationship: _____

c. The quantity demanded for good X increases from 100 to 101 units as the price of good Y increases from

$8 to $15. Coefficient: _____ Relationship: _____

6. Use the information in the table below to identify the income characteristic of each product A–E using the following labels: N = normal (or superior); I = inferior.

Product	% change in income	% change in quantity demanded	Income type (N or I)
A	10	10	———
B	1	15	———
C	5	– 12	———
D	5	– 2	———
E	10	1	———

■ **SELF-TEST**

Circle the T if the statement is true; the F if it is false.

1. If the relative change in price is greater than the relative change in quantity demanded, the price elasticity coefficient is greater than one.   **T   F**

2. If the quantity demanded for a product increases from 100 to 150 units when the price decreases from $14 to

$10, the price elasticity of demand for this product in this price range is 1.2. **T F**

3. A product with a price elasticity of demand equal to 1.5 is described as price inelastic. **T F**

4. The flatness or steepness of a demand curve is based on absolute changes in price and quantity, while elasticity is based on relative or percentage changes in price and quantity. **T F**

5. Demand tends to be inelastic at higher prices and elastic at lower prices. **T F**

6. Price elasticity of demand and the slope of the demand curve are two different things. **T F**

7. If the price of a product increases from $5 to $6 and the quantity demanded decreases from 45 to 25, then according to the total revenue test, the product is price inelastic in this price range. **T F**

8. Total revenue will not change when price changes if the price elasticity of demand is unitary. **T F**

9. When the absolute value of the price elasticity coefficient is greater than 1 and the price of the product decreases, then the total revenue will increase. **T F**

10. The demand for most agricultural products is inelastic. Consequently, an increase in supply will reduce the total income of producers of agricultural products. **T F**

11. A state government seeking to increase its excise-tax revenues is more likely to increase the tax rate on restaurant meals than on automobile tires. **T F**

12. In general, the larger the portion of a household budget required to buy a product, the greater will tend to be the price elasticity of demand for the product. **T F**

13. An empirical study of commuter rail transportation in the Philadelphia area indicates that the "short-run" commuter response is price elastic, while the "long-run" response is price inelastic. **T F**

14. If the demand for soybeans is highly inelastic, a bumper crop may reduce farm incomes. **T F**

15. If an increase in product price results in no change in the quantity supplied, supply is perfectly elastic. **T F**

16. The immediate market period is a time so short that producers cannot respond to a change in demand and price. **T F**

17. The price elasticity of supply will tend to be more inelastic in the long run. **T F**

18. A constant-cost industry has a vertical or near-vertical long-run supply curve. **T F**

19. Cross elasticity of demand is measured by the per-

centage change in quantity demanded over the percentage change in income. **T F**

20. A negative cross elasticity of demand for two goods indicates that they are complements. **T F**

21. Inferior goods have a positive income elasticity of demand. **T F**

22. If the government imposes a price ceiling below what would be the free-market price of a commodity, a shortage of the commodity will develop. **T F**

23. A price floor set by government will raise the equilibrium price and quantity in a market. **T F**

24. If the legal price floor is above the equilibrium price, shortages will develop in the market. **T F**

25. A legal ceiling on interest rates charged by issuers of bank credit cards would probably lead to actions by the issuers to reduce costs or to increase revenues. **T F**

Circle the letter that corresponds to the best answer.

1. If when the price of a product rises from $1.50 to $2, the quantity demanded of the product decreases from 1000 to 900, the price elasticity of demand coefficient is:
(a) 3.00
(b) 2.71
(c) 0.37
(d) 0.33

2. If a 1% fall in the price of a commodity causes the quantity demanded of the commodity to increase 2%, demand is:
(a) inelastic
(b) elastic
(c) of unitary elasticity
(d) perfectly elastic

3. In the diagram below, D_1 is a:

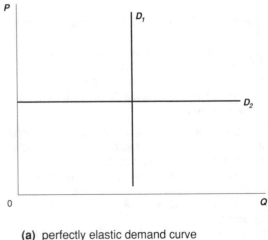

(a) perfectly elastic demand curve
(b) perfectly inelastic demand curve

(c) unitary elastic demand curve

(d) a "long-run" demand curve

4. Compared to the lower-right portion, the upper-left portion of most demand curves tends to be:

(a) more inelastic

(b) more elastic

(c) unitary elastic

(d) perfectly inelastic

5. In which range of the demand schedule is demand price inelastic?

Price	Quantity demanded
$11	50
9	100
7	200
5	300
3	400

(a) $11–$9

(b) $9–$7

(c) $7–$5

(d) $5–$3

6. When a business increased the price of its product from $7 to $8 when the price elasticity of demand was inelastic, then:

(a) total revenues decreased

(b) total revenues increased

(c) total revenues remain unchanged

(d) total revenues were perfectly inelastic

7. You are the sales manager for a pizza company and have been informed that the price elasticity demand for your most popular pizza is greater than one. To increase total revenues, you should:

(a) increase the price of the pizza

(b) decrease the price of the pizza

(c) hold pizza prices constant

(d) decrease demand for your pizza

8. Which of the following is *not* characteristic of a commodity the demand for which is elastic?

(a) the price elasticity coefficient is less than unity

(b) total revenue decreases if price rises

(c) buyers are relatively sensitive to price changes

(d) the relative change in quantity is greater than the relative change in price

9. The demand for Nike basketball shoes is more price elastic than the demand for basketball shoes as a whole. This is best explained by the fact that:

(a) Nike basketball shoes are a luxury good, not a necessity

(b) Nike basketball shoes are the best made and widely advertised

(c) there are more complements for Nike basketball shoes than for basketball shoes as a whole

(d) there are more substitutes for Nike basketball shoes than for basketball shoes as a whole

10. Which of the following is *not* characteristic of a good the demand for which is inelastic?

(a) there are a large number of good substitutes for the good for consumers

(b) the buyer spends a small percentage of his total income on the good

(c) the good is regarded by consumers as a necessity

(d) the period of time for which demand is given is very short

11. An empirical study of commuter rail transportation in the Philadelphia area indicated that price elasticity of demand is:

(a) elastic in the "short run" and the "long run"

(b) inelastic in the "short run" and the "long run"

(c) elastic in the "short run" but inelastic in the "long run"

(d) inelastic in the "short run" but elastic in the "long run"

12. If a 5% fall in the price of a commodity causes quantity supplied to decrease by 8%, supply is:

(a) inelastic

(b) of unitary elasticity

(c) elastic

(d) perfectly inelastic

13. In the diagram below, what is the price elasticity of supply between points **A** and **C**?

(a) 1.33

(b) 1.67

(c) 1.85

(d) 2.46

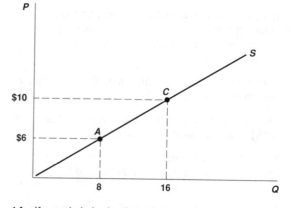

14. If supply is inelastic and demand decreases, the total revenue of sellers will:

(a) increase

(b) decrease

(c) decrease only if demand is elastic

(d) increase only if demand is inelastic

15. The chief determinant of the price elasticity of supply of a product is:
   (a) the number of good substitutes the product has
   (b) the length of time sellers have to adjust to a change in price
   (c) whether the product is a luxury or a necessity
   (d) whether the product is a durable or a nondurable good

16. The long-run supply curve in a constant-cost industry will be:
   (a) perfectly elastic
   (b) perfectly inelastic
   (c) unit elastic
   (d) income elastic

17. The slope of the long-run supply curve in an increasing-cost industry would be:
   (a) vertical
   (b) horizontal
   (c) upsloping
   (d) downsloping

18. If a 5% increase in the price of one good results in a decrease of 2% in the quantity demanded of another good, then it can be concluded that the two goods are:
   (a) complements
   (b) substitutes
   (c) independent
   (d) normal

19. Most goods can be classified as **normal** goods rather than inferior goods. The definition of a normal good means that:
   (a) the percentage change in consumer income is greater than the percentage change in price of the normal good
   (b) the percentage change in quantity demanded of the normal good is greater than the percentage change in consumer income
   (c) as consumer income increases, consumer purchases of a normal good increase
   (d) the income elasticity of demand is negative

20. Based on the information in the table, which product would be an inferior good?

Product	% change in income	% change in quantity demanded
A	− 10	+ 10
B	+ 10	+ 10
C	+ 5	+ 5
D	− 5	− 5

   (a) Product A
   (b) Product B
   (c) Product C
   (d) Product D

21. In the diagram below, a legal price floor of $9.00 will result in:

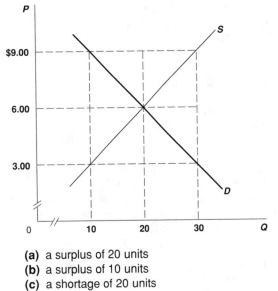

   (a) a surplus of 20 units
   (b) a surplus of 10 units
   (c) a shortage of 20 units
   (d) no shortage or surplus

The next three questions (22, 23, and 24) relate to the table below that shows a hypothetical supply and demand schedule for a product.

Quantity demanded (pounds)	Price (per pound)	Quantity supplied (pounds)
200	$4.40	800
250	4.20	700
300	4.00	600
350	3.80	500
400	3.60	400
450	3.40	300
500	3.20	200

22. The equilibrium price and quantity is:
   (a) $4.00 and 600 pounds
   (b) $3.80 and 350 pounds
   (c) $3.60 and 400 pounds
   (d) $3.40 and 300 pounds

23. If a legal price floor is established at $4.20, there will be a:
   (a) shortage of 450 pounds
   (b) surplus of 450 pounds
   (c) shortage of 300 pounds
   (d) surplus of 300 pounds

24. A shortage of 150 pounds of the product will occur if a legal price is established at:
   (a) $3.20
   (b) $3.40
   (c) $3.80
   (d) $4.00

25. Which of the following would be an example of a price floor?

  (a) controls on apartment rent in major cities
  (b) limiting interest charged by credit card companies
  (c) price controls during World War II
  (d) price supports for agricultural products

■ **DISCUSSION QUESTIONS**

1. Define and explain the price elasticity of demand concept in terms of each of the following:

  (a) the relative sensitiveness of quantity demanded to changes in price;
  (b) the behavior of total revenue when price changes;
  (c) the elasticity coefficient; and
  (d) the relationship between the relative (percentage) change in quantity demanded and the relative (percentage) change in price.

2. What is meant by perfectly elastic demand? By perfectly inelastic demand? What does the demand curve look like when demand is perfectly elastic and when it is perfectly inelastic?

3. In computing the price elasticity coefficient, it usually makes a considerable difference whether the higher price and lower quantity or the lower price and higher quantity are used as a point of reference. What have economists done to eliminate the confusion which would arise if the price elasticity of demand coefficient varied and depended upon whether a price rise or fall were being considered?

4. Demand seldom has the same elasticity at all prices. What is the relationship between the price of most commodities and the price elasticity of demand for them?

5. What is the relationship, if there is a relationship, between the price elasticity of demand and the slope of the demand curve?

6. When the price of a commodity declines, the quantity demanded of it increases. When demand is elastic, total revenue is greater at the lower price; but when demand is inelastic, total revenue is smaller. Explain why total revenue will sometimes increase and why it will sometimes decrease.

7. What are the factors which together determine the price elasticity of demand for a product?

8. Of what practical importance is the price elasticity of demand? Cite examples of its importance to business firms, workers, farmers, and governments.

9. Explain what determines the price elasticity of supply of an economic good or service.

10. Why does the government from time to time impose price ceilings and minimum prices on certain goods and services? What are the consequences of these ceilings and minimums if they are not set at the price which would prevail in the free market?

■ **ANSWERS**

Chapter 7 Demand and Supply: Elasticities and Applications

FILL-IN QUESTIONS

  1. fully, allocated; *a.* latter, micro-; *b.* market, prices

  2. inelastic, elastic

  3. percentages, comparisons

  4. inelastic, vertical, perfectly elastic, horizontal

  5. average, average

  6. varies, unsound

  7. *a.* greater than; *b.* less than; *c.* equal to

  8. inversely, directly

  9. elastic: greater than 1, decrease, increase; inelastic: less than 1, increase, decrease; of unitary elasticity: equal to 1, remain constant, remain constant

  10. *a.* the number of good substitute products available; *b.* the relative importance of the product in the total budget of the buyer; *c.* whether the good is a necessity or a luxury; *d.* the period of time in which demand is being considered

  11. quantity supplied, price

  12. the amount of time which a seller has to respond to a price change, less

  13. cross, income

  14. substitutes, complements, independent

  15. normal or superior, inferior

  16. *a.* 7.00, 15,000; *b.* shortage, 4000; *c.* surplus, 2000.

  17. war, shortages, rationing

  18. minimum wages, agricultural price supports

  19. surplus, attempt to reduce supply or increase demand, purchase the surplus and store or dispose of it

  20. rationing

PROBLEMS AND PROJECTS

1. total revenue: $300, 360, 400, 420, 420, 400, 360; elasticity coefficient: $2\frac{5}{7}$ (2.71), $1\frac{8}{9}$ (1.89), $1\frac{4}{11}$ (1.36), 1, $\frac{11}{15}$ (0.73), $\frac{9}{17}$ (0.53); character of demand: elastic, elastic, elastic, unitary elasticity, inelastic, inelastic

2. *a.* elastic, increases; *b.* unitary, remains the same; *c.* inelastic, decreases

3. Elasticity coefficient: $1\frac{4}{15}$ (1.27), $1\frac{4}{13}$ (1.31), $1\frac{4}{11}$ (1.36), $1\frac{4}{9}$ (1.44), $1\frac{4}{7}$ (1.57), $1\frac{4}{5}$ (1.8); character of supply: elastic, elastic, elastic, elastic, elastic, elastic

4. *a.* (1) S_3; (2) S_2; (3) S_1; *b.* p_1, q_1; *c.* (1) p_4, remain at q_1; (2) p_3, q_2; (3) p_2, q_3; *d.* more; *e.* less, greater

5. *a.* .43, substitute; *b.* $-.71$ complement; *c.* .02, independent

6. N, N, I, I, N

SELF-TEST

1. F, p. 106
2. T, p. 107
3. F, p. 107
4. T, p. 108
5. F, p. 108
6. T, p. 108
7. F, pp. 109–110
8. T, p. 110
9. T, p. 109
10. T, p. 113
11. F, p. 113
12. T, p. 111
13. F, pp. 111–112
14. T, p. 113
15. F, p. 114
16. T, p. 114
17. F, p. 115
18. F, p. 116
19. F, p. 116
20. T, p. 116
21. F, p. 116
22. T, p. 117
23. F, p. 119
24. F, p. 119
25. T, p. 118

1. *c*, p. 106
2. *b*, p. 107
3. *b*, p. 107
4. *b*, p. 108
5. *d*, pp. 109–110
6. *b*, p. 109
7. *b*, p. 109
8. *a*, p. 111
9. *d*, pp. 110–111
10. *a*, pp. 110–111
11. *d*, pp. 111–112
12. *c*, p. 114
13. *a*, p. 114
14. *b*, pp. 114–115
15. *b*, p. 114
16. *a*, p. 116
17. *c*, pp. 115–116
18. *a*, p. 116
19. *c*, p. 116
20. *a*, p. 116
21. *a*, p. 119
22. *c*, p. 117
23. *b*, p. 119
24. *b*, p. 117
25. *d*, p. 119

DISCUSSION QUESTIONS

1. pp. 105–107
2. p. 107
3. pp. 107–108
4. p. 108
5. p. 108
6. pp. 109–110
7. pp. 110–111
8. pp. 112–114
9. pp. 114–115
10. pp. 117–119

CHAPTER 8

Consumer Behavior and Utility Maximization

Previous chapters explained that consumers typically buy more of a product as its price decreases and less of a product as its price increases. Chapter 8 looks behind this law of demand to explain why consumers behave in this way.

Two explanations for the law of demand are presented in the chapter. The first explanation is a general and simple one that is based on income and substitution effects. From this perspective, a change in the price of a product changes the amount consumed because of a change in the real income and because of a change in the price of this good relative to other products that could be purchased. The other explanation is more detailed and abstract because it is based on the concept of marginal utility. In this view, the additional satisfaction (or marginal utility) that a consumer obtains from the consumption of each additional unit of a product will tend to decline, and therefore a consumer will only have an incentive to purchase additional units of a product if its price falls. (A third explanation of consumer demand that is more complete than the first two is based on the use of indifference curves, but this more complex discussion is placed in the appendix to the chapter.)

The majority of the chapter presents the marginal-utility view of consumer behavior. This explanation requires that you first understand the concepts and assumptions upon which this theory of consumer behavior rests, and second, do some rigorous reasoning using these concepts and assumptions. It is an exercise in logic, but be sure that you follow the reasoning. To aid you, several problems are provided so that you can work things out for yourself.

Of course no one believes that consumers actually perform these mental gymnastics before they spend their incomes or make a purchase. But the marginal-utility approach to consumer behavior is studied because the consumers behave "as if" they made their purchases on the basis of very fine calculations. Thus, this approach explains what we do in fact observe, and makes it possible for us to predict with a good deal of precision how consumers will react to changes in their incomes and in the prices of products.

The consumption of any good or service requires that the consumer use scarce and valuable time. The final section of the chapter will show you how the value of the time required for the consumption of a product can be put into the marginal-utility theory; and what the implications of this modification of the theory are.

■ CHECKLIST

When you have studied this chapter you should be able to:

☐ Define and distinguish between the income and the substitution effects of a price change.
☐ Use the income and the substitution effects to explain why a consumer will buy more of a product when its price falls and why a consumer will buy less of a product when its price rises.
☐ Define marginal utility, total utility, and the law of diminishing marginal utility.
☐ Explain the relationship of the law of diminishing marginal utility to demand and to elasticity.
☐ List four assumptions made in the theory of consumer behavior.
☐ State the utility-maximizing rule.
☐ Use the utility-maximizing rule to determine how a consumer would spend his fixed income when you are given the utility and price data.
☐ Derive a consumer's demand for a product from utility, income, and price data.
☐ Explain how the value of time is incorporated into the theory of consumer behavior; and several of the implications of this modification of the theory.

■ CHAPTER OUTLINE

1. The law of consumer demand can be explained by employing either the income-effect and substitution-effect concepts, or the concept of marginal utility.

   a. Consumers buy more of a commodity when its price falls because their money income will go further (the income effect) and because the commodity is now less expensive relative to other commodities (the substitution effect).

b. The essential assumption made in the alternative explanation is that the more the consumer buys of any commodity, the smaller becomes the marginal (extra) utility obtained from it.

2. The assumption (or law) of diminishing marginal utility is the basis of the theory that explains how a consumer will spend his or her income.

a. The typical consumer, it is assumed, is rational, knows his or her marginal-utility schedules for the various goods available, has a limited money income to spend, and must pay a price to acquire each of the goods which yield utility.

b. Given these assumptions, the consumer maximizes the total utility obtained when the marginal utility of the last dollar spent on each commodity is the same for all commodities.

c. Algebraically, total utility is a maximum when the marginal utility of the last unit of a commodity purchased divided by its price is the same for all commodities (that is, marginal utility per dollar is equal for all commodities).

3. To find a consumer's demand for a product the utility-maximizing rule is applied to determine the amount of the product the consumer will purchase at different prices, income, and tastes and the prices of other products remaining constant.

4. The marginal-utility theory includes the fact that consumption takes time and time is a scarce resource.

a. The full price of any consumer good or service is equal to its market price plus the value of time taken to consume it (the income the consumer could have earned had he used that time for work).

b. The inclusion of the value of consumption time in theory of consumer behavior has several significant implications.

■ IMPORTANT TERMS

Income effect
Substitution effect
Utility
Marginal utility

Law of diminishing
marginal utility
Rational
Budget restraint
Utility-maximizing rule

■ FILL-IN QUESTIONS

1. A fall in the price of a product tends to (increase, decrease) _____ the *real* income of a consumer, and a rise in its prices tends to _____

real income. This is called the _____ effect.

2. When the price of a product increases, the product becomes relatively (more, less) _____ expensive than it was and the prices of other products become relatively (higher, lower) _____ than they were; the consumer will, therefore, buy (less, more) _____ of the product in question and _____ of the other products. This is called the _____ effect.

3. The law of diminishing marginal utility is that marginal utility will (increase, decrease) _____ as a consumer increases the quantity of a particular commodity consumed.

4. Assuming that all other things are equal, if the marginal utility of a product decreases rapidly as additional units are consumed, then demand is likely to be (elastic, inelastic) _____, but if marginal utility decreases slowly as consumption increases then it suggests that demand is _____

5. The marginal-utility theory of consumer behavior assumes that the consumer is _____ and has certain _____ for various goods.

6. A consumer cannot buy all he or she wishes of every good and service because income is _____ and goods and services have _____; these two facts are called the _____

7. When the consumer is maximizing the utility which his income will obtain for him, the _____ _____ is the same for all the products he buys.

8. If the marginal utility of the last dollar spent on one product is greater than the marginal utility of the last dollar spent on another product, the consumer should (increase, decrease) _____ her purchases of the first and _____ her purchases of the second product.

9. Assume there are only two products, X and Y, a consumer can purchase with a fixed income. The consumer is maximizing utility algebraically when:

(a) _____   (c) _____

_____ = _____

(b) _____   (d) _____

10. In deriving a consumer's demand for a particular product the two factors (other than the tastes of the consumer) which are held constant are:

a. _____

b. _____

11. The consumption of any product requires _____
a. This is a valuable economic resource because it is

_____

b. Its value is equal to _____

_____

c. And the full price to the consumer of any product is,

therefore, _____ plus _____

■ **PROBLEMS AND PROJECTS**

1. Suppose that when the price of bread is a dollar per loaf, the Robertson family buys six loaves of bread in a week.
a. When the price of bread falls to 80 cents, the Robertson family will increase its bread consumption to seven loaves.

(1) Measured in terms of bread, the fall in the price of bread will _____ their real income by _____ loaves. (**Hint:** How many loaves of bread **could** they now buy without changing the amount they spend on bread?)
(2) Is the Robertsons' demand for bread elastic or inelastic? _____
b. When the price of bread rises from a dollar to $1.20 per loaf, the Robertson family will decrease its bread consumption to four loaves.
(1) Measured in terms of bread, this rise in the price of bread will _____ their real income by _____ loaf.
(2) Is the Robertson's demand for bread elastic or inelastic? _____

2. Assume that Palmer finds only three goods, A, B, and C, are for sale; and that the amounts of utility which their consumption will yield him are as shown in the table below. Compute the marginal utilities for successive units of A, B, and C and enter them in the appropriate columns.

Good A			Good B			Good C		
Quantity	Utility	Marginal utility	Quantity	Utility	Marginal utility	Quantity	Utility	Marginal utility
1	21	_____	1	7	_____	1	23	_____
2	41	_____	2	13	_____	2	40	_____
3	59	_____	3	18	_____	3	52	_____
4	74	_____	4	22	_____	4	60	_____
5	85	_____	5	25	_____	5	65	_____
6	91	_____	6	27	_____	6	68	_____
7	91	_____	7	28.2	_____	7	70	_____

3. Using the marginal-utility data for goods A, B, and C which you obtained in problem 2, assume that the prices of A, B, and C are $5, $1, and $4, respectively, and that Palmer has an income of $37 to spend.
a. Complete the following table by computing the **marginal utility per dollar** for successive units of A, B, and C.
b. Palmer would **not** buy 4 units of A, 1 unit of B, and

4 units of C because _____
c. Palmer would **not** buy 6 units of A, 7 units of B, and

4 units of C because _____

d. When Palmer is maximizing his utility he will buy:

(1) _____ units of A, (2) _____

units of B, (3) _____ units of C; his total

utility will be _____ and the marginal utility of the last dollar spent on each good will

be _____
e. If Palmer's income increased by $1, he would spend

it on good _____, assuming he can buy frac-

tions of a unit of a good, because _____

	Good A		Good B		Good C
Quantity	Marginal utility per dollar	Quantity	Marginal utility per dollar	Quantity	Marginal utility per dollar
1	_____	1	_____	1	_____
2	_____	2	_____	2	_____
3	_____	3	_____	3	_____
4	_____	4	_____	4	_____
5	_____	5	_____	5	_____
6	_____	6	_____	6	_____
7	_____	7	_____	7	_____

4. Ms. Thompson has an income of $36 to spend each week. The only two goods she is interested in purchasing are H and J. The marginal-utility schedules for these two goods are shown in the table below.

	Good H					Good J	
Quantity	MU	MU/$6	MU/$4	MU/$3	MU/$2	MU/$1.50	MU	MU/$4
1	45	7.5	11.25	15	22.5	30	40	10
2	30	5	7.5	10	15	20	36	9
3	20	3.33	5	6.67	10	13.33	32	8
4	15	2.5	3.75	5	7.5	10	28	7
5	12	2	3	4	6	8	24	6
6	10	1.67	2.5	3.33	5	6.67	20	5
7	9	1.5	2.25	3	4.5	6	16	4
8	7.5	1.25	1.88	2.5	3.75	5	12	3

The price of J does not change from week to week and is $4. The marginal utility per dollar from J is also shown in the table.

But the price of H varies from one week to the next. The marginal utility per dollar from H when the price of H is $6, $4, $3, $2, and $1.50 is shown in the table.

a. Complete the table below to show how much of H Ms. Thompson will buy each week at each of the five possible prices of H.

Price of H	Quantity of H demanded
$6.00	_____
4.00	_____
3.00	_____
2.00	_____
1.50	_____

b. What is the table you completed in *a* called?

_____

5. Assume that a consumer can purchase only two goods. These two goods are *R* (recreation) and *M* (ma-

terial goods). The market price of *R* is $2 and the market price of *M* is $1. The consumer spends all her income in such a way that the marginal utility of the last unit of *R* she buys is 12 and the marginal utility of the last unit of *M* she buys is 6.

a. If we ignore the time it takes to consume *R* and *M*, is the consumer maximizing the total utility she obtains from two two goods? _____

b. Suppose it takes 4 hours to consume each unit of *R* and 1 hour to consume each unit of *M*; and the consumer can earn $2 an hour when she works.

(1) The full price of a unit of *R* is $_____

(2) The full price of a unit of *M* is $_____

c. If we take into account the full price of each of the commodities, is the consumer maximizing her total utility? _____ How do you know this? _____

d. If the consumer is not maximizing her utility, should she increase her consumption of *R* or of *M*? _____

Why should she do this? _____

e. Will she use more or less of her time for consuming *R*? _____

■ SELF-TEST

Circle the T if the statement is true; the F if it is false.

1. An increase in the real income of a consumer will result from an increase in the price of a product which the consumer is buying.   **T F**

2. The income and substitution effects will induce the consumer to buy more of normal good Z when the price of Z increases.   **T F**

3. Utility and usefulness are not synonymous.   **T F**

4. Marginal utility is the change in total utility from consuming one more unit of a product.   **T F**

5. Because utility cannot actually be measured, the marginal-utility theory cannot really explain how consumers will behave.   **T F**

6. A consumer's demand curve for a product is down-sloping because total utility decreases as more of the product is consumed.   **T F**

7. If total utility is increasing, then marginal utility is positive and may be either increasing or decreasing.   **T F**

8. There is a significant, positive relationship between the rate of decrease in marginal utility and the price elasticity of demand.   **T F**

9. When marginal utility falls slowly as more of a good is consumed, then demand will tend to be *inelastic*.   **T F**

10. The theory of consumer behavior assumes that consumers act rationally to "get the most from their money."   **T F**

11. All consumers are subject to the budget restraint.   **T F**

12. To find a consumer's demand for a product, the price of the product is varied while tastes and income and the prices of other products remain unchanged.   **T F**

13. The theory of consumer behavior assumes that consumers attempt to maximize marginal utility.   **T F**

14. If the marginal utility per dollar spent on product A is greater than the marginal utility per dollar spent on product B, then to maximize utility the consumer should purchase less of A and more of B.   **T F**

15. When the consumer is maximizing total utility, the marginal utilities of the last unit of every product he buys are identical.   **T F**

16. The marginal utility of product X is 15 and its price is $5, while the marginal utility of product Y is 10 and its price is $2. The utility-maximizing rule suggests that there should be *less* consumption of product Y.   **T F**

17. In most cases, a change in incomes will cause a change in the portfolio of goods and service of purchased by consumers.   **T F**

18. A consumer can earn $10 an hour when she works. It takes 2 hours to consume a product. The value of the time required for the consumption of the product is $5.   **T F**

19. The marginal utility of leisure time appears to decrease as the quantity of available leisure time increases.   **T F**

20. A decrease in the productivity of labor will tend over time to increase the value of time.   **T F**

Circle the letter that corresponds to the best answer.

1. The reason the substitution effect works to encourage a consumer to buy more of a product when its price decreases is:
   (a) the real income of the consumer has been increased
   (b) the real income of the consumer has been decreased
   (c) the product is now relatively less expensive than it was
   (d) other products are now relatively less expensive than they were

2. Karen Hansen buys only two goods, food and clothing. Both are normal goods for Karen. Suppose the price of food decreases. Karen's consumption of clothing will:
   (a) decrease due to the income effect
   (b) increase due to the income effect
   (c) increase due to the substitution effect
   (d) decrease due to the substitution effect

3. Which of the following best expresses the law of diminishing marginal utility?
   (a) the more a person consumes of a product, the smaller becomes the utility which he receives from its consumption
   (b) the more a person consumes of a product, the smaller becomes the additional utility which he receives as a result of consuming an additional unit of the product
   (c) the less a person consumes of a product, the smaller becomes the utility which he receives from its consumption
   (d) the less a person consumes of a product, the smaller becomes the additional utility which he receives as a result of consuming an additional unit of the product

The table below shows a hypothetical total utility schedule for a consumer of chocolate candy bars.

Number consumed	Total utility
0	0
1	9
2	19
3	27
4	35
5	42

4. This consumer begins to experience diminishing marginal utility when he consumes the:
(a) first candy bar
(b) second candy bar
(c) third candy bar
(d) fourth candy bar

5. Other things being equal, demand is likely to be *elastic* if the marginal utility of a product:
(a) decreases rapidly as additional units are consumed
(b) decreases slowly as additional units are consumed
(c) increases rapidly as additional units are consumed
(d) increases slowly as additional units are consumed

6. Which of the following is *not* an essential assumption of marginal-utility theory of consumer behavior?
(a) the consumer has a small income
(b) the consumer is rational
(c) goods and services are not free
(d) goods and services yield decreasing amounts of marginal utility as the consumer buys more of them

7. A consumer is making purchases of products A and B such that the marginal utility of product A is 20 and the marginal utility of product B is 30. The price of product A is $10 and the price of product B is $20. The utility-maximizing rule suggests that this consumer should increase consumption of product:
(a) B and decrease consumption of product A
(b) B and increase consumption of product A
(c) A and decrease consumption of product B
(d) make no change in consumption of A or B

Answer the next three questions (8, 9, and 10) based on the table below showing the marginal-utility schedules for goods X and Y for a hypothetical consumer. The price of good X is $1 and the price of good Y is $2. The income of the consumer is $9.

Good X		Good Y	
Quantity	MU	Quantity	MU
1	8	1	10
2	7	2	8
3	6	3	6
4	5	4	4
5	4	5	3
6	3	6	2
7	2	7	1

8. To maximize utility, the consumer will buy:
(a) 7X and 1Y
(b) 5X and 2Y
(c) 3X and 3Y
(d) 1X and 4Y

9. When the consumer purchases the utility-maximizing combination of goods X and Y, total utility will be:
(a) 36
(b) 45
(c) 48
(d) 52

10. Suppose that the consumer's income increased from $9 to $12. What would be the utility-maximizing combination of goods X and Y?
(a) 5X and 2Y
(b) 6X and 3Y
(c) 2X and 5Y
(d) 4X and 4Y

11. Suppose that the prices of A and B are $3 and $2, respectively, that the consumer is spending his entire income and buying 4 units of A and 6 units of B, and that the marginal utility of both the 4th unit of A and the 6th unit of B is 6. It can be concluded that:
(a) the consumer is in equilibrium
(b) the consumer should buy more of A and less of B
(c) the consumer should buy less of A and more of B
(d) the consumer should buy less of both A and B

12. A decrease in the price of product Z will:
(a) increase the marginal utility per dollar spent on Z
(b) decrease the marginal utility per dollar spent on Z
(c) decrease the total utility per dollar spent on Z
(d) cause no change in the marginal utility per dollar spent on Z

13. Robert Woods is maximizing his satisfaction consuming two goods, X and Y. If the marginal utility of X is half that of Y, what is the price of X if the price of Y is $1.00?
(a) $0.50
(b) $1.00
(c) $1.50
(d) $2.00

14. Summing the marginal utilities of each unit consumed will determine total:
(a) cost
(b) revenue
(c) utility
(d) consumption

Answer the next four questions (15, 16, 17, and 18) on the basis of the following total utility data for products A and B. Assume that the prices of A and B are $6 and $8, respectively, and that consumer income is $36.

Units of A	Total utility	Units of B	Total utility
1	18	1	32
2	30	2	56
3	38	3	72
4	42	4	80
5	44	5	84

15. What is the level of total utility for the consumer in equilibrium?
(a) 86
(b) 102
(c) 108
(d) 120

16. How many units of the two products will the consumer buy?
(a) 1 of A and 4 of B
(b) 2 of A and 2 of B
(c) 2 of A and 3 of B
(d) 3 of A and 4 of B

17. If the price of A decreases to $4, then the utility-maximizing combination of the two products is:
(a) 2 of A and 2 of B
(b) 2 of A and 3 of B
(c) 3 of A and 3 of B
(d) 4 of A and 4 of B

18. Which of the following represents the demand curve for A?

(a)		(b)		(c)		(d)	
P	Q_d	P	Q_d	P	Q_d	P	Q_d
$6	1	$6	2	$6	2	$6	2
4	4	4	5	4	3	4	4

19. The full price of a product to a consumer is:
(a) its market price
(b) its market price plus the value of its consumption time
(c) its market price less the value of its consumption time
(d) the value of its consumption time less its market price

20. A consumer has two basic choices: rent a videotape movie for $4.00 and spend two hours of time watching it, or spend $15 for dinner at a restaurant that takes an hour of time. If the marginal utilities of the movie and the dinner are the same, and the consumer values time at $15 an hour, the rational consumer will most likely:
(a) rent more movies and buy fewer restaurant dinners
(b) buy more restaurant dinners and rent fewer movies
(c) buy fewer restaurant dinners and rent fewer movies
(d) make no change in the consumption of both

DISCUSSION QUESTIONS

1. Explain, employing the income-effect and substitution-effect concepts, the reasons consumers buy more of a product at a lower price than at a higher price, and vice versa.

2. Why is utility a "subjective concept"? How does the subjective nature of utility limit the practical usefulness of the marginal-utility theory of consumer behavior?

3. What is the relationship of marginal utility to the price elasticity of demand?

4. What essential assumptions are made about consumers and the nature of goods and services in developing the marginal-utility theory of consumer behavior? What is meant by "budget restraint"?

5. When is the consumer in equilibrium and maximizing total utility? Explain why any deviation from this equilibrium will decrease the consumer's total utility.

6. Using the marginal-utility theory of consumer behavior, explain how an individual's demand schedule for a particular consumer good can be obtained. Why does a demand schedule obtained in this fashion almost invariably result in an inverse or negative relationship between price and quantity demanded?

7. Explain how a consumer might determine the value of his or her time. How does the value of time affect the full price the consumer pays for a good or service?

8. What does taking time into account explain that the traditional approach to consumer behavior does not explain?

ANSWERS

Chapter 8 Consumer Behavior and Utility Maximization

FILL-IN QUESTIONS

1. increase, decrease, income
2. more, lower, less, more, substitution
3. decrease
4. inelastic, elastic
5. rational, preferences
6. limited, prices, budget restraint
7. ratio of the marginal utility of the last unit purchased of a product to its price
8. increase, decrease

9. *a.* MU of product X; *b.* price of X; *c.* MU of product Y; *d.* price of Y

10. *a.* the income of the consumer; *b.* the prices of other products

11. time; *a.* scarce; *b.* the income that can be earned by using the time for work; *c.* market price, value of the consumption time

PROBLEMS AND PROJECTS

1. *a.* (1) increase, 1½; (2) inelastic; *b.* (1) decrease, 1; (2) elastic

2. marginal utility of good A: 21, 20, 18, 15, 11, 6, 0; marginal utility of good B: 7, 6, 5, 4, 3, 2, 1.2; marginal utility of good C: 23, 17, 12, 8, 5, 3, 2

3. *a.* marginal utility per dollar of good A: 4⅕, 4, 3⅗, 3, 2⅕, 1⅕, 0; marginal utility per dollar of good B: 7, 6, 5, 4, 3, 2, 1⅕; marginal utility per dollar of good C, 5¾, 4¼, 3, 2, 1¼, ¾, ½; *b.* the marginal utility per dollar spent on good B (7) is greater than the marginal utility per dollar spent on good A (3), and the latter is greater than the marginal utility per dollar spent on good C (2); *c.* he would be spending more than his $37 income; *d.* (1) 4; (2) 5; (3) 3; 151, 3; *e.* A, he would obtain the greatest marginal utility for his dollar (2⅕)

4. *a.* 2, 3, 4, 6, 8; *b.* the demand schedule (for good H)

5. *a.* yes; *b.* (1) 10, (2) 3; *c.* no, the marginal utility to price ratios are not the same for the two goods; *d.* of M, because its MU/P ratio is greater; *e.* less

SELF-TEST

DISCUSSION QUESTIONS

Appendix to Chapter 8 Indifference Curve Analysis

This brief appendix contains the third explanation or approach to the theory of consumer behavior. In it you are introduced first to the budget line and then to the indifference curve. These two geometrical concepts are next combined to explain when a consumer is purchasing the combination of two products that maximizes the total utility

obtainable with his or her income. The last step is to vary the price of one of the products to find the consumer's demand (schedule or curve) for the product.

■ CHECKLIST

When you have studied this appendix you should be able to:

☐ Define the concept of a budget line.
☐ Explain how to measure the slope of a budget line and determine the location of the budget line.
☐ Define the concept of an indifference curve.
☐ State two characteristics of indifference curves.
☐ Explain the meaning of an indifference map.
☐ Given an indifference map, determine which indifference curves bring more or less total utility to consumers.
☐ Use indifference curves to identify which combination of two products maximizes the total utility of consumers.
☐ Derive a consumer's demand for a product using indifference curve analysis.
☐ Compare and contrast the marginal-utility and the indifference curve analyses of consumer behavior.

■ APPENDIX OUTLINE

1. A budget line shows graphically the different combinations of two products a consumer can purchase with a particular money income; and it has a negative slope.
   a. An increase (decrease) in the money income of the consumer will shift the budget line to the right (left) without affecting its slope.
   b. An increase (decrease) in the prices of both products shifts it to the left (right); but an increase (decrease) in the price of the product the quantity of which is measured horizontally (the price of the other product remaining constant) pivots the budget line around a fixed point on the vertical axis in a clockwise (counterclockwise) direction.

2. An indifference curve shows graphically the different combinations of two products which bring a consumer the same total utility.
   a. An indifference curve is downsloping; if utility is to remain the same when the quantity of one product increases the quantity of the other product must decrease.
   b. An indifference curve is also convex to the origin; the more a consumer has of one product the smaller is the quantity of a second product he is willing to give up to obtain an additional unit of the first product.
   c. The consumer has an indifference curve for every level of total utility; and the nearer (farther) a curve is to (from) the origin in this indifference map the smaller (larger) is the utility of the combinations on that curve.

3. The consumer is in equilibrium and purchasing the combination of two products that brings the maximum utility to him where the budget line is tangent to an indifference curve.

4. In the marginal-utility approach to consumer behavior it is assumed that utility is measurable; but in the indifference curve approach it need only be assumed that a consumer can say whether a combination of products has more utility than, less utility than, or the same amount of utility as another combination.

5. The demand (schedule or curve) for one of the products is derived by varying the price of that product and shifting the budget line, holding the price of the other product and the consumer's income constant, and finding the quantity of the product the consumer will purchase at each price when in equilibrium.

■ **IMPORTANT TERMS**

Budget line   **Indifference map**
Indifference curve   **Equilibrium position**
**Marginal rate of
substitution**

■ **FILL-IN QUESTIONS**

1. A budget line shows the various combinations of two products that can be purchased with a given _____; and, when quantities of X are measured horizontally and quantities of Y vertically, it has a slope equal to the ratio of _____ to the _____

2. When:
  a. a consumer's income increases the budget line moves to the (right, left) _____
  b. quantities of E are measured horizontally and quantities of F vertically, an increase in the price of E will fan the budget line (outward, inward) _____ around a fixed point on the _____ axis.

3. An indifference curve shows the various combinations of two products that give a consumer the same _____
  a. An indifference curve slopes (upward, downward) _____ and the slope of an indifference curve is equal to the marginal _____ of _____

  b. It is (concave, convex) _____ to the origin.

4. The more a consumer has of one product, the (greater, smaller) _____ is the quantity of a second product he or she will give up to obtain an additional unit of the first product: as a result the marginal rate of substitution of the first for the second product (increases, decreases) _____ as a consumer moves from left to right (or downward) along an indifference curve.

5. The farther from the origin an indifference curve lies, the (greater, smaller) _____ is the total utility obtained from the combinations of products on that curve.

6. A consumer obtains the greatest attainable total utility or satisfaction when he or she purchases that combination of two products at which his or her budget line is _____ _____. At this point the consumer's marginal rate of substitution is equal to _____ _____

7. Were a consumer to purchase a combination of two products which lies on her budget line and at which her budget line is steeper than the indifference curve intersecting that point, she could increase her satisfaction by trading (down, up) _____ her budget line.

8. The marginal-utility approach to consumer behavior requires that we assume utility (is, is not) _____ numerically measurable; and the indifference curve approach (does, does not) _____ require we make this assumption.

9. When quantities of product X are measured along the horizontal axis, a decrease in the price of X:
  a. fans the budget line (inward, outward) _____ and to the (right, left) _____;
  b. puts the consumer, when in equilibrium, on a (higher, lower) _____ indifference curve;
  c. and normally induces the consumer to purchase (more, less) _____ of product X.

10. Using indifference curves and different budget lines to determine how much of a particular product an individual consumer will purchase at different prices makes it possible to derive that consumer's _____ curve or schedule for that product.

■ PROBLEMS AND PROJECTS

1. Following are the schedules for three indifference curves.

Indifference schedule 1		Indifference schedule 2		Indifference schedule 3	
A	B	A	B	A	B
0	28	0	36	0	45
1	21	1	28	1	36
2	15	2	21	2	28
3	10	3	15	3	21
4	6	4	10	4	15
5	3	5	6	5	10
6	1	6	3	6	6
7	0	7	1	7	3
		8	0	8	1
				9	0

a. On the graph below, measure quantities of A along the horizontal axis (from 0 to 9) and quantities of B along the vertical axis (from 0 to 45).

(1) Plot the 8 combinations of A and B from indifference schedule 1 and draw through the 8 points a curve which is in no place a straight line. Label this curve IC 1.

(2) Do the same for the 9 points in indifference schedule 2 and label it IC 2.

(3) Repeat the process for the 10 points in indifference schedule 3 and label the curve IC 3.

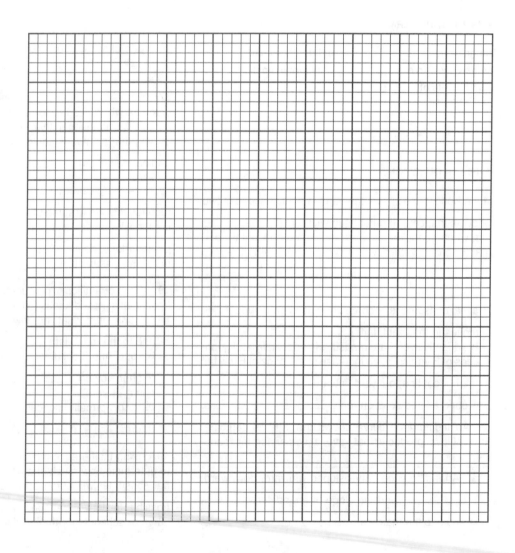

b. Assume the price of A is $12, the price of B is $2.40, and a consumer has an income of $72.

(1) Complete the table below to show the quantities of A and B this consumer is able to purchase.

A	B
0	____
1	____
2	____
3	____
4	____
5	____
6	____

(2) Plot this budget line on the graph you completed in part *a* (above).

(3) This budget line has a slope equal to _____
c. To obtain the greatest satisfaction or utility from his income of $72 this consumer will:

(1) purchase _____ units of A and _____ of B;

(2) and spend $_____ on A and $_____ on B.

2. Shown below is a graph with three indifference curves and three budget lines. This consumer has an income of $100 and the price of Y remains constant at $5.

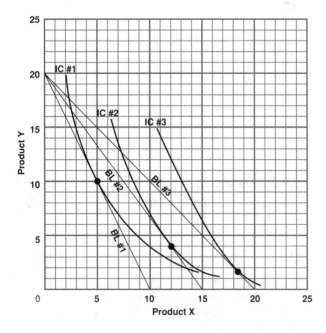

a. When the price of X is $10 the consumer's budget line is BL #1 and the consumer:

(1) purchases _____ X and _____ Y;

(2) and spends $_____ on X and $_____ on Y.
b. If the price of X is $6⅔ the budget line is BL #2 and the consumer:

(1) purchases _____ X and _____ Y;

(2) and spends $_____ for X and $_____ for Y.
c. And when the price of X is $5, the consumer has budget line BL #3 and:

(1) buys _____ X and _____ Y; and

(2) spends $_____ on X and $_____ on Y.
d. On the graph below plot the quantities of X demanded at the three prices.

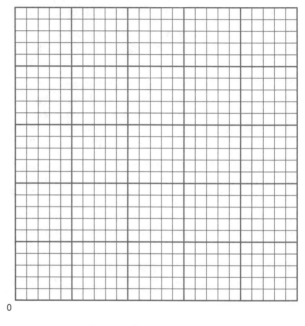

e. Between $10 and $5 this consumer's demand for X is (elastic, inelastic) _____ and for him products X and Y are (substitutes, complements) _____

■ **SELF-TEST**

Circle the T if the statement is true; the F if it is false.

1. The slope of the budget line when quantities of F are measured horizontally and quantities of G vertically is equal to the price of G divided by the price of F.   **T   F**

2. An increase in the money income of a consumer shifts the budget line to the right.   **T   F**

3. The closer to the origin an indifference curve lies the smaller is the total utility a consumer obtains from the combinations of products on that indifference curve.　T　F

4. If a consumer moves from one combination (or point) on an indifference curve to another combination (or point) on the same curve the total utility obtained by the consumer does not change.　T　F

5. A consumer maximizes total utility when he or she purchases the combination of the two products at which his or her budget line crosses an indifference curve.　T　F

6. A consumer is unable to purchase any of the combinations of two products which lie below (or to the left) of the consumer's budget line.　T　F

7. An indifference curve is concave to the origin.　T　F

8. A decrease in the price of a product normally enables a consumer to reach a higher indifference curve.　T　F

9. It is assumed in the marginal-utility approach to consumer behavior that utility is numerically measurable.　T　F

10. In both the marginal-utility and indifference curve approaches to consumer behavior it is assumed that a consumer is able to say whether the total utility obtained from combination A is greater than, equal to, or less than the total utility obtained from combination B.　T　F

11. The budget line shows all combinations of two products which the consumer can purchase, given money income and the prices of the products.　T　F

12. On an indifference map, the further from the origin, the lower the level of utility associated with each indifference curve.　T　F

13. The marginal rate of substitution shows the rate, at the margin, at which the consumer is prepared to substitute one good for the other so as to remain equally satisfied.　T　F

14. On an indifference map, the consumer's equilibrium position will be where the slope of the highest attainable indifference curve equals the slope of the budget line.　T　F

15. There can be an intersection of consumer indifference curves.　T　F

Circle the letter that corresponds to the best answer.

1. Suppose a consumer has an income of $8, the price of R is $1, and the price of S is $0.50. Which of the following combinations is on the consumer's budget line?
(a) 8R and 1S
(b) 7R and 1S

(c) 6R and 6S
(d) 5R and 6S

2. If a consumer has an income of $100, the price of U is $10, and the price of V is $20, the maximum quantity of U the consumer is able to purchase is:
(a) 5
(b) 10
(c) 20
(d) 30

3. When the income of a consumer is $20, the price of T is $5, the price of Z is $2, and the quantity of T is measured horizontally, the slope of the budget line is:
(a) $\frac{2}{5}$
(b) $2\frac{1}{2}$
(c) 4
(d) 10

4. An indifference curve is a curve which shows the different combinations of two products that:
(a) give a consumer equal marginal utilities
(b) give a consumer equal total utilities
(c) cost a consumer equal amounts
(d) have the same prices

5. In the schedule for an indifference curve below, how much of G is the consumer willing to give up to obtain the third unit of H?
(a) 3
(b) 4
(c) 5
(d) 6

Quantity of G	Quantity of H
18	1
12	2
7	3
3	4
0	5

6. The slope of the indifference curve measures the:
(a) slope of the budget line
(b) total utility of a good
(c) space on an indifference map
(d) marginal rate of substitution

7. To derive the demand curve of a product, the price of the product is varied. For the indifference curve analysis, the:
(a) budget line is held constant
(b) money income of the consumer changes
(c) tastes and preferences of the consumer are held constant
(d) prices of other products the consumer might purchase changes

The next four questions (8, 9, 10, and 11) are based on the diagram below.

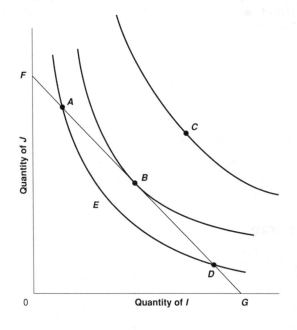

The next four questions (12, 13, 14, and 15) are based on the diagram below.

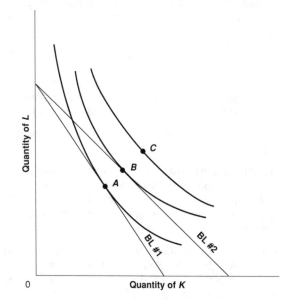

8. The budget line is best represented by line:
(a) *AB*
(b) *AD*
(c) *FG*
(d) *DG*

9. Which combination of goods *I* and *J* will the consumer purchase?
(a) *A*
(b) *B*
(c) *C*
(d) *E*

10. Suppose the price of good *I* increases. The budget line will shift:
(a) inward around a point on the *J* axis
(b) outward around a point on the *J* axis
(c) inward around a point on the *I* axis
(d) outward around a point on the *I* axis

11. If the consumer chooses the combination of goods *I* and *J* represented by point *E*, then the consumer could:
(a) obtain more goods with the available money income
(b) not obtain more goods with the available money income
(c) shift the budget line outward so that it is tangent with point *C*
(d) shift the budget line inward so that it is tangent with point *E*

12. If the budget line shifts from BL #1 to BL #2, it is because the price of:
(a) *K* increased
(b) *K* decreased
(c) *L* increased
(d) *L* decreased

13. If the budget line shifts from BL #2 to BL #1, it is because the price of:
(a) *K* increased
(b) *K* decreased
(c) *L* increased
(d) *L* decreased

14. When the budget line shifts from BL #2 to BL #1, the consumer will buy:
(a) more of *K* and *L*
(b) less of *K* and *L*
(c) more of *K* and less of *L*
(d) less of *K* and more of *L*

15. Point *C* on indifference curve IC #3 can be an attainable combination of products *K* and *L*, if:
(a) the price of *K* increases
(b) the price of *L* increases
(c) money income increases
(d) money income decreases

■ DISCUSSION QUESTIONS

1. Explain why the slope of the budget line is negative and why the slope of an indifference curve is negative and convex to the origin.

2. How will each of the following events affect the budget line?
   (a) A decrease in the money income of the consumer;
   (b) an increase in the prices of both products; and
   (c) a decrease in the price of one of the products.

3. Explain why the budget line can be called "objective" and an indifference curve "subjective."

4. Suppose a consumer purchases a combination of two products that is on his or her budget line but the budget line is not tangent to an indifference curve at that point. Of which product should the consumer buy more and of which should he or she buy less? Why?

5. Explain how the indifference map of a consumer and the budget line are utilized to derive the consumer's demand for one of the products. In deriving demand, what is varied and what is held constant?

6. What is the "important difference between the marginal utility theory and the indifference curve theory of consumer demand"?

■ ANSWERS

Appendix to Chapter 8 Indifference Curve Analysis

FILL-IN QUESTIONS

1. income, the price of X, price of Y

2. *a.* right; *b.* inward, F

3. total satisfaction (utility); *a.* downward, rate, substitution; *b.* convex

4. smaller, decreases

5. greater

6. tangent to an indifference curve, the ratio of the price of the product measured on the horizontal axis to the price of the product measured on the vertical axis

7. up

8. is, does not

9. *a.* outward, right; *b.* higher; *c.* more

10. demand

PROBLEMS AND PROJECTS

1. *b.* (1) 30, 25, 20, 15, 10, 5, 0; (3) 5; *c.* (1) 3, 15; (2) 36, 36

2. *a.* (1) 5, 10; (2) 50, 50; *b.* (1) 12, 4; (2) 80, 20; *c.* (1) 19, 1; (2) 95, 5; *e.* elastic, substitutes

SELF-TEST

1. F, p. 134	**9.** T, p. 137
2. T, p. 134	**10.** T, p. 136
3. T, p. 136	**11.** T, p. 134
4. T, p. 135	**12.** F, p. 136
5. F, p. 136	**13.** T, p. 135
6. F, p. 136	**14.** T, pp. 136–137
7. F, p. 135	**15.** F, p. 136
8. T, p. 136	

1. *d,* p. 134	**9.** *b,* p. 136
2. *b,* p. 134	**10.** *a,* pp. 134–135
3. *b,* p. 134	**11.** *a,* p. 136
4. *b,* p. 135	**12.** *b,* p. 134
5. *c,* p. 135	**13.** *a,* p. 134
6. *d,* p. 135	**14.** *b,* p. 136
7. *c,* pp. 137–138	**15.** *c,* p. 136
8. *c,* p. 134	

DISCUSSION QUESTIONS

1. pp. 134–135	**4.** p. 136
2. pp. 134–135	**5.** pp. 137–138
3. pp. 134–135	**6.** p. 137

CHAPTER 9

The Costs of Production

In previous chapters, the factors which influence the demand for a product purchased by consumers were examined in some detail. Chapter 9 turns to the other side of the market and begins the investigation of the forces which determine the amount of a particular product a business firm will produce and the price it will charge for that product.

The factors that determine the output of a firm and the price of the product are the costs of producing the product **and** the structure of the market in which the product is sold. In addition there is the demand for the product. In the next four chapters you will learn how costs and demand determine price and output in four different kinds of market structures: pure competition, pure monopoly, monopolistic competition, and oligopoly. Because Chapter 9 is an examination of the way in which the costs of the firm change as the output of the firm changes, this chapter is extremely important if the four chapters which follow it are to be understood. For this reason it is necessary for you to master the material dealing with the costs of the firm.

You will probably find that you have some difficulty with the new terms and concepts. Particular attention, therefore, should be given to them. These new terms and concepts are used in the explanation of the costs of the firm and will be used over and over again in later chapters. If you try to learn them in the order in which you encounter them you will have little difficulty because the later terms build on the earlier ones.

After the new terms and concepts are well fixed in your mind, understanding the generalizations made about the relationships between cost and output will be much simpler. Here the important things to note are (1) that the statements made about the behavior of costs are **generalizations** (they do not apply to any particular firm or enterprise, but are more or less applicable to every business firm); and (2) that the generalizations made about the relationships between particular types of cost and the output of the firm are fairly precise generalizations. When attempting to learn these generalizations, you will find it worthwhile to draw rough graphs (with cost on the vertical and output on the horizontal axis) which describe the cost relationships. Try it especially with the following types of costs: **short-run** fixed, variable, total, average fixed, average variable, average total, and marginal costs; and **long-run** average cost.

One last cue: In addition to learning **how** the costs of the firm vary as its output varies, be sure to understand **why** the costs vary the way they do. In this connection note that the behavior of short-run costs is the result of the law of diminishing returns and that the behavior of long-run costs is the consequence of economies and diseconomies of scale.

■ CHECKLIST

When you have studied this chapter you should be able to:

☐ Define economic cost.
☐ Distinguish between an explicit and an implicit cost.
☐ Explain the difference between normal profit and economic profit and why the former is a cost and the latter is not a cost.
☐ Distinguish between the short run and the long run in production.
☐ State the law of diminishing returns and explain its rationale with examples.
☐ Compute marginal and average product when you are given the necessary data.
☐ Explain the relationship between marginal and average product.
☐ Explain the difference between a fixed cost and a variable cost and between average cost and marginal cost.
☐ Compute and graph average fixed cost, average variable cost, average total cost, and marginal cost when you are given total-cost data.
☐ State the relationship between average product and average variable cost and between marginal product and marginal cost.
☐ Explain why cost curves might shift.
☐ Explain the difference between short-run costs and long-run costs.
☐ State why the long-run average cost curve is expected to be U-shaped.

☐ List the causes of the economies and the diseconomies of scale.
☐ Indicate the relationship between long-run average costs and the structure and competitiveness of an industry.
☐ Describe the relevance of economies and diseconomies of scale.
☐ Explain the concept of minimum efficient scale.

■ CHAPTER OUTLINE

1. Because resources are scarce and may be employed to produce many different products, the economic cost of using resources to produce any one of these products is an opportunity cost: the amount of other products that cannot be produced.

a. In money terms, the costs of employing resources to produce a product are also an opportunity cost: the payments a firm must make to the owners of resources to attract these resources away from their best alternative opportunities for earning incomes; and these costs may be either explicit or implicit.

b. *Normal* profit is an implicit cost and is the minimum payment that entrepreneurs must receive for performing the entrepreneurial functions for the firm.

c. *Economic*, or pure, profit is the revenue a firm receives in excess of all its explicit and implicit economic (opportunity) costs. (The firm's accounting profit is its revenue less only its *explicit* costs.)

d. The firm's economic costs vary as the firm's output varies; and the way in which costs vary with output depends upon whether the firm is able to make short-run or long-run changes in the amounts of resources it employs. The firm's plant is a fixed resource in the short run and a variable resource in the long run.

2. In the short run the firm cannot change the size of its plant and can vary its output only by changing the quantities of the variable resources it employs.

a. The law of diminishing returns determines the manner in which the costs of the firm change as it changes its output in the short run.

b. The total short-run costs of a firm are the sum of its fixed and variable costs. As output increases:
(1) the fixed costs do not change;
(2) at first the variable costs increase at a decreasing rate, and then increase at an increasing rate;
(3) and at first total costs increase at a decreasing rate and then increase at an increasing rate.

c. Average fixed, variable, and total costs are equal, respectively, to the firm's fixed, variable, and total costs divided by the output of the firm. As output increases:
(1) average fixed cost decreases;
(2) at first average variable cost decreases and then increases;

(3) and at first average total cost also decreases and then increases.

d. Marginal cost is the extra cost incurred in producing one additional unit of output.
(1) Because the marginal product of the variable resource increases and then decreases (as more of the variable resource is employed to increase output), marginal cost decreases and then increases as output increases.
(2) At the output at which average variable cost is a minimum, average variable cost and marginal cost are equal; and at the output at which average total cost is a minimum, average total cost and marginal cost are equal.
(3) On a graph, marginal cost will always intersect average variable cost at its minimum point, and marginal cost will always intersect average total cost at its minimum point. These intersections will always have marginal cost approaching average variable cost and average total cost from below.
(4) Changes in either resource prices or technology will cause the cost curves to shift.

3. In the long run, all the resources employed by the firm are variable resources, and, therefore, all its costs are variable costs.

a. As the firm expands its output by increasing the size of its plant, average cost tends to fall at first because of the economies of large-scale production; but as this expansion continues, sooner or later, average cost begins to rise because of the diseconomies of large-scale production.

b. The economies and diseconomies encountered in the production of different goods are important factors influencing the structure and competitiveness of various industries.
(1) Minimum efficient scale (MES) is the smallest level of output at which a firm can minimize long-run average costs. This concept explains why relatively large and small firms could coexist in an industry and be viable when there is an extended range of constant returns to scale.
(2) In other industries the long-run average cost curve will decline over a range of output. Given consumer demand, efficient production will be achieved only with a small number of large firms.
(3) When economies of scale extend beyond the market size, the conditions for a natural monopoly are produced, wherein unit costs are minimized by having a single firm produce a product.

■ IMPORTANT TERMS

Economic cost	**Implicit cost**
Opportunity cost	**Economic (pure) profit**
Explicit cost	**Short run**

Long run
Law of diminishing returns
Normal profit
Marginal product
Average product
Fixed resource
Variable resource
Fixed cost
Variable cost
Total cost
Average fixed cost

Average variable cost
Total product
Average (total) cost
Marginal cost
Economies of (large) scale
Diseconomies of (large) scale
Constant returns to scale
Minimum efficient scale (MES)
Natural monopoly

■ FILL-IN QUESTIONS

1. The cost of producing a particular product is the quantity of _____ products that cannot be produced. The value or worth of any resource is what it can earn in its best alternative use and is called the (out-of-pocket, opportunity) _____ cost of that resource.

2. The money cost of producing a product is the amount of money the firm must pay to resource owners to _____ these resources away from alternative employments in the economy; and these costs may be either _____ or _____ costs.

3. Normal profit is a cost because it is the payment which the firm must make to obtain the services of the _____
   a. Economic profit is not a cost and is equal to the firm's total _____ less its total _____
   b. Accounting profit is equal to the firm's total revenue less its (explicit, implicit) _____ costs.

4. In the short run the firm can change its output by changing the quantity of the (fixed, variable) _____ resources it employs; but it cannot change the quantity of the _____ resources. This means that the firm's plant capacity is fixed in the (short, long) _____ run and variable in the _____ run.

5. The law of diminishing returns is that as successive units of a (fixed, variable) _____ resource are added to a _____ resource beyond some point the (total, marginal) _____ product of the former resource will decrease. The law

assumes that all units of input are of (equal, unequal) _____ quality.

6. When the total product:
   a. increases at an increasing rate, the marginal product is (rising, falling) _____;
   b. increases at a decreasing rate, the marginal product is (positive, negative, zero) _____, but (rising, falling) _____ before;
   c. is at a maximum, the marginal product is (positive, negative, zero) _____;
   d. decreases, the marginal product is (positive, negative, zero) _____

7. When the marginal product of any input:
   a. exceeds its average product the average product is (rising, falling) _____;
   b. is less than its average product the average product is _____;
   c. is equal to its average product the average product is a (minimum, maximum) _____

8. On the graph below sketch the way in which the average product and the marginal product of a resource change as the firm increases its employment of that resource.

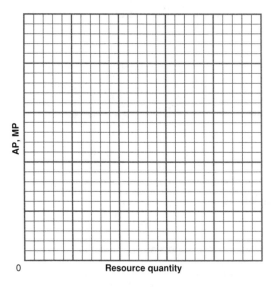

9. The short-run costs of a firm are either _____ costs or _____ costs, but in the long run all costs are _____ costs.

10. On the graph on the next page sketch the manner in which fixed cost, variable cost, and total cost change as the output the firm produces in the short run changes.

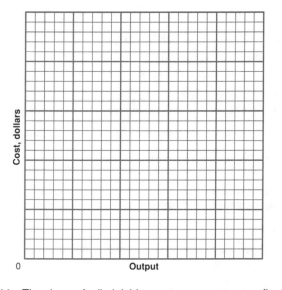

11. The law of diminishing returns causes a firm's

_____ cost, _____

cost, and _____ cost to decrease at first
and then to increase as the output of the firm increases.
Sketch these three cost curves on the graph below in such
a way that their proper relationship to each other is shown.

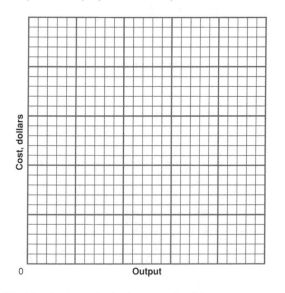

12. Marginal cost is the increase in either _____

_____ cost or _____
which occurs when the firm increases its output by one
unit.

13. If marginal cost is less than average variable cost,
average variable cost will be (rising, falling, constant)

_____ but if average variable cost is less than

marginal cost, average variable cost will be _____

14. Assume that labor is the only variable input in the
short run and that the wage rate paid to labor is constant.
   a. When the marginal product of labor is rising, the
   marginal cost of producing a product is (rising, falling)

   _____

   b. When the average variable cost of producing a
   product is falling, the average product of labor is

   _____

   c. At the output at which marginal cost is a minimum,
   the marginal product of labor is a (minimum, maximum)

   _____

   d. At the output at which the average product of labor
   is a maximum, the average variable cost of producing

   the product is a _____
   e. At the output at which average variable cost is a
   minimum:

   (1) average variable cost and _____ cost

   are _____

   (2) average product and _____ product are

   _____

15. The long-run average cost of producing a product is
equal to the lowest of the short-run costs of producing that
product after the firm has had all the time it requires
to make the appropriate adjustments in the size of its

_____

16. Below are the short-run average-cost curves of producing a product with three different sizes of plants, plant
1, plant 2, and plant 3. Draw the firm's long-run average
cost on this graph.

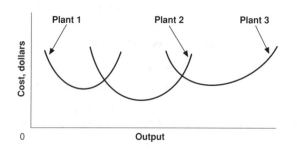

17. List below four important types of economy of large
scale:

   a. _____

   b. _____

   c. _____

   d. _____

18. The factor which gives rise to diseconomies of large scale is _____

19. Economies and diseconomies of scale are significant in the American economy because they affect the _____ and the _____ of the firms in a particular industry.

20. The smallest level of output at which a firm can minimize long-run average costs is _____. Relatively large and small firms could coexist in this type of industry and be equally viable when there is an extended range of _____

21. In some industries, the long-run average cost curve will (increase, decrease) _____ over a long range of output and efficient production will be achieved with only a few (small, large) _____ firms. The conditions for a _____ are created when unit costs are minimized by having a single firm produce a product, so that (economies, diseconomies) _____ of scale extend beyond the market's size.

■ **PROBLEMS AND PROJECTS**

1. The table below shows the total production of a firm as the quantity of labor employed increases. The quantities of all other resources employed are constant.
  a. Compute the marginal products of the first through the eighth unit of labor and enter them in the table.
  b. Now compute the average products of the various quantities of labor and enter them in the table.

Units of labor	Total production	Marginal product of labor	Average product of labor
0	0		0
1	80	_____	_____
2	200	_____	_____
3	330	_____	_____
4	400	_____	_____
5	450	_____	_____
6	480	_____	_____
7	490	_____	_____
8	480	_____	_____

c. There are increasing returns to labor from the first through the _____ unit of labor and decreasing returns from the _____ through the eighth unit.
  d. When total production is increasing, marginal product is (positive, negative) _____ and when total production is decreasing, marginal product is _____
  e. When marginal product is greater than average product, then average product will (rise, fall) _____, and when marginal product is less than average product, then average product will _____

2. Assume that a firm has a plant of fixed size and that it can vary its output only by varying the amount of labor it employs. The table at the top of the next page shows the relationships between the amount of labor employed, the output of the firm, the marginal product of labor, and the average product of labor.
  a. Assume each unit of labor costs the firm $10. Compute the total cost of labor for each quantity of labor the firm might employ, and enter these figures in the table.
  b. Now determine the marginal cost of the firm's product as the firm increases its output. Divide the ***increase*** in total labor cost by the ***increase in total output*** to find the marginal cost. Enter these figures in the table.
  c. When the marginal product of labor:
  (1) Increases, the marginal cost of the firm's product (increases, decreases) _____
  (2) Decreases, the marginal cost of the firm's product _____
  d. If labor is the only variable input, the total labor cost and total variable cost are equal. Find the average variable cost of the firm's product (by dividing the total labor cost by total output) and enter these figures in the table.
  e. When the average product of labor:
  (1) Increases, the average variable cost (increases, decreases) _____
  (2) Decreases, the average variable cost _____

Quantity of labor employed	Total output	Marginal product of labor	Average product of labor	Total labor cost	Marginal cost	Average variable cost
0	0	—	—	$_____	—	—
1	5	5	5	_____	$_____	$_____
2	11	6	5½	_____	_____	_____
3	18	7	6	_____	_____	_____
4	24	6	6	_____	_____	_____
5	29	5	4⅘	_____	_____	_____
6	33	4	5½	_____	_____	_____
7	36	3	5⅐	_____	_____	_____
8	38	2	4¾	_____	_____	_____
9	39	1	4⅓	_____	_____	_____
10	39	0	3⁹⁄₁₀	_____	_____	_____

3. In the table below you will find a schedule of a firm's fixed cost and variable cost.

   a. Complete the table by computing total cost, average fixed cost, average total cost, and marginal cost.

b. On the first graph on page 95, plot and label fixed cost, variable cost, and total cost.

c. On the second graph on page 95, plot average fixed cost, average variable cost, average total cost, and marginal cost; label the four curves.

Output	Total fixed cost	Total variable cost	Total cost	Average fixed cost	Average variable cost	Average total cost	Marginal cost
$ 0	$200	$ 0	$_____				
1	200	50	_____	$_____	$50.00	$_____	$_____
2	200	90	_____	_____	45.00	_____	_____
3	200	120	_____	_____	40.00	_____	_____
4	200	160	_____	_____	40.00	_____	_____
5	200	220	_____	_____	44.00	_____	_____
6	200	300	_____	_____	50.00	_____	_____
7	200	400	_____	_____	57.14	_____	_____
8	200	520	_____	_____	65.00	_____	_____
9	200	670	_____	_____	74.44	_____	_____
10	200	900	_____	_____	90.00	_____	_____

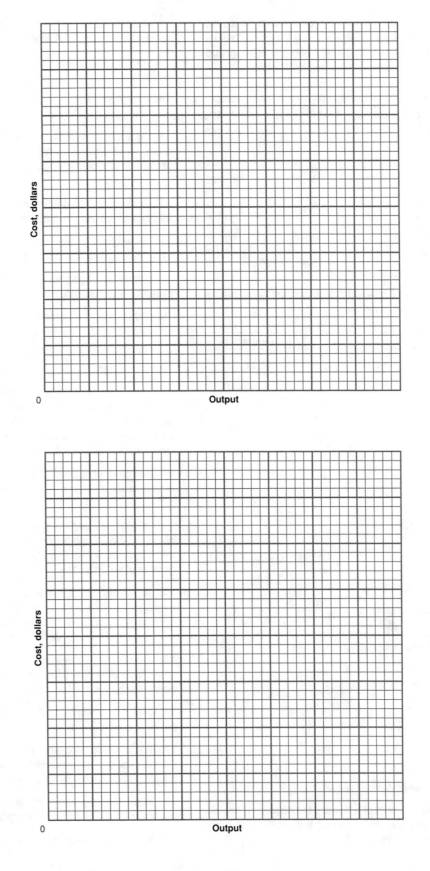

4. Below are the short-run average-total-cost schedules for three plants of different size which a firm might build to produce its product. Assume that these are the only possible sizes of plants which the firm might build.

Plant size A		Plant size B		Plant size C	
Output	ATC	Output	ATC	Output	ATC
10	$ 7	10	$17	10	$53
20	6	20	13	20	44
30	5	30	9	30	35
40	4	40	6	40	27
50	5	50	4	50	20
60	7	60	3	60	14
70	10	70	4	70	11
80	14	80	5	80	8
90	19	90	7	90	6
100	25	100	10	100	5
110	32	110	16	110	7
120	40	120	25	120	10

a. Complete the **long-run** average-cost schedule for the firm in the table below.

Output	Average cost
10	$____
20	____
30	____
40	____
50	____
60	____
70	____
80	____
90	____
100	____
110	____
120	____

b. For outputs between:

(1) _____ and _____, the firm should build plant A.

(2) _____ and _____, the firm should build plant B.

(3) _____ and _____, the firm should build plant C.

■ **SELF-TEST**

Circle the T if the statement is true; the F if it is false.

1. The economic costs of a firm are the payments it must make to resource owners to attract their resources from alternative employments. **T F**

2. Economic or pure profit is an explicit cost, while normal profit is an implicit cost. **T F**

3. In the short run the size (or capacity) of a firm's plant is fixed. **T F**

4. The resources employed by a firm are all variable in the long run and all fixed in the short run. **T F**

5. The law of diminishing returns is that as successive amounts of a variable resource are added to a fixed resource, beyond some point total output will diminish. **T F**

6. An assumption of the law of diminishing returns is that all units of variable inputs are of equal quality. **T F**

7. When total product is increasing at a decreasing rate, marginal product is positive and increasing. **T F**

8. When average product is falling, marginal product is greater than average product. **T F**

9. When marginal product is negative, total production (or output) is decreasing. **T F**

10. The larger the output of a firm, the smaller is the fixed cost of the firm. **T F**

11. If the fixed cost of a firm increases from one year to the next (because the premium it must pay for the insurance on the buildings it owns has been increased) while its variable-cost schedule remains unchanged, its marginal-cost schedule will also remain unchanged. **T F**

12. Marginal cost is equal to average variable cost at the output at which average variable cost is a minimum. **T F**

13. When the marginal product of a variable resource increases, the marginal cost of producing the product will decrease; and when marginal product decreases, marginal cost will increase. **T F**

14. If the price of a variable input should increase, the average variable cost, average total cost, and marginal cost curves would all shift upward, but the position of the average fixed cost curve would remain unchanged. **T F**

15. One of the explanations of why the long-run average-cost curve of a firm rises after some level of output has been reached is the law of diminishing returns. **T F**

16. The primary cause of diseconomies of scale is increased specialization of labor. **T F**

17. If a firm has constant returns to scale in the long run the total costs of producing its product do not change when it expands or contracts its output. **T F**

18. Many firms appear to be larger than is necessary for them to achieve the minimum efficient scale. **T F**

19. If a firm increases all its inputs by 30% and its output increases by 20%, the firm is encountering economies of scale.   **T F**

20. Minimum efficient scale occurs at the largest level of output at which a firm can minimize long-run average costs.   **T F**

Circle the letter that corresponds to the best answer.

1. Suppose that a firm produces 100,000 units a year and sells them all for $5 each. The explicit costs of production are $350,000 and the implict costs of production are $100,000. The firm has an accounting profit of:
  (a) $200,000 and pure economic profit of $25,000
  (b) $150,000 and pure economic profit of $50,000
  (c) $125,000 and pure economic profit of $75,000
  (d) $100,000 and pure economic profit of $50,000

2. Pure economic profit for a firm is defined as the total revenues of the firm minus its:
  (a) accounting profit
  (b) explict costs of production
  (c) implicit cost of production
  (d) opportunity cost of all inputs

3. The law of diminishing returns is most useful for explaining the:
  (a) shape of the short-run marginal cost curve
  (b) shape of the long-run average cost curve
  (c) decline in average fixed costs as output increases
  (d) decline in total fixed costs as output increases

*Use the table below to answer the next two questions (**4** and **5**). Assume that the only variable resource used to produce output is labor.*

Amount of labor	Amount of output
1	3
2	8
3	12
4	15
5	17
6	18

4. The marginal product of the fourth unit of labor is:
  (a) 3 units of output
  (b) 3¾ units of output
  (c) 4 units of output
  (d) 15 units of output

5. When the firm hires four units of labor the average product of labor is:
  (a) 3 units of output
  (b) 3¾ units of output
  (c) 4 units of output
  (d) 15 units of output

6. Because the average product of a variable resource initially increases and later decreases as a firm increases its output:

  (a) average variable cost decreases at first and then increases
  (b) average fixed cost declines as the output of the firm expands
  (c) variable cost at first increases by increasing amounts and then increases by decreasing amounts
  (d) marginal cost at first increases and then decreases

7. Because the marginal product of a resource at first increases and then decreases as the output of the firm increases:
  (a) average fixed cost declines as the output of the firm increases
  (b) average variable cost at first increases and then decreases
  (c) variable cost at first increases by increasing amounts and then increases by decreasing amounts
  (d) total cost at first increases by decreasing amounts and then increases by increasing amounts

*For the next three questions (**8, 9,** and **10**) use the data given in the table below. The fixed cost of the firm is $500 and the firm's total variable cost is indicated in the table.*

Output	Total variable cost
1	$ 200
2	360
3	500
4	700
5	1,000
6	1,800

8. The average variable cost of the firm when 4 units of output are produced is:
  (a) $175
  (b) $200
  (c) $300
  (d) $700

9. The average total cost of the firm when 4 units of output are being produced is:
  (a) $175
  (b) $200
  (c) $300
  (d) $700

10. The marginal cost of the sixth unit of output is:
  (a) $200
  (b) $300
  (c) $700
  (d) $800

11. Marginal cost and average variable cost are equal at the output at which:
  (a) marginal cost is a minimum
  (b) marginal product is a maximum
  (c) average product is a maximum
  (d) average variable cost is a maximum

12. Average variable cost may be either increasing or decreasing when:
(a) marginal cost is decreasing
(b) marginal product is increasing
(c) average fixed cost is decreasing
(d) average total cost is decreasing

The next four questions (13, 14, 15, and 16) are based on the following figure.

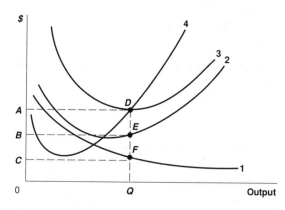

13. In the figure, curves 1, 3, and 4, respectively, represent:
(a) average variable cost, marginal cost, and average total cost
(b) average total cost, average variable cost, and marginal cost
(c) avarage fixed cost, average total cost, and marginal cost
(d) marginal cost, average total cost, and average variable cost

14. At output level **Q**, the average fixed cost is measured by vertical distance represented by:
(a) **DE**
(b) **DF**
(c) **DQ**
(d) **EF**

15. As output increases beyond the level represented by **Q**:
(a) marginal product is rising
(b) marginal product is falling
(c) total fixed costs are rising
(d) total costs are falling

16. If the firm is producing at output level **Q**, then the total variable costs of production are represented by area:
(a) 0**QFC**
(b) 0**QEB**
(c) 0**QDC**
(d) **CFEB**

17. At an output of 10,000 units per year, a firm's total

variable costs are $50,000 and its average fixed costs are $2. The total costs per year for the firm are:
(a) $50,000
(b) $60,000
(c) $70,000
(d) $80,000

18. A firm has total fixed costs of $4,000 a year. The average variable cost is $3.00 for 2000 units of output. At this level of output, its average total costs are:
(a) $2.50
(b) $3.00
(c) $4.50
(d) $5.00

19. If the short-run average variable costs of production for a firm are falling, then this indicates that:
(a) average variable costs are above average fixed costs
(b) marginal costs are below average variable costs
(c) average fixed costs are constant
(d) total costs are falling

20. Which of the following is most likely to be a long-run adjustment for a firm which manufactures jet fighter planes on an assembly-line basis?
(a) an increase in the amount of steel the firm buys
(b) a reduction in the number of "shifts" of workers from three to two
(c) a changeover from the production of one type of jet fighter to the production of a later-model jet fighter
(d) a changeover from the production of jet fighters to the production of sports cars

Answer the next two questions (21 and 22) using the following table. Three short-run cost schedules are given for three plants of different sizes which a firm might build in the long run.

Plant 1		Plant 2		Plant 3	
Output	ATC	Output	ATC	Output	ATC
10	$10	10	$15	10	$20
20	9	20	10	20	15
30	8	30	7	30	10
40	9	40	10	40	8
50	10	50	14	50	9

21. What is the **long-run** average cost of producing 40 units of output?
(a) $7
(b) $8
(c) $9
(d) $10

22. At what output is long-run average cost a minimum?
(a) 20
(b) 30
(c) 40
(d) 50

23. Which of the following is *not* a factor which results in economies of scale?
 (a) more efficient utilization of the firm's plant
 (b) increased specialization in the use of labor
 (c) greater specialization in the management of the firm
 (d) utilization of more efficient equipment

24. The long-run average costs of producing a particular product are one of the factors that determine:
 (a) the competition among the firms producing the product
 (b) the number of firms in the industry producing the product
 (c) the size of each of the firms in the industry producing the product
 (d) all of the above

25. A firm is encountering constant returns to scale when it increases all of its inputs by 20% and its output increases by:
 (a) 10%
 (b) 15%
 (c) 20%
 (d) 25%

■ **DISCUSSION QUESTIONS**

1. Explain the meaning of the opportunity cost of producing a product and the difference between an explicit and an implicit cost. How would you determine the implicit money cost of a resource?

2. What is the difference between normal and economic profit? Why is the former an economic cost? How do you define accounting profit?

3. What type of adjustments can a firm make in the long run that it cannot make in the short run? What adjustments can it make in the short run? How long is the short run?

4. Why is the distinction between the short run and the long run important?

5. State precisely the law of diminishing returns. Exactly what is it that diminishes, and why does it diminish?

6. Distinguish between a fixed cost and a variable cost. Why are short-run total costs partly fixed and partly variable costs, and why are long-run costs entirely variable?

7. Why do short-run variable costs increase at first by decreasing amounts and later increase by increasing amounts? How does the behavior of short-run variable cost influence the behavior of short-run total costs?

8. Describe the way in which short-run average fixed cost, average variable cost, average total cost, and marginal cost vary as the output of the firm increases.

9. What is the connection between marginal product and marginal cost and between average product and average variable cost? How will marginal cost behave as marginal product decreases and increases? How will average variable cost change as average product rises and falls?

10. What is the precise relationship between marginal cost and minimum average variable cost and between marginal cost and minimum average total cost? Why are these relationships necessarily true?

11. What happens to the average total costs, average variable cost, average fixed cost, and marginal cost curves when the price of a variable input increases or decreases? Describe what other factor can cause short-run cost curves to shift.

12. What does the long-run average-cost curve of a firm show? What relationship is there between long-run average cost and the short-run average-total-cost schedules of the different-sized plants which a firm might build?

13. Why is the long-run average-cost curve of a firm U-shaped?

14. What is meant by an economy of scale? What are some of the more important types of such an economy?

15. What is meant by and what causes diseconomies of large scale?

16. Why are the economies and diseconomies of scale of great significance, and how do they influence the size of firms in an industry and the number of firms in an industry?

■ **ANSWERS**

Chapter 9 The Costs of Production

FILL-IN QUESTIONS

1. other, opportunity
2. attract, explicit, implicit
3. entrepreneur(s); *a.* revenues, costs; *b.* explicit
4. variable, fixed, short, long
5. variable, fixed, marginal, equal
6. *a.* rising; *b.* positive, falling; *c.* zero; *d.* negative
7. *a.* rising; *b.* falling; *c.* maximum
8. see Figure 9–2(b) of the text
9. fixed, variable, variable
10. see Figure 9–3 of the text
11. average variable, average total, marginal; see Figure 9–6 of the text
12. total variable, total cost
13. falling, rising
14. *a.* falling; *b.* rising; *c.* maximum; *d.* minimum; *e.* (1) marginal, equal, (2) marginal, equal

15. plant

16. see Figure 9–8 of the text

17. *a.* increased specialization in the use of labor; *b.* better utilization of and increased specialization in management; *c.* more efficient productive equipment; *d.* better utilization of by-products

18. managerial complexities (problems)

19. size, number

20. minimum efficient scale, constant returns to scale

21. decrease, large, natural monopoly, economies

PROBLEMS AND PROJECTS

1. *a.* 80, 120, 130, 70, 50, 30, 10, −10; *b.* 80, 100, 110, 100, 90, 80, 70, 60; *c.* third, fourth; *d.* positive, negative; *e.* rise, fall

2. *a.* $0, 10, 20, 30, 40, 50, 60, 70, 80, 90, 100; *b.* $2.00, 1.67, 1.43. 1.67, 2.00, 2.50, 3.33, 5.00, 10.00; *c.* (1) decreases, (2) increases; *d.* 2.00, 1.82, 1.67. 1.67, 1.72, 1.82, 1.94, 2.11, 2.31, 2.56; *e.* (1) decreases, (2) increases

3. *a.*

Total cost	Average fixed cost	Average total cost	Marginal cost
$ 200	—	—	—
250	$200.00	$250.00	$ 50
290	100.00	145.00	40
320	66.67	106.67	30
360	50.00	90.00	40
420	40.00	84.00	60
500	33.33	83.33	80
600	28.57	85.71	100
720	25.00	90.00	120
870	22.22	96.67	150
1,100	20.00	110.00	230

4. *a.* $7.00, 6.00, 5.00, 4.00, 4.00, 3.00, 4.00, 5.00, 6.00, 5.00, 7.00, 10.00; *b.* (1) 10, 40; (2) 50, 80; (3) 90, 120

SELF-TEST

1. T, p. 140
2. F, p. 141
3. T, p. 142
4. F, p. 142
5. F, p. 142
6. T, p. 143
7. F, pp. 143–144
8. F, p. 144
9. T, p. 144
10. F, p. 145
11. T, p. 150
12. T, p. 149
13. T, pp. 148–149
14. T, p. 150
15. F, p. 151
16. F, p. 154
17. F, p. 154
18. T, p. 155
19. F, p. 154
20. F, p. 155

1. *b,* p. 141
2. *d,* p. 141
3. *a,* p. 142
4. *a,* p. 143
5. *b,* pp. 143–144
6. *a,* pp. 144–145
7. *d,* p. 145
8. *a,* p. 146
9. *c,* p. 147
10. *d,* pp. 147–148
11. *c,* pp. 148–149
12. *c,* p. 147
13. *c,* pp. 147; 149
14. *a,* p. 146
15. *b,* p. 149
16. *b,* pp. 146–147
17. *c,* p. 147
18. *d,* p. 147
19. *b,* p. 149
20. *d,* p. 142
21. *b,* pp. 150–151
22. *b,* pp. 150–151
23. *a,* pp. 152–153
24. *d,* pp. 155–156
25. *c,* p. 154

DISCUSSION QUESTIONS

1. p. 140
2. p. 141
3. p. 142
4. pp. 142–143
5. p. 145
6. pp. 145–146
7. pp. 146–148
8. pp. 148–149
9. p. 149
10. p. 150
11. pp. 150–151
12. p. 151
13. p. 151
14. pp. 151–153
15. p. 154
16. pp. 154–155

CHAPTER **10**

Price and Output Determination: Pure Competition

Chapter 10 is the first of four chapters which bring together the demand for a product and the production costs studied in Chapter 9. Each of the four chapters combines demand and production costs in a *different* market structure and analyzes and draws conclusions for that particular kind of product market. The questions which are analyzed and for which *both short-run* and *long-run* answers are sought are the following. Given the costs of the firm, what output will it produce; what will be the market price of the product; what will be the output of the entire industry; what will be the profit received by the firm; and what relationships will exist between price, average total cost, and marginal cost?

In addition to finding the answers to these questions you should learn *why* the questions are answered the way they are in each of the market models and in what way the answers obtained in one model *differ* from those obtained in the other models.

Actually, the answers are obtained by applying logic to different sets of assumptions. It is important, therefore, to note specifically what the assumptions are and how the assumptions made in one model differ from those of other models. Each model assumes that every firm is guided in making its decisions solely by the desire to maximize its profits, and that the costs of the firm are not materially affected by the type of market in which it *sells* its output. The important differences in the models which account for the differing answers involve (1) such characteristics of the market as the number of sellers, the ease of entry into and exodus from the industry, and the kind of product (standardized or differentiated) produced; and (2) the way in which the *individual firm* sees the demand for its product.

Chapter 10 begins by describing the three major characteristics of each of the four basic types of market models. From this point on it focuses its attention entirely on the purely competitive model. There are several good reasons for studying pure competition. Not the least of these reasons is that in the long run, pure competition—subject to certain exceptions—results in an ideal or perfect allocation of resources. After obtaining the answers to the questions listed in the first paragraph above, the authors return at the end of the chapter to explain in what sense competitive resource allocation is ideal and in what cases it may be less than ideal. In Chapters 11 and 12, which concern monopoly and monopolistic competition, respectively, it will be found that in these market situations resource allocation is less than ideal. You, therefore, should pay special attention in Chapter 10 to what is meant by an ideal allocation of resources and why pure competition results in this perfect allocation.

■ **CHECKLIST**

When you have studied this chapter you should be able to:

☐ List the five characteristics of each of the four basic market models.

☐ Give examples of industries that reflect the characteristics of the four basic market models.

☐ Explain why a purely competitive firm is a "price taker."

☐ Describe the firm's view of the demand for its product and the marginal revenue from the sale of additional units.

☐ Compute average, total, and marginal revenue when you are given the demand schedule faced by a purely competitive firm.

☐ Use the total-revenue and total-cost approach to determine the output that a purely competitive firm will produce in the short run under three different conditions; and explain *why* the firm will produce this output.

☐ Use the marginal-revenue and marginal-cost approach to determine the output that a purely competitive firm will produce in the short run under three different conditions; and explain *why* the firm will produce this output.

☐ Compare and contrast the total and marginal approaches to the determination of output in the short run.

☐ Find the *firm's* short-run supply curve when you are given the firm's short-run cost schedules.

☐ Find the *industry's* short-run supply curve (or schedule) when you are given the typical firm's short-run cost schedules.

☐ Determine, under short-run conditions, the price at which the product will sell, the output of the industry, and the output of the individual firm.

☐ Determine, under long-run conditions, the price at which the product will sell, the output of the firm, and the output of the industry.

☐ Explain the role played by the entry and exit of firms in a purely competitive industry in achieving equilibrium in the long run.

☐ Describe the characteristics and rationale for the long-run supply curve in a constant-cost industry, in an increasing-cost industry, and in a decreasing-cost industry.

☐ Distinguish between productive and allocative efficiency.

☐ Explain the significance of (MR) P = AC = MC.

☐ Identify four potential barriers for achieving allocative and productive efficiency in a competitive market.

■ **CHAPTER OUTLINE**

1. The *price* a firm charges for the good or service it produces and its *output* of that product depend not only on the demand for and the cost of producing it but on the character (or structure) of the market (industry) in which it sells the product.

2. The models of the markets in which firms sell their products are pure competition, pure monopoly, monopolistic competition, and oligopoly; and these four models are defined in terms of the number of firms in the industry, whether the product they sell is standardized or differentiated, and how easy it is for new firms to enter the industry.

3. This chapter examines pure competition in which a large number of independent firms, no one of which is able by itself to influence market price, sell a standardized product in a market which firms are free to enter and to leave in the long run. Although pure competition is rare in practice, there are at least three good reasons for studying this "laboratory case."

4. A firm selling its product in a purely competitive industry cannot influence the price at which the product sells; and is a price taker.

  a. The demand for its product is, therefore, perfectly price elastic.

  b. Average revenue (or price) and marginal revenue are equal and constant at the fixed (equilibrium) market price; and total revenue increases at a constant rate as the firm increases its output.

  c. The demand (average revenue) and marginal revenue curves faced by the firm are horizontal and identical at the market price; and the total revenue curve has a constant positive slope.

5. There are two complementary approaches to the analysis of the output that the purely competitive firm will produce in the short run.

  a. Employing the total-revenue-total-cost approach, the firm will produce the output at which total economic profit is the greatest or total loss is the least, provided that the loss is less than the firm's fixed costs (that is, provided that total revenue is greater than total variable cost). If the firm's loss is greater than its fixed cost, it will minimize its loss by producing no output.

  b. Employing the marginal-revenue-marginal-cost approach, the firm will produce the output at which marginal revenue (or price) and marginal cost are equal, provided price is greater than average variable cost. If price is less than average variable cost, the firm will shut down to minimize its loss. The short-run supply curve of the individual firm is that part of its short-run marginal-cost curve which is above average variable cost.

  c. Table 10-8 in the text summarizes the principles which the competitive firm follows when it decides what output to produce in the short run.

  d. The short-run supply curve of the industry (which is the sum of the supply curves of the individual firms) and the total demand for the product determine the short-run equilibrium price and equilibrium output of the industry; and the firms in the industry may be either prosperous or unprosperous in the short run.

6. In the long run the price of a product produced under conditions of pure competition will equal the minimum average total cost, and firms in the industry will neither have economic profits nor suffer economic losses.

  a. If economic profits are being received in the industry during the short run, firms will enter the industry in the long run (attracted by the profits), increase total supply, and thereby force price down to the minimum average total cost, leaving only a normal profit.

  b. If losses are being suffered in the industry during the short run, firms will leave the industry in the long run (seeking to avoid losses), reduce total supply, and thereby force price up to the minimum average total cost, leaving only a normal profit.

  c. If an industry is a constant-cost industry, the entry of new firms will not affect the average-total-cost schedules or curves of firms in the industry.

  (1) An increase in demand will result in no increase in the long-run equilibrium price, and the industry will be able to supply larger outputs at a constant price.

  (2) Graphically, the long-run supply curve in a constant-cost industry is horizontal at the minimum of the average-total-cost curve, indicating that firms make only normal profits, but not economic profits.

  d. If an industry is an increasing-cost industry, the entry of new firms will raise the average-total-cost schedules or curves of firms in the industry.

(1) An increase in demand will result in an increase in the long-run equilibrium price, and the industry will be able to supply larger outputs only at higher prices.

(2) Graphically, the long-run supply curve in an increasing-cost industry is upsloping at the minimum of the average-total-cost curve, indicating that firms make only normal profits, but not economic profits.

e. If an industry is a decreasing-cost industry, the entry of new firms will lower the average-total-cost schedules or curves of firms in the industry.

(1) An increase in demand will result in a decrease in the long-run equilibrium price, and the industry will be able to supply larger outputs only at lower prices.

(2) Graphically, the long-run supply curve in a decreasing-cost industry is downsloping at the minimum of the average-total-cost curve, indicating that firms make only normal profits, but not economic profits.

7. In the long run, each purely competitive firm is compelled by competition to produce that output at which price, marginal revenue, average cost, and marginal cost are equal and average cost is a minimum.

a. An economy in which all industries were purely competitive would use its resources efficiently.

(1) Goods are efficiently **produced** when the average total cost of producing them is at a minimum; buyers benefit most from this efficiency when they are charged a price just equal to minimum average total cost.

(2) Resources are efficiently **allocated** when goods are produced in such quantities that the total satisfaction obtained from the economy's resources is at a maximum; or when the price of each good is equal to its marginal cost.

b. Even in a purely competitive economy, the allocation of resources may not, for at least four reasons, be the most efficient.

(1) The distribution of income provided by the competitive market system may be quite unequal and create distortions in allocation of resources and the production of goods and services.

(2) Spillover costs and benefits and the production of public goods may not be taken into account in the allocation of resources in the competitive market model.

(3) The rate of technological advance may be slower and use of the best-known productive techniques may be less widespread in purely competitive industries.

(4) The range of consumer choice and the development of new products may be restricted in a purely competitive economy.

IMPORTANT TERMS

Pure competition

Pure monopoly

Monopolistic competition

Oligopoly

Imperfect competition

Price-taker

Total revenue

Average revenue

Marginal revenue

Total-receipts-total-cost approach

Marginal-revenue-marginal-cost approach

The profit-maximizing case

Break-even point

The loss-minimizing case

The close-down case

MR = MC rule

P = MC rule

The firm's short-run supply curve (schedule)

The competitive industry's short-run supply curve (schedule)

Short-run competitive equilibrium

Long-run competitive equilibrium

Constant-cost industry

Increasing-cost industry

Long-run supply

Productive efficiency

Allocative efficiency

FILL-IN QUESTIONS

1. The four market models examined in this and the next three chapters:

a. are _____,
_____,
_____, and
_____;

b. differ in terms of _____ of firms in the industry; whether the product is _____ or _____; control over _____; how easy or difficult it is for new firms to _____ the industry; and nonprice _____

2. What are the four specific conditions which characterize pure competition?

a. _____

b. _____

c. _____

d. _____

3. The individual firm in a purely competitive industry is a price-(maker, taker) _____; and finds that the demand for its product is perfectly (elastic, inelastic) _____ and that marginal revenue is (less than, greater than, equal to) _____ the price of the product.

4. Economic profit is equal to _____

5. The two approaches which may be used to determine the most profitable output for any firm are the _____ approach and _____ approach.

6. A firm should produce in the short run only if it can obtain a _____ or suffer an economic loss which is no greater than its _____
Provided it produces any output at all:

a. It will produce that output at which its profit is a (maximum, minimum) _____ or its loss is a _____

b. Or, said another way, the output at which marginal _____ and marginal _____ are equal.

7. A firm will produce at an economic loss in the short run if the price which it receives is greater than its average (fixed, variable, total) _____ cost.

8. In the short run the individual firm's supply curve is _____;
the short-run market supply curve is _____
_____

9. The short-run equilibrium price for a product produced by a purely competitive industry is the price at which _____
and _____ are equal; the equilibrium quantity is _____

10. In a purely competitive industry in the short run the number of firms in the industry and the sizes of their plants are (fixed, variable) _____; but in the long run they are _____

11. When a purely competitive industry is in long-run equilibrium the price which the firm is paid for its product is equal not only to marginal revenue but to long-run _____ cost and to long-run _____ cost; and long-run average cost is a (maximum, minimum, neither) _____

12. Firms tend to enter industry in the long run if _____ and leave it if _____
_____

13. If the entry of new firms into an industry tends to raise the costs of all firms in the industry, the industry is said to be a(n) (constant-, increasing-, decreasing-) _____ cost industry; and its long-run supply curve is (horizontal, downsloping, upsloping) _____

14. If an economy is to make the best use of its scarce resources it is necessary that it achieve both _____ and _____ efficiency.

15. The purely competitive economy achieves productive efficiency in the long run because price and _____ cost are equal and the latter is a (maximum, minimum) _____

16. In the long run the purely competitive economy is allocatively efficient because price and _____ cost are equal.

17. List four reasons why resource allocation in a purely competitive economy may be less than efficient.

a. _____

b. _____

c. _____

d. _____

■ **PROBLEMS AND PROJECTS**

1. Employing the following set of terms, complete the table at the top of page 105 by inserting the appropriate letter or letters in the blanks.

a. one
b. few
c. many
d. a very large number
e. standardized
f. differentiated
g. some

h considerable
i. very easy
j. blocked
k. fairly easy
l. fairly difficult
m. none
n. unique

2. Below is the demand schedule facing the individual firm.

Price	Quantity demanded	Average revenue	Total revenue	Marginal revenue
$10	0	$_____	$_____	—
10	1	_____	_____	$_____
10	2	_____	_____	_____
10	3	_____	_____	_____
10	4	_____	_____	_____
10	5	_____	_____	_____
10	6	_____	_____	_____

Market characteristics	Market model			
	Pure competition	Pure monopoly	Monopolistic competition	Oligopoly
Number of firms	——	——	——	——
Type of product	——	——	——	——
Control over price	——	——	——	——
Conditions of entry	——	——	——	——
Nonprice competition	——	——	——	——

a. Complete the table by computing average revenue, total revenue, and marginal revenue.

b. Is this firm operating in a market which is purely competitive? _____ How can you tell?

c. The coefficient of the price elasticity of demand is the same between every pair of quantities demanded. What is it? _____

d. What relationship exists between average revenue and marginal revenue? _____

_____

e. On the following graph plot the demand schedule, average revenue, total revenue, and marginal revenue; label each of these curves.

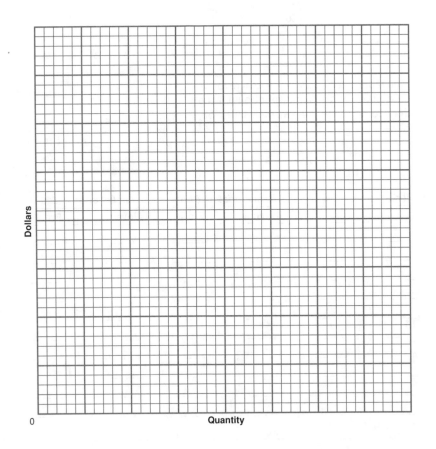

Dollars

0   Quantity

f. The demand, average-revenue, and marginal-revenue curves are all _____ lines at a price of $_____ across all quantities.

g. The total-revenue curve is an upsloping line with a _____ slope because marginal revenue is _____

3. Assume that a purely competitive firm has the schedule of costs given in the table below.

Output	TFC	TVC	TC
0	$300	$ 0	$ 300
1	300	100	400
2	300	150	450
3	300	210	510
4	300	290	590
5	300	400	700
6	300	540	840
7	300	720	1,020
8	300	950	1,250
9	300	1,240	1,540
10	300	1,600	1,900

a. Complete the table below to show the total revenue and total profit of the firm at each level of output the firm might produce. Assume market prices of $55, $120, and $200.

b. Indicate what output the firm would produce and what its profits would be at a:

(1) Price of $55: output of _____ and profit of _____

(2) Price of $120: output of _____ and profit of _____

(3) Price of $200: output of _____ and profit of _____

c. Plot the cost data for total variable cost and total cost in the graph on the opposite page. Then plot the total revenue when the price is $55, $120, and $200. For each price indicate the level of output and the economic profit or loss on the graph.

Output	Market price = $55 Revenue	Profit	Market price = $120 Revenue	Profit	Market price = $200 Revenue	Profit
0	$____	$____	$____	$____	$____	$____
1	____	____	____	____	____	____
2	____	____	____	____	____	____
3	____	____	____	____	____	____
4	____	____	____	____	____	____
5	____	____	____	____	____	____
6	____	____	____	____	____	____
7	____	____	____	____	____	____
8	____	____	____	____	____	____
9	____	____	____	____	____	____
10	____	____	____	____	____	____

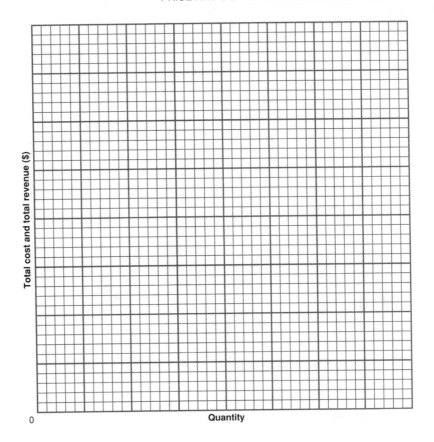

Quantity

0

4. Now assume that the same purely competitive firm has the schedule of average and marginal costs given in the table below.

Output	AFC	AVC	ATC	MC
0				
1	$300	$100	$400	$100
2	150	75	225	50
3	100	70	170	60
4	75	73	148	80
5	60	80	140	110
6	50	90	140	140
7	43	103	146	180
8	38	119	156	230
9	33	138	171	290
10	30	160	190	360

a. At a price of $55, the firm would produce _____ units of output. At a price of $120, the firm would pro-

duce _____ units of output. At a price of $200, the

firm would produce _____ units of output. Compare your answers to those you gave in problem 3.

b. The *per unit* economic profit (or loss) is calculated

by subtracting _____ at a particular

level of output from the product price. This *per unit* economic profit is then multiplied by the number of units

of _____ to determine the economic profit for the competitive firm.

(1) At the product price of $200, the average total costs

are $_____, so *per unit* economic profit is $_____. Multiplying this amount by the number of units of output

results in an economic profit of $ _____

(2) At the product price of $120, the average total costs

are $_____, so *per unit* economic losses are

$_____. Multiplying this amount by the number of

units of output results in an economic loss of $_____

(3) Compare your answers to those you gave in problem 3b (2) and 3b (3).

b. Plot the data for average and marginal cost in the graph on the next page. Then plot the marginal revenue when the price is $55, $120, and $200. For each price, indicate the level of output and the economic profit or loss on the graph. Compare your answers and graph to those you gave in problem 3.

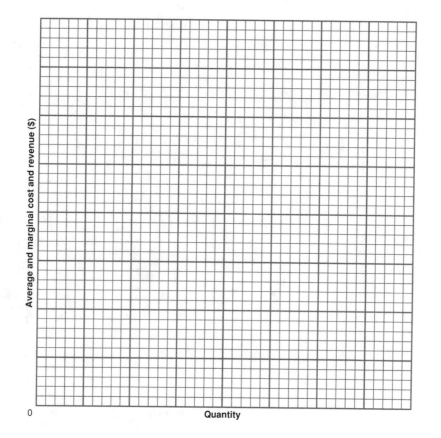

5. Use the total cost data in problem 3 or the average and marginal cost data in problem 4 in your work on problem 5.

a. In the table below, complete the supply schedule for the competitive firm and state what the economic profit will be at each price.

Price	Quantity supplied	Profit
$360	_____	$_____
290	_____	_____
230	_____	_____
180	_____	_____
140	_____	_____
110	_____	_____
80	_____	_____
60	_____	_____

b. If there are 100 firms in the industry and all have the same cost schedule:

(1) Complete the market supply schedule in the table.

Quantity demanded	Price	Quantity supplied
400	$360	_____
500	290	_____
600	230	_____
700	180	_____
800	140	_____
900	110	_____
1,000	80	_____

(2) Using the demand schedule given in (1):

(a) what will the market price of the product be?
$_____;

(b) what quantity will the individual firm produce?
_____;

(c) how large will the firm's profit be? $_____;

(d) will firms tend to enter or leave the industry in the long run? _____ Why? _____
_____

6. If the total costs assumed for the individual firm in problem 3 were long-run total costs and if the industry were a constant-cost industry:

    a. What would be the market price of the product in the long run? $_____

    b. What output would each firm produce when the industry was in long-run equilibrium? _____

    c. Approximately how many firms would there be in the industry in the long run, given the present demand for the product? _____

    d. If the table below was the market demand schedule for the product, how many firms would there be in the long run in the industry? _____

Price	Quantity demanded
$360	500
290	600
230	700
180	800
140	900
110	1,000
80	1,100

    e. On the graph below draw a long-run supply curve of

    (1) a constant-cost industry

    (2) an increasing-cost industry

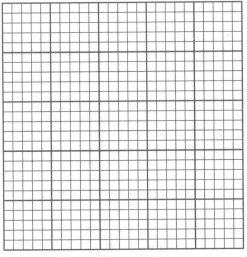

0

■ **SELF-TEST**

Circle the T if the statement is true; the F if it is false.

1. The structures of the markets in which business firms sell their products in the American economy are all pretty much the same. **T F**

2. A large number of sellers does not necessarily mean that the industry is purely competitive. **T F**

3. Only in a purely competitive industry do individual firms have no control over the price of their product. **T F**

4. Imperfectly competitive markets are defined as all markets except those which are purely competitive. **T F**

5. One of the reasons for studying the pure competition model is that many industries are almost purely competitive. **T F**

6. The purely competitive firm views an average-revenue schedule as identical to its marginal-revenue schedule. **T F**

7. The demand curves for firms in a purely competitive industry are perfectly inelastic. **T F**

8. If a firm can cover its variable costs and some fixed costs, then the firm should continue to operate in the short run. **T F**

9. Given the short-run costs of firms in a purely competitive industry, the profits of these firms depend solely upon the level of the total demand for the product. **T F**

10. A purely competitive firm will produce in the short run the output at which marginal cost and marginal revenue are equal provided that the price of the product is greater than its average variable cost of production. **T F**

11. If a purely competitive firm is producing an output less than its profit-maximizing output, marginal revenue is greater than marginal cost at that output. **T F**

12. The short-run supply curve of a purely competitive firm tends to slope upward from left to right because of the law of diminishing returns. **T F**

13. A firm wishing to maximize its economic profits or minimize economic losses will always produce that output at which marginal costs and marginal revenue are equal. **T F**

14. The long-run supply curve for a competitive, increasing-cost industry is upwardsloping. **T F**

15. When firms in a purely competitive industry are earning profits which are less than normal, the supply of the product will tend to decrease in the long run. **T F**

16. If a purely competitive firm is in short-run equilibrium and its marginal cost is grater than is average total cost, then firms will leave the industry in the long run.   **T   F**

17. Pure competition, if it could be achieved in all industries in the economy, would result in the most efficient allocation of resources.   **T   F**

18. Under conditions of pure competition, firms are forced to employ the most efficient production methods available to survive.   **T   F**

19. The marginal costs of producing a product are society's measure of the marginal worth of alternative products.   **T   F**

20. There is no scientific basis for determining which distribution of total money income results in the greatest satisfaction of wants in the economy.   **T   F**

Circle the letter that corresponds to the best answer.

1. The four models of the markets (industries) in which business firms sell their products differ in terms of:
   (a) the number of firms in the industry
   (b) how easy or difficult it is for new firms to enter the industry
   (c) whether the product is standardized or differentiated
   (d) all of the above

2. Which of the following is *not* characteristic of pure competition?
   (a) large number of sellers
   (b) differentiated product
   (c) easy entry
   (d) no advertising

3. If the product produced by an industry is standardized, the market structure can be:
   (a) pure competition or monopolistic competition
   (b) pure competition or oligopoly
   (c) monopolistic competition or oligopoly
   (d) pure competition, monopolistic competition, or oligopoly

4. Into which of the following industries is entry least difficult?
   (a) pure competition
   (b) pure monopoly
   (c) monopolistic competition
   (d) oligopoly

5. Which of the following industries comes *closest* to being purely competitive?
   (a) wheat
   (b) shoes
   (c) retailing
   (d) farm implements

6. In which of the following market models is the individual seller of a product a "price-taker"?
   (a) pure competition
   (b) pure monopoly
   (c) monopolistic competition
   (d) oligopoly

7. In a purely competitive industry:
   (a) each of the existing firms will engage in various forms of nonprice competition
   (b) new firms are free to enter and existing firms are able to leave the industry very easily
   (c) individual firms have a "price policy"
   (d) each of the firms produces a differentiated (non-standardized) product

8. The demand schedule or curve confronted by the individual purely competitive firm is:
   (a) perfectly inelastic
   (b) inelastic but not perfectly inelastic
   (c) perfectly elastic
   (d) elastic but not perfectly elastic

9. A firm will be willing to produce at a loss in the short run if:
   (a) the loss is no greater than its total fixed costs
   (b) the loss is no greater than its average fixed costs
   (c) the loss is no greater than its total variable costs
   (d) the loss is no greater than its average variable cost

10. The individual firm's short-run supply curve is that part of its marginal-cost curve lying above its:
   (a) average-total-cost curve
   (b) average-variable-cost curve
   (c) average-fixed-cost curve
   (d) average-revenue curve

11. If a single purely competitive firm's most profitable output in the short run were an output at which it was neither receiving an economic profit nor suffering an economic loss, one of the following would *not* be true. Which one?
   (a) marginal cost and average total cost are equal
   (b) marginal cost and average variable cost are equal
   (c) marginal cost and marginal revenue are equal
   (d) marginal cost and average revenue are equal

12. Which one of the following statements is true of a purely competitive industry in short-run equilibrium?
   (a) price is equal to average total cost
   (b) total quantity demanded is equal to total quantity supplied
   (c) profits in the industry are equal to zero
   (d) output is equal to the output at which average total cost is a minimum

13. Suppose that when 2000 units of output are produced, the marginal cost of the 2001st unit is $5. This amount is equal to the minimum of average total cost, and marginal cost is rising. If the optimal level of output in the short run is 2500 units, then at that level:

(a) marginal cost is greater than $5 and marginal cost is less than average total cost

(b) marginal cost is greater than $5 and marginal cost is greater than average total cost

(c) marginal cost is less than $5 and marginal cost is greater than average total cost

(d) marginal cost is equal to $5 and marginal cost is equal to average total cost

14. The Zebra, Inc., is selling in a purely competitive market. Its output is 250 units which sell for $2 each. At this level of output, marginal cost is $2 and average variable cost is $2.25. The firm should:

(a) produce zero units of output

(b) decrease output to 200 units

(c) continue to produce 250 units

(d) increase output to maximize profits

The next four questions (15, 16, 17 and 18) are based on the following graph.

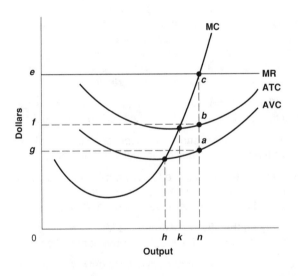

15. If the firm is producing at output level 0**n**, the rectangular area **fecb** is:

(a) total variable cost

(b) total fixed costs

(c) total revenue

(d) total economic profit

16. At the profit-maximizing output, average fixed cost is:

(a) **ab**

(b) **ac**

(c) **na**

(d) **nb**

17. At the profit-maximizing output, the total variable costs are equal to the area:

(a) 0**fbn**

(b) 0**ecn**

(c) 0**gan**

(d) **gfba**

18. The demand curve for this firm is equal to:

(a) MR, and the supply curve is the portion of the MC curve where output is greater than level **n**

(b) MR, and the supply curve is the portion of the MC curve where output is greater than level **k**

(c) MR, and the supply curve is the portion of the MC curve where output is greater than level **h**

(d) MR, and the supply curve is the portion of the ATC curve where output is greater than level **k**

Answer the next five questions (19, 20, 21, 22, and 23) on the basis of the following cost data for a firm that is selling in a purely competitive market.

Output	AFC	AVC	ATC	MC
1	$300	$100	$400	$100
2	150	75	225	50
3	100	70	170	60
4	75	73	148	80
5	60	80	140	110
6	50	90	140	140
7	43	103	146	180
8	38	119	156	230
9	33	138	171	290
10	30	160	190	360

19. If the market price for the firm's product is $140, the competitive firm will produce:

(a) 5 units at an economic loss of $150

(b) 6 units and "break even"

(c) 7 units and "break even"

(d) 8 units at an economic profit of $74

20. If the market price for the firm's product is $290, the competitive firm will produce:

(a) 7 units at an economic profit of $238

(b) 8 units at an economic profit of $592

(c) 9 units at an economic profit of $1071

(d) 10 units at an economic profit of $1700

21. If the product price is $179, then **per unit** economic profit at the profit-maximizing output is:

(a) $15

(b) $23

(c) $33

(d) $39

22. The total fixed costs are:

(a) $100

(b) $200

(c) $300

(d) $400

Assume there are 100 identical firms in this industry and total or market demand is shown below.

Price	Quantity demanded
$360	600
290	700
230	800
180	900
140	1000
110	1100
80	1200

23. The equilibrium price will be:
(a) $140
(b) $180
(c) $230
(d) $290

24. Assume that the market for wheat is purely competitive. Currently, each of the firms growing wheat are experiencing economic losses. In the long run, we can expect this market's:
(a) supply curve to increase
(b) demand curve to increase
(c) supply curve to decrease
(d) demand curve to decrease

25. The long-run supply curve under pure competition will be:
(a) downsloping in an increasing-cost industry and upsloping in a decreasing-cost industry
(b) horizontal in a constant-cost industry and upsloping in a decreasing-cost industry
(c) horizontal in a constant-cost industry and upsloping in an increasing-cost industry
(d) upsloping in an increasing-cost industry and vertical in a constant-cost industry

26. Increasing-cost industries find that their costs rise as a consequence of an increased demand for the product because of:
(a) the diseconomies of scale
(b) diminishing returns
(c) higher resource prices
(d) a decreased supply of the product

27. When a purely competitive industry is in long-run equilibrium, one of the following statements is *not* true. Which one?
(a) firms in the industry are earning normal profits
(b) price and long-run average total cost are equal to each other
(c) long-run marginal cost is at its minimum level
(d) long-run marginal cost is equal to marginal revenue

28. It is contended that which of the following triple identities results in the most efficient use of resources?
(a) $P = AC = MC$
(b) $P = AR = MR$
(c) $P = MR = MC$
(d) $AC = MC = MR$

29. An economy is producing the goods most wanted by society when, for each and every good, its:
(a) price and average cost are equal
(b) price and marginal cost are equal
(c) marginal revenue and marginal cost are equal
(d) price and marginal revenue are equal

30. The operation of a purely competitive market system accurately measures:
(a) both spillover costs and spillover benefits
(b) spillover costs but not spillover benefits
(c) spillover benefits but not spillover costs
(d) neither spillover costs nor spillover benefits

■ **DISCUSSION QUESTIONS**

1. What are the four market models (or situations) which economists employ and what are the major characteristics of each type of market?

2. If pure competition is so rare in practice, why are students of economics asked to study it?

3. Explain how the firm in a purely competitive industry sees the demand for the product it produces in terms of
(a) the price elasticity of demand;
(b) the relation of average to marginal revenue; and
(c) the behavior of total, average, and marginal revenues as the output of the firm increases.

4. Why is a firm willing to produce at a loss in the short run if the loss is no greater than the fixed costs of the firm?

5. Explain how the short-run supply of an individual firm and of the purely competitive industry are determined.

6. What determines the equilibrium price and output of a purely competitive industry in the short run? Will economic profits in the industry be positive or negative?

7. Why do the MC = MR rule and MC = *P* rule mean the same thing under conditions of pure competition?

8. What are the important distinctions between the short run and the long run and between equilibrium in the short run and in the long run in a competitive industry?

9. When is the purely competitive industry in long-run equilibrium? What forces the purely competitive firm into this position?

10. What is a constant-cost industry? What is an increasing-cost industry? Under what economic conditions is each likely to be found? What will be the nature of the long-run supply curve in each of these industries?

11. When has an economy achieved the most efficient use of its scarce resources? What two kinds of efficiency are necessary if the economy is to make the most efficient use of its resources?

12. Why is it said that a purely competitive economy is an efficient economy?

13. What did Adam Smith mean when he said that self-interest and competition bring about results which are in the best interest of the economy as a whole without government regulation or interference?

14. Even if an economy is purely competitive, the allocation of resources may not be ideal. Why?

15. Does pure competition *always* promote both the use of the most efficient technological methods of production and the development of better methods?

■ ANSWERS

Chapter 10 Price and Output Determination: Pure Competition

FILL-IN QUESTIONS

1. *a.* pure competition, pure monopoly, monopolistic competition, oligopoly (any order); *b.* number, standardized, differentiated (either order), price, enter, competition

2. *a.* a large number of independent sellers; *b.* a standardized product; *c.* no single firm supplies enough to influence market price; *d.* no obstacles to the entry of new firms or the exodus of old firms

3. taker, elastic, equal to

4. total revenue minus total cost

5. total-revenue-total-cost, marginal-revenue-marginal-cost

6. profit, fixed costs; *a.* maximum, minimum; *b.* cost, revenue (either order)

7. variable

8. that portion of the firm's marginal-cost curve which lies above the average-variable-cost curve, the sum of the short-run supply curves of all firms in the industry

9. total quantity demanded, total quantity supplied (either order), the quantity demanded and supplied at the equilibrium price

10. fixed, variable

11. average, marginal (either order), minimum

12. the firms in the industry are realizing profits in the short run, the firms in the industry are realizing losses in the short run

13. increasing-, upsloping

14. productive, allocative (either order)

15. average, minimum

16. marginal

17. *a.* the competitive price system does not necessarily result in an ideal distribution of money income in the economy; *b.* the competitive price system does not accurately measure costs and benefits when spillover costs and benefits are significant or provide social goods; *c.* the competitive price system does not entail the use of the most efficient productive techniques; *d.* the competitive price system may not provide for a sufficient range of consumer choice or for the development of new products

PROBLEMS AND PROJECTS

1. number of firms: d, a, c, b; type of product: e, n, f, e, or f; control over price: m, h, g, g; entry: i, j, k, l; nonprice competition: m, g, h, g or h

2. *a.* average revenue: all are $10.00; total revenue: $0, 10.00, 20.00, 30.00, 40.00, 50.00, 60.00; marginal revenue: all are $10,000; *b.* yes, because price (average revenue) is constant and equal to marginal revenue; *c.* infinity; *d.* they are equal; *e.* see Figure 10-1 of text for an example; *f.* horizontal, $10; *g.* constant, constant

3. *a.* (see table below); *b.* (1) 0, −$300; (2) 5, −$100; (3) 7, $380; *c.* see Figure 10-2 of the text for an example

4. *a.* 0, 5, 7 (same answers as in **3***b*); *b.* average total cost; output; (1) $146 ($200−$146 = $54), ($54 × 7 = $378); (2) $140, ($120 − $140 = −$20), (−$20 × 5 = −$100); (3) same answers but $2 difference in **3***b*(3) and **4***b*(1) due to rounding; *c.* see Figure 10-3 of text for an example

Market price = $55		Market price = $120		Market price = $200	
Revenue	Profit	Revenue	Profit	Revenue	Profit
$ 0	$ − 300	$ 0	$ − 300	$ 0	$ − 300
55	− 345	120	− 280	200	− 200
110	− 340	240	− 210	400	− 50
165	− 345	360	− 150	600	90
220	− 370	480	− 110	800	210
275	− 425	600	− 100	1,000	300
330	− 510	720	− 120	1,200	360
385	− 635	840	− 180	1,400	380
440	− 810	960	− 290	1,600	350
495	− 1,045	1,080	− 460	1,800	260
550	− 1,350	1,200	− 700	2,000	100

5. *a.* see table below

Price	Quantity supplied	Profit
$360	10	$1,700
290	9	1,070
230	8	590
180	7	240
140	6	0
110	5	−150
80	4	−270
60	0	−300

b. (1) quantity supplied: 1000, 900, 800, 700, 600, 500, 400; (2) (*a*) 180; (*b*) 7; (*c*) 240; (*d*) enter, profits in the industry will attract them into the industry

6. *a.* 140; *b.* 6; *c.* 133 = 800 (the total quantity demanded at $140) ÷ 6 (the output of each firm); *d.* 150 = 900 ÷ 6; *e.* (1) the curve is a horizontal line (see Figure 10–10 in the text), (2) the curve slopes upward (see Figure 10–11 in the text)

SELF-TEST

1. F, p. 160
2. T, p. 161
3. T, p. 161
4. T, p. 161
5. F, p. 162
6. T, p. 163
7. F, p. 162
8. T, p. 164
9. T, p. 173
10. T, p. 171
11. T, p. 167
12. T, p. 172
13. F, p. 167
14. T, p. 168
15. T, p. 176
16. F, p. 176
17. F, p. 179
18. T, p. 179
19. T, p. 180
20. T, pp. 181–182

1. *d*, p. 161
2. *b*, p. 161
3. *b*, p. 161
4. *a*, p. 161
5. *a*, p. 161
6. *a*, p. 161
7. *b*, pp. 161–162
8. *c*, p. 162
9. *a*, p. 164
10. *b*, p. 172
11. *b*, p. 173
12. *b*, pp. 173–174
13. *b*, pp. 171–172
14. *a*, pp. 170–171
15. *d*, p. 169
16. *a*, p. 170
17. *c*, p. 170
18. *c*, p. 172
19. *b*, p. 167
20. *c*, p. 168
21. *d*, p. 169
22. *c*, p. 170
23. *c*, p. 173
24. *c*, p. 176
25. *c*, pp. 177–178
26. *c*, p. 178
27. *c*, p. 179
28. *a*, p. 179
29. *b*, p. 180
30. *d*, p. 183

DISCUSSION QUESTIONS

1. p. 161
2. p. 162
3. pp. 162–164
4. p. 164
5. pp. 171–173
6. pp. 173–174
7. pp. 173; 180
8. p. 174
9. pp. 174–175
10. pp. 178–179
11. pp. 179–180
12. pp. 179–180
13. p. 181
14. pp. 181–183
15. pp. 179–183

Price and Output Determination: Pure Monopoly

Chapter 11 is the second of the four chapters which deal with specific market models and is concerned with what economists call pure monopoly. Like pure competition, pure monopoly is rarely found in the American economy. But there are industries which are close to being pure monopolies, and these industries produce about 5% of the GDP; an understanding of pure monopoly is helpful in understanding the more realistic situation of oligopoly.

It is only possible for pure monopoly, approximations of pure monopoly, and oligopoly to exist if firms are prevented in some way from entering an industry in the long run. Anything which tends to prevent entry is referred to as a "barrier to entry." The second part of Chapter 11 is devoted to a description of the more important types of barriers to entry. Remember that barriers to entry not only make it possible for monopoly to exist in the economy but also explain why so many markets are oligopolies (which you will study in Chapter 13).

Like the preceding chapter, this chapter tries to answer certain questions about the firm. These are: what output will the firm produce; what price will it charge; what will be the profit received by the firm; and what will be the relationship between price and average cost and between price and marginal cost? In answering these questions for the monopoly firm and in comparing pure competition and pure monopoly note the following:

1. Both the competitive and monopoly firm try to maximize profits by producing that output at which marginal cost and marginal revenue are equal.

2. The individual firm in a perfectly competitive industry sees a perfectly price elastic demand for its product at the going market price because it is but one of many firms in the industry; but the monopolist sees a market demand schedule which is less than perfectly price elastic because the monopolist *is* the industry. The former, therefore, has *only* an output policy and is a price-taker; but the latter is able to determine the price at which it will sell its product and is a price-maker.

3. When demand is perfectly price elastic, price is equal to marginal revenue and is constant; but when demand is less than perfectly price elastic, marginal revenue is less

than price and both decrease as the output of the firm increases.

4. Because entry is blocked in the long run, firms cannot enter a monopolistic industry to compete away profits as they can under conditions of pure competition.

In addition to determining the price the monopolist will charge, the quantity of its product it will produce, and the size of its profits, Chapter 11 has three other goals. It examines the economic effects of monopoly by comparing it with pure competition. Chapter 11 also explains what is meant by price discrimination, the conditions which must prevail if a monopolist is to engage in price discrimination. The final section of Chapter 11 introduces you to the problem a government agency faces when it must determine the maximum price a public utility will be allowed to charge for its product.

■ CHECKLIST

When you have studied this chapter you should be able to:

☐ Define pure monopoly based on five characteristics.
☐ List and explain four potential barriers that would prevent or deter the entry of new firms into an industry.
☐ Describe the demand curve or schedule for the product produced by a pure monopolist and cite three implications.
☐ Compute marginal revenue when you are given the demand for the monopolist's product.
☐ Explain the relationship between the price the monopolist charges and the marginal revenue from the sale of an additional unit of the product.
☐ State the principle which explains what output the monopolist will produce and the price that will be charged.
☐ Determine the profit-maximizing output and price for the pure monopolist when you are given the demand and cost data.
☐ Explain why there is no supply curve for the pure monopolist.
☐ Discuss three popular misconceptions about the pricing behavior of pure monopolists.

☐ Describe the economic effects of monopoly on the price of the product, the quantity of output produced, the allocation of the economy's resources, and the distribution of income.

☐ Explain the complications caused by economies of scale, X-inefficiency, and rent-seeking expenditures in comparing the costs of firms operating in competitive and monopoly industries.

☐ Define technological progress (or dynamic efficiency) and compare technological progress in competitive and monopoly models.

☐ Define price discrimination and list three conditions which are necessary for it to exist.

☐ Explain the economic consequences of price discrimination.

☐ Use graphical analysis to identify the socially optimal price and the fair return price for the regulated monopoly (public utility).

☐ Explain the dilemma of regulation based on your graphical analysis of regulated monopoly.

■ CHAPTER OUTLINE

1. Pure monopoly is a market situation in which a single firm sells a product for which there are no close substitutes. While it is rare in practice, the study of monopoly provides an understanding of firms which are "almost" monopolies and is useful in understanding monopolistic competition and oligopoly.

2. Pure monopoly (and oligopoly) can exist in the long run only if potential competitors find there are barriers which prevent their entry into the industry.
    a. There are at least four types of entry barriers: economies of scale; natural monopolies (public utilities); legal barriers (patents and licenses); and ownership of essential resources.
    b. Entry barriers are seldom perfect in preventing the entry of new firms, and efficient production may, in some cases, require that firms be prevented from entering an industry.

3. The demand curve of the monopolist is downsloping because the monopolist is the industry. By contrast, the purely competitive firm has a horizontal (perfectly price elastic) demand curve because it is only one of many small firms in an industry. The implications of the downsloping shape monopolist's demand curve are several:
    a. The monopolist can only increase sales by lowering product price; thus price will exceed marginal revenue for every unit of output but the first.
    b. The monopolist will have a pricing policy, or is a "price-maker"; the purely competitive firm has no price policy and is a "price-taker."
    c. The monopolist will avoid setting price in the inelas-

tic segment of its demand curve because total revenue will be decreasing and marginal revenue will be negative; price will be set in the elastic portion of the demand curve.

4. The output and price determination of the profit-maximizing monopolist entails several considerations:
    a Monopoly power in the sale of a product does not necessarily affect the prices that the monopolist pays for resources or the costs of production; an assumption is made in this chapter that the monopolist hires resources in a competitive market and uses the same technology as competitive firms.
    b. The monopolist produces that output at which marginal cost and marginal revenue are equal, and charges a price at which this profit-maximizing output can be sold.
    c. The monopolist has no supply curve because there is no unique relationship between price and quantity supplied; price and quantity supplied will change when demand and marginal revenue change. By contrast, a purely competitive firm has a supply curve that is the portion of the marginal cost curve above average variable cost, and there is a unique relationship between price and quantity supplied.
    d. Three popular misconceptions about monopolists are that they charge as high a price as is possible, that they seek maximum profit *per unit* of output, and that they are always profitable and never experience losses.

5. The existence of pure monopoly has significant effects on the economy as a whole.
    a. Because it produces smaller outputs and charges higher prices than would result under conditions of pure competition and because price is greater than both average total and marginal cost, monopoly misallocates resources (results in neither productive nor allocative efficiency).
    b. Monopoly contributes to income inequality in the economy.
    c. A monopolist may have lower or higher average costs than a pure competitor producing the same product would have.
    (1) If there are economies of scale in the production of the product, the monopolist is able to produce the good or service at a lower long-run average cost than a large number of small pure competitors could produce it.
    (2) But if a monopolist is more susceptible to X-inefficiency than a purely competitive firm, its long-run average costs at every level of output are higher than what those of a purely competitive firm would be.
    (3) Rent-preserving expenditures in the form of legal fees, lobbying, and public-relations expenses to obtain or maintain a monopoly position add nothing to output, but increase costs.

d. A monopolist may also be more or less efficient over time than pure competitors in developing new lower-cost techniques of producing existing products and in developing new products.

6. To increase profits a pure monopolist may engage in price discrimination by charging different prices to different buyers of the same product (when the price differences do not represent differences in the costs of producing the product).

  a. To discriminate the seller must have some monopoly power; be capable of separating buyers into groups which have different price elasticities of demand; and be able to prevent the resale of the product from one group to another group.

  b. The seller charges each group the highest price that group would be willing to pay for the product rather than go without it. Discrimination increases not only the profits but also the output of the monopolist.

  c. Price discrimination is common in the American economy.

7. The prices charged by monopolists are often regulated by governments to reduce the misallocation of resources.

  a. A ceiling price determined by the intersection of the marginal-cost and demand schedules is the socially optimum price and improves the allocation of resources.

  b. This ceiling may force the firm to produce at a loss; and so government may set the ceiling at a level determined by the intersection of the average-cost and demand schedules to allow the monopolist a fair return.

  c. The dilemma of regulation is that the socially optimum price may cause losses for the monopolist, and that a fair-return price results in a less efficient allocation of resources.

■ **IMPORTANT TERMS**

Pure monopoly	Dynamic efficiency
Barrier to entry	Price discrimination
Natural monopoly	Socially optimal price
X-inefficiency	Fair-return price
Rent-seeking behavior	Dilemma of regulation

■ **FILL-IN QUESTIONS**

1. Pure monopoly is an industry in which a single firm is the sole producer of a product for which are are no (substitutes, close substitutes) _____ and into which entry in the long run is (easy, difficult, blocked) _____

2. What are the four most important types of barrier to entry?

  a. _____

  b. _____

  c. _____

  d. _____

3. If there are substantial economies of scale in the production of a product, a small-scale firm will find it difficult to enter into and survive in an industry because its average costs will be (greater, less) _____ than those of established firms; and a firm will find it difficult to start out on a large scale because it will be nearly impossible to acquire the needed (labor, money capital) _____

4. Public utility companies tend to be _____ _____ monopolies, and they receive their franchises from and are _____ by governments.

5. The demand schedule confronting the pure monopolist is _____ perfectly elastic; this means that marginal revenue is (greater, less) _____ than average revenue (or price) and that both marginal revenue and average revenue (increase, decrease) _____ as output increases.

6. When demand is price elastic, a decrease in price will (increase, decrease) _____ total revenue, but when demand is price inelastic, a decrease in price will _____ total revenue. The demand curve for the purely competitive firm is (horizontal, downsloping) _____, but it is _____ for the monopolist. The profit maximizing monopolist will want to set price in the price (elastic, inelastic) _____ portion of its demand curve.

7. The supply curve for a purely competitive firm is the portion of the (average variable cost, marginal cost) _____ curve that lies above the _____ curve. The supply curve for the monopolist (is the same, does not exist) _____

8. When the profits of a monopolist are a maximum, _____ and _____ are equal; and price (or average revenue) is (greater, less) _____ than marginal cost.

9. Three common fallacies about pure monopoly are that:

  a. It charges the _____ price.

  b. Its average (or per unit) profit is _____

  _____

  c. It always receives a _____

10. The output produced by a monopolist is inefficiently *produced* because the average total cost of producing the product is not _____ and resources are not efficiently *allocated* because _____ is not equal to _____

11. Monopoly seems to result in a greater inequality in the distribution of income because the owners of monopolies are largely in the (upper, middle, lower) _____ income groups.

12. Resources can be said to be more efficiently allocated by pure competition than by pure monopoly only if the purely competitive firm and the monopoly have the same _____ and they will not be the same if the monopolist:

  a. by virtue of being a large firm enjoys economies of _____ not available to a pure competitor; or

  b. is more susceptible to _____ than pure competitors, and

  c. may need to make _____ expenditures to obtain or maintain monopoly privileges granted by government; this expense increases costs.

13. Monopolists are more dynamically efficient than pure competitors if they improve the _____ of producing existing products (and thereby lower the _____ of producing them) and develop new _____ over time more rapidly than pure competitors.

14. There is price discrimination whenever a product is sold at different _____ and these differences are not equal to the differences in the _____ of producing the product.

15. Price discrimination is possible only when the following three conditions are found:

  a. _____

  b. _____

  c. _____

16. The two economic consequences of a monopolist's engagement in price discrimination are a(n) (increase, decrease) _____ in the profits and a(n) _____ in the output of the monopolist.

17. The misallocation of resources that results from monopoly can be *eliminated* if a ceiling price for the monopolist's product is set equal to _____; such a price is, however, usually less than _____

18. If a regulated monopolist is allowed to earn a fair return, the ceiling price for the product is set equal to _____; such a price reduces but does not eliminate the _____ of resources caused by monopoly.

■ **PROBLEMS AND PROJECTS**

1. The demand schedule for the product produced by a monopolist is given in the table below.
  a. Complete the table by computing total revenue, marginal revenue, and the price elasticity of demand (use midpoints formula).

Quantity demanded	Price	Total revenue	Marginal revenue	Price elasticity
0	$700	$_____		
1	650	_____	$_____	_____
2	600	_____	_____	_____
3	550	_____	_____	_____
4	500	_____	_____	_____
5	450	_____	_____	_____
6	400	_____	_____	_____
7	350	_____	_____	_____
8	300	_____	_____	_____
9	250	_____	_____	_____
10	200	_____	_____	_____
11	150	_____	_____	_____
12	100	_____	_____	_____
13	50	_____	_____	_____
14	0	_____	_____	_____

  b. The relationships in the table indicate that:

(1) total revenue rises from $0 to a maximum of $_____ as price falls from $700 to $_____. Then, as price falls to zero, total revenue falls from its maximum to $_____;

(2) the relationship between price and total revenue suggests that demand is price (elastic, inelastic) _____ when quantity demanded is between a zero and 7 units of output, but that demand is price (elastic, inelastic) _____ when quantity demanded is between 7 units and 14 units;

(3) When demand is price elastic and total revenue rises from $0 to a maximum, marginal revenue is (negative, positive) _____, but when demand is price inelastic and total revenue falls from its maximum, marginal revenue is _____

c. Use the data in the table on page 118 to plot and graph the demand curve and the marginal revenue curve for the monopolist. Indicate the portion of the demand curve that is price elastic and the portion that is price inelastic.

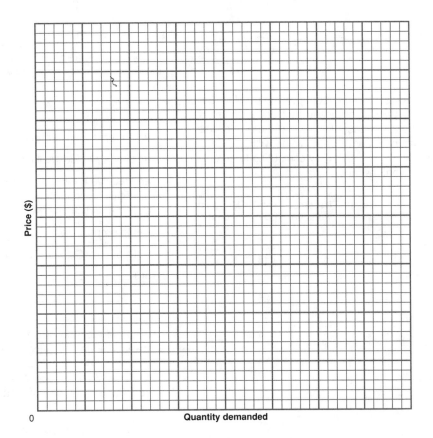

2. In the table on the next page are demand and cost data for a pure monopolist.

a. Complete the table by filling in the column for total revenue, marginal revenue, and marginal cost.

b. Answer the next three questions using the data you calculated in the table.

(1) What output will the monopolist produce? _____

(2) What price will the monopolist charge? _____

(3) What total profit will the monopolist receive at the profit-maximizing level of output? _____

Quantity	Price	Total revenue	Marginal revenue	Total cost	Marginal cost
0	$17	$____		$10	
1	16	____	$____	18	$____
2	15	____	____	23	____
3	14	____	____	25	____
4	13	____	____	27	____
5	12	____	____	28	____
6	11	____	____	32	____
7	10	____	____	40	____
8	9	____	____	50	____
9	8	____	____	64	____
10	7	____	____	80	____

3. Now assume that the pure monopolist in problem 2 is able to engage in price discrimination and sell each unit of the product at a price equal to the maximum price the buyer of that unit of the produce would be willing to pay.

a. Complete the table below by computing total revenue and marginal revenue.

Quantity	Price	Total revenue	Marginal revenue	Total cost	Marginal cost
0	$17	$____		$10	
1	16	____	$____	18	$____
2	15	____	____	23	____
3	14	____	____	25	____
4	13	____	____	27	____
5	12	____	____	28	____
6	11	____	____	32	____
7	10	____	____	40	____
8	9	____	____	50	____
9	8	____	____	64	____
10	7	____	____	80	____

b. From the table it can be seen that:
(1) the marginal revenue which the discriminating monopolist obtains from the sale of an additional unit is equal to the _____

(2) Using the same table of costs, the discriminating monopolist would produce _____ units of the product, charge the buyer of the last unit of product produced a price of $_____, and obtain a total economic profit of $_____

(3) If the pure monopolist is able to engage in price discrimination its profits will be (larger, smaller, the same) _____ and it will produce an output that is (larger, smaller, the same) _____

4. In the table below are cost and demand data for a pure monopolist.

Quantity demanded	Price	Marginal revenue	Average cost	Marginal cost
0	$17.50			
1	16.00	$16.00	$24.00	$24.00
2	14.50	13.00	15.00	6.00
3	13.00	10.00	11.67	5.00
4	11.50	7.00	10.50	7.00
5	10.00	4.00	10.00	8.00
6	8.50	1.00	9.75	8.50
7	7.00	−2.00	9.64	9.00
8	5.50	−5.00	9.34	9.25
9	4.00	−8.00	9.36	9.50

a. An unregulated monopolist would produce _____ units of a product, sell it at a price of $_____, and receive a total profit of $_____

b. If this monopolist were regulated and the maximum price it could charge were set equal to marginal cost, it would produce _____ units of a product, sell it at a price of $_____, and receive a total profit of $_____. Such regulation would either _____ the firm or require that the regulating government _____ the firm.

c. If the monopolist were not regulated and were allowed to engage in price discrimination by charging the maximum price it could obtain for each unit sold it would produce 6 units (because the marginal revenue from the 6th unit and the marginal cost of the 6th unit would both be $8.50). Its total revenue would be $_____, its total costs would be $_____, and its total profit would be $_____

d. If the monopolist were regulated and allowed to charge a fair-return price, it would produce _____ units of product, charge a price of $_____, and receive a profit of $_____

e. From which situation—*a*, *b*, or *d*—does the most efficient allocation of resources result? _____ From which situation does the least efficient allocation result? _____ In practice, government would probably select situation _____

■ **SELF-TEST**

Circle the T if the statement is true; the F if it is false.

1. The pure monopolist produces a product for which there are no substitutes. **T F**

2. The weaker the barriers to entry into an industry, the more competition there will be in the industry, other things being equal. **T F**

3. Barriers to entry are rarely complete for the monopolist. **T F**

4. Monopoly is always undesirable unless it is regulated by the government. **T F**

5. The monopolist can increase the sale of its product if it charges a lower price. **T F**

6. As a monopolist increases its output, it finds that its total revenue at first decreases, and that after some output level is reached, its total revenue begins to increase. **T F**

7. A purely competitive firm is a price-taker but a monopolist is a price-maker. **T F**

8. A monopolist will not voluntarily sell at a price at which the demand for its product is inelastic. **T F**

9. The monopolist determines the profit-maximizing output by producing that output at which marginal cost and marginal revenue are equal and sets the product price equal to marginal cost and marginal revenue at that output. **T F**

10. The monopolist maximizing total profit is also producing that output at which per unit (or average) profit is a maximum. **T F**

11. A monopolist "will charge the highest price it can get." **T F**

12. Pure monopoly guarantees economic profits. **T F**

13. A monopolist seeks maximum total profits, not maximum unit profits. **T F**

14. Resources are misallocated by monopoly because price is not equal to marginal cost. **T F**

15. One of the economic effects of monopoly is less income inequality. **T F**

16. When there are substantial economies of scale in the production of a product, the monopolist may charge a price that is lower than the price that would prevail if the product were produced by a purely competitive industry. **T F**

17. The purely competitive firm is more likely to be affected by X-inefficiency than a monopolist. **T F**

18. Rent-seeking expenditures that monopolists make to obtain or maintain monopoly privilege have no effect on the firm's costs. **T F**

19. Economists are agreed that monopolies are less dynamically efficient than competitive firms. **T F**

20. In a society in which technology is not changing and the economies of scale can be employed by both pure competitors and monopolists, the purely competitive firm will use the more efficient methods of production. **T F**

21. Price discrimination occurs when a given product is sold at more than one price and these price differences are not justified by cost differences. **T F**

22. A discriminating monopolist will produce a larger output than a nondiscriminating monopolist. **T F**

23. The regulated utility is likely to make economic profit when price is set to achieve the most efficient allocation of resources (P = MC). **T F**

24. A "fair return" price for a regulated utility would have price set to equal average cost. **T F**

25. The dilemma of monopoly regulation is that the production by a monopolist of an output that causes no misallocation of resources may force the monopolist to suffer an economic loss. **T F**

Circle the letter that corresponds to the best answer.

1. Which of the following is the **best** example of a pure monopoly?
(a) your neighborhood grocer
(b) the telephone company in your community
(c) the manufacturer of a particular brand of toothpaste
(d) an airline furnishing passenger service between two major cities

2. Which of the following is an important characteristic of a natural monopoly?
(a) economies of scale throughout the range of market demand
(b) competition would be less expensive for the consumer
(c) it is a public utility
(d) it has low fixed costs

3. Monopoly can probably exist over a long period of time only if:
(a) it is based on the control of raw materials
(b) it controls the patents on the product
(c) cut-throat competition is employed to eliminate rivals
(d) government assists the monopoly and prevents the establishment of rival firms

4. Which of the following is true with respect to the demand data confronting a monopolist?
(a) marginal revenue is greater than average revenue
(b) marginal revenue decreases as average revenue decreases

(c) demand is perfectly price elastic
(d) average revenue (or price) increases as the output of the firm increases

5. When the monopolist is maximizing total profits *or* minimizing losses:
(a) total revenue is greater than total cost
(b) average revenue is greater than average total cost
(c) average revenue is greater than marginal cost
(d) average total cost is less than marginal cost

6. At which of the following combinations of price and marginal revenue is the price elasticity of demand less than 1?
(a) price equals $102, marginal revenue equals $42
(b) price equals $92, marginal revenue equals $22
(c) price equals $82, marginal revenue equals $2
(d) price equals $72, marginal revenue equals −$18

7. Monopolists' profits may be positive, negative, or zero:
(a) in the short run
(b) in the long run
(c) in both the short run and long run
(d) where marginal cost equals marginal revenue and where average total cost is less than demand

8. At present ouput a monopolist determines that its marginal cost is $18 and its marginal revenue is $21. The monopolist will maximize profits or minimize losses by:
(a) increasing price while keeping output constant
(b) decreasing price and increasing output
(c) decreasing both price and output
(d) increasing both price and output

*Answer the next four questions (**9, 10, 11,** and **12**) based on the demand and cost data for a pure monopolist given in the table below.*

Output	Price	Total cost
0	$1,000	$ 500
1	600	520
2	500	580
3	400	700
4	300	1,000
5	200	1,500

9. How many units of output will the profit-maximizing monopolist produce?
(a) 1
(b) 2
(c) 3
(d) 4

10. The profit-maximizing monopolist would set its price at:
(a) $120
(b) $200
(c) $233
(d) $400

11. If the monopolist could sell each unit of the product at the maximum price the buyer of that unit would be willing to pay for it and if the monopolist sold 4 units, total revenue would be:
(a) $1200
(b) $1800
(c) $2000
(d) $2800

12. If the monopolist were forced to produce the socially optimal output by the imposition of a ceiling price, the ceiling price would have to be:
(a) $200
(b) $300
(c) $400
(d) $500

13. The supply curve for a pure monopolist:
(a) is the portion of the marginal cost curve that lies above the average variable cost curve
(b) is perfectly price elastic at the market price
(c) is upsloping
(d) does not exist

14. A monopolist at the equilibrium level of output does not *produce* the product as efficiently as is possible because:
(a) the average total cost of producing it is not a minimum
(b) the marginal cost of producing the last unit is less than its price
(c) it is earning a profit
(d) average revenue is greater than the cost of producing an extra unit of output

15. X-inefficiency means that a firm fails to:
(a) produce an output at the lowest average cost possible
(b) produce an output at the lowest total cost possible
(c) employ resources in their least-cost combination to produce an output
(d) do all of the above

16. Dynamic efficiency refers to:
(a) the achievement of economies of scale in producing products
(b) the development over time of more efficient (less costly) techniques of producing products and the improvement of these products
(c) the avoidance of X-inefficiency
(d) the avoidance of allocative inefficiency

17. Over time monopoly *may* result in greater technological improvement than would be forthcoming under conditions of pure competition for several reasons. Which of the following is *not* one of these reasons?
(a) technological advance will lower the costs and enhance the profits of the monopolist, and these increased profits will not have to be shared with rivals

(b) technological advance will act as a barrier to entry and thus allow the monopolist to continue to be a monopolist

(c) technological advance requires research and experimentation, and the monopolist is in a position to finance them out of profits

(d) technological advance is apt to make existing capital equipment obsolete, and the monopolist can reduce costs by speeding up the rate at which its capital becomes obsolete

18. Which of the following is **not** one of the conditions which must be realized before a seller finds price discrimination is workable?

(a) the buyer must be unable to resell the product
(b) the product must be a service
(c) the seller must have some degree of monopoly power
(d) the seller must be able to segment the market

19. If a monopolist engages in price discrimination rather than charging all buyers the same price its:

(a) profits and its output are greater
(b) profits and its output are smaller
(c) profits are greater and its output is smaller
(d) profits are smaller and its output is greater

Answer the next four questions (20, 21, 22, and 23) based on the demand and cost data for a pure monopolist given in the table below.

Quantity demanded	Price	Total cost
0	$700	$ 300
1	650	400
2	600	450
3	550	510
4	500	590
5	450	700
6	400	840
7	350	1,020
8	300	1,250
9	250	1,540
10	200	1,900

20. The profit-maximizing output and price for this monopolist would be:

(a) 5 units and a $450 price
(b) 6 units and a $400 price
(c) 7 units and a $350 price
(d) 8 units and a $300 price

In answering the next two questions (21 and 22), assume this monopolist is able to engage in price discrimination and sell each unit of the product at a price equal to the maximum price the buyer of that unit would be willing to pay.

21. The marginal revenue that the price discriminating monopolist obtains from the sale of an additional unit is equal to:

(a) total revenue
(b) average cost
(c) unit cost
(d) price

22. The profit maximizing output and price for the price discriminating monopolist would be:

(a) 6 units and a $400 price
(b) 7 units and a $350 price
(c) 8 units and a $300 price
(d) 9 units and a $250 price

23. How much greater would the total economic profits be for the discriminating monopolist than the nondiscriminating monopolist?

(a) $720
(b) $830
(c) $990
(d) $1070

The next question (24) is based on the graph below.

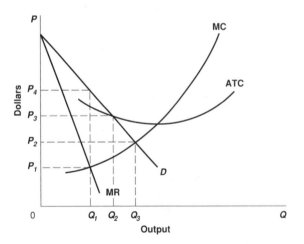

24. The price and output combination for the unregulated profit maximizing monopoly compared with the socially optimal price and output combination for the regulated monopoly would be, respectively:

(a) P_4 and Q_1 versus P_3 and Q_2
(b) P_4 and Q_1 versus P_2 and Q_3
(c) P_3 and Q_2 versus P_4 and Q_1
(d) P_2 and Q_3 versus P_3 and Q_2

25. A monopolist who is limited by the imposition of a ceiling price to a fair return sells the product at a price equal to:

(a) average total cost
(b) average variable cost
(c) marginal cost
(d) average fixed cost

■ DISCUSSION QUESTIONS

1. What is pure monopoly? Why is it studied if it is so rare in practice?

2. What is meant by a barrier to entry? What kinds of such barriers are there? How important are they in pure competition, pure monopoly, monopolistic competition, and oligopoly?

3. Why are the economies of scale a barrier to entry?

4. Why are most natural monopolies also public utilities? What does government hope to achieve by granting exclusive franchises to and regulating such natural monopolies?

5. How do patents and licenses create barriers to entry? Cite examples.

6. Compare the pure monopolist and the individual pure competitor with respect to:
    (a) the demand schedule;
    (b) the marginal-revenue schedule;
    (c) the relationship between marginal revenue and average revenue;
    (d) price policy; and
    (e) the ability to administer (or set) price.

7. Explain why marginal revenue is always less than average revenue when demand is less than perfectly elastic.

8. Suppose a pure monopolist discovered it was producing and selling an output at which the demand for its product was inelastic. Explain why a decrease in its output would increase its economic profits.

9. What output will the monopolist produce? What price will it charge?

10. Why does the monopolist not charge the highest possible price for the product? Why does the monopolist not set the price for the product in such a way that average profit is a maximum? Why are some monopolies unprofitable?

11. In what sense is resource allocation and production more efficient under conditions of pure competition than under monopoly conditions?

12. How does monopoly allegedly affect the distribution of income in the economy and why does monopoly seemingly have this effect on income distribution in the American economy?

13. What are the three complications that may result in a monopolist having lower or higher average costs than a competitive firm? How do each of these complications affect the average costs of a monopolist and what evidence is there to support the belief that these two complications lower or raise the average costs of a monopolist?

14. Does monopoly, when compared with pure competition, result in more or less dynamic efficiency (technological progress)? What are the arguments on **both** sides of this question? What evidence is there to support the two views?

15. What is meant by price discrimination and what conditions must be realized before it is workable? Explain how a monopolist who discriminates would determine what price to charge for each unit of the product sold (or to charge each group of buyers) and how discrimination would affect the profits and the output of the monopolist.

16. How do public utility regulatory agencies attempt to eliminate the misallocation of resources that results from monopoly? Explain the dilemma that almost invariably confronts the agency in this endeavor; and explain why a fair-return policy only reduces but does not eliminate misallocation.

■ ANSWERS

Chapter 11 Price and Output Determination: Pure Monopoly

FILL-IN QUESTIONS

1. close substitutes, blocked

2. *a.* the economies of scale; *b.* natural monopolies; *c.* patents and licenses; *d.* ownership of essential raw materials

3. greater, money capital

4. natural, regulated

5. less than, less, decrease

6. increase, decrease, horizontal, downsloping, elastic

7. marginal cost, average variable cost, does not exist

8. marginal revenue, marginal cost, greater

9. *a.* highest possible; *b.* a maximum; *c.* pure profit

10. a minimum, price (or average revenue), marginal cost

11. upper

12. costs (or cost schedules); *a.* scale; *b.* X-inefficiency; rent-preserving

13. techniques (technology), costs (or cost schedules), products

14. prices, cost

15. *a.* the seller has some monopoly power; *b.* the seller is able to separate buyers into groups which have different elasticities of demand for the product; *c.* the original buyers cannot resell the product

16. increase, increase

17. marginal cost, average (total) cost

18. average (total) cost, misallocation

PROBLEMS AND PROJECTS

1. *a.* total revenue: $0, 650, 1200, 1650, 2000, 2250, 2400, 2450, 2400, 2250, 2000, 1650, 1200, 650, 0; marginal revenue: $650, 550, 450, 350, 250, 150, 50, −50, −150, −250, −350, −400, −550, −650; price elasticity: 27, 8.33, 4.60, 3.00, 2.11, 1.54, 1.15, .87, .65, .47, .33, .22, .12, .04 *b.* (1) $2450, $350, 0; (2) elastic, inelastic; (3) positive, negative *c.* see Figure 11−2 in the text as an example

2. *a.* total revenue: $0, 16, 30, 42, 52, 60, 66, 70, 72, 72, 70; marginal revenue: $16, 14, 12, 10, 8, 6, 4, 2, 0, −2; marginal cost: $8, 5, 2, 2, 1, 4, 8, 10, 14, 16 *b.* (1) 6; (2) $11; (3) $34 (TR of $66 minus TC of $32)

3. *a.* total revenue: $0, 16, 31, 45, 58, 70, 81, 91, 100, 108, 115; marginal revenue: $16, 15, 14, 13, 12, 11, 10, 9, 8, 7; marginal cost: $8, 5, 2, 2, 1, 4, 8, 10, 14, 16; *b.* (1) price; (2) 7 units; $10; $51 (TR of $91 minus TC of $40); (3) larger, larger

4. *a.* 4, 11.50, 4.00; *b.* 6, 8.50, −7.50, bankrupt, subsidize; *c.* 73.50, 58.50, 15.00; *d.* 5, 10.00, zero; *e.* b, a, d

SELF-TEST

1. F, p. 187	**14.** T, p. 197
2. T, p. 188	**15.** F, p. 198
3. T, p. 188	**16.** T, p. 198
4. F, p. 191	**17.** F, pp. 198−199
5. T, p. 191	**18.** F, p. 199
6. F, p. 191	**19.** F, p. 200
7. T, pp. 187; 193	**20.** T, p. 200
8. T, p. 193	**21.** T, p. 201
9. F, pp. 193−195	**22.** T, p. 202
10. F, p. 196	**23.** F, p. 203
11. F, p. 196	**24.** T, p. 203
12. F, p. 196	**25.** T, pp. 203−204
13. T, p. 196	

1. *b*, p. 188	**14.** *a*, p. 197
2. *a*, p. 189	**15.** *d*, pp. 198−199
3. *d*, p. 191	**16.** *b*, p. 200
4. *b*, p. 192	**17.** *d*, p. 200
5. *c*, pp. 194−195	**18.** *b*, p. 201
6. *d*, p. 193	**19.** *a*, p. 202
7. *a*, p. 196	**20.** *b*, pp. 193−195
8. *b*, p. 195	**21.** *d*, p. 202
9. *c*, pp. 193−195	**22.** *c*, p. 202
10. *d*, pp. 193−195	**23.** *c*, p. 202
11. *b*, p. 202	**24.** *b*, p. 203
12. *b*, p. 203	**25.** *a*, p. 203
13. *d*, p. 196	

DISCUSSION QUESTIONS

1. pp. 187−188	**9.** pp. 193−195
2. pp. 189−191	**10.** p. 196
3. p. 189	**11.** p. 197
4. pp. 189−190	**12.** p. 198
5. p. 190	**13.** pp. 198−199
6. pp. 191−193	**14.** p. 200
7. pp. 189−192	**15.** pp. 201−202
8. p. 193	**16.** pp. 203−204

CHAPTER 12

Price and Output Determination: Monopolistic Competition

Chapter 12 is the third of the four chapters which deal with specific market situations. As its name implies, monopolistic competition is a blend of pure competition and pure monopoly. One of the reasons for studying those relatively unrealistic market situations was to prepare you for this realistic study of monopolistic competition.

It must be pointed out that monopolistic competition is not a description of all markets. The study of it, however, will help you to understand the many markets which are nearly monopolistically competitive. It will also help you to understand, as you will learn in the next chapter, why oligopoly is prevalent in the American economy and how oligopoly differs from monopolistic competition.

The first task is to learn exactly what is meant by monopolistic competition. Next you should examine the demand curve which the monopolistically competitive firm sees for its product and note how and why it differs from the demand curves faced by the purely competitive firm and by the monopolist. In this connection it is also important to understand that as the individual firm changes the character of the product it produces or changes the extent to which it promotes the sale of its product, both the costs of the firm and the demand for its product will change. A firm confronts a different demand curve every time it alters its product or its promotion of the product.

With the product and promotional campaign of the firm *given*, the price-output analysis of the monopolistic competitor is relatively simple. In the short run this analysis is identical with the analysis of the price-output decision of the pure monopolist in the short run. It is only in the long run that the competitive element makes itself apparent: The entry (or exit) of firms forces the price the firm charges down (up) *toward* the level of average cost. This price is not equal either to *minimum* average cost or to marginal cost; and consequently monopolistic competition, on these two scores, can be said to be less efficient than pure competition.

A relatively large part of Chapter 12 is devoted to a discussion of nonprice competition. This explanation is given for very good reasons. In monopolistically competitive industries a part of the competitive effort of individual firms is given over to product differentiation, product de-

velopment, and product advertising. Each firm has three things to manipulate—price, product, and advertising—in trying to maximize its profits. While monopolistic competition may not be as economically efficient as pure competition in terms of a *given* product and the promotion of it, when all the economic effects—good and bad—of differentiation, development, and advertising are considered this shortcoming may or may not be offset. Whether it is actually offset is an unanswerable question.

If Chapter 12 has one central idea it is this: monopolistic competition cannot be compared with pure competition solely on the basis of prices charged at any given moment of time; it must also be judged in terms of whether it results in better products, in a wider variety of products, in better-informed consumers, in lower-priced radio and television programs, magazines, and newspapers, and other socially redeeming features.

The study of monopolistic competition is a realistic study and for that reason it is a difficult study. Many factors have to be considered in explaining how such a group of firms behaves and in appraising the efficiency with which such an industry allocates scarce resources.

■ CHECKLIST

When you have studied this chapter you should be able to:

☐ List the four characteristics of monopolistic competition.
☐ Describe the four forms that product differentiation may take in the marketplace.
☐ Compare the firm's demand curve under monopolistic competition with a firm's demand curve in pure monopoly and in pure competition.
☐ Determine the output of and the price charged by a monopolistic competitor (producing a given product and engaged in a given amount of sales promotion) in the short run when you are given the cost and demand data.
☐ Explain why the price charged by a monopolistic competitor (producing a given product and engaged in a given

amount of sales promotion) will in the long run tend to equal average cost.

☐ Identify the "wastes of monopolistic competition" and explain why product differentiation may "offset" these wastes.

☐ Enumerate the three principal types of nonprice competition.

☐ Present the major arguments in the cases for and against advertising.

☐ Discuss the empirical evidence in support of the traditional and new perspective views of advertising.

☐ Explain why monopolistic competition is more complex in practice than is suggested by the graphical analysis represented in the chapter.

■ **CHAPTER OUTLINE**

1. A monopolistically competitive industry is one in which a fairly large number of independent firms produces differentiated products, in which both price and various forms of nonprice competition occur, and into which entry is relatively easy in the long run. Many American industries approximate monopolistic competition.

2. Assume that the products the firms in the industry produce and the amounts of promotional activity in which they engage are given.

  a. The demand curve confronting each firm will be highly but not perfectly price elastic because each firm has many competitors who produce close but not perfect substitutes for the product it produces.

  (1) Comparing the demand curve for the monopolistic competitor to other market structures suggests that it is not perfectly elastic as is the case with the pure competitor, but it is also more elastic than the demand curve of the pure monopolist.

  (2) The degree of elasticity, however, for each monopolistic competitor will depend on the number of rivals and the extent of product differentiation.

  b. In the short run the individual firm will produce the output at which marginal cost and marginal revenue are equal and charge the price at which that output can be sold; either profits or losses may result in the short run.

  c. In the long run the entry and exodus of firms will *tend* to change the demand for the product of the individual firm in such a way that profits are eliminated (price and average costs are made equal to each other).

3. Monopolistic competition among firms producing a given product and engaged in a given amount of promotional activity results in less economic efficiency and more waste than does pure competition.

  a. The average cost of each firm is equal in the long run to its price, but the industry does not realize allo-

cative efficiency because output is smaller than the output at which marginal cost and price are equal.

  b. The industry does not realize productive efficiency because the output is smaller than the output at which average cost is a minimum.

4. In addition to setting its price and output so that its profit is maximized, each individual firm also attempts to differentiate its product and to promote or advertise it to increase the firm's profit; these additional activities give rise to nonprice competition among firms.

  a. Product differentiation means that the monopolistically competitive firms will offer consumers a wide range of types, style, brands, and quality variants of a product; this expansion of consumer choice may offset the wastes of monopolistic competition.

  b. Product development is an attempt by firms to improve a product, and it serves as a form of nonprice competition; to the extent that improved products contribute to consumer welfare, this type of nonprice competition among monopolistic firms may also offset some of the wastes of competition.

5. Whether the advertising of differentiated products results in economic waste or in greater efficiency is debatable; there are good arguments on both sides of this question and there is no clear answer to it.

  a. The arguments focus on three major questions: whether advertising is persuasion or information, whether advertising promotes economic concentration or competition, and whether advertising contributes to economic waste or economic efficiency.

  b. Empirical evidence on the economic effects of advertising has produced two schools of thought:

  (1) The traditional view argues and presents evidence in support of the idea that advertising reduces active competition among existing firms and serves as a barrier to entry to new firms. Higher prices to consumers and enhanced profits for existing firms result.

  (2) The new perspective view and evidence indicate that advertising acts as a relatively inexpensive means of increasing the number of substitute products known to buyers; thus, this information makes an industry more competitive.

  c. The monopolistically competitive firm tries to adjust its price, its product, and its promotion of the product so that the amount by which the firm's total revenue exceeds the total cost of producing and promoting its product is at a maximum.

■ **IMPORTANT TERMS**

Monopolistic competition
Product differentiation
Nonprice competition

Wastes of monopolistic competition
Traditional and new perspective views of advertising

■ FILL-IN QUESTIONS

1. In a monopolistically competitive market a (few, relatively large number of) _____ producers sell (standardized, differentiated) _____ _____ products; these producers (do, do not) _____ collude; and they engage in both _____ and _____ competition. In the long run entry into the industry is (difficult, fairly easy) _____

2. Because monopolistically competitive firms sell differentiated products each firm has (no, limited, complete) _____ control over the price of its product and there is _____ between the firms.

3. List the four forms that product differentiation may take:

a. _____

b. _____

c. _____

d. _____

4. Given the product being produced and the extent to which that product is being promoted, in the **short run**:
a. The demand curve confronting the monopolistically competitive firm will be (more, less) _____ elastic than that facing a monopolist and _____ elastic than that facing a pure competitor.
b. The elasticity of this demand curve will depend upon _____ and _____
c. The firm will produce the output at which _____ and _____ are equal.

5. In the long run, the **entry** of new firms into a monopolistically competitive industry will (expand, reduce) _____ the demand for the product produced by each firm in the industry and (increase, decrease) _____ the elasticity of that demand.

6. In the long run, **given** the product and the amount of product promotion, the price charged by the individual firm will tend to equal _____, its economic profits will tend to equal _____, and its average cost will

be _____ than the minimum average cost of producing and promoting the product.

7. Although representative firms in monopolistic competition tend to earn (economic, normal) _____ profits in the long run, there can be complications that may result in firms earning _____ profits or losses in the long run.
a. Some firms may achieve a degree of product _____ that cannot be duplicated by other firms that contribute to _____ profits.
b. There may be _____ to entry that prevent penetration of the market by other firms that contribute to _____ profit.
c. Some firms may attempt to maintain a "_____ of life," and consequently experience _____ losses.

8. Given the product and the extent of product promotion, monopolistic competition is wasteful because _____ and because _____

9. In the long run, the monopolistic competitor cannot protect and increase profits by varying the product's price or output but it can try to protect and increase profits by _____ and _____

10. Product differentiation and product development tend to result in the consumer being offered a wider _____ of goods at any given time and an improved _____ of goods over a period of time.

11. The debate over advertising focuses on three critical areas:

a. _____ or _____?

b. _____ or _____?

c. _____ or _____?

12. The traditional view of advertising is that it will alter consumer preferences in favor of a product, or _____ consumers, but the new perspective contends that consumers get important _____ from advertising.

13. The creation of "brand loyalty" is a traditional view of advertising that suggests it promotes economic _____ industries because advertising

makes product (demand, supply) _____ (more, less) _____ elastic. The counter view is that advertising promotes _____ because it makes consumers more aware of substitutes and decreases (demand, supply) _____ for a particular product.

14. Advertising has long been thought to be wasteful because it prevents the realization of _____ and _____ efficiency, but the newer view of advertising contends that it is efficient because it provides important _____ for consumer and reduces _____ costs of consumers.

15. The different case studies of the economic effects of advertising indicate that in the U.S. it is (procompetitive, anticompetitive, both pro- and anticompetitive) _____

16. In attempting to maximize its profits the monopolistic competitor will vary the price, the _____, and the _____ of the product until the firm feels no further change in these three variables will result in greater profit.

■ **PROBLEMS AND PROJECTS**

1. Listed below are several industries. Indicate in the space after each whether you believe it is monopolistically competitive (MC) or not monopolistically competitive (N). If you indicate the latter, explain why you think the industry is not a monopolistically competitive one.

a. The production of automobiles in the United States.

_____

b. The retail distribution of automobiles in the United States. _____

_____

c. Grocery supermarkets in a city of 500,000 people.

_____

d. The retail sale of gasoline in a city of 500,000 people.

_____

e. The production of low-priced shoes in the United States. _____

_____

f. The mail-order sale of men's clothes. _____

_____

_____

2. Assume that the short-run cost and demand data given in the table below confront a monopolistic competitor selling a given product and engaged in a given amount of product promotion.

Output	Total cost	Marginal cost	Quantity demanded	Price	Marginal revenue
0	$ 50		0	$120	
1	80	$_____	1	110	$_____
2	90	_____	2	100	_____
3	110	_____	3	90	_____
4	140	_____	4	80	_____
5	180	_____	5	70	_____
6	230	_____	6	60	_____
7	290	_____	7	50	_____
8	360	_____	8	40	_____
9	440	_____	9	30	_____
10	530	_____	10	20	_____

a. Compute the marginal cost and marginal revenue of each unit of output and enter these figures in the table.

b. In the short run the firm will (1) produce _____ units of output, (2) sell its output at a price of $_____, and (3) have a total economic profit of $_____

c. In the long run, (1) the demand for the firm's product will _____, (2) until the price of the product equals _____ and (3) the total economic profits of the firm are _____

3. Match the following descriptions to the correct graph on the next page. Indicate on each graph, the area of economic profit or loss, or state if the firm is just making normal profits.

a. a purely competitive firm in earning economic profits in the short run   Graph _____

b. a purely competitive firm in long-run equilibrium

Graph _____

c. a natural monopoly   Graph _____

d. a monopolistically competitive firm earning economic profits in the short run   Graph _____

e. a monopolistically competitive firm experiencing economic losses in the short run   Graph _____

f. a monopolistically competitive firm in long-run equilibrium   Graph _____

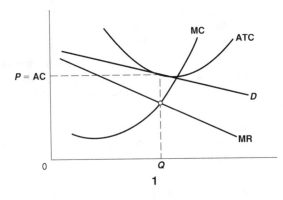

1

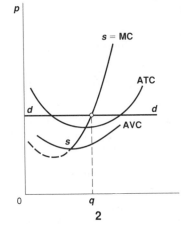

2

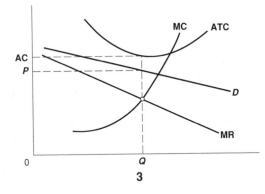

3

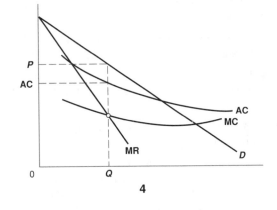

4

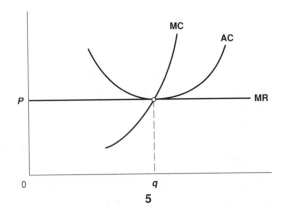

5

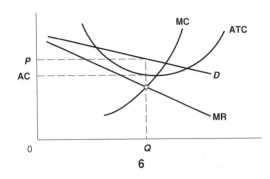

6

■ **SELF-TEST**

Circle the T if the statement is true; the F if it is false.

1. Monopolistic competitors have no control over the price of their products.　　　　　　　　　**T　F**

2. The publisher of McConnell/Brue *Microeconomics* and this *Study Guide* is a monopolistic competitor.　**T　F**

3. The firm's reputation for servicing or exchanging its product is a form of product differentiation under monopolistic competition.　　　　　　　　　　　**T　F**

4. Entry is relatively easy in pure competition but there are significant barriers to entry in monopolistic competition.　　　　　　　　　　　　　　**T　F**

5. There are thousands of competitors in a monopolistically competitive industry.　　　　　　　**T　F**

6. The smaller the number of firms in an industry and the greater the extent of product differentiation, the greater will be the elasticity of the individual seller's demand curve.　　　　　　　　　　　　　　　**T　F**

7. The demand curve of the monopolistic competitor is most likely to be less elastic than the demand curve of the pure monopolist.　　　　　　　　　　**T　F**

8. In the short run, firms that are monopolistically competitive may earn economic profits or incur losses.　**T　F**

9. The long-run equilibrium position in monopolistic competition would be where price is equal to marginal cost.　　　　　　　　　　　　　　**T　F**

10. Representative firms in a monopolistically competitive market earn economic profits in the long run.　　**T　F**

11. One reason why monopolistic competition is wasteful, given the products the firms produce and the extent to which they promote them, is that the average cost of producing the product is greater than the minimum average cost at which the product could be produced.　**T　F**

12. The wider the range of differentiated products offered to consumers by a monopolistically competitive industry the less excess capacity there will be in that industry.　　　　　　　　　　　　　　　**T　F**

13. A firm will improve the quality of its product only if it expects that the additional revenue which it will receive will be greater than the extra costs involved.　　**T　F**

14. Successful product improvement by one firm has little or no effect on other firms under monopolistic competition.　　　　　　　　　　　**T　F**

15. Cash rebates are a common form of nonprice competition.　　　　　　　　　　　　**T　F**

16. Through product development and advertising expenditures, a monopolistically competitive firm may strive to increase the demand for its product more than these forms of nonprice competition increase its costs.　**T　F**

17. Those who contend that advertising contributes to the growth of economic concentration in the economy argue that the advertising by established firms creates barriers to the entry of new firms into an industry.　　**T　F**

18. The new perspective on advertising would be that advertising increases knowledge of available products so that consumers are more aware of substitutes.　**T　F**

19. There tends to be rather general agreement among both critics and defenders of advertising that advertising increases the average cost of producing and promoting the product.　　　　　　　　　　　**T　F**

20. Empirical evidence clearly indicates that advertising reduces competition and leads to a misallocation of the economy's resources.　　　　　　　　　**T　F**

Circle the letter that corresponds to the best answer.

1. Which of the following would be most characteristic of monopolistic competition?
　(a) thousands of firms in the industry
　(b) product standardization
　(c) collusion among firms
　(d) nonprice competition

2. All the following are forms that product differentiation can take in monopolistic competition ***except:***
　(a) promotion and packaging of the product
　(b) sale of the homogeneous product at a standard price
　(c) physical or qualitative differences in the products
　(d) services and the conditions involving the sale of the product

3. In the short run, a representative monopolistically competitive firm:
　(a) obtains an economic profit
　(b) breaks even
　(c) suffers an economic loss
　(d) may have an economic profit or loss or break even

4. A monopolistically competitive firm is producing at an output level in the short run where average total cost is $3.50, price is $3.00, marginal revenue is $1.50, marginal cost is $1.50. This firm is operating:
　(a) with an economic loss in the short run
　(b) with an economic profit in the short run
　(c) at the break-even level of output in the short run
　(d) at an inefficient level of output in the short run

5. If firms enter a monopolistically competitive industry, then we would expect the firm's demand curve to:
　(a) increase and the firm's price to increase
　(b) decrease and the firm's price to decrease
　(c) remain the same but the firm's price to increase

(d) remain the same and the firm's price to remain the same

Answer the next four questions (*6, 7, 8,* and *9*) on the basis of the following diagram for a monopolistically competitive firm in short-run equilibrium. Assume the firm is part of an increasing-cost industry.

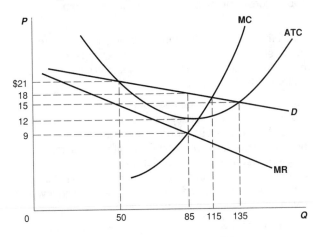

6. The firm's profit maximizing price will be:
(a) $9
(b) $12
(c) $15
(d) $18

7. The equilibrium output for this firm will be:
(a) 50
(b) 85
(c) 115
(d) 135

8. This firm will realize an economic profit of:
(a) $510
(b) $765
(c) $1021
(d) $1170

9. If firms enter this industry in the long run the:
(a) average total cost curve will shift upward and demand will decrease
(b) average total cost curve will shift downward and demand will increase
(c) marginal revenue curve will shift upward and demand will decrease
(d) marginal revenue curve will shift upward and demand will increase

Answer the next three questions (*10, 11,* and *12*) based on the demand and cost schedules for a monopolistic competitor given in the table at the top of the next column.

Price	Quantity demanded	Total cost	Output
$10	1	$14	1
9	2	17	2
8	3	22	3
7	4	29	4
6	5	38	5
5	6	49	6

10. What output will the monopolistic competitor produce?
(a) 2
(b) 3
(c) 4
(d) 5

11. What will be the economic profit or loss for this monopolistic competitor at the profit-maximizing level of output?
(a) $-$1
(b) $1
(c) $2
(d) $3

12. *In the long run,* the number of firms in this monopolistic competitive industry will most likely:
(a) stay the same
(b) decrease
(c) increase
(d) cannot be determined from the information

13. Given the product the firm is producing and the extent to which the firm is promoting it, *in the long run:*
(a) the firm will produce that output at which marginal cost and price are equal
(b) the elasticity of demand for the firm's product will be less than it was in the short run
(c) the number of firms in the industry will be greater than it was in the short run
(d) the economic profits being earned by the firms in the industry will tend to equal zero

14. Which of the following is *not* one of the features of monopolistic competition which may offset the wastes associated with such a market structure?
(a) a wider variety of products is offered to consumers
(b) much advertising is self-canceling
(c) the quality of products improves over time
(d) consumers are better informed of the availability and prices of products

15. If an industry is to be economically efficient it is necessary that:
(a) price equal average cost
(b) price equal marginal cost
(c) average cost equal marginal cost
(d) all of the above

16. Were a monopolistically competitive industry in long-run equilibrium a firm in that industry might be able to increase its economic profits by:

(a) increasing the price of its product

(b) increasing the amounts it spends to advertise its product

(c) decreasing the price of its product

(d) decreasing the output of its product

17. The traditional view of advertising argues that advertising:

(a) makes the firm's demand curve less elastic and helps the firm reduce prices to consumers

(b) makes the firm's demand curve less elastic and helps the firm increase profits

(c) gives a new firm an opportunity to overcome barriers to entry created by an established firm

(d) gives consumers information on products to increase the known number of substitutes to buyers

18. Which of the following would be closest to recent empirical evidence supporting the new perspective on advertising? A study that showed that:

(a) above average levels of advertising produced below average rates of increases in output

(b) above average rates of increases in prices produced below average levels of advertising

(c) below average rates of output increases produced above average levels of advertising

(d) above average levels of advertising produced below average rates of increases in prices

19. Which of the following can be fairly concluded with respect to the economic effects of advertising?

(a) advertising helps to maintain a high level of aggregate demand in the economy

(b) evidence on the economic effects of advertising is mixed because of the difficulties of determining cause and effect in studies

(c) advertising in the American economy leads almost invariably to higher product prices

(d) lower unit costs and lower prices result when a firm advertises because advertising increases the size of the firm's market and promotes economies of scale

20. In seeking to maximize its profits the three variables which the monopolistically competitive firm must consider are:

(a) price, product, and promotion

(b) price, publicity, and promotion

(c) price, product, and publicity

(d) product, publicity, and promotion

■ **DISCUSSION QUESTIONS**

1. What are the chief characteristics of a monopolistic competitive market? In what sense is there competition and in what sense is there monopoly in such a market?

2. What is meant by product differentiation? By what methods can products be differentiated? How does product differentiation affect the kind of competition in, and inject an element of monopoly into, markets?

3. Comment on the elasticity of the demand curve faced by the monopolistically competitive firm in the short run. Assume that the firm is producing a given product and is engaged in a given amount of promotional activity. What two factors determine just how elastic that demand curve will be?

4. What output will the monopolistic competitor produce in the short run, and what price will it charge for its product? What determines whether the firm will earn profits or suffer losses in the short run?

5. In the long run what level of economic profits will the individual monopolistically competitive firm *tend* to receive? Why is this just a tendency? What forces economic profits toward this level, and why will the firm produce a long-run output which is smaller than the most "efficient" output? (Again assume, in answering this question, that the firm is producing a given product and selling it with a given amount of promotional activity.)

6. In what two senses is monopolistic competition wasteful or a misallocation of resources?

7. What methods, other than price cutting, can an individual monopolistic competitor employ to attempt to protect and increase its economic profits in the long run?

8. To what extent and how do product differentiation and product development offset the "wastes" associated with monopolistic competition?

9. Does advertising result in a waste of resources, or does it promote a more efficient utilization of resources? What arguments can be presented to support the contention that it is wasteful and detrimental, and what claims are made to support the view that it is beneficial to the economy?

10. What is the empirical evidence in support of the traditional and new perspective views of advertising? What conclusion can be drawn about the economic effects of advertising?

11. When is a monopolistic competitor in long-run equilibrium not only with respect to the price it is charging but also with respect to the product it is producing and the extent to which it is promoting its product?

■ **ANSWERS**

Chapter 12 Price and Output Determination: Monopolistic Competition

FILL-IN QUESTIONS

1. relatively large number of, differentiated, do not, price, non-price, fairly easy

2. limited, rivalry

3. *a.* product quality; *b.* services; *c.* location; *d.* promotion and packaging

4. *a.* more, less; *b.* number of rivals the firm has, the degree of product differentiation; *c.* marginal cost, marginal revenue

5. reduce, increase

6. average cost, zero, greater

7. normal, economic; *a.* differentiation, economic; *b.* barriers, economic; *c.* way, economic

8. average cost is greater than minimum average cost, price is greater than marginal cost

9. product differentiation, product promotion

10. variety, quality

11. *a.* persuasion or information; *b.* concentration or competition; *c.* wasteful or efficient

12. persuade (or manipulate), information

13. concentration, demand, less, competition, demand

14. allocative, productive (either order); information, search

15. both

16. product, promotion

PROBLEMS AND PROJECTS

1. *a.* N; *b.* MC; *c.* MC; *d.* MC; *e.* N; *f.* MC

2. *a.* marginal cost: $30, 10, 20, 30, 40, 50, 60, 70, 80, 90; marginal revenue: $110, 90, 70, 50, 30, 10, −10, −30, −50, −70;

b. (1) 4; (2) $80; (3) $180; *c.* (1) decrease; (2) average cost; (3) equal to zero

3. *a.* 2; *b.* 5; *c.* 4; *d.* 6; *e.* 3; *f.* 1

SELF-TEST

1. F, p. 208
2. T, p. 208
3. T, p. 208
4. F, p. 209
5. F, pp. 207–208
6. F, p. 209
7. F, p. 209
8. T, p. 208
9. F, p. 210
10. F, p. 210
11. T, p. 211
12. F, pp. 211–212
13. T, p. 213
14. F, p. 213
15. F, p. 212
16. T, pp. 212–213
17. T, p. 214
18. T, p. 214
19. F, p. 215
20. F, p. 215

1. *d*, p. 209
2. *b*, p. 208
3. *d*, p. 210
4. *a*, p. 210
5. *b*, p. 210
6. *d*, p. 210
7. *b*, p. 210
8. *a*, p. 210
9. *a*, p. 210
10. *b*, p. 211
11. *c*, p. 210
12. *c*, p. 210
13. *d*, pp. 210–211
14. *b*, p. 211
15. *d*, p. 211
16. *b*, p. 213
17. *b*, p. 214
18. *d*, pp. 215–216
19. *b*, p. 215
20. *a*, p. 217

DISCUSSION QUESTIONS

1. pp. 207–208
2. pp. 208–209
3. p. 209
4. pp. 210–211
5. pp. 210–211
6. p. 211
7. pp. 212–213
8. pp. 211–212
9. pp. 214–215
10. pp. 215–216
11. p. 217

CHAPTER 13

Price and Output Determination: Oligopoly

This chapter is the last of four chapters on market structures, and in some ways it is the most difficult. Oligopoly is one of those topics of study in economics that offer few definite conclusions. The ambiguity resulting from the analysis of oligopoly often makes it frustrating for students to study. By contrast, economists do draw fairly definite conclusions and make strong generalizations about price and output determination under conditions of pure competition, pure monopoly, and monopolistic competition, as you have learned in the last three chapters.

Oligopoly, however, is the most realistic market structure that you will examine. Many economists believe that it is the most prevalent type of market structure—or at least the most important—in the American economy. This realism and the different examples of oligopoly that can be found throughout the American economy make the study of oligopoly more difficult and complex than is the case with other market structures. Despite these problems, there are insights about oligopoly that you *can* and *should* learn.

The concept of oligopoly is fairly easy to grasp—a few firms that are mutually interdependent and that dominate the market for a product. The underlying causes of oligopoly are economies of scales, barriers to entry, and mergers, which are subjects you have read about before. Economists use concentration ratios to measure the degree of firm dominance of an industry, but as with most economic measures you have studied in previous chapters, they are subject to several shortcomings.

What is more difficult to grasp is oligopoly behavior. The game theory overview should help you understand *what is meant* by mutual interdependence and *why it exists* in an oligopoly. If you can do this, you will be well on the road to understanding why specific conclusions cannot be reached about the price and output determination of individual firms. You will also see why oligopolists are loath to engage in price competition and why they frequently resort to *collusion* to set prices and sometimes use nonprice competition to determine market share. Collusion does not give firms complete protection from the rigors of competition because there are incentives to cheat on collusive agreements.

There is no standard model of oligopoly because of the diversity of markets and the uncertainty caused by mutual interdependence among firms. Chapter 13, however, does present four variants of oligopoly models that cover the range of market situations. The kinked-demand curve model is the first of these variants. It explains why, in the absence of collusion, oligopolists will not raise or lower their prices even when their costs change. But the kinked-demand curve does not explain what price oligopolists will set; it only explains why price, once set, will be relatively inflexible.

The second model examines how oligopolists resort to collusion to set price. The collusion can be overt, as in a cartel agreement, or the collusion can be covert, as in a gentlemen's agreement. The history of the OPEC international cartel provides a classic example of how covert collusion can work in practice, and how obstacles to collusion can eventually weaken the power of a cartel.

Two other models of oligopoly are also worthy of note. In some industries there is a dominant firm that serves as the price leader for the other firms. In this price leadership model there is no overt collusion, only tacit collusion, among firms involved in setting prices in this industry. The fourth model is based on "cost-plus pricing" where an oligopolist estimates the cost of production and uses a standard percentage "markup" to determine price. This pricing scheme is especially helpful to multiproduct oligopolists.

Whether oligopoly is economically efficient is a difficult question given the various models of oligopoly. Nevertheless, you should take time to evaluate the allocative and productive efficiency of a collusive oligopoly (or cartel) and compare it to pure competition or pure monopoly. A more controversial question, however, is whether oligopoly is desirable in the long run for technological progress. Both the competitive and Schumpeter-Galbraith views are presented on this question along with the empirical evidence.

In the final section of the chapter the American automobile industry is examined to illustrate a real-world oligopoly in action. Here you will see that three firms dominated an industry characterized by high barriers to entry, price-leadership, and nonprice competition in the three decades following World War II. But you will also discover that the American automobile industry, like the Old Gray Mare, "ain't what she used to be." Over the past twenty-five years, foreign competition weakened the oligopolistic structure of the domestic automobile industry; GM, Ford, and Chrysler now account for only about 65% of domestic car sales. The industry responded to this foreign competition by lobbying Congress for import protection and by participating in joint ventures with foreign producers, both actions serving to preserve the market power of the oligopoly as it entered a new era.

■ **CHECKLIST**

When you have studied this chapter you should be able to:

☐ Define oligopoly and distinguish between homogeneous and differentiated oligopolies.
☐ Describe concentration ratios and list five shortcomings of this measure.
☐ Use the Herfindahl index to assess the distribution of market power among dominant firms in an oligopoly.
☐ Identify the three most significant causes of oligopoly and explain how each of these tends to result in oligopolistic industries.
☐ Explain why it is difficult to predict what price will be charged and what output will be produced by an oligopolist.
☐ Describe three characteristics of oligopoly using a game theory perspective.
☐ Employ the kinked demand curve to explain why oligopoly prices tend to be inflexible.
☐ Explain two criticisms of kinked-demand analysis.
☐ Describe the price that would be set and the output that would be produced by oligopolists who were producing a homogeneous product with identical cost and demand curves.
☐ Give examples of overt and covert collusion.
☐ List six obstacles to collusion.
☐ Use the history of OPEC to illustrate how cartels can work to benefit oil producers and how obstacles to collusion eventually weakened OPEC.
☐ Describe the price leadership model of oligopoly and three tactics used by a price leader.
☐ Describe how a firm (such as General Motors) employs cost-plus pricing to determine the prices it will charge for its products.
☐ Explain the role played by nonprice competition in oligopolistic industries and two reasons why oligopolists emphasize nonprice competition.
☐ Compare oligopoly to other market structures in terms of allocative and productive efficiency.
☐ Compare the Schumpeter-Galbraith view with the competitive view of oligopoly, and explain whether the empirical evidence does or does not support each viewpoint.

☐ Describe the American automobile industry in terms of the number of sellers and their market shares, the height and kinds of barriers to entry, the method employed to set prices, the types of nonprice competition, the level of profits, and the rate of technological progress.
☐ Explain the effects of foreign competition on the domestic automobile industry.

■ **CHAPTER OUTLINE**

1. Oligopoly is frequently encountered in the American economy.
   a. It is composed of a few firms that dominate an industry and that sell a standardized or differentiated product.
   b. Concentration ratios are used to measure the degree of market dominance.
   (1) If the top four firms control 40% or more of the total market, the industry is considered to be oligopolistic.
   (2) But concentration ratios have shortcomings and must be interpreted with care because of problems with defining markets, interindustry competition, world trade, the distribution of market power, and actual market performance.
   c. The existence of oligopoly is usually the result of economies of scale, other barriers to entry, and the advantages of merger.

2. Insight into the pricing behavior of oligopolists can be gained by thinking of the oligopoly situation as a game of strategy. This game theory overview leads to three conclusions.
   a. Firms in an oligopolistic industry are "mutually interdependent" and must consider the actions of rivals when they make price decisions.
   b. Oligopoly often leads to overt or covert collusion among the firms to fix prices or to coordinate pricing because competition among oligopolists results in low prices and profits; collusion helps maintain higher prices and profits.
   c. Collusion creates incentive to cheat among oligopolists.

3. The economic analysis of oligopoly is difficult because the "oligopoly" actually covers many different market situations and because mutual interdependence makes it difficult for an oligopolist to estimate a demand curve. Nevertheless, two important characteristics of oligopoly are inflexible prices and simultaneous price changes by oligopolistic firms. An analysis of four oligopoly models helps explain the various pricing practice of oligopolists.
   a. In the kinked-demand curve model there is no collusion.
   (1) Each firm believes that when it lowers its price its rivals will lower their prices; and when it increases its price its rivals will not increase their prices.

(2) The firm is, therefore, reluctant to change its price for fear of decreasing its profits.

(3) But the model has two shortcomings: it does not explain how the going price gets set; prices are not as rigid as implied by the model.

b. The game theory perspective suggests that "mutual interdependence" of oligopolists encourages firms to collude to maintain or to increase prices and profits.

(1) Firms that collude tend to set their prices and joint output at the same level a pure monopolist would set them.

(2) The method of collusion employed by the firms may be covert, as in a cartel agreement, or covert, as in a gentlemen's agreement.

(3) There are at least six obstacles that make it difficult for firms to collude or maintain collusive arrangements: difference in demand and cost among firms; the number of firms in the arrangement; incentives to cheat; changing economic conditions; potential for entry by other firms; and legal restrictions and penalties.

(4) The OPEC cartel provides an example of collusion working to increase price and profits during the 1970s and the obstacles to collusion that reduced the market power of the cartel during the 1980s.

c. Price leadership is a form of covert collusion or gentlemen's agreement in which one firm initiates price changes and the other firms in the industry follow the lead. Three price leadership tactics have been observed.

(1) Price adjustments tend to be made infrequently as cost and demand condition change to a significant degree.

(2) The price leader announces the price change in various ways, through speeches, announcement, or other such activities.

(3) The price set may not maximize short-run profits for the industry, especially if the industry wants to prevent entry by other firms.

d. In the cost-plus pricing model a firm determines its price by adding a percentage markup to its average cost of production.

(1) Actions taken by firms under model are also consistent with outcomes from collusion and price leadership models of oligopoly.

(2) Cost-markup pricing is especially appealing to multiproduct oligopolists who find it difficult and costly to estimate demand on many products.

4. Oligopolistic firms often avoid price competition but engage in nonprice competition to determine each firm's market share for two reasons: price cuts are easily duplicated, but nonprice competition is more unique; oligopolists have greater financial resources to devote to advertising and product development.

5. To compare the efficiency of an oligopolist with that of a pure competitor is difficult.

a. Many economists believe that oligopoly is neither allocatively efficient (P = MC) nor productively efficient (P = minimum ATC).

b. The competitive view is that oligopoly has much the same result as monopoly; but Schumpeter and Galbraith believe that oligopoly is needed if there is to be rapid technological progress (dynamic efficiency).

c. While the evidence is not conclusive, it appears that most of the important inventions have not been made by large firms; and the structure of the industry may not affect its technological progress.

6. The automobile industry in the United States is an example of an oligopoly in which are found a few large firms and significant barriers to entry; price leadership; styling competition among the sellers; and significant import competition from foreign producers.

■ **IMPORTANT TERMS**

Oligopoly	Kinked demand curve
Fewness	Price war
Homogeneous oligopoly	Collusion
Differentiated oligopoly	Cartel
Concentration ratio	Gentlemen's agreement
Interindustry competition	Price leadership
Import competition	Cost-plus pricing
Herfindahl index	Traditional view (of oligopoly)
Game theory model	
Mutual interdependence	Schumpeter-Galbraith view (of oligopoly)
Noncollusive oligopoly	

■ **FILL-IN QUESTIONS**

1. In an oligopoly a _____ firms produce either a _____ or a _____ product, and entry into such an industry is _____

2. The percentage of the total industry sales accounts for the top four firms in an industry is known as a _____. An industry is generally considered to be oligopolistic when the top four firms control ____% or more of the market. The distribution of market power among the dominant firms, however, is measured by the _____; it is calculated by summing the _____ of each firm in the industry.

3. The three major underlying causes of oligopoly are _____,

_____, and

_____

4. The basics of the pricing behavior of oligopolists can be understood from a _____ theory perspective that leads to three insights.

  a. Oligopoly consists of a _____ number of firms that are _____. This means that when setting the price of its product each producer must consider the _____ of rivals. The monopolist does not face this problem because it has _____ rivals; and the pure competitor and monopolistic competitor do not face it because they have _____ rivals.

  b. The characteristics of oligopoly create a tendency for _____ among firms to set prices and restrict competition.

  c. But, _____ creates incentive to _____ on agreements to increase market share or profits.

5. Formal economic analysis cannot be easily used to explain the prices and outputs of oligopolists because oligopoly is in fact (one, a small number of, many) _____ specific market situation(s); and when firms are mutually interdependent each firm is (certain, uncertain) _____ about how its rivals will react when it changes the price of its product.

6. Oligopoly prices tend to be (flexible, inflexible) _____ and oligopolists tend to change their prices (independently, simultaneously) _____

7. The kinked demand curve which the individual non-colluding oligopolist sees for its product is highly (elastic, inelastic) _____ at prices above the current or going price and tends to be only slightly _____ or _____ below that price.

8. The kinked demand curve for a noncolluding oligopolist is drawn on the assumption that if the oligopolist raises its price its rivals will _____ and if it lowers its prices its rivals will _____

9. Because the oligopolist who confronts a kinked demand curve finds that there is a _____ in

its marginal-revenue curve, small changes in the marginal-cost curve do not change the _____

_____

10. When oligopolists collude, the prices they set and their combined output tend to be the same as would be set (in a purely competitive industry, by a pure monopolist) _____

11. A cartel is a formal agreement among sellers in which the _____ and the total _____ of the product and each seller's _____ of the market are specified.

12. A gentlemen's agreement is (a formal, an informal) _____ agreement on _____; each firm's share of the market is determined by _____

13. Six obstacles to collusion among oligopolists are:

  a. _____
  b. _____
  c. _____
  d. _____
  e. _____
  f. _____

14. _____ is an international oil cartel whose market power has declined in recent years because of three obstacles to (kinked-demand, collusion) _____

  a. One reason for the decline is the (increase, decrease) _____ in oil prices during the 1970s that (attracted, discouraged) _____ new entrants into oil production.

  b. A second reason is the (increase, decrease) _____ in the demand for oil during the early 1980s because of recession and (increased, decreased) _____ use of alternative energy sources.

  c. A third reason is (fair-play, cheating) _____ among the (thirteen, thirty) _____ cartel members and the (similarity, diversity) _____ of economic circumstances among the members.

15. When one firm in an oligopoly is almost always the first to change its price and the other firms change their prices after it has changed its price the oligopoly model is called _____

16. When a firm employs a cost-plus formula to determine the price it will charge for a product it adds a percentage _____ to the _____ cost of producing the product.

17. There tends to be very little (price, nonprice) _____ competition among oligopolists and a great deal of _____ competition which they use to determine each firm's _____
The two reasons for the emphasis on this kind of competition are:

    a. _____

    b. _____

18. Although it is difficult to evaluate the economic efficiency of oligopoly, when comparisons are made to pure competition the conclusion drawn is that there will neither be _____ nor _____ efficiency under oligopoly. The price and output behavior of the oligopolist is more likely to be similar to that found under pure _____

19. The competitive view of oligopoly is that it results in (lower, higher) _____ prices and profits, _____ outputs, and a rate of technological progress that is (slower, faster) _____ than would be found if the industry were more competitive.

20. In the Schumpeter-Galbraith view of oligopoly:

    a. Only oligopolists have both the _____ and the _____ to be technologically progressive;
    b. Over time oligopolists will bring about a more rapid rate of _____, lower _____ and _____, and perhaps greater _____ and _____ than the same industry competitively organized.

21. The empirical evidence seems to indicate that the large oligopolists (have, have not) _____ been the major source of technological progress in the United States.

22. The market structure of the automobile industry in the United States can be characterized as (monopolistic, oligopolistic) _____, with price

_____ and nonprice competition that has focused on _____

    a. In recent decades, (import, export) _____ _____ competition reduced the market power of the domestic industry. The industry responded by lobbying government for _____ _____ quotas on Japanese cars during the early 1980s.
    b. The industry also arranged joint ventures with (domestic, foreign) _____ producers, thereby serving to (increase, decrease) _____ mutual interdependence worldwide among automobile producers.

    c. Foreign competition has also altered the _____ role that was traditionally played by General Motors.

■ **PROBLEMS AND PROJECTS**

1. Consider the following payoff matrix in which the numbers indicate the profit in millions of dollars for a duopoly based either a high-price or a low-price strategy.

		Firm X	
		High-price	Low-price
Firm Y	High-price	X = $200 Y = $200	X = $250 Y = $ 50
	Low-price	X = $ 50 Y = $250	X = $ 50 Y = $ 50

    a. *Situation 1:* Each firm chooses a high-price strategy. *Result:* Each firm will earn $_____ million in profit for a total of $_____ million for the two firms.
    b. *Situation 2:* Firm X chooses a low-price strategy while Firm Y maintains a high-price strategy. *Result:* Firm X will earn $_____ million and Firm Y will earn $_____. Compared to Situation 1, Firm X has an incentive to cut prices because it will earn $_____ million more in profit and Firm Y will earn $_____ million less in profit. Together, the firms will earn $_____ million in profit, which is $_____ less than in Situation 1.
    c. *Situation 3:* Firm Y chooses a low-price strategy while Firm X maintains a high-price strategy. *Result:* Firm Y has an incentive to cut prices because it will earn $_____ million and Firm X will earn $_____. Compared to Situation 1, Firm Y will earn $_____ million more in profit and Firm X will earn $_____ million less in profit.

Together, the firms will earn $_____ million in profit, which is $_____ less than in Situation 1.

d. *Situation 4:* Each firm chooses a low-price strategy. *Result:* Each firm will earn $_____ million in profit for a total of $_____ million for the two firms. This total is $_____ less than in Situation 1.

e. *Conclusions:*

(1) The two firms have a strong incentive to collude and adopt the high-price strategy because there is the potential for $_____ million more in profit for the two firms than with a low-price strategy (Situation 4), or the potential for $_____ million more for the two firms than with a mixed-price strategy (Situations 2 or 3).

(2) There is also a strong incentive for each firm to cheat on the agreement and adopt a low-price strategy when the other firm maintains a high-price strategy because this situation will produce $_____ more in profit for the cheating firm compared to honoring a collusive agreement for a high-price strategy.

2. The kinked-demand schedule which an oligopolist believes confronts the firm is given in the table in the next column.

Price	Quantity demanded	Total revenue	Marginal revenue per unit
$2.90	100	$_____	
2.80	200	_____	$_____
2.70	300	_____	_____
2.60	400	_____	_____
2.50	500	_____	_____
2.40	525	_____	_____
2.30	550	_____	_____
2.20	575	_____	_____
2.10	600	_____	_____

a. Compute the oligopolist's total revenue at each of the nine prices, and enter these figures in the table.

b. Also compute marginal revenue *for each unit* between the nine prices and enter these figures in the table.

c. What is the current, or going, price for the oligopolist's product? $_____ How much is it selling? _____

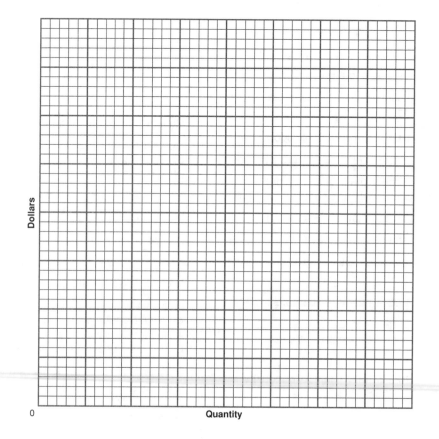

d. On the graph on the previous page, plot the oligopolist's demand curve and marginal-revenue curve. Connect the demand points and the marginal-revenue points with as straight a line as possible. (***Be sure*** to plot the marginal-revenue figures at the average of the two quantities involved, that is, at 150, 250, 350, 450, 512½, 537½, 562½, and 587½.)

e. Assume that the marginal-cost schedule of the oligopolist is given in columns (1) and (2) of the table below. Plot the marginal-cost curve on the graph on which demand and marginal revenue were plotted.

(1) Output	(2) MC	(3) MC′	(4) MC″
150	$1.40	$1.90	$.40
250	1.30	1.80	.30
350	1.40	1.90	.40
450	1.50	2.00	.50
512½	1.60	2.10	.60
537½	1.70	2.20	.70
562½	1.80	2.30	.80
587½	1.90	2.40	.90

(1) Given demand and marginal cost, what price should the oligopolist charge to maximize profits?

$_____ How many units of product will it sell

at this price? _____
(2) If the marginal-cost schedule changed from that shown in columns (1) and (2) to that shown in columns

(1) and (3), what price should it charge? $_____

What level of output will it produce? _____
How have profits changed as a result of the change in

costs? _____
Plot the new marginal-cost curve on the graph.
(3) If the marginal-cost curve schedule changed from that shown in columns (1) and (2) to that shown in col-

umns (1) and (4), what price should it charge? $____

What level of output will it produce? _____
How have profits changed as a result of the change in

costs? _____
Plot the new marginal-cost curve on the graph.

3. An oligopoly producing a homogeneous product is composed of three firms. Assume that these three firms have identical cost schedules. Assume also that if any one of these firms sets a price for the product, the other two firms charge the same price. As long as they all charge the same price they will share the market equally; and the quantity demanded of each will be the same.

At the bottom of the page is the total-cost schedule of one of these firms and the demand schedule that confronts it when the other firms charge the same price as this firm.

a. Complete the marginal-cost and marginal-revenue schedules facing the firm.
b. What price would this firm set if it wished to maxi-

mize its profits? _____
c. How much would:

(1) It sell at this price? _____

(2) Its profits be at this price? $_____
d. What would be the industry's:

(1) Total output at this price? _____

(2) Joint profits at this price? $_____
e. Is there any other price this firm can set, assuming that the other two firms charge the same price, which

would result in a greater joint profit for them? _____

If so, what is that price? $_____
f. If these three firms colluded in order to maximize their joint profit, what price would they charge?

$_____

Output	Total cost	Marginal cost	Price	Quantity demanded	Marginal revenue
0	$ 0		$140	0	
1	30	$____	130	1	$____
2	50	____	120	2	____
3	80	____	110	3	____
4	120	____	100	4	____
5	170	____	90	5	____
6	230	____	80	6	____
7	300	____	70	7	____
8	380	____	60	8	____

4. A firm producing automobiles has $4 billion invested in capital and its average total cost schedule is shown below.

Output (cars per year)	Average total cost
1,100,000	$14,000
1,200,000	10,000
1,300,000	8,000
1,400,000	7,000
1,500,000	6,500
1,600,000	6,250
1,700,000	6,600
1,800,000	7,200

a. If the objective of the firm is to have an annual return *after* taxes equal to 10% of its invested capital it must earn $_____ million after taxes each year.

b. To earn this amount after taxes when its earnings are taxed at a 50% rate it must earn $_____ million *before* taxes.

c. When the firm estimates that its most likely annual output (its "standard volume") is 1,500,000 automobiles:

(1) to achieve its objective of a 10% after-tax return on its investment it must earn $_____ per automobile. (*Hint*: Divide the required return before taxes by its annual output.)

(2) to earn this amount per automobile it must set the price of an automobile at $_____

(3) the markup is approximately _____%.

■ **SELF-TEST**

Circle the T if the statement is true; the F if it is false.

1. The products produced by the firms in an oligopolistic industry may be either homogeneous (standardized) or differentiated.   **T   F**

2. Oligopolistic industries contain a few large firms that act independently of one another.   **T   F**

3. The greeting card industry is an example of a differentiated oligopoly.   **T   F**

4. Concentration ratios are low in those industries which are oligopolies.   **T   F**

5. Concentration ratios include adjustments for interindustry competition in measuring concentration in an industry.   **T   F**

6. The monopoly power of domestic producers is overstated by concentration ratios because import competition from foreign suppliers is not taken into account.   **T   F**

7. The uncertainty which exists in oligopolies is the uncertainty faced by each firm on how its rivals will react if it changes its price.   **T   F**

8. The kinked-demand curve is an economic tool which can be used to explain how the current market price of an oligopolistic product is determined.   **T   F**

9. One of the shortcomings of kinked-demand analysis is that it does not explain how the going oligopoly price was established in the first place.   **T   F**

10. Collusion occurs when firms in an industry reach an overt or covert agreement to fix prices, divide or share the market, and in some way restrict competition among the firms.   **T   F**

11. Secret price concessions and other forms of cheating will strengthen collusion.   **T   F**

12. A cartel is usually a written agreement among firms which sets the price of the product and determines each firm's share of the market.   **T   F**

13. The practice of price leadership is almost always based on a formal written or oral agreement.   **T   F**

14. An oligopolist utilizing a cost-plus pricing formula typically adds a percentage markup to what its unit cost would be if it operated at full capacity.   **T   F**

15. Price competition between firms is an important characteristic of oligopoly.   **T   F**

16. Nonprice competition is the typical method of determining each oligopolist's share of the total market.   **T   F**

17. It is often argued that oligopolists typically possess both the means and the incentives for technological progress, and that the means are the substantial profits received by them.   **T   F**

18. Almost all the important technological advances in the United States between 1880 and 1965 can be attributed to the research and development activities of large business firms.   **T   F**

19. The American automobile industry is a fairly good example of a differentiated oligopoly.   **T   F**

20. Foreign competition has altered the price leadership pattern that characterized the American automobile industry in past decades.   **T   F**

Circle the letter that corresponds to the best answer.

1. The number of firms in an oligopolistic industry is:
   (a) one
   (b) a few
   (c) many
   (d) very many

2. Which of the following products is produced in an industry that best illustrates the concept of a homogeneous oligopoly?
- **(a)** lead
- **(b)** beer
- **(c)** automobiles
- **(d)** breakfast cereal

3. Concentration ratios take into account:
- **(a)** interindustry competition
- **(b)** import competition
- **(c)** the existence of separate local markets for products
- **(d)** none of the above

4. Industry A is dominated by four large firms that hold market shares of 40, 30, 20, and 10. The Herfindahl index for this industry is:
- **(a)** 100
- **(b)** 1000
- **(c)** 3000
- **(d)** 4500

5. Which of the following contributes to the existence of oligopoly in an industry?
- **(a)** low barriers to entry
- **(b)** standardized products
- **(c)** economies of scale
- **(d)** elastic demand

The next three questions (6, 7, and 8) are based on the following payoff matrix for a duopoly in which the numbers indicate the profit in thousands of dollars for a high-price or a low-price strategy.

		Firm A	
		High-price	Low-price
Firm B	**High-price**	A = $425 B = $425	A = $525 B = $275
	Low-price	A = $275 B = $525	A = $200 B = $200

6. If both firms collude to maximize joint profits, the total profits for the two firms will be:
- **(a)** $400,000
- **(b)** $800,000
- **(c)** $850,000
- **(d)** $950,000

7. Assume that Firm B adopts a low-price strategy while Firm A maintains a high-price strategy. Compared to the results from a high-price strategy for both firms, Firm B will now:
- **(a)** lose $150,000 in profit and Firm A will gain $150,000 in profit
- **(b)** gain $100,000 in profit and Firm A will lose $150,000 in profit
- **(c)** gain $150,000 in profit and Firm A will lose $100,000 in profit
- **(d)** gain $525,000 in profit and Firm A will lose $275,000 in profit

8. If both firms operate independently and do not collude, the most likely profit is:
- **(a)** $200,000 for Firm A and $200,000 for Firm B
- **(b)** $525,000 for Firm A and $275,000 for Firm B
- **(c)** $275,000 for Firm A and $525,000 for Firm B
- **(d)** $425,000 for Firm A and $425,000 for Firm B

9. Mutual interdependence is only characteristic of:
- **(a)** pure and monopolistic competition
- **(b)** monopolistic competition and oligopoly
- **(c)** pure competition and oligopoly
- **(d)** oligopoly

10. Mutual interdependence means that:
- **(a)** each firm produces a product similar but not identical to the products produced by its rivals
- **(b)** each firm produces a product identical to the products produced by its rivals
- **(c)** each firm must consider the reactions of its rivals when it determines its price policy
- **(d)** each firm faces a perfectly elastic demand for its product

11. The prices of products produced by oligopolies tend to be:
- **(a)** relatively flexible and when firms change prices they are apt to change them at the same time
- **(b)** relatively inflexible and when firms change prices they are not apt to change them at the same time
- **(c)** relatively inflexible and when firms change prices they are apt to change them at the same time
- **(d)** relatively flexible and when firms change prices they are not apt to change them at the same time

12. The demand curve confronting an oligopolist tends to be:
- **(a)** elastic
- **(b)** of unitary elasticity
- **(c)** inelastic
- **(d)** one which depends upon the prices charged by his rivals

13. If an individual oligopolist's demand curve is "kinked," it is necessarily:
- **(a)** inelastic below the going price
- **(b)** inelastic above the going price
- **(c)** elastic above the going price
- **(d)** of unitary elasticity at the going price

Use the following diagram to answer the next question (14).

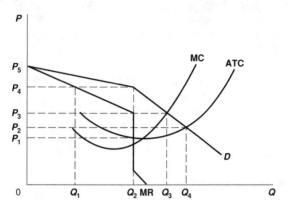

14. The profit maximizing price and output for this oligopolistic firm is:
(a) P_5 and Q_2
(b) P_4 and Q_2
(c) P_3 and Q_3
(d) P_2 and Q_4

15. Below is the demand schedule confronting an oligopolist. Which one of the eight prices seems to be the "going" price of the product produced by the firm?
(a) $4.50
(b) $4
(c) $3.50
(d) $3

Price	Quantity demanded
$5.00	10
4.50	20
4.00	30
3.50	40
3.00	42
2.50	44
2.00	46
1.00	48

16. Which of the following is *not* a means of colluding?
(a) a cartel
(b) a kinked demand curve
(c) a gentlemen's agreement
(d) price leadership

17. To be successful, collusion requires that oligopolists be able to:
(a) keep prices and profits as low as possible
(b) block or restrict the entry of new producers
(c) reduce legal obstacles that protect market power
(d) keep the domestic economy from experiencing high inflation

18. Oligopolists tend to collude because collusive control over the price they charge permits them to:
(a) increase their profits
(b) decrease their uncertainties

(c) deter the entry of new firms into their industry
(d) do all of the above

19. When oligopolists collude the results are generally:
(a) greater output and higher price
(b) greater output and lower price
(c) smaller output and lower price
(d) smaller output and higher price

20. Which of the following constitutes an obstacle to collusion among oligopolists?
(a) a general business recession
(b) a small number of firms in the industry
(c) a homogeneous product
(d) the patent laws

21. Oligopolistic firms that produce a variety of products and do not wish to estimate demand for products would tend to use which price strategy?
(a) price wars
(b) price leadership
(c) cost-plus pricing
(d) price inflexibility

22. Market shares in oligopolistic industries are usually determined on the basis of:
(a) covert collusion
(b) nonprice competition
(c) gentlemen's agreements
(d) joint profit maximization

23. Many economists would conclude that in a highly oligopolistic market there is:
(a) allocative efficiency, but not productive efficiency
(b) productive efficiency, but not allocative efficiency
(c) both allocative and productive efficiency
(d) neither allocative nor productive efficiency

24. It is the belief of Schumpeter and Galbraith that an industry organized oligopolistically when compared with the same industry organized competitively would over time:
(a) foster more rapid improvement in the quality of the good or service produced
(b) bring about a greater reduction in the average cost of producing the product
(c) lower the price of the product by a larger percentage
(d) all of the above

25. A factor that has increased mutual interdependence in the worldwide automobile industry has been:
(a) lobbying of Congress by United States automobile producers for import quotas on Japanese cars
(b) the creation of a Japanese export cartel after the expiration of import quotas imposed by the United States
(c) joint ownership arrangement and joint ventures between Japanese and United States automobile producers

(d) price competition by Japanese automobile producers to increase market share of the small-car market in the United States

■ DISCUSSION QUESTIONS

1. What are the essential characteristics of an oligopoly? How does it differ from monopolistic competition?

2. Explain how the concentration ratio in a particular industry is computed. What is the relationship between this ratio and fewness?

3. What are the shortcomings of the concentration ratio as a measure of the extent of competition in an industry?

4. What are the underlying causes of oligopoly?

5. How can game theory be used to explain price behavior under oligopoly? What do "mutual interdependence" and "collusion" mean with respect to oligopoly?

6. Why is it difficult to use one standard model to explain the prices charged by and the outputs of oligopolists?

7. Explain what the kinked demand curve is, its most important characteristics, the assumptions upon which it is based, and the kind of marginal-revenue curve to which it gives rise. How can the kinked demand curve be used to explain why oligopoly prices are relatively inflexible? Under what conditions will oligopolists acting independently raise or lower their prices even though their demand curves may be kinked?

8. Why do oligopolists find it advantageous to collude? What are the obstacles to collusion?

9. Suppose a few firms produce a homogeneous product, have identical cost curves, and charge the same price. How will the price they set, their combined output of the product, and their joint profit compare with what would be found in the same industry if it were a pure monopoly with several plants?

10. Explain:
   (a) a cartel;
   (b) a gentlemen's agreement;
   (c) price leadership, and
   (d) cost-plus pricing.

11. Why do oligopolists engage in little price competition and in extensive nonprice competition?

12. Contrast the Schumpeter-Galbraith views on the dynamic economic efficiency of oligopoly with the competitive view.

13. What does the empirical evidence have to say about sources of technological progress in the United States?

14. Using the following criteria, describe the American automobile industry: (1) number of firms and their market shares; (2) the barriers to entry; (3) the means used to establish the prices of automobiles; (4) the role of nonprice competition; (5) profits; and (6) technological progress.

15. Explain the causes of and the effects of foreign competition on the American automobile industry during the past two decades. How has competition in the market for automobiles in the United States been affected?

■ ANSWERS

Chapter 13 Price and Output Determination: Oligopoly

FILL-IN QUESTIONS

1. few, standardized, differentiated, difficult

2. concentration ratio; 40; Herfindahl index, squared market shares

3. the economies of scale, other barriers to entry, the advantages of merger

4. game; *a.* few, mutually interdependent, reactions, no, many; *b.* collusion; *c.* collusion, cheat

5. many, uncertain

6. inflexible, simultaneously

7. elastic, elastic, inelastic

8. not raise their prices, lower their prices

9. gap, price the oligopolist will charge

10. by a pure monopolist

11. price, output, share

12. an informal, prices, the ingenuity of each seller (i.e., nonprice competition)

13. *a.* demand and cost differences; *b.* a large number of firms; *c.* cheating (secret price cutting); *d.* a recession; *e.* potential entry; *f.* legal obstacles (antitrust laws)

14. OPEC (Organization of Petroleum Exporting Countries), collusion; *a.* increase, attracted; *b.* decrease, increased; *c.* cheating, thirteen, diversity

15. price leadership

16. markup, average

17. price, nonprice, share of the market, *a.* price cuts can be quickly matched by rival firms; *b.* oligopolists tend to have the greater financial resources required to engage in nonprice competition

18. allocative, productive, monopoly

19. higher, lower, slower

20. *a.* means, incentives; *b.* product improvement, costs, prices, output, employment

21. have not

22. oligopolistic, leadership, styling and technology; *a.* import, import; *b.* foreign, increase; *c.* price leadership

PROBLEMS AND PROJECTS

1. *a.* 200, 400; *b.* 250, 50, 50, 150, 300, 100; *c.* 250, 50, 50, 150, 300, 100; *d.* 50, 100, 300; *e.* (1) 300, 100; (2) 50

2. *a.* total revenue: 290, 560, 810, 1040, 1250, 1260, 1265, 1265, 1260; *b.* marginal revenue: 2.70, 2.50, 2.30, 2.10, 0.40, 0.20, 0, −0.20; *c.* 2.50, 500; *e.* (1) 2.50, 500; (2) 2.50, 500, they have decreased; (3) 2.50, 500, they have increased.

3. *a.* marginal cost: $30, 20, 30, 40, 50, 60, 70, 80; marginal revenue: $130, 110, 90, 70, 50, 30, 10, −10; *b.* $90; *c.* (1) 5; (2) $280; *d.* (1) 15; (2) $840; *e.* no; *f.* $90

4. *a.* 400; *b.* 800; *c.* (1) 533.33, (2) 7033.33, (3) 8.2

1. *b*, p. 220
2. *a*, p. 220
3. *d*, p. 221
4. *c*, pp. 221−222
5. *c*, p. 222
6. *c*, pp. 223−224
7. *b*, pp. 223−224
8. *a*, pp. 223−224
9. *d*, p. 223
10. *c*, p. 223
11. *c*, p. 225
12. *d*, p. 225
13. *c*, p. 225
14. *b*, p. 226
15. *c*, pp. 225−226
16. *b*, p. 225
17. *b*, p. 227
18. *d*, p. 227
19. *d*, p. 227
20. *a*, p. 229
21. *c*, p. 231
22. *b*, p. 232
23. *d*, pp. 232−233
24. *d*, p. 233
25. *c*, p. 238

SELF-TEST

1. T, p. 220
2. F, p. 220
3. T, p. 221
4. F, p. 221
5. F, p. 221
6. T, p. 221
7. T, p. 223
8. F, p. 226
9. T, p. 226
10. T, p. 227
11. F, p. 229
12. T, p. 228
13. F, p. 230
14. F, p. 231
15. F, p. 232
16. T, p. 232
17. T, p. 233
18. F, p. 233
19. T, p. 234
20. T, pp. 235−238

DISCUSSION QUESTIONS

1. pp. 220−221
2. p. 221
3. p. 221
4. p. 222
5. pp. 223−224
6. pp. 224−225
7. pp. 225−226
8. pp. 227−228
9. p. 232
10. pp. 228−229
11. p. 232
12. pp. 232−233
13. pp. 233−234
14. pp. 234−235
15. pp. 235−238

CHAPTER 14

Production and the Demand for Resources

Chapter 14 is the first of a group of three chapters which examine the markets for resources. Resource markets are markets in which employers of resources (demanders) and the owners of these resources (suppliers) determine the prices at which resources will be employed and the quantities of these resources that will be hired.

These resources—you should recall—are labor, land, capital, and entrepreneurial ability. The prices of resources have particular names. The price paid for labor is called a wage, the price paid for the use of land is rent, the price paid for the use of capital is interest, and the price paid for entrepreneurial ability is profit.

The employers of resources are business firms who use resources to produce their products. When the number of employers and the number of owners of a resource are large the market for that resource is a purely competitive market; and—as you already know—the demand for and the supply of that resource will determine its price and the total quantity of it that will be employed.

Chapter 14 begins the examination of resource markets by looking at the business firm and the demand (or employer) side of the resource market. The material in this chapter is *not* an explanation of what determines the demand for a *particular* resource; but it is an explanation of what determines the demand for *any* resource. In Chapters 15 and 16 the other sides of the resource markets and particular resources are examined in detail.

The list of important terms for Chapter 14 is relatively short, but included in the list are two very important concepts—**marginal revenue product** and **marginal resource cost**—which you must grasp if you are to understand how much of a resource a firm will hire. These two concepts are similar to, but not identical with, the marginal-revenue and marginal-cost concepts employed in the study of product markets and in the explanation of the quantity of output a firm will produce.

Marginal revenue and marginal cost are, respectively, the change in the firm's total revenue and the change in the firm's total cost when it produces and sells an additional unit of **output**; marginal revenue product and marginal resource cost are, respectively, the change in the firms' total revenue and the change in the firm's total cost when it hires an additional unit of an **input**. You should note that the two new concepts deal with changes in revenue and costs as a consequence of hiring more of a **resource**.

When a firm wishes to maximize its profits, it produces that **output** at which marginal revenue and marginal cost are equal. But how much of each resource does it hire if it wishes to maximize its profits? It hires that amount of each *resource* at which the marginal revenue product and the marginal resource cost of that resource are equal. And a firm that employs the amount of each resource that maximizes its profits **also** produces the output that maximizes its profits. (If you doubt this statement, see footnote number 4 in the text.)

There is another similarity between the output and the input markets insofar as the firm is concerned. You will recall that the competitive firm's **supply** curve is a portion of its **marginal-cost** curve. The purely competitive firm's **demand** curve for a resource is a portion of its **marginal-revenue-product** curve. Just as cost is the important determinant of supply, the revenue derived from the use of a resource is the important factor determining the demand for that resource.

■ CHECKLIST

When you have studied this chapter you should be able to:

☐ Present four reasons for studying resource pricing.
☐ Explain why the demand for an economic resource is a derived demand.
☐ Define marginal revenue product.
☐ Determine the marginal revenue product schedule of a resource used to produce a product which is sold in a purely competitive market when you are given the relevant data.
☐ Define marginal resource cost.
☐ State the rule employed by a profit-maximizing firm to determine how much of a resource it will employ.
☐ Apply the MRP = MRC rule to determine the quantity

of a resource a firm will hire when you are given the necessary data.

☐ Explain why the marginal revenue product schedule of a resource is the firm's demand for the resource.

☐ Find the marginal revenue product schedule of a resource used to produce a product which is sold in an imperfectly competitive market when you are given the necessary data.

☐ Derive the market demand for a resource.

☐ List the three factors which would change a firm's demand for a resource.

☐ Predict the effect of an increase or decrease in each of the three factors affecting resource demand on the demand of a firm for a resource.

☐ Enumerate the four determinants of the price elasticity of demand for a resource.

☐ Describe how a change in each of the four determinants of the resource price elasticity would change the price elasticity of demand for a resource.

☐ State the rule employed by a firm to determine the least-cost combination of resources.

☐ Use the least-cost rule to find the least-cost combination of resources for production when you are given the necessary data.

☐ State the rule employed by a profit-maximizing firm to determine how much of each of several resources to employ.

☐ Apply the profit-maximizing rule to determine the quantity of each resource a firm will hire when you are given the necessary data.

☐ Explain the "marginal productivity theory of income distribution."

☐ Give two criticisms of the marginal productivity theory of income distribution.

■ **CHAPTER OUTLINE**

1. The study of what determines the prices of resources is important because resource prices: influence the size of individual incomes and the resulting distribution of income; allocate scarce resources; affect the way in which firms combine resources to produce their products; and raise ethical questions about the distribution of income.

2. Economists generally agree upon the basic principles of resource pricing, but the complexities of different resources markets make these principles difficult to apply.

3. The demand for a single resource depends upon (or is derived from) the demand for the goods and services it can produce.

  a. Because resource demand is a derived demand, the demand for a single resource depends upon the marginal productivity of the resource and the market price of the good or service it is used to produce.

  b. Marginal revenue product combines these two fac-

tors—the marginal product of a resource and the market price of the product it produces—into a single useful tool.

  c. A firm will hire a resource up to the quantity at which the marginal revenue product of the resource is equal to its marginal resource cost.

  d. The firm's marginal-revenue-product schedule for a resource is that firm's demand schedule for the resource.

  e. If a firm sells its output in an imperfectly competitive market, the more the firm sells the lower becomes the price of the product. This causes the firm's marginal-revenue-product (resource demand) schedule to be less elastic than it would be if the firm sold its output in a purely competitive market.

  f. The market (or total) demand for a resource is the horizontal summation of the demand schedules of all firms employing the resource.

4. Changes in the demand for the product being produced, changes in the productivity of the resource, and changes in the prices of other resources will tend to change the demand for a resource.

  a. A change in the demand for a product produced by a resource such as labor will change the demand of a firm for labor in the same direction.

  b. A change in the productivity of a resource such as labor (caused by an increase in the quantity of other resources such as capital, technological improvements, and improvement in resource quality) will change the demand of a firm for the resource in the same direction.

  c. A change in the price of a

  (1) **substitute** resource will change the demand for a resource such as labor in the same direction if the substitution effect outweighs the output effect, and in the opposite direction if the output effect outweighs the substitution effect;

  (2) **complementary** resource will change the demand for a resource such as labor in the opposite direction.

5. The price elasticity of resource demand measures the sensitivity of producers to changes in resource prices.

  a. There are four possible factors that affect the price elasticity of resource demand:

  (1) the rate at which the marginal product of the resource declines—the slower the rate, the more elastic the resource demand;

  (2) the ease of substitution of other resources—the more good substitute resources that are available, the more elastic the demand for the resource;

  (3) the elasticity of the demand for the product that the resource produces—the more elastic the product demand, the more elastic the resource demand;

  (4) the ratio of labor cost to total cost—the greater the ratio of labor cost to total cost, the greater the price elasticity of demand for labor.

6. Firms typically employ more than one resource in producing a product.

    a. The firm employing resources in purely competitive markets is hiring resources in the least-cost combination when the ratio of the marginal product of a resource to its price is the same for all the resources the firm hires.

    b. The firm is hiring resources in the most profitable combination if it hires resources in a purely competitive market when the marginal revenue product of each resource is equal to the price of that resource.

    c. A numerical example illustrates the least-cost and profit-maximizing rules for a firm that employs resources in purely competitive markets.

7. The marginal productivity theory of income distribution seems to result in an equitable distribution of income because each unit of a resource receives a payment equal to its marginal contribution to the firm's revenue; but the theory has at least two serious faults.

    a. The distribution of income will be unequal because resources are unequally distributed among individuals in the economy.

    b. The income of those who supply resources will not be based on their marginal productivities if there is monopsony or monopoly in the resource markets of the economy.

■ **IMPORTANT TERMS**

Derived demand	Least-cost rule
Marginal revenue product	(combination)
Marginal resource cost	Profit-maximizing rule
MRP = MRC rule	(combination)
Substitution effect	Marginal productivity theory of income distribution
Output effect	

■ **FILL-IN QUESTIONS**

1. Resource prices allocate _____ and are one of the factors that determine the (incomes, costs) _____ of households and the _____ of business firms.

2. The demand for a resource is a _____ demand and depends upon the _____ of the resource and the _____ of the product produced from the resource.

3. A firm will find it profitable to hire units of a resource up to the quantity at which the _____

and the _____ of the resource are equal; and if the firm hires the resource in a purely competitive market, the _____ and the _____ of the resource will be equal.

4. A firm's demand schedule for a resource is the firm's _____ schedule for that resource because both indicate the quantities of the resource the firm will employ at various resource _____

5. A producer that sells its product in an imperfectly competitive market finds that the more of a resource it hires, the (higher, lower) _____ becomes the price at which it can sell its product. As a consequence, the marginal-revenue-product (or demand) schedule for the resource is (more, less) _____ elastic than it would be if the output were sold in a purely competitive market.

6. The market demand curve for a resource is obtained by _____

7. The demand for a resource will change if the demand for the _____ changes, if the _____ of the resource changes, or if the _____ of other resources change.

8. In the space to the right of each of the following, indicate whether the change would tend to increase ($+$) or decrease ($-$) a firm's demand for a particular resource.

    a. An increase in the demand for the firm's product.

    _____

    b. A decrease in the amounts of all other resources the firm employs. _____

    c. An increase in the productivity of the resource.

    _____

    d. An increase in the price of a substitute resource when the output effect is greater than the substitution effect. _____

    e. A decrease in the price of a complementary resource. _____

9. The output of the firm being constant, a decrease in the price of resource A will induce the firm to hire (more, less) _____ of resource A and _____ of other resources; this is called the _____ effect. But if the decrease in the price of A results in lower total costs and an increase in output, the firm may hire _____ of both resources; this is called the _____ effect.

10. Four determinants of the price elasticity of demand for a resource are the rate at which the _____ of the resource decreases, the ease with which other resources can be _____ for it, the _____ of demand for the product which it is used to produce, and the _____

11. Suppose a firm employs resources in purely competitive markets. If the firm wishes to produce any given amount of its product in the least costly way, the ratio of the _____ of each resource to its _____ must be the same for all resources.

12. A firm that hires resources in purely competitive markets is employing the combination of resources which will result in maximum profits for the firm when the _____ of every resource is equal to its _____

13. When the marginal revenue product of a resource is equal to the price of that resource, the marginal revenue product of the resource divided by its price is equal to _____

14. In the marginal productivity theory the distribution of income is an equitable one because each unit of each resource is paid an amount equal to its _____ _____

15. The marginal productivity theory rests on the assumption of (competitive, imperfect) _____ markets. In the real world, there are market imperfections because of monopsony or monopoly power, so wage rates and other resource prices (do, do not) _____ measure contributions to national output.

■ PROBLEMS AND PROJECTS

1. The table at the bottom of the page shows the total production a firm will be able to obtain if it employs varying amounts of resource A while the amounts of the other resources the firm employes remain constant.
  a. Compute the marginal product of each of the seven units of resource A and enter these figures in the table.
  b. Assume the product the firm produces sells in the market for $1.50 per unit. Compute the total revenue of the firm at each of the eight levels of output and the marginal revenue product of each of the seven units of resource A. Enter these figures in the table at the bottom of the page.
  c. On the basis of your computations complete the firm's demand schedule for resource A by indicating in the table below how many units of resource A the firm would employ at the given prices.

Price of A	Quantity of A demanded
$21.00	_____
18.00	_____
15.00	_____
12.00	_____
9.00	_____
6.00	_____
3.00	_____
1.50	_____

2. In the table on the next page are the marginal product data for resource B. Assume that the quantities of other resources employed by the firm remain constant.
  a. Compute the total product (output) of the firm for each of the seven quantities of resource B employed and enter these figures in the table.
  b. Assume that the firm sells its output in an imperfectly competitive market and that the prices at which

Quantity of resource A employed	Total product	Marginal product of A	Total revenue	Marginal revenue product of A
0	0		$_____	
1	12	_____	_____	$_____
2	22	_____	_____	_____
3	30	_____	_____	_____
4	36	_____	_____	_____
5	40	_____	_____	_____
6	42	_____	_____	_____
7	43	_____	_____	_____

it can sell its product are those given in the table. Compute and enter in the table:
(1) Total revenue for each of the seven quantities of B employed.
(2) The marginal revenue product of each of the seven units of resource B.
c. How many units of B would the firm employ if the market price of B were:

(1) $25: _____

(2) $20: _____

(3) $15: _____

(4) $9: _____

(5) $5: _____

(6) $1: _____

Quantity of resource B employed	Marginal product of B	Total product	Product price	Total revenue	Marginal revenue product of B
0	—	0		$0.00	—
1	22	____	$1.00	____	$____
2	21	____	.90	____	____
3	19	____	.80	____	____
4	16	____	.70	____	____
5	12	____	.60	____	____
6	7	____	.50	____	____
7	1	____	.40	____	____

3. In the table below are the marginal-product and marginal-revenue-product schedules for resource C and resource D. Both resources are variable and are employed in purely competitive markets. The price of C is $2 and the price of D is $3.

Quantity of resource C employed	Marginal product of C	Marginal revenue product of C	Quantity of resource D employed	Marginal product of D	Marginal revenue product of D
1	10	$5.00	1	21	$10.50
2	8	4.00	2	18	9.00
3	6	3.00	3	15	7.50
4	5	2.50	4	12	6.00
5	4	2.00	5	9	4.50
6	3	1.50	6	6	3.00
7	2	1.00	7	3	1.50

a. The least-cost combination of C and D that would enable the firm to produce:

(1) 64 units of its product is _____ C and _____ D.

(2) 99 units of its product is _____ C and _____ D.
b. The profit-maximizing combination of C and D is

_____ C and _____ D.
c. When the firm employs the profit-maximizing combination of C and D, it is also employing C and D in the

least-cost combination because _____

equals _____

d. Examination of the figures in the table reveals that

the firm sells its product in a _____

competitive market at a price of $_____
e. Employing the profit-maximizing combination of C and D, the firm's:

(1) Total output is _____

(2) Total revenue is $_____

(3) Total cost is $_____

(4) Total profit is $_____

■ **SELF-TEST**

Circle the T if the statement is true; the F if it is false.

1. In the resource markets of the economy resources are demanded by business firms and supplied by households. **T F**

2. The prices of resources are an important factor in the determination of the supply of a product. **T F**

3. The market demand for a particular resource is the sum of the individual demands of all firms that employ that resource. **T F**

4. A resource which is highly productive will always be in great demand. **T F**

5. A firm's demand schedule for a resource is the firm's marginal-revenue-product schedule for the resource.
T F

6. It will be profitable for a firm to hire additional units of labor resources up to the point where the marginal revenue product of labor is equal to its marginal resource cost. **T F**

7. A firm with one worker can produce 30 units of a product that sells for $4 a unit, but the same firm with two workers can produce 70 units of that product. The marginal revenue product of the second worker is $400. **T F**

8. The marginal revenue product of a purely competitive seller will fall because marginal product diminishes and product price falls. **T F**

9. A producer's demand schedule for a resource will be more elastic if the firm sells its product in a purely competitive market than it would be if it sold the product in an imperfectly competitive market. **T F**

10. When two resources are substitutes for each other both the substitution effect and the output effect of a decrease in the price of one of these resources operate to increase the quantity of the other resource employed by the firm. **T F**

11. The output effect of an increase in the price of a resource is to increase the quantity demanded of that resource. **T F**

12. If two resources are complementary, an increase in the price of one of them will reduce the demand for the other. **T F**

13. An increase in the price of a resource will cause the demand for the resource to decrease. **T F**

14. The demand curve for labor will increase when the demand for (and price of) the product produced by that labor increases. **T F**

15. There is an inverse relationship between the productivity of labor and the demand for labor. **T F**

16. The faster the rate at which the marginal product of a variable resource declines, the greater will be the price elasticity of demand for that resource. **T F**

17. The demand for labor will be less elastic when labor is a smaller proportion of the total cost of producing a product. **T F**

Use the following information as the basis for answering questions 18 and 19. The marginal revenue product and price of resource A are $12 and a constant $2, respectively; and the marginal revenue product and price of resource B are $25 and a constant $5, respectively. The firm sells its product at a constant price of $1.

18. The firm should decrease the amount of A and increase the amount of B it employs if it wishes to decrease its total cost without affecting its total output. **T F**

19. If the firm wishes to maximize its profits, it should increase its employment of both A and B until their marginal revenue products fall to $2 and $5, respectively. **T F**

20. The marginal productivity theory of income distribution results in an equitable distribution only if resource markets are competitive. **T F**

Circle the letter that corresponds to the best answer.

1. The prices paid for resources affect:
(a) the money incomes of households in the economy
(b) the allocation of resources among different firms and industries in the economy
(c) the quantities of different resources employed to produce a particular product
(d) all of the above

2. The study of the pricing of resources tends to be complex because:
(a) supply and demand do not determine resource prices
(b) economists do not agree on the basic principles of resource pricing
(c) the basic principles of resource pricing must be varied and adjusted when applied to particular resource markets
(d) resource pricing is essentially an ethical question

3. The demand for a resource is ***derived*** from:
(a) the marginal productivity of the resource and price of the good or service produced from it
(b) the marginal productivity of the resource and the price of the resource
(c) the price of the resource and the price of the good or service produced from it
(d) the price of the resource and the quantity of the resource demanded

4. As a firm that sells its product in an imperfectly competitive market increases the quantity of a resource it employs, the marginal revenue product of that resource falls because:
   (a) the price paid by the firm for the resource falls
   (b) the marginal product of the resource falls
   (c) the price at which the firm sells its product falls
   (d) both the marginal product and the price at which the firm sells its product fall

5. The law of diminishing returns explains why:
   (a) the MRP of an input in a purely competitive market decreases as a firm increases the quantity of an employed resource
   (b) the MRC of an input in a purely competitive market decreases as a firm increases the quantity of an employed resource
   (c) resource demand is a derived demand
   (d) there are substitution and output effects for resources

Use the following total-product and marginal-product schedules for a resource to answer the next four questions (6, 7, 8, and 9). Assume that the quantities of other resources the firm employs remain constant.

Units of resource	Total product	Marginal product
1	8	8
2	14	6
3	18	4
4	21	3
5	23	2

6. If the product the firm produces sells for a constant $3 per unit, the marginal revenue product of the 4th unit of the resource is:
   (a) $3
   (b) $6
   (c) $9
   (d) $12

7. If the firm's product sells for a constant $3 per unit and the price of the resource is a constant $15, the firm will employ how many units of the resource?
   (a) 2
   (b) 3
   (c) 4
   (d) 5

8. If the firm can sell 14 units of output at a price of $1 per unit and 18 units of output at a price of $0.90 per unit, the marginal revenue product of the 3rd unit of the resource is:
   (a) $4
   (b) $3.60
   (c) $2.20
   (d) $0.40

9. If the firm can sell 8 units at a price of $1.50, 14 units at a price of $1.00, 18 units at a price of $0.90, 21 units at a price of $0.70, and 23 units at a price of $0.50, then the firm is:
   (a) maximizing profits at a product price of $0.50
   (b) minimizing its costs at a product price of $1.00
   (c) selling in an imperfectly competitive market
   (d) selling in a purely competitive market

10. Which of the following would increase a firm's demand for a particular resource?
   (a) an increase in the prices of complementary resources used by the firm
   (b) a decrease in the demand for the firm's product
   (c) an increase in the productivity of the resource
   (d) a decrease in the price of the particular resource

11. In finding the substitution effect of a change in the price of a particular resource, which of the following is assumed to be constant?
   (a) the total output of the firm
   (b) the total expenditures of the firm
   (c) the employment of all other resources
   (d) the MPs of all resources

12. Suppose resource A and resource B are substitutes and the price of A increases. If the output effect is greater than the substitution effect:
   (a) the quantity of A employed by the firm will increase and the quantity of B employed will decrease
   (b) the quantity of both A and B employed by the firm will decrease
   (c) the quantity of both A and B employed will decrease
   (d) the quantity of A employed will decrease and the quantity of B employed will increase

13. Two resource inputs, capital and labor, are complementary and used in fixed proportions. A decrease in the price of capital will:
   (a) increase the demand for labor
   (b) decrease the demand for labor
   (c) decrease the quantity demanded for labor
   (d) have no effect because the relationship is fixed

14. Which of the following would result in an increase in the elasticity of demand for a particular resource?
   (a) an increase in the rate at which the marginal product of that resource declines
   (b) a decrease in the elasticity of demand for the product which the resource helps to produce
   (c) an increase in the percentage of the firm's total costs accounted for by the resource
   (d) a decrease in the number of other resources which are good substitutes for the particular resource

15. A firm is allocating its expenditure for resources in a way that will result in the least total cost of producing any given output when:

(a) the amount the firm spends on each resource is the same
(b) the marginal revenue product of each resource is the same
(c) the marginal product of each resource is the same
(d) the marginal product per dollar spent on the last unit of each resource is the same

16. A business is employing inputs such that the marginal product of labor is 20 and the marginal product of capital is 45. The price of labor is $10 and the price of capital is $15. If the business wants to minimize costs, then it should:
(a) use more labor and less capital
(b) use less labor and less capital
(c) use less labor and more capital
(d) make no change in resource use

17. Assume that a profit-maximizing computer disk manufacturer is employing resources so that the MRP of the last unit hired for resource X is $240 and the MRP of the last unit hired for resource Y is $150. The price of resource X is $80 and the price of resource Y is $50. The firm should:
(a) hire more of resource X and less of resource Y
(b) hire less of resource X and more of resource Y
(c) hire less of both resource X and resource Y
(d) hire more of both resource X and resource Y

18. A firm that hires resources in a purely competitive market is **not necessarily** maximizing its profits when:
(a) the marginal revenue product of every resource is equal to 1
(b) the marginal revenue product of every resource is equal to its price
(c) the ratio of the marginal revenue product of every resource to its price is equal to 1
(d) the ratio of the price of every resource to its marginal revenue product is equal to 1

*Answer the next three questions (**19**, **20**, and **21**) on the basis of the information in the following table for a purely competitive market.*

Number of workers	Total product	Product price ($)
0	0	4
1	16	4
2	26	4
3	34	4
4	40	4
5	44	4

19. At a wage rate of $15, the firm will choose to employ:
(a) 2 workers
(b) 3 workers
(c) 4 workers
(d) 5 workers

20. At a wage rate of $30, the firm will choose to employ:
(a) 2 workers
(b) 3 workers
(c) 4 workers
(d) 5 workers

21. If the product price increases to a constant $8, then at a wage rate of $30, the firm will choose to employ:
(a) 2 workers
(b) 3 workers
(c) 4 workers
(d) 5 workers

22. The demand for labor would most likely become more inelastic as a result of an increase in the:
(a) elasticity of the demand for the product that the labor produces
(b) time for employers to make technological changes or purchase new equipment
(c) proportion of labor costs to total costs
(d) rate at which marginal revenue product declines

23. Assume that a purely competitive firm uses two resources, labor (**L**) and capital (**C**), to produce a product. In which situation would the firm be maximizing profit?

	MRP_L	MRP_C	P_L	P_C
(a)	10	20	30	40
(b)	10	20	10	20
(c)	15	15	10	10
(d)	30	40	10	5

24. In the marginal productivity theory of income distribution when all markets are purely competitive, each unit of each resource receives a money payment equal to:
(a) its marginal product
(b) its marginal revenue product
(c) the needs of the resource-owner
(d) the payments received by each of the units of the other resources in the economy

25. A major criticism of the marginal productivity theory of income distribution is that:
(a) labor markets are often subject to imperfect competition
(b) the theory suggests that there eventually will be equality in incomes
(c) purely competitive firms are only interested in profit maximization
(d) the demand for labor resources are price elastic

■ **DISCUSSION QUESTIONS**

1. Why is it important to study resource pricing?

2. Why is resource demand a derived demand, and upon what two factors does the strength of this derived demand depend?

3. Explain why firms that wish to maximize their profits follow the MRP = MRC rule.

4. What constitutes a firm's demand schedule for a resource? Why? What determines the total, or market, demand for a resource?

5. Why is the demand schedule for a resource less elastic when the firm sells its product in an imperfectly competitive market than when it sells it in a purely competitive market?

6. Explain what will cause the demand for a resource to increase and what will cause it to decrease.

7. Explain the difference between the "substitution effect" and the "output effect."

8. What determines the elasticity of the demand for a resource? Explain the exact relationship between each of these four determinants and elasticity.

9. Assuming a firm employs resources in purely competitive markets, when is it spending money on resources in such a way that it can produce a given output for the least total cost?

10. When is a firm that employs resources in purely competitive markets utilizing these resources in amounts that will maximize the profits of the firm?

11. What *is* the marginal productivity theory of income distribution? What ethical proposition must be accepted if this distribution is to be fair and equitable? What are the two major shortcomings of the theory?

■ **ANSWERS**

Chapter 14 Production and the Demand for Resources

FILL-IN QUESTIONS

1. resources, incomes, costs

2. derived, productivity, value (price)

3. marginal revenue product, marginal resource cost, price, marginal resource cost (either order)

4. marginal revenue product, prices

5. lower, less

6. adding the demand curves for the resource of all the firms hiring the resource

7. product, productivity, prices

8. *a.* +; *b.* −; *c.* +; *d.* −; *e.* +

9. more, less, substitution, more, output

10. marginal product, substituted, price-elasticity, portion of total production costs accounted for by the resource

11. marginal product, price

12. marginal revenue product, price

13. one

14. marginal revenue product (marginal contribution to the firm's revenue)

15. competitive, do not

PROBLEMS AND PROJECTS

1. *a.* marginal product of A: 12, 10, 8, 6, 4, 2, 1; *b.* total revenue: 0, 18.00, 33.00, 45.00, 54.00, 60.00, 63.00, 64.50; marginal revenue product of A: 18.00, 15.00, 12.00, 9.00, 6.00, 3.00, 1.50; *c.* 0, 1, 2, 3, 4, 5, 6, 7

2. *a.* total product: 22, 43, 62, 78, 90, 97, 98; *b.* (1) total revenue: 22.00, 38.70, 49.60, 54.60, 54.00, 48.50, 39.20; (2) marginal revenue product of B: 22.00, 16.70, 10.90, 5.00, −0.60, −5.50, −9.30; *c.* 0, 1, 2, 3, 4, 4

3. *a.* (1) 1, 3; (2) 3, 5; *b.* 5, 6; *c.* the marginal product of C divided by its price, the marginal product of D divided by its price; *d.* purely, $.50; *e.* (1) 114; (2) $57; (3) $28; (4) $29

SELF-TEST

1. T, p. 240	**11.** F, p. 246
2. T, p. 241	**12.** T, p. 247
3. T, p. 245	**13.** F, p. 247
4. F, p. 242	**14.** T, p. 247
5. T, p. 243	**15.** F, p. 245
6. T, p. 242	**16.** F, p. 247
7. F, p. 242	**17.** T, p. 248
8. F, p. 243	**18.** F, p. 248
9. T, p. 244	**19.** T, p. 249
10. F, p. 246	**20.** F, p. 251

1. *d*, p. 241	**14.** *c*, p. 248
2. *c*, p. 241	**15.** *d*, p. 248
3. *a*, pp. 241–242	**16.** *c*, p. 248
4. *d*, p. 243	**17.** *d*, p. 249
5. *a*, p. 242	**18.** *a*, p. 249
6. *c*, p. 242	**19.** *d*, pp. 242–243
7. *a*, pp. 242–243	**20.** *b*, pp. 242–243
8. *c*, pp. 243–244	**21.** *d*, pp. 242–243
9. *c*, pp. 243–244	**22.** *d*, p. 247
10. *c*, p. 245	**23.** *b*, p. 249
11. *a*, p. 246	**24.** *b*, p. 251
12. *b*, p. 246	**25.** *a*, p. 252
13. *a*, p. 246	

DISCUSSION QUESTIONS

1. p. 241	**7** p. 246
2. pp. 241–242	**8.** pp. 247–248
3. pp. 242–243	**9.** pp. 248–249
4. p. 243	**10.** pp. 249–250
5. pp. 243–245	**11.** pp. 251–252
6. pp. 245–247	

The Pricing and Employment of Resources: Wage Determination

The preceding chapter of the text defined marginal revenue product and marginal resource cost. It also explained what determines the demand for *any* resource. Chapter 15 builds upon these explanations and applies them to the study of a particular resource, labor, and the wage rate, the price paid for labor.

But as you learned in Chapters 10 through 13, it requires more than an understanding of supply and demand to explain the price of a product and the output of a firm and an industry. An understanding of the competitiveness of the market in which the product is sold is also required. It was for this reason that purely competitive, monopolistic, monopolistically competitive, and oligopolistic markets were examined in detail. The same is true of labor markets. The competitiveness of labor markets must be examined if the factors which determine wage rates and the quantity of labor employed are to be understood.

Following comments on the meanings of certain terms, the general level of wages, and the reasons for the high wage level in the United States, Chapter 15 explains how wage rates are determined in particular types of labor markets. Six kinds of labor markets are studied: (1) the competitive market in which the number of employers is large and labor is nonunionized; (2) the monopsony market in which a single employer hires labor under competitive (nonunion) conditions; (3) a market in which a union controls the supply of labor, the number of employers is large, and the union attempts to increase the total demand for labor; (4) a similar market in which the union attempts to reduce the total supply of labor; (5) another similar market in which the union attempts to obtain a wage rate that is above the competitive-equilibrium level by threatening to strike; and (6) the bilateral monopoly market, in which a single employer faces a labor supply controlled by a single union.

It is, of course, important for you to learn the characteristics of and the differences between each of these labor markets. It is also important that you study each of them carefully to see *how* the characteristics of the market affect the wage rate that will be paid in these markets. In the first two types of markets, the wage rate which will be paid is quite definite, and here you should learn exactly what level of wages and employment will prevail.

When unions control the supply of labor, wage and employment levels are less definite. If the demand for labor is competitive, the wage rate and the amount of employment will depend upon how successful the union is in increasing the demand for labor, in restricting the supply of labor, or in setting a wage rate which employers will accept. If there is but a single employer, wages and employment will fall within certain limits; exactly where they occur within these limits will depend upon the bargaining strength of the union and of the firm. You should, however, know what the limits are.

The sections explaining wages in particular labor markets are the more important parts of the chapter. But the sections which examine the effects of minimum wage laws on employment and wage rates, the reasons why different workers receive different wage rates, and pay and performance are also important. You should, therefore, pay attention to (1) the case against, the case for, and the real-world effects of the minimum wage; (2) the several causes of wage differentials; and (3) the principal agent problem and different schemes that are used by employers to prevent shirking or to tie worker pay to performance.

■ **CHECKLIST**

When you have studied this chapter you should be able to:

☐ Define wages (or the wage rate); and distinguish between nominal and real wages.
☐ Identify two major factors that contribute to the general level of wages in the United States.
☐ List at least five reasons for high productivity in the United States.
☐ Describe the long-run relationship between real wages and productivity in the United States.
☐ Define the difference between a competitive labor market and a monopsonistic labor market.

☐ Use graphs to explain wage rates and the level of employment in competitive labor markets.
☐ Use graphs to explain wage rates and the level of employment in monopolistic labor markets.
☐ List three techniques labor unions use to increase the demand for labor.
☐ Enumerate the ways in which exclusive or craft unions try to decrease the supply of labor.
☐ Explain and illustrate graphically the effects of actions taken by craft unions to decrease the supply of labor on wages and the employment of workers.
☐ Explain and illustrate graphically how the organization of workers by an industrial union in a previously competitive labor market would affect the wage rate and the employment level.
☐ Describe evidence on the effect of unions on wage increases and two reasons that might mitigate unemployment effects from wage increases.
☐ Use a graph to explain why the equilibrium wage rate and employment level is indeterminate when a labor market is a bilateral monopoly; and to predict the range within which the wage rate will be found.
☐ Present the case for, and the case against, a legally established minimum wage.
☐ List the three major factors which explain why wage differentials exist.
☐ Describe two reasons why groups of workers in the labor force with similar characteristics may earn different wages.
☐ Explain the nonmonetary aspect of job differences.
☐ Cite three reasons for labor market imperfections.
☐ Describe the principal agent problem.
☐ Identify five different pay schemes that have been used by employers to prevent shirking or to tie worker pay to performance.

■ **CHAPTER OUTLINE**

1. A wage (or the wage rate) is the price paid per unit of time for any type of labor and can be measured either in money or in real terms. Earnings are equal to the wage multiplied by the amount of time worked.

2. The general (or average) level of real wages in the United States is among the highest in the world because the demand for labor in the United States has been great relative to the supply of labor.
   a. The demand for labor in the United States has been strong because labor has been highly productive; and it has been highly productive for several major reasons—substantial quantities of capital goods and natural resources, technological advancement, improvements in labor quality, and other factors (management

techniques, business environment, and size of the domestic market).
   b. The real hourly wage rate and output per hour of labor are closely and directly related to each other; and real income per worker can increase only at the same rate as output per worker.
   c. The increases in the demand for labor that have resulted from the increased productivity of labor over time have been greater than the increase in the supply of labor in the United States; and as a result the real wage rate in the United States has increased in the long run.

3. The wage rate received by a specific type of labor depends upon the demand for and the supply of that labor, and upon the competitiveness of the market in which that type of labor is hired.
   a. In a purely competitive and nonunionized labor market the total demand for and the total supply of labor determine the wage rate; from the point of view of the individual firm the supply of labor is perfectly elastic at this wage rate (that is, the marginal labor cost is equal to the wage rate) and the firm will hire the amount of labor at which the marginal revenue product of labor is equal to its marginal labor cost.
   b. In a monopsonistic and nonunionized labor market the firm's marginal labor costs are greater than the wage rates it must pay to obtain various amounts of labor; and it hires the amount of labor at which marginal labor cost and the marginal revenue product of labor are equal. Both the wage rate and the level of employment are less than they would be under purely competitive conditions.
   (1) Note that if the firm employs resources in imperfectly competitive markets, it is hiring resources in the least-cost combination when the ratio of the marginal product of a resource to its marginal resource cost is the same for all resources; and,
   (2) it is hiring resources in the most profitable combination when the marginal revenue product of each resource is equal to its marginal resource cost.
   c. In labor markets in which labor unions represent workers, the unions attempt to raise wage rates by
   (1) increasing the demand for labor by increasing the demands for the products produced by the union workers, by increasing the productivity of these workers, and by increasing the prices of resources which are substitutes for the labor provided by the members of the union;
   (2) reducing the supply of labor; or
   (3) imposing upon employers wage rates in excess of the equilibrium wage rate which would prevail in a purely competitive market.
   d. Labor unions are aware that actions taken by them to increase wage rates may also increase the unemployment of their members and may, therefore, limit

their demands for higher wages; but the unemployment effect of higher wages is lessened by increases in and a relatively inelastic demand for labor.

e. In a labor market characterized by bilateral monopoly, the wage rate depends, within certain limits, on the relative bargaining power of the union and of the employer.

f. Whether minimum wage laws reduce poverty is a debatable question; but the evidence suggests that while they increase the incomes of employed workers they also reduce the number of workers employed.

4. Differences in wages exist among workers for three major reasons.

a. Workers are not homogeneous and they can be thought of as falling into many **noncompeting** occupational groups. The wages for each group differs because of:

(1) differences in the abilities or skills possessed by workers, the number of workers in each group, and the demand for those abilities or skills in the labor market; and

(2) investment in human capital by workers through education and training.

b. Jobs also vary in difficulty and attractiveness, and thus higher wages may be necessary to compensate for less desirable aspects of some jobs.

c. Workers are not perfectly mobile because of geographic, institutional, and sociological conditions or situations.

5. Wage payments in labor markets are often more complex in practice and are often designed to make a connection between worker pay and performance.

a. A **principal-agent problem** arises when the interests of agents (workers) diverge from the interest of principal (firms). For example, **shirking** on the job can occur if workers give less than the desired level of performance for pay received.

b. Firms can try to reduce shirking by monitoring worker activity, but this monitoring is costly; therefore, **incentive pay** plans are adopted by firms to tie worker compensation more closely to performance. Among the various incentive schemes are:

(1) piece rate payments, commissions, royalties, bonuses, and profit sharing plans;

(2) seniority pay to give junior workers an incentive to work harder to achieve the benefits of senority; and

(3) efficiency wages that pay workers above-market wages to get greater effort.

b. Wage decisions are often more complex than indicated in the models of wage and employment determination discussed in this chapter; decisions over the most effective incentive scheme directly affect worker performance and the monitoring costs of employers.

■ **IMPORTANT TERMS**

Wage (rate)	Inclusive unionism
Earnings	Industrial union
Nominal wage (rate)	Bilateral monopoly
Real wage (rate)	Minimum wage
Marginal resource (labor) cost	Wage differential
	Noncompeting groups
Competitive labor market	Equalizing differences
Monopsony	Human capital investment
Oligopsony	Principal-agent problem
Exclusive unionism	Shirking
Craft union	Incentive pay plan
Occupational licensure	

■ **FILL-IN QUESTIONS**

1. A wage rate is the price paid for labor per unit of _____ and the earnings of labor are equal to the _____ multiplied by _____; nominal wages are an amount of money, while real wages are _____

_____

2. The general level of wages is higher in the United States than in most foreign countries because:

a. The demand for labor in the U.S. is (strong, weak) _____ relative to the supply of labor;

b. American labor tends to be highly productive, among other reasons, because it has relatively large amounts of _____ and _____ with which to work and employs a generally superior _____ to produce goods and because of the high _____ of the American labor force.

3. In a competitive labor market:

a. the supply curve slopes upward from left to right because it is necessary for employers to pay higher _____ to attract workers from _____. The market supply curve rises because it is an _____ curve.

b. the demand is the sum of the _____ _____ of all firms hiring this type of labor;

c. the wage rate will equal the rate at which the

_____ and the

_____ are equal.

4. Insofar as an individual firm hiring labor in a competitive market is concerned, the supply of labor is

_____ elastic because the individual firm is

unable to affect the _____ it must pay.

5. The individual employer who hires labor in a competitive market hires that quantity of labor at which the

_____ of labor is equal to the

_____ or the _____

6. A monopsonist employing labor in a market which is competitive on the supply side will hire that amount of labor

at which _____

_____ and

_____ are equal. And because

the marginal labor cost is (greater, less) _____

_____ than the wage rate in such a market the employer will pay a wage rate which is less than both the

_____ of labor and the marginal

_____

a. It is employing the combination of resources that enables it to produce any given output in the least

costly way when the _____ of every resource

divided by its _____ is the same for all resources.

b. It is employing the combination of resources that

maximizes its profits when the _____ of

every resource is equal to its _____ (or

when the _____ of each resource di-

vided by its _____ is equal to _____)

7. When compared with a competitive labor market, a market dominated by a monopsonist results in (higher,

lower) _____ wage rates and in (more,

less) _____ employment.

8. The basic objective of labor unions is to

_____; they

attempt to accomplish this goal either by increasing the

_____ for labor, restricting

the _____ of labor, or imposing

_____ wage rates on employers.

9. Craft unions typically try to increase wages by

_____ while industrial unions

try to increase wages by _____

a. If they are successful, employment in the craft or industry is (decreased, increased, not affected)

_____

b. This effect on the employment of their members

may lead unions to (increase, decrease) _____
their wage demands.

c. But unions will not worry too much about the effect on employment of higher wage rates if the economy is

(growing, contracting, stationary) _____
or if the demand for labor is relatively (elastic, inelastic)

_____

10. Labor unions can increase the demand for the services of their members by increasing the demand for

_____, by increasing the _____

of their members, and by increasing the _____ of resources which are substitutes for the services supplied by their members.

11. In a labor market which is a bilateral monopoly, the monopsonist will not pay a wage greater than

_____; the union will ask for some wage

greater than the _____.
Within these limits the wage rate will depend on

_____

12. The effect of the imposition of effective minimum wage rates, ignoring any shock effects, in:

a. competitive labor markets is to (increase, decrease)

_____ the wage rate and to _____
employment.

b. monopsonistic labor markets is to _____

the wage rate and to _____ employment.

13. After a minimum wage increase workers will (in-

crease, decrease) _____ their income, but the em-

ployment of certain groups will _____, and the in-

comes of these workers will _____. It is estimated

that a _____% increase in the minimum wage will re-
duce employment of teenage workers by 1 to 3%. An increase in the minimum wage will also tend to reduce em-

ployment among _____ adults, _____, and

_____ because they are employed in a dispropor-
tionate share of low-wage occupations. The antipoverty

effect of the minimum wage is a _____ one for the economy.

14. Actual wage rates received by different workers tend to differ because workers are not _____, because jobs vary in _____, and because labor markets are _____

15. The total labor force is composed of a number of _____ groups of workers. Wages differ among these groups as a consequence of differences in innate _____ and because of different investments in _____ through training and education.

16. Within each of these noncompeting groups, some workers receive higher wages than others to compensate these workers for the less desirable _____ aspects of a job. These wage differentials are called _____

17. Another reason that workers performing identical jobs often receive different wages is due to _____, which are of three basic types: _____, _____, and _____

18. Parties, such as workers, who are hired to advance the firm's interests can be regarded as the firm's _____, and firms may be regarded as _____, or parties who hire others to achieve their objectives. The objective of a firm is to maximize _____ and workers help a firm achieve that objective in return for _____, but when the interests of a firm and the workers diverge, a _____ problem is created.

19. An example of this type of problem is _____, a situation where workers provide less than the agreed amount of work effort on the job. To prevent this situation, firms can closely _____ job performance, but this is costly; therefore, firms offer different _____ plans. Examples of such plans include _____ rate payments, _____ and royalties, and bonuses and _____ sharing.

20. Two other pay plans used by firms are _____ pay, which is designed to give the young worker an incentive to work hard for job tenure, and _____ wages, which means that workers are paid above equilibrium wages to encourage greater work effort.

■ **PROBLEMS AND PROJECTS**

1. Suppose a single firm has for a particular type of labor the marginal revenue product schedule given in the following table.

Number of units of labor	MRP of labor
1	$15
2	14
3	13
4	12
5	11
6	10
7	9
8	8

a. Assume there are 100 firms with the same marginal-revenue-product schedules for this particular type of labor. Compute the total or market demand for this labor by completing column 1 in the table below.

(1) Quantity of labor demanded	(2) Wage rate	(3) Quantity of labor supplied
_____	$15	850
_____	14	800
_____	13	750
_____	12	700
_____	11	650
_____	10	600
_____	9	550
_____	8	500

b. Using the supply schedule for labor given in columns 2 and 3:

(1) What will be the equilibrium wage rate? $_____

(2) What will be the total amount of labor hired in the market? _____

c. The individual firm will:

(1) have a marginal labor cost of $_____

(2) employ _____ units of labor.

(3) pay a wage of $_____

d. On the graph on the next page plot the market demand and supply curves for labor and indicate the equilibrium wage rate and the total quantity of labor employed.

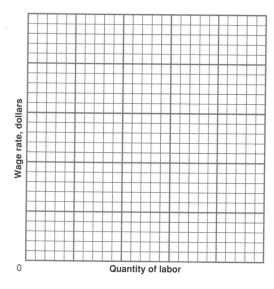

0   Quantity of labor

(1) Number of labor units	(2) MRP of labor	(3) Wage rate	(4) Total labor cost	(5) Marginal labor cost
0		$ 2	$____	
1	$36	4	____	$____
2	32	6	____	____
3	28	8	____	____
4	24	10	____	____
5	20	12	____	____
6	16	14	____	____
7	12	16	____	____
8	8	18	____	____

a. Compute the firm's total labor costs at each level of employment and the marginal labor cost of each unit of labor, and enter these figures in columns 4 and 5.

b. The firm will:

(1) hire _____ units of labor.

(2) pay a wage of $_____

(3) have a marginal revenue product for labor of

$_____ for the last unit of labor employed.

c. Plot the marginal revenue product of labor, the supply curve for labor, and the marginal-labor-cost curve on the following graph and indicate the quantity of labor the firm will employ and the wage it will pay.

e. On the graph below plot the individual firm's demand curve for labor, the supply curve for labor, and the marginal-labor-cost curve which confronts the individual firm; and indicate the quantity of labor the firm will hire and the wage it will pay.

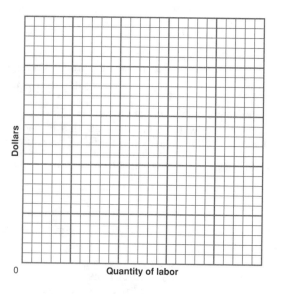

0   Quantity of labor

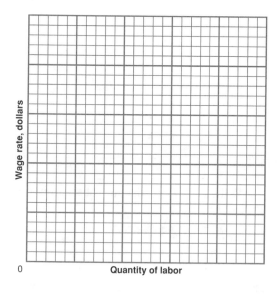

0   Quantity of labor

f. The imposition of a $12 minimum wage rate would change the total amount of labor hired in this market to

_____

2. In the table at the top of the page, assume a monopsonist has the marginal-revenue-product schedule for a particular type of labor given in columns 1 and 2 and that the supply schedule for labor is that given in columns 1 and 3.

d. If this firm hired labor in a competitive labor market,

it would hire at least _____ units and pay a wage of at least $_____

3. Assume that the employees of the monopsonist in problem 2 organize a strong industrial union. The union demands a wage rate of $16 for its members, and the monopsonist decides to pay this wage because a strike would be too costly.

a. In the table below compute the supply schedule for labor which now confronts the monopsonist by completing column 2.

(1) Number of labor units	(2) Wage rate	(3) Total labor cost	(4) Marginal labor cost
1	$____	$____	
2	____	____	$____
3	____	____	____
4	____	____	____
5	____	____	____
6	____	____	____
7	____	____	____
8	____	____	____

b. Compute the total labor cost and the marginal labor cost at each level of employment and enter these figures in columns 3 and 4.

c. The firm will:

(1) hire _____ units of labor.

(2) pay a wage of $_____

(3) pay total wages of $_____

d. As a result of unionization the wage rate has _____, the level of employment has _____, and the earnings of labor have _____

e. On the graph below plot the firm's marginal revenue product of labor schedule, the labor supply schedule, and the marginal-labor-cost schedule. Indicate also the wage rate the firm will pay and the number of workers it will hire.

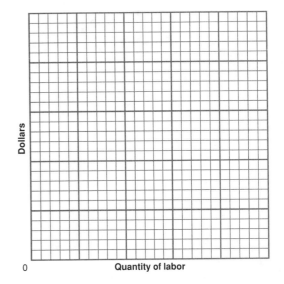

Dollars

0   **Quantity of labor**

4. Match the following descriptions to the correct graph below.

    a. A bilateral monopoly.   Graph _____

    b. The supply and demand for labor for a purely competitive firm.   Graph _____

    c. The labor strategy used by a craft union to raise wages.   Graph _____

    d. A monopsonistic labor market.   Graph _____

    e. The strategy used by an industrial union to raise wages above a competitive level.   Graph _____

    f. A strategy used by a union to get people to "buy union made products."   Graph _____

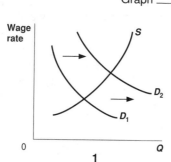

1

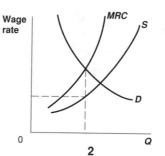

2

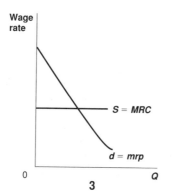

3

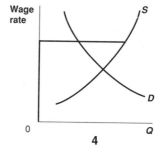

4

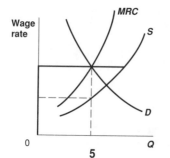

5

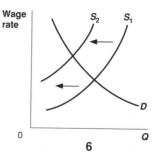

6

■ **SELF-TEST**

Circle the T if the statement is true; the F if it is false.

  1. The general level of real wages is higher in the United States than in many foreign countries because the supply of labor is large relative to the demand for it.   **T F**

  2. The average real income per workers and the average real output per worker in an economy are two names for the same thing.   **T F**

  3. If an individual firm employs labor in a competitive market, it finds that its marginal labor cost is equal to the wage rate in that market.   **T F**

4. Given a purely competitive employer's demand for labor, a lower wage will result in more workers being hired.
T F

5. Both monopsonists and firms hiring labor in purely competitive markets hire labor up to the quantity at which the marginal revenue product of labor and marginal labor cost are equal.
T F

6. Increasing the productivity of labor will tend to increase the demand for labor.
T F

7. One strategy used by unions to bolster the demand for union workers is to lobby against a higher minimum wage for nonunion workers.
T F

8. Restricting the supply of labor is a means of increasing wage rates more commonly used by craft unions than by industrial unions.
T F

9. Occupational licensure has been one of the principal means employed by the Federal government to increase the number of blacks and Hispanics in certain skilled occupations and trades.
T F

10. The imposition of an above-equilibrium wage rate will cause employment to fall off more when the demand for labor is inelastic than it will when the demand is elastic.
T F

11. Union members are paid wage rates which on the average are greater by 10% or more than the wage rates paid to nonunion members.
T F

12. The actions of both exclusive and inclusive unions that raise the wage rates paid to them by competitive employers of labor also cause, other things remaining constant, an increase in the employment of their members.
T F

13. In a bilateral monopoly the negotiated wage will be below the competitive equilibrium wage in that labor market.
T F

14. If a labor market is purely competitive, the imposition of an effective minimum wage will increase the wage rate paid and decrease employment in that market.
T F

15. When an effective minimum wage is imposed upon a monopsonist the wage rate paid by the firm will increase and the number of workers employed by it may also increase.
T F

16. An increase in the minimum wage rate in the American economy tends to increase the unemployment of teenagers and of others in low-wage occupations. **T F**

17. Actual wage rates received in different labor markets tend to differ because the demands for particular types of labor relative to their supplies differ.
T F

18. Wage differentials that are used to compensate workers for unpleasant aspects of a job are called efficiency wages.
T F

19. "Ben Robbins is a skilled artisan of a particular type, is unable to obtain membership in the union representing that group of artisans, and is, therefore, unable to practice his trade." This is an example of institutional immobility.
T F

20. Shirking is an example of a principal-agent problem.
T F

Circle the letter that corresponds to the best answer.

1. Real wages would decline if the:
(a) prices of goods and services rose more rapidly than money-wage rates
(b) prices of goods and services rose less rapidly than money-wage rates
(c) prices of goods and services and wage rates both rose
(d) prices of goods and services and wage rates both fell

2. Which of the following has **not** led to the generally high productivity of American workers?
(a) the high level of real wage rates in the United States
(b) the superior quality of the American labor force
(c) the advanced technology utilized in American industries
(d) the large quantity of capital available to assist the average worker in the United States

3. A characteristic of a purely competitive labor market would be:
(a) firms hiring different types of labor
(b) workers supplying labor under a union contract
(c) "wage taker" behavior by the firms
(d) "price maker" behavior by the firms

4. The supply curve for labor in a purely competitive market rises because:
(a) it is an opportunity cost curve
(b) the marginal resource cost is constant
(c) the wage rate paid to workers falls
(d) the marginal revenue product rises

5. The individual firm which hires labor under purely competitive conditions faces a supply curve for labor which:
(a) is perfectly inelastic
(b) is of unitary elasticity
(c) is perfectly elastic
(d) slopes upward from left to right

6. All of the following are characteristics of a monopsonist **except**:
(a) the firm's employment is a large portion of the total employment of that type of labor
(b) the type of labor is relatively immobile
(c) the wage rate it must pay workers varies directly with the number of workers it employs
(d) the supply curve is the marginal resource cost curve

7. A monopsonist pays a wage rate which is:
(a) greater than the marginal revenue product of labor
(b) equal to the marginal revenue product of labor
(c) equal to the firm's marginal labor cost
(d) less than the marginal revenue product of labor

8. If a firm employs resources in imperfectly competitive markets, to maximize its profits the marginal revenue product of each resource must equal:
(a) its marginal product
(b) its marginal resource cost
(c) its price
(d) one

9. Compared with a purely competitive labor market, a monopsonistic market will result in:
(a) higher wage rates and a higher level of employment
(b) higher wage rates and a lower level of employment
(c) lower wage rates and a higher level of employment
(d) lower wage rates and a lower level of employment

10. The labor market for nurses in a small community that has two hospitals would be best described as:
(a) monopolistically competitive
(b) a bilateral monopoly
(c) an oligopsony
(d) an oligopoly

11. Higher wage rates and a higher level of employment are the usual consequences of:
(a) inclusive unionism
(b) exclusive unionism
(c) an above-equilibrium wage rate
(d) an increase in the productivity of labor

12. Which of the following would *not* increase the demand for a particular type of labor?
(a) an increase in the productivity of that type of labor
(b) an increase in the prices of those resources which are substitutes for that type of labor
(c) an increase in the prices of those resources which are complements to that type of labor
(d) an increase in the demand for the products produced by that type of labor

13. Occupational licensing laws have the economic effect of
(a) increasing the demand for labor
(b) decreasing the supply of labor
(c) strengthening the bargaining position of an industrial union
(d) weakening the bargaining position of a craft union

14. Industrial unions typically attempt to increase wage rates by:
(a) imposing an above-equilibrium wage rate upon employers
(b) increasing the demand for labor

(c) decreasing the supply of labor
(d) forming a bilateral monopoly

Answer the next three questions (15, 16, and 17) using the data in the table below.

Wage rate	Quantity of labor supplied	Marginal labor cost	Marginal revenue product of labor
$10	0	—	$18
11	100	$11	17
12	200	13	16
13	300	15	15
14	400	17	14
15	500	19	13
16	600	21	12

15. If the firm employing labor were a monopsonist the wage rate and the quantity of labor employed would be, respectively:
(a) $14 and 300
(b) $13 and 400
(c) $14 and 400
(d) $13 and 300

16. But if the market for this labor were purely competitive the wage rate and the quantity of labor employed would be, respectively:
(a) $14 and 300
(b) $13 and 400
(c) $14 and 400
(d) $13 and 300

17. If the firm employing labor were a monopsonist and the workers were represented by an industrial union, the wage rate would be:
(a) between $13 and $14
(b) between $13 and $15
(c) between $14 and $15
(d) below $13 or above $15

Answer the next four questions (18, 19, 20, and 21) on the basis of the following labor market diagram, where D is the demand curve for labor, S is the supply curve for labor, and MRC is the marginal resource (labor) cost.

18. If this were a purely competitive labor market, the number of workers hired and the wage rate in equilibrium would be:
(a) 4000 and $14
(b) 4000 and $8
(c) 6000 and $10
(d) 8000 and $12

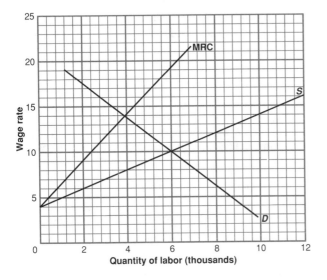

24. Shirking can be considered to be principal-agent problem because:

    (a) work objectives of the principals (the workers) diverge from the profit objectives of the agent (the firm)

    (b) profit objectives of the principal (the firm) diverge from the work objectives of the agents (the workers)

    (c) the firm is operating in an oligopsonistic labor market

    (d) the firm pays efficiency wages to workers in a labor market

25. A firm pays an equilibrium wage of $10.00 an hour and the workers produce 10 units of output an hour. If the firm adopts an efficiency wage and it is successful, then the wage rate for these workers will:

    (a) rise and output will fall

    (b) fall and output will rise

    (c) rise and output will rise

    (d) fall and output will fall

19. If this were a monopsonistic labor market, the number of workers hired and the wage rate in equilibrium would be:

    (a) 4000 and $14

    (b) 4000 and $8

    (c) 6000 and $10

    (d) 8000 and $12

20. An inclusive union seeks to maximize the employment of workers with the monopsonist. If successful, the number of workers employed and the wage rate would be:

    (a) 4000 and $14

    (b) 6000 and $12

    (c) 6000 and $10

    (d) 8000 and $12

21. If the market was characterized as a bilateral monopoly, the number of workers hired and the wage rate in equilibrium would be:

    (a) 6000 and $10

    (b) 4000 and $14

    (c) 4000 and $8

    (d) indeterminant

22. The fact that a baseball player receives a wage of $4,000,000 a year can **best** be explained in terms of:

    (a) noncompeting labor groups

    (b) equalizing differences

    (c) labor immobility

    (d) imperfections in the labor market

23. The fact that unskilled construction workers receive higher wages than gas-station attendants is **best** explained in terms of:

    (a) noncompeting labor groups

    (b) equalizing differences

    (c) labor immobility

    (d) imperfections in the labor market

■ **DISCUSSION QUESTIONS**

1. Why is the general level of real wages higher in the United States than in most foreign nations? Why has the level of real wages continued to increase even though the supply of labor has continually increased?

2. Explain why the productivity of the American labor force increased in the past to its present high level.

3. In the competitive model what determines the market demand for labor and the wage rate? What kind of supply situation do all firms as a group confront? What kind of supply situation does the individual firm confront? Why?

4. In the monopsony model what determines employment and the wage rate? What kind of supply situation does the monopsonist face? Why? How does the wage rate paid and the level of employment compare with what would result if the market were competitive?

5. In what sense is a worker who is hired by a monopsonist "exploited" and one who is employed in a competitive labor market "justly" rewarded? Why do monopsonists wish to restrict employment?

6. When supply is less than perfectly elastic, marginal labor cost is greater than the wage rate. Why?

7. What basic methods do labor unions employ to try to increase the wages received by their members? If these methods are successful in raising wages, what effect do they have upon employment?

8. What three methods might labor employ to increase the demand for labor? If these methods are successful, what effects do they have upon wage rates and employment?

9. When labor unions attempt to restrict the supply of labor to increase wage rates, what devices do they employ to do this for the economy as a whole and what means do they use to restrict the supply of a given type of worker?

10. How do industrial unions attempt to increase wage rates, and what effect does this method of increasing wages have upon employment in the industry affected?

11. Both exclusive and inclusive unions are able to raise the wage rates received by their members. Why might unions limit or temper their demands for higher wages? What two factors determine the extent to which they will or will not reduce their demands for higher wages?

12. What is bilateral monopoly? What determines wage rates in a labor market of this type?

13. What is the effect of minimum wage laws upon wage rates and employment in:
(a) competitive labor markets;
(b) monopsony labor markets; and
(c) the economy as a whole?

14. How:
(a) do the wage rates paid to union members differ from those paid to nonunion employees; and
(b) do minimum wage rates affect the employment of workers in high- and low-wage occupations?

15. What is meant by the term "noncompeting" groups in a labor market? What two factors tend to explain wage differentials in noncompeting groups?

16. How are wages used to equalize differences in the characteristics of jobs? Give examples.

17. Describe three types of immobilities that give rise to imperfections in labor markets. Discuss how these immobilities contribute to wage differentials.

18. Explain what is meant by the principal-agent problem and relate it to shirking. What are the different pay incentive plans that are correct for shirking on the job. How does seniority pay reduce shirking? What is the reason for efficiency wages?

■ **ANSWERS**

Chapter 15 The Pricing and Employment of Resources: Wage Determination

FILL-IN QUESTIONS

1. time, wage rate, the amount of time worked, the goods and services nominal wages will purchase

2. a. strong; b. capital equipment, natural resources, technology, quality

3. a. wages, alternative employment, opportunity cost; b. marginal-revenue-product (demand) schedules; c. total quantity of labor demanded, total quantity of labor supplied (either order)

4. perfectly, wage rate

5. marginal revenue product, wage rate, marginal labor cost

6. marginal revenue product, marginal labor cost, greater, marginal revenue product, labor cost; a. marginal product, marginal resource cost; b. marginal revenue product, marginal resource cost, marginal revenue product, marginal resource cost, one

7. lower, less

8. increase wages, demand, supply, above-equilibrium

9. restricting the supply of labor, imposing above-equilibrium wage rates; a. decreased; b. decrease; c. growing, inelastic

10. products they produce, productivity, prices

11. marginal revenue product of labor, competitive and monopsonistic equilibrium wage, the relative bargaining strength of the union and the monopsonist

12. a. increase, decrease; b. increase, increase

13. increase, decrease, increase, 10, young, blacks, women, mixed (or ambivalent)

14. homogeneous (the same), attractiveness, imperfect

15. noncompeting, abilities, human capital

16. nonmonetary, equalizing differences

17. immobilities, geographic, institutional, sociological

18. agents, principals, profits, wages (or income), principal-agent

19. shirking, monitor, incentive pay, piece, commissions, profit

20. seniority, efficiency

PROBLEMS AND PROJECTS

1. a. quantity of labor demanded: 100, 200, 300, 400, 500, 600, 700, 800; b. (1) 10.00; (2) 600; c. (1) 10.00; (2) 6; (3) 10.00; f. 400

2. a. total labor cost: 0, 4.00, 12.00, 24.00, 40.00, 60.00, 84.00, 112.00, 144.00; marginal labor cost: 4.00, 8.00, 12.00, 16.00, 20.00, 24.00, 28.00, 32.00; b. (1) 5; (2) 12.00; (3) 20.00; d. 6, 14.00

3. a. wage rate: 16.00, 16.00, 16.00, 16.00, 16.00, 16.00, 16.00, 18.00; b. total labor cost: 16.00, 32.00, 48.00, 64.00, 80.00, 96.00, 112.00, 144.00; marginal labor cost: 16.00, 16.00, 16.00, 16.00, 16.00, 16.00, 16.00; c. (1) 6; (2) 16.00; (3) 96.00; d. increased, increased, increased

4. a. 5; b. 3; c. 6; d. 2; e. 4; f. 1

SELF-TEST

1. F, p. 256
2. T, p. 257
3. T, p. 258
4. T, pp. 258–259
5. T, p. 261
6. T, p. 263
7. F, p. 263
8. T, p. 263
9. F, pp. 263–264
10. F, p. 265

11. T, p. 265
12. F, p. 265
13. F, pp. 265–266
14. T, p. 266
15. T, p. 266

16. T, pp. 266–267
17. T, pp. 267–268
18. F, p. 268
19. T, p. 269
20. T, p. 271

21. *d*, p. 265
22. *a*, p. 267
23. *b*, p. 268

24. *b*, pp. 270–271
25. *c*, p. 272

1. *a*, p. 256
2. *a*, p. 256
3. *c*, p. 257
4. *a*, p. 258
5. *c*, p. 259
6. *d*, p. 259
7. *d*, p. 261
8. *b*, p. 261
9. *d*, p. 261
10. *c*, p. 260

11. *d*, pp. 256–257
12. *c*, pp. 262–263
13. *b*, p. 263
14. *a*, p. 264
15. *d*, p. 261
16. *c*, p. 258
17. *b*, pp. 265–266
18. *c*, p. 258
19. *b*, p. 260
20. *c*, p. 262

DISCUSSION QUESTIONS

1. p. 256
2. pp. 256–257
3. pp. 257–258
4. pp. 259–261
5. pp. 258–261
6. p. 260
7. pp. 262–265
8. pp. 262–265
9. pp. 263–265

10. pp. 264–265
11. p. 265
12. pp. 265–266
13. p. 266
14. pp. 265–266
15. pp. 267–268
16. p. 268
17. pp. 267–269
18. pp. 270–272

CHAPTER 16

The Pricing and Employment of Resources: Rent, Interest, and Profits

Chapter 16 concludes the study of the prices of resources by examining rent, interest, and profits. Compared with the study of wage rates in Chapter 15, each of the first three major sections in Chapter 16 is considerably briefer and a good deal simpler. You might do well to treat these sections as if they were actually three minichapters.

There is nothing especially difficult about Chapter 16. By now you should understand that the marginal revenue product of a resource determines the demand for that resource and that this understanding can be applied to the demand for land and capital. It will be on the supply side of the land market that you will encounter whatever difficulties there are. The supply of land is unique because it is perfectly *inelastic*: changes in rent do not change the quantity of land which will be supplied. Demand, given the quantity of land available, is thus the sole determinant of rent. Of course land varies in productivity and can be used for different purposes, but these are merely the factors which explain why the rent on all lands is not the same.

Capital, as the economist defines it, means capital goods. Is the rate of interest, then, the price paid for the use of capital goods? No, not quite. Capital is not one kind of good; it is many different kinds. In order to be able to talk about the price paid for the use of capital goods there must be a simple way of adding up different kinds of capital goods. The simple way is to measure the quantity of capital goods in terms of money. The rate of interest is, then, the price paid for the use of money (or of financial capital).

The rate of interest is determined by the demand for and supply of loanable funds in the economy. In a simplified model, businesses are the primary demanders of loanable funds because they want to use this financial capital to buy capital goods (e.g., equipment, machinery, factories, etc.). As with the demand for any good or service, the greater the price of using loanable funds (the interest rate), the smaller the amount of loanable funds that firms will be able and willing to borrow. A business will most likely borrow funds and make an investment in capital goods if the expected rate of return on the investment is greater than the interest rate. Therefore, the lower the interest rate, the greater the opportunities for profitable in-

vestments and the greater the amount of loanable funds demanded.

On the supply side, households are the typical suppliers of loanable funds. At a higher rate of interest, households are willing to supply more loanable funds than at lower interest rates. The reason has to do with the weighing of present consumption to future consumption. Most consumers prefer present consumption, but they would be willing to forgo this current use of funds and make them available for loan if there is compensation in the form of interest payments. Thus, the greater the interest rate, the more saving there will be by households, which in turn creates a greater supply of loanable funds.

The intersection of the demand curve and the supply curve for loanable funds determines the equilibrium rate of interest, or the price of loanable funds, and the equilibrium quantity. This relationship is illustrated in Figure 16-2. The demand and supply curves of loanable funds can also shift due to a variety of factors. For example, there could be an increase in the rates of return on investments, which would increase the demand for loanable funds at each and every interest rate; changes in the tax laws could make savings more attractive and this change would increase the supply of loanable funds. You should also note that, while in the simplified model businesses are the demanders and households the suppliers of loanable funds, in reality these sectors can operate on both sides of the market.

When it comes to profits, supply and demand analysis fails the economist. Profits are not merely a wage for a particular type of labor; rather they are rewards for taking risks and the gains of the monopolist. Such things as "the quantity of risk taken" or "the quantity of effort required to establish a monopoly" simply can't be measured; consequently it is impossible to talk about the demand for or the supply of them. Nevertheless, profits are important in the economy. They are largely rewards for doing things that have to be done if the economy is to allocate resources efficiently and to progress and develop; they are the lure or the bait which makes people willing to take the risks that result in efficiency and progress.

The final section of Chapter 16 answers two questions about the American economy. What part of the national income goes to workers and what part goes to capitalists—those who provide the economy with land, capital goods, and entrepreneurial ability? And have the shares going to workers and to capitalists changed in the past eighty or so years? The student may be surprised to learn that the lion's share—about 80%—of the national income goes to workers today and went to workers at the beginning of the century; and that capitalists today and in 1900 got about 20%. There is, in short, no evidence to support the belief that workers get less and capitalists more or the opposite belief that workers obtain a greater part and capitalists a smaller part of the national income today than they did about ninety years ago in the United States.

■ **CHECKLIST**

When you have studied this chapter you should be able to:

☐ Define economic rent and explain what determines the amount of economic rent paid.

☐ Explain why economic rent is a surplus (or unearned income).

☐ State the means Henry George and the socialists would use to recover this surplus.

☐ Explain why the owners of land do not all receive the same economic rent.

☐ Explain why, if economic rent is a surplus, a firm must pay rent.

☐ Define interest and state two aspects about it.

☐ Explain why there is a positive relationship between the interest rate and the supply of loanable funds.

☐ Identify the inverse relationship between the interest rate and the demand for loanable funds.

☐ Describe how the equilibrium rate of interest is established given the demand for and supply of loanable funds.

☐ State how much loanable funds (or financial capital) an individual business will tend to borrow at the equilibrium interest rate.

☐ Distinguish between a change in the quantity demanded and a change in the demand for loanable funds; distinguish between a change in the quantity supplied and a change in the supply of loanable funds.

☐ Explain how the level of the interest rate affects investment spending and the aggregate level of national output and employment in the economy; and the allocation of capital goods among firms (the composition of the production of physical capital).

☐ Define economic profit and distinguish between economic profit and normal profit.

☐ Identify the potential sources of profit for firms.

☐ Explain the functions of profits in the American economy.

☐ State the current relative size of labor's and of capital's share of the national income and describe what has happened to these shares in the U.S. economy since 1900.

■ **CHAPTER OUTLINE**

1. Economic rent is the price paid for the use of land or natural resources whose supply is perfectly inelastic.

   a. Demand is the active determinant of economic rent because changes in the level of economic rent do not change the quantity of land supplied; and economic rent is, therefore, a payment which in the aggregate need not be paid to ensure that the land will be available.

   b. Some people have argued that land rents are unearned incomes, and that either land should be nationalized or rents should be taxed away; and the single tax advocated by Henry George would have no effect on resource allocation in the economy.

   (1) Thus the case for taxing land can be made on the basis of equity and efficiency considerations.

   (2) But critics have pointed out four disadvantages of such a tax.

   c. Economic rents on different types of land vary because land differs in its productivity.

   d. Land has alternative uses; and rent is a cost to a firm because it must pay rent to lure land away from alternative employments.

2. The interest rate is the price paid for the use of money. The loanable funds theory of interest describes how the interest rate is determined by the demand for and supply of loanable funds.

   a. The supply of loanable funds is generally provided by households through savings. There is a positive relationship between the interest rate and the quantity of loanable funds supplied.

   b. The demand for loanable funds typically comes from businesses for investment in capital goods. There is an inverse relationship between the interest rate and the quantity of loanable funds demanded. Lower interest rates provided more profitable investment opportunities; higher interest rates reduce investment.

   c. The intersection of the demand for and supply of loanable funds determines the equilibrium interest rate and the quantity of funds loaned.

   d. There are some extensions to the simplified model of the loanable funds market:

   (1) factors can shift the demand for and supply of loanable funds. For example, the supply can shift because of changes in the savings behavior of households, or, the demand can shift because of changes in technology that change the rate of return on investments;

   (2) households and businesses can operate on both sides of the markets—as demanders and suppliers; and,

(3) the quantity of loanable funds supplied may not be very responsive to changes in the interest rate.

e. While it is convenient to speak as if there were but a single interest rate, there are actually a number of different rates of interest. The rates vary because of four loan factors—risk, maturity, size, and taxability—and because of market imperfections.

f. The interest rate plays two roles.

(1) Because of the inverse relationship between the interest rate and the demand for loanable funds, the level of the interest rate affects the level of investment in capital goods, and, therefore, the aggregate level of national output and employment in the economy.

(2) The interest rate rations (allocates) financial and physical capital among competing firms and determines the composition of the output of capital goods.

3. Economic profit is what remains of the firm's revenues after all its explicit and implicit opportunity costs have been deducted.

a. Profit is a payment for entrepreneurial ability, which involves combining and directing the use of resources in an uncertain and innovating world.

b. Profits are:

(1) rewards for assuming the risks in an economy in which the future is uncertain and subject to change;

(2) rewards for assuming the risks and uncertainties inherent in innovation; and

(3) surpluses which business firms obtain from the exploitation of monopoly power.

c. The expectation of profits motivates business firms to innovate, and profits (and losses) guide business firms to produce products and to use resources in the way desired by society.

4. National income data for the American economy indicate the following.

a. In the period 1982–1990 wages and salaries were 74% of the national income, but using a broader definition of labor income (wages and salaries plus proprietors' income—which is mostly a payment for labor), labor's share was about 80% and capital's share (rent, interest, and corporate profits) was about 20% of national income.

b. Since the years 1900–1909 wages and salaries have increased from 55 to about 74%.

(1) But labor's share, employing the broader definition of labor income, has remained at about 80% and capital's share at about 20% of the national income because of the structural changes which occurred in the American economy.

(2) The growth of labor unions in the United States does not explain the increases in the wages and salaries received by workers.

■ **IMPORTANT TERMS**

Economic rent	Rate of return
Incentive function	Normal profit
Single-tax movement	Economic (pure) profit
Truth in Lending Act	Static economy
The (*or* pure) rate of interest	Insurable risk
	Uninsurable risk
The loanable funds theory of interest	

■ **FILL-IN QUESTIONS**

1. Rent is the price paid for the use of _____

_____

and _____

and their total supply is _____

2. The active determinant of rent is (demand, supply) _____ and the passive determinant is _____. Because rent does ***not*** perform a(n) (rationing, incentive) _____ function economists consider it to be a _____

_____

3. Socialists argue that land rents are (earned, unearned) _____ incomes and that land should be _____ so that these incomes can be used for the good of society as a whole. Proponents of the _____ argue that economic rent could be completely taxed away without affecting the amount of land available for productive purposes.

4. Rents on different pieces of land are not the same because _____

_____.

And while rent from the viewpoint of the economy as a whole is a surplus, rent is a cost to _____ users of land which must be paid because land has

_____

5. Interest is the price paid for the use of _____ _____; and interest is typically stated as a _____ of the amount of money borrowed. Money (is, is not) _____ an eco-

nomic resource because money _____
productive.

6. Money or financial capital is obtained in the loanable funds market. The equilibrium rate of interest is determined by the intersection of the _____ curve and the _____ curve for loanable funds; the quantity demanded for loanable funds is (greater than, less than, or equal to) _____ the quantity supplied at the equilibrium rate of interest.

7. The quantity supplied of loanable funds is (inversely, directly) _____ related to the interest rate. In this case, the higher the interest rate, the (more, less) _____ funds households are willing to save and make available for loan.

8. The quantity demanded of loanable funds is (directly, inversely) _____ related to the interest rate. In this case, the higher the interest rate, the (more, less) _____ the quantity demanded for loanable funds because there are _____ opportunities for profitable investment. An investment is considered profitable if the _____ is greater than the interest rate.

9. A change in the thriftiness of households will cause a (movement along, change in) _____ the (demand, supply) _____ curve for loanable funds. A change in the rate of return on potential investments from an improvement in technology will cause a (movement along, change in) _____ the (demand, supply) _____ curve for loanable funds.

10. In the less simplified model of the loanable funds market, households can be both _____ and _____; businesses can be both _____ and _____. Also, some economists think that the supply curve for loanable funds may be highly (elastic, inelastic) _____

11. Give five reasons why the interest rates on different loans would differ.

a. _____

b. _____

c. _____

d. _____

e. _____

12. The interest rate performs two important functions. It helps determine how much _____ will occur in the economy and then _____ it among various firms and industries.

13. Normal profits are a payment for the resource called (land, labor, capital, entrepreneurial ability) _____ _____ and this resource performs four functions: It combines the other _____ to produce goods and services, makes (routine, nonroutine) _____ decisions for the firm, (invents, innovates) _____ new products and production processes, and bears the economic (costs, risks, criticisms) _____ associated with the other three functions.

14. When the future is _____, businesses necessarily assume risks, some of which are _____ and some of which are _____. The risks which businesses cannot avoid arise either because the _____ is changing or because the firm itself deliberately engages in _____

15. Profits:
   a. Are important in the American economy because the expectation of profits stimulates firms to innovate, and the more innovation there is, the higher will be the levels of _____, _____, and _____ in the economy;
   b. and losses promote the efficient _____ of resources in the economy unless the profits are the result of (competition, monopoly) _____

16. Defining labor income broadly to include both wages and salaries and proprietors' income:
   a. Labor's share of the national income is today about _____%;
   b. The capitalists' share is the sum of _____ _____, _____, and _____; and is today about _____% of the national income;
   c. Since the beginning of the twentieth century:
   (1) Labor's share has (increased, decreased, remained constant) _____
   (2) Capital's share has _____

■ **PROBLEMS AND PROJECTS**

1. Assume that the quantity of a certain type of land available is 300,000 acres and the demand for this land is that given in the table below.

Pure land rent, per acre	Land demanded, acres
$350	100,000
300	200,000
250	300,000
200	400,000
150	500,000
100	600,000
50	700,000

a. The pure rent on this land will be $_____

b. The total quantity of land rented will be _____

_____ acres.

c. On the graph below, plot the supply and demand curves for this land and indicate the pure rent for land and the quantity of land rented.

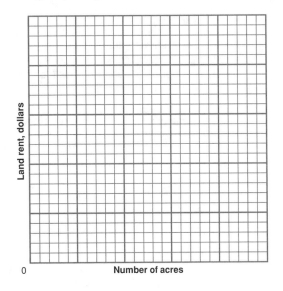

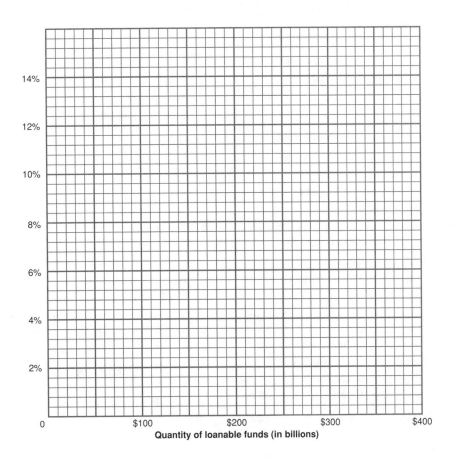

d. If landowners were taxed at a rate of $250 per acre for their land, the pure rent on this land after taxes would be $_____ but the number of acres rented would be _____

2. The schedule below shows interest rates (column 1), the associated quantity demand of loanable funds (column 2), and the quantity supplied of loanable funds (column 4) in billions of dollars at those interest rates.

Interest rate (1)	Quantity demanded		Quantity supplied	
	(2)	(3)	(4)	(5)
12%	50	____	260	____
10	100	____	240	____
8	150	____	220	____
6	200	____	200	____
4	250	____	180	____
2	300	____	160	____

a. Plot the demand and supply schedules on the graph at the bottom of page 177. (The interest rate is measured along the vertical axis and the quantity demanded or supplied is measured on the horizontal axis.)

(1) The equilibrium interest rate is _____%. The quantity demanded is $_____ billion and the quantity supplied is $_____ billion.
(2) At an interest rate of 10%, the quantity demanded of loanable funds is $_____ billion and the quantity supplied of loanable funds is $_____ billion. There is an excess of loanable funds of $_____ billion.
(3) At an interest rate of 4%, the quantity demanded of loanable funds is $_____ billion and the quantity supplied of loanable funds is $_____ billion. There is a shortage of loanable funds of $_____ billion.

b. If technology improves and the demand for loanable funds increases by $70 billion at each interest rate, then the new equilibrium interest rate will be _____% and the equilibrium quantity of loanable funds will be $_____ billion. Fill in the new demand schedule in column 3 of the table above and plot this new demand curve on the graph.

c. Then, because of changes in the tax laws, households become more thrifty by $140 at each interest rate.

The new equilibrium interest rate will be _____% and the equilibrium quantity of loanable funds will be $_____ billion. Fill in the new supply schedule

in column 5 and plot this new supply curve on the graph.

3. Firms make investment decisions based on the rate of return and the interest rate.
a. In each of the following simple cases, calculate the rate of return on an investment.
(1) You invest in a new machine that costs $2,000 but which is expected to increase total revenues by $2,075 in one year.
(2) You invest in a new piece of equipment that costs $150,000, but which is expected to increase total revenues in one year by $160,000.
(3) You invest in a new plant that costs $3 million and which is expected to increase total revenues in one year by $3.5 million.

b. Given each of the following interest rates would you make an investment in situations 1, 2, and 3 of above.
(1) An interest rate of 5%.
(2) An interest rate of 8%.
(3) An interest rate of 15%.

4. The following table shows estimated wages and salaries, proprietors' income, corporate profits, interest, rent, and the national income of the United States in 1990.

Wages and salaries	$3290 billion
Proprietors' income	373 billion
Corporate profits	319 billion
Interest	490 billion
Rent	− 13 billion
National income	4460 billion

a. Wages and salaries were _____% of the national income.
b. Labor's share of the national income was _____% and capital's share was _____%.

■ **SELF-TEST**

Circle the T if the statement is true; the F if it is false.

1. Rent is the price paid for the use of land and other property resources.   **T F**

2. The determination of economic rent for land and other natural resources is based on a demand curve that is perfectly inelastic.   **T F**

3. Rent is a surplus because it does not perform an incentive function.   **T F**

4. Rent is unique because it is not determined by demand and supply.   **T F**

5. Henry George argued in *Progress and Poverty* that the increasing land rents would produce more unearned income for landowners which could then be taxed by government.   **T   F**

6. Critics of the single tax on land argue that it would bring in too much revenue for the government.   **T   F**

7. For individual producers, rental payments are a surplus, but for society they are a cost.   **T   F**

8. Money is an economic resource and the interest rate is the price paid for this resource.   **T   F**

9. The quantity of loanable funds demanded is inversely related to the interest rate.   **T   F**

10. The quantity of loanable funds supplied is directly related to the interest rate.   **T   F**

11. An increase in the demand for loanable funds would tend to increase the interest rate.   **T   F**

12. An increase in the rate of return on investments would most likely increase the supply of loanable funds.   **T   F**

13. Other things equal, long-term loans usually command lower rates of interest than do short-term loans.   **T   F**

14. The pure rate of interest is best approximated by the interest paid on long-term bonds with very low risk, such as the thirty-year U.S. Treasury bond.   **T   F**

15. A normal profit is the minimum payment the entrepreneur must expect to receive to induce him or her to provide a firm with entrepreneurial ability.   **T   F**

16. If the economists' definition of profits were used, total profit in the economy would be greater than they would be if the accountants' definition were used.   **T   F**

17. The expectation of profits is the basic motive for innovation, while actual profits and losses aid in the efficient allocation of resources.   **T   F**

18. The increasing importance of the corporation in the American economy is a part of the explanation of why wages and salaries have increased as shares of the national income.   **T   F**

19. The growth of labor unions is the main cause of the expansion of wages and salaries as a share of the national income.   **T   F**

20. Over the past ninety years there has been a shift from labor-intensive to capital- and land-intensive production.   **T   F**

Circle the letter that corresponds to the best answer.

1. Which of the following is considered by economists to be a productive economic resource?

(a) money capital
(b) capital goods
(c) interest
(d) profit

2. The price paid for a natural resource that is completely fixed in supply is:
(a) profit
(b) interest
(c) rent
(d) a risk payment

3. In total, the supply of land is:
(a) perfectly inelastic
(b) of unitary elasticity
(c) perfectly elastic
(d) elastic but not perfectly elastic

4. Which of the following is **not** characteristic of the tax proposed by Henry George?
(a) it would be equal to 100% of all land rent
(b) it would be the only tax levied by government
(c) it would not affect the supply of land
(d) it would reduce rents paid by the amount of the tax

5. A single tax on land in the United States would:
(a) bring in tax revenues sufficient to finance all current government spending
(b) be impractical because it is difficult to distinguish between payments for the use of land and those for the use of capital
(c) tax all "unearned" incomes in the economy at a rate of 100%
(d) be or do all of the above

6. Which of the following is **not** true?
(a) the greater the demand for land, the greater will be the economic rent paid for the use of land
(b) a "windfall profits" tax on the increases in the profits of petroleum producers which have resulted from the rise in oil prices is an example of a tax on economic rent
(c) individual users of land have to pay a rent to its owners because that land has alternative uses
(d) the less productive a particular piece of land is, the greater will be the rent its owner is able to earn from it

7. The economic rent from land will increase, **ceteris paribus**, whenever the:
(a) price of land decreases
(b) demand for land increases
(c) demand for land decreases
(d) supply curve for land increases

8. When the supply curve for land lies entirely to the right of the demand curve:
(a) landowners will receive an economic rent
(b) landowners will not receive an economic rent
(c) the interest rate on land will increase
(d) the interest rate on land will decrease

9. Which of the following would tend to result in a lower interest rate?
(a) the greater the risk involved
(b) the shorter the length of the loan
(c) the smaller the amount of the loan
(d) the greater the imperfections in the money market

10. What is the most likely reason why a lender would prefer a high-quality municipal bond that pays a 6% rate of interest as compared to a high-quality corporate bond paying 8%?
(a) the municipal bond is tax-exempt
(b) the municipal bond is a long-term investment
(c) the corporate bond is safer than the municipal bond
(d) the municipal bond is easier to purchase than a corporate bond

11. In the competitive market for loanable funds, when the quantity of funds demanded exceeds the quantity supplied, then the:
(a) interest rate will decrease
(b) interest rate will increase
(c) demand curve will increase
(d) supply curve will decrease

12. A decrease in the productivity of capital goods will, ceteris paribus:
(a) increase the supply of loanable funds
(b) decrease the supply of loanable funds
(c) increase the demand for loanable funds
(d) decrease the demand for loanable funds

13. If the annual rate of interest were 18% and the rate of net profit a firm expects to earn annually by building a new plant were 20%, the firm would:
(a) not build the new plant
(b) build the new plant
(c) have to toss a coin to decide whether to build the new plant
(d) not be able to determine from these figures whether to build the plant

*The next two questions (**14** and **15**) refer to the following data.*

Expected rate of net profit	Amount of capital goods investment (in billions)
19%	$220
17	250
15	300
13	360
11	430
9	500

14. If the interest rate is 13%:
(a) $300 billion of investment will be undertaken
(b) $360 billion of investment will be undertaken
(c) $430 billion of investment will be undertaken
(d) $500 billion of investment will be undertaken

15. An increase in the interest rate from 15% to 17% would:
(a) increase investment by $40 billion
(b) increase investment by $50 billion
(c) decrease investment by $50 billion
(d) decrease investment by $40 billion

16. Which of the following is an economic cost?
(a) uninsurable risk
(b) normal profit
(c) economic profit
(d) monopoly profit

17. Which of the following would **not** be a function of the entrepreneur?
(a) the introduction of a new product on the market
(b) the making of decisions in a static economy
(c) the incurring of unavoidable risks
(d) the combination and direction of resources in an uncertain environment

18. Business firms obtain economic profits because:
(a) not all risks are insurable
(b) not all markets are competitive
(c) the economy is dynamic
(d) all of these

19. The monopolists who obtain an economic profit are able to do so because:
(a) they are innovators
(b) all their risks are insurable
(c) uncertainty has been reduced to the minimum
(d) most of their decisions are nonroutine

20. Since around 1900:
(a) capital's share of national income has increased
(b) labor's share has increased
(c) labor's share has decreased
(d) capital's share has been almost constant

■ **DISCUSSION QUESTIONS**

1. Explain what determines the economic rent paid for the use of land. What is unique about the supply of land?

2. Why is land rent a "surplus"? What economic difficulties would be encountered if the government adopted Henry George's single tax proposal as a means of confiscating this surplus? What do the critics think of the concept of a single tax on land?

3. Even though land rent is an economic surplus it is also an economic cost for the individual user of land. Why and how can it be both an economic surplus and an economic cost?

4. Explain what determines (a) the amount of loanable funds that households are willing to supply; (b) the amount that businesses wish to demand; and (c) how these desires are resolved in the market for loanable funds.

5. How might a change in productivity affect the interest rate? How might a change in the tax laws affect household savings and the interest rate. What are the implications if the supply curve for loanable funds is highly inelastic?

6. What is the connection between the rate of return on a capital goods investment and the interest rate? Give examples of possible investment situations.

7. Why are there actually many different rates at any given time? Identify factors that may explain the reasons for the differences.

8. What two important functions does the rate of interest perform in the economy?

9. What are profits? For what resource are they a payment, and what tasks does this resource perform?

10. Why would there be no economic profits in a purely competitive static economy?

11. "The risks which an entrepreneur assumes arise because of uncertainties which are external to the firm and because of uncertainties which are developed by the initiative of the firm itself." Explain.

12. What two important functions do profits or the expectation of profits perform in the economy? How does monopoly impede the effective performance of these functions?

13. Monopoly results in profits and reduces uncertainty. Is it possible that monopolists may undertake more innovation as a result? Why?

14. What part of the American national income is wages and salaries and what part is labor income? Why do your answers to these questions differ? What part of the national income is the income of capitalists? What kinds of income are capitalist income?

15. What have been the historical trends in the shares of national income that are wages and salaries, labor income, and capitalist income? What changes in the American economy can account for these trends?

16. Explain why the growth of labor unions is not a good explanation of the expanding share of the national income going for wages and salaries.

■ **ANSWERS**

Chapter 16 The Pricing and Employment of Resources: Rent, Interest, and Profits

FILL-IN QUESTIONS

1. land, natural resources, fixed (perfectly inelastic)

2. demand, supply, incentive, surplus

3. unearned, nationalized, single tax

4. land differs in productivity (quality), individual, alternative uses

5. money; percentage, is not, is not

6. demand, supply (either order); equal to

7. directly, more

8. inversely, less, less, rate of return

9. change in, supply, change in, demand

10. demanders, suppliers (either order); demanders, suppliers (either order); inelastic

11. *a.* risk; *b.* length of loan; *c.* amount of loan; *d.* tax status of loan (or investment); *e.* market imperfections

12. investment, rations

13. entrepreneurial ability, resources, nonroutine, innovates, risks

14. uncertain, insurable, uninsurable, economy as a whole, innovation

15. *a.* investment, employment, output; *b.* allocation, monopoly

16. *a.* 80; *b.* rent, interest, corporate profit, 20; *c.* (1) remained constant, (2) remained constant

PROBLEMS AND PROJECTS

1. *a.* 250; *b.* 300,000; *d.* 0, 300,000

2. *a.* (1) 6%, 200, 200; (2) 100, 240, 140; (3) 250, 180, 70; *b.* 8%, 220; *c.* 4%, 320. The completed table would be:

Interest rate (1)	Quantity demanded		Quantity supplied	
	(2)	(3)	(4)	(5)
12%	50	120	260	400
10	100	170	240	380
8	150	220	220	360
6	200	270	200	340
4	250	320	180	320
2	300	370	160	300

3. *a.* (1) 3.8%; (2) 6.7%; (3) 16.7%; *b.* (1) no, yes, yes; (2) no, no, yes; (3) no, no, yes

4. *a.* 73.8; *b.* 81.3, 18.7

SELF-TEST

1. F, p. 275
2. F, p. 276
3. T, pp. 276–277
4. F, p. 276
5. T, p. 277
6. F, p. 277
7. F, p. 278
8. F, p. 279
9. T, pp. 279–280
10. T, p. 279
11. T, p. 280
12. F, pp. 279–280
13. F, p. 281
14. T, p. 281
15. T, p. 283
16. F, p. 282
17. T, pp. 284–285
18. T, pp. 285–286
19. F, pp. 285–286
20. F, pp. 285–286

1. *b*, p. 279
2. *c*, p. 275
3. *a*, p. 276
4. *d*, p. 277
5. *b*, p. 277
6. *d*, p. 276
7. *b*, p. 276
8. *b*, p. 276
9. *b*, p. 281
10. *a*, p. 281

11. *b*, p. 280
12. *d*, p. 282
13. *b*, p. 282
14. *b*, p. 282
15. *c*, p. 282
16. *b*, p. 283
17. *b*, p. 283
18. *d*, pp. 283–284
19. *c*, p. 284
20. *d*, pp. 285–286

DISCUSSION QUESTIONS

1. pp. 275–276
2. pp. 276–277
3. p. 279
4. pp. 280–281
5. pp. 280–281
6. pp. 279–280
7. p. 281
8. p. 282

9. pp. 282–283
10. pp. 283–284
11. pp. 283–284
12. pp. 284–285
13. p. 284
14. pp. 285–286
15. pp. 285–286
16. p. 286

CHAPTER 17

General Equilibrium: The Market System and Its Operation

Chapter 17 provides a conclusion to the previous ten chapters and ties together many of the things you have already learned about microeconomics. By this time you have read a large amount of material concerning the operation of supply and demand in product and resource markets and under different market conditions. You may have lost sight of the fact—emphasized in Chapter 5—that the American economy is a *system* of markets and prices. This means that *all* prices and *all* markets are linked together.

The chief purpose of Chapter 17 is to help you understand why and how these markets are linked together, connected, and interrelated. The theory which explains the relationships between different markets and different prices is called *general* equilibrium analysis. (By way of contrast, the theory which explains a single product or resource market and the price of the one good or service bought and sold in that market is called *partial* equilibrium analysis.) An understanding of general equilibrium is necessary in order to understand how the market system as a whole operates to allocate its scarce resources.

Three approaches are used to enable the student to grasp the essentials and the importance of general equilibrium analysis. First, the chapter illustrates how general equilibrium works using supply and demand analysis in product and resource markets. Here you learn what the effects are of an increase in the demand for hypothetical product X accompanied by a decrease in the demand for product Y. This explanation includes a description of the short- and long-run effects on the products X and Y, and a discussion of the effects on the markets in which the producers employ resources. There are other adjustments that stem from the initial change. These further adjustments involve the markets for complementary and substitute products, the markets in which resources are used to produce these other products, and the distribution of income in the economy. You should also note that, although the competitive market system tends to promote economic efficiency and maximize consumer satisfaction, in the real world there are complications for the achievement of those objectives because markets may be imperfectly competitive.

Second, to help you understand the interrelationships between the different sectors of the economy, an input-output table is used. The table lists the producing sectors and the total output from each sector. It also shows how many inputs are required by each sector to produce its level of output. The interdependent nature of sectors in the economy is demonstrated by following the repercussions of a change in the output of a commodity with the aid of an input-output table.

Third, the chapter makes general equilibrium analysis more concrete by describing two recent examples of how one change in the economy leads to many other changes. The first example focuses on both the domestic and worldwide implications of a significant increase in the price of oil during the 1970s. This economic event had ramifications for many product and resource markets that are interrelated through the market system. You should spend time trying to understand through this example how a change in the price of a product in one market had a "ripple" effect on other markets and on the overall performance of the United States and world economy.

The second example illustrates how a change in the characteristics of our population, not just a change in price, sets off other changes in product and resource markets. The greater longevity and declining birth rates means that the American population is growing older. This important development increases the demand for various medical care—doctors, nursing homes, and prescription drugs— and also reduces the demand for products that would be bought by younger adults—housing, education, and children's household goods. In the resource markets, there is likely to be a slowing in the growth of the labor force, which has other implications for macroeconomic factors such as unemployment rates and microeconomic factors such as the demand for older workers.

What you should learn from this chapter, and the examples it presents, is that general equilibrium analysis is valuable because it provides a deeper and more analytical understanding of a variety of changes in our society. Many interrelations among markets and prices do exist in both the domestic and world economy, and it is important for you to see the connections. To be able to do this means that you must trace the total effect of a change in price or in economic policy throughout the economy, or you must investigate the full consequences of a change in such factors as consumer tastes, population, the availability of resources, or technology on the society.

When you finish Chapter 17, you are ready to examine economic issues or problems related to government and the operation of the market system. This discussion will give you more insight into the problems encountered in allocating scarce resources in our economic system whether it be by government or by the private sector. These topics are examined in the next six chapters.

■ **CHECKLIST**

When you have studied this chapter you should be able to:

☐ Distinguish between partial and general equilibrium analysis.
☐ Identify the four concepts which underlie the demand and supply curves in the product and resource markets of the economy.
☐ Explain, using graphs if you wish, both the immediate and secondary effects of a change in tastes, technology, or the availability of resources upon equilibrium prices and quantities in the product and resource markets; and upon the distribution of income in the economy.
☐ State three reasons why the competitive market system makes efficient use of resources.
☐ Identify three potential complications with the efficient operation of the competitive market economy in the real world.
☐ Specify what is shown along the left side, along the top, and in each of the boxes of an input-output table.
☐ Find the effects, when you are given an input-output table, of a change in the output of one industry upon the outputs of other industries in the economy.
☐ Cite examples of how the increase in the price of oil during the 1970s led to changes in resource and product markets in the United States economy.
☐ Describe the effects from the increase in the price of oil during the 1970s on world economy.
☐ Explain the product market implications of an aging population for the United States.
☐ Identify two reasons for the project decline in the growth of the labor force.
☐ Make five predictions about the labor market in the United States based on the projected decline in the growth of the labor force.

■ **CHAPTER OUTLINE**

1. Partial equilibrium analysis is the study of equilibrium prices and quantities in specific product and resource markets which form the price-market system. General equilibrium analysis is the study of the interrelations among these markets.

2. To understand the effects of an increase in consumer demand for product X accompanied by a decrease in consumer demand for product Y, imagine that the industry producing X uses only type A labor and that the industry producing Y uses only type B labor.
    a. Assume also that the demand curve for each product has a negative slope because of diminishing marginal utility and the supply curve has a positive slope because of increasing marginal cost; and assume that the demand curve for each type of labor has a negative slope because of diminishing marginal product and the supply curve has a positive slope because of the work-leisure preferences of workers.
    b. Beginning with all markets in long-run equilibrium, the short-run effects are an increased (decreased) output and price and economic profits (losses) in industry X (Y), an increased (decreased) derived demand for type A (type B) labor, and increased (decreased) wage rates and employment for type A (type B) labor.
    c. The long-run adjustments are the entry (exit) of firms in industry X (Y); an increase (decrease) in the supply of X (Y); a higher (lower) price than existed initially in industry X (Y), assuming increasing-cost industries; an increase (decrease) in the supply of A (B); and higher (lower) wage rates for A (B) than initially existed.
    d. In addition to these adjustments there will also be:
    (1) An increase (decrease) in the demand for and the prices and outputs of products which are substitutes (complements) for X or complements (substitutes) for Y; and an increased (decreased) demand for the resources used to produce those products whose outputs increase (decrease).
    (2) An increase (decrease) in the demand for the other resources used along with A (B).
    (3) A redistribution of income from workers and entrepreneurs in industry Y to those in industry X.
    e. In summary, any initial change in tastes, in the supply of resources, or in technology will not only have an immediate effect upon equilibrium price and quantity in a specific market, but will also have secondary effects in other markets and upon other equilibrium prices and quantities.
    f. There are also implications for economic efficiency in competitive markets:
    (1) In the ideal case, competitive markets will produce an allocation of an economy's resources and output of goods and services that is allocatively efficient, productively efficient, and that maximizes the satisfactions of

consumers, given the distribution of income and free choice by consumers.

(2) In the real world, however, there can be complications from:

(a) the underproduction of public goods and goods with spillover benefits, or the overproduction of goods with spillover costs;

(b) a distribution of income that may not be viewed as just or equitable; and

(c) markets that may be only imperfectly competitive, and therefore less efficient and slow to respond to change.

3. The input-output table indicates the specific relationships that exist among the outputs of the various sectors of the economy.

a. The outputs of each sector are the inputs of the other sectors; and the inputs of each sector are the outputs of the other sectors.

b. Because of this interdependence, any change in the output of one sector will alter the outputs of the other sectors.

4. Oil prices rose during the 1970s because of the actions taken by the OPEC cartel. This change in the price of one resource had a significant effect on many other resource and product markets beyond just the oil market. This example illustrates the difference between partial equilibrium analysis, which considers the impact on just the oil market, and general equilibrium, which considers the repercussions on markets for many oil-related products and resources.

a. In the product market, for example, the increase in the price of oil:

(1) increased the demand for substitute products that were energy-efficient, such as fuel-efficient automobiles or insulation, and decreased the demand for complementary goods and services that require gasoline consumption, such as recreational vehicles or automobile travel (tourism); and

(2) decreased the supply of some products, such as gasoline or fertilizer, because of higher oil costs to produce these products, and increased the supply of other products, such as energy-conserving equipment, because productivity improved in firms making this type of equipment.

b. In the resource market, for example, the increase in the price of oil:

(1) increased the demand for alternative energy sources such as coal or natural gas, and decreased the demand for capital goods that required oil-related energy; and

(2) decreased the supply of labor in the Snow Belt and increased it in the Sun Belt.

c. There were national and international effects from the increase in oil prices.

(1) The national economy experienced a rising tide of imports from fuel-efficient vehicles and more expensive oil that contributed to a decline in net exports and spendable income, thereby reducing aggregate demand; the oil price "shocks" also shifted aggregate supply, leading to cost-push inflation and less domestic output.

(2) On the international level, the increase in oil prices made the United States trade deficits worse, thereby reducing the international value of the dollar and contributing to domestic inflation; less-developed countries that did not produce oil suffered less favorable terms of trade that retarded economic growth.

5. The increase in the average age of the population in the United States has many economic consequences in both the product market and the labor market.

a. In the product market, there will be an increase in the demand for health-related goods and services, and a decrease in demand for child-related goods and services; and the rate of saving is likely to increase because the relative level of consumption and debt is less among an older population that a younger population that is raising children.

b. In the labor market, there will be a decline in the growth of the labor force caused by a drop in the birth rate during the 1960s and 1970s after the "baby boom" years, and by a slowing in the expected rate of participation of women in the work force. These developments are the basis for five predictions about the labor market—lower unemployment rates, higher real wages, retention of older workers, increased immigration, and more emphasis on the growth of productivity.

■ **IMPORTANT TERMS**

Market system	Input-output analysis
Partial equilibrium analysis	Input-output table
General equilibrium analysis	

■ **FILL-IN QUESTIONS**

1. Partial equilibrium analysis is concerned with prices and outputs in _____ markets in the economy, and general equilibrium analysis is concerned with the _____ among markets and prices.

2. General equilibrium exists in an economy where there is _____ in all the _____ and _____ markets in the economy.

3. When studying the markets for products and for resources, we assume that the demand curves slope _____ and the supply curves slope

_____

a. The slope of the demand curve for:

(1) products is due to _____

(2) resources is due to _____

b. The slope of the supply curve for:

(1) products is due to _____

(2) labor is due to _____

4. Assume the demand for consumer good P increases while the demand for consumer good Q decreases. In the short run:

a. The price and output of P will (increase, decrease)

_____ and the price and output of Q will

_____

b. Profits in industry _____ will increase and profits in industry _____ will decrease.

c. If the only resource used in industry P is type C labor and the only resource used in industry Q is type D labor, the demand for C will (increase, decrease)

_____ and the demand for D

will _____

d. Wage rates and the quantity of labor employed in

the market for _____ will increase while

those in the market for _____ will decrease.

5. Using the same assumptions made in **4** above, if the two industries are increasing-cost industries, the increase in the demand for P along with the decrease in the demand for Q will in the long run:

a. Cause firms to enter industry _____

and to leave industry _____

b. Cause the supply of P to (increase, decrease)

_____ and the supply of Q

to _____

c. Bring about a(n) _____ in the price

of P and a(n) _____ in the price of Q.

d. Increase the supply of type _____

labor and decrease the supply of type _____ labor.

e. _____ the employment of type C

labor and _____ the employment of type D labor.

6. Still using the assumptions made in **4** and **5** above, the increase in the price of P and the decrease in the price of Q will:

a. Increase the demand for products which are (sub-

stitutes, complements) _____ for P and

decrease the demand for _____

b. (Increase, Decrease) _____ the de-mand for those resources used along with type C labor

and _____ the demand for those re-sources used along with type D labor.

c. Redistribute income from workers and entrepre-

neurs in industry _____ to those in

industry _____

7. The economic changes or disturbances which may set off a complex economic chain reaction are of three

basic types: changes in _____,

changes in _____,

and changes in _____

8. Given the distribution of income, purely competitive product and resource markets bring about the production of a combination of goods and services which maximizes

the _____ of the consumers of the economy.

9. The ability of a purely competitive price system to al-locate resources efficiently is open to question for three reasons:

a. It fails to take into account the _____

_____ and the

_____ of the goods and services produced and it neglects or ignores the production of

_____ goods.

b. It does not necessarily result in an ideal

_____ of income.

c. Product and resource markets in the real world are

actually _____ competitive. As a result

the allocation of resources is less than _____ and adjustments to changes in tastes, technology, and

the availability of resources are _____

and _____

10. Listed down the left side of an input-output table are

the _____ sectors of the economy and

listed across the top of the table are the _____ sectors. The output of any sector is a(n) _____ of other sectors; and the inputs of any sector are the _____ of other sectors.

11. Assuming constant returns to scale, if industry X sells 30% of its product to industry Y and if industry Y increases its production by 25%, then industry X will have to increase its production by _____%.

12. According to the partial equilibrium analysis, the actions of the OPEC cartel to reduce the output of oil caused the supply of oil to (increase, decrease) _____, equilibrium price to _____, and equilibrium output to _____

13. From a general equilibrium perspective, however, the change in oil prices produced changes in product and resource markets and in the national economy:

   a. In the product market, the demand for large, domestic automobiles (increased, decreased) _____; the demand for fuel-efficient foreign automobiles _____. The demand for recreational travel and resorts _____; the demand for insulation and weather stripping _____

   b. The prices of products derived from oil (increased, decreased) _____ contributing to (higher, lower) _____ prices for producers that used these products as inputs.

   c. In the resource markets, the demand for labor in domestic automobile production (increased, decreased) _____; the demand for labor in the energy conservation industry _____. The supply of capital goods requiring substantial energy inputs for production _____

   d. For the national economy, net exports and aggregate demand showed a(n) (increase, decrease) _____ and aggregate supply showed a(n) _____, causing the price level to _____ and domestic output to _____

   e. For the world economy, the rise in oil prices (increased, decreased) _____ the trade deficit of the United States, _____ the international value of the dollar, and _____ the debts of less-developed countries that do not produce oil.

14. The aging of the American population has many economic consequences in both the product market and in the labor market:

   a. In the product market, there will be (an increase, a decrease) _____ in the demand for health-related goods and services, and _____ in demand for child-related goods and services; the rate of saving is likely to show _____ because there is usually _____ in the rate consumption and debt as adults finish raising families.

   b. In the labor market, there will be _____ in the growth of the labor force caused by a drop in the birth rate and a slowing of growth in the labor force participation of women.

15. The slowing in the growth of the labor force sets the basis for five predictions about future labor markets. There will be (higher, lower) _____ unemployment rates, _____ real wages, (less, more) _____ retention of older workers, _____ immigration, and _____ emphasis on the growth of productivity in the economy.

■ **PROBLEMS AND PROJECTS**

1. Below are three types of economic change which can occur in the economy. In the spaces allotted following each change, indicate what you think the effect will be— increase (+), decrease (−), no change (0), or an indeterminate change (?)—on demand or supply, price, and output or employment in the markets affected by the initial change.

   No answers to this problem will be found in the "Answers" section because the answer to each question depends upon such things as whether the short run or the long run is considered, whether the industry is an increasing- or constant-cost industry, and whether you consider only the "immediate-secondary effect" of the initial change. The purpose of this exercise is to get you to **attempt** to trace through the economy the full effect of an initial change and to see the extent and complexity of price-market interrelations.

   a. Decrease in the demand for consumer good X but no **initial** change in the demand for other consumer goods.

   (1) Effect on the price of and the quantity of good X produced.   _____

(2) Effect on the demand for, the price of, and the output of goods which are substitutes for good X. _____
(3) Effect on the demand for, the price of, and the output of goods which are complements for good X.

_____

(4) Effect on the demand for, the price of, and the employment of resources used in the production of good X. _____
(5) Effect on the supply of, the price of, and the output of goods which employ the same resources used in the production of good X. _____
(6) Effect on the demand for, the price of, and the employment of resources which are substitutes for the resources used to produce good X. _____

b. Decrease in the supply of resource Y.
(1) Effect on the price of and the employment of resource Y. _____
(2) Effect on the supply of, the price of, and the output of goods which employ resource Y in the production process. _____
(3) Effect on the demand for, the price of, and the employment of resources which are complementary to resource Y. _____
(4) Effect on the demand for, the price of, and the output of those goods which are substitutes for the goods produced with resource Y. _____
(5) Effect on the demand for, the price of, and the output of those goods which are complements for goods produced with resource Y. _____
(6) Effect on the demand for, the price of, and the employment of resources which are substitutes for resource Y. _____

c. Improvement in the technology of producing good Z.
(1) Effect on the supply of, the price of, and the output of good Z. _____
(2) Effect on the demand for, the price of, and the output of goods which are substitutes for good Z. _____
(3) Effect on the demand for, the price of, and the output of goods which are complements for good Z.

_____

(4) Effect on the demand for, the price of, and the employment of resources used to produce good Z. _____
(5) Effect on the supply of, the price of, and the output of those goods which also employ the resources used to produce good Z. _____

2. Below is an incomplete input-output table for an economy with five sectors. All the figures in the table are physical units rather than dollars.

Producing sectors	Using sectors					Total outputs
	A	B	C	D	E	
A	100	150	75	—	25	425
B	30	20	70	80	200	—
C	10	60	—	20	20	110
D	205	35	40	10	—	300
E	—	140	60	35	80	390

a. Complete the table by computing (by addition or subtraction) the missing input-output figures.
b. Assume that sector B wishes to expand its output by 100 units. By what percentage does sector B wish to expand its output? _____%
c. Assuming constant returns to scale in all sectors of the economy, by how many *units* will each of the following sectors of the economy have to expand its output if sector B is to expand its output by 100 units?

(1) Sector A: _____

(2) Sector C: _____

(3) Sector D: _____

(4) Sector E: _____
d. By what *percentage* will each of these sectors have to expand its output?

(1) Sector A: _____%

(2) Sector C: _____%

(3) Sector D: _____%

(4) Sector E: _____%
e. What further adjustments in the outputs of the various sectors of the economy will follow those given in (*c*) and (*d*) above?

_____

_____

■ **SELF-TEST**

Circle the T if the statement is true; the F if it is false.

1. General equilibrium analysis is the same thing as macroeconomics. **T F**

2. The study of the effect of an increase in the demand for product C, other things remaining equal, upon the price and the output of product C is an example of partial equilibrium analysis. **T F**

3. General equilibrium analysis gives a broader picture of the economic consequences of economic changes and economic policies than partial equilibrium analysis even though some of these consequences turn out to be insignificant. **T F**

4. The demand curve for labor is downsloping because of diminishing marginal utility. **T F**

5. The supply curve for a product slopes upward in the short run because of the diminishing marginal productivity of variable resources and increasing marginal cost. **T F**

Use the following data for the next three questions (6, 7, and 8) and for multiple-choice questions 7 and 8. Initially there is general equilibrium, and then the demand for consumer good W increases and the demand for consumer good Z decreases. Both industries are increasing-cost industries in the long run. Industry W employs only type G labor, and Z employs only type H labor.

6. In the short run, price, output, and profits will increase in industry Z and decrease in industry W. **T F**

7. In the long run, the quantity of type G labor employed will increase and the quantity of type H labor employed will decrease. **T F**

8. Income will be redistributed from workers and entrepreneurs in industry Z to those in industry W. **T F**

9. A change in demand, a change in technology, or a change in resource supply can set off a chain reaction of economic changes in the economy. **T F**

10. Given the distribution of income in the economy, purely competitive product and resource markets lead to the production of a collection of products which maximizes the satisfaction of consumer wants. **T F**

11. In the real world, product and resource markets tend to be purely competitive. **T F**

12. In an input-output table, the inputs of each sector are the outputs of the other sectors. **T F**

13. An input-output table is constructed so that a change in one sector will not produce a change in another sector. **T F**

14. Higher price for oil during the 1970s increased the demand for domestic cars. **T F**

15. The use of capital goods is not affected by higher energy prices because they have already been produced. **T F**

16. The short-term demand for gasoline is price elastic. **T F**

17. During the 1970s, the increased expenditure by the United States for imported oil increased the supply of dollars relative to demand in foreign exchange markets. **T F**

18. The aging of the American population will tend to cause a decrease in the demand for prescription drugs. **T F**

19. The level of consumption and consumer debt is likely to increase with the increase in the average age of the population in the United States. **T F**

20. One prediction that can be made based on the aging of the American population is that less emphasis will need to be given to productivity in the economy. **T F**

Circle the letter that corresponds to the best answer.

1. An economist that studies the economic effects of an increase in a tariff on imported automobiles on producers and consumers, both foreign and domestic, and on national and foreign economies would best be described as conducting:
(a) partial equilibrium analysis
(b) general equilibrium analysis
(c) resource market analysis
(d) product market analysis

2. The concept of increasing marginal cost serves to explain the:
(a) downward slope of the product demand curve
(b) downward slope of the resource demand curve
(c) upward slope of the product supply curve
(d) upward slope of the labor supply curve

3. The downward slope of the demand curve for a product is the result of:
(a) diminishing marginal utility
(b) diminishing marginal productivity
(c) increasing marginal cost
(d) the work-leisure preferences of workers

4. The upward slope of the supply curve of labor is the result of:
(a) diminishing marginal utility
(b) increasing marginal productivity
(c) decreasing marginal cost
(d) rising opportunity cost

5. If the demand for consumer good A increased, which one of the following would **not** be a possible consequence?
(a) increase in the price of A
(b) increase in the demand for resources used to produce A
(c) increase in the supply of those goods which are substitutes for A
(d) increase in the prices of other goods which employ the same resources used to produce A

6. If the supply of resource B increased, which one of the following would **not** be a possible consequence?

(a) decrease in the price of B

(b) decrease in the demand for those goods produced from B

(c) decrease in the demand for those resources which are substitutes for resource B

(d) decrease in the demand for those goods which are substitutes for the goods produced with resource B

*Use the data preceding true-false question **6** to answer the following two questions (**7** and **8**).*

7. When the new long-run general equilibrium is reached:

(a) the wage rate for type G labor will be higher than it was originally

(b) the wage rate for type G labor will be lower than it was originally

(c) wage rates in both labor markets will be the same as they were originally

(d) it is impossible to tell what will have happened to wage rates

8. As a result of the changes in the demands for W and Z:

(a) the demand for products which are substitutes for Z will have increased

(b) the demand for products which are complements for W will have increased

(c) the demand for products which are substitutes for Z will have decreased

(d) the demand for products which are complements for Z will have decreased

9. A highly complex chain reaction of economic events can be set off in the economy by an initial change in:

(a) demand

(b) technology

(c) resource supply

(d) all of the above

10. Which of the following is a disadvantage with purely competitive product and resource markets?

(a) the maximization of consumer satisfaction

(b) spillover costs and benefits

(c) allocative efficiency

(d) productive efficiency

11. In the construction of an input-output table:

(a) the outputs of each sector are the outputs of the other sectors

(b) the inputs of each sector are the inputs of the other sectors

(c) the outputs of each sector are the inputs of the other sectors

(d) the input of each sector is equal to the output of each sector

*Use the following input-output table to answer the next two questions (**12** and **13**).*

Producing sectors	Using sectors					Total outputs
	A	B	C	D	E	
A	20	15	35	25	60	155
B	45	55	90	10	20	220
C	40	15	80	10	5	150
D	65	10	25	20	40	160
E	100	75	80	45	10	310

12. If sector C were to decrease its output by 50 units, and assuming constant returns to scale in all sectors, the **initial** impact on sector B would be a decrease in its output of:

(a) 5 units

(b) $13\frac{6}{7}$ units

(c) $26\frac{2}{3}$ units

(d) 30 units

13. If sector C is to increase its output by 50 units, and assuming constant returns to scale, sector E's output will have to increase initially by:

(a) 8.6%

(b) 19.4%

(c) 20%

(d) 37.5%

14. When the price of oil rose during the 1970s, it resulted in what changes in the **resource** market?

(a) less demand for domestic cars and more demand for fuel-efficient foreign cars

(b) more demand for Thermopane windows for homes and less demand for recreational travel

(c) more demand for labor in the installation of insulation and less demand for labor in the production of domestic cars

(d) less demand for motor oil by consumers and more demand for public transportation

15. The price elasticity of demand for gasoline is estimated to be about .20 to .40. This means that:

(a) a 10% increase in price will result in a 2 to 4% increase in consumption

(b) a 10% increase in price will result in a 2 to 4% decrease in consumption

(c) a 1% increase in price will result in a 2 to 4% decrease in consumption

(d) a 2 to 4% increase in price will result in a 10% increase in consumption

16. The best example of an international effect from the increase in oil prices during the 1970s is:
  (a) a boom in the economies of oil-producing states in the United States
  (b) an increase in the debts of less developed countries that did not produce oil
  (c) an increase in the demand for energy-efficient capital goods made in China
  (d) a decrease in the imports of fuel-efficient cars from Japan

17. Larger expenditures by the United States for imported oil during the 1970s caused the international value of the United States dollar to:
  (a) depreciate because of an increase in the supply of dollars relative to demand
  (b) depreciate because of an increase in the demand for dollars relative to the supply
  (c) appreciate because of an increase in the supply of dollars relative to the demand
  (d) appreciate because of an increase in the demand for dollars relative to the supply

18. The trend toward an older population in the United States will tend to:
  (a) increase demand for starter homes and decrease demand for toys
  (b) increase demand for consumer credit and increase demand for rental apartments
  (c) decrease demand for nurses and increase the demand for furniture
  (d) decrease demand for jeans and increase the demand for prescription drugs

19. The aging of the American population suggests that in future labor markets there will be:
  (a) an increase in unemployment rates
  (b) an increase in real wages
  (c) a decrease in emphasis on productivity
  (d) a decrease in immigration from other nations

20. Which statements would be the best example of the type of insight provided by general equilibrium analysis?
  (a) a decrease in the supply of oil will raise the price of oil and reduce the equilibrium output
  (b) tariff-inspired expansion of the auto industry will entail a contraction in the productioin of many other goods in a full-employment economy
  (c) input-output analysis guarantees that planned production targets will be met in less-developed nations
  (d) partial equilibrium analysis shows the "little ripples" whereas general equilibrium shows the "big splash" from an oil price increase

■ **DISCUSSION QUESTIONS**

1. Explain the difference between partial equilibrium and general equilibrium analysis.

2. Why is general equilibrium analysis so important?

3. Suppose the demand for television sets decreases at the same time that the demand for airline travel increases. What would be:
  (a) the short-run effects of these changes in the markets for television-set production workers and airline workers;
  (b) the long-run effects in these markets;
  (c) the long-run effects in the markets for complementary and substitute products and in the markets for other resources; and
  (d) the effect upon the distribution of income?

4. Imagine that the availability of iron ore used to produce steel increased or the technology of steel making improved. What would be the short- and long-run effects upon:
  (a) the steel industry;
  (b) steelworkers;
  (c) the automobile industry;
  (d) the aluminum industry;
  (e) the machine tool industry; and
  (f) the coal industry?

5. Why is a purely competitive price system "conducive to an efficient allocation of resources"?

6. When a market system is less than purely competitive, what are the economic consequences?

7. Explain precisely what an input-output table is and the kind of information it contains.

8. In addition to indicating the interrelationships between the various sectors of the economy, an input-output table can be used for what purposes?

9. Describe the multitude of effects on product and resource markets in the United States from the significant increase in oil prices created by the OPEC cartel during the 1970s. How does this event illustrate the value of general equilibrium analysis compared with a partial equilibrium analysis?

10. What was the impact of the oil price increases during the 1970s on the international economy? Give examples of economic events.

11. What changes in the product market and in consumption and saving will result from an increase in the average age of the population.

12. What two factors have contributed to the slowdown in the growth of the labor force? What predictions about labor markets are suggested by this development?

■ ANSWERS

Chapter 17 General Equilibrium: The Market System and Its Operation

FILL-IN QUESTIONS

1. specific, interrelationships

2. equilibrium, product, resource

3. downward, upward: *a.* (1) diminishing marginal utility, (2) diminishing marginal productivity; *b.* (1) increasing marginal cost, (2) rising opportunity cost

4. *a.* increase, decrease; *b.* P, Q; *c.* increase, decrease; *d.* C, D

5. *a.* P, Q; *b.* increase, decrease; *c.* increase, decrease; *d.* C, D; *e.* increase, decrease

6. *a.* substitutes, complements; *b.* increase, decrease; *c.* Q, P

7. tastes, availability of resources, technology

8. satisfaction or utility

9. *a.* spillover costs, spillover benefits, public; *b.* distribution; *c.* imperfectly, ideal, incomplete, slow

10. producing, consuming (using), input, outputs

11. 7.5

12. decrease, increase, decrease

13. *a.* decreased, increased, decreased, increased; *b.* increased, higher; *c.* decreased, increased, decreased; *d.* decrease, decrease, increase, decrease; *e.* increased, decreased, increased

14. *a.* increase, decrease, decrease, increase; *b.* decrease

15. lower, lower, more, more, more

PROBLEMS AND PROJECTS

2. *a.* From left to right: 75, 0, 75, 10, 400; *b.* 25; *c.* (1) 37.5; (2) 15; (3) 8.75; (4) 35; *d.* (1) 8.8; (2) 13.6; (3) 2.9; (4) 8.97; *e.* each sector will have to increase its inputs in order to increase its output, and this will require still further increases in the outputs of the various sectors

SELF-TEST

1. F, pp. 290–291
2. T, p. 290
3. T, p. 291
4. F, p. 291
5. T, p. 291
6. F, pp. 291–292
7. T, p. 293
8. T, p. 293
9. T, p. 293
10. T, p. 294
11. F, p. 294
12. T, pp. 294–295
13. F, p. 295
14. F, p. 296
15. F, p. 296
16. F, p. 296
17. T, p. 297
18. F, p. 298
19. F, p. 298
20. F, pp. 299–300

1. *b*, p. 291
2. *c*, p. 291
3. *a*, p. 291
4. *d*, p. 291
5. *c*, p. 293
6. *b*, p. 293
7. *d*, p. 293
8. *c*, p. 293
9. *d*, p. 293
10. *b*, p. 294
11. *c*, p. 295
12. *d*, p. 295
13. *a*, p. 295
14. *c*, p. 296
15. *b*, p. 296
16. *b*, p. 297
17. *a*, p. 297
18. *d*, p. 298
19. *b*, p. 299
20. *b*, pp. 290–291

DISCUSSION QUESTIONS

1. pp. 290–291
2. p. 291
3. pp. 291–293
4. pp. 291–293
5. p. 294
6. p. 294
7. pp. 294–295
8. p. 295
9. pp. 296–297
10. p. 297
11. pp. 297–298
12. pp. 298–299

CHAPTER 18

Government and Market Failure: Public Goods, the Environment, and Information Problems

This chapter is the first of two chapters that takes a more extensive look at the economic role of government that was introduced in Chapter 6. The primary focus of this chapter is **market failures** that occur in our economy. These failures often result in government intervention in the economy to provide public goods and services, to address externality problems such as pollution, and to improve the quality and amount of information for buyers and sellers in private markets.

The chapter begins by reviewing the characteristics of public goods. You should recall from Chapter 6 that a private good is divisible and subject to the exclusion principle, whereas a public good is indivisible and not subject to exclusion. What is new in Chapter 18 is that you are shown how the demand curve and schedule for a public good are constructed and how the optimal allocation of a public good is determined. You should also note how the demand and supply curves for a public good are related to collective marginal benefits and marginal costs.

Governments employ benefit-cost analysis to determine whether they should or should not undertake some specific action—a particular project or program. This type of analysis forces government to estimate both the marginal costs and the marginal benefits of the project or program; to expand its activities only where the additional benefits exceed the added costs; and to reduce or eliminate programs and projects when the marginal costs exceed the marginal benefits. This analysis, however, depends on the ability to measure benefits and costs with some degree of accuracy. This may not be possible in some cases, thereby limiting the application of benefit-cost analysis.

The second topic of the chapter is externalities, a situation where a cost is incurred or a benefit is obtained by a party that was not involved in the market transactions. You learned in Chapter 6 that one role of government is to reduce the spillover costs to society from negative externalities and to increase the spillover benefits to society from positive externalities. This general point is now modified by the **Coase theorem** that suggests that there are situations where government intervention is not required. Individual bargaining can settle most externality problems when there is clear ownership of property rights, the number of people involved is small, and the costs of bargaining are minimal. When these conditions do not hold, then government action with direct controls or specific taxes may be necessary to solve the problem. You discover that it may even be possible for the government to create a **market** for externality rights, and that there is a rule for the optimal reduction of an externality.

Pollution is a prime example of a negative externality and it is the focus of a case study. There are many types of pollution, but their causes stem from the **law of conservation of matter and energy**. The production of goods and services uses resources that ultimately become waste (matter or energy) that our environment is not able to reabsorb. Over the years, the government has developed a number of antipollution policies. In this chapter you will learn about two national ones—the Superfund law of 1980 and the Clean Air Act of 1990. You will also discover how the market forces of supply and demand in the recycling market help to reduce some of the demands for the dumping of solid waste in landfills.

The third major type of failure that you will encounter in this chapter is information. You probably never thought about the role of information in the functioning of markets, but in this last section of the chapter you will discover how important information is to both buyers and sellers. For example, buyers need some assurance about the measurement standards or quality of products that they purchase, be it gasoline or medical care. The government may intervene in some markets to ensure that this information is made available.

Inadequate information in markets creates problems for sellers, too. In certain markets, such as insurance, sellers experience a **moral hazard problem** because buyers change their behavior and become less careful, and the change in behavior makes it more costly to sellers. There is also an **adverse selection** problem in the insurance market because those buyers most likely to benefit (higher-risk buyers) are more likely to purchase the insurance, and therefore this group imposes higher costs on sellers than if the riskers were more widely spread among the population. Actions of sellers to screen buyers means that fewer people will be covered by insurance, and it creates a situation that may lead to the provision of social insurance by government. Government may also provide better information about workplace safety or enforce safety standards to address information problems in resource markets.

You should not finish this chapter with the sole thought that all market failures require government intervention and direct control. Some problems do require a specific government action, but other problems may be handled in a more efficient or optimal way through individual negotiations, through lawsuits or through the use of market incentives. What is important for you to understand is the range of solutions to different market and information failures, and the rationale for government intervention to correct them.

■ **CHECKLIST**

When you have studied this chapter you should be able to:

☐ Compare the characteristics of a public good with a private good.
☐ Calculate the demand for a public good when given tabular data.
☐ Explain how marginal costs and marginal benefits are reflected in the demand for or the supply of a public good.
☐ Identify on a graph where there is an overallocation, an underallocation, and an optimal allocation of a public good.
☐ Use benefit-cost analysis to determine the extent to which government should apply resources to a project or program when you are given the cost and benefit data.
☐ Define and give examples of positive and negative externalities (spillovers).
☐ State the conditions that are necessary for the Coase theorem and give an example of its use.
☐ Explain how liability rules and lawsuits are used to resolve externality problems.
☐ Identify two means used by government to achieve allocative efficiency when there are negative externalities.
☐ Determine the price a government agency should charge in a market for pollution rights when you are given the necessary data.
☐ Compare the advantages of a market for pollution rights to direct controls.
☐ Explain and illustrate with a graph a rule for determining the optimal reduction of a negative externality.
☐ Describe the dimensions of the pollution problem.
☐ Cite four major causes of the pollution problem.
☐ Discuss the purpose of the Superfund law of 1980.
☐ Identify five major provisions of the Clean Air Act of 1990.
☐ Explain how pollution rights are traded under the Clean Air Act.

☐ Describe the solid waste disposal problem and the reason for interest in recycling.
☐ Define the meaning of "information failures."
☐ Explain how inadequate information about sellers can cause market failures and give two examples of ways that the government resolves these problems.
☐ Describe how inadequate information about buyers can cause moral hazard, adverse selection, and workplace safety problems and give examples.
☐ Cite an example of a way that information difficulties are overcome without government intervention.

■ **CHAPTER OUTLINE**

1. The characteristics of a private good are that it is divisible and subject to the exclusion principle, where those who are unable to pay for the good or service are excluded from enjoying the benefits of the provision of the good or service; in contrast, a public (collective) good such as national defense is indivisible and not subject to exclusion— once it is provided for one person it is available for all.
  a. The demand for a public good is determined by summing the prices that people are willing to pay collectively for the last unit of the public good at each quantity demanded, whereas the demand for a private good is determined by summing the quantities demanded at each price.
  b. In the market for public goods:
  (1) The demand curve is downsloping because of the law of diminishing marginal utility; it reflects the monetary value of the perceived benefits of additional units that are equally available to people for joint consumption.
  (2) The supply curve is upsloping because of the law of diminishing returns; additional units supplied reflect increasing marginal costs.
  (3) The optimal allocation is determined by the intersection of the supply and demand curves:
  (a) if the marginal benefit exceeds the marginal cost, there is an underallocation of a public good;
  (b) but if the marginal benefit exceeds the marginal cost there will be an overallocation.
  (c) Only when the marginal benefits equal the marginal costs is there an optimal allocation of public goods.
  c. Benefit-cost analysis may be employed by government to determine whether it should employ resources for a project and to decide on the total quantity of resources it should devote to a project.
  (1) Additional resources should be devoted to a project only so long as the marginal benefit to society from using the additional resources for the project exceeds the marginal costs to society of the additional resources, or where the total benefits minus the total costs are at a maximum.

(2) Government encounters the problem of accurately measuring the benefits and the costs in this type of analysis.

2. Market failure can arise from externalities or spillovers, where a third party bears a portion of the cost associated with the production or consumption of a good or service. Negative externalities result in the overallocation of resources to a commodity and positive externalities lead to an underallocation of resources.

a. Individual bargaining can be used to correct negative externalities or to encourage positive externalities. The *Coase theorem* suggests that private negotiations rather than government intervention should be the course of action if there is clear ownership of the property, the number of people involved is small, and the costs of bargaining is minimal. When these conditions do not hold, however, it may be necessary for government intervention.

b. It is possible to resolve disputes that arise from externalities through the legal system. This system defines property rights and specifies liability rules that can be used for lawsuits to cover externality disputes. This method also has limitations because of expense, length of time to resolve the dispute, and the uncertainty of the outcomes.

c. When there is the potential for severe harm to common resources, such as air or water, and when the situation involves a large number of people, two types of government intervention may be necessary.

(1) Direct controls uses legislation to ban or to limit the activities that produce a negative externality. These actions reduce the supply of the products that create the negative externalities to levels that are allocatively efficient.

(2) Specific taxes are also applied to productive activity that create negative externalities. These taxes increase the cost of production, and thus decrease the supply to levels that are allocatively efficient.

d. Another solution has been to create a market for externality rights, or to internalize the spillover cost or benefit in a private market. For example, with a pollution problem in a region:

(1) The government (a pollution-control agency) might set the limit for the amount of pollution permitted, which means that the supply curve is perfectly inelastic (vertical) at some level of pollution;

(2) The demand curve would reflect the willingness of polluters to pay for the right to pollute at different prices for pollution rights;

(3) and the price for pollution rights would be determined by the intersection of the demand and supply curves.

(4) Given a fixed supply curve, an increase in demand, because of economic growth in the region, would increase the price of pollution rights.

e. In most cases, it is not allocatively efficient to eliminate completely the production of goods that create negative externalities. From society's perspective, the optimal reduction of a negative externality occurs where the marginal cost to society and the marginal benefit of reducing the externality are equal (**MB** = **MC**). Over time, there may be shifts in the marginal cost and marginal benefit curves that change the optimal level.

3. Pollution provides a prime example of a major negative externality for our industrial society.

a. The dimensions of the problem are extensive, and include air pollution, water pollution, toxic waste, solid-waste disposal, oil spills, and potential changes to the climate.

b. The causes of the pollution problem relate to the *law of conservation of matter and energy*. Matter used for production of goods and services ultimately gets transformed into waste (in the form of matter or energy) after it is consumed. The waste creates a problem if there is an imbalance between it and the capacity of the environment to reabsorb the waste. Population density, rising income, changing technology, and economic incentives are all factors contributing to the pollution problem.

c. Antipollution policy in the United States is complex.

(1) The *Superfund law of 1980* uses direct controls and specific taxes to correct the toxic waste problem.

(2) The *Clean Air Act of 1990* uses direct controls through uniform emission standards to limit the amount of air pollution. The act covers toxic chemicals, urban smog, motor vehicle emissions, ozone depletion, and acid rain. The act also permits some trading of pollution rights to reduce acid rain.

d. Solid waste is usually deposited in garbage dumps or it is incinerated. Dumps and incinerators, however, create negative externalities, and they are becoming increasingly expensive. The situation has created a market for recycled items to help reduce this pollution problem. Government can use either demand or supply incentives to encourage recycling as an alternative to dumping or incineration of solid waste.

4. Economic inefficiency from information failures can occur in markets.

a. When information about sellers is incomplete, inaccurate, or very costly, then there will be market failures. For example, in the market for gasoline, consumers need accurate information about the amount and quality of gasoline they purchase. In the market for medical service, it is important that consumers have some assurances about the credentials of physicians. These information failures are remedied by government through such actions as the establishment measurement standards, and by testing and licensing.

b. Inadequate information about buyers creates market failures.

(1) A market may produce less than the optimal amount of goods and services from society's perspective because of a moral hazard problem. This problem results when buyers alter their behavior and increase the costs of sellers. For example, the provision of insurance may cause the insured to be less cautious.

(2) There is also an adverse selection problem that occurs in many markets. In the case of insurance, the buyers most likely to need or benefit from insurance are the ones most likely to purchase it. These higher-risk buyers impose higher costs on sellers. Sellers then screen out the higher-risk buyers, but this action reduces the population covered by insurance in the private market. In some cases, government may establish a social insurance system that is designed to cover a much broader group of the population than would be covered by the private insurers, such as with social security.

(3) Market failures occur in resource markets when there is inadequate information for workers about the health hazards or safety of a workplace. Government can act to correct these problems by publishing health and safety information, or by forcing businesses to provide more information. The more typical approach to this problem has been the enforcement of standards for health and safety on the job.

c. Government does not always need to intervene in the private market to address information problems. Businesses can adopt policies to correct these problems, and some firms or other organizations can specialize in providing important market information for buyers or sellers.

■ **IMPORTANT TERMS**

Public good

Benefit-cost analysis

Marginal cost equals marginal benefit rule

Positive or negative externality (spillover)

Coase theorem

Market for externality rights

Optimal amount of externality reduction

Law of conservation of matter and energy

Superfund law of 1980

Clean Air Act of 1990

Moral hazard problem

Adverse selection problem

■ **FILL-IN QUESTIONS**

1. A public good:

a. is one which is _____ and for which the _____ principle does not apply; and

b. has a market demand curve that will either be _____ or significantly _____ because people will not make voluntary payments for public goods in the marketplace;

c. but, if you knew people's preferences for a public good, you could determine the demand for it by adding the _____ people collectively are willing to pay for the last unit of the public good at each quantity demanded.

2. The demand curve for a public good slopes downward because of the law of diminishing marginal (returns, utility) _____; the supply curve for a public good is upsloping because of the law of diminishing marginal _____. The collective demand curve is based on perceived marginal (benefits, costs) _____ that are equally available to people for joint consumption; the supply curve for a public good reflects marginal _____

3. The optimal quantity of a public good will be shown by the _____ of the collective demand curve and the supply curve for a public good, which means that _____ equals _____. When the perceived marginal benefit for a public good is greater than the marginal cost, there will be an (overallocation, underallocation) _____ of the public good; but when the perceived marginal benefit is less than the marginal cost, there will be an _____ of the public good.

4. In applying benefit-cost analysis, government should employ more resources in the production of public goods if the marginal (costs, benefits) _____ from the additional public goods exceed the marginal _____ that result from having fewer private goods. The _____ rule will determine which plan from a benefit-cost analysis will result in the (maximum, minimum) _____ net benefit to society.

5. When government employs benefit-cost analysis, it often finds it difficult to _____ the benefits and costs of a program, which means that the analysis can be difficult to apply.

6. One of the objectives of government is to correct for externalities or _____ that result in a cost or a benefit for an individual or a group that is a third party to a market transaction. When negative

_____ are present there will be an (over-allocation, underallocation) _____ of resources going to the production of that good, whereas there will be an _____ of resources for the production of that good with positive _____ _____.

7. The _____ theorem suggests when there are negative or positive _____ in situations where the _____ of property is defined, the number of people involved is _____, and the costs of bargaining are _____, then government intervention (is, is not) _____ required.

8. This legal system is also important for settling externality disputes between individuals because settling it defines _____ rights and specifies _____ rules that can be used for lawsuits. This method has limitations because of the dollar _____, the length of time, and _____ of the result.

9. Government may intervene to resolve externality problems by using direct _____ in the form of legislation that restricts business activity. In other cases, the government may impose specific _____ or _____ charges.

10. One solution to a negative externality problem such as pollution is to create a _____ for externality rights.
 a. For example, in a region there might be a set amount of air pollution accepted, so the supply curve for the air pollution rights would be perfectly (elastic, inelastic) _____.
 b. The demand curve for air pollution rights would be _____sloping and would intersect the supply curve to determine the _____ for the right to pollute the air in that area.
 c. If the demand for air pollution rights increased over time, then _____ would rise but the quantity supplied would _____.

11. Reducing negative externalities comes at a "_____" and therefore society must decide how much of a decrease it wants to "_____." The optimal

reduction of a negative externality occurs where the society's marginal _____ is equal to society's marginal _____.

12. The pollution problem stems from the law of _____. Matter used for production of goods and services ultimately gets transformed into _____, which is another form of matter or energy that the environment may not be able to re-_____. This pollution problem is the result of increases in population _____, rising _____, changes in _____, and the absence of economic _____ to refrain from polluting.

13. To correct a toxic waste problem, Congress passed the _____ law of 1980. The _____ Act of 1990 imposes uniform _____ standards to limit the amount of air pollution. The act also permits some _____ of pollution rights to reduce acid rain.

14. An alternative to the dumping or incineration of solid waste is _____. Government policies can be enacted to provide incentives on the _____-side or the _____-side of the market.

15. Markets can produce information failures when information about sellers is incomplete or obtaining the information is very _____. For example, in a market for gasoline, the government establishes _____ for measurement or quality. In the medical market, the government protects consumers by _____ physicians.

16. Inadequate information about buyers can lead to two problems. First, if a market situation arises where buyers alter their behavior and increase the cost to sellers, then a moral _____ problem has been created. Second, if buyers withhold information from sellers that would impose a large cost on sellers, then an adverse _____ problem has been created. The first problem occurs (at the same time, after) _____ a person makes a purchase, but the second problem occurs _____ the buyer makes a purchase.

17. Another example of information failure occurs in labor markets where there is incomplete or inadequate information about workplace _____. The government will intervene in these situations to publish _____ or to enforce _____

18. Private businesses overcome some information problems about the reliability or quality through such actions as _____ for products, or the _____ of businesses that makes them more uniform. Some businesses and organizations also collect and _____ product information that is useful for buyers. Despite these actions, there may still be need for government actions to correct information problems and to promote an _____ allocation of society's scarce resources.

■ PROBLEMS AND PROJECTS

1. Data on two individuals' preferences for a public good are reflected in the table below. P_1 and P_2 represent the prices individuals 1 and 2, the only two people in the society, are willing to pay for each quantity.

Quantity	P_1	P_2
1	$6	$6
2	5	5
3	4	4
4	3	3
5	2	2
6	1	1

a. Complete the table below showing the collective demand for the public good in this society.

Q_d	Price	Q_s
1	$_____	7
2	_____	6
3	_____	5
4	_____	4
5	_____	3
6	_____	2

b. Given the supply schedule for this public good as shown by the Q_s column, the optimal quantity of this public good is _____ units and the optimal price is $_____

c. When 3 units of this public good are produced, the perceived marginal benefit is $_____ and the marginal cost is $_____; there will be an (overallocation, underallocation) _____ of resources to this public good.

d. When 6 units of this public good are produced, the perceived marginal benefit is $_____ and the marginal cost is $_____; there is an (underallocation, overallocation) _____ of resources to this public good.

2. Imagine that a state government is considering the construction of a new highway to link its two largest cities. Its estimate of the total costs and the total benefits of building 2, 4, 6, and 8 lane highways between the two cities are shown in the table at the bottom of the page. (All figures are in millions of dollars.)

a. Compute the marginal cost and the marginal benefit of the 2, 4, 6, and 8 lane highways.

b. Will it benefit the state to allocate resources to construct a highway? _____

c. If the state builds a highway:

(1) It should be a _____ lane highway.

(2) The total cost will be $_____

(3) The total benefit will be $_____

(4) The net benefit to the state will be $_____

3. Assume the atmosphere of Cuyahoga County, Ohio (the Cleveland metropolitan area), is able to reabsorb 1500 tons of pollutants per year. The schedule at the top of the next page shows the price polluters would be willing to pay for the right to dispose of 1 ton of pollutants per year and the total quantity of pollutants they would wish to dispose of at each price.

a. If there were no emission fee, polluters would put _____ tons of pollutants in the air each year; and this quantity of pollutants would exceed the

Project	Total cost	Marginal cost	Total benefit	Marginal benefit
No highway	$ 0		$ 0	
2 lane highway	500	$_____	650	$_____
4 lane highway	680	_____	750	_____
6 lane highway	760	_____	800	_____
8 lane highway	860	_____	825	_____

Price (per ton of pollutant rights)	Total quantity of pollutant rights demanded (tons)
$ 0	4,000
1,000	3,500
2,000	3,000
3,000	2,500
4,000	2,000
5,000	1,500
6,000	1,000
7,000	500

ability of nature to reabsorb them by _____ tons.

b. To reduce pollution to the capacity of the atmosphere to recycle pollutants, an emission fee of $_____ per ton should be set.

c. Were this emission fee set, the total emission fees set would be $_____

d. Were the quantity of pollution rights demanded at each price to increase by 500 tons, the emission fee could be increased by $_____ and total emission fees collected would increase by $_____

■ **SELF-TEST**

Circle the T if the statement is true; the F if it is false.

1. The exclusion principle applies to public goods but it does not apply to private goods. **T F**

2. When determining the demand for a public good you add the prices people are willing to pay collectively for the last unit of the public good at each quantity demanded. **T F**

3. When the marginal benefit of a public good exceeds the marginal cost there will be an overallocation of resources to that public good use. **T F**

4. The optimal allocation of a public good is determined by the rule that marginal cost (MC) equals marginal revenue (MR). **T F**

5. Reducing government spending is the same as economy in government. **T F**

6. In practice is it usually quite simple to estimate the costs and benefits of a project financed by government. **T F**

7. There is an overallocation of resources to the production of a commodity when negative externalities are present. **T F**

8. The Coase theorem suggests that government intervention is required whenever there are negative or positive externalities. **T F**

9. Lawsuits and liability rules create externality problems instead of helping to resolve them. **T F**

10. Taxes that are imposed on businesses which create an externality will lower the marginal cost of production and increase supply. **T F**

11. One solution to the negative externalities caused by pollution is to create a market for pollution rights where the social costs of pollution are turned into private costs. **T F**

12. In the market for pollution rights, if a government agency sets a fixed level for pollution, the supply curve of pollution rights will be perfectly elastic. **T F**

13. If a society has marginal costs for pollution abatement of $10 and the marginal benefit of pollution abatement is $8, then to achieve an optimal amount of the pollution it should increase the amount of pollution abatement. **T F**

14. Pollution is caused almost exclusively by profit-seeking business firms. **T F**

15. The Superfund law of 1980 uses direct controls and specific taxes to address the problem of toxic waste. **T F**

16. The Clean Air Act of 1990 permits the trading of emission credits between electric utilities and the trading of pollution rights between polluters. **T F**

17. If the government provides a subsidy to producers of recycled paper products, then the demand for recycled paper *products* should increase. **T F**

18. The inspection of meat products by the Federal government for quality is justified on the grounds that it reduces the costs of obtaining information in the market for meat. **T F**

19. If the provision of government health insurance encourages people to take more health risks, then it has created a moral hazard. **T F**

20. Adverse selection problems primarily result when the government begins enforcing standards for safety in the workplace. **T F**

Circle the letter that corresponds to the best answer.

1. How do public goods differ from private goods? Public goods:
   (a) are divisible
   (b) are subject to the exclusion principle
   (c) are divisible and subject to the exclusion principle
   (d) are *not* divisible and *not* subject to the exclusion principle

Answer the next four questions (2, 3, 4, and 5) on the basis of the following information for a public good. P₁ and P₂ represent the prices individuals 1 and 2, the only two people in the society are willing to pay for each quantity of a public good. Qₛ represents the supply curve for the public good in the society.

Quantity	P₁	P₂	Qₛ
0	0	0	6
1	0	1	5
2	1	2	4
3	2	3	3
4	3	4	2
5	4	5	1
6	5	6	0

2. This society is willing to pay what amount for the third unit of the public good?
  (a) $7
  (b) $6
  (c) $5
  (d) $4

3. This society is willing to pay what amount for the fifth unit of the public good?
  (a) $11
  (b) $10
  (c) $9
  (d) $8

4. Given the supply curve **Qₛ**, the optimal price and quantity of the public good in this society will be:
  (a) $9 and 5 units
  (b) $7 and 4 units
  (c) $5 and 3 units
  (d) $3 and 2 units

5. If this good were a private good instead of a public good, the total quantity demanded at the $4 price would be:
  (a) 9 units
  (b) 8 units
  (c) 7 units
  (d) 6 units

Answer the next three questions (6, 7, and 8) for a public good on the basis of the graph at the top of the next column.

6. Where the marginal benefits equal the collective marginal costs is represented by point:
  (a) *b*
  (b) *c*
  (c) *d*
  (d) *e*

7. Which line segment would indicate the amount by which the marginal benefit of this public good is less than the marginal cost?
  (a) *ab*
  (b) *bc*

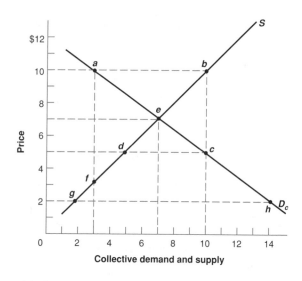

Collective demand and supply

  (c) *fa*
  (d) *gh*

8. If 3 units of this public good are produced there will be an:
  (a) overallocation of resources to this public good because the marginal cost of $10 is greater than the marginal benefit of $3
  (b) overallocation of resources to this public good because the marginal cost of $10 is greater than the marginal benefit of $5
  (c) underallocation of resources to this public good because the marginal benefit of $10 is greater than the marginal cost of $5
  (d) underallocation of resources to this public good because the marginal benefit of $10 is greater than the marginal benefit of $3

9. Assume that a government is considering a new antipollution program and it may choose to include in this program any number of four different projects. The marginal cost and the marginal benefits of each of the four projects are given below. What total amount should this government spend on the antipollution program?
  (a) $2 million
  (b) $7 million
  (c) $17 million
  (d) $37 million

Project	Marginal cost	Marginal benefit
# 1	$ 2 million	$ 5 million
# 2	5 million	7 million
# 3	10 million	9 million
# 4	20 million	15 million

10. One condition for the Coase theorem to hold is that there be:
  (a) clear ownership of the property rights
  (b) a large number of people involved in the dispute

(c) active government intervention to solve the externality problem

(d) a sizeable cost for bargaining to settle the dispute between the private parties

11. Which of the following would be the most effective strategy for addressing a problem such as acid rain which stems from the pollution of coal-burning electric utilities?

(a) private negotiations between property owners and the utilities

(b) lawsuits filed against the utilities by property owners

(c) asking consumers to reduce electricity consumption

(d) government taxes on utility emissions

12. If government were to sell pollution rights, an increase in the demand for pollution rights will:

(a) increase both the quantity of pollutants discharged and the market price of pollution rights

(b) increase the quantity discharged and have no effect on the market price

(c) have no effect on the quantity discharged and increase the market price

(d) have no effect on either the quantity discharged or the market price

Use the following table to answer the next three questions (13, 14, and 15). The data in the table show the marginal costs and marginal benefits to a city for five different levels of pollution abatement.

Quantity of pollution abatement	Marginal cost	Marginal benefit
500 tons	$500,000	$100,000
400 tons	300,000	150,000
300 tons	200,000	200,000
200 tons	100,000	300,000
100 tons	50,000	400,000
0 tons	25,000	800,000

13. If the city seeks an optimal reduction of the externality, then it will select how many tons of pollution abatement?

(a) 0
(b) 300
(c) 400
(d) 500

14. If the marginal benefit of pollution abatement increased by $150,000 at each level because of the community's desire to attract more profitable and cleaner industry, then the optimal level of pollution abatement in tons would be:

(a) 200
(b) 300
(c) 400
(d) 500

15. What would cause the optimal level of pollution abatement to be 200 tons?

(a) technological improvement in production that decreases marginal costs by $150,000 at each level

(b) an increase in the health risk from this pollution that increases marginal benefits by $200,000 at each level

(c) the need to replace old pollution monitoring equipment with new equipment that increases marginal costs by $200,000 at each level

(d) reduction in the public demand for pollution control that decreases marginal benefits by $100,000 at each level

16. Which of the following has **not** contributed to the pollution problem in the United States?

(a) increasing population density
(b) rising prices for gasoline and oil
(c) an improved standard of living
(d) more use of plastic and aluminum containers

17. Results from the Superfund law of 1980 indicate that it:

(a) reduced major sources of pollution by 20%, but the fund is now exhausted and reauthorization is uncertain

(b) raised $10 billion from the chemical industry to treat toxic waste, but progress is slow and legal negotiations over dump sites drain funds

(c) made recycling the most economical method for handling waste in many communities, but citizen compliance is limited and depends on economic incentives

(d) established uniform emission standards that are being paid for out of the fund, but legal action is sometimes necessary to get cooperation from companies

18. The acid-rain provisions of the Clean Air Act of 1990:

(a) permit the exchange of pollution rights within firms and between firms in an area

(b) set stricter limits on the discharge of chlorofluorocarbons (CFCs) for the 1990s

(c) fund research on applications of the law of conservation of matter and energy

(d) force companies to install "maximum achievable control technologies" by the year 2000

19. Which of the following would tend to increase the demand for recycled paper?

(a) an increase in the price of regular paper
(b) an increase in taxes on all paper production
(c) a decrease in interest in protecting the environment
(d) a decrease in subsidies for all paper production

20. If Congress adopted an increase in government insurance on bank deposits, this action would create a moral hazard problem because it may:

(a) lead to careful screening of depositors and the source of their funds

(b) restrict the amount of deposits made by bank customers

(c) encourage bank officers to make riskier loans
(d) reduce bank investments in real estate

■ DISCUSSION QUESTIONS

1. What are the basic characteristics of public goods? How do public goods differ from private goods? Contrast how you construct the demand curve for a public good with the procedure for constructing the demand curve for a private good using individual demand schedules.

2. Explain the relationship between the marginal cost and benefit of a public good when there is an underallocation, an overallocation, and an optimal allocation of resources for the provision of the public good.

3. Describe benefit-cost analysis and state the rules used to make decisions from a marginal and a total perspective. What is the major problem encountered when benefit-cost analysis is utilized by government?

4. What are externalities and spillovers? Give examples of positive externalities and negative externalities.

5. Under what conditions might it be worthwhile for the government to intervene or not to intervene to settle a spillover problem? Should the government intervene in an externality dispute between two property owners over the use of one party's land? Should government intervene in the case of acid rain?

6. How do lawsuits and liability rules resolve externality problems? What type of actions would the government take to reduce externalities? How would these actions be justified?

7. How do you create a market for externality rights in the case of pollution? What are some advantages and limitations of this approach to the pollution problem?

8. What rule can society use to determine the optimal level of pollution abatement? What are the problems with this approach?

9. Outline the dimensions of the pollution problem in the United States. Why has this problem developed? What is the specific cause of the pollution problem?

10. Discuss the major features of the Superfund law of 1980 and the Clean Air Act of 1990. What features of a market for externalities are built into the Clean Air Act?

11. Why is solid waste disposal of national concern? How does recycling serve as a partial alternative to it? How does a market for recyclable items work?

12. Describe how inadequate information about sellers creates market problems for buyers. Give examples.

13. Explain what is meant by a "moral hazard problem" and describe how it affects sellers. What are some examples of the application of this problem?

14. How can the market for insurance result in an adverse selection problem? What actions might government take to correct this information problem?

15. In what way does workplace safety become an information problem? How might this problem be resolved by government or by businesses?

■ ANSWERS

Chapter 18 Government and Market Failure: Public Goods, the Environment, and Information Problems

FILL-IN QUESTIONS

1. *a.* indivisible, exclusion; *b.* nonexistent, understated; *c.* prices

2. utility, returns, benefits, costs

3. intersection, marginal benefit, marginal cost (either order); underallocation, overallocation

4. benefits, costs, marginal benefit–marginal cost, maximum

5. measure

6. spillovers, externalities (spillovers), overallocation, underallocation, externalities

7. Coase, externalities (spillovers), ownership, small, negligible (minor), is not

8. property, liability, cost, uncertainty

9. controls, taxes, emissions

10. market, *a.* inelastic; *b.* down, price; *c.* price, remain constant (stays the same)

11. price, buy, benefit, cost (either order for last two)

12. conservation of matter and energy, waste, absorb, density, incomes, technology, incentives

13. Superfund, Clean Air, emission, trading

14. recycling, demand, supply (either order for last two)

15. costly, standards, licensing

16. hazard, selection, after, at the same time

17. safety, information, standards

18. warranties, franchising, publish, efficient

PROBLEMS AND PROJECTS

1. *a.* $12, 10, 8, 6, 4, 2; *b.* 4, 6; *c.* 8, 4, underallocation; *d.* 2, 10, overallocation

2. *a.* marginal cost: $500, $180, $80, $100; marginal benefit: $650, $100, $50, $25; *b.* yes; *c.* (1) 2, (2) $500, (3) $650, (4) $150

3. *a.* 4,000, 2,500; *b.* 5,000; *c.* 7,500,000; *d.* 1,000, 1,500,000

SELF-TEST

1. F, p. 304
2. T, pp. 304–305
3. F, p. 305
4. F, p. 305
5. F, p. 306
6. F, p. 307
7. T, p. 307
8. F, p. 307
9. F, p. 308
10. F, p. 309

11. T, p. 309
12. F, p. 309
13. F, p. 311
14. F, p. 313
15. T, p. 313
16. T, p. 314
17. F, p. 316
18. T, p. 317
19. T, p. 318
20. F, p. 318

1. *d*, p. 304
2. *a*, pp. 304–305
3. *c*, pp. 304–305
4. *b*, p. 305
5. *a*, p. 304
6. *d*, p. 306
7. *b*, p. 306
8. *d*, p. 306
9. *b*, p. 306
10. *a*, p. 307

11. *d*, p. 308
12. *c*, p. 310
13. *b*, p. 311
14. *c*, p. 311
15. *c*, p. 311
16. *b*, p. 312
17. *b*, p. 313
18. *a*, p. 314
19. *a*, p. 315
20. *c*, p. 318

DISCUSSION QUESTIONS

1. p. 304
2. pp. 305–306
3. pp. 304–307
4. p. 307
5. pp. 307–308
6. pp. 308–309
7. pp. 309–310
8. pp. 310–311

9. pp. 312–313
10. pp. 313–314
11. pp. 314–316
12. p. 317
13. p. 318
14. pp. 318–319
15. p. 319

Public Choice Theory and Taxation

Although both Chapters 18 and 19 analyze the role of government in the economy, the two chapters look at government from an opposite perspective. Chapter 18 discussed market failure issues and what actions government takes to correct these market problems. Chapter 19 now examines government failure, or why government makes inefficient use of the scarce resources. For this explanation, you will first be introduced to *public choice theory*, or the economic analysis of public decision making. Later in the chapter you will learn more about *public finance*, which covers such topics as the principles of taxation and the economic effects of specific taxes.

Many public decisions are made by majority voting, but this decision-making procedure may distort the true preferences of society. In the first section of the chapter you will find out how majority voting may lead to inefficient outcomes in the provision of public goods. In some choices, the benefits of a public good are greater than the costs, but the majority votes against it. In other choices, the benefits outweigh the costs, but the provision of the public good is supported by the majority vote. Although actions by interest groups and the use of logrolling may tend to reduce inefficiencies created by majority rule, the final result depends on the circumstances of the decision.

There is also a paradox from majority voting that you should note. Depending on how a vote or election is arranged, it is possible for majority rule to produce choices that are inconsistent with the ranking of preferences among voters. You should spend time working through the example in the textbook so you understand how opposing outcomes can result from majority rule. You should also learn why the median voters strongly influence the result of a vote or an election when there is majority rule. In fact, the median-voter model is very useful for explaining why the middle position on issues is often adopted in public decisions.

The second section of Chapter 19 discusses other reasons for inefficiencies by government. Here you will learn that: (1) special-interest effects and rent-seeking behavior impair public decisions; (2) politicians often have a strong incentive to adopt an economic policy that has clear benefits to voters, but hidden or uncertain costs; (3) public choice is more limited and less flexible than private choice because it entails voting for or accepting a "bundle" of programs, some good and some bad; and (4) bureaucratic inefficiencies in the public sector arise from the lack of the economic incentives and competitive pressures found in the private sector.

Chapter 19 then switches from public choice theory to public finance for further insights about government, and, in particular, about taxation. In the third section of the chapter you learn the economic principles used in levying taxes. You also learn about the regressive, progressive, and proportional classifications for taxes, and how the major taxes of the United States fit into this classification scheme.

The incidence and efficiency loss of a tax are described in the fourth section of the chapter. Incidence means "who ends up paying the tax." As you will discover, the elasticities of demand and of supply determine how much of the tax will be paid by buyers and how much of it will be paid by sellers. No matter who pays the tax, however, there is an efficiency loss to society from the tax, the size of which is also affected by the elasticities of demand and of supply. With this knowledge, you are now ready to study the probable incidence of five taxes—personal income, corporate income, sales, excise, and property—that are used to raise most of the tax revenue for government in the United States.

The fifth and sixth sections of the chapter discuss the American tax structure and explore the question of whether an increase in the size of the role of government reduces or expands the freedoms of individuals. The authors present the conservative case of those who argue that expanded government reduces personal freedom and the liberal case of those who contend that it may create individual freedom.

■ CHECKLIST

When you have studied this chapter you should be able to:

☐ Explain the purpose of public choice theory and the topics it covers.

☐ Illustrate how majority voting procedures can produce inefficient outcomes either when the vote is "yes" or the vote is "no."

☐ Describe how interest groups and political logrolling affect the efficiency of outcomes from voting.

☐ Give an example of the paradox of voting.

☐ Describe the median-voter model, its applicability to the real world, and two implications of the model.

☐ Explain the meaning of the phrase "public sector failure" and cite examples.

☐ Give an example of a special-interest effect and an example of rent-seeking behavior.

☐ Describe the economic problem that arises when there are clear benefits and hidden costs to a political decision.

☐ Compare the type of choices made by consumers in the private market with the type of choices made by citizens.

☐ Contrast the incentives for economic efficiency in private business with those found in the public agencies and bureaucracies.

☐ Distinguish between the ability-to-pay principle of taxation and the benefits-received principle of taxation.

☐ Determine whether a tax is regressive, progressive, or proportional when you are given the necessary data.

☐ Describe the progressivity, regressivity, and proportionality of the five major kinds of taxes used in the United States.

☐ Illustrate with the use of a supply and demand graph how the price elasticity of demand and supply affect tax incidence.

☐ Describe the efficiency loss of a tax using a supply and demand graph.

☐ Explain the effects of price elasticity of demand or supply on the efficiency loss of a tax.

☐ Evaluate the probable incidence of the personal income, corporate income, sales and excise, and property taxes.

☐ Describe recent estimates of the tax burden in the American economy, the progressivity of the tax structure, and the effect of changes in the tax system on the distribution of income.

☐ Explain two major tax issues that have been discussed in recent years.

☐ Present the case for and present the case against the proposition that an expanded public sector reduces personal freedom.

■ IMPORTANT TERMS

Public choice theory
Public finance
Logrolling
Paradox of voting
Median-voter model

Public sector failure
Special-interest effect
Rent-seeking behavior
Benefits-received principle
Ability-to-pay principle

Average tax rate
Progressive tax
Regressive tax
Proportional tax
Personal income tax
Sales tax
Excise tax
Corporate income tax
Payroll tax

Property tax
Elasticity
Tax incidence
Excess burden of a tax
Tax Reform Act (TRA) of 1986
Value-added tax (VAT)
Fallacy of limited decisions

■ CHAPTER OUTLINE

1. Critics of the government argue that it has failed to find solutions for many problems of society and that it is very inefficient in its use of society's scarce resources. This chapter first analyzes economic decisions made by government from a *public choice* perspective, and then turns to the issue of *public finance*, and examines the economics of taxation.

2. Most decisions about government activity are made collectively through majority voting, but the procedure is not without problems:

a. Voting outcomes may be economically inefficient in cases where voters reject a public good whose total benefits exceed total costs, or fail to reject a public good whose total costs are greater than the total benefits. These inefficiencies can be resolved sometimes by:

(1) the formation of special interest groups that work to overcome inefficient outcomes,

(2) or, through the use of logrolling, where votes are traded to secure a favorable and efficient decision;

(3) but logrolling can also lead to inefficient decisions.

b. The paradox of voting suggests that the public may not be able to make consistent choices that reflect its preferences.

c. Based on the median-voter model it is suggested that the person or groups holding the middle position on an issue will likely determine the outcome from a majority rule election. Public decisions tend to reflect the median view.

3. Public choice theory suggests that the public sector has failed because the process it uses to make decisions is inherently weak and results in an economically inefficient allocation of resources.

a. The weakness of the decision-making process in the public sector and the resulting inefficient allocation of resources is often the result of pressures exerted on Congress and the bureaucracy by special interests and may be fostered by a system which might encourage rent-seeking behavior, whereby wealth is transferred to one group at the expense of another group or to society as a whole.

b. Those seeking election to public office frequently favor (oppose) programs whose benefits (costs) are clear and immediate and whose costs (benefits) are uncertain and deferred, even when the benefits are less (greater) than the costs.

c. When the citizen must vote for candidates who represent different but complete programs, the voter is unable to select those parts of a program which he or she favors and to reject the other parts of the program.

d. It is argued that the public sector (unlike the private sector) is inefficient because those employed there are offered no incentive to be efficient; and because there is no way to measure efficiency in the public sector.

e. Just as the private or market sector of the economy does not allocate resources perfectly, the public sector does not perform its functions perfectly; and the imperfections of both sectors make it difficult to determine which sector will provide a particular good or service more efficiently.

4. The financing of public goods and services through taxation also raises an important question about how the tax burden is allocated among people.

a. The benefits-received principle and the ability-to-pay principle are widely employed to determine how the tax bill should be apportioned among the economy's citizens.

(1) The benefits-received principle suggests that those people who benefit most from public goods should pay for them.

(2) The ability-to-pay principle states that taxes for the support of public goods should be tied to the income and wealth of people, or their ability to pay.

b. Taxes can be classified as progressive, regressive, or proportional according to the way in which the average tax *rate* changes as incomes change.

(1) The average tax rate increases as income increases with a progressive tax, it decreases as income increases with a regressive tax, and it remains the same as income increases with a proportional tax.

(2) In the United States, the personal income tax tends to be mildly progressive, the corporate income tax is proportional, and the payroll and property taxes are regressive.

5. Tax incidence and the efficiency loss of a tax are also important in discussion of public finance.

a. The price elasticities of demand and supply determine the incidence of a sales or excise tax.

(1) The imposition of such a tax on a commodity decreases the supply of the commodity and increases its price. The amount of the price increase is the portion of the tax paid by the buyer; the seller pays the rest.

(2) The price elasticities of demand and supply affect the portions paid by buyers and sellers: the more elastic (inelastic) the demand for the commodity, the greater (smaller) is the portion paid by the seller; the more elas-

tic (inelastic) the supply of the commodity, the greater (smaller) is the portion paid by the buyer.

b. There is an efficiency loss from taxation. This loss occurs because there is a reduction in output, despite the fact that the marginal benefits of that output are greater than the marginal cost. Thus, the consumption and production of the taxed commodity has been reduced below the optimal level by the tax.

(1) The degree of the efficiency loss of a sales or an excise tax depends on the elasticities of supply and demand: other things equal, the greater the elasticity of supply and demand, the greater the efficiency loss of a sales or an excise tax; consequently, the total tax burden to society may not be equal even though two taxes produce equal tax revenue.

c. A tax levied upon one person or group of persons may be shifted partially or completely to another person or group; and to the extent that a tax can be shifted or passed on through lower prices paid or higher prices received, its incidence is passed on. The incidence of the four major types of taxes is only probable and is not known for certain.

d. Because some taxes levied in the American economy and progressive and some are regressive it appears that the American tax system is only slightly progressive, has very little effect on the distribution of income in the United States, and has become less progressive over the past 20 years; but estimates of the progressivity of the tax system depend on the assumed incidence of the various taxes; and the transfer payments made by governments do reduce income inequality in the United States.

6. In recent years two tax-related issues have been debated in the United States.

a. How to "reindustrialize" the American economy by significantly increasing spending for modern machinery is the first of these issues; and it has been suggested that the corporate income tax be reduced and a *value-added tax* on consumer goods be levied.

b. Whether higher tax rates or new taxes are required to reduce large and persistent Federal budget deficits is the second tax-related issue.

7. The nature and amount of government activity and the extent of individual freedom may be related to each other.

a. Conservatives argue that the cost of government entails not only the economic cost from a growing public sector, but also a cost in terms of reduced economic freedom for the individual because government now makes more of the decisions over economic activity.

b. Liberals counter that the conservative position is subject to the fallacy of limited decisions. If government activity expands, that does not necessarily mean that there is less private decision making because the range of choices can be expanded by increased governmental activity.

■ FILL-IN QUESTIONS

1. The economic analysis of government decisions and the economic problems created by the public sector are topics studied under the theory of public (finance, choice) _____, while the study of public spending and taxation would be the subject of public _____

2. Many collective decisions are made on the basis of majority voting, which has two problems:

   a. This system of voting leads to economic _____, where there might be an _____ or a _____ devoted to a particular public good; but the problem might be resolved through the influence of _____ groups or possibly through _____;

   b. the other problem is the _____, a situation where the public may not be able to rank its preferences with consistency.

3. There are also insights into majority voting based on the _____ model, where the person holding the _____ position is likely to determine the outcome from an election.

4. When governments use resources to attempt to solve social problems and the employment of these resources does not result in solutions to these problems there has been _____ sector _____

5. Four possible reasons for inefficiency in the public sector are:

   a. that government instead of promoting the general interests (or welfare) of its citizens may promote the _____ interest of small groups in the economy and may promote _____ behavior;

   b. that the benefits from a program or project are often (clear, hidden) _____ and its costs are frequently _____;

   c. that individual voters are unable to _____ _____ the particular quantities of each public good and service they wish the public sector to provide;

   d. that there are weak _____ to be efficient in the public sector and no way to _____ the efficiency of the public sector.

6. Despite the recognition of inefficiency in the public sector:

   a. It should be recognized that there is also inefficiency in the _____ of the economy;

   b. the institutions employed in both sectors to allocate resources are _____

   c. It is, therefore, difficult to determine to which sector the production of a particular good or service should be _____

7. The two philosophies of apportioning the tax burden which are most evident in the American economy are the _____ principle and the _____ principle.

8. As income increases: if a tax is proportional the average tax rate _____; if it is progressive the average rate _____; and if it is regressive the average rate _____

9. Indicate in the space to the right of each of the following taxes whether that tax (as applied in the United States) is regressive (R) or progressive (P) or whether it is uncertain (U) which it is.

   a. Personal income tax   _____

   b. Sales tax   _____

   c. Payroll tax   _____

   d. Property tax   _____

   e. Corporation income tax   _____

10. When an excise tax is levied on a commodity the amount of the tax borne by buyers of the commodity is equal to the amount the _____ of the commodity rises as a result of the tax. The incidence of such a tax depends on the price elasticity of demand and of supply.

   a. The buyer's portion of the tax is larger the (more, less) _____ elastic the demand and the _____ elastic the supply.

   b. The seller's portion of the tax is larger the _____ elastic the demand and the _____ elastic the supply.

11. When an excise tax reduces the consumption and production of the taxed product below their allocatively efficient levels, there is an _____ of the tax. Other things equal, the greater the elasticity of supply and demand, the (greater, less) _____ the

_____ of the tax.

12. What is the probable incidence of each of the following taxes?

   a. Personal income tax: _____

   b. Sales and excise tax: _____

   c. Corporate income tax: _____

   d. Property tax: _____

_____

13. The American tax structure is mildly (regressive, progressive) _____

   a. As a result it has a (small, great) _____ effect on the distribution of income in the United States.
   b. But these conclusions depend on the assumed

_____ of the various taxes used in the American economy.
   c. Over the last 20 years the American tax structure

has become (more, less) _____ progressive.
   d. Income inequality in the United States is, however,

reduced by the system of _____ payments made by governments.

14. The Tax Reform Act of 1986 (increased, decreased)

_____ the number of tax brackets, (raised, low-

ered) _____ tax rates, and (narrowed, broad-

ened) _____ the tax base of the Federal personal income tax.

15. In recent years, two major issues related to taxes have been:
   a. reindustrializing the U.S. economy and increasing

the _____ of American workers.
   (1) This would require that consumption be (increased,

decreased) _____ and investment

be _____

   (2) This might be accomplished by lowering the (per-

sonal, corporate) _____ income tax and

establishing a _____ tax on consumption;

   b. whether there should be (higher, lower) _____
tax rates or new taxes to contain large and persistent Federal budget deficits. One option is to introduce

_____; the other option is to increase the pro-

gressivity of the personal _____

16. Many conservatives argue that a larger public sector

also diminishes _____.
Liberals counter that to believe that more governmental activity necessarily decreases private decision-making and economic activity is an example of the fallacy of

_____

■ **PROBLEMS AND PROJECTS**

1. In the table below are the demand and supply schedules for copra in the New Hebrides Islands.

Quantity demanded (pounds)	Price (per pound)	Before-tax quantity supplied (pounds)	After-tax quantity supplied (pounds)
150	$4.60	900	___
200	4.40	800	___
250	4.20	700	___
300	4.00	600	___
350	3.80	500	___
400	3.60	400	___
450	3.40	300	0
500	3.20	200	0
550	3.00	100	0

a. Before a tax is imposed on copra, its equilibrium price is $_____

b. The government of New Hebrides now imposes an excise tax of $.60 per pound on copra. Complete the after-tax supply schedule in the right-hand column of the table.

c. After the imposition of the tax, the equilibrium price of copra is $_____

d. Of the $.60 tax, the amount borne by

(1) the buyer is $_____ or _____%

(2) the seller is $_____ or _____%

2. On the graph below draw a perfectly elastic demand curve and a normal upsloping supply curve for a commodity. Now impose an excise tax on the commodity, and draw the new supply curve that would result.

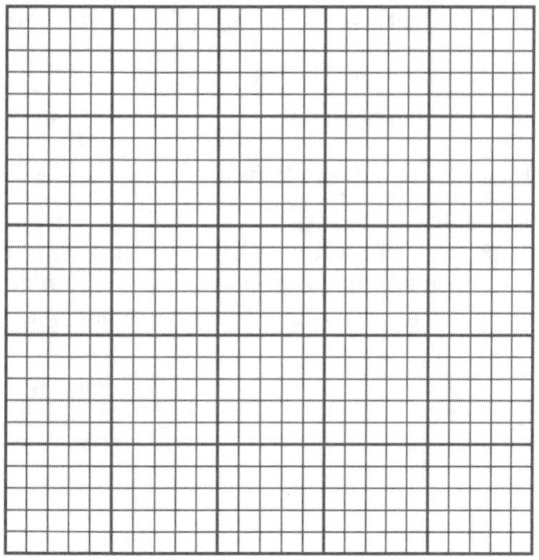

0

a. As a consequence of the tax, the price of the commodity has _____

b. It can be concluded that when demand is perfectly elastic, the buyer bears _____ of the tax and the seller bears _____ of the tax.

c. Thus the *more* elastic, the demand, the _____ _____ is the portion of the tax borne by the buyer and the _____ is the portion borne by the seller.

d. But the *less* elastic the demand, the _____ _____ is the portion borne by the buyer and

the _____ is the portion borne by the seller.

3. On the graph below draw a perfectly elastic supply curve and a normal downsloping demand curve. Impose an excise tax on the commodity and draw the new supply curve.

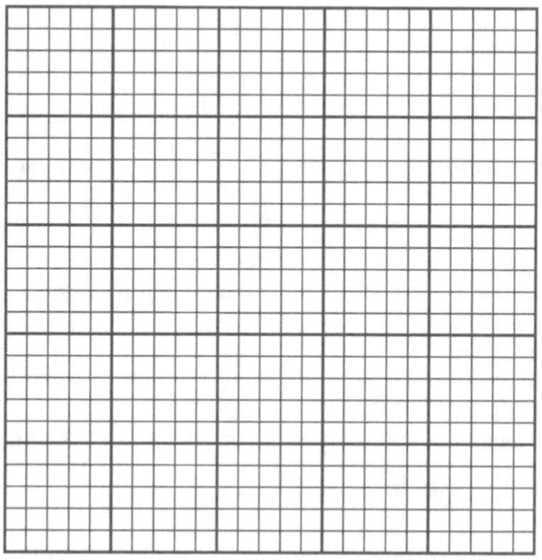

0

a. As a result of the tax, the price of the commodity has _____

b. From this it can be concluded that when supply is perfectly elastic, the buyer bears _____ of the tax and the seller bears _____ of the tax.

c. Thus the *more* elastic the supply, the _____ _____ is the portion of the tax borne by the buyer and the _____ is the portion borne by the seller.

d. But the *less* elastic the supply, the _____ _____ is the portion borne by the buyer and the _____ is the portion borne by the seller.

4. In the table at the top of the next page are five levels of taxable income and the amount that would be paid at each of the five levels under three tax laws: A, B, and C. Compute for each of the three tax laws the *average* rate of taxation at each of the four remaining income levels and indicate whether the tax is regressive, proportional, progressive, or some combination thereof.

Income	Tax A		Tax B		Tax C	
	Tax paid	Av. tax rate %	Tax paid	Av. tax rate %	Tax paid	Av. tax rate %
$ 1,500	45.00	3 %	30.00	2 %	135.00	9 %
3,000	90.00	_____	90.00	_____	240.00	_____
5,000	150.00	_____	150.00	_____	350.00	_____
7,500	225.00	_____	187.50	_____	450.00	_____
10,000	300.00	_____	200.00	_____	500.00	_____
Type of tax:	_____		_____		_____	

5. Assume a state government levies a 4% sales tax on all consumption expenditures. Consumption expenditures at six income levels are shown in the table below.

Income	Consumption expenditures	Sales tax paid	Average tax rate, %
$35,000	$5,000	$200	4.0
6,000	5,800	232	3.9
7,000	6,600	_____	_____
8,000	7,400	_____	_____
9,000	8,200	_____	_____
10,000	9,000	_____	_____

a. Compute the sales tax paid at the next four incomes.
b. Compute the average tax rate at these incomes.
c. Using income as the tax base, the sales tax is a

_____ tax.

■ **SELF-TEST**

Circle the T if the statement is true; the F if it is false.

1. Majority voting may produce outcomes that are economically inefficient because it fails to take into account the strength of preferences of the individual voter. **T F**

2. Logrolling will always diminish economic efficiency in government. **T F**

3. The paradox of voting is that majority voting will result in consistent choices that reflect the preferences of the public. **T F**

4. The proposition that the person holding the middle position on an issue will likely determine the outcome of an election is suggested by the median-voter model. **T F**

5. There is a failure in the public sector whenever a governmental program or activity has been expanded to the level at which the marginal social cost exceeds the marginal social benefit. **T F**

6. The special-interests effect, it is argued by those concerned with public choice theory, tends to reduce public sector failures because the pressures exerted on government by one special-interest group are offset by the pressures brought to bear by other special-interest groups. **T F**

7. When the costs of programs are hidden and the benefits are clear vote-seeking politicians tend to reject economically justifiable programs. **T F**

8. The limited choice of citizens refers to the inability of individual voters to select the precise bundle of social goods and services that best satisfies the citizen's wants when he or she must vote for a candidate and the candidate's entire program. **T F**

9. The chief difficulty in applying the benefits-received principle of taxation is determining who receives the benefit of many of the goods and services which government supplies. **T F**

10. The state and Federal taxes on gasoline are good examples of taxes levied on the benefits-received principle. **T F**

11. A tax is progressive when the average tax rate decreases as income increases. **T F**

12. A general sales tax is considered to be a proportional tax with respect to income. **T F**

13. When an excise tax is placed on a product bought and sold in a competitive market, the portion of the tax borne by the seller equals the amount of the tax less the rise in the price of product due to the tax. **T F**

14. The more elastic the demand for a good, the greater will be the portion of an excise tax on the good borne by the seller. **T F**

15. The efficiency loss of an excise tax is the gain in net benefits for the producers from the increase in the price of the product. **T F**

16. The degrees of efficiency loss from an excise tax varies from market to market and depends on the elasticities of supply and demand. **T F**

17. Estimates of the overall structure of the American tax system depend on the assumed incidence of taxes. **T F**

18. A value-added tax is a tax on the difference between the value of goods sold by a firm and the value of the goods it purchased from other firms.　　　**T F**

19. Advocates of "reindustrializing" the American economy have proposed increasing the tax rate imposed by the Federal government on corporate incomes to force corporations to be more efficient.　　　**T F**

20. Both liberals and conservatives agree that the expansion of government's role in the economy has reduced personal freedom in the United States.　　　**T F**

Circle the letter that corresponds to the best answer.

1. Deficiencies in the processes used to make collective decisions in the public sector and economic inefficiencies caused by government are the primary focus of:
(a) public finance
(b) public choice theory
(c) the study of tax incidence
(d) the study of tax shifting

2. The trading of votes to secure favorable outcomes on decisions which otherwise would be adverse is referred to as:
(a) logrolling, and it increases economic efficiency
(b) logrolling, and it may increase or decrease economic efficiency
(c) rent-seeking behavior and it decreases economic efficiency
(d) rent-seeking behavior and it may increase or decrease economic efficiency

Answer the next four questions (3, 4, 5, and 6) on the basis of the following table which shows the rankings of the public goods by three voters: A, B, and C.

Public good	Voter A	Voter B	Voter C
Dam	1	2	3
School	3	1	2
Road	2	3	1

3. In a choice between a dam and the school:
(a) a majority of voters favor the dam
(b) a majority of voters favor the school
(c) a majority of voters favor both the dam and the school
(d) there is not a majority of votes for either the dam or the school

4. In a choice between a road and a dam:
(a) a majority of voters favor the dam
(b) a majority of voters favor the road
(c) a majority of voters favor both the dam and the road
(d) there is not a majority of votes for either the road or the dam

5. In a choice between a school and a road:
(a) a majority of voters favor the road
(b) a majority of voters favor the school
(c) a majority of voters favor both the road and the school
(d) there is not a majority of votes for either the road or the school

6. What do the rankings in the table indicate about choices made under majority rule? Majority voting:
(a) reflects irrational preferences
(b) produces inconsistent choices
(c) produces consistent choices in spite of irrational preferences
(d) results in economically efficient outcomes because they have been influenced by special interests

7. The idea that the person holding the middle position will in a sense determine the outcome of an election is suggested by the:
(a) rent-seeking behavior
(b) paradox of voting
(c) median-voter model
(d) fallacy of limited decisions

8. Which of the following is *not* one of the reasons for the alleged greater efficiency of the private sector?
(a) the least efficient workers in the economy gravitate to the public sector
(b) strong incentives to be efficient are largely absent in the public sector
(c) there is no simple way to measure or test efficiency in the public sector
(d) there is a tendency in the public sector to increase the budgets of agencies that have failed to perform efficiently

9. It is difficult to determine whether provision for a particular good or service should be assigned to the private or public sector of the economy because:
(a) the institutions in both sectors function efficiently
(b) the markets function efficiently and the agencies of government perform imperfectly
(c) the markets are faulty and government agencies function with much greater efficiency
(d) the institutions in both sectors are imperfect

10. Which of the following is true of the ability-to-pay principle as applied in the United States?
(a) it is less widely applied than the benefits-received principle
(b) tax incidence is generally taken as the measure of the ability to pay
(c) gasoline taxes are based on this principle
(d) as the tax base increases, taxes paid increase both absolutely and relatively

11. Taxing people according the principle of ability-to-pay would be most characteristic of:
  (a) a payroll tax
  (b) a value-added tax
  (c) a general sales tax
  (d) a progressive income tax

12. When the income of a taxpayer increases and a tax is regressive, the amount of the tax paid by the taxpayer:
  (a) increases
  (b) decreases
  (c) remains unchanged
  (d) may do any of the above

13. Which of the following tends to be a progressive tax in the United States?
  (a) income tax
  (b) property tax
  (c) sales tax
  (d) payroll tax

14. In a competitive market the portion of an excise tax borne by a buyer is equal to:
  (a) the amount the price of the product rises as a result of the tax
  (b) the amount of the tax
  (c) the amount of the tax less the amount the price of the product rises as a result of the tax
  (d) the amount of the tax plus the amount the price of the product rises as a result of the tax

15. Which of the following statements is correct?
  (a) the more elastic the supply, the greater the portion of an excise tax borne by the seller
  (b) the more elastic the demand, the greater the portion of an excise tax borne by the seller
  (c) the more inelastic the supply, the greater the portion of an excise tax borne by the buyer
  (d) the more inelastic the demand, the greater the portion of an excise tax borne by the seller

Answer the next four questions (16, 17, 18, and 19) based on the graph of an excise tax imposed by government, as shown in the next column.

16. What is the amount of the excise tax paid by the seller in terms of price per unit sold?
  (a) $1.00
  (b) $2.00
  (c) $3.00
  (d) $4.00

17. The amount of the excise tax paid by the consumer is:
  (a) $2.00
  (b) $6.00
  (c) $12.00
  (d) $16.00

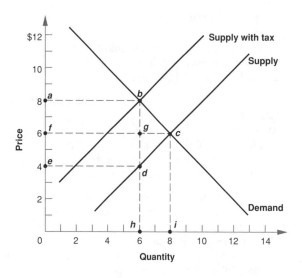

18. The tax revenue for government is represented by area:
  (a) *abde*
  (b) *abgf*
  (c) *fgde*
  (d) *abcde*

19. The efficiency loss of the tax is represented by area:
  (a) *bgc*
  (b) *bdc*
  (c) *abcf*
  (d) *hbci*

20. The efficiency loss of an excise tax is:
  (a) greater, the greater the elasticity of supply and demand
  (b) greater, the less the elasticity of supply and demand
  (c) less, the greater the elasticity of supply and demand
  (d) not affected by the elasticity of supply and demand

21. Which of the following taxes can be least easily shifted?
  (a) personal income tax
  (b) corporation income tax
  (c) sales tax
  (d) business property tax

22. A recent study of the American tax structure shows it to be:
  (a) very progressive
  (b) slightly progressive
  (c) slightly regressive
  (d) very regressive

23. The advocates of "reindustrializing" the American economy argue that:
  (a) the production of consumer goods must be increased

(b) the productivity of American workers must be improved

(c) corporate income taxes should be increased

(d) the production of investment goods needs to be reduced by a substantial amount

24. A value-added tax as used by many countries would basically tax a firm's:

(a) revenues from the sale of a product

(b) purchases of resources to produce the product

(c) revenue from the firm's sales less the resource cost

(d) capital goods and land held by the firm

25. The statement that "government extends the range of free choice for members of a society when it provides public goods and services" would serve to illustrate:

(a) rent-seeking behavior

(b) the median-voter model

(c) the benefits-received principle

(d) the fallacy of limited decisions

■ **DISCUSSION QUESTIONS**

1. Explain the difference between public choice theory and public finance. Why has there been dissatisfaction with government decisions?

2. What is the relationship between majority voting and the efficiency of outcomes from an election? How do special interest groups or the use of logrolling influence the efficiency of outcomes?

3. Why is there a paradox with majority voting? Do the outcomes from majority voting suggest that voters are irrational in their preferences?

4. Describe how median voters influence the election results and debates over public issues? What factors make the median voter model imperfect?

5. Explain what is meant by "public sector failure." Is it related to market failure and externalities?

6. Public choice theory suggests that there are a number of reasons for public sector failures. What are the reasons? Explain how each would tend to result in the inefficient allocation of the economy's resources.

7. It is generally agreed that "national defense must lie in the public sector while wheat production can best be accomplished in the private sector." Why isn't there agreement on where many other goods or services should be produced?

8. What are the two basic philosophies for apportioning the tax burden in the United States? Explain each. What are the difficulties encountered in putting these philosophies into practice?

9. Explain the differences among progressive, regressive, and proportional taxes. Which taxes fall into each of these three categories?

10. Explain the effect which the imposition of an excise tax has on the supply of a commodity bought and sold in a competitive market. How do you find what part of the tax is passed on to the buyer and what part is borne by the seller? What determines the division of the tax between the buyer and the seller?

11. What is the relationship between the price elasticity of demand for a commodity and the portion of an excise tax on a commodity borne by the buyer and by the seller? What is the relationship between the price elasticity of supply and the incidence of the tax?

12. How does an excise tax produce an efficiency loss for society? How is this efficiency loss affected by the elasticity of supply or demand? All else equal, shouldn't the total tax burden be equal for two taxes that produce equal revenues?

13. Which of the following taxes tends to be shifted?

(a) personal income tax

(b) corporate income tax

(c) sales and excise taxes

(d) property tax

From whom is the tax shifted and upon whom is the tax incidence?

14. What can be said about the progressivity or regressivity of the overall structure of the American tax system?

15. What does the term "reindustrialize" mean when applied to the American economy? Why do the proponents of reindustrialization feel the economy is in need of it and what steps would they take to accomplish it?

16. Why might higher tax rates or new taxes be needed for the Federal government? What options might be considered?

17. Do you think government limits or expands personal freedom? Do you think that government's role in the economy should be increased or decreased? What is meant by the "fallacy" of limited decisions?

■ **ANSWERS**

Chapter 19 Public Choice Theory and Taxation

FILL-IN QUESTIONS

1. choice, finance

2. *a.* inefficiency, overallocation, underallocation, special interest, logrolling; *b.* paradox of voting

3. median-voter, middle

4. public, failure

5. *a.* special, rent-seeking; *b.* clear, hidden; *c.* select; *d.* incentives, test (measure)

6. *a.* private sector; *b.* imperfect; *c.* assigned

7. benefits-received, ability-to-pay

8. is constant, increases, decreases

9. *a.* P; *b.* R; *c.* R; *d.* R; *e.* U

10. price; *a.* less, more; *b.* more, less

11. efficiency loss, greater, efficiency loss

12. *a.* the persons upon whom it is levied; *b.* those who buy the taxed product; *c.* either the firm or its customers; *d.* owners when they occupy their own residences, tenants who rent residences from the owners, consumers who buy the products produced on business property

13. progressive; *a.* small; *b.* incidence; *c.* less; *d.* transfer

14. decreased, lowered, broadened

15. *a.* productivity, (1) decreased, increased, (2) corporate, value-added; *b.* higher, VAT, income tax.

16. economic freedom, limited decisions

PROBLEMS AND PROJECTS

1. *a.* $3.60; *b.* (reading down) 600, 500, 400, 300, 200, 100; *c.* $4.00; *d.* (1) $.40, 67; (2) $.20, 33

2. *a.* not changed; *b.* none, all; *c.* smaller, larger; *d.* larger, smaller

3. *a.* increased by the amount of the tax; *b.* all, none; *c.* larger, smaller; *d.* smaller, larger

4. Tax A: 3, 3, 3, 3, proportional; Tax B: 3, 3, 2.5, 2, combination; Tax C: 8, 7, 6, 5, regressive

5. *a.* $264, 296, 328, 360; *b.* 3.8, 3.7, 3.64, 3.6; *c.* regressive

SELF-TEST

1. T, p. 325	**11.** F, p. 332
2. F, p. 325	**12.** F, p. 332
3. F, p. 326	**13.** T, pp. 333–335
4. T, p. 327	**14.** T, p. 335
5. T, p. 328	**15.** F, pp. 335–336
6. F, p. 328	**16.** T, p. 336
7. F, p. 329	**17.** T, p. 336
8. T, p. 329	**18.** T, p. 338
9. T, p. 331	**19.** F, p. 338
10. T, p. 331	**20.** F, pp. 339–340

1. *b*, p. 324	**14.** *a*, p. 334
2. *b*, p. 325	**15.** *b*, p. 334
3. *b*, p. 326	**16.** *b*, pp. 333–334
4. *a*, p. 326	**17.** *c*, pp. 333–334
5. *a*, p. 326	**18.** *a*, p. 335
6. *b*, pp. 326–327	**19.** *b*, p. 335
7. *c*, p. 327	**20.** *a*, p. 336
8. *a*, p. 329	**21.** *a*, p. 336
9. *d*, p. 330	**22.** *b*, p. 337
10. *d*, p. 331	**23.** *b*, p. 337
11. *d*, p. 332	**24.** *c*, pp. 338–339
12. *d*, p. 332	**25.** *d*, pp. 340–341
13. *a*, p. 332	

DISCUSSION QUESTIONS

1. pp. 323–324	**10.** pp. 333–334
2. pp. 324–325	**11.** p. 334
3. p. 326	**12.** pp. 335–336
4. p. 327	**13.** pp. 336–337
5. p. 328	**14.** pp. 337–338
6. p. 328	**15.** p. 338
7. pp. 329–330	**16.** p. 339
8. pp. 331–332	**17.** pp. 339–341
9. p. 332	

Antitrust and Regulation

This is the third of six chapters which deal with government and current problems in the American economy and is one of the two chapters which concern the monopoly problem. Chapter 20 examines the monopoly problem in output markets, and Chapter 23 examines the monopoly problem in labor markets. It should be noted that the term "monopoly" as used here does **not** mean pure or absolute monopoly; instead it means control of a large percentage of the total supply by one or a few suppliers—industrial concentration. Actually there is no such thing as pure monopoly, just degrees of industrial concentration.

Whether industrial concentration is a real threat to efficient resource allocation and technological progress in the United States is certainly a debatable question. It is a question that will be argued from time to time by the American people and their representatives in Congress. Chapter 20 does not attempt to answer the question. It is important, however, for you to see that it is a debatable question and to see that there are good and plausible arguments on both sides of the question.

A part of Chapter 20 is devoted to an examination of the ways in which the Federal government has attempted to reduce industrial concentration and to limit the use of monopoly power. In this section you will find a discussion of a number of Federal laws, and the question which a student almost always raises is, "Am I expected to know these laws?" The answer is yes, you should have a general knowledge of these laws. Another question which students often raise with respect to these laws is, "What good is there in knowing them anyhow?" In examining any important current problem it is important to know how the problem arose, what steps have already been taken to solve it, how successful the attempts were, and why the problem is still not solved. A more general answer to the same question is that an informed citizenry is necessary if a democracy is to solve its problems. And most of these laws continue in force and are enforced; many of you will work for business firms which are subject to their provisions.

After looking at the case for and the defense of industrial concentration and at the antitrust laws enacted by the Federal government, Chapter 20 presents the two major issues that have arisen in the interpretation of the antitrust laws; asks how effective these laws have been; and observes that the Federal government has in several ways promoted and fostered industrial concentration and restricted competition in the United States.

In addition to restricting and to fostering industrial concentration, the Federal government has also undertaken to regulate, beginning with the railroads in 1887, industries that appeared to be natural monopolies. This regulation by agencies and commissions has, however, at least three serious problems of which you should be aware. One of these problems is that some of the regulated industries may not be natural monopolies at all and would be competitive industries if they were left unregulated. From this problem comes the legal cartel theory of regulation: many industries desire to be regulated so that competition among the firms in the industry will be reduced and the profits of these firms increased. A consequence of the problems encountered in regulating industries has been the trend in recent years to deregulate a few of the industries previously regulated by agencies or commissions. One of the industries which has been deregulated in the United States is the airline industry; and the case of the airlines is examined in a section of the text. Here you will see that despite the predictions of the critics of deregulation, deregulation has been generally beneficial for consumers and the economy.

Beginning in the early 1960s a host of new agencies and commissions began to engage in regulation which is different from the regulation of the prices charged by and the services offered by specific industries. Critics of social regulation contend that it is costly, and that the marginal costs exceed the benefits. Although social regulation does increase product prices and indirectly reduces worker productivity, supporters of this type of regulation argue that the social benefits over time will exceed the costs. You should spend time understanding both sides of this issue.

When you finish this chapter, you should conclude that antitrust, industrial regulation, and social regulation are trouble spots for the American economy. Antitrust and regulation raise important issues and questions about the role of government maintaining competition and restricting certain business practices in a market economy. How we deal with the issues or answer the questions will affect how good or bad our lives are now and will be in the future.

■ **CHECKLIST**

When you have studied this chapter you should be able to:

☐ Define the term industrial concentration and explain how it is used in this chapter.
☐ Cite four arguments in the case against industrial concentration.
☐ State four arguments in defense of industrial concentration.
☐ Outline the major provisions of each of the following:
  ● Sherman Act
  ● Clayton Act
  ● Federal Trade Commission Act
  ● Wheeler-Lea Act
  ● Celler-Kefauver Act
☐ Contrast the behavior and structural approaches to the enforcement of antitrust laws for judging the competitiveness of an industry.
☐ Explain the importance of market definition in the interpretation of antitrust laws.
☐ Generalize about the application of antitrust laws to existing market structure, mergers, and price fixing.
☐ Distinguish between a horizontal, vertical, and conglomerate merger.
☐ Explain the use the Herfindahl index for merger guidelines.
☐ Cite recent examples of price fixing and two major consequences of price fixing.
☐ List three groups which have been exempted from the provisions of the antitrust laws, and list two laws or policies which tend to restrict competition in the United States.
☐ Define a natural monopoly; and explain how it is related to the public interest theory of regulation.
☐ State the three problems that have been encountered in the economic regulation of industries by agencies and commissions.
☐ Distinguish between the public interest and legal cartel theories of regulation.
☐ Describe the principal economic effects of the deregulation of the airline industry in the United States; and compare these effects with the effects predicted by the critics of deregulation.
☐ Contrast industrial (or economic) regulation with social regulation; and state the principal concerns and the three distinguishing features of the latter.
☐ Present the case against social regulation made by its critics.
☐ Describe three economic implications of social regulation.
☐ Make the case for social regulation by discussing the benefits and citing data.

■ **CHAPTER OUTLINE**

1. The term "industrial concentration," as used in this chapter, means a situation in which a small number of firms control all or a substantial percentage of the total output of a major industry. Business firms may be large in either an absolute or a relative sense, and in many cases they are large in both senses. Chapter 33 is concerned with firms large in both senses.

2. Whether industrial concentration is beneficial or detrimental to the American economy is debatable. A case can be made against industrial concentration; but industrial concentration can also be defended.
  a. Many argue that industrial concentration results in a misallocation of resources; it is not needed for firms to achieve the economics of mass production and it does not lead to technological progress; it contributes to income inequality in the economy; and it is politically dangerous.
  b. But others argue that industrial concentration is often faced by interindustry and foreign competition; that it offers superior products; that large firms are necessary if they are to achieve the economies of scale in producing goods and services; and that monopolistic or concentrated industries promote a high rate of technological progress.

3. Government policies toward industrial concentration have not been clear and consistent; legislation and policy, however, have for the most part been aimed at restricting concentration and promoting competition.
  a. Following the Civil War, the expansion of the American economy brought with it the creation of trusts (or industrial concentration) in many industries; and the fear of the trusts resulted in the enactment of antitrust legislation.
  b. The Sherman Antitrust Act of 1890 was the first antitrust legislation and made monopolization and restraint of trade criminal offenses.
  c. In 1914 the Clayton Antitrust Act outlawed a number of specific techniques by which monopolies or oligopolies had been created.
  d. During the same year Congress passed the Federal Trade Commission Act which established the Federal Trade Commission to investigate unfair practices that might lead to the development of monopoly power; and in 1938 it amended this act by passing the Wheeler-Lea Act to prohibit deceptive practices (including false and misleading advertising and misrepresentation of products).
  e. And in 1950 passage of the Celler-Kefauver Act plugged a loophole in the Clayton Act and prohibited mergers that might lead to a substantial reduction in competition.

4. The effectiveness of the antitrust laws in preventing monopoly and maintaining competition has depended upon the zeal with which the Federal government has enforced the laws and upon the interpretation of these laws by the Federal courts; and two major issues have arisen in the interpretation of the antitrust laws.

a. The first of these issues is whether an industry should be judged on the basis of its highly concentrated structure or on the basis of its market behavior; and this issue has resulted in controversy and in two different approaches to the application of the antitrust laws.

b. The second issue is whether to define the market in which firms sell their products narrowly or broadly.

c. Whether the antitrust laws have been effective is a difficult question to answer. The application of the laws to existing market structures, to the three types of mergers, and to price fixing has ranged from lenient to strict:

(1) for existing market structures, it has been lenient;

(2) for horizontal, vertical, or conglomerate mergers, it usually varies by the type of merger and the particulars of a case, but merger guidelines are based on the Herfindahl index (the sum of the squared values of market shares within an industry);

(3) for price fixing, it has been strict, and as a consequence it is now often done in secret or through the use of informal collusion in the form of price leadership or cost-plus pricing.

d. The United States government has also restricted competition:

(1) by exempting labor unions, agricultural cooperatives, and certain occupational groups (at the state and local levels) from the provisions of the antitrust laws;

(2) by granting monopoly power to the producers of patented products; and

(3) by imposing tariffs and other trade barriers to protect American producers in some industries from foreign competition.

5. In addition to the enactment of the antitrust laws, government has undertaken to regulate natural monopolies.

a. If a single producer can provide a good or service at a lower average cost (because of economies of scale) than several producers, then competition is not economical and a natural monopoly exists. Government may either produce the good or service or (following the public interest theory) regulate private producers of the product for the benefit of the public.

b. The effectiveness of the regulation of business firms by regulatory agencies has been criticized for three principal reasons.

(1) Regulation, it is argued, increases costs and leads to an inefficient allocation of resources and higher prices.

(2) The regulatory agencies, it is also contended, have been "captured" by the regulated industries and protect them rather than the public.

(3) And some of the regulated industries, it can be argued, are not natural monopolies and would be competitive if they were not regulated.

c. The legal cartel theory of regulation is that potentially competitive industries want and support the regulation of their industries in order to increase the profits of the firms in the industries by limiting competition among them.

6. The three criticisms of the regulation of industries and the legal cartel theory of regulation led during the 1970s and 1980s to the deregulation of a number of industries in the United States. In particular, the deregulation of the airlines in 1978 had a number of economic effects:

a. Air fares rose less than the general level of prices and are lower than before deregulation because of increased competition among airlines to reduce unit labor costs.

b. Air service to most communities, even smaller ones, was maintained or expanded, but there have been delays on some routes because of the nature of the "spoke and hub" system; although deregulation raised concerns about air safety, the evidence is at worst mixed.

c. The number of air carriers initially increased, but recent consolidation of the industry has raised new concerns about concentration in the industry; also airport congestion and the competitive practices of airlines make the entry of new firms difficult.

d. Overall, airline deregulation contributed about $100 billion in net benefit to the economy during the 1980s, but growing concentration in the industry will need monitoring and possibly antitrust actions.

7. Beginning in the early 1960s, social regulation developed and resulted in the creation of additional regulatory agencies.

a. This regulation differed in several ways from the older regulation of specific industries and aimed to improve the quality of life in the United States.

b. While the objectives of the new regulation are desirable, the overall costs for both program administration and compliance costs can be high; most of the costs, however, are compliance costs which are about 20 times administrative costs.

c. Critics argue that the marginal costs of this regulation exceed its marginal benefit and it is, therefore, inefficient because:

(1) regulatory standards and objectives are poorly drawn and targeted;

(2) the rules and regulations are made based on limited and inadequate information;

(3) there are unintended secondary effects from the regulation that boost product costs;

(4) regulatory agencies tend to attract "overzealous" workers who believe in regulation.

d. The economic consequences of social regulation are that it increases product prices, it may slow the rate of product innovation, and it may lessen competition.

e. The defenders of social regulation contend that it is needed to fight serious and neglected problems, such as job and auto safety or environment pollution; and that the social benefits, if they can be measured, will over time exceed the costs.

■ IMPORTANT TERMS

Industrial concentration	Rule of reason
Big business	Alcoa case
Interindustry competition	DuPont Cellophane case
Foreign competition	Horizontal merger
Potential competition	Vertical merger
Regulatory agency	Conglomerate merger
Sherman Act	Per se violations
Treble damages	Patent laws
Clayton Act	Natural monopoly
Tying agreement	Public utility
Interlocking directorate	Public interest theory of regulation
Federal Trade Commission Act	
Federal Trade Commission	Legal cartel theory of regulation
Cease-and desist order	Airline Deregulation Act
Wheeler-Lea Act	Industrial (economic) regulation
Celler-Kefauver Act	Social regulation
U.S. Steel case	

■ FILL-IN QUESTIONS

1. As used in this chapter, industrial concentration means that (many firms, a few firms) _____ control all or a substantial portion of the output of a major industry; and this chapter is concerned with firms that are large (absolutely, relatively, both absolutely and relatively) _____

2. Those who argue the case against industrial concentration assert that it results in a _____ of resources, (slows, speeds) _____ the rate of technological progress, contributes to the _____ distribution of income, and creates political _____ in the United States.

3. Those who defend industrial concentration contend that the monopoly power was the result of offering _____ to the market, that their power is limited by _____ and _____ competition, that large firms are necessary to achieve economies of _____, and that the large firms are conducive to a rapid rate of _____

4. Federal legislation and policies have mostly attempted to maintain (competition, monopoly) _____ _____, but at times they have fostered the development of _____

5. The Sherman Act of 1890 made it illegal to _____-ize or to restrain _____ between the states or between nations.

6. The Clayton Act of 1914 prohibited such practices as price _____, acquisition of the _____ of competing corporations, _____ contracts, and _____ directorates.

7. The Federal Trade Commission was set up under the act of that name in 1914 to investigate _____ competitive practices, hold public _____ on such complaints, and to issue _____ orders.

8. The _____ Act had the effect of prohibiting false and misleading advertising.

9. The _____ Act banned the acquisition of the assets of one firm by another, and the _____ Act prohibited the acquisition of the **stock** of one firm by another when the result would be reduced competition.

10. The two basic issues in applying the antitrust laws are whether the extent of industrial concentration in a particular industry should be judged on the basis of that industry's behavior or its _____; and whether the size of the market in which a firm sells its products should be defined _____ or _____

    a. The courts judged the steel industry on the basis of its behavior in 1920 when they applied the rule of _____ in the U.S. Steel case; but used the other method of judging an industry in 1945 in the _____ case.

    b. In 1956 they ruled that although DuPont sold nearly all the Cellophane produced in the United States it did not dominate the market for flexible _____

11. A merger between two competitors selling similar products in the same market is a (vertical, horizontal, conglomerate) _____ merger. A _____ merger occurs among firms at different stages in the production process of the same industry. A _____ merger results when a firm in one industry is purchased by a firm in an unrelated industry. The _____ index is used as a guideline for mergers.

12. The Federal government promotes the growth of monopoly and restricts competition when it exempts certain industries or practices from the provisions of the _____ laws.

    a. Federal legislation has exempted _____ _____ and _____ cooperatives.

    b. The _____ laws have the effect of granting inventors legal monopolies on their products; and _____ and other barriers to trade shelter American producers from foreign competition.

13. When a single firm is able to supply the entire market at a lower average cost than a number of competing firms, there is a _____ monopoly. In the United States many of these monopolies are controlled by regulatory _____ or _____.

14. The three major criticisms of regulation of industries by an agency or commission are

    a. The reguated firms have no incentive to reduce their _____ because the commission will then require them to lower their prices; and, because the prices they are allowed to charge are based on the value of their capital equipment, firms tend to make uneconomical substitutions of (labor, capital) _____ for _____.

    b. The regulatory commission has been "captured" or is controlled by _____

    c. Regulation has been applied to industries which are not _____ monopolies and which in the absence of regulation would be _____.

15. The public interest theory of regulation assumes that the objective of regulating an industry is to protect society from abuses of _____ power; but an alternative theory assumes that the firms wish to be regulated because it enables them to form, and the commission helps them to create, a profitable and legal _____

16. Airline deregulation (increased, decreased) _____ airfares in the 1980s in part because competition _____ costs. There were

_____ concerns about airline safety because airport congestion _____.
Since deregulation, the number of air carriers initially _____ but they have now _____, which _____ concerns about industrial concentration in the airline industry. Overall, the deregulation of airlines _____ the net benefit to society by about $100 billion during the 1980s.

17. The basic reason for social regulation and the creation and growth of the regulatory agencies has been the desire to improve the (quantity, quality) _____ of life in the United States.

    a. It is concerned with the _____ under which goods and services are produced, the impact of their production upon _____, and the physical _____ of the goods.

    b. And it differs in several ways from the older form of regulation which is labeled _____ or _____ regulation.

18. The costs of social regulation include _____ _____ costs, such as salaries paid to employees of regulatory agencies, and _____ costs incurred by businesses and state and local governments in meeting the requirements of the regulatory laws. The latter costs have been estimated to be about _____ times those of the former. Critics of social legislation contend that its marginal costs are (greater, less) _____ than its marginal benefits.

19. The economic effects of social regulation are several: it tends to (increase, decrease) _____ product prices and tends to _____ worker productivity; it also may _____ the rate of innovation and may _____ competition in the economy.

20. Supporters of social regulation hold that there are serious and substantial _____ that must be dealt with by society; that the relevant economic test is whether the _____ if social regulation is to be judged as worthwhile; and that _____ tend to be taken for granted or are difficult to measure, or may require time to accrue.

21. The dispute over social regulation (is, is not) _____ over whether the regulation should occur. It _____ over how and when regulation should be used and it _____ over how we can improve the system of regulation.

■ **PROBLEMS AND PROJECTS**

1. Below is a list of Federal laws. Following this list is a series of provisions found in Federal laws. Match each of the laws with the appropriate provision by placing the appropriate capital letter after each of the provisions.
   A. Sherman Act
   B. Clayton Act
   C. Federal Trade Commission Act
   D. Wheeler-Lea Act
   E. Celler-Kefauver Act
   a. Established a commission to investigate and prevent unfair methods of competition. _____
   b. Made monopoly and restraint of trade illegal and criminal. _____
   c. Prohibited the acquisition of the assets of a firm by another firm when such an acquisition will lessen competition. _____
   d. Had the effect of prohibiting false and misleading advertising and the misrepresentation of products. _____
   e. Clarified the Sherman Act and outlawed specific techniques or devices used to create monopolies and restrain trade. _____

2. Indicate with the letter L for *leniently* (or permissively) and the letter S for *strictly* how the antitrust laws tend to be applied to each of the following.
   a. Vertical mergers in which each of the merging firms sells a small portion of the total output of its industry _____
   b. Price fixing by a firm in an industry _____
   c. Conglomerate mergers _____
   d. Existing market structures in which no firm sells 60% or more of the total output of its industry _____
   e. Horizontal mergers in which the merged firms would sell a large portion of the total output of their industry and no one of the firms is on the verge of bankruptcy _____
   f. Action by firms in an industry to divide up sales _____
   g. Horizontal mergers where one of the firms is on the verge of bankruptcy _____

3. In the table below are data on five different industries and the market shares for each of the firms in the industry. Assume that there is no foreign competition, entry into the industry is difficult, and that no firm in each industry is on the verge of bankruptcy.

Industry	Market share of firms in industry						Herfindahl index
	1	2	3	4	5	6	
A	35	25	15	11	10	4	_____
B	30	25	25	20	—	—	_____
C	20	20	20	15	15	10	_____
D	60	25	15	—	—	—	_____
E	22	21	20	18	12	7	_____

   a. In the column to the right of the table, calculate the Herfindahl index.
   b. The industry with the most monopoly power is Industry _____ and the industry with the least monopoly power is Industry _____.
   c. If the *sixth* firm in Industry A sought to merge with the *fifth* firm in that industry, then the government (would, would not) _____ be likely to challenge the merger. The Herfindahl index for this industry is _____, which is higher than the merger guideline of _____ points used by the government, but the merger increases the index by only _____ points.
   d. If the *fourth* firm in Industry B sought to merge with the *third* firm in that industry, then the government (would, would not) _____ be likely to challenge the merger. The Herfindahl index for this industry is _____, which is higher than the merger guideline of the government, and the merger increases the index by _____ points.
   e. A *conglomerate* merger between the *fourth* firm in Industry C and the *fourth* firm in Industry E (would, would not) _____ likely be challenged by the government. The Herfindahl index would (increase, remain the same) _____ with this merger.
   f. If a *vertical* merger between the *first* firm in Industry B with the *first* firm in Industry D lessened competition in each industry, then the merger (would, would not) _____ likely be challenged by the government, but the merger _____ likely be challenged if it did not lessen competition in each industry.

■ **SELF-TEST**

Circle the T if the statement is true, the F it is false.

1. The term "industrial concentration" in this chapter is taken to mean a situation in which a single firm or a small number of firms control the major portion of the output of an important industry. **T   F**

2. It is clear that on balance, industrial concentration is detrimental to the functioning of the American economy. **T   F**

3. Those who defend industrial concentration contend that it is technologically more progressive than smaller firms. **T   F**

4. Potential competition acts as a restraint on the price and output decisons of firms possessing market power. **T   F**

5. The Federal government has consistently passed legislation and pursued policies designed to maintain competition. **T   F**

6. Industrial concentration and "trusts" developed in the American economy during the two decades preceding the American Civil War. **T   F**

7. The courts in 1920 applied the rule of reason to the U.S. Steel Corporation and decided that the corporation possessed monopoly power and had unreasonably restrained trade. **T   F**

8. Those who believe an industry should be judged on the basis of its structure contend that any industry with a monopolistic structure must behave like a monopolist. **T   F**

9. The market for DuPont's product was broadly defined by the courts in the DuPont Cellophane case of 1956. **T   F**

10. The Reagan and Bush administrations were committed to a more vigorous enforcement of the antitrust laws in the areas of market structure and mergers. **T   F**

11. To gain a conviction under **per se violations**, the party making the charge must show that the conspiracy to fix prices actually succeeded or caused damage. **T   F**

12. Occupational licensure and patent have been most beneficial in promoting competition in markets. **T   F**

13. Public ownership rather than public regulation has been the primary means utilized in the United States to ensure that the behavior of natural monopolists is socially acceptable. **T   F**

14. The rationale underlying the public interest theory of regulation of natural monopolies is to allow the consumers of their goods or services to benefit from the economies of scale. **T   F**

15. Regulated firms, because the prices they are allowed to charge are set to enable them to earn a "fair" return over their costs, have a strong incentive to reduce their costs. **T   F**

16. From the perspective of the legal cartel theory of regulation, firms want to be regulated by government. **T   F**

17. The deregulation of airlines in the United States generally lowered prices to consumers of airline services during the 1980s. **T   F**

18. Those who favor social regulation believe that it is needed in order to improve the quality of life in the United States. **T   F**

19. Critics of the social regulation argue that its marginal costs exceed its marginal benefits. **T   F**

20. Social regulation tends to lower product prices and raise worker productivity. **T   F**

Circle the letter that corresponds to the best answer.

1. "Industrial concentration" in this chapter refers to which one of the following?
  (a) firms that are absolutely large
  (b) firms that are relatively large
  (c) firms that are either absolutely or relatively large
  (d) firms that are both absolutely and relatively large

2. Which of the following is **not** a part of the case **against** industrial concentration?
  (a) highly concentrated industries are larger than they need to be to benefit from economies of scale
  (b) highly concentrated industries earn economic profits which they use for research and technological development
  (c) monopoly power leads to the misallocation of resources
  (d) monopoly power leads to greater income inequality

3. An essential part of the defense of industrial concentration is that the power of big business is limited by:
  (a) interindustry competition
  (b) foreign competition
  (c) potential competition from new firms in the industry
  (d) all of the above

4. Which one of the following laws stated that contracts and conspiracies in restraint of trade, monopolies, attempts to monopolize, and conspiracies to monopolize are illegal?
  (a) Sherman Act
  (b) Clayton Act
  (c) Federal Trade Commission Act
  (d) Wheeler-Lea Act

5. Which one of the following acts specifically outlawed tying contracts and interlocking directorates?
(a) Sherman Act
(b) Clayton Act
(c) Federal Trade Commission Act
(d) Wheeler-Lea Act

6. Which one of the following acts has given the Federal Trade Commission the task of preventing false and misleading advertising and the misrepresentation of products?
(a) Sherman Act
(b) Clayton Act
(c) Federal Trade Commission Act
(d) Wheeler-Lea Act

7. Which of the following acts banned the acquisition of the assets of a firm by a competing firm when the acquisition would tend to reduce competition?
(a) Celler-Kefauver Act
(b) Wheeler-Lea Act
(c) Clayton Act
(d) Federal Trade Commission Act

8. The argument that an industry which is highly concentrated will behave like a monopolist and the Alcoa court case of 1945 suggest that the application of antitrust laws should be based on industry:
(a) behavior
(b) structure
(c) efficiency
(d) rule of reason

9. The merger of a firm in one industry with a firm in an unrelated industry is called a:
(a) horizontal merger
(b) vertical merger
(c) secondary merger
(d) conglomerate merger

10. Toward which of the following has the application of the antitrust laws been the most strict in recent years?
(a) existing market structures
(b) conglomerate mergers
(c) mergers in which one of the firms is on the verge of bankruptcy
(d) price fixing

11. An industry has four firms, each with a market share of 25%. There is no foreign competition, entry into the industry is difficult, and no firm is on the verge of bankruptcy. If two of the firms in the industry sought to merger, this action would most likely be opposed by the government because the Herfindahl index for the industry is:
(a) 2000 and the merger would increase the index by 1000
(b) 2500 and the merger would increase the index by 1000

(c) 2500 and the merger would increase the index by 1250
(d) 3000 and the merger would increase the index by 1250

12. When the government or other party making the charge can show that there was a conspiracy to fix prices, even if the conspiracy did not succeed, then this would be an example of:
(a) a tying contract
(b) a per se violation
(c) the rule of reason
(d) the legal cartel theory

13. Which of the following does *not* restrict competition in the American economy?
(a) the exemption of labor unions and agricultural co-operatives from the antitrust laws
(b) protective tariffs and other barriers to international trade
(c) the difficulties many new firms encounter in obtaining charters that allow them to become corporations
(d) American patent laws

14. An example of industrial or economic regulation would be the:
(a) Federal Communications Commission
(b) Food and Drug Administration
(c) Occupational Safety and Health Administration
(d) Environmental Protection Agency

15. Legislations designed to regulate "natural monopolies" would be based on which theory of regulation?
(a) cartel
(b) public interest
(c) X-inefficiency
(d) public ownership

16. Those who oppose the regulation of industry by regulatory agencies contend that:
(a) many of the regulated industries are natural monopolies
(b) the regulatory agencies have been "captured" by the firms they are supposed to regulate
(c) regulation contributes to an increase in the number of mergers in industries
(d) regulation helps to moderate costs and improves efficiency in the production of a good or service produced by the regulated industry

17. The legal cartel theory of regulation:
(a) would allow the forces of demand and supply to determine the rates (prices) of the good or service
(b) would attempt to protect the public from abuses of monopoly power
(c) assumes that the regulated industry wishes to be regulated

(d) assumes that both the demand for and supply of the good or service produced by the regulated industry are perfectly inelastic

18. Critics of the deregulation of industry argue that (among other things) deregulation will lead to:
   (a) higher prices for the products produced by the industry
   (b) the monopolization of the industry by a few large firms
   (c) a decline in the quantity or the quality of the product produced by the industry
   (d) all of the above

19. Deregulation of airlines in the United States has resulted in:
   (a) higher air fares
   (b) the monopolization of the airline industry by two large firms
   (c) a reduction in the availability of air services in the larger communities
   (d) lower wage rates for airline employees

20. The contestability of markets in the airline industry was probably:
   (a) increased by the use of "frequent flyer" programs by airlines
   (b) increased by the improvement in safety and airline regulation
   (c) decreased in the short term by a lack of airport capacity
   (d) decreased in the short term by a reduction in the quality of airline service

21. Which of the following is *not* a concern of the social regulation?
   (a) the prices charged for goods
   (b) the physical characteristics of goods produced
   (c) the conditions under which goods are manufactured
   (d) the impact upon society of the production of goods

22. Those costs incurred by businesses and state and local government in meeting the requirement of regulatory commissions are referred to as:
   (a) administrative costs
   (b) compliance costs
   (c) containment costs
   (d) per unit costs

23. Which one of the following is engaged in social regulation?
   (a) the Federal Trade Commission
   (b) the Interstate Commerce Commission
   (c) the Environmental Protection Agency
   (d) the Federal Energy Regulatory Commission

24. Which of the following is one of the major criticisms leveled against social regulation by its opponents?

(a) it is procompetitive
(b) it will decrease the rate of innovation in the economy
(c) it will increase the amount of price fixing among businesses
(d) it will require too long a time for it to achieve its objectives

25. Supporters of social regulation contend that:
   (a) there is a pressing need to reduce the number of mergers in American business
   (b) the presence of natural monopoly requires strong regulatory action by government
   (c) the social benefits will over time exceed the social costs
   (d) administrative and compliance costs are often exaggerated

■ **DISCUSSION QUESTIONS**

1. Explain the difference between the way the term "monopoly" is used in this chapter and the way it is used in Chapter 11. How is "industrial concentration" defined? How is the expression used in this chapter?

2. What are the chief arguments in the case against industrial concentration? In what two ways is the term *unprogressive* used in these arguments?

3. What are the chief arguments advanced in defense of industrial concentration?

4. What are the historical background to and the main provisions of the Sherman Act?

5. The Clayton Act and the Federal Trade Commission Act amended or elaborated the provisions of the Sherman Act, and both aimed at preventing rather than punishing monopoly. What were the chief provisions of each of these acts, and how did they attempt to prevent monopoly? In what two ways is the FTC Act important?

6. What loophole in the Clayton Act was plugged by the Celler-Kefauver Act in 1950 and how did it alter the coverage of the antitrust laws with respect to mergers?

7. Contrast the two different approaches to the application of the antitrust laws that are illustrated by the decisions of the courts in the U.S. Steel and Alcoa cases.

8. Why is defining the market an important issue in the application of the antitrust laws? How did the courts define the market in the case brought against DuPont for monopolizing the market for Cellophane?

9. How are the antitrust laws applied today to (*a*) existing market structures; (*b*) horizontal mergers; (*c*) vertical mergers; (*d*) conglomerate mergers; and (*e*) price fixing? What are the guidelines used for mergers?

10. In what ways has the Federal government restricted competition and fostered monopoly in the American economy?

11. What is a natural monopoly and what are the two alternative ways that can be used to ensure that it behaves in a socially acceptable fashion?

12. Explain the three major criticisms leveled against public interest regulation as it is practiced by commissions and agencies in the United States.

13. What is the legal cartel theory of regulation? Contrast it with the public interest theory of regulation.

14. Why were a number of industries in the American economy deregulated in the 1970s and 1980s? What did the proponents and the critics of deregulation predict would be the economic effects of deregulation?

15. How has deregulation affected the airline industry in terms of fares, service, safety, and industry structure? Why might antitrust enforcement be needed in this industry?

16. How does the social regulation differ from the industrial (or economic) regulation? What is the objective of this type of regulation, its three principal concerns, and its three distinguishing features?

17. What are the two types of costs of regulation? How do these costs compare?

18. Why do critics of regulation argue that the marginal costs exceed the marginal benefits?

19. What are three economic implications of social regulation?

20. What arguments do supporters of social regulation give?

■ **ANSWERS**

Chapter 20 Antitrust and Regulation

FILL-IN QUESTIONS

1. a few firms, both absolutely and relatively

2. misallocation, slows, unequal, dangers

3. superior products, interindustry, foreign (either order), scale, technological progress

4. competition, monopoly

5. monopol-, trade

6. discrimination, stock, tying, interlocking

7. unfair, hearings, cease-and-desist

8. Wheeler-Lea

9. Celler-Kefauver, Clayton

10. structure, narrowly, broadly (either order); a. reason, Alcoa; b. packaging materials

11. horizontal, vertical, conglomerate, Herfindahl

12. antitrust; a. (labor) unions, agricultural; b. patent, tariffs

13. natural, agencies, commissions (either order)

14. a. costs, capital, labor; b. the industry (firms) it is supposed to regulate; c. natural, competitive

15. monopoly, cartel

16. decreased, decreased, increased, increased, increased, decreased, increased, increased

17. quality; a. conditions, society, character; b. industrial, economic (either order)

18. administrative, compliance, 20, greater

19. increase, decrease, decrease, decrease

20. problems, benefits exceed the costs, benefits

21. is not, is, is

PROBLEMS AND PROJECTS

1. a. C; b. A; c. E; d. D; e. B

2. a. L; b. S; c. L; d. L; e. S; f. S; g. L

3. a. 2312, 2550, 1750, 4450, 1842; b. D, C; c. would not, 2312 1800, 80; d. would, 2550, 1000; e. would not, remain the same; f. would, would not

SELF-TEST

1. T, pp. 343–344	6. F, p. 346	11. F, p. 349	16. T, p. 352
2. F, p. 344	7. F, p. 347	12. F, p. 350	17. T, p. 353
3. T, p. 345	8. T, p. 347	13. F, p. 351	18. T, p. 355
4. T, p. 345	9. T, p. 348	14. F, p. 351	19. T, pp. 355–356
5. F, p. 346	10. F, p. 350	15. F, p. 352	20. F, pp. 356–357

1. d, p. 344	8. b, p. 347	14. a, pp. 351; 355	20. c, p. 354
2. b, p. 344	9. d, p. 348	15. b, p. 351	21. a, p. 355
3. d, p. 345	10. d, p. 349	16. b, p. 352	22. b, p. 355
4. a, p. 346	11. c, p. 349	17. c, p. 352	23. c, p. 355
5. b, p. 346	12. b, p. 349	18. d, p. 353	24. b, p. 357
6. d, p. 347	13. c, p. 350	19. d, p. 354	25. c, p. 357
7. a, p. 347			

DISCUSSION QUESTIONS

1. pp. 343–344	6. p. 347	11. p. 351	16. p. 355
2. p. 344	7. pp. 347–348	12. p. 352	17. pp. 355–356
3. p. 345	8. p. 348	13. pp. 351–352	18. p. 356
4. pp. 345–346	9. pp. 348–350	14. p. 353	19. pp. 356–357
5. pp. 346–347	10. p. 350	15. pp. 353–354	20. p. 357

CHAPTER 21

Agriculture: Economics and Policy

Agriculture is a large and vital part of the American and world economy, and therefore it merits the special attention it receives in Chapter 21. As you will learn, the economics of agriculture and farm policies of the Federal government are of concern not only to those directly engaged in farming, but also to American consumers and businesses who purchase farm products, and to American taxpayers who subsidize farm incomes. Agriculture is also important in the world economy because each nation must find a way to feed its population, and because domestic farm policies designed to enhance farm incomes often lead to distortions in world trade and economic inefficiency in world agricultural production.

The chapter begins by examining both the short-run and the long-run problem in American agriculture. The short-run problem is that farm prices and incomes have fluctuated sharply from year to year. The long-run problem is that agriculture is a declining industry, and as a consequence farm incomes fell over time. To understand the causes of each of these problems you will have to make use of the concept of inelastic demand and to employ your knowledge of how demand and supply determine price in a competitive market. The effort which you put into the study of these tools in previous chapters will now pay a dividend: understanding the causes of a real-world problem and the policies designed to solve the problem.

The agricultural policies of the Federal government have been directed at enhancing and stabilizing farm incomes by supporting farm prices. In connection with the support of farm prices you are introduced to the concept of parity. Once you understand parity and recognize that the parity price has in the past been above what the competitive price would have been you will come to some important conclusions. Consumers paid higher prices for and consumed smaller quantities of the various farm products; and at the prices supported by the Federal government there were surpluses of these products. The Federal government bought these surpluses to keep the price above the competitive market price. The purchases of the surpluses were financed by American taxpayers. To eliminate these surpluses, government looked for ways to increase the demand for or to decrease the supply of these commodities. Programs to increase demand and decrease supply were put into effect, but they failed to eliminate the annual surpluses.

Over the past half century, farm policies have not worked well and have been criticized for several reasons. First, the policies confuse the **symptions** of the problem (low farm prices and incomes) with the **causes** of the problem (resource allocation). Second, the costly farm subsidizes are also misguided because they tend to benefit the high-income instead of the low-income farmer. Third, some policies of the Federal government contradict or offset other policies designed to help farmers. Fourth, changes in the scale of farming and in domestic and world markets contribute to the declining effectiveness of domestic agricultural programs.

Despite the many reasons for criticizing farm policy, you will also learn that a public choice perspective provides insights into why costly farm programs have been subsidized by the Federal government over the years. Government subsidies for agriculture, however, are likely to decline in the future because of a falling farm population and less effective farm lobby, pressures to balance the Federal budget, negative public opinion about farm subsidies, and efforts to develop world agricultural policies.

In recent years, negotiations have been started to reduce world trade barriers to agricultural products. In this section of the chapter you will learn that a high level of domestic support for the price of farm products has severe negative effects on international trade and the economic efficiency in agricultural production worldwide. Although the United States has taken steps to reduce these trade barriers through international negotiations and recent changes in domestic farm policy, much remains to be done.

In the long run, it may be futile to try to enhance farm incomes in an economy in which the basic problem is too many farmers; and it may be better to allow farm prices and farm incomes to drift downward toward their long-run equilibrium levels in a free market. This would accelerate the movement of farmers out of agriculture and improve the allocation of the economy's resources. But to prevent unstable farm prices and farm incomes, the Federal government should try to stabilize farm prices in the short run as they move toward their long-run free market (or competitive) levels. This could be accomplished by the proposed free-market stabilization policy examined in the text.

The final section surveys what the pessimists and the optimists say about the possibility of worldwide shortages of agricultural products (that is, food) in the next century. The question is one of feast or famine during the years in which you will live the greater part of your life.

■ CHECKLIST

When you have studied this chapter you should be able to:

☐ Give five reasons for studying the economics of American agriculture.

☐ Explain the four causes of the short-run problem in agriculture.

☐ Identify two major factors contributing to long-run problems in agriculture.

☐ Use a supply and demand graph to illustrate the long-run problem in agriculture.

☐ Give cost estimates of the size of farm subsidies in the United States in recent years.

☐ Present several arguments which are made in support of Federal assistance to agriculture.

☐ Define the parity ratio and explain its significance to agricultural policy.

☐ Use a supply and demand graph to identify the economic effects of price supports for agricultural products on output, farm income, consumer and taxpayer expenditures, economic efficiency, and international trade.

☐ Give examples of how the Federal government restricts supply and bolsters demand for farm products.

☐ Present four criticisms of American agricultural policy.

☐ Use four insights from public choice theory to discuss the politics of agricultural legislation and expenditures by the Federal government for farm programs.

☐ Give four reasons to support a prediction that farm subsidies will decline in the future.

☐ Explain the effects of agricultural policy in the European Community (EC) and in the United States on world trade in agricultural products.

☐ List three proposals of the United States in the negotiations of the General Agreement on Tariffs and Trade (GATT).

☐ Identify three objectives of the Farm Act of 1990.

☐ Describe the characteristics, operation, and advantages of a market-oriented policy designed to stabilize farm product prices and farm income.

☐ List the contentions of the pessimists and the responses of the optimists on the issue of whether the world will be able to feed itself fifty years from now.

■ CHAPTER OUTLINE

1. The economic analysis of American agriculture is important for at least five reasons: it is the nation's largest industry; it is a real-world example of the purely competitive model; it illustrates the economic effects of government intervention in markets; it reflects changes in global markets; and it highlights aspects of public choice theory.

2. The farm problem is both a short-run and a long-run problem: the short-run problem is the frequent sharp changes in the incomes of farmers from one year to the next; the long-run problem is the tendency for farm prices and incomes to lag behind the upward trend of prices and incomes in the rest of the economy.

   a. The causes of the short-run (income-instability) problem are the inelastic demand for farm products, fluctuations in the output of agricultural products, fluctuations in the domestic demand, and the unstable foreign demand which result in relatively large changes in agricultural prices and farm incomes.

   b. The causes of the long-run problem (low farm income and farm prices) stem from two basic factors:
(1) the supply of agricultural products increased significantly over most of this century because of technological advance in agriculture; and
(2) the demand for agricultural products failed to match the large increase in supply even though there were large increases in income (and population) because the demand for agricultural products is *income* inelastic (that is, increases in income lead to less than proportionate increases in expenditures on farm products).

3. Since the 1930s, farmers have been able to obtain various forms of public aid, but the primary purpose of the Federal government programs has been to enhance and stabilize farm prices and incomes.

   a. Federal government support of agricultural programs is costly (estimated to be $40 to $55 billion from 1990–1994); several arguments are used to justify these expenditures, such as the poor incomes of farmers, the importance of the "family farm," the hazards of farming, and market power problems.

   b. The cornerstone of Federal policy to raise farm prices is the concept of parity (or the parity price) which would give the farmer year after year the same real income per unit of output.

   c. Historically farm policy supported farm prices at some percentage of the parity price. But because the supported price was almost always above the market price, government had to support the price by purchasing and accumulating surpluses of agricultural products; and while farmers gained from this policy, there were losses for consumers and for society, and problems were created in the international sector. To reduce the annual and accumulated surpluses, government attempted:

(1) to reduce the output (or supply) of farm products by acreage-allotment and soil bank programs; and

(2) to expand the demand for farm products by finding new uses for farm products, expanding domestic demand, and increasing the foreign demand for agricultural commodities.

4. Agricultural policies designed to stabilize farm income and prices have not worked well over the past half century, and are subject to four major criticisms.

　a. Farm programs have confused the **symptoms** of the problem (low farm product and low farm incomes) with the **causes** of the problem (resource allocation), and have encouraged people to stay in agriculture.

　b. The major benefits from farm programs are misguided because low-income farmers often receive small government subsidies while high-income farmers often receive large government subsidies; price supports also affect land values and become a subsidy for owners of farm land who rent their land and do not farm.

　c. The various farm programs of the Federal government have often offset or contradicted each other.

　d. Domestic farm policy is becoming less effective in its goal of enhancing farm incomes because of the increased size of farm operations, and because of the significant effects on farm incomes from changes in interest rates or the international value of the dollar.

5. The politics of farm policy explain why costly and extensive farm programs have persisted in the United States despite a decline in the farm population and in the farm vote.

　a. Four insights from public choice theory serve to explain this development: **rent-seeking behavior** by farm groups; the **special-interest effect** that impairs public decision-making; political **logrolling** to turn negative outcomes into a positive outcomes; and the **clear benefits and hidden costs** of farm programs.

　b. But farm subsidies are likely to decline in the future because of continuing declines in the farm population, pressures to balance the Federal budget, the excesses and negative publicity from farm subsidies, and conflicts between domestic and world agricultural policies.

6. The move to reduce trade barriers to agricultural products on a worldwide basis is a significant development of recent years.

　a. Increased domestic support for the price of farm products often has negative effects on trade.

　(1) For example, price support policies by the European Community led to higher trade barriers (tariffs or quotas) to restrict the agricultural imports, gave incentives for domestic overproduction led to demands for export subsidies, and caused problems for American farmers.

　(2) From a world perspective, trade barriers for agricultural products are economically inefficient, distort the patterns of world trade, create frictions in international relations, and are costly (about $35 billion per year).

　b. The United States government proposed a reduction in agricultural tariffs, export subsidies for farm products, and domestic farm supports that distort world trade in recent negotiations of the **General Agreements on Tariffs and Trade** (GATT), but no progress has been made because of opposition from other nations.

　c. The **Farm Act of 1990** has sought to reduce the cost of farm subsidies through reductions in acreage covered by farm programs and by increasing the role of the market in determining farm product prices.

　d. In the long run, it is likely that farm policy will shift from the goal of **enhancing** farm income to the goal of **stabilizing** farm incomes by such government actions as buying farm products when they fall below the long-run trend in the market, or by selling accumulated surpluses when prices rise above the long-run trend; several advantages are cited by proponents of this **market-oriented income stabilization policy**.

7. The American economy has produced agricultural surpluses over the years, but other nations have been plagued by chronic shortages of food; a pessimistic or an optimistic answer can be given to the question of whether the world will be able to feed itself in the future.

■ **IMPORTANT TERMS**

Short-run farm problem	Acreage allotment programs
Long-run farm problem	
Agricultural Adjustment Act of 1933	Soil bank program
	Food for Peace program
Parity concept	Farm Act of 1990
Parity ratio	Market-oriented income stabilization
Price support	

■ **FILL-IN QUESTIONS**

　1. It is important to study the economics of American agriculture for at least five reasons: it is the _____ industry in the nation; it provides a real-world example of the _____ model; it demonstrates the effects of government _____; it reflects the _____ agricultural markets; and it illustrates aspects of _____ theory.

　2. The basic cause of the short-run problem in agriculture is the _____ demand for farm products. This demand occurs because farm products have few

good _____, and because of rapidly diminishing
_____

3. The inelastic demand for farm products contributes to unstable farm prices and incomes because relatively (large, small) _____ changes in the output of farm products results in relative _____ changes in prices and incomes; and because relatively _____ changes in domestic or foreign demand result in relatively _____ changes in prices and incomes.

4. From a long-run perspective, the (demand for, supply of) _____ agricultural products increased greatly over the past twenty-five years because of technological progress, but the _____ agricultural products did not increase by as much, in large part because food demand is income (elastic, inelastic) _____ and because the rate of population increase has not matched the increase in production.

5. Since the 1930s, the Federal government has primarily developed programs to enhance or to stabilize the _____ and _____ of farmers. Federal support for agricultural programs is estimated to cost $_____ to $_____ billion under the five-year farm bill adopted in 1990.

6. Four arguments used to justify these expenditures are: the _____ income of farmers; the importance to the "_____" farm as an American institution; the "_____" of farming from many natural disasters; and the fact that the farmers sell their output in (purely competitive, imperfectly competitive) _____ markets, and purchase their inputs in _____ markets.

7. If farmers were to receive a parity price for a product, year after year a given output would enable them to acquire a (fixed, increased) _____ amount of goods and services.

8. If the government supports farm prices at an above-equilibrium level, the result will be (shortages, surpluses) _____ which the government must _____ in order to maintain prices at their support level.

a. Farmers benefit from this price-support program because it increases their _____

b. But consumers are hurt by it because they must pay

higher _____ and consume (more, less) _____ of the product.

c. Society (gains, loses) _____ because taxpayers will pay (higher, lower) _____ taxes to finance the purchase of the surplus by government; and because there is economic _____ _____ from the (overallocation, underallocation) _____ of resources to agriculture.

d. There are also _____ costs from distortion in worldwide supply and demand for agricultural products, the increased potential for _____ barriers, and a (positive, negative) _____ effect on less developed countries.

9. To bring the equilibrium level of prices in the market up to their support level, government has attempted to (increase, decrease) _____ the demand for and to _____ the supply of farm products.

10. Two types of programs that have been used by the Federal government to reduce agricultural production are acreage-_____ and _____ programs. The Federal government has also attempted to find new _____ for agricultural commodities, and to increase domestic and foreign _____ for agricultural products through the domestic food _____ program or the foreign _____ program.

11. Agricultural policies to stabilize farm income and prices (have, have not) _____ worked well over the past sixty years for at least four reasons:

a. They have confused the _____ of the farm problem (low prices and incomes) with the _____ of the problem (misallocation of resources);

b. Much of the benefits from farm subsidies go to (high, low) _____-income farmers instead of _____-income farmers;

c. Farm programs of the Federal government have offset or _____ each other;

d. Domestic farm policy is (increasing, decreasing) _____ in its effectiveness in enhancing farm incomes because of the _____ scale of farm operations; and because of the significant effects on farm incomes from changes in domestic _____ rates

or the international value of the _____

12. Despite these criticisms, farm policies have received strong support in Congress over the years, the result of which can be explained by insights from _____ theory. Farm groups are exhibiting _____ behavior when they lobby for programs that transfer income to them. There is also a _____ effect because the costs to individual taxpayers is (large, small) _____ but the benefits to farmers is _____ from farm programs. Agricultural groups or farm-state politicians can turn negative outcomes into positive outcomes by political _____. The benefits of farm programs are (clear, hidden) _____, but the costs are _____

13. Farm subsidies are likely to decline in the future because of declines in the farm _____, pressures to balance the Federal _____, negative publicity from the excesses of farm _____, and domestic and world agricultural _____ conflicts.

14. The effects of higher supports for the prices of agricultural products by the European Community have been (increased, decreased) _____ trade barriers, _____ incentives for domestic production in the member nations, _____ export subsidies for farm products in member nations, and _____ sales of American agricultural products to the European Community.

15. World barriers to free trade in agricultural products _____ trade and contribute to economic _____ in the allocation of world resources to agriculture. The estimate benefits from free trade in world agriculture are $_____ billion per year.

16. The American proposals in recent negotiations under the General Agreements on _____ called for (an increase, a decrease) _____ in agricultural tariffs, _____ export subsidies for farm products, and _____ domestic price supports for agricultural commodities that distort world trade, but the negotiations collapsed because of strong opposition from other nations.

17. The *Farm Act of 1990* aimed to decrease the cost of farm subsidies through reductions in _____ covered by farm programs, and by making more use of the _____ to determine prices for agricultural commodities.

18. The market-oriented income stabilization policy:
   a. would have the Federal government (buy, sell) _____ agricultural commodities when their market prices fell below and _____ agricultural commodities when their market prices rose above their long-run trends of prices.
   b. would, its proponents contend, (expand, contract) _____ government involvement in agriculture, improve the _____ of resources in the long run, reduce the costs of the farm programs to _____, and stimulate the _____ of agricultural commodities.

19. There is a global dimension to farm problems:
   a. The pessimistic view is one of possible famine as (supply, demand) _____ outpaces _____ because:
   (1) the quantity of arable land is _____ and its quality is _____;
   (2) urban sprawl reduces the availability of (agricultural, nonagricultural) _____ land;
   (3) the underground water system is being depleted by increasing _____;
   (4) world _____ continues to increase; and
   (5) future agricultural production may be affected by long-run changes in the _____
   b. Optimists contend global famine is not a serious prospect because:
   (1) the arable land for production can be _____ _____;
   (2) agricultural _____ continues to rise, especially in _____ countries;
   (3) the rate of world _____ growth is diminishing; and
   (4) any food shortages would produce adjustments in _____ system.

■ PROBLEMS AND PROJECTS

1. In columns 1 and 2 in the following table is a demand schedule for agricultural product X.

(1) Price	(2) Bushels of X demanded	(3) Bushels of X demanded
$2.00	600	580
1.80	620	600
1.60	640	620
1.40	660	640
1.20	680	660
1.00	700	680
.80	720	700
.60	740	720

a. Is demand elastic or inelastic in the price range given? _____

b. If the amount of X produced should increase from 600 to 700 bushels, the income of producers of X would _____ from $_____ to $_____; an increase of _____% in the amount of X produced would cause income to _____ by _____%.

c. If the amount of X produced were 700 bushels and the demand for X decreased from that shown in columns 1 and 2 to that shown in columns 1 and 3, the price of X would _____ from $_____ to $_____; the income of farmers would _____ from $_____ to $_____.

d. Assume that the government supports a price of $1.80, that the demand for X is that shown in columns 1 and 2, and that farmers grow 720 bushels of X.

(1) At the supported price there will be a surplus of _____ bushels of X.

(2) If the government buys this surplus at the support price the cost to the taxpayers of purchasing the surplus is $_____

(3) The total income of the farmers producing product X when they receive the support price of $1.80 per bushel for their entire crop of 720 bushels is $_____

(4) Had farmers to sell the crop of 720 bushels at the free-market price, the price of X would be only $_____ per bushel; and the total income of these farmers would be $_____

(5) The gain to farmers producing X from the price-support program is, therefore, $_____

(6) In addition to the cost to taxpayers of purchasing the surplus, consumers pay a price that is $_____

greater than the free-market price and receive a quantity of X that is _____ bushels less than they would have received in a free market.

2. The following table gives the index of prices farmers paid in three different years. The price farmers received in year 1, the base year, for a certain agricultural product was $3.50 per bushel.

a. Compute the parity price of the product in years 2 and 3 and enter them in the table.

Year	Index of prices paid	Parity price	Price received	Parity ratio
1	100	$3.50	$3.50	100%
2	120	_____	3.78	_____%
3	200	_____	5.25	_____%

b. The prices received for the product in each year are also shown in the table. Complete the table by computing the parity *ratio* in years 2 and 3. (*Hint:* It is *not* necessary to construct an index of prices received in order to compute the parity ratio. This ratio can be computed by dividing the price received by the parity price.)

3. The demand schedule for agricultural product Y is given in columns 1 and 2 of the following table.

(1) Price	(2) Bales of Y demanded	(3) Bales of Y demanded
$5.00	40,000	41,000
4.75	40,200	41,200
4.50	40,400	41,400
4.25	40,600	41,600
4.00	40,800	41,800
3.75	41,000	42,000
3.50	41,200	42,200

a. If farmers were persuaded by the government to reduce the size of their crop from 41,000 to 40,000 bales, the income of farmers would _____ from $_____ to $_____

b. If the crop remained constant at 41,000 bales and the demand for Y increased to that shown in columns 1 and 3, the income of farmers would _____ from $_____ to $_____

4. Suppose the demand for sow jowls during a certain period of time was that shown in the table on the next page, and the Federal government wished to stabilize the price of sow jowls at $.70 a pound.

Price (per pound)	Quantity demanded (pounds)
$1.00	1000
.90	1020
.80	1040
.70	1060
.60	1080
.50	1100
.40	1120

a. If the output of sow jowls were 1100 pounds during that period of time, the market price of sow jowls would

be $_____ and the Federal government

would (buy, sell) _____ (how many)

_____ pounds of sow jowls.

b. But if the output were 1000 pounds during that period of time, the market price of sow jowls would be

$_____ and the Federal government

would _____ (how many) _____
pounds of sow jowls.

■ **SELF-TEST**

Circle the T if the statement is true; the F if it is false.

1. The short-run farm problem is the sharp year-to-year fluctuations in farm prices and farm incomes that frequently occur.   **T F**

2. The demand for farm products is price elastic. **T F**

3. The quantities of agricultural commodities produced tend to be fairly *insensitive* to changes in agricultural prices because a large percentage of farmers' total costs are variable.   **T F**

4. The foreign demand for farm products is relatively stable.   **T F**

5. Appreciation of the dollar will tend to increase the demand for farm products.   **T F**

6. The supply of agricultural products has tended to increase more rapidly than the demand for these products in the United States.   **T F**

7. Most of the recent technological advances in agriculture have been initiated by farmers.   **T F**

8. The demand for farm products is income elastic.   **T F**

9. The long-run farm problem is that the incomes of farmers have been low relative to incomes in the economy as a whole.   **T F**

10. The size of the farm population in the United States

has declined in both relative and absolute terms since about 1930.   **T F**

11. The major aim of agricultural policy in the United States has been to enhance and stabilize farm prices and farm incomes.   **T F**

12. Federal expenditures for farm price and income support programs are relatively small and cost only $1 billion a year.   **T F**

13. If the prices paid by farmers were 500% higher than in the base year and the price received by farmers were 400% higher than in the base year, the parity ratio would be 125%.   **T F**

14. Application of the parity concept to farm prices causes farm prices to decline and results in agricultural surpluses.   **T F**

15. When government supports farm prices at above-equilibrium levels it can reduce the annual surpluses of agricultural commodities either by increasing the supply or by decreasing the demand for them.   **T F**

16. The acreage-allotment and soil bank programs were designed to decrease the supply of farm products. **T F**

17. Restricting the number of acres which farmers employ to grow agricultural products has not been a very successful method of reducing surpluses because farmers tend to cultivate their land more intensively when the acreage is reduced.   **T F**

18. Public policy has been effective in alleviating the resource allocation problem in agriculture.   **T F**

19. The price-income support programs for agriculture have most benefited those farmers who least need the government assistance.   **T F**

20. A farm organization lobbying Congress for an increase in farm subsidies is an example of political *logrolling*.   **T F**

21. One reason to predict that farm subsidies will decline in the future is that there is a declining farm population.
   T F

22. Domestic agricultural support programs are not harmful to world agricultural trade and contribute to the efficiency allocation of worldwide resources to agriculture.
   T F

23. The Farm Bill of 1990 called for an increase in farm subsidies and reduced reliance on markets to determine the prices of agricultural products.   **T F**

24. A market-oriented income stabilization policy would shift the goal of farm policy from enhancing to stabilizing farm incomes.   **T F**

25. There are no strong counterarguments to the position that "unless the nations of the world adopt new agricultural policies there will be a worldwide famine fifty years from now."   **T   F**

Circle the letter that corresponds to the best answer.

1. If the demand for agricultural products is price inelastic, a relatively small increase in supply will result in:
   (a) a relatively small increase in farm prices and incomes
   (b) a relatively small decrease in farm prices and a relatively large increase in farm incomes
   (c) a relatively large decrease in farm prices and incomes
   (d) a relatively large increase in farm prices and a relatively small decrease in farm incomes

2. The year-to-year instability of farm prices and farm incomes is the result of fluctuations in:
   (a) the outputs of farmers
   (b) the domestic demand for farm products
   (c) the foreign demand for agricultural commodities
   (d) all of the above

3. If over time increases in the supply of farm products are much greater than the increases in demand for farm products, then the supply and demand model for farm products would suggest that price:
   (a) and quantity will both increase
   (b) and quantity will both decrease
   (c) will increase, but the quantity will decrease
   (d) will decrease, but the quantity will increase

4. Which one of the following is *not* a reason why the increases in demand for agricultural commodities have been relatively small?
   (a) the population of the United States has not increased so rapidly as the productivity of agriculture
   (b) the increased per capita incomes of American consumers have resulted in less than proportionate increases in their expenditures for farm products
   (c) the demand for agricultural products is inelastic
   (d) the standard of living in the United States is well above the level of bare subsistence

5. The market system has failed to solve the long-run problem of low farm incomes because:
   (a) the demand for agricultural products is relatively inelastic
   (b) the supply of agricultural products is relatively elastic
   (c) agricultural products have relatively few good substitutes
   (d) agricultural resources are relatively immobile

6. The farm bill passed in 1990 is expected to cost, over a five-year period, about:

   (a) $5 billion
   (b) $20 billion
   (c) $40–$55 billion
   (d) $100–$115 billion

7. Which of the following is *not* one of the arguments used in support of public aid for agriculture in the United States?
   (a) farmers are relative poor and need help to maintain a "way of life"
   (b) farmers are subject to hazards to which other industries are not subject
   (c) farmers sell their products in highly competitive markets and buy resources in highly imperfect markets
   (d) farmers are more affected by competition from foreign producers than other parts of the economy

8. Farm parity means that:
   (a) the real income of the farmer remains constant
   (b) a given output will furnish the farmer with a constant amount of real income
   (c) the purchasing power of the farmer's nominal income remains constant
   (d) the nominal income of the farmer will buy a constant amount of goods and services

9. If the index of prices paid by farmers was 1000 and the prices received by farmers was 600, then the parity ratio would be:
   (a) 2.1
   (b) 1.7
   (c) 0.6
   (d) 0.4

10. The necessary consequence of the government's supporting farm prices at an above-equilibrium level is:
   (a) a surplus of agricultural products
   (b) increased consumption of agricultural products
   (c) reduced production of agricultural products
   (d) the destruction of agricultural products

11. Another consequence of having government support farm prices at an above-equilibrium level is that consumers pay higher prices for farm products and:
   (a) consume more of these products and pay higher taxes
   (b) consume less of these products and pay higher taxes
   (c) consume more of these products and pay lower taxes
   (d) consume less of these products and pay lower taxes

Use the diagram on the next page to answer the next three questions (12, 13, and 14). D is the demand for and S is the supply of a certain product.

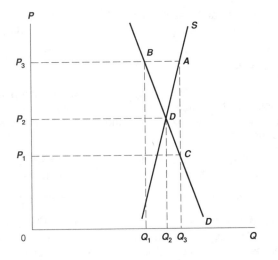

12. If the Federal government supported the price of this product at P_3, the total amount it would have to spend to purchase the surplus of the product would be:
(a) $0Q_3AP_3$
(b) Q_1Q_3AB
(c) P_1CAP_3
(d) $0Q_1BP_3$

13. With a support price of P_3, the total income of producers of the product will be:
(a) $0Q_3AP_3$
(b) $0Q_1BP_3$
(c) $0Q_3CP_1$
(d) $0Q_2DP_2$

14. With a support price of P_3, the amount spent by consumers will be:
(a) $0Q_3AP_3$
(b) $0Q_1BP_3$
(c) $0Q_2DP_2$
(d) Q_1Q_3AB

*Answer the next three questions (**15, 16,** and **17**) on the basis of the demand and supply schedules for agricultural product Z as shown below.*

Pounds of Z demanded	Price	Pounds of Z supplied
850	$1.30	1150
900	1.20	1100
950	1.10	1050
1000	1.00	1000
1050	.90	950
1100	.80	900
1150	.70	850

15. If the Federal government supports the price of Z at $1.30 a pound, then at this price, there is:
(a) a surplus of 200 pounds of **Z**
(b) a surplus of 300 pounds of **Z**

(c) a surplus of 400 pounds of **Z**
(d) a shortage of 400 pounds of **Z**

16. With a Federal price support of $1.30 a pound, consumers spend:
(a) $1,040, the Federal government spends $410, and farmers receive income from product **Z** of $1,450
(b) $1,105, the Federal government spends $390, and farmers receive income from product **Z** of $1,495
(c) $1,296, the Federal government spends $240, and farmers receive income from product **Z** of $1,320
(d) $1,045, the Federal government spends $110, and farmers receive income from product **Z** of $1,155

17. If instead of supporting the price the Federal government took actions to increase demand by 150 units at each price and to decrease supply by 150 units at each price, then the equilibrium price would be:
(a) $1.00 and the income of farmers would be $1000
(b) $1.10 and the income of farmers would be $1320
(c) $1.20 and the income of farmers would be $1260
(d) $1.30 and the income of farmers would be $1300

18. Which one of the following is **not** a reason why farm programs have generally failed to accomplish their aims?
(a) the farm programs have not eliminated the basic cause of the problem
(b) restricting agricultural output increases farm prices but reduces farm income when demand is inelastic
(c) the farm program has become increasingly more costly and less effective
(d) the principal beneficiaries of government aid have been farmers with high, not low, incomes

19. Which of the following can diminish the effectiveness of farm programs?
(a) changes in interest rates in the economy
(b) changes in the international value of the dollar
(c) the accessibility of foreign markets to farmers
(d) all of the above

20. When farmers and farm organizations lobby Congress for a larger appropriation for agricultural price and income programs, then according to public choice theory this action would be an example of:
(a) confusing symptoms with causes
(b) misguided subsidies
(c) rent-seeking behavior
(d) political logrolling

21. Which of the following has been a consequence of protective trade barriers for agriculture established by the nations of the European Community (EC)?
(a) restriction of exports of EC farm products
(b) subsidization of imports of U.S. farm products
(c) overproduction of farm products in the EC
(d) underproduction of farm products in the EC

22. The goal of a market-oriented income stabilization policy would be:

(a) to prevent farm prices and incomes from falling in the long run

(b) to prevent sharp fluctuations in farm prices and incomes from one year to the next

(c) to increase farm prices and incomes in the long run

(d) to prevent both sharp year-to-year fluctuations and falling long-run farm prices and incomes

23. In a market-oriented income stabilization policy the Federal government would:

(a) sell surplus farm commodities when their prices fall below their long-run trend of prices

(b) buy surplus farm commodities when their prices rise above their long-run trend of prices

(c) sell surplus farm commodities when their prices rise above their long-run trend

(d) buy surplus farm commodities when their market prices fall

24. Which of the following is *not* one of the advantages its proponents see in a market-oriented income stabilization policy?

(a) an expansion in the employment of resources in the agricultural sector of the economy

(b) an expansion in the exports of the agricultural sector of the ecoomy

(c) a reduction in the costs to taxpayers of the farm program

(d) a reduction in government involvement in agriculture

25. A good reason for an optimistic view of the capacity of the world to feed itself fifty years from now would be that:

(a) the population of the world is increasing

(b) the climate of the world is changing

(c) agricultural productivity is rising

(d) land is being put to more productive uses in urban areas

■ **DISCUSSION QUESTIONS**

1. Why are the economics of agriculture and agriculture policy important topics for study?

2. What is the short-run farm problem and what are its causes?

3. Why does the demand for agricultural products tend to be inelastic? What are the implications for agriculture?

4. What have been the specific causes of the large increases in the supply of agricultural products since World War I?

5. Why has the demand for agricultural products failed to increase at the same rate as the supply of these products?

6. Explain why the farm population tends to be relatively immobile.

7. What is meant by "the farm program"? What particular aspect of the farm problem has traditionally received the major attention of farmers and their representatives in Congress?

8. Why do agricultural interests claim that farmers have a special right to aid from the Federal government?

9. Explain the concept of parity and the parity ratio.

10. Why is the result of government-supported prices invariably a surplus of farm commodities? How do supported prices affect consumers and farmers?

11. What programs has the government used to try to restrict farm production? Why have these programs been relatively unsuccessful in limiting agricultural production?

12. How has the Federal government tried to increase the demand for farm products?

13. Why has farm policy not been successful in preventing falling farm prices and incomes, surpluses, and the disparity in farm incomes?

14. What insights does public choice theory provide about the persistence of Federal government support for farm programs?

15. What are the reasons to suggest that the Federal government support for farm programs will decline in the future?

16. Explain the economic effects of high trade barriers for agricultural products on a domestic economy and on the world economy using the nations of the European Community as the example of a domestic economy. What are the estimated costs to the world economy of trade barriers in agriculture?

17. Discuss the proposal of the United States in the agricultural trade negotiations of the General Agreements on Tariffs and Trade (GATT).

18. What is the direction of farm policy in the United States as reflected in the Farm Act of 1990?

19. Explain

(a) how the market-oriented income stabilization policy would shift the emphasis from enhancing to stabilizing farm prices and incomes

(b) how the Federal government would stabilize farm prices and incomes if it adopted this policy

(c) what advantages the proponents of this policy believe it would have

20. What are the arguments of the pessimists and of the optimists on the issue of whether the world will be able to feed itself in the next century?

■ ANSWERS

Chapter 21 Agriculture: Economics and Policy

FILL-IN QUESTIONS

1. largest, purely competitive, policies, globalization, public choice

2. inelastic, substitutes, marginal utility

3. small, large, small, large

4. supply of, demand for, inelastic

5. prices, income (either order), 40, 55

6. low (or poor), family, hazards, purely competitive, imperfectly competitive

7. fixed

8. surpluses, purchase; *a.* incomes; *b.* prices, less; *c.* loses, higher, inefficiency, overallocation; *d.* international, trade, negative

9. increase, decrease

10. allotments, soil bank, uses, demand, stamps, Food for Peace

11. have not, *a.* symptoms, causes; *b.* high, low; *c.* contradicted; *d.* decreasing, large, interest, dollar

12. public choice, rent-seeking, special interest, small, large, logrolling, clear, hidden

13. population, budget, subsidies, policy

14. increased, increased, increased, decreased

15. distort, inefficiency, 35

16. Tariffs and Trade, a decrease, a decrease, a decrease

17. acreage, market

18. *a.* buy, sell; *b.* contract, allocation, taxpayers, export

19. *a.* demand, supply; (1) fixed, poor, (2) agricultural, (3) irrigation, (4) population, (5) climate; *b.* (1) increased, (2) productivity, less developed, (3) population, (4) price (market)

PROBLEMS AND PROJECTS

1. *a.* inelastic; *b.* decrease, 1,200.00, 700.00, 16⅔, decrease, 41⅔; *c.* fall, 1.00, 0.80, fall, 700.00, 560.00; *d.* (1) 100, (2) 180, (3) 1296, (4) 0.80, 576, (5) 720, (6) 1.00, 100

2. *a.* 420, 7.00; *b.* 90, 75

3. *a.* increase, 153,750.00, 200,000.00; *b.* increase, 153,750.00, 205,000.00

4. *a.* .50, buy, 40; *b.* 1.00, sell, 60

SELF-TEST

1. T, p. 362	**14.** F, p. 368
2. F, pp. 362–363	**15.** F, p. 368
3. F, p. 363	**16.** T, p. 369
4. F, p. 364	**17.** T, p. 369
5. F, p. 364	**18.** F, p. 370
6. T, pp. 364–365	**19.** T, p. 370
7. F, p. 365	**20.** F, p. 371
8. F, p. 365	**21.** T, p. 372
9. T, pp. 365–366	**22.** F, p. 372
10. T, p. 366	**23.** F, p. 373
11. T, p. 366	**24.** T, p. 373
12. F, p. 366	**25.** F, p. 375
13. F, p. 368	

1. *c*, p. 363	**14.** *b*, p. 368
2. *d*, pp. 363–364	**15.** *b*, p. 368
3. *d*, p. 365	**16.** *b*, p. 368
4. *c*, p. 365	**17.** *d*, pp. 368–369
5. *d*, p. 366	**18.** *b*, p. 370
6. *c*, p. 366	**19.** *d*, p. 371
7. *d*, p. 367	**20.** *c*, p. 371
8. *b*, p. 367	**21.** *c*, p. 372
9. *c*, p. 368	**22.** *b*, p. 373
10. *a*, p. 368	**23.** *c*, pp. 373–374
11. *b*, p. 368	**24.** *a*, p. 374
12. *b*, p. 368	**25.** *c*, p. 375
13. *a*, p. 368	

DISCUSSION QUESTIONS

1. p. 362	**11.** p. 369
2. pp. 362–363	**12.** pp. 369–370
3. p. 363	**13.** pp. 370–371
4. p. 365	**14.** pp. 371–372
5. p. 365	**15.** p. 372
6. pp. 365–366	**16.** pp. 372–373
7. pp. 366–367	**17.** p. 373
8. p. 367	**18.** p. 373
9. pp. 367–368	**19.** pp. 373–374
10. p. 368	**20.** pp. 374–375

CHAPTER 22

Income Inequality and Poverty

Chapter 22 examines another current problem in the economy of the United States: the unequal distribution of total income and the poverty of many families in the nation.

The things which you should learn from this chapter are found in the checklist below. In addition, the following ideas have an important bearing on the discussion of inequality and poverty. First, you will recall from Chapter 6 that one of the functions of government in the American economy is to modify the economic results which a *pure* market system would yield: it is the market system and the institutions of capitalism which bring about an unequal distribution of income, and government in the United States has worked to reduce—but not eliminate—this unequal distribution.

Second, the critics of the market system attack the system because it has unequally distributed income. But American capitalism has replied by repairing many of its faults. It is for this reason that people and groups advocating drastically different economic systems have met with little success in the United States or in other nations of the world.

Third, the single most effective method of reducing the importance of income inequality and the extent of poverty in the United States has been the maintenance of full employment and an expanding average standard of living. Other programs have aided in the achievement of this goal, but the best cure has been the high and increasing output of the American economy.

Fourth, very few people advocate an absolutely equal distribution of income; the question to be decided is not one of inequality or equality, but of how much or how little inequality there should be. The question can be looked at either ethically or economically, and the economist has nothing to offer on the ethical question but a personal value judgment. From the economic point of view it is the task of the economist to observe that less income inequality may result in a smaller domestic output and a lower employment rate. This is the fundamental "tradeoff" confronting the economy and it requires that the people of the United States make a choice. The pros and cons of the income-inequality issue represent no more than different opinions on the degree to which we should reduce our economic efficiency (total output and employment) in order to reduce income inequality.

Finally, while poverty is caused by many forces, it is essentially an economic problem. Any attack on poverty will have to be an economic attack. Over the years a variety of programs have been established to provide income support for people in the United States. At the end of the chapter you will learn about the major features of the programs. Despite these established programs, there is still dissatisfaction with the income maintenance system. The final topic of the chapter focuses on comprehensive and partial proposals for reform of public assistance.

■ CHECKLIST

When you have studied this chapter you should be able to:

☐ Present data from the textbook to support the conclusion that there is considerable income inequality in the United States.

☐ Report what has happened to the distribution of income in the United States in three time periods since 1929.

☐ State what is measured on each axis when a Lorenz curve is used to describe the degree of income inequality; and what area measures the extent of income inequality.

☐ Explain the two ways in which Census Bureau data on income inequality have been adjusted; and what the adjusted data reveal about the degree of and the trends in income equality in the United States.

☐ Describe the effects of taxes and of transfer payments on the extent of inequality in the distribution of income and poverty in the American economy.

☐ Enumerate seven causes of an unequal distribution of income.

☐ State the case *for* and the case *against* income equality.

☐ Explain the trade-off between equality and efficiency that is at the heart of the debate over how much income inequality is desirable.

☐ Define poverty using current government standards.

☐ Identify the groups in which poverty is concentrated.

☐ Describe the trends in the poverty rate since 1960.

☐ Explain the "black underclass" view of ghetto poverty and poverty programs.

☐ Give three reasons why poverty tends to be invisible.

☐ Contrast social insurance with public assistance (welfare); and list the three programs in the former and the four programs in the latter category.

☐ State three major criticisms of the welfare system.

☐ Explain how a negative income tax (NIT) might be employed to reform the welfare system and the two crucial elements in any NIT plan.

☐ List the three goals of any NIT plan and explain why it is impossible to devise a program in which these three goals do not conflict.

☐ State five reasons why the AFDC program was subject to calls for reform.

☐ Explain what *workfare* means and describe the Family Support Act of 1988.

■ CHAPTER OUTLINE

1. There is considerable income inequality in the American economy.

   a. The extent of the inequality can be seen by examining a personal-distribution-of-income table.

   b. Since 1929 the real incomes received by all income classes have increased; and between 1929 and 1947 the relative distribution of personal income changed to reduce income inequality. From 1947–1969 there was a slight increase in the equality of income distribution, but from 1969–1990, the distribution of income moved to less equality. Comparing 1947 to 1990, the distribution of income has been relatively constant.

   c. The Lorenz curve is a geometric device for portraying the extent of inequality in any group at any time, for comparing the extent of inequality among different groups, and for contrasting the extent of inequality at different times.

2. The data published annually by the Bureau of the Census may overstate the extent of income inequality in the United States.

   a. By broadening the concept of income to include in-kind transfers, education provided by government, and capital gains, and by subtracting Federal personal income and payroll taxes, Browning concluded that inequality in the distribution of income is less than assumed and has lessened with the passage of time.

   b. By looking at earnings over a lifetime rather than in a single year Paglin found that there is less income inequality than census data indicate and that income equality has lessened since World War II.

3. The tax system and the transfer payments of govern-ment in the United States significantly reduce the extent of income inequality and of poverty in the American economy.

4. The impersonal market system does not necessarily result in a just or fair distribution of income; at least seven factors explain why income inequality exists:

   (1) the distribution of abilities and skills of people;

   (2) differences in education and training;

   (3) preferences of certain types of jobs and willingness to accept risk on the job;

   (4) discrimination in labor markets;

   (5) inequalities in the ownership of property and in the accumulation of wealth;

   (6) market power in either resource or product markets; and

   (7) other factors such as luck, personal connections, and misfortunes.

5. The important question which society must answer is not whether there will or will not be income inequality but what is the best amount of inequality.

   a. Those who argue for equality contend that it leads to the maximum satisfaction of consumer wants (utility) in the economy.

   b. But those who argue for inequality contend that equality would reduce the incentives to work, save, invest, and take risks; and that these incentives are needed if the economy is to be efficient: to produce as large an output (and income) as it is possible for it to produce from its available resources.

   c. In the United States there is a trade-off between economic equality and economic efficiency. A more nearly equal distribution of income results in less economic efficiency (a smaller domestic output) and greater economic efficiency leads to a more unequal distribution of income. The debate over the right amount of inequality depends, therefore, upon how much output society is willing to sacrifice to reduce income inequality.

6. Aside from inequality in the distribution of income, there is great concern today with the problem of poverty in the United States.

   a. Using the generally accepted definition of poverty, 13.5% of the people in the American economy live in poverty.

   b. The poor tend to be concentrated among certain groups, such as blacks, Hispanics, female-headed families, and children.

   c. The poverty rate decreased significantly between 1960 and 1968, remained relatively constant from 1969–1978, increased in the early 1980s, and has gradually declined since then. When alternative poverty rates are calculated that take into account the monetary value of noncash transfer, the estimated rate for 1990 was 9.8%.

d. Some observers contend that ghettos produce a "black underclass" and a culture of poverty that cannot be corrected by antipoverty programs, and thus the poor must help themselves out of poverty. Critics of this view counter that it is simplistic, blames the victim, and fails to focus on larger social and economic problems; they think the poverty problem can be partially addressed by better jobs, work experiences, and income-maintenance programs.

e. Poverty in the United States tends to be invisible because the pool of poor people changes, the poor are isolated in large cities, and the poor do not have a political voice.

7. The income-maintenance system of the United States is intended to reduce poverty and includes both social insurance and public assistance (welfare) programs.

a. OASDI ("social security") and Medicare are the principal social insurance programs and are financed by taxes levied on employers and employees.

b. The unemployment insurance programs maintained by the states and financed by taxes on employers are also a part of the social insurance program of the United States.

c. The public assistance programs include SSI, AFDC, food stamps, and Medicaid.

d. The social security (or welfare) system has been criticized in recent years. Its critics argue that it is costly to administer, is inequitable, impairs incentives to work, and creates family problems.

8. One comprehensive approach to income maintenance would employ a negative income tax (NIT) to subsidize families whose incomes are below a certain level.

a. In any NIT plan a family would be guaranteed a minimum income and the subsidy to a family would decrease as its earned income increases. But a comparison of three alternative plans reveals that the guaranteed income, the (benefit-loss) rate at which the subsidy declines as earned income increases, and the (break-even) income at which the subsidy is no longer paid may differ.

b. The comparison of the plans also indicates there is a conflict among the goals of taking families out of poverty, maintaining incentives to work, and keeping the costs of the plan at a reasonable level; and that a trade-off among the three goals is necessary because no one plan can achieve all three goals.

9. A more recent, but more piecemeal, approach to welfare reform is **workfare**. This reform plan has focused primarily on the AFDC program. Under this plan, welfare recipients would be provided with education, training, and work activities to help move them from public assistance to employment. This welfare-to-work plan was enacted in the Family Assistance Act of 1988.

■ **IMPORTANT TERMS**

Income inequality

Lorenz curve

In-kind transfer

Optimal distribution of income

Equality vs. efficiency trade-off

Poverty rate

Income-maintenance system

Social security programs

Public assistance (welfare) programs

Old age, survivors, and disability insurance (OASDI)

Medicare

Unemployment insurance (compensation)

Supplemental security income (SSI)

Aid to Families with Dependent Children (AFDC)

Food stamp program

Medicaid

Negative income tax (NIT)

Guaranteed income

Benefit-loss rate

Break-even income

Workfare plans

Family Support Act of 1988

■ **FILL-IN QUESTIONS**

1. It can fairly be said that the extent of income inequality in the United States is _____

a. The percentage of total personal income received by the highest quintile has since 1929 (increased, decreased) _____ and the percentage received by the lowest two quintiles has _____; and these changes can fairly be said to have been (slight, significant) _____

b. But since the close of World War II the distribution of personal income in the United States (has, has not) _____ changed significantly.

2. Income inequality can be portrayed graphically by drawing a _____ curve.

a. When such a curve is plotted, the cumulative percentage of (income, families) _____ is measured along the horizontal and the cumulative percentage of _____ is measured along the vertical axis.

b. The curve which would show a completely (perfectly) equal distribution of income is a diagonal line which would run from the (lower, upper) _____ left to the _____ right corner of the graph.

c. The extent or degree of income inequality is measured by the area which lies between the _____ and the _____

3. Two major criticisms of the census data on the distribution of income in the United States are that the income concept used in the census is too (narrow, broad) _____ and that the income-accounting period is too (short, long) _____. When the data are adjusted to take account of these two criticisms the distribution of income is (more, less) _____ unequal and over time the inequality has become (greater, smaller) _____

4. The tax system and the transfer programs in the American economy significantly (reduce, expand) _____ the degree of inequality in the distribution of income.

5. The important factors which explain (or cause) income inequality are differences in _____; in _____ and _____; in job _____ and risk; in labor market _____; in the ownership of _____; in market _____; and in luck, connections, misfortune, and discrimination.

6. Those who argue for the:
   a. equal distribution of income contend that it results in the maximization of total (income, utility) _____ in the economy;
   b. unequal distribution of income believe it results in a greater total (income, utility) _____

7. The fundamental trade-off is between economic _____ and economic _____ This means that:
   a. less income inequality leads to a (greater, smaller) _____ total output; and
   b. a larger total output requires (more, less) _____ income inequality.
   c. The problem for a society that wants more equality is how to (minimize, maximize) _____ the adverse effects on economic efficiency. Recent studies suggest that the (gain, loss) _____ from the redistribution of income may be higher than originally thought.

8. Using the more or less official definition of poverty,
   a. The poor includes any family of four with less than $_____ and any individual with less than $_____ a year to spend.

b. Approximately _____% of the population and about _____ million people are poor.

9. Poverty tends to be concentrated:
   a. among the (young, elderly) _____
   b. among (whites, blacks and Hispanics) _____
   c. in families headed by _____

10. Alleviating ghetto poverty is difficult.
   a. One view holds that city ghettos are spawning a _____ which traps people in a permanent cycle of poverty; the responsibility for solving this poverty problem largely rests with _____ and not with government programs or laws.
   b. Critics of this view contend that it is _____ _____ and blames the _____ of poverty. They suggest that poverty in ghettos may be alleviated by providing residents with more and better _____, improved _____ and _____; and that a program of income _____ be instituted.

11. In the affluent economy of the United States much of the poverty in the country is (visible, invisible) _____ _____ because the poverty _____ changes from year to year, the poor are isolated in large _____, and the poor do not have a _____ voice.

12. The income-maintenance system in the United States consists of social _____ programs and public _____ programs.
   a. In the first category of programs are
   (1) _____ and medi-_____; and
   (2) _____ compensation.
   b. In the second category are
   (1) (use initials) _____ and _____;
   (2) the _____ program; and
   (3) medi-_____

13. Critics of the income-maintenance system often refer to "the welfare mess" and point to its three *ins*: they contend that it is administratively *in*-_____, is *in*-_____, and impairs work

in-_____

14. The two critical elements of any negative income tax plan are a _____ income below which family incomes would not be allowed to fall and a _____rate which specifies the rate at which the subsidy would be reduced if earned income increases.

15. The three goals of any negative income tax plan:

  a. are to get families out of _____,

  provide _____ to work, and ensure

  the _____ of the program are reasonable;

  b. are (complementary, conflicting) _____

16. Recent reforms of the income supplement system have focused on _____ because among other reasons the program tends to encourage family

_____, encourage or at least subsidize

_____, and promote a _____ of poverty.

17. The criticisms of AFDC have resulted in a variety of

_____ proposals, where people on welfare would receive help through education, training, and work

to move from public assistance to _____.

In 1988, the _____ Act was passed to reform welfare in this manner.

■ PROBLEMS AND PROJECTS

1. The distribution of personal income among families in a hypothetical economy is shown in the table below.

  a. Complete the table by computing:
  (1) The percentage of all families in each income class and all lower classes; enter these figures in column 4.
  (2) The percentage of total income received by each income class and all lower classes; enter these figures in column 5.

  b. From the distribution of income data in columns 4 and 5 it can be seen that:
  (1) Consumer units with less than $15,000 a year income constitute the lowest _____% of all families and receive _____% of the total income.
  (2) Families with incomes of $50,000 a year or more constitute the highest _____% of all families and receive _____% of the total income.

  c. Use the figures you entered in columns 4 and 5 to draw a Lorenz curve on the graph on the next page. (Plot the seven points and the zero-zero point and connect them with a smooth curve.) Be sure to label the axes.
  (1) On the same graph draw a diagonal line which would indicate complete equality in the distribution of income.
  (2) Shade the area of the graph that shows the degree of income inequality.

(1) Personal income class	(2) Percentage of all families in this class	(3) Percentage of total income received by this class	(4) Percentage of all families in this and all lower classes	(5) Percentage of total income received by this and all lower classes
Under $10,000	18	4	_____	_____
$10,000–$14,999	12	6	_____	_____
$15,000–$24,999	14	12	_____	_____
$25,000–$34,999	17	14	_____	_____
$35,000–$49,000	19	15	_____	_____
$50,000–$74,999	11	20	_____	_____
$75,000 and over	9	29	_____	_____

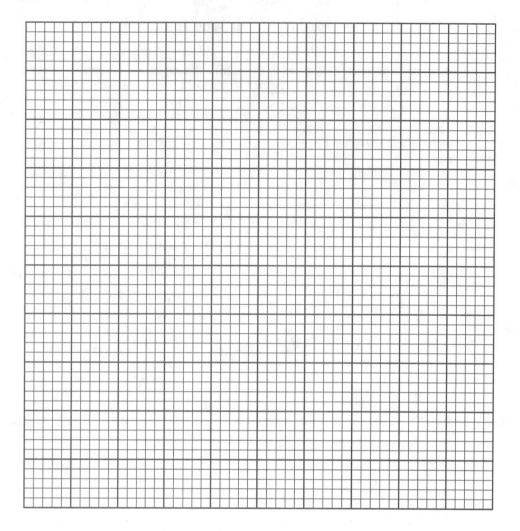

2. The table below contains different possible earned incomes for a family of a certain size.

Earned income	NIT subsidy	Total income
$ 0	$5,000	$5,000
5,000	_____	_____
10,000	_____	_____
15,000	_____	_____
20,000	_____	_____
25,000	_____	_____

a. Assume that $5,000 is the guaranteed income for a family of this size and that the benefit-loss rate is 20%. Enter the NIT subsidy and the total income at each of the five remaining earned-income levels. (*Hint*: 20% of $5,000 is $1,000.)

(1) This NIT program retains strong incentives to work because whenever the family earns an additional $5,000 its total income increases by $_____

(2) But this program is costly because the family receives a subsidy until its earned income, the break-even income, is $_____

b. To reduce the break-even income the benefit-loss rate is raised to 50%. Complete the table below.

Earned income	NIT subsidy	Total income
$ 0	$5,000	$5,000
2,500	_____	_____
5,000	_____	_____
7,500	_____	_____
$10,000	_____	_____

(1) This program is less costly than the previous one because the family only receives a subsidy until it earns the break-even income of $_____;

(2) but the incentives to work are less because whenever the family earns an additional $5,000 its total income increases by only $_____

c. Both of the previous two NIT programs guaranteed an income of only $5,000. Assume that that guaranteed income is raised to $7,500 and the benefit-loss rate is kept at 50%. Complete the table below.

Earned income	NIT subsidy	Total income
$ 0	$7,500	$7,500
3,000	_____	_____
6,000	_____	_____
9,000	_____	_____
12,000	_____	_____
15,000	_____	_____

(1) This program is more costly than the previous one because the break-even income has risen to

$_____

(2) The incentives to earn additional income are no better in this program than in the previous one. But to improve these incentives by reducing the benefit-loss rate to 40% would raise the break-even income to (divide the guaranteed income by the benefit-loss rate)

$_____

d. To summarize:

(1) given the guaranteed income, the lower the benefit-loss rate the (greater, less) _____ are the incentives to earn additional income and the

(greater, less) _____ is the break-even income and the cost of the NIT program;

(2) and given the benefit-loss rate, the greater the guaranteed income, the (greater, less) _____ is the break-even income and the cost of the program;

(3) but to reduce the break-even income and the cost of the program requires either a(n) (increase, decrease)

_____ in the benefit-loss rate or a(n)

_____ in the guaranteed income.

■ **SELF-TEST**

Circle the T if the statement is true; the F if it is false.

1. According to the authors of the text, there is considerable income inequality in the United States.   **T F**

2. Since 1929 the percentage of total personal income received by families in the highest income quintile has decreased.   **T F**

3. There was a significant increase in income inequality in the 1929–1947 period.   **T F**

4. The distribution of income has been relatively stable when you compare 1947 with 1990.   **T F**

5. In a Lorenz curve, the percentage of families in each income class is measured along the horizontal axis and the percentage of the total income received by those families is measured on the vertical axis.   **T F**

6. After the adjustments made by Edgar Browning in the Census Bureau data, the distribution of personal income in the United States is less unequal, and there is a trend over time toward less inequality.   **T F**

7. Adjustments for differences in the ages of receivers of income seem to make the distribution of personal income in the United States more unequal.   **T F**

8. The distribution of income in the United States *after* taxes and transfers are taken into account is less unequal than it is before they are taken into account.   **T F**

9. Differences in "job tastes" is one explanation for income differences in the United States.   **T F**

10. Those who favor equality in the distribution of income contend that equality will lead to stronger incentives to work, save, invest, and take risks and to a greater national output and income.   **T F**

11. In the tradeoff between equality and economic efficiency, an increase in efficiency requires a decrease in inequality.   **T F**

12. Using the semiofficial definition of poverty, about 13.5% of the population of the United States is poor.   **T F**

13. The incidence of poverty is extremely high among female-headed families.   **T F**

14. Including the value of noncash transfers in poverty rate calculations tends to decrease the estimate of the poverty rate.   **T F**

15. OASDI, Medicare, and unemployment compensation are public assistance (or welfare) programs.   **T F**

16. Those who have been critical of the American system of income maintenance contend that the welfare system impairs incentives to work.   **T F**

17. In a NIT program, the benefit-loss rate is the rate at which subsidy benefits decrease as the earned income of a family increases.   **T F**

18. The lower the benefit-loss rate the smaller are the incentives to earn additional income.   **T F**

19. Workfare plans are basically designed to provide public funds for transportation so that people on welfare can get to work. **T F**

20. In 1988 Congress passed the Family Support Act, which revised the welfare provisions of OASDHI. **T F**

Circle the letter that corresponds to the best answer.

1. According to the Census Bureau statistics, families making less than $10,000 a year account for about:
(a) 6% of all families and receive about 1% of total personal income
(b) 9% of all families and receive about 1% of total personal income
(c) 12% of all families and receive about 2% of total personal income
(d) 15% of all families and receive about 4% of total personal income

2. In 1990, the top 5% of families received about what percentage of total income before taxes?
(a) 13%
(b) 18%
(c) 21%
(d) 25%

3. Which of the following would be evidence of a decrease in income inequality in the United States?
(a) a decrease in the percentage of total personal income received by the lowest quintile
(b) an increase in the percentage of total personal income received by the highest quintile
(c) an increase in the percentage of total personal income received by the four lowest quintiles
(d) a decrease in the percentage of total personal income received by the four lowest quintiles

4. In the post-World War II period there has been;
(a) a significant decrease in the percentage of total personal income received by the highest quintile
(b) a significant increase in the percentage of total personal income received by the lowest quintile
(c) a significant increase in the percentage of total personal income received by the middle three quintiles
(d) no significant change in the percentage of total personal income received by any of the five quintiles

5. When a Lorenz curve has been drawn, the degree of income inequality in an economy is measured by:
(a) the slope of the diagonal that runs from the southwest to the northeast corner of the diagram
(b) the slope of the Lorenz curve
(c) the area between the Lorenz curve and the axes of the graph
(d) the area between the Lorenz curve and the southwest-northeast diagonal

Use the graph below to answer the next four questions (6, 7, 8, and 9). The graph shows four different Lorenz curves (1, 2, 3, and 4).

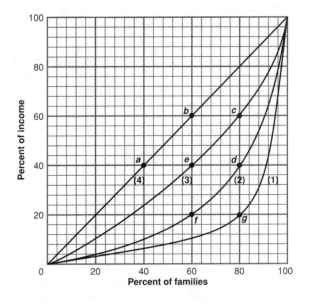

6. The greatest increase in income equality would occur with a shift in a Lorenz curve from:
(a) 1 to 2
(b) 1 to 4
(c) 4 to 1
(d) 3 to 1

7. What point indicates that 80% of the families receive only 40% of the income?
(a) *c*
(b) *d*
(c) *e*
(d) *g*

8. The movement from point *b* to point *f* in the graph would indicate that:
(a) 60% of families now receive 40% of income instead of 60% of income
(b) 60% of income goes to 20% of families instead of 60% of families
(c) 20% of income goes to 20% of families instead of 60% of families
(d) 60% of families now receive 20% of income instead of 60% of income

9. Which change would indicate that there has been an increase in income *inequality*? A movement from point:
(a) *b* to *a*
(b) *g* to *d*
(c) *g* to *f*
(d) *e* to *d*

10. Suppose that Laura earns $5000 in year 1 and $50,000 in year 2, while Kristin earns $50,000 in year 1 and only $5000 in year 2. Is there income inequality for the two individuals?
(a) both the annual and the two-year data indicate equality
(b) both the annual and the two-year data indicate inequality
(c) the annual data indicate inequality, but two-year data indicate equality
(d) the annual data indicate equality, but two-year data indicate inequality

11. The empirical data indicate that the tax system and the transfer programs of the government:
(a) significantly reduces the degree of inequality in the distribution of income
(b) produces only a slight reduction in the degree of inequality in the distribution of income
(c) significantly increases the degree of inequality in the distribution of income
(d) produces only a slight increase in the degree of inequality in the distribution of income

12. Which of the following is *not* one of the causes of the unequal distribution of income in the United States?
(a) the unequal distribution of property
(b) in-kind transfers
(c) the inability of the poor to invest in human capital
(d) luck and the unequal distribution of misfortune

13. Suppose that Ms. Anne obtains 5 units of utility from the last dollar of income received by her and that Mr. Charles obtains 8 units of utility from the last dollar of his income. Those who favor an equal distribution of income would:
(a) advocate redistributing income from Charles to Anne
(b) advocate redistributing income from Anne to Charles
(c) be content with this distribution of income between Anne and Charles
(d) argue that any redistribution of income between them would increase total utility

14. The case for income inequality is primarily made on the basis that income inequality:
(a) is reduced by the transfer payment programs for the poor
(b) is necessary to maintain incentives to work and produce output
(c) depends on luck and chance, which cannot be corrected by government action
(d) is created by education and training programs that distort the distribution of income

15. The debate over income redistribution focuses on the tradeoff between equality and:
(a) efficiency
(b) unemployment
(c) economic growth
(d) economic freedom

16. The leaky-bucket analogy is used to describe the:
(a) welfare reform mess
(b) trends in the poverty rate
(c) economic loss from income redistribution programs
(d) piecemeal approach toward income maintenance programs

17. Poverty does not have a precise definition, but the officially accepted poverty line for a family of four in 1990 was about:
(a) $ 6,652
(b) $ 7,300
(c) $ 9,100
(d) $13,359

18. In 1990, which group had the largest percentage in poverty?
(a) Hispanics
(b) families headed by women
(c) children under 18 years of age
(d) the elderly (65 years and older)

19. Which of the following would best characterize the trend in the poverty rate in the 1980s?
(a) it decreased steadily during the 1980s
(b) it increased steadily during the 1980s
(c) it increased during the early 1980s and then decreased
(d) it decreased during the early 1980s and then increased

20. The position that city ghettos create a culture of poverty that is not alleviated by social programs and that require the self-help of the poor is most closely associated with which view of ghetto poverty?
(a) workfare
(b) black underclass
(c) income maintenance
(d) "invisible poor"

21. An example of a social insurance program would be:
(a) Medicare
(b) Medicaid
(c) food stamps
(d) Aid to Families with Dependent Children

22. Which of the following is designed to provide a nationwide minimum income for the aged, the blind, and the disabled?
(a) SSI
(b) FFS

(c) AFDC
(d) OASDI

23. The income maintenance system has been criticized for a number of reasons. What is *not* one of the criticisms?
(a) the system is dependent on a costly and large bureaucracy for administration
(b) freedom of consumer choice is enhanced with the use of noncash transfer payments
(c) there are inequities in the program benefits for those with similar needs
(d) the programs is detrimental to incentives to work and may keep people on welfare

24. Negative income tax plans have been criticized because it is difficult to construct a plan that:
(a) provides reasonable income levels and incentives to work for the poor, but is not too costly
(b) is not subject to substantial administrative costs and bureaucratic red tape
(c) does not discriminate against those individuals with similar circumstances, but who have similar needs
(d) promotes family unity and does not create a "culture of poverty" among the participants in the program

25. Workfare proposals, as incorporated into the Family Support Act of 1988, would:
(a) provide a reasonable level of guaranteed income for low-income working families
(b) provide education and job training opportunities for welfare recipients to help and require them to become employed
(c) decrease the level of support for social security programs and transfer the funds to improve the Aid to Families with Dependent Children program
(d) substitute the payment of cash for the use of food stamps for those willing that are willing to go to work

■ **DISCUSSION QUESTIONS**

1. How much income inequality is there in the American economy? Cite figures to support your conclusion. What causes income inequality in American capitalism?

2. Has the distribution of income changed in the United States during the past 60 to 65 years? If it has, in what way, to what extent, and why has it changed? Has income distribution changed in the past 45 to 50 years?

3. What is measured along each of the two axes when a Lorenz curve is drawn?
(a) If the distribution of income were completely equal, what would the Lorenz curve look like?
(b) If one family received all of the income of the economy, what would the Lorenz curve look like?
(c) After the Lorenz curve for an economy has been

drawn, how is the degree of income inequality in that economy measured?

4. How does the Bureau of the Census measure income in its published data on the distribution of income in the United States. What are the two major criticisms of these data?

5. How did:
(a) Edgar Browning and
(b) Morton Paglin adjust the census data on the distribution of income? What do their adjusted figures reveal about the distribution of income in the United States?

6. What effect do taxes and transfers have upon the distribution of income in the United States? How much of this change in the distribution of income is the result of the transfer payments made by government?

7. What are seven factors contributing to income inequality in the United States?

8. State the case for an equal distribution of income and the case for an unequal distribution. What would be traded for what in the fundamental "tradeoff"? Describe the leaky-bucket analogy.

9. What is the currently accepted and more or less official definition of poverty? How many people and what percentage of the American population are poor if we use this definition of poverty?

10. What characteristics—other than the small amounts of money they have to spend—do the greatest concentrations of the poor families of the nation *tend* to have?

11. What have been the trends in the poverty rate since 1960? In the 1980s?

12. What is the black underclass view of poverty? What do critics of this view think can be done to alleviate ghetto poverty?

13. Why does poverty in the United States tend to be invisible or hidden?

14. Explain the difference between social insurance and public assistance (or welfare). List and briefly describe the three social insurance and the four public assistance programs that constitute the income-maintenance system of the United States.

15. State at least three basic reasons why the income maintenance system has been criticized. Are there other criticisms of the system?

16. Explain how poverty and the unequal distribution of income would be reduced by a negative income tax. Be sure to include in your explanation definitions of guaranteed income, the benefit-loss rate, and break-even income.

17. What are the three goals or objectives of any NIT plan? Explain why there is a conflict among these objectives—why all three goals cannot be achieved simultaneously.

18. What were some of the problems with AFDC? How was this program changed by the Family Support Act of 1988?

■ **ANSWERS**

Chapter 22 Income Inequality and Poverty

FILL-IN QUESTIONS

1. considerable; *a.* decreased, increased, significant; *b.* has not

2. Lorenz; *a.* families, income; *b.* lower, upper; *c.* Lorenz curve, line of complete equality (either order)

3. narrow, short, less, smaller

4. reduce

5. ability, education, training, tastes, discrimination, property, power

6. *a.* utility; *b.* income

7. equality, efficiency (either order); *a.* smaller; *b.* more; *c.* minimize, loss

8. *a.* 13,359, 6,652; *b.* 13.5, 34

9. *a.* young; *b.* blacks and Hispanics; *c.* women

10. *a.* black underclass, the poor; *b.* simplistic, victims, jobs, education, training, maintenance

11. invisible, pool, cities, political

12. insurance, assistance; *a.* (1) OASDI, care, (2) unemployment; *b.* (1) SSI, AFDC (either order), (2) food-stamp, (3) caid

13. efficient, equitable, centives

14. guaranteed, benefit-loss

15. *a.* poverty, incentives, costs; *b.* conflicting

16. AFDC, dissolution, illegitimate births, culture

17. workfare, employment (work), Family Support (Welfare Reform)

PROBLEMS AND PROJECTS

1. *a.* (1) column 4: 18, 30, 44, 61, 80, 91, 100; (2) column 5: 4, 10, 22, 36, 51, 71, 100; *b.* (1) 30, 10; (2) 20, 49

2. *a.* NIT subsidy: 4,000, 3,000, 2,000, 1,000, 0; Total income: 9,000, 13,000, 17,000, 21,000, 25,000; (1) 4,000, (2) 25,000; *b.* NIT subsidy: 3,750, 2,500, 1,250, 0; Total income 6,250, 7,500, 8,750, 10,000; (1) 10,000 (2) 2,500; *c.* NIT subsidy; 6,000, 4,500, 3,000, 1,500, 0; Total income: 9,000, 10,500, 12,000, 13,500, 15,000; (1) 15,000, (2) 18,750; *d.* (1) greater, greater, (2) greater, (3) increase, decrease

SELF-TEST

1. T, p. 378
2. T, p. 379
3. F, p. 379
4. T, pp. 379–380
5. T, p. 380
6. T, p. 381
7. F, pp. 381–382
8. T, p. 382
9. T, p. 382
10. F, p. 384
11. F, pp. 385–386
12. T, p. 386
13. T, p. 386
14. T, p. 387
15. F, pp. 388–389
16. T, p. 390
17. T, p. 391
18. F, p. 391
19. F, p. 392
20. F, p. 392

1. *b*, p. 379
2. *b*, p. 380
3. *c*, p. 380
4. *d*, pp. 379–380
5. *d*, p. 380
6. *b*, pp. 380–381
7. *b*, pp. 380–381
8. *d*, pp. 380–381
9. *d*, pp. 380–381
10. *c*, pp. 381–382
11. *a*, p. 381
12. *b*, pp. 382–383
13. *b*, p. 384
14. *b*, pp. 384–385
15. *a*, p. 385
16. *c*, p. 386
17. *d*, p. 386
18. *b*, p. 386
19. *c*, p. 387
20. *b*, pp. 387–388
21. *a*, p. 388
22. *a*, p. 390
23. *b*, p. 390
24. *a*, p. 392
25. *b*, p. 392

DISCUSSION QUESTIONS

1. p. 379
2. pp. 379–380
3. p. 380
4. pp. 381–382
5. pp. 381–382
6. p. 382
7. pp. 382–383
8. pp. 384–385
9. p. 386
10. pp. 386–387
11. p. 387
12. pp. 387–388
13. p. 388
14. pp. 388–389
15. p. 390
16. pp. 391–392
17. p. 392
18. pp. 392–393

Labor-Market Issues: Unionism, Discrimination, and Immigration

Chapter 23 completes the examination of government and current economic problems by looking at three major issues in labor markets—unionism, discrimination, and immigration. Most of the chapter focuses on unionism and labor-management relations. This topic is almost always in the news for one reason or another—strikes, new labor legislation, wage increases, employee "wage concessions," union demands, and collective bargaining. Discrimination was cited as a factor contributing to poverty in Chapter 22, but Chapter 23 now extends the discussion by analyzing discrimination in labor markets. Finally, you learn in Chapter 23 that labor is a resource that can move between nations and you learn how this movement can affect the market for labor in nations.

The labor union is an important institution in American capitalism. But labor unions did not always occupy the position in the economy that they now do. The first part of Chapter 23 is devoted to a historical review of their development in the Unites States and is separated into three periods. The important thing for you to see is that the growth and power of unions in each of these periods clearly depended upon the rights and recognition given to them by Federal law. At first the law repressed them, then it encouraged them, and finally it has sought to curb and control their greatly increased power.

Until 1955 the labor movement in the United States was divided into those unions affiliated with the AFL and those affiliated with the CIO. But in 1955 the labor movement was united when the AFL and CIO merged. Since then, however, unionism in the American economy has declined: the percentage of the labor force organized in unions has declined; and in more recent years the number of union members has decreased. The second section of Chapter 23 examines two possible hypotheses which separately or together might explain this decline in unionism in the U.S.

In Chapter 15 you learned how unions directly and indirectly seek to influence wage rates. The impact of the union upon its own membership, upon employers, and upon the rest of the economy is more than just a matter of wages, however. The third section of Chapter 23 examines the contents usually found in a contract between a union and an employer. The purpose of this examination is to give you some idea of the goals which unions seek and other issues over which employers and employees bargain and upon which they must reach an agreement. Another extremely important idea which you will find in the section is this: Labor-management relations mean more than the periodic signing of a contract; they also mean the day-to-day working relations between the union and the employer and the new problems and issues not specifically settled in the contract which must be resolved under the general provisions of that contract.

The fourth section of the chapter examines the economic effects or impact of unions on the economy. Unions affect the economy in four principle ways: they affect the wage rates of their members relative to the wage rates of nonunionized workers; the productivity of labor and, therefore, the efficiency with which the economy uses its resources; the inequality with which the earnings of labor are distributed among workers; and the rate of inflation in the economy. Just how unions affect these four economic variables is, to a large extent, uncertain and debatable. The authors of the text present you with both sides of the issues, however, and draw whatever conclusions can be obtained from the empirical evidence.

Discrimination has always been present in labor markets and is therefore one of the three major topics studied in the fifth section of this chapter. The section first looks at the four forms of economic discrimination—wage, employment, human-capital, and occupational—to give you an understanding of the dimension of the problem. The analysis then focuses on occupational segregation and presents the crowding model which is similar to the one presented earlier in the chapter to study the efficiency effects of unions. After a brief comment on the discrimination costs, the section ends by discussing the topic of comparable worth and some nondiscriminatory factors.

The third major topic discussed in the final section of the chapter is immigration. The migration of workers from a poor nation (such as Mexico) to a rich nation (such as the United States) creates economic effects on wage rates, output and employment, and business incomes in the two nations. The method employed to find the effects of this immigration is similar to the analysis of unions and discrimination you studied earlier in the chapter. The conclusions drawn about immigration using the supply and demand analysis are definite and you should be sure you understand them. The conclusions, however, are only approximations of reality. The real world is more complicated than a supply-and-demand model. Be sure you understand the four complications which are introduced toward the end of this section and how these complications modify the conclusions obtained by using supply and demand.

■ **CHECKLIST**

When you have studied this chapter you should be able to:

☐ Describe the attitudes and behavior of the courts and business toward labor unions during the repression phase.
☐ Identify the three fundamental ideas of Samuel Gompers.
☐ Explain how the Norris-LaGuardia Act and the Wagner Act contributed to the revival and rapid growth of the labor movement during the encouragement phase.
☐ Contrast the beliefs of John L. Lewis and the founders of the CIO with those of the leaders of the AFL during the 1930s.
☐ Identify the four headings into which the provisions of the Taft-Hartley Act can be put.
☐ Outline the provisions of the Landrum-Griffin Act.
☐ State the extent to which unionism in the United States has declined over the past 35 years; and present two hypotheses to explain this decline.
☐ Enumerate and explain the contents of the four basic areas of a collective-bargaining agreement.
☐ Describe the effects unions have on the wages of their members, on the wages of unorganized (nonunion) workers, and on the average level of real wages in the American economy; and state the size of the wage advantage of unionized workers.
☐ List the three ways in which unions might have a negative impact and the three ways in which they might have a positive impact on efficiency in the economy.
☐ Explain in detail how the unionization of a particular labor market leads to the misallocation of labor and a decline in the domestic output.
☐ Identify a way in which unions increase and the two ways in which they decrease, the inequality with which the earnings of labor are distributed.
☐ Contrast the causes of inflation in the demand-pull and cost-push models; discuss wage increases as an inflationary factor.
☐ List four kinds of discrimination.
☐ Use the crowding model to explain why women and blacks receive lower wages and why the labor resources of the economy are more efficiently allocated when occupational discrimination is eliminated.

☐ Estimate how much racial or other kinds of discrimination costs the United States each year.
☐ State the comparable worth doctrine and three objections to using it to set wages for women.
☐ List a few of the nondiscriminatory factors that have resulted in women receiving lower incomes than men.
☐ Recount briefly the history of immigration into the United States and the estimates of the number of legal and illegal immigrants entering the U.S. in recent years.
☐ Use a supply-and-demand model to explain the effects of the migration of workers from a poor to a rich nation on wage rates, output, and business incomes in the two nations.
☐ Explain how the four complicating factors modify the effects of migration on the two economies.
☐ Describe other economic and noneconomic complexities about immigration.

■ **CHAPTER OUTLINE**

1. The history of labor unions in the United States can be divided into three periods or phrases.
  a. During the *repression* phase, between 1790 and 1930, the growth of unions was severely limited by the judicial application of the criminal conspiracy doctrine and by the refusal of many firms to recognize and bargain with unions; but between 1886 and 1930 the AFL, following the union philosophy of Samuel Gompers, was able to organize many crafts and expand its membership.
  b. Between 1930 and 1947, the *encouragement* phase, labor union membership grew rapidly, encouraged by pro-labor legislation; and the CIO was formed to unionize industrial workers.
  c. In the *intervention* phase from 1947 onward, government regulation and control of labor-management relations increased with the passage of the Taft-Hartley and Landrum-Griffin acts.

2. The merger of the AFL and the CIO in 1955 reunited the American labor movement, but since then membership in unions as a percentage of the labor force has declined; and there are two complementary explanations of the relative decline in union membership.
  a. The structural-change explanation (or hypothesis) is that a number of changes in the structure of the economy and of the labor force have occurred and these changes have not been favorable to the expansion of union membership.
  b. The managerial-opposition hypothesis is that the opposition of management to unions has increased and become more aggressive in recent years, and the legal and illegal tactics employed by management against unions have decreased union membership.

3. Collective bargaining between labor and management results in collective-bargaining (or work) agreements between them.

a. This bargaining and the resulting agreements are more often than not the result of compromise; strikes and violence are actually quite rare.

b. The work agreements reached take many different forms; but the agreement between the employer and the union usually covers four basic areas: union status and managerial prerogatives, wages and hours, seniority and the control of job opportunities, and the grievance procedure.

4. Labor unions may increase wage rates, increase or decrease economic efficiency, make the distribution of income more or less unequal, and contribute to inflation.

a. While unions have increased the wages of their members relative to the wages of nonunion members, they have had little or no effect on the average level of real wages in the economy.

b. Whether unions result in more or less efficiency and an increase or a decrease in the productivity of labor in the economy is a question with two sides.

(1) The negative view is that they decrease efficiency by their featherbedding and work rules, by engaging in strikes, and by fostering a misallocation of labor resources.

(2) The positive view is that they increase efficiency by having a shock effect on the performance of management, by reducing worker turnover, and by the informal transfer of skills from the more- to the less-skilled workers fostered by the seniority system.

(3) The empirical evidence shows that unions have increased labor productivity in some industries and decreased it in other industries; but this evidence has not led to any general conclusion on the effect of unionization on the productivity of labor in the economy.

c. There is also no agreement on the effect of unions on the distribution of earnings among workers.

(1) Some economists argue that unions increase earnings and reduce employment in the labor markets which are unionized; but this increases the supply of labor and lowers earnings in the labor markets which are not unionized: the result is an increase in the inequality with which earnings are distributed.

(2) Other economists observe that unions try to obtain equal wage rates for all workers performing the same jobs both within a single firm and among different firms; and that the effect is to decrease the inequality with which earnings are distributed.

d. Whether unions generate cost-push inflation is a controversial issue.

(1) In the demand-pull model of inflation increases in wage rates are a result (or the effect) of an increase in aggregate demand and not the cause of inflation; but in the cost-push model of inflation union-imposed increases in wage rates greater than the increases in the productivity of labor lead to higher price levels in the economy.

(2) Most experts would agree that inflation in the past has been the result of increases in aggregate demand or of supply-side shocks and has not been the result of increases in wage rates.

5. The greater incidence of poverty among blacks, Hispanics, and women is in part the result of discrimination.

a. This discrimination is found in the wage, employment, human-capital, and occupational discrimination to which these groups are subject.

b. Women and blacks have been subjected to occupational discrimination which has crowded them into a small number of occupations in which the supply of workers is large relative to the demand for them and wage rates and incomes are, therefore, lower; and the crowding model illustrates these effects and the effects of the elimination of this discrimination.

c. The costs of this discrimination to the economy are estimated at 4% of the domestic output.

d. It is necessary to add to the examination of income inequality, poverty, and discrimination in the United States that

(1) the comparable worth doctrine has been suggested as a further method of reducing occupational discrimination against women; and while his suggestion has been subjected to several criticisms, it will be an important public-policy issue in the future; and

(2) the differences between the incomes of men and women and between those of whites and nonwhites are not all due to discrimination and are instead partly due to nondiscriminatory factors.

6. The immigration of workers into the United States is a controversial issue because this international movement of labor has economic effects on the American economy.

a. Largely unimpeded until World War I but then curtailed by law until liberalized after World War II, annual entry into the United States now consists of approximately 700,000 legal and 500,000 illegal immigrants.

b. In a simple model, the movement of workers from one economy into another economy lowers the average level of wage rates, expands the domestic output, and increases business incomes in the latter economy; has the opposite effects in the former economy; and increases output in the world.

c. These conclusions must, however, be modified to take into account the costs of migration, remittances and backflows, the levels of employment in the two economies, and the effects on tax revenues and government spending in the economy receiving the immigrants.

d. In addition to its economic effects, immigration raises several noneconomic issues in the United States.

■ IMPORTANT TERMS

Criminal-conspiracy
doctrine

Injunction

Discriminatory discharge

Blacklisting

Lockout

Yellow-dog contract

Company union

Business unionism

American Federation
of Labor

Norris-LaGuardia Act
of 1932

Wagner (National Labor
Relations) Act of 1935

National Labor Relations
Board

Congress of Industrial
Organizations

Taft-Hartley (Labor-
Management Relations)
Act of 1947

Jurisdictional strike

Sympathy strike

Secondary boycott

Featherbedding

Closed shop

Landrum-Griffin (Labor-
Management Reporting
and Disclosure) Act
of 1959

Structural-change
hypothesis

Managerial-opposition
hypothesis

Union shop

Open shop

Nonunion shop

Right-to-work law

Managerial prerogatives

Cost-of-living adjustment
(COLA)

Grievance procedure

Seniority

Fringe benefit

Collective voice

Exit mechanism

Voice mechanism

Wage discrimination

Employment
discrimination

Human-capital
discrimination

Occupational
discrimination

Crowding model
of occupational
discrimination

Comparable worth
doctrine

Legal immigrant

Illegal immigrant

Simpson-Rodino Act
of 1986

Remittances

Backflows

Two terms for review:

Craft unionism

Industrial unionism

■ FILL-IN QUESTIONS

1. About _____ million workers belong to labor unions in the United States. This is approximately what percentage of the civilian labor force? _____

2. During the repression phase of labor union history, union growth was slow because of the hostility of the _____ toward labor unions and the reluctance of American businesses to _____ and _____ with labor unions.

3. Unions were limited in their growth between 1790 and 1930 by courts which applied the _____ doctrine to labor unions and issued _____ to prevent strikes, picketing, and boycotts.

4. Employers used the following nonjudicial means of retarding the growth of labor unions in the repression phase: _____, _____, _____, _____, _____, _____, and _____

5. The philosophy of the AFL under the leadership of Samuel Gompers was _____ _____, _____, and _____

6. In the encouragement phase of labor union history, unions grew as a consequence of such favorable legislation as the _____ and _____ acts; and the (AFL, CIO) _____, based on the principle of (craft, industrial) _____ unionism, was formed to organize (skilled, both skilled and unskilled) _____ workers in a particular industry or group of related industries.

7. The National Labor Relations Act of 1935 guaranteed the "twin rights" of labor; the right to _____ and the right to _____; in addition it established the _____ Board and listed a number of unfair labor practices by (management, unions) _____

8. Three important events that occurred in the history of labor unions after 1946 were the passage of the _____ and _____ acts and the _____ of the AFL and the CIO.

9. Since the merger of the AFL and CIO in 1955 union membership as a percentage of the labor force has (increased, decreased, remained constant) _____

_____ and the number of unionized workers has

_____

10. The two complementary hypotheses which can be used to explain the changes in the size of the union membership are the _____ and the _____ hypotheses.

11. A typical work agreement between a union and an employer covers the following four basic areas:

a. _____

b. _____

c. _____

d. _____

12. Unionization of workers in the American economy has tended to (increase, decrease, have no effect on) _____ the wage rates of union members, to _____ the wage rates of nonunion workers, and to _____ the average level of real wage rates received by all workers.

13. Unions have a
a. negative effect on productivity and efficiency in the economy to the extent that they

(1) engage in _____ and impose _____ rules on their employers,

(2) engage in _____ against their employers, or

(3) impose (above-, below-) _____ equilibrium wage rates on employers that lead to the _____ of labor resources;
b. positive effect on productivity and efficiency in the economy to the extent that

(1) the wage increases they obtain have a _____ effect that induces employers to substitute (labor, capital) _____ for _____ and to hasten their search for technologies that (increase, decrease) _____ the costs of production,

(2) they (increase, decrease) _____ labor turnover, or

(3) the _____ system results in the (formal, informal) _____ training of (younger, older) _____ by _____ employees.

14. Unionization has the effect of:
a. increasing the inequality with which labor earnings are distributed when it displaces workers from (high, low) _____-wage employment in (unionized, nonunionized) _____ labor markets to _____-wage employment in _____ labor markets;
b. decreasing the inequality with which labor earnings are distributed if it results in a wage rate for a particular job that is (the same, different) _____ within the firm and is _____ among firms.

15. In the:
a. demand-pull model of inflation increases in wage rates are the (result, cause) _____ of inflation; and in the cost-push model of inflation increases in wage rates in excess of increases in the productivity of labor are the _____ of inflation;
b. American economy the major episodes of rapid inflation have been the result of expansions in aggregate (demand, supply) _____ or shocks on the _____ side.

16. The four principal kinds of *economic* discrimination are:

a. _____

b. _____

c. _____

d. _____

17. The occupational discrimination that pushes women and blacks into a small number of occupations in which the supply of labor is large relative to the demand for it is explained by the _____ model.
a. Because supply is large relative to demand, wages and incomes in these occupations are (high, low) ____
b. The reduction or elimination of this occupational discrimination would result in a (more, less) _____ efficient allocation of the labor resources of the economy, and a(n) (expansion, contraction) _____ in the national income and output.

18. The number of legal immigrants to the U.S. under current legislation is about _____ a year, and the number of illegal immigrants in recent years is estimated to be about _____ a year.

19. The movement of workers from a poor nation to a rich nation tends:

  a. in the rich nation to (increase, decrease) _____

  _____ the national output, to

  _____ wage rates, and to

  _____ business incomes;

  b. in the poor nation to _____ national

  output, to _____ wage rates, and

  to _____ business incomes; and

  c. in the world to _____ the real output of goods and services.

20. List the four complications that may modify the conclusions reached in question 19 above.

  a. _____

  b. _____

  c. _____

  d. _____

■ **PROBLEMS AND PROJECTS**

1. Below is a list of frequently employed terms, and following the terms is a series of identifying phrases. Match the term with the phrase by placing the appropriate letter after each of the phrases. *Note:* All the terms will not be needed.

  A. Injunction
  B. Blacklisting
  C. Lockout
  D. Yellow-dog contract
  E. Company union
  F. Business union
  G. Jurisdictional strike
  H. Sympathy strike
  I. Secondary boycott
  J. Featherbedding
  K. Closed shop
  L. Union shop
  M. Open shop
  N. Nonunion shop
  O. Checkoff
  P. Craft union
  Q. Industrial union

  1. A worker must be a member of the union before he or she is eligible for employment. _____

  2. A worker agrees when employed not to join a union. _____

  3. A union open to all workers employed by a given firm or in a given industry. _____

  4. A union organized and encouraged by an employer to prevent the formation of a union which might make "unreasonable" demands. _____

  5. The refusal of a labor union to buy or to work with the products produced by another union or group of nonunion workers. _____

  6. A dispute between two unions over whose members are to perform a certain job. _____

  7. A court order which forbids a person or group of persons to perform some act. _____

  8. The closing of the place of employment by the employer as a means of preventing the formation of a union. _____

  9. Concern of unions with better pay, hours, and working conditions rather than with plans for social and economic reform. _____

  10. Payment of workers for work not actually performed. _____

2. Below is a list of provisions found in four important pieces of labor legislation. Identify the act in which the provision is found by putting either **(N)** for the Norris-La-Guardia Act, **(W)** for the Wagner Act, **(T)** for the Taft-Hartley Act, or **(L)** for the Landrum-Griffin Act in the space following each provision.

  a. Specified that contracts between a union and an employer must contain a termination or reopening clause.

  b. Established a board to investigate unfair labor practices and to conduct elections among workers. _____

  c. Guaranteed to workers the right to organize unions to bargain collectively. _____

  d. Declared that yellow-dog contracts were unenforceable and limited the use of injunctions against unions.

  e. Regulated union elections and finances and guaranteed certain rights to union members in their dealings with the union and its officers. _____

  f. Outlawed the closed shop, jurisdictional and certain sympathy strikes, secondary boycotts, and featherbedding. _____

  g. Provided a procedure whereby strikes affecting the health and safety of the nation might be delayed.

  _____

h. Outlawed company unions, antiunion discrimination in hiring and discharging workers, and interfering with the rights of workers to form unions. _____

3. Suppose there are two identical labor markets in the economy. The supply of workers and the demand for workers in each of these markets are shown in the table below.

Quantity of labor demanded	Wage rate (MRP of labor)	Quantity of labor supplied
10	$100	70
20	90	60
30	80	50
40	70	40
50	60	30
60	50	20
70	40	10

a. In each of the two labor markets the equilibrium wage rate in a competitive labor market would be

$_____ and employment would be

_____ workers.

b. Now suppose that in the first of these labor markets workers form a union and the union imposes an above-equilibrium wage rate of $90 on employers.

(1) Employment in the unionized labor market will (rise, fall) _____ to _____ workers; and

(2) the output produced by workers employed by the firms in the unionized labor market will (expand, contract) _____ by $_____

c. If the workers displaced by the unionization of the first labor market all enter and find employment in the second labor market which remains nonunionized and competitive.

(1) the wage rate in the second labor market will (rise, fall) _____ to _____

(2) the output produced by the workers employed by firms in the second labor market will (expand, contract) _____ by $_____

d. While the total employment of labor in the two labor markets has remained constant, the total output produced by the employers in the two labor markets has (expanded, contracted) _____ by

$_____

4. Suppose there are only three labor markets in the economy and each of these markets is perfectly competitive. The table at the top of the next column contains the demand (or marginal-revenue-product) schedule for labor in each of these three markets.

Wage rate (marginal revenue product of labor per hour)	Quantity of labor (millions per hour)
$11	4
10	5
9	6
8	7
7	8
6	9
5	10
4	11
3	12

a. Assume there are 24 million homogeneous workers in the economy and that one-half of these workers are male and one-half are female.

(1) If the 12 million female workers can be employed only in labor market Z, for all of them to find employment the hourly wage rate must be $_____

(2) If of the 12 million male workers, 6 million are employed in labor market X and 6 million are employed in labor market Y, the hourly wage rate in labor markets X and Y will be $_____

b. Imagine now that the impediment to the employment of females in labor markets X and Y is removed; and that as a result (and because the demand and marginal revenue product of labor is the same in all three markets) 8 million workers find employment in each labor market.

(1) in labor market Z (in which only females had previously been employed):

(a) the hourly wage rate will rise to $_____

(b) the *decrease* in national output that results from the decrease in employment from 12 to 8 million workers is equal to the loss of the marginal revenue products of the workers no longer employed; and it totals

$_____

(2) In labor market X and in labor market Y (in each of which only males had previously been employed):

(a) the hourly wage rate will fall to $_____

(b) the *increase* in national output that results from the increase in employment from 6 to 8 million workers is equal to the marginal revenue products of the additional workers employed; and the gain in *each* of these markets is $ _____ million and the total gain in the two markets is $_____

(c) the *net* gain to society from the reallocation of female workers is $_____ million.

5. In the tables on the next page are the demands for labor and the levels of domestic output that can be produced at each level of employment in two countries.

| Country A | | |
Wage rate	Quantity of labor demanded	Real output
$20	95	$1900
18	100	1990
16	105	2070
14	110	2140
12	115	2200
10	120	2250
8	125	2290

| Country B | | |
Wage rate	Quantity of labor demanded	Real output
$20	10	$200
18	15	290
16	20	370
14	25	440
12	30	500
10	35	550
8	40	590

a. If there were full employment in both countries and if:

(1) the labor force in Country A were 110, the wage rate in Country A would be $_____

(2) the labor force in Country B were 40, the wage rate in Country B would be $_____

b. With these labor forces and wage rates:

(1) total wages paid in A would be $_____ and the incomes of businesses (capitalists) in A would be $_____. (*Hint:* Subtract the total wages paid from the real output.)

(2) total wages paid in B would be $_____ and business incomes in B would be $_____

c. Assume the difference between the wage rates in the two countries induces 5 workers to migrate from B to A. So long as both countries maintain full employment,

(1) the wage rate in A would (rise, fall) _____ to $_____;

(2) and the wage rate in B would _____ to $_____

d. The movement of workers from B to A would

(1) (increase, decrease) _____ the output of A by $_____;

(2) _____ the output of B by $_____

(3) _____ their combined (and the world's) output by $_____

e. This movement of workers from B to A also (in-

creased, decreased) _____ business incomes in A by $_____ and _____ business incomes in B by $_____

■ **SELF-TEST**

Circle the T if the statement is true; the F if it is false.

1. An injunction is a court order which declares that combinations of workers to raise wages are illegal.   T F

2. Blacklisting was a device employed by early labor unions to cut off a firm's labor supply.   T F

3. The CIO was based on the principle of industrial unionism while the AFL was operated on the craft union philosophy.   T F

4. The Taft-Hartley Act lists a number of unfair labor practices on the part of management.   T F

5. Under the provisions of the Labor-Management Relations Act of 1947 yellow-dog contracts and featherbedding are prohibited.   T F

6. The merger of the AFL and CIO in 1945 was one of the main causes of a feeling that labor unions had become too powerful that led to the enactment of the Taft-Hartley Act in 1947.   T F

7. Union membership has increased in every year since the end of World War II.   T F

8. Strikes precede nearly 25% of the contracts negotiated by labor unions and management.   T F

9. Collective bargaining between labor and management means no more than deciding upon the wage rates employees will receive during the life of the contract.   T F

10. The four-points criteria employed by unions in arguing for higher wages can also be used by management to resist higher wages and to argue for decreased wages.   T F

11. Seniority means that the worker with the longest continuous employment by a firm is the last to be laid off and the first to be recalled from a layoff.   T F

12. The wages of union members exceed the wages of nonunion members on the average by more than 40%.   T F

13. Strikes in the American economy result in fairly little lost work time and reductions in total output.   T F

14. The imposition of an above-equilibrium wage rate in a particular labor market tends to reduce the employment of labor in that market.   T F

15. The loss of output in the American economy that is the result of increases in wage rates imposed by unions on employers is relatively large. T F

16. Reduced labor turnover tends to decrease the productivity of labor. T F

17. The seniority system, its advocates argue, expands the informal training of less-skilled, younger workers and improves the productivity of a firm's work force. T F

18. It is generally agreed that unions decrease the productivity of labor in the American economy. T F

19. An authoritative study concludes that unionization, on balance, increases income inequality by about 3%. T F

20. In the demand-pull model of inflation increased wage rates are the result of increases in aggregate demand that increase the demand for labor in the economy. T F

21. The cost of discrimination against blacks in the United States is equal to approximately 4% of the national output. T F

22. The difference between the average earnings of full-time female and male workers is only partly the result of occupational discrimination. T F

23. The annual number of *illegal* immigrants entering the United States in recent years may be as large as 500,000. T F

24. The movement of workers from low- to high-average-income nations tends to increase the world's real output of goods and services. T F

25. Remittances to their families in Mexico from Mexican workers who have migrated to the United States expands the gain in the national output of the United States and expands the loss of national output in Mexico. T F

Circle the letter that corresponds to the best answer.

1. About what percentage of all civilian workers are members of unions?
 (a) 5%
 (b) 16%
 (c) 24%
 (d) 27%

2. Which of the following would *not* be used by a firm to prevent the organization of a genuine union among its employees?
 (a) lockout
 (b) featherbedding
 (c) company union
 (d) yellow-dog contract

3. Which one of the following was an essential part of Samuel Gompers' union philosophy?
 (a) industrial unionism

 (b) support of the Democratic Party at the polls
 (c) establishment of producer cooperatives operated by labor and management
 (d) business unionism

4. The Norris-LaGuardia Act outlawed:
 (a) yellow-dog contracts
 (b) the closed shop
 (c) company unions
 (d) blacklisting

5. The Wagner Act outlawed:
 (a) company unions
 (b) the closed shop
 (c) featherbedding
 (d) injunctions against unions

6. The Taft-Hartley Act outlawed:
 (a) the nonunion shop
 (b) the open shop
 (c) the union shop
 (d) the closed shop

7. Which one of the following is *not* a provision of the Landrum-Griffin Act?
 (a) allows a worker to sue a union if the union denies the member certain rights
 (b) unions are prohibited from making political contributions in elections for Federal offices
 (c) requires regularly scheduled union elections and the use of secret ballots
 (d) guarantees union members the right to attend union meetings, to vote and to participate in the meeting, and to nominate union officers

8. Which one of the following is *not* presently an unfair practice?
 (a) the refusal of either unions or companies to bargain in good faith
 (b) the coercion of employees by unions to join and by companies not to join unions
 (c) the practices of company and business unionism
 (d) both jurisdictional strikes and secondary boycotts

9. The decline in union membership in the United States in recent years can be explained by the:
 (a) managerial-growth hypothesis
 (b) structural-change hypothesis
 (c) relative-income hypothesis
 (d) complementary-expansion hypothesis

10. If workers at the time they are hired have a choice of joining the union and paying dues or of not joining the union and paying no dues, there exists:
 (a) a union shop
 (b) an open shop
 (c) a nonunion shop
 (d) a closed shop

11. Unionization has tended to:
(a) increase the wages of union workers and decrease the wages of nonunion workers
(b) increase the wages of nonunion workers and decrease the wages of union workers
(c) increase the wages of both union and nonunion workers
(d) increase the average level of real wages in the economy

12. Which of the following tends to decrease (to have a negative effect on) productivity and efficiency in the economy?
(a) reduced labor turnover
(b) featherbedding and union-imposed work rules
(c) the seniority system
(d) the shock effect of higher union-imposed wage rates

13. The higher wages imposed on employers in a unionized labor market tend to result in:
(a) lower wage rates in nonunionized labor markets and a decline in national output
(b) lower wage rates in nonunionized labor markets and an expansion in national output
(c) higher wage rates in nonunionized labor markets and a decline in national output
(d) higher wage rates in nonunionized labor markets and an expansion in national output

14. The reallocation of labor from employment where its MRP is $50,000 to employment where its MRP is $40,000 will:
(a) increase the output of the economy by $10,000
(b) increase the output of the economy by $90,000
(c) decrease the output of the economy by $10,000
(d) decrease the output of the economy by $90,000

15. Which of the following tends to increase (have a positive effect on) productivity and efficiency in the economy?
(a) reduced labor turnover
(b) featherbedding and union-imposed work rules
(c) strikes
(d) the unionization of a particular labor market

16. A wage increase imposed by unions on employers has a shock effect if it induces employers to:
(a) accelerate the substitution of capital for labor
(b) hasten their search for productivity-increasing technologies
(c) speed their employment of productive techniques that reduce their costs
(d) do any or all of the above

17. Unions tend to reduce labor turnover by providing workers with all but one of the following. Which one?
(a) an exit mechanism
(b) a voice mechanism
(c) a collective voice
(d) a wage advantage

18. The effect of union-imposed wage increases in the unionized labor markets of the economy is to:
(a) decrease inequality in the distribution of labor earnings
(b) leave unchanged the distribution of labor earnings
(c) increase inequality in the distribution of labor earnings
(d) destabilize the distribution of earnings between unionized and nonunionized workers

19. In the cost-push model of inflation, increases in nominal-wage rates that exceed increases in the productivity of labor:
(a) increase aggregate supply and the price level in the economy
(b) increase aggregate supply and decrease the price level in the economy
(c) decrease aggregate supply and the price level in the economy
(d) decrease aggregate supply and increase the price level in the economy

20. Most of the sustained and rapid inflation in the United States has *not* been the result of:
(a) increases in aggregate demand
(b) supply-side shocks
(c) increases in the money supply
(d) increases in money-wage rates

21. The average weekly earnings of full-time female workers is about what percentage of the average annual earnings of full-time male employees?
(a) 70%
(b) 75%
(c) 90%
(d) 95%

22. Which of the following is *not* one of the four dimensions of *economic* discrimination?
(a) wage discrimination
(b) racial and sexual discrimination
(c) occupational discrimination
(d) human-capital discrimination

23. The crowding of women and minorities into certain occupations:
(a) is the result of occupational discrimination
(b) results in the misallocation of resources
(c) explains the lower wage rates in the crowded occupations
(d) all of the above

24. If there is full employment in both nations, the effect of the migration of workers from a poor to a rich nation is to increase:
(a) the average wage rate in the rich nation
(b) the output in the rich nation
(c) business incomes in the poor nation
(d) the total wages received by nonmigrant workers in the poor nation

25. Which of the following would increase the gains realized in the world from the migration of workers?

(a) the explicit and implicit costs of migration

(b) the remittances of workers to their native countries

(c) the migration of unemployed workers to nations in which they find employment

(d) the migration of employed workers to nations in which the taxes they pay are less than the welfare benefits they receive

■ **DISCUSSION QUESTIONS**

1. What are the three phases in the history of labor unions in the United States? What was the law with respect to unions, what was the extent of unionization, and what were the principal events in each of these periods?

2. How were the courts able to retard the growth of unions between 1790 and 1930? How did employers attempt to limit union growth?

3. Explain the union philosophy of Samuel Gompers.

4. What were the chief provisions of the Norris-La-Guardia Act and the Wagner Act?

5. Explain how the principles of the CIO differed from those on which the AFL was based.

6. Contrast the philosophy and policy embodied in the Wagner Act with that found in the Taft-Hartley Act.

7. What are the four main sections of the Taft-Hartley Act? What specific practices are outlawed by the act and what specific things are required of unions, union officers, and bargaining agreements?

8. Explain the major provisions of the Landrum-Griffin Act.

9. What evidence is there that the labor movement in the United States has declined? What are two possible causes of this decline?

10. What are the four basic areas usually covered in the collective-bargaining agreement between management and labor?

11. What are the four arguments employed by labor (management) in demanding (resisting) higher wages? Why are these arguments "two-edged"?

12. How large is the union wage advantage in the United States? How has the unionization of many labor markets affected the average level of real wages in the American economy?

13. By what basic means do unions have a positive and a negative effect on economic efficiency in the economy? What appears to have been the overall effect of unions on economic efficiency in the American economy?

14. What effect does the unionization of a particular labor market have upon:

(a) the wage rate in that market,

(b) the wage rates in other labor markets, and

(c) the total output of the economy?

15. Explain how unions:

(a) reduce labor turnover and

(b) improve the skills of younger workers.

16. How and in what ways do unions affect

(a) the distribution of earnings among workers and

(b) the price level (the rate of inflation)?

17. What is meant by economic discrimination and what are the four major types of such discrimination? How does this discrimination affect the earnings of blacks (and other minorities) and women relative to the earnings of white men in the United States?

18. If labor markets were competitive, what would be the effect of reducing or eliminating occupational discrimination in these labor markets upon the wage rates received by men and women and upon the national output?

19. What:

(a) are the comparable worth doctrine and the objections to it; and

(b) are the factors other than discrimination that lead to differences in the earnings of men and women in the United States?

20. Construct a supply-and-demand model to explain the effects of the migration of labor from a poor to a rich nation on the average wage rate, output, and business income in the two nations. What is the effect of this migration on the real output of the world?

21. What four complications make it necessary to modify the conclusions you reached in question 20? Explain how each of these complications alters your conclusions.

22. How do the types of workers who immigrate and economic conditions in the economy to which they migrate change the benefits from immigrants to the nation into which workers migrate?

■ **ANSWERS**

Chapter 23 Labor-Market Issues: Unionism, Discrimination, and Immigration

FILL-IN QUESTIONS

1. 17, 16

2. courts, recognize, bargain

3. criminal conspiracy, injunctions

4. discriminatory discharge, blacklisting, lockout, strikebreakers, yellow-dog contracts, paternalism, company unions

5. business unionism, political neutrality, craft unionism

6. Norris-LaGuardia, Wagner, CIO, industrial, both skilled and unskilled

7. organize, bargain collectively, National Labor Relations, management

8. Taft-Hartley, Landrum-Griffin, merger

9. decreased, decreased

10. structural-change, managerial-opposition (any order)

11. *a.* the degree of recognition and status accorded the union and the prerogatives of management; *b.* wages and hours; *c.* seniority and job opportunities; *d.* a procedure for settling grievances (any order)

12. increase, decrease, have no effect on

13. *a.* (1) featherbedding, work, (2) strikes, (3) above-, misallocation; *b.* (1) shock, capital, labor, decrease, (2) decrease, (3) seniority, informal, younger, older

14. *a.* high, unionized, low, nonunionized; *b.* the same, the same

15. *a.* result, cause; *b.* demand, supply

16. *a.* wage discrimination; *b.* employment discrimination; *c.* human-capital discrimination; *d.* occupational discrimination

17. crowding; *a.* low; *b.* more, expansion

18. 700,000, 500,000

19. *a.* increase, decrease, increase; *b.* decrease, increase, decrease; *c.* increase

20. *a.* including the costs of migration; *b.* remittances and backflows; *c.* the amounts of unemployment in the two nations; *d.* the fiscal aspects in the country receiving the immigrants

PROBLEMS AND PROJECTS

1. 1. K; 2. D; 3. Q; 4. E; 5. I; 6. G; 7. A; 8. C; 9. F; 10. J

2. *a.* T; *b.* W; *c.* W; *d.* N; *e.* L; *f.* T; *g.* T; *h.* W

3. *a.* 70, 40; *b.* (1) fall, 20, (2) contract, 150; *c.* (1) fall, 50 (2) expand, 110; *d.* contracted, 40

4. *a* (1) 3, (2) 9; *b* (1) (*a*) 7, (*b*) 18, (2) (*a*) 7, (*b*) 15, 30 (*c*) 12

5. *a.* (1) 14, (2) 8; *b.* (1) 1540, 600, (2) 320, 270; *c.* (1) fall, 12, (2) rise, 10; *d.* (1) increase, 60, (2) decrease, 40, (3) increase, 20; *e.* increased, 220, decreased, 70

SELF-TEST

1. F, p. 397	**14.** T, p. 406
2. F, p. 398	**15.** F, p. 406
3. T, p. 400	**16.** F, p. 407
4. F, p. 399	**17.** T, p. 407
5. F, p. 400	**18.** F, p. 407
6. F, p. 401	**19.** F, p. 408
7. F, p. 401	**20.** T, p. 408
8. F, p. 402	**21.** T, p. 412
9. F, p. 402	**22.** T, p. 412
10. T, p. 403	**23.** T, p. 413
11. T, p. 403	**24.** T, p. 414
12. F, p. 404	**25.** F, p. 415
13. T, p. 406	

1. *b*, p. 396	**14.** *c*, p. 406
2. *b*, p. 398	**15.** *a*, p. 407
3. *d*, p. 398	**16.** *d*, p. 407
4. *a*, p. 399	**17.** *a*, p. 407
5. *a*, p. 399	**18.** *c*, p. 408
6. *d*, pp. 400–401	**19.** *d*, pp. 408–409
7. *b*, p. 401	**20.** *d*, p. 409
8. *c*, p. 400	**21.** *a*, p. 409
9. *b*, p. 401	**22.** *b*, p. 410
10. *b*, p. 403	**23.** *d*, p. 411
11. *a*, p. 404	**24.** *b*, p. 414
12. *b*, p. 405	**25.** *c*, p. 415
13. *a*, pp. 405–406	

DISCUSSION QUESTIONS

1. pp. 396–397	**12.** p. 404
2. pp. 397–398	**13.** pp. 405–407
3. pp. 398–399	**14.** pp. 402–404
4. p. 399	**15.** p. 407
5. p. 400	**16.** pp. 408–409
6. pp. 400–401	**17.** pp. 409–410
7. p. 401	**18.** pp. 411–412
8. p. 401	**19.** p. 412
9. pp. 401–402	**20.** pp. 413–414
10. pp. 402–403	**21.** pp. 415–416
11. p. 403	**22.** pp. 414–415

International Trade: Comparative Advantage and Protectionism

This is the first of two chapters dealing with international trade and finance. International trade is a subject with which most people have little firsthand experience. For this reason many of the terms, concepts, and ideas encountered in these chapters will be unfamiliar and may not be readily grasped. However, most of this material is fairly simple if you will take some pains to examine it. The ideas and concepts employed are new, but they are not especially complex or difficult.

At the beginning it is essential to recognize that international trade is important to the United States. Exports from and imports into the American economy were $519 and $612 billion in 1991. The United States *absolutely* is the greatest exporting and importing nation in the world. In *relative* terms, other nations have exports and imports which are larger percentages of their GDPs. They may export and import more than 35 percent of GDP, while the United States exports and imports only about 11% to 13% of GNP. It is equally important for you to understand from the beginning that international trade differs from the trade that goes on within nations. Different nations use different monies, not just one money; resources are less mobile internationally than they are *intra*nationally; and nations place more political restrictions on international trade than they do on intranational trade.

But while foreign trade differs from domestic trade, nations trade for the same basic reason that people within a nation trade: to take advantage of the benefits of specialization. Nations specialize in and export those goods and services in the production of which they have a comparative advantage. A comparative advantage means that the opportunity cost of producing a particular good or service is lower in that nation than in another nation. These nations will avoid the production of and import the goods and services in the production of which other nations have a comparative advantage. In this way all nations are able to obtain products which are produced as inexpensively as possible. Put another way, when nations specialize in those products in which they have a comparative advantage, the world as a whole can obtain more goods and services from its resources; and each of the nations of the world can enjoy a standard of living higher than it would have if it did not specialize and export and import.

But regardless of the advantages of specialization and trade among nations, people in the United States and throughout the world have for well over 200 years debated whether free trade or protection was the better policy for their nation. Economists took part in this debate and, with few exceptions, argued for free trade and against protection. Those who favor free trade contend that free trade benefits both the nation and the world as a whole. "Free traders" argue that tariffs, import quotas, and other barriers to international trade prevent or reduce specialization and decrease both a nation's and the world's production and standard of living.

But nations have and continue to erect barriers to trade with other nations. The questions upon which the latter part of this chapter focuses attention are (1) what motivates nations to impose tariffs and to limit the quantities of goods imported from abroad; (2) what effects do protection have upon a nation's own prosperity and upon the prosperity of the world; and (3) what kinds of arguments do those who favor protection employ to support their position—on what grounds do they base their contention that their nation will benefit from the erection of barriers which reduce imports from foreign nations.

The chapter's final major section is a brief review of American policy toward trade barriers since 1934. That year began a series of gradual but substantial tariff-rate reductions which have continued almost up to the present year under the General Agreement on Tariffs and Trade (GATT). There has also been economic integration among nations in an area that reduces trade restrictions. The European Economic Community, or Common Market, the United States–Canadian Free-Trade Agreement and more recently, the proposal for a North American free-trade zone are examples of economic integration. Despite this progress in decreasing the barriers to trade with other nations, protectionism is not dead. Advocates of protection are alive—though not quite well—and the causes and costs of this rebirth of protectionism in the United States conclude the chapter.

Whether free trade or protection will be the policy of the United States in the years to come may well depend upon whether you understand that free trade helps everyone and that protection is costly for a nation and for the world economy.

■ **CHECKLIST**

When you have studied this chapter you should be able to:

☐ Explain the importance of international trade to the American economy in terms of volume, dependence, trade patterns, and output effects.

☐ Identify three features of international trade which distinguish it from the trade that takes place within a nation.

☐ State the two economic circumstances which make it desirable for nations to specialize and trade.

☐ Explain the basic principle of comparative advantage based on an individual example.

☐ Compute the costs of producing two commodities when you are given the necessary data in a two-nation example.

☐ Determine which nation has the comparative advantage in the production of each commodity using the cost data you computed for the two-nation example.

☐ Calculate the range in which the terms of trade will occur in the two-nation example.

☐ Explain how nations benefit from trade and specialization based on the two-nation example.

☐ Restate the case for free trade.

☐ Identify the four principal types of artificial barriers to international trade and the motive for erecting these barriers.

☐ Explain the economic effects of a protective tariff on resource allocation, the price of the commodity, the total production of the commodity, and the outputs of foreign and domestic producers of the commodity.

☐ Analyze the economic effects of an import quota and compare them with the economic effects of a tariff.

☐ Enumerate six arguments used to support the case for protection and find the weakness in each of these arguments.

☐ List the major provisions of the Reciprocal Trade Agreements Act of 1934 and of the General Agreement on Tariffs and Trade (GATT) of 1947; and explain why the former was a sharp change in the trade policy of the United States.

☐ Describe the recent focus of GATT negotiations.

☐ Identify the four major goals of the European Economic Community (the Common Market).

☐ Explain the features and the economic significance of the United States–Canadian Free-Trade Agreement of 1988.

☐ Discuss the proposal for a North American free-trade zone.

☐ Identify the causes of the rebirth of protectionism in the United States, give examples of it, and discuss its cost.

■ **CHAPTER OUTLINE**

1. Trade among nations is large enough and unique enough to warrant special attention.

   a. While the relative importance of international trade to the United States is less than it is to other nations:

   (1) this country's imports and exports are about 11% to 13% of its GDP (about $519 billion imports and $612 billion exports in 1991), and the United States is the largest trading nation in the world;

   (2) the American economy depends on this trade for important raw materials and markets for its finished goods;

   (3) the United States imports more from the rest of the world as a whole, Japan, and the OPEC nations than it exports to them, most American trade is with other developed nations, and Canada is the largest trading partner; and

   (4) changes in the net exports (exports minus imports) have a multiplier effect on American output, employment, and prices.

   b. International trade has three characteristics that distinguish it from domestic trade: resources are less mobile, the nations use different currencies (or money), and the trade is subjected to more political restrictions.

2. Specialization and trade among nations is advantageous because the world's resources are not evenly distributed and the efficient production of different commodities necessitates different methods and combinations of resources.

3. Two simple hypothetical examples explain comparative advantage and the gains from trade.

   a. In an individual example, suppose that an accountant wants to have his house painted, but the accountant can either do it himself (he is a skilled painter) or hire a professional painter to do the job.

   (1) The law of comparative advantage suggests that the accountant will specialize in that work where the opportunity cost is lower relative to the work where the opportunity cost is higher.

   (2) The same principle applies to the professional painter in deciding whether to prepare his own tax return, or specialize in painting and hire an accountant to prepare the tax return for him.

   (3) Given the hypothetical labor time and wage data in the textbook example, both the accountant and the painter reduce their opportunity costs when they specialize in their respective jobs and exchange money for other services they desire.

   b. In an international trade example, suppose the world is composed of only two nations, each of which is capable of producing two different commodities and in which the production possibilities curves are different straight lines (whose opportunity cost ratios are constant but different).

(1) With different opportunity cost ratios, each nation will have a comparative (cost) advantage in the production of one of the two commodities; and if the world is to use its resources economically each nation must specialize in the commodity in the production of which it has a comparative advantage.

(2) The ratio at which one product is traded for another—the terms of trade—lies between the opportunity cost ratios of the two nations.

d. Each nation gains from this trade because specialization permits a greater total output from the same resources and a better allocation of the world's resources.

e. If opportunity cost ratios in the two nations are not constant, specialization may not be complete.

f. The basic argument for free trade among nations is that it leads to a better allocation of resources and a higher standard of living in the world; but it also increases competition and deters monopoly in these nations.

4. Nations, however, retard international trade by erecting artificial barriers; and tariffs, import quotas, a variety of nontariff barriers, and voluntary export restrictions are the principal barriers to trade.

a. Special interest groups within nations benefit from protection and persuade their nations to erect trade barriers; but the costs to consumers of this protection exceed the benefits to the economy.

b. The imposition of a tariff on a good imported from abroad has both direct and indirect effects on an economy.

(1) The tariff increases the domestic price of the good, reduces its domestic consumption, expands its domestic production, decreases foreign production, and transfers income from domestic consumers to government.

(2) It also reduces the income of foreign producers and the ability of foreign nations to purchase goods and services in the nation imposing the tariff, causes the contraction of relatively efficient industries in that nation, decreases world trade, and lowers the real output of goods and services.

c. The imposition of a quota on an imported product has the same direct and indirect effects as that of a tariff on that product, with the exception that a tariff generates revenue for government use whereas an import quota transfers that revenue to foreign producers.

5. The arguments for protectionism are many but they often are of questionable validity.

a. The military self-sufficiency argument can be challenged because it is difficult to determine which industry is "vital" to national defense and must be protected; it

would be more efficient economically to provide a direct subsidy to military producers rather than impose a tariff.

b. Trade barriers do not necessarily increase domestic employment because:

(1) imports may eliminate some jobs, but create others; therefore, imports may only change the composition of employment, not the overall level of employment;

(2) the exports of one nation become the imports of another; tariffs barriers can be viewed as "beggar thy neighbor" policies;

(3) there is likely to be retaliation from other nations from the imposition of trade barriers that will reduce domestic output and employment; and,

(4) they create a less efficient allocation of resources by shielding protected domestic industries from the rigors of competition.

c. Using tariff barriers to permit diversification for stability in economy is not necessary for advanced economies such as the United States and there may be economic costs to diversification in less developed nations.

d. It is alleged that infant-industries need protection until they are sufficiently large to compete. But the argument may not apply to developed economies; it is difficult to select which industries will prosper; protectionism tends to persist long after it is needed; and direct subsidies may be more economically efficient. A variant of this argument for advanced nations is "strategic trade policy" to justify barriers that protect the investment in high risk, growth industries for a nation, but these policies often lead to retaliation and smaller policies from other trading nations.

e. Sometimes protection is sought against the "dumping" of excess foreign goods on American markets. Dumping is a legitimate concern and is restricted under United States trade law, but to use dumping as an excuse for widespread tariff protection is unjustified and the number of documented cases is few. If foreign companies are more efficient (low cost) producers, what may appear to be dumping may actually be comparative advantage at work.

f. Protection is sometimes sought because of the cheap foreign labor argument; it should be realized that nations gain from trade based on comparative advantage and without trade living standards will be lower.

g. In summary, most of the protectionist arguments are fallacious or based on half-truths. The only points that have some validity, under certain conditions, are the infant-industry and military-sufficiency arguments, but both are subject to abuse. The historical evidence suggests that free trade promotes and protectionism deters prosperity and economic growth in the world.

6. International trade policies have changed over the years.

a. Until 1934, the United States steadily increased tariff rates to protect private-interest groups. Since the passage of the Reciprocal Trade Agreement Act of 1934, tariff rates have been substantially reduced.

b. Many nations, including the United States, signed the General Agreement on Tariffs and Trade (GATT) in an attempt to eliminate trade barriers. The Uruguay "round" of negotiations, begun in 1986, is the current forum for multination trade negotiations and they involve reducing agricultural subsidies worldwide, removal of trade barriers in services, ending restrictions on foreign investments, and establishing worldwide recognition for patents, copyrights, and trademarks. GATT negotiations temporarily collapsed in 1990 mainly over issues related to agricultural subsidies for domestic production and exports.

c. Economic integration, or the combining of markets of two or more nations into free trade zones, is another method for trade liberalization. There are three examples of economic integration:

(1) The European Common Market sought the economic integration of thirteen Western European nations to create mass markets and increase economic growth; a number of specific goals were set for 1992; but the success of the integration creates problems for non-member nations such as the United States because of potential tariff barriers.

(2) The United States–Canadian Free-Trade Agreement of 1989 eliminated many trade restrictions between the two nations and should be a benefit to both countries given the volume of trade between them.

(3) A proposed North American free-trade zone would add Mexico to the free-trade zone created by the United States and Canada in 1989. The three nations would constitute a sizable trading bloc to counter the development of the European Common Market. Proponents cite the usual advantages of free trade, while critics worry about job losses from the United States to Mexico and the potential for abuse of the agreement by trading partners.

d. In recent years pressures for protection from goods produced abroad have reemerged in the United States.
(1) There are several interrelated causes of these pressures including a backlash from past tariff reductions, more firms are affected by foreign competition, other nations are now more competitive with the United States, and American imports have exceeded exports in recent years.
(2) There are examples of restrictions placed on imports into the United States, and although tariffs overall are low, some very high tariffs and restrictions have been placed on a select list of goods.
(3) The costs to consumers in the United States of protection are high; protection is similar to a regressive tax because it redistributes income from the lowest to the highest income groups; the gains that trade barriers create for protected industries produce a much greater loss for the overall economy.

■ **IMPORTANT TERMS**

Labor- (land-, capital-) intensive commodity

Cost ratio

Comparative advantage

Specialization

Terms of trade

Trading possibilities line

Tariff

Revenue tariff

Protective tariff

Import quota

Nontariff barriers (NTBs)

Voluntary export restrictions (VERs)

Smoot-Hawley Tariff Act of 1930

Dumping

Reciprocal Trade Agreements Act of 1934

Most-favored-nation clause

General Agreement on Tariffs and Trade (GATT)

Export subsidies

Economic integration

European Common Market (European Economic Community)

United States–Canadian Free-Trade Agreement

North American free-trade zone

■ **FILL-IN QUESTIONS**

1. Trade is important to the United States in many ways.
   a. The imports of the United States amount to about

   _____% of the economy's GNP and exports amount to about _____%. In absolute volume of imports and exports the United States is the world's

   _____ trading nation.

   b. The United States is _____ on world trade and the bulk of its trade is with (less developed, developed) _____ nations. The largest trading partner of the United States is (Japan, Canada) _____

   c. Changes in net exports have _____ effects on the level of national income, employment, and prices.

2. Special attention is devoted to international trade because resources are (more, less) _____ mobile between nations than within a nation; because each nation employs a different _____; and because international trade is subject to a (greater, smaller) _____ number of political interferences and controls than domestic trade.

3. Nations tend to trade among themselves because the distribution of economic resources among them is (even, uneven) _____ and because the efficient production of various goods and services necessitates (the same,

different) _____
technologies or combinations of resources.

4. The nations of the world tend to specialize in those goods in the production of which they have a _____, to export those goods, and to import those goods in the production of which they do not have a _____

5. If the cost ratio in country X is 4 Panama hats equal 1 pound of bananas, while in country Y, 3 Panama hats equal 1 pound of bananas:

   a. In country X hats are relatively (expensive, inexpensive) _____ and bananas relatively _____

   b. In country Y hats are relatively _____ and bananas relatively _____

   c. X has a comparative advantage and should specialize in the production of _____ and Y has a comparative advantage and should specialize in the production of _____

   d. When X and Y specialize and trade, the terms of trade will be somewhere between _____ and _____ hats for each pound of bananas; and will depend upon _____

   e. When the actual terms of trade turn out to be 3½ hats for 1 pound of bananas, the cost of obtaining:

   (1) 1 Panama hat has been decreased from _____ to _____ pounds of bananas in Y.

   (2) 1 pound of bananas has been decreased from _____ to _____ Panama hats in X.

   f. This international specialization will not be complete if the cost of producing either good (increases, decreases, remains constant) _____ as a nation produces more of it.

6. The basic argument for free trade is that it results in a better _____ of resources and a higher _____ of living.

7. The barriers to international trade include _____, _____ quotas, the non _____ barriers, and _____ restrictions.

8. Nations erect barriers to international trade to benefit the economic positions of _____ groups even though these barriers (increase, decrease)

_____ economic efficiency and trade among nations, and the benefits to a nation are (greater, less) _____ than the costs to it.

9. When the United States imposes a tariff on a good which is imported from abroad:

   a. the price of that good in the United States will (increase, decrease) _____

   b. the total purchases of the good in the United States will _____

   c. the output of:

   (1) American producers of the good will _____ _____

   (2) foreign producers will _____

   d. the ability of foreigners to buy goods and services in the United States will _____ and, as a result, output and employment in American industries that sell goods and services abroad will _____

10. When comparing the effects of a tariff with the effects of a quota to restrict the U.S. imports of a product, the basic difference is that with a (tariff, quota) _____ the U.S. government will receive revenue, but with a _____ foreign producers will receive the revenue that would have gone to the U.S. government.

11. List the six arguments which protectionists employ to justify trade barriers.

   a. _____

   b. _____

   c. _____

   d. _____

   e. _____

   f. _____

12. The only two protectionism arguments containing any reasonable justification for protection are the _____ argument and the _____ argument.

13. Until 1930 the trend of tariff rates in the United States was (upward, downward) _____; but since the passage of the _____ Act in 1934 the trend has been _____. This act empowered the President to lower _____ rates by up to _____% in return for a reduction in foreign restrictions on American goods and incorporated _____ clauses in American trade agreements.

14. The three main principles set down in the General Agreement on Tariffs and Trade are:

a. _____

b. _____

c. _____

15. The Uruguay _____ negotiations is focused on proposals to eliminate trade barriers and domestic subsidies in _____; to remove barriers to trade in _____; to end restrictions on foreign economic _____; and to establish and enforce _____, _____, and _____ rights on an international basis; but the negotiations temporarily broke down in 1990 primarily over issues related to subsidies in _____.

16. The specific aims of the European Common Market were the abolition of _____ _____ among member nations, the establishment of common tariffs on goods imported from _____ nations, the free movement of _____ and _____ among member nations, and common policies with respect to other matters.

17. A recent example of economic integration in the Western hemisphere was the _____ of 1989. Under terms of the agreement all trade restrictions will be eliminated over a _____-year period. It has been estimated that the agreement will produce annual gains to each nation of $_____ to $_____ billion when fully implemented.

18. A recent proposal for a free-trade zone in North America would include three nations: _____, _____, and _____. Supporters contend that it would increase total output from scarce resources in each nation because of specialization according to _____, but U.S. critics complain about the potential loss of _____

19. What are four interrelated factors which have resulted in the recent resurgence of pressures for the protection of American industries?

a. _____

b. _____

c. _____

d. _____

20. The costs of protecting American producers from foreign competition are equal to the rise in the _____ American consumers have to pay for the protected goods.

a. These costs are (greater, less) _____ than the benefits to American producers.

b. The costs of protection were borne mostly by those consumers in the (highest, lowest) _____ income group.

■ **PROBLEMS AND PROJECTS**

1. Shown on the next page are the production possibilities curves for two nations: the United States and Chile. Suppose these two nations do not currently engage in international trade or specialization, and suppose that points **A** and **a** show the combinations of wheat and copper they now produce and consume.

a. The straightness of the two curves indicates that the cost ratios in the two nations are (changing, constant) _____

b. Examination of the two curves reveals that the cost ratio in:

(1) The United States is _____ million tons of wheat for _____ thousand pounds of copper.

(2) Chile is _____ million tons of wheat for _____ thousand pounds of copper.

c. If these two nations were to specialize and trade wheat for copper,

(1) The United States would specialize in the production of wheat because _____

_____

(2) Chile would specialize in the production of copper because _____

d. The terms of trade, if specialization and trade occur, will be greater than 2 and less than 4 million tons of wheat for 1 thousand pounds of copper because _____

_____

e. Assume the terms of trade turn out to be 3 million tons of wheat for 1 thousand pounds of copper. Draw in the trading possibilities curve for the United States and Chile.

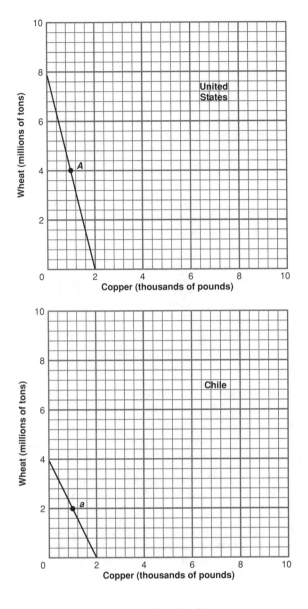

Copper (thousands of pounds)

ferent prices (P). Also shown in the table are the quantities of woolen gloves that would be supplied by American producers (S_a) and the quantities that would be supplied by foreign producers (S_f) at the nine different prices.

P	D	S_a	S_f	S_t	S'_f	S'_t
$2.60	450	275	475	_____	_____	_____
2.40	500	250	450	_____	_____	_____
2.20	550	225	425	_____	_____	_____
2.00	600	200	400	_____	_____	_____
1.80	650	175	375	_____	_____	_____
1.60	700	150	350	_____	_____	_____
1.40	750	125	325	_____	_____	_____
1.20	800	0	300	_____	_____	_____
1.00	850	0	0	_____	_____	_____

a. Compute and enter in the table the total quantities that would be supplied (S_t) by American and foreign producers at each of the prices.

b. If the market for woolen gloves in the United States is a competitive one the equilibrium price for woolen

gloves is $_____ and the equilibrium quantity is

_____

c. Suppose now that the United States government imposes an 80 cent ($0.80) per pair of gloves tariff on all gloves imported into the United States from abroad. Compute and enter into the table the quantities that would be supplied (S'_f) by foreign producers at the nine different prices. (**Hint**: If foreign producers were willing to supply 300 pairs at a price of $1.20 when there was no tariff they are now willing to supply 300 pairs at $2.00, the $0.80 per pair tariff plus the $1.20 they will receive for themselves. The quantities supplied at each of the other prices may be found in a similar fashion.)

d. Compute and enter into the table the total quantities that would be supplied (S'_t) by American and foreign producers at each of the nine prices.

e. As a result of the imposition of the tariff the equilibrium price has risen to $_____ and the equilibrium quantity has fallen to _____

f. The number of pairs sold by:

(1) American producers has (increased, decreased)

_____ by _____

(2) foreign producers has (increased, decreased)

_____ by _____

g. The total revenues (after the payment of the tariff) of:

(1) American producers—who **do not** pay the tariff—

have (increased, decreased) _____ by $_____

f. With these trading possibilities curves, suppose the United States decides to consume 5 million tons of wheat and 1 thousand pounds of copper while Chile decides to consume 3 million tons of wheat and 1 thousand pounds of copper. The gains from trade to:

(1) The United States are _____ million

tons of wheat and _____ thousand pounds of copper.

(2) Chile are _____ million tons of

wheat and _____ thousand pounds of copper.

2. The following table shows the quantities of woolen gloves demanded (**D**) in the United States at several dif-

(2) foreign producers—who **do** pay the tariff—have (increased, decreased) _____ by $_____

h. The total amount spent by American buyers of woolen gloves has _____ by $_____

i. The total number of dollars earned by foreigners has _____ by $_____; and, as a result, the total foreign demand for goods and services produced in the United States will _____ by $_____

j. The tariff revenue of the United States government has _____ by $_____

k. If an import quota was imposed that had the same effect as the tariff on price and output, the amount of the tariff revenue, $_____, would now be received as revenue by _____ producers.

■ **SELF-TEST**

Circle the T if the statement is true; the F if it is false.

1. Since 1975 the dollar volume of U.S. imports has increased and the dollar volume of its exports has decreased.　　T　F

2. The American economy's share of world trade has decreased since 1947.　　T　F

3. The United States exports and imports goods and services with a dollar value greater than any other nation in the world.　　T　F

4. The United States is completely dependent on trade for certain commodities which cannot be obtained in domestic markets.　　T　F

5. Canada is the most important trading partner for the United States in terms of the volume of exports and imports.　　T　F

Use the following production possibilities to answer the next five questions (6, 7, 8, 9, and 10).

NEPAL PRODUCTION POSSIBILITIES TABLE

Product	A	B	C	D	E	F
Yak fat	0	4	8	12	16	20
Camel hides	40	32	24	16	8	0

Production alternatives

KASHMIR PRODUCTION POSSIBILITIES TABLE

Product	A	B	C	D	E	F
Yak fat	0	3	6	9	12	15
Camel hides	60	48	36	24	12	0

Production alternatives

6. In Kashmir the cost of 1 camel hide is 3 units of yak fat.　　T　F

7. Nepal has a comparative advantage in producing camel hides.　　T　F

8. The best terms of trade for Nepal and Kashmir are 5 camel hides for 1 yak fat.　　T　F

9. With specialization and trade, the trading possibilities curves of both nations would move to the right of their production possibilities curves.　　T　F

10. Assume that prior to specialization and trade, Nepal and Kashmir produced combination B. If these two nations now specialized by comparative advantage, the total gains from specialization and trade would be 60 camel hides.　　T　F

11. Increasing production costs tend to prevent specialization among trading nations from being complete.　T　F

12. Trade among nations tends to bring about a more efficient use of the world's resources and a greater world output of goods and services.　　T　F

13. Free trade among nations tends to increase monopoly and lessen competition in these nations.　　T　F

14. A tariff on coffee in the United States is an example of a protective tariff.　　T　F

15. The imposition of a tariff on a good imported from abroad will raise the price of the good and lower the quantity of it bought and sold.　　T　F

16. The major difference between a tariff and a quota on an imported product is that a quota produces revenue for the government.　　T　F

17. To advocate tariffs which would protect domestic producers of goods and materials essential to national defense is to substitute a political-military objective for the economic objectives of efficiently allocating resources.　　T　F

18. An increase in a nation's imports will, other things remaining constant, expand aggregate demand, real output, and employment in that nation.　　T　F

19. The Smoot-Hawley Tariff Act of 1930 reduced tariffs in the United States to the lowest level ever in an attempt to pull the nation out of the Great Depression.　T　F

20. One crop economies may be able to make themselves more stable and diversified by imposing tariffs on goods imported from abroad; but these tariffs are apt also to lower the standard of living in these economies.　T　F

21. Protection against the "dumping" of foreign goods at low prices on the American market is one good reason for widespread, permanent tariffs.　　T　F

22. The only argument for tariffs that has, in the appropriate circumstances, any economic justification is the increase-domestic-employment argument. **T F**

23. If the United States concludes a tariff agreement which lowers the tariff rates on goods imported from another nation and that trade agreement contains a most-favored-nation clause, the lower tariff rates are then applied to those goods when they are imported from (most) other nations in the world. **T F**

24. Export subsidies are government payments to reduce the price of a product to buyers from other nations. **T F**

25. The members of the European Economic Community have experienced freer trade since they formed the Common Market in 1958. **T F**

26. The economic integration of nations creates larger markets for firms within the nations that integrate and makes it possible for these firms and their customers to benefit from the economies of large-scale (mass) production. **T F**

27. The formation of the European Economic Community (Common Market) has made it more difficult for American firms to compete with firms located within the Community for customers there. **T F**

28. The United States–Canadian Free-Trade Agreement of 1988 is an example of the gains to be obtained from voluntary export restrictions. **T F**

29. The proposed North American free-trade zone also includes Central American nations. **T F**

30. The cost of protecting American firms and employees from foreign competition is the rise in the prices of products produced in the United States, and this cost almost always exceeds its benefits. **T F**

Circle the letter that corresponds to the best answer.

1. In 1991 the imports of the United States amounted to approximately what percentage of the United States' GDP?
(a) 5%
(b) 7%
(c) 9%
(d) 13%

2. Which nation is our most important trading partner in terms of the quantity of trade volume?
(a) Japan
(b) Canada
(c) Germany
(d) United Kingdom

3. Which of the following is *not* true?
(a) the greater part of the export-import trade in merchandise is with the less developed nations

(b) the U.S. imports more merchandise from the OPEC nations than it exports to them
(c) the U.S. imports more merchandise from Japan than it exports to it
(d) the merchandise imports of the U.S. exceed its exports of merchandise

4. In recent years the total exports and imports of goods and services of the U.S have been about:
(a) $200 and $300 billion
(b) $300 and $400 billion
(c) $400 and $500 billion
(d) $500 and $600 billion

5. International trade is a special and separate area of economic study because:
(a) international trade involves the movement of goods over greater distances than trade within a nation
(b) resources are more mobile internationally than domestically
(c) countries engaged in international trade use different monies
(d) international trade is based on comparative advantage

6. Nations would not need to engage in trade if:
(a) all products were produced from the same combinations of resources
(b) world resources were evenly distributed among nations
(c) world resources were perfectly mobile
(d) all of the above

*Use the tables preceding true-false question **6** to answer the following four questions (**7, 8, 9** and **10**).*

7. The data in the table show that production in:
(a) both Nepal and Kashmir are subject to increasing opportunity costs
(b) both Nepal and Kashmir are subject to constant opportunity costs
(c) Nepal is subject to increasing opportunity costs and Kashmir to constant opportunity costs
(d) Kashmir to increasing opportunity costs and Nepal to constant opportunity costs

8. If Nepal and Kashmir engage in trade, the terms of trade will be:
(a) between 2 and 4 camel hides for 1 unit of yak fat
(b) between ⅓ and ½ units of yak fat for 1 camel hide
(c) between 3 and 4 units of yak fat for 1 camel hide
(d) between 2 and 4 units of yak fat for 1 camel hide

9. Assume that prior to specialization and trade Nepal and Kashmir both choose production possibility "C." Now if each specializes according to its comparative advan-

tage, the resulting gains from specialization and trade will be:
- **(a)** 6 units of yak fat
- **(b)** 8 units of yak fat
- **(c)** 6 units of yak fat and 8 camel hides
- **(d)** 8 units of yak fat and 6 camel hides

10. Each nation produced only one product in accordance with its comparative advantage and the terms of trade were set at 3 camel hides for 1 yak fat. In this case, the Nepal could obtain a maximum combination of 8 yak fat and:
- **(a)** 12 camel hides
- **(b)** 24 camel hides
- **(c)** 36 camel hides
- **(d)** 48 camel hides

11. Which one of the following is characteristic of tariffs?
- **(a)** they prevent the importation of goods from abroad
- **(b)** they specify the maximum amounts of specific commodities which may be imported during a given period of time
- **(c)** they often protect domestic producers from foreign competition
- **(d)** they enable nations to reduce their exports and increase their imports during periods of depression

12. The motive for the erection by a nation of barriers to the importation of goods and services from abroad is to:
- **(a)** improve economic efficiency in that nation
- **(b)** protect and benefit special interest groups in that nation
- **(c)** reduce the prices of the goods and services produced in that nation
- **(d)** expand the export of goods and services to foreign nations

13. When a tariff is imposed on a good imported from abroad:
- **(a)** the demand for the good increases
- **(b)** the demand for the good decreases
- **(c)** the supply of the good increases
- **(d)** the supply of the good decreases

Answer the next five questions (14, 15, 16, 17, and 18) on the basis of the following diagram, where S_d and D_d are the domestic supply and demand for a product and P_w is the world price of that product.

14. In a closed economy (without international trade), the equilibrium price would be:
- **(a)** $0P_d$ but in an open economy, the equilibrium price will be $0P_t$
- **(b)** $0P_d$ but in an open economy, the equilibrium price will be $0P_w$
- **(c)** $0P_w$ but in an open economy, the equilibrium price will be $0P_d$

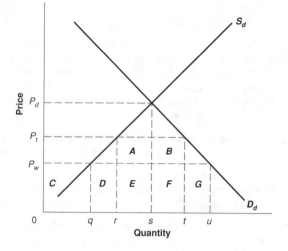

- **(d)** $0P_w$ but in an open economy, the equilibrium price will be $0P_t$

15. If there is free trade in this economy and no tariffs, the total revenue going to the foreign producers is represented by:
- **(a)** area C
- **(b)** areas A and B combined
- **(c)** areas $A, B, E,$ and F combined
- **(d)** areas $D, E, F,$ and G combined

16. If a per unit tariff was imposed in the amount of P_wP_t, then domestic producers would supply:
- **(a)** $0q$ units and foreign producers would supply qu units
- **(b)** $0s$ units and foreign producers would supply su units
- **(c)** $0r$ units and foreign producers would supply rt units
- **(d)** $0t$ units and foreign producers would supply tu units

17. Given a per unit tariff in the amount of P_wP_t, the amount of the tariff revenue paid by consumers of this product is represented by:
- **(a)** area A
- **(b)** area B
- **(c)** areas A and B combined
- **(d)** areas $D, E, F,$ and G combined

18. Assume an import quota of rt units is imposed on the foreign nation producing this product. The amount of **total** revenue going to foreign producers is represented by areas:
- **(a)** $A + B$
- **(b)** $E + F$
- **(c)** $A + B + E + F$
- **(d)** $D + E + F + G$

19. Tariffs lead to:
- **(a)** the contraction of relatively efficient industries

(b) an overallocation of resources to relatively efficient industries

(c) an increase in the foreign demand for domestically produced goods

(d) an underallocation of resources to relatively inefficient industries

20. "The nation needs to protect itself from foreign countries that sell their products in our domestic markets at less than the cost of production." This quotation would be most closely associated with which protectionist argument?

(a) diversification for stability

(b) increase domestic employment

(c) protection against dumping

(d) cheap foreign labor

21. Which one of the following arguments for protection is the least fallacious and most pertinent in the United States today?

(a) the military self-sufficiency argument

(b) the increase-domestic-employment argument

(c) the cheap foreign labor argument

(d) the infant-industry argument

22. Which of the following is the likely result of the United States employing tariffs to protect its high wages and standard of living from cheap foreign labor?

(a) an increase in U.S. exports

(b) a rise in the American real GDP

(c) a decrease in the average productivity of American workers

(d) a decrease in the quantity of labor employed by industries producing the goods on which tariffs have been levied

23. Which of the following is a likely result of imposing tariffs to increase domestic employment?

(a) a short-run increase in domestic employment

(b) retaliatory increases in the tariff rates of foreign nations

(c) a long-run decline in exports

(d) all of the above

24. The infant-industry argument for tariffs:

(a) is especially pertinent for the European Economic Community

(b) generally results in tariffs that are removed after the infant industry has matured

(c) makes it rather easy to determine which infant industries will become mature industries with comparative advantages in producing their goods

(d) might better be replaced by an argument for outright subsidies for infant industries

25. Which one of the following specifically empowered the President of the United States to reduce its tariff rates up to 50% if other nations would reduce their tariffs on American goods?

(a) the Underwood Act of 1913

(b) the Hawley-Smoot Act of 1930

(c) the Trade Agreements Act of 1934

(d) the General Agreement on Tariffs and Trade of 1947

26. Which of the following is **not** characteristic of the General Agreement on Tariffs and Trade? Nations signing the agreement were committed to:

(a) the elimination of import quotas

(b) the reciprocal reduction of tariffs by negotiation

(c) the nondiscriminatory treatment of all trading nations

(d) the establishment of a world customs union

27. One important topic for discussion during the Uruguay round of GATT was:

(a) removing voluntary export restraints in manufacturing

(b) eliminating trade barriers and subsidies in agriculture

(c) abolishing the need for patent, copyright, and trademark protection

(d) increasing tariff barriers on services but reducing tariff barriers on foreign economic investments

28. The European Common Market:

(a) is designed to eliminate tariffs and import quotas among its members

(b) aims to allow the eventual free movement of capital and labor within the member nations

(c) imposes common tariffs on goods imported into the member nations from outside the Common Market area

(d) does all of the above

29. An example of economic integration would be the:

(a) Smoot-Hawley Tariff Act

(b) United States–Canadian Free-Trade Agreement

(c) Reciprocal Trade Agreements Act

(d) General Agreements on Tariffs and Trade

30. Pressures for the protection of American industries have increased in recent years because of:

(a) previous decreases in the barriers to trade

(b) persistent trade deficits in the United States

(c) increased competition from imported products

(d) all of the above

■ **DISCUSSION QUESTIONS**

1. In relative and absolute terms, how large is the volume of the international trade of the United States? What has happened to these figures over the past thirty or so years?

2. What are the principal exports and imports of the American economy? What commodities used in the economy come almost entirely from abroad and what American industries sell large percentages of their outputs abroad?

3. Which nations are the principal "trading partners" of the United States? How much of this trade is with the developed and how much of it is with the less developed nations of the world?

4. Are the American economy's exports of merchandise to greater or less than its imports of merchandise from:
(a) Japan,
(b) the OPEC nations, and
(c) the rest of the world?

5. In what ways is international trade different from the trade which takes place within a nation?

6. Why do nations specialize in certain products and export their surplus production of these goods at the same time that they are importing other goods? Why do they not use the resources employed to produce the surpluses which they export to produce the goods which they import?

7. What two facts—one dealing with the distribution of the world's resources and the other related to the technology of producing different products—are the basis for the trade among nations?

8. Explain:
(a) the theory or principle of comparative advantage;
(b) what is meant by and what determines the terms of trade; and
(c) the gains from trade.

9. What is the "case for free trade"?

10. What motivates nations to erect barriers to the importation of goods from abroad and what types of barriers do they erect?

11. Suppose the United States were to increase the tariff on automobiles imported from Germany (and other foreign countries). What would be the effect of this tariff-rate increase on:
(a) the price of automobiles in the United States;
(b) the total number of cars sold in the United States during a year;
(c) the number of cars produced by and employment in the German automobile industry;
(d) production by and employment in the American automobile industry;
(e) German income obtained by selling cars in the United States;
(f) the German demand for goods produced in the U.S.;
(g) the production of and employment in those American industries which now export goods to Germany;
(h) the standards of living in the U.S. and in Germany;
(i) the allocation of resources in the American economy; and
(j) the allocation of the world's resources?

12. Compare and contrast the economic effects of a tariff with the economic effects of an import quota on a product. Give an example of a recent import quota and explain how it affected foreign producers.

13. Critically evaluate the military self-sufficiency and infant-industry arguments (including strategic trade policy) as a basis for protectionism.

14. Is there a "strong case" for protectionism that can be made on the basis of one of the following reasons: increasing domestic employment, diversifying for stability, defending against the "dumping" of products, or shielding domestic workers from competition from "cheap" foreign labor? Summarize the case for and the case against protectionism.

15. What was the tariff policy of the United States between 1920 and 1930? What has been the policy since 1934? Explain the basic provisions of the Reciprocal Trade Agreements Act.

16. How has the United States cooperated with other nations since 1945 to reduce trade barriers? What were the three cardinal principles contained in the General Agreements on Tariffs and Trade? What were the basic objectives and what were the results of the "Uruguay Round" of GATT negotiations?

17. What were the four main goals of the European Economic Community? How does the achievement of these goals bring about an increased standard of living within the Community? What problems and what benefits does the success of the EC create for the United States?

18. What was the United States–Canadian Free-Trade Agreement and what is its economic significance?

19. What recent actions have been taken to create a free-trade zone? What are the pros and cons of this proposal?

20. Why have the pressures for the protection of American firms and workers increased in the last few years? What:
(a) are several examples of this increased protection; and
(b) are the costs to the American economy of protection?

■ **ANSWERS**

Chapter 24 International Trade: Comparative Advantage and Protectionism

FILL-IN QUESTIONS

1. *a.* 13, 11, largest; *b.* dependent, developed, Canada; *c.* multiple

2. less, money (currency), greater

3. uneven, different

4. comparative advantage, comparative advantage

5. *a.* inexpensive, expensive; *b.* expensive, inexpensive; *c.* hats, bananas; *d.* 3, 4, world demand and supply for hats and bananas; *e.* (1) ⅓, ²⁄₇, (2) 4, 3½; *f.* increases

6. allocation, standard

7. tariffs, import, tariff, voluntary export

8. special interest, decrease, less

9. *a.* increase; *b.* decrease; *c.* (1) increase, (2) decrease; *d.* decrease, decrease

10. tariff, quota

11. *a.* military self-sufficiency; *b.* infant industry; *c.* increase domestic employment; *d.* diversification for stability; *e.* protection against dumping; *f.* cheap foreign labor

12. military self-sufficiency, infant-industry

13. upward, Reciprocal Trade Agreements, downward, tariff, 50, most-favored-nation

14. *a.* equal, nondiscriminatory treatment of all trading nations; *b.* reduction of tariffs by negotiation; *c.* elimination of import quotas

15. Round, agriculture, services, investments, patents, copyrights, trademarks, agriculture

16. tariffs and import quotas, nonmember, capital, labor

17. United States–Canadian Free-Trade Agreement, 10, 1, 3

18. United States, Canada, Mexico; comparative advantage, jobs (or employment)

19. *a.* the freer trade that resulted from past reductions in trade barriers; *b.* the increased competition from abroad that resulted from a more open economy; *c.* the increased competitiveness of foreign products that resulted from lower labor costs and prices abroad; *d.* persistent trade deficits

20. prices; *a.* greater; *b.* lowest

PROBLEMS AND PROJECTS

1. *a.* constant; *b.* (1) 8, 2, (2) 4, 2; *c.* (1) it has a comparative advantage in producing wheat (its cost of producing wheat is less than Chile's), (2) it has a comparative advantage in producing copper (its cost of producing copper is less than the United States), *d.* one of the two nations would be unwilling to trade if the terms of trade are outside this range; *f.* (1) 1, 0, (2) 1, 0

2. *a.* 750, 700, 650, 600, 550, 500, 450, 300, 0; *b.* $2.00, 600; *c.* 375, 350, 325, 300, 0, 0, 0, 0, 0; *d.* 650, 600, 550, 500, 175, 150, 125, 0, 0; *e.* $2.20, 550; *f.* (1) increased, 25, (2) decreased, 75; *g.* (1) increased, $95, (2) decreased, $345; *h.* increased, $10; *i.* decreased, $345, decrease, $345; *j.* increased, $260; *k.* $260, foreign

CHAPTER 25

Exchange Rates, the Balance of Payments, and Trade Deficits

In the last chapter you learned **why** nations engage in international trade and **why** they erect barriers to trade with other nations. In Chapter 25 you will learn **how** nations using different monies (or currencies) are able to trade with each other.

The means nations employ to overcome the difficulties that result from the use of different monies is fairly simple. When the residents of a nation (its consumers, business firms, or governments) wish to buy goods or services or real or financial assets from, make loans or gifts to, or pay interest and dividends to the residents of other nations they **buy** some of the money used in that nation. They pay for the foreign money with some of their own money. In other words, they **exchange** their own money for foreign money.

When the residents of a nation sell goods or services or real or financial assets to, receive loans or gifts from, or are paid dividends or interest by the residents of foreign nations and obtain foreign money they **sell** this foreign money—often called foreign exchange—in return for some of their own money. That is, they **exchange** foreign money for their own money.

The markets in which one money is sold and is paid for with another money are called foreign exchange markets. The price that is paid (in one money) for a unit of another money is called the foreign exchange rate (or the rate of exchange). And like most prices, the foreign exchange rate for any foreign currency is determined by the demand for and the supply of that foreign currency.

As you know from Chapter 24, nations buy and sell large quantities of goods and services across national boundaries. But the residents of these nations also buy and sell such financial assets as stocks and bonds and such real assets as land and capital goods in other nations; and the governments and individuals in one nation make gifts (remittances) in other nations. At the end of a year, nations summarize their foreign transactions with the rest of the world. This summary is called the nation's international balance of payments: a record of how it obtained foreign money during the year and what it did with this foreign money.

Of course, all foreign money obtained was used for some purpose—it did not evaporate—and consequently the balance of payments **always** balances. The international balance of payments is an extremely important and useful device for understanding the amounts and kinds of international transactions in which the residents of a nation engage. But it also enables us to understand the meaning of a balance of payments imbalance (a deficit or a surplus), the causes of these imbalances, and how to deal with them.

Probably the most difficult section of this chapter is concerned with balances of payments deficits and surpluses. A balance of payments deficit (surplus) is found when the receipts of foreign money are less (greater) than the payments of foreign money and the nation must reduce (expand) its official reserves to make the balance of payments balance. You should pay particular attention to the way in which a system of **flexible** exchange rates and the way in which a system of **fixed** exchange rates will correct balance of payments deficits and surpluses; and the advantages and disadvantages of these two alternative methods of eliminating imbalances.

As examples of these two types of exchange rate systems you will find in the third section of the chapter an examination of the gold standard, of the Bretton Woods system, and of the managed floating exchange rate system. In the first two systems exchange rates are fixed; and in the third system exchange rates are fixed in the short run (to obtain the advantages of fixed exchange rates) and flexible in the long run (to enable nations to correct balance of payments deficits and surpluses).

The final section of the chapter examines trade deficits of the United States of the 1980s and early 1990s. The problem is that during the early 1980s the United States imported goods and services with a dollar-and-cents value greater than the value of the goods and services it exported; and it incurred very large current-account deficits in those years. It was able to do this only by increasing its debts to (by borrowing from) the rest of the world; and by 1985 it owed more to foreigners than they owed to people in the United States. The primary (though not the only) cause of the trade deficit was the high international value of (exchange rate for) the American dollar during the mid-1980s. The high exchange rate for the dollar meant that the exchange rates for foreign currencies were low. The low exchange rates for other currencies and the high exchange rate for the dollar expanded American imports, contracted American exports, and produced the foreign-trade problem in the United States.

The relatively high exchange rate for the dollar in the mid-1980s was the result of real interest rates which were higher in the United States than in the rest of the world. Real interest rates were higher in the American economy than in the rest of the world because the large budget deficits of the Federal government forced it to borrow in the American money market; and these high real interest rates in the United States increased the attractiveness to foreigners of financial investment (buying bonds or lending) in the U.S., increased the foreign demand for dollars in the foreign exchange markets, and drove the price of the dollar upward in these markets. Although the value of the dollar fell over the 1985–1987 period, the trade deficit persisted for several reasons, and only in mid-1988 did the deficit begin to fall. Even today, however, the trade deficit remains large.

The undesirable effects of the trade deficit have led to a search for policy options. Two are worthy of note while five others are more limited remedies. First, it is thought by many economists that a reduction in the budget deficit of the Federal government would help reduce real interest rates in the United States relative to other nations, increase foreign investment in the United States and the demand for dollars, and cause the value of the dollar to fall. Putting the nation's "fiscal house" in order would help reduce the value of the dollar and move exports and imports to balance in a way that would be more acceptable to the major trading partners of the United States. Second, it is thought that if nations with large trade surpluses with the United States, such as Japan and Germany, would take actions to increase their rate of economic growth, this condition would help increase exports from the United States to those nations.

One last word for you. This chapter is filled with new terms. Some of these are just special words used in international economies to mean things with which you are already familiar. Be very sure you learn what all of the new terms mean. It will simplify your comprehension of this chapter and enable you to understand more readily the foreign trade "crisis" of the United States examined at the end of the chapter.

■ CHECKLIST

When you have studied this chapter you should be able to:

☐ Explain how American exports create a demand for dollars and generate a supply of foreign exchange; and how American imports create a demand for foreign exchange and generate a supply of dollars.

☐ Define each of the five balances found in a nation's international balance of payments; and distinguish between a deficit and a surplus in each of these five balances.

☐ Explain the relationship between the current and capital account balances; and between the balance of payments and changes in the official reserves of a nation.

☐ Using a supply and demand graph, illustrate how a foreign exchange market works to establish the price and quantity of a currency.

☐ Identify the five principal determinants of the demand for and supply of a particular foreign money.

☐ Explain how a change in each of these determinants would affect the rate of exchange for that foreign money.

☐ Provide an explanation of how flexible (floating) exchange rates function to eliminate payments deficits and surpluses; and enumerate the three disadvantages of this method of correcting imbalances.

☐ Enumerate the four means by which a nation may fix (or "peg") foreign exchange rates.

☐ Explain how a nation with a payments deficit might employ its international reserves to prevent a rise in foreign exchange rates.

☐ Describe how a nation with a payments deficit might use trade policies, fiscal and monetary policies, and exchange controls to eliminate the deficit.

☐ List the three conditions which a nation had to fulfill if it was to be on the gold standard.

☐ Explain how gold flows operated to reduce payments deficits and surpluses; and identify its basic advantages and its disadvantages.

☐ Explain how the Bretton Woods system stabilized exchange rates and attempted to provide for orderly changes in exchange rates to eliminate payments imbalances.

☐ Define the international monetary reserves of nations in the Bretton Woods system.

☐ Explain why the United States had to incur balance of payments deficits to expand these reserves, and describe the dilemma this created for the United States.

☐ Describe how the United States severed the link between gold and the international value of the dollar in 1971 that led to the floating of the dollar and brought to an end the old Bretton Woods system.

☐ Explain what is meant by a system of managed floating exchange rates.

☐ Enumerate its two alleged virtues and three alleged shortcomings of a system of managed floating exchange rates.

☐ Contrast the adjustments necessary to correct payments deficits and surpluses when exchange rates are flexible and when they are fixed.

☐ Describe and explain the causes of the large trade deficits of the 1980s and early 1990s.

☐ Analyze the effects of the trade deficit on output and employment and prices in the United States and on the indebtedness of Americans to foreigners.

☐ State what two major policies are proposed for reducing the foreign-trade deficit of the United States.
☐ Discuss five other "remedies" for large trade deficits.

■ **CHAPTER OUTLINE**

1. Trade between two nations differs from domestic trade because the nations use different monies; but this problem is resolved by the existence of foreign-exchange markets in which the money used by one nation can be purchased and paid for with the money of the other nation.

  a. American exports create a demand for dollars and generate a supply of foreign money in the foreign-exchange markets; increase the money supply in the United States and decrease foreign money supplies; and earn monies that can be used to pay for American imports.

  b. American imports create a supply of dollars and generate a demand for foreign money in foreign-exchange markets; decrease the money supply in the United States and increase foreign money supplies; and use monies obtained by exporting.

2. The international balance of payments for a nation is an annual record of all its transactions with the other nations in the world; and it records all the payments received from and made to the rest of the world.

  a. The current-account section of a nation's international balance of payments records its trade in currently produced goods and services; and within this section:
  (1) the trade balance of the nation is equal to its exports of goods (merchandise) less its imports of goods (merchandise), and the nation has a trade surplus (deficit) if the exports are greater (less) than the imports;
  (2) the balance on goods and services is equal to its exports of goods and services less its imports of goods and services; and
  (3) the balance on the current account is equal to its balance on goods and services plus its net investment income (dividends and interest) from other nations and its net private and public transfers to other nations, and this balance may be either a surplus or a deficit.

  b. The capital-account section of a nation's international balance of payments records its sales of real and financial assets (which earn it foreign money) and its purchases of real and financial assets (which use up foreign money), and the nation has a capital-account surplus (deficit) if its sales are greater (less) than its purchases of real and financial assets.

  c. The current and capital accounts in a nation's international balance of payments are interrelated: a nation with a current-account deficit can finance the deficit by borrowing or selling assets abroad (with a capital-account surplus) and a nation with a current-account

surplus can lend or buy assets abroad (incur a capital-account deficit).

  d. The official reserves of a nation are the foreign currencies (monies) owned by its central bank: these reserves a nation uses to finance a net deficit on its current and capital accounts, and these reserves increase when a nation has a net surplus on its current and capital accounts; and in this way the nation's total outpayments and inpayments are made to equal each other (to balance).

  e. A nation is said to have a balance-of-payments surplus (deficit) when the current and capital account balance is positive (negative) and its official reserves increase (decrease).

  f. The merchandise or trade deficit of a nation implies its producers are losing their competitiveness in foreign markets, but is beneficial to consumers in that nation who receive more goods (imports) from abroad than they must pay for (export); and a balance-of-payments deficit is undesirable to the extent that the nation's official reserves are limited and require the nation to take painful macroeconomic adjustments to correct it.

3. The kinds of adjustments a nation with a balance-of-payments deficit or surplus must make to correct the imbalance depends upon whether exchange rates are flexible (floating) or fixed.

  a. If foreign exchange rates float freely the demand for and the supply of foreign exchange determine foreign exchange rates; and the exchange rate for any foreign money is the rate at which the quantity of that money demanded is equal to the quantity of it supplied.
  (1) A change in the demand for or supply of a foreign money will cause the exchange rate for that money to rise or fall; and when there is a rise (fall) in the price paid in dollars for a foreign money it is said that the dollar has depreciated (appreciated) and that the foreign money has appreciated (depreciated).

A HELPFUL HINT

The application of the terms *depreciate* and *appreciate* to foreign exchange confuses many students. Here are some hints that will help reduce the confusion.
  First:
  ● depreciate means decrease; and appreciate means increase.
  Second: what decreases when Country A's currency depreciates and increases when its currency appreciates is
  ● the quantity of Country B's currency that can be purchased for *one unit* of Country A's currency.
  Third: when the exchange rate for B's currency:
  ● *rises* the quantity of B's currency that can be purchased for one unit of A's currency *decreases* (just as a rise in the price of cigars decreases the number of cigars that can be bought for a dollar) and A's currency has *depreciated;*
  ● *falls* the quantity of B's currency that can be purchased for one unit of A's currency *increases* (just as a fall in the price of cigars increases the number of cigars that can be bought for a dollar) and A's currency has *appreciated.*

(2) Changes in the demand for or supply of a foreign currency are largely the result of changes in tastes, relative income changes, relative price changes, changes in relative real interest rates, and speculation.

(3) When a nation has a payments deficit (surplus), foreign exchange rates will rise (fall); this will make foreign goods and services more (less) expensive, decrease (increase) imports, make a nation's goods and services less (more) expensive for foreigners to buy, increase (decrease) its exports; and these adjustments in foreign exchange rates and in imports and exports correct the nation's payments deficit (surplus).

(4) But flexible exchange rates increase the uncertainties faced by exporters, importers, and investors (and reduce international trade); change the terms of trade; and destabilize economies (by creating inflation or unemployment).

b. When nations fix (or "peg") foreign exchange rates, the governments of these nations must intervene in the foreign exchange markets to prevent shortages and surpluses of foreign monies.

(1) One way for a nation to stabilize foreign exchange rates is for its government to sell (buy) a foreign money in exchange for its own money (or gold) when there is a shortage (surplus) of the foreign money.

(2) A nation with a payments deficit might also discourage imports by imposing tariffs, import quotas, and special taxes; and encourage exports by subsidizing them.

(3) To eliminate a payments deficit a nation might require exporters who earn foreign exchange to sell it to the government; and the government would then ration the available foreign exchange among importers and make the value of imports equal to the value of exports.

(4) Another way for a nation to stabilize foreign exchange rates is to employ fiscal and monetary policies to reduce its national income and price level and to raise interest rates relative to those in other nations; and, thereby, reduce the demand for and increase the supply of the different foreign monies.

4. The nations of the world in their recent history have employed three different exchange rate systems.

a. Between 1879 and 1934 (with the exception of the World War I years) the operation of the gold standard kept foreign exchange rates relatively stable.

(1) A nation was on the gold standard when it:

(a) defined its monetary unit in terms of a certain quantity of gold;

(b) maintained a fixed relationship between its stock of gold and its money supply; and

(c) allowed gold to be exported and imported without restrictions.

(2) Foreign exchange rates between nations on the gold standard would fluctuate only within a narrow range (determined by the cost of packing, insuring, and shipping gold from country to country); and if a foreign exchange rate rose (fell) to the upper (lower) limit of the range gold would flow out of (into) a nation.

(3) But if a nation has a balance-of-payments deficit (surplus) and gold flowed out of (into) the country, its money supply would decrease (increase); this would raise (lower) interest rates and reduce (expand) aggregate demand, national output, employment, and prices in that country; and the balance-of-payments deficit (surplus) would be eliminated.

(4) The gold standard resulted in nearly stable foreign-exchange rates (which by reducing uncertainty stimulated international trade), and automatically corrected balance-of-payments deficits and surpluses; but it required that nations accept such unpleasant adjustments as recession and inflation to eliminate their balance-of-payments deficits and surpluses.

(5) During the worldwide Great Depression of the 1930s nations felt that remaining on the gold standard threatened their recoveries from the Depression, and the devaluations of their currencies (to expand exports and reduce imports) led to the breakdown and abandonment of the gold standard.

b. From the end of World War II until 1971 the Bretton Woods system, committed to the adjustable-peg system of exchange rates and managed by the International Monetary Fund (IMF), kept foreign-exchange rates relatively stable.

(1) The adjustable-peg system required the United States to sell gold to other member nations at a fixed price and the other members of the IMF to define their monetary units in terms of either gold or dollars (which established fixed exchange rates among the currencies of all member nations); and for the other member nations to keep the exchange rates for their currencies from rising by selling foreign currencies, selling gold, or borrowing on a short-term basis from the IMF.

(2) The system also provided for orderly changes in exchange rates to correct a fundamental imbalance (persistent and sizable balance-of-payments deficits) by allowing a nation to devalue its currency (increase its defined gold or dollar equivalent).

(3) The other nations of the world used gold and dollars as their international monetary reserves in the Bretton Woods system: for these reserves to grow the United States had to continue to have balance-of-payments deficits, but to continue the convertibility of dollars into gold it had to reduce the deficits; and, faced with this dilemma, the United States in 1971 suspended the convertibility of the dollar, brought an end to the Bretton Woods system of fixed exchange rates, and allowed the exchange rates for the dollar and the other currencies to float.

c. Exchange rates today are managed by individual nations to avoid short-term fluctuations and allowed to float in the long term to correct balance-of-payments deficits and surpluses; and this new system of managed floating exchange rates is favored by some and criticized by others.

(1) Its proponents contend that this system has not led to any decrease in world trade and it has enabled the world to adjust to severe economic shocks.

(2) Its critics argue that it has resulted in volatile exchange rates and has not reduced balance-of-payments deficits and surpluses; and that it is a "nonsystem" that a nation may employ to achieve its own domestic economic goals.

5. During the 1980s and into the 1990s, the United States has been running large trade deficits because its exports grew slowly but its imports grew rapidly. There are now large merchandise and current-account deficits.

a. These deficits have had three major causes.

(1) The international value of the dollar rose from 1980–1985 because of large Federal-budget deficits, a tighter monetary policy during the early 1980s, and lower rates of inflation in the United States and higher real interest rates than in the rest of the world. The value of the dollar declined from 1985–1987 because of intervention by five industrial nations to supply dollars to the foreign exchange market and the increasing demand for foreign currency to purchase imports. The dollar's fall helped increase American exports, but imports continued to rise until mid-1988 in part because foreign producers kept price increases low by accepting low per unit profits.

(2) The more rapid recover of the American economy from the 1980–1982 recession increased its imports by large amounts; and the less rapid recovery of the rest of the world increased. American exports by only small amounts.

(3) American exports to the less developed nations fell and its imports from them rose because they used restrictive monetary and fiscal policies and devalued their currencies to cope with their international debts to the developed nations.

b. The trade deficits of the United States lowered real output and employment, restrained inflation, lessened the prices of imported goods in the United States, and increased the indebtedness of Americans to foreigners; had the opposite effects on its industrialized trading partners.

c. To deal with the trade deficit several policies have been considered:

(1) It is argued that a decline in the Federal-budget deficits will lower the real rate of interest in the United States compared to other nations; G-7 nations would like the United States to "put its fiscal house in order" rather than just relying on "managed" depreciation of the dollar to ease the trade imbalance.

(2) The adoption of expansionary monetary and fiscal policies by the major trading partners of the United States would tend to increase economic growth in those nations and thereby increase exports from the United States to those nations.

(3) Other "remedies"—easy money, protective tariffs, recession, increasing competitiveness, and direct foreign investment—are possible but some have limitations and drawbacks.

■ **IMPORTANT TERMS**

Financing exports and imports

Foreign exchange market

Export transaction

Import transaction

Rate of exchange (foreign exchange rate)

International balance of payments

Current account

Trade balance

Trade surplus

Trade deficit

Balance on goods and services

Balance on current account

Net investment income

Net transfers

Capital account

Capital inflow

Capital outflow

Balance on the capital account

Current account deficit

Current account surplus

Capital account deficit

Capital account surplus

Official reserves

Balance of payments deficit

Balance of payments surplus

Flexible (floating) exchange rate

Fixed exchange rate

Exchange rate (currency) depreciation

Exchange rate (currency) appreciation

Purchasing power parity

Exchange control

Gold standard

Gold flow

Gold export point

Gold import point

Devaluation

Bretton Woods system

Adjustable pegs

International Monetary Fund

International monetary reserves

Managed floating exchange rate

G-7 nations

■ **FILL-IN QUESTIONS**

1. The rate of exchange for the French franc is the number of (francs, dollars) _____ which an American must pay to obtain one (franc, dollar) _____

2. When the rate of exchange for the Saudi Arabian riyal is 30 American cents, the rate of exchange for the American dollar is _____ riyals.

3. American:

a. exports create a (demand for, supply of) _____ foreign money, generate a _____ dollars, (increase, decrease) _____ the money supply in the United States, and _____ money supplies abroad;

b. imports create a _____ foreign money, generate a _____ dollars, and _____ the money supply in the United States, and _____ money supplies abroad.

4. In addition to the demand for foreign currency by American firms that wish to import goods from foreign countries, Americans also demand foreign money to purchase _____ and _____ services abroad and to pay _____ and _____ on foreign investments in the United States.

5. The balance of payments of a nation records all payments its residents make to and receive from residents in _____

a. Any transaction that *earns* foreign exchange for that nation is a (debit, credit) _____ and is shown with a (+, −) _____ sign.
b. A transaction that *uses up* foreign exchange is a _____ and is shown with a _____ sign.

6. When a nation has a:
a. balance of trade deficit its exports are (greater, less) _____ than its imports of _____;
b. balance-on-goods-and-services surplus its exports are _____ than its imports of goods and services;
c. current-account deficit its balance on goods and services plus its net _____ income and net _____ is (positive, negative) _____

7. The capital account records the capital inflows and capital outflows of a nation.
a. The capital inflows are the expenditures made (in that nation, abroad) _____ by residents of (that nation, other nations) _____; and the capital outflows are the expenditures made _____ by residents of _____ for _____ and _____ assets.
b. A nation has a capital-account surplus when its capital-account inflows are (greater, less) _____ than its outflows.

8. A nation:
a. may finance a current-account deficit by (buying, selling) _____ assets or by (borrowing, lending) _____ abroad; and
b. may use a capital-account surplus to (buy, sell) _____ assets or to (borrow, lend) _____ abroad.

9. The official reserves of a nation are the quantities of (foreign monies, its own money) _____ owned by its _____ bank. If that nation has
a. a deficit on the current and capital accounts its official reserves (increase, decrease) _____;
b. a surplus on the current and capital accounts its official reserves _____;
c. either a current and capital account deficit or surplus, the sum of the current and capital balances and the increases or decreases in its official reserves total _____

10. A country has a balance-of-payments deficit if the sum of its current and capital accounts balance is (positive, negative) _____ and its official reserves (increase, decrease) _____; and a payments surplus when the sum of its current and capital accounts balance is _____ and its official reserves _____

11. If foreign exchange rates float freely and a nation has a balance of payments *deficit:*
a. that nation's money in the foreign exchange markets will (appreciate, depreciate) _____ and foreign monies will _____
b. as a result of these changes in foreign exchange rates, the nation's imports will (increase, decrease) _____, its exports will _____, and the size of its deficit will _____

12. What effect (depreciation or appreciation) would each of the following have upon the French franc in the foreign exchange market (*ceteris paribus*)?
a. The increased preference in the United States for domestic wines over wines produced in France: _____
b. A rise in the national income of the United States: _____
c. An increase in the price level in France: _____
_____

d. A rise in real interest rates in the United States: _____

e. The belief of speculators in France that the dollar will appreciate in the foreign exchange market: _____

13. There are three disadvantages of freely floating foreign exchange rates: The risks and uncertainties associated with flexible rates tend to (expand, diminish) _____ trade between nations; when a nation's currency depreciates, its terms of trade with other nations are (worsened, bettered) _____; and fluctuating exports and imports can destabilize an economy and result in _____ or in _____ in that economy.

14. To fix or "peg" the rate of exchange for the German mark when:
   a. the exchange rate for the mark is rising, the United States would (buy, sell) _____ marks in exchange for dollars;
   b. the exchange rate for the mark is falling, the United States would _____ marks in exchange for dollars.

15. Under a fixed exchange rate system, a nation with a balance of payments deficit:
   a. might attempt to eliminate the deficit by (taxing, subsidizing) _____ imports or by _____ exports;
   b. might employ exchange controls and ration foreign exchange among those who wish to (export, import) _____ goods and services and require all those who _____ goods and services to sell the foreign exchange they earn to the _____

16. If the United States has a payments deficit with Japan and the exchange rate for the Japanese yen is rising, then under a fixed exchange rate system the United States might employ (expansionary, contractionary) _____ fiscal and monetary policies to reduce the demand for the yen; but this would bring about (inflation, recession) _____ in the United States.

17. A nation is on the gold standard when it defines its money in terms of _____, maintains a fixed relationship between its _____ supply and gold _____, and allows gold to be freely _____

from and _____ into the nation.

18. When the nations of the world were on the gold standard
   a. exchange rates were relatively (stable, unstable) _____,
   b. but when a nation had a payments deficit:
   (1) gold flowed (into, out of) _____ the nation;
   (2) its money supply and price level (increased, decreased) _____ and its interest rates _____;
   (3) its payments deficit (rose, fell) _____ and it experienced (inflation, recession) _____ _____

19. The Bretton Woods system was established to bring about (flexible, fixed) _____ exchange rates; and, to accomplish this, if employed the _____ system of exchange rates. Under the Bretton Woods system;
   a. a member nation defined its monetary unit in terms of _____ or _____;
   b. each member nation stabilized the exchange rate for its currency and prevented it from rising by (buying, selling) _____ foreign currency which it obtained from its _____ fund, by (buying, selling) _____ gold, or by (borrowing from, lending to) _____ the International Monetary Fund;
   c. a nation with a deeply rooted payments deficit could (devalue, revalue) _____ its currency;
   d. international monetary reserves included both _____ and _____;
   e. it was hoped that exchange rates in the short run would be (stable, flexible) _____ enough to promote international trade and in the long run would be _____ enough to correct balance of payments imbalances.

20. The role of the dollar as a component of international monetary reserves produced a dilemma:
   a. For these reserves to grow the United States had to incur balance of payments (surpluses, deficits) _____
   b. This resulted in an increase in the foreign holding

of American dollars and in a decrease in the American

reserves (stock) of _____

c. The ability of the United States to convert dollars into gold and the willingness of foreigners to hold dollars (because they were "as good as gold") therefore

(increased, decreased) _____

d. For the dollar to remain an acceptable international monetary reserve the U.S. payments deficits had to be

(eliminated, continued) _____;
but for international monetary reserves to grow the U.S.

payments deficits had to be _____

21. The United States completed the destruction of the Bretton Woods system in 1971 when it suspended the

convertibility of dollars into _____ and
allowed the value of the dollar to be determined by

_____.
Since then the international monetary system has moved from exchange rates which (for all practical purposes)

were (fixed, floating) _____ to ex-

change rates which are _____

22. The system of exchange rates which has developed

since 1971 has been labeled a system of _____
exchange rates. This means that individual nations will:
   a. in the short term buy and sell foreign exchange to

   keep exchange rates _____
   b. in the long term allow exchange rates to rise or fall

   to correct payments _____

23. The advantages of the current system of exchange

rates are that it did not reduce the _____ of
trade over the years and it has survived much economic

_____, but its disadvantages are the

_____ of the system, and the lack of clear rules

and guidelines for nations that make it a "_____"

24. The major problem with foreign trade in the United States concerns the American merchandise and current-

account (surpluses, deficits) _____ which
were brought about by the sharp increases in its (exports,

imports) _____ and the small increases in

its _____

25. The three causes of the trade deficits during the 1980s were
   a. the (strong, weak) _____ dollar,

b. the (slow, rapid) _____ growth of the American economy, and

c. the (expanded, reduced) _____ exports of the United States to less developed nations.

26. Changes in the international value of the dollar contributed to the trade deficit problem.
   a. From 1980–1985, the rise in the value of the dollar

made American goods (more, less) _____ ex-

pensive and foreign goods _____ expensive,

(increased, decreased) _____ American ex-

ports, and _____ American imports and

   b. was the result of relatively (high, low) _____
real interest rates in the United States caused by large

Federal-budget (surpluses, deficits) _____,

a (light, easy) _____ monetary policy, and

relatively (high, low) _____ rates of inflation in the United States.
   c. From 1985–1987, the value of the dollar (rose, fell)

_____ but imports continued to
rise because foreign producers accepted lower per unit

_____ and in 1987 _____ nations
agreed to halt the decline of the dollar.
   d. Finally, from 1988–1991 the deficit began to (in-

crease, decrease) _____

27. American:
   a. imports increased sharply in the mid-1980s be-

cause its national income (rose, fell) _____
rapidly after the 1980–1982 recession.
   b. exports to many less developed nations declined because their foreign debt problem forced them to

apply (expansionary, restrictive) _____
monetary and fiscal policies to their economies and to

(revalue, devalue) _____ their currencies in

order to expand their (exports, imports) _____

and reduce their _____

28. The effects of the large American foreign-trade defi-

cits have been to (expand, contract) _____
real domestic output and employment in the United States,

to (speed, slow) _____ its rate of inflation, to

(raise, lower) _____ the prices of goods it im-

ported, and to (increase, decrease) _____
American indebtedness to foreigners. It has also

changed the United States from a net (creditor, debtor)

_____ to a net _____ nation.

29. Two policies to correct the trade deficit include a(n)

(expansion, contraction) _____ in the budget deficit of the Federal government to help lower real interest rates in the United States relative to other nations,

and a(n) _____ in the economies of major trading partners, such as Japan and Germany, to help increase demand for exports for the United States.

30. Other "remedies" for large trade deficits include:

_____ money, protective _____, forced

_____, increased _____ of American

products, and direct foreign _____.

■ **PROBLEMS AND PROJECTS**

1. Assume an American exporter sells $3 million worth of wheat to an importer in Colombia. If the rate of exchange for the Colombian peso is $0.02 (two cents), the wheat has a total value of 150 million pesos.

a. There are two ways the importer in Colombia may pay for the wheat. It might write a check for 150 million pesos drawn on its bank in Botogá and send it to the American exporter.

(1) The American exporter would then sell the check to its bank in New Orleans and its demand deposit there

would increase by $_____ million.

(2) This New Orleans bank now sells the check for 150 million pesos to a correspondent bank (an American commercial bank that keeps an account in the Botogá bank).

(a) The New Orleans bank's account in the correspondent bank increases by _____ million

(dollars, pesos) _____; and

(b) the correspondent bank's account in the Botogá bank increases by _____ million (pesos,

dollars) _____.

b. The second way for the importer to pay for the wheat is to buy from its bank in Botogá a draft on an American bank for $3 million, pay for this draft by writing a check for 150 million pesos drawn on the Botogá bank, and send the draft to the American exporter.

(1) The American exporter would then deposit the draft in its account in the New Orleans bank and its demand

deposit account there would increase by $_____ million.

(2) The New Orleans bank collects the amount of the

draft from the American bank on which it is drawn through the Federal Reserve Banks.

(a) Its account at the Fed increases by $_____ million; and

(b) the account of the bank on which the draft was

drawn decreases by $_____ million.

c. Regardless of the way employed by the Colombian importer to pay for the wheat:

(1) The export of the wheat created a (demand for, supply of) _____ dollars

and a _____ pesos

(2) The number of dollars owned by the American exporter has (increased, decreased) _____ and the number of pesos owned by the Colombian importer has _____.

2. The table below contains hypothetical international balance of payments data for the United States. All figures are in billions.

Current account	
(1) U.S. merchandise exports	$+150
(2) U.S. merchandise imports	−200
(3) Balance of trade	____
(4) U.S. exports of services	+75
(5) U.S. imports of services	−60
(6) Balance on goods and services	____
(7) Net investment income	+12
(8) Net transfers	−7
(9) Balance on current account	____
Capital account	
(10) Capital inflows to the U.S.	+80
(11) Capital outflows from the U.S.	−55
(12) Balance on capial account	____
(13) Current and capital account balance	____
(14) Official reserves	____
	$____0

a. Compute with the appropriate sign (+ or −) and enter in the table the six missing items.

b. The United States had a payments (deficit, surplus)

_____ of $_____.

3. In the table below are the supply and demand schedules for the British pound.

Quantity of pounds supplied	Price	Quantity of pounds demanded
400	$5.00	100
360	4.50	200
300	4.00	300
286	3.50	400
267	3.00	500
240	2.50	620
200	2.00	788

a. If the exchange rates are flexible:

(1) What will be the rate of exchange for the pound?

$_____

(2) What will be the rate of exchange for the dollar?

£_____

(3) How many pounds will be purchased in the market?

_____

(4) How many dollars will be purchased in the market?

_____

b. If the government of the United States wished to fix or "peg" the price of the pound at $5.00 it would have to (buy, sell) _____ (how many) _____ pounds for $_____

c. And if the British government wishes to fix the price of the dollar at £⅖ it would have to (buy, sell) _____ (how many) _____ pounds for $_____

■ **SELF-TEST**

Circle the T if the statement is true; the F if it is false.

1. The importation of goods and services by Americans from abroad creates a supply of dollars in the foreign exchange market. **T F**

2. American exports expand foreign money supplies and reduce the supply of money in the United States. **T F**

3. The international balance of payments of the United States records all the payments its residents receive from and make to the residents of foreign nations. **T F**

4. Exports are a debit item and are shown with a plus sign ($+$) and imports are a credit item and are shown with a minus sign ($-$) in the international balance of payments of a nation. **T F**

5. The United States had a balance of trade deficit in 1990. **T F**

6. The balance on goods and services of the United States in 1990 was positive (a surplus). **T F**

7. In 1990 the United States had positive net investment income and negative net transfers from the rest of the world. **T F**

8. In 1990 there was a net capital outflow from the United States and the United States had a capital-account deficit. **T F**

9. The United States would have a balance of payments surplus if the balance on its current and capital accounts were positive. **T F**

10. Any nation with a balance of payments deficit must reduce its official reserves. **T F**

11. The sum of a nation's current-account balance, its capital-account balance, and the change in its official reserves in any years is always equal to zero. **T F**

12. A large trade deficit in Brazil is harmful to consumers in Brazil. **T F**

13. If a nation has a balance of payments deficit and exchange rates are flexible, the price of that nation's money in the foreign exchange markets will fall and this will reduce its imports and increase its exports. **T F**

14. The purchasing power parity theory basically explains why there is an inverse relationship between the price of dollars and the quantity demanded. **T F**

15. The expectations of speculators in the United States that the exchange rate for the Japanese yen will fall in the future will increase the supply of yen in the foreign exchange market and decrease the exchange rate for the yen. **T F**

16. Were the United States' terms of trade with Nigeria to worsen, Nigeria would obtain a greater quantity of American goods and services for every barrel of oil it exported to the United States. **T F**

17. If a nation wishes to fix (or "peg") the foreign exchange rate for the Swiss franc, it must buy Swiss francs with its own currency when the rate of exchange for the Swiss franc rises. **T F**

18. If exchange rates are stable or fixed and a nation has a payments surplus, prices and money incomes in that nation will tend to rise. **T F**

19. A nation using exchange controls to eliminate a balance of payments surplus might depreciate its currency. **T F**

20. If country A defined its money as worth 100 grains of gold and country B defined its money as worth 20 grains of gold, then, ignoring packing, insuring, and shipping charges, 5 units of country A's money would be worth 1 unit of country B's money. **T F**

21. When nations were on the gold standard, foreign exchange rates fluctuated only within limits determined by the cost of moving gold from one nation to another. **T F**

22. If a nation maintains an exchange stabilization fund it would purchase its own money with gold or foreign monies when the value of its money falls in foreign exchange markets. **T F**

23. In the Bretton Woods system a nation could not devalue its currency by more than 10% without the permission of the International Fund.　　**T　F**

24. In the Bretton Woods system a nation with persistent balance of payments surpluses had an undervalued currency and should have increased the pegged value of its currency.　　**T　F**

25. Because the world's stock of gold did not grow very rapidly it became necessary for the United States to have payments deficits if international monetary reserves were to increase.　　**T　F**

26. One of the basic shortcomings of the Bretton Woods system was its inabiity to bring about the changes in exchange rates needed to correct persistent payments deficits and surpluses.　　**T　F**

27. Another basic shortcoming of the Bretton Woods system was its failure to maintain stable foreign exchange rates.　　**T　F**

28. The United States shattered the Bretton Woods system in August 1971 by raising tariff rates on nearly all the goods it imported by an average of 40%.　　**T　F**

29. Using the managed floating system of exchange rates, a nation with a persistent balance of payments surplus should allow the value of its currency in foreign exchange markets to decrease.　　**T　F**

30. Two criticisms of the current managed floating exchange rate system are its potential for volatility and its lack of clear policy rules or guidelines for nations to manage exchange rates.　　**T　F**

31. The foreign-trade deficits experienced by the American economy in the 1980s were caused by sharp increases in American exports and slight increases in American imports.　　**T　F**

32. The principal reason for the strong dollar in the early 1980s was the high real interest rates in the United States.　　**T　F**

33. High real interest rates in the United States would tend to increase the attractiveness of financial investment in the United States to foreigners and the foreign demand for American dollars.　　**T　F**

34. The rapid growth of the American economy after 1982 lessened foreign-trade deficits because exports were directly related to national income.　　**T　F**

35. The strong international value of the dollar in the mid-1980s imposed special hardships on American firms dependent on export markets and those that competed with imported goods.　　**T　F**

36. The negative net exports of the United States have increased the indebtedness of Americans to foreigners.　　**T　F**

37. In 1985 the status of the United States was changed from net-debtor to net-creditor nation.　　**T　F**

38. The major trading partners in the United States contend that it must work to reduce the Federal budget deficit if it is to achieve a better balance of international trade.　　**T　F**

39. Improved economic growth in the major economies of the major trading partners of the United States would tend to worsen the trade deficit.　　**T　F**

40. Under the right circumstances, an easy money policy can help reduce a trade deficit.　　**T　F**

Circle the letter that corresponds to the best answer.

1. If an American could buy £25,000 for $100,000, the rate of exchange for the pound would be:
(a) $40
(b) $25
(c) $4
(d) $.25

2. American residents demand foreign currencies in order:
(a) to pay for goods and services imported from foreign countries
(b) to receive interest payments and dividends on their investments outside the United States
(c) to make real and financial investments in foreign nations
(d) to do all of the above

3. A nation's balance of trade is equal to its:
(a) exports less its imports of merchandise (goods)
(b) exports less its imports of goods and services
(c) exports less its imports of goods and services plus its net investment income and net transfers
(d) exports less its imports of goods, services, and capital

4. A nation's balance on the current account is equal to its:
(a) exports less its imports of merchandise (goods)
(b) exports less its imports of goods and services
(c) exports less its imports of goods and services plus its net investment income and net transfers
(d) exports less its imports of goods, services, and capital

5. The net investment income of the United States in its international balance of payments is:
(a) the interest income it receives from foreign residents

(b) the dividends it receives from foreign residents
(c) the interest payments and dividends it receives from foreign residents
(d) the interest payments, dividends, and transfers it receives from foreign residents

6. Capital flows into the United States include the purchase by foreign residents of:
   (a) a factory building owned by Americans
   (b) shares of stock owned by Americans
   (c) bonds owned by Americans
   (d) all of the above

7. An American current account deficit may be financed by:
   (a) borrowing abroad
   (b) selling real assets to foreigners
   (c) selling financial assets to foreigners
   (d) doing any of the above

8. The official reserves of the United States are:
   (a) the stock of gold owned by the Federal government
   (b) the foreign currencies owned by the Federal Reserve Banks
   (c) the money supply of the United States
   (d) all of the above

9. A nation may be able to correct or eliminate a persistent (long-term) balance of payments deficit by:
   (a) lowering the barriers on imported goods
   (b) reducing the international value of its currency
   (c) expanding its national income
   (d) reducing its official reserves

10. If exchange rates float freely the exchange rate for any currency is determined by:
    (a) the demand for it
    (b) the supply of it
    (c) the demand for and the supply of it
    (d) the official reserves that "back" it

11. If a nation had a balance of payments surplus and exchange rates floated freely:
    (a) the foreign exchange rate for its currency would rise, its exports would increase, and its imports would decrease
    (b) the foreign exchange rate for its currency would rise, its exports would decrease, and its imports would increase
    (c) the foreign exchange rate for its currency would fall, its exports would increase, and its imports would decrease
    (d) the foreign exchange rate for its currency would fall, its exports would decrease, and its imports would increase

12. Assuming exchange rates are flexible, which of the following should increase the dollar price of the Swedish krona?

    (a) a rate of inflation greater in Sweden than in the United States
    (b) real interest-rate increases greater in Sweden than in the United States
    (c) national-income increases greater in Sweden than in the United States
    (d) the increased preference of Swedes for American over Swedish automobiles

13. Which of the following would be one of the results associated with the use of freely floating foreign exchange rates to correct a nation's balance of payments surplus?
    (a) the nation's terms of trade with other nations would be worsened
    (b) importers in the nation who had made contracts for the future delivery of goods would find that they had to pay a higher price than expected for the goods
    (c) if the nation were at full employment the decrease in exports and the increase in imports would be inflationary
    (d) exporters in the nation would find their sales abroad had decreased

14. When exchange rates are fixed and a nation at full employment has a balance of payments surplus, the result in that nation will be:
    (a) a declining price level
    (b) falling money income
    (c) inflation
    (d) rising real income

15. The use of exchange controls to eliminate a nation's balance of payments deficit results in:
    (a) decreasing the nation's imports
    (b) decreasing the nation's exports
    (c) decreasing the nation's price level
    (d) decreasing the nation's income

16. A nation with a balance of payments surplus might attempt to eliminate this surplus by employing:
    (a) import quotas
    (b) higher tariffs
    (c) subsidies on items which the nation exports
    (d) none of the above

17. Which one of the following conditions did a nation **not** have to fulfill if it was to be one under the gold standard?
    (a) use only gold as a medium of exchange
    (b) maintain a fixed relationship between its gold stock and its money supply
    (c) allow gold to be freely exported from and imported into the nation
    (d) define its monetary unit in terms of a fixed quantity of gold

18. If the nations of the world were on the gold standard and one nation has a balance of payments surplus:
    (a) foreign exchange rates in that nation would rise toward the gold import point

(b) gold would tend to be imported into that country
(c) the level of prices in that country would tend to fall
(d) employment and output in that country would tend to fall

19. Under the gold standard a nation with a balance of payments deficit would experience all but one of the following. Which one?
(a) gold would flow out of the nation
(b) the nation's money supply would contract
(c) interest rates in the nation would fall
(d) real national output, employment, and prices in the nation would decline

20. Which of the following was the principal disadvantage of the gold standard?
(a) unstable foreign exchange rates
(b) persistent payments imbalances
(c) the uncertainties and decreased trade that resulted from the depreciation of gold
(d) the domestic macroeconomic adjustments experienced by a nation with a payments deficit or surplus

21. All but one of the following were elements in the adjustable-peg system of foreign exchange rates. Which one?
(a) each nation defined its monetary unit in terms of gold or dollars
(b) nations bought and sold their own currencies to stabilize exchange rates
(c) nations were allowed to devalue their currencies freely within a range when faced with persistent payments deficits
(d) the gold deposits of all member nations were held by the IMF

22. Which one of the following was *not* characteristic of the International Monetary Fund in the Bretton Woods system?
(a) made short-term loans to member nations with balance of payments deficits
(b) tried to maintain relatively stable exchange rates
(c) required member nations to maintain exchange stabilization funds
(d) extended long-term loans to less developed nations for the purpose of increasing their productive capacities

23. The objective of the adjustable-peg system was exchange rates which were:
(a) adjustable in the short run and fixed in the long run
(b) adjustable in both the short and long run
(c) fixed in both the short and long run
(d) fixed in the short run; adjustable in the long run

24. Which of the following is the best definition of international monetary reserves in the Bretton Woods system?
(a) gold
(b) dollars

(c) gold and dollars
(d) gold, dollars, and British pounds

25. The dilemma created by the U.S. payments deficits was that:
(a) to maintain the status of the dollar as an acceptable international monetary reserve the deficit had to be reduced and to increase these reserves the deficits had to be continued
(b) to maintain the status of the dollar the deficit had to be continued and to increase reserves the deficit had to be eliminated
(c) to maintain the status of the dollar the deficit had to be increased and to expand reserves the deficit had to be reduced
(d) to maintain the status of the dollar the deficit had to be reduced and to expand reserves the deficit had to be reduced

26. "Floating" the dollar means:
(a) the value of the dollar is determined by the demand for and the supply of the dollar
(b) the dollar price of gold has been increased
(c) the price of the dollar has been allowed to crawl upward at the rate of one-fourth of 1% a month
(d) the IMF decreased the value of the dollar by 10%

27. A system of managed floating exchange rates:
(a) allows nations to stabilize exchange rates in the short term
(b) requires nations to stabilize exchange rates in the long term
(c) entails stable exchange rates in both the short and long term
(d) none of the above

28. Floating exchange rates:
(a) tend to correct balance of payments imbalances
(b) reduce the uncertainties and risks associated with international trade
(c) increase the world's need for international monetary reserves
(d) tend to expand the volume of world trade

29. The foreign-trade problem facing the United States is:
(a) its merchandise and current-account surpluses
(b) its merchandise deficit and current-account surplus
(c) its merchandise and current-account deficit
(d) its merchandise surplus and current-account deficit

30. Which of the following is *not* one of the causes of the growth of American trade deficits during the 1980s?
(a) the strong dollar
(b) the rapid growth of the American economy

(c) the reduced imports of heavily indebted less developed nations from the United States

(d) the high rate of inflation experienced by the American economy relative to rates in other nations

31. High real interest rates in the United States during the mid-1980s were the result of all but one of the following. Which one?

(a) the budget deficits of the Federal government

(b) the low demand of foreign investors for the dollar

(c) the tight money policy of the Federal Reserve Banks

(d) the relatively low rate of inflation in the United States

32. The external debt problems of less developed nations forced many of them to apply:

(a) restrictive monetary and fiscal policies and to devalue their currencies

(b) restrictive monetary and fiscal policies and to revalue their currencies

(c) expansionary monetary and fiscal policies and to devalue their currencies

(d) expansionary monetary and fiscal policies and to revalue their currencies

33. The effect of the trade deficit in the United States during the early and mid-1980s was to:

(a) increase the rate of inflation

(b) increase output and employment

(c) decrease aggregate demand

(d) decrease the international value of the dollar

34. One policy solution for large trade deficits is a reduction in the Federal budget deficit because this change would tend to:

(a) increase real interest rates and increase the demand for dollars in the United States

(b) decrease real interest rates and increase the demand for dollars in the United States

(c) decrease real interest rates and decrease the demand for dollars in the United States

(d) increase real interest rates and decrease the demand for dollars in the United States

35. It is suggested that the large trade deficits of the United States can best be reduced with:

(a) an easy money policy in the United States

(b) an expansionary fiscal policy in the United States

(c) economic policies that increase the rate of growth in the G-7 nations

(d) an appreciation in the value of the currencies of less developed nations

■ **DISCUSSION QUESTIONS**

1. What is foreign exchange and the foreign exchange rate? Who are the demanders and suppliers of a particular foreign exchange, say, the French franc? Why is a buyer (demander) in the foreign exchange markets always a seller (supplier) also?

2. What is meant when it is said that "a nation's exports pay for its imports"? Do nations pay for all their imports with exports?

3. What is an international balance of payments? What are the principal sections in a nation's international balance of payments and what are the principal "balances" to be found in it?

4. How can a nation finance a current account deficit and what can it do with a current account surplus? How does a nation finance a balance of payments deficit and what does it do with a balance of payments surplus?

5. Is it good or bad for a nation to have a balance of payments deficit or surplus?

6. What types of events cause the exchange rate for a foreign currency to appreciate or to depreciate? How will each of these events affect the exchange rate for a foreign money and for a nation's own money?

7. How can freely floating foreign exchange rates eliminate balance of payments deficits and surpluses? What are the problems associated with this method of correcting payments imbalances?

8. How may a nation employ its international monetary reserves to fix or "peg" foreign exchange rates? Be precise. How does a nation obtain or acquire these monetary reserves?

9. What kinds of trade controls may nations with payments deficits employ to eliminate their deficits?

10. How can foreign exchange controls to be used to restore international equilibrium? Why do such exchange controls necessarily involve the rationing of foreign exchange? What effect do these controls have upon prices, output, and employment in nations that use them?

11. If foreign exchange rates are fixed, what kind of domestic macroeconomic adjustments are required to eliminate a payments deficit? To eliminate a payments surplus?

12. When was a nation on the gold standard? How did the international gold standard correct payments imbalances? What were the disadvantages of this method of eliminating payments deficits and surpluses?

13. Why does the operation of the international gold standard ensure relatively stable foreign exchange rates, that is, rates which fluctuate only within very narrow limits? What are limits and what are the advantages of stable exchange rates?

14. What is the "critical difference" between the adjustments necessary to correct payments deficits and surpluses under the gold standard and those necessary when exchange rates are flexible? How did this difference lead to the demise of the gold standard during the 1930s?

15. Explain:
(a) why the International Monetary Fund was established and what the objectives of the adjustable-peg (or Bretton Woods) system were
(b) what the adjustable-peg system was and the basic means it employed to stabilize exchange rates in the short run; and
(c) when and how the system was to adjust exchange rates in the long run.

16. What did nations use as international monetary reserves under the Bretton Woods system? Why was the dollar used by nations as an international money and how could they acquire additional dollars?

17. Explain the dilemma created by the need for expanding international monetary reserves and for maintaining the status of the dollar.

18. Why and how did the United States shatter the Bretton Woods system in 1971? If the international value of the dollar is no longer determined by the amount of gold for which it can be exchanged, what does determine its value?

19. Explain what is meant by a managed floating system of foreign exchange rates. When are exchange rates managed and when are they allowed to float?

20. Explain the arguments of the proponents and the critics of the managed floating system.

21. What was the foreign-trade problem of the United States during the 1980s and early 1990s? What were
(a) its causes; and
(b) its effects on the American economy?

22. What two major policies are suggested for reducing the large trade deficits in the United States? How would such policies affect national output and employment? What other five remedies have also been discussed?

■ **ANSWERS**

Chapter 25 Exchange Rates, the Balance of Payments, and Trade Deficits

FILL-IN QUESTIONS

1. francs, dollar

2. $3\frac{1}{3}$

3. *a.* supply of, demand for, increase, decrease; *b.* demand for, supply of, decrease, increase

4. transportation, insurance (either order), interest, dividends (either order)

5. the other nations of the world: *a.* credit, +; *b.* debit, −

6. *a.* less, merchandise; *b.* greater; *c.* investment, transfers, negative

7. *a.* in that nation, other nations, in other nations, that nation, real, financial (either order); *b.* greater

8. *a.* selling, borrowing; *b.* buy, lend

9. foreign monies, central; *a.* decrease; *b.* increase; *c.* zero

10. negative, decrease, positive, increase

11. *a.* depreciate, appreciate; *b.* decrease, increase, decrease

12. *a.* depreciate; *b.* appreciate; *c.* depreciate; *d.* depreciate; *e.* depreciate

13. diminish, worsened, recession, inflation (either order)

14. *a.* sell; *b.* buy

15. *a.* taxing, subsidizing; *b.* import, export, government

16. contractionary, recession

17. gold, money, stock, exported, imported

18. *a.* stable; *b.* (1) out of, (2) decreased, rose, (3) fell, recession

19. fixed, adjustable-peg; *a.* gold, dollars (either order); *b.* buying, exchange-stabilization, selling, borrowing from; *c.* devalue; *d.* gold, dollars (either order); *e.* stable, flexible

20. *a.* deficits; *b.* gold; *c.* decreased; *d.* eliminated, continued

21. gold, market forces (demand and supply), fixed, floating

22. managed floating; *a.* stable; *b.* imbalances

23. growth, turbulence, volatility, nonsystem

24. deficits, imports, exports

25. *a.* strong; *b.* rapid; *c.* reduced

26. *a.* more, less, decreased, increased; *b.* high, deficits, tight, low; *c.* fell, profits, G-7; *d.* decrease

27. *a.* rose; *b.* restrictive, devalue, exports, imports

28. contract, slow, lower, increase, creditor, debtor

29. contraction, expansion

30. easy, tariffs, recession, competitiveness, investment

PROBLEMS AND PROJECTS

1. *a.* (1) 3, (2) (a) 3, dollars, (b) 150, pesos; *b.* (1) 3, (2) (a) 3, (b) 3; *c.* (1) demand for, supply of, (2) increased, decreased

2. *a.* −50, −35, −30, +25, −5, +5; *b.* deficit, 5

3. *a.* (1) 4.00, (2) ¼, (3) 300, (4) 1200; *b.* buy, 300, 1500; *c.* sell, 380, 950

SELF-TEST

1. T, pp. 445–446
2. F, pp. 445–446
3. T, pp. 446–447
4. F, p. 447
5. T, p. 447
6. F, p. 447
7. T, p. 447
8. F, p. 447
9. T, pp. 447–449
10. T, pp. 447–449
11. T, pp. 447–449
12. F, p. 449
13. T, pp. 452–453
14. F, p. 452
15. T, p. 452
16. T, p. 454
17. F, p. 454
18. T, p. 455
19. F, p. 455
20. F, p. 456
21. T, p. 456
22. T, pp. 456–457
23. T, pp. 458–459
24. T, pp. 458–459
25. T, pp. 459–460
26. T, pp. 459–460
27. F, pp. 459–460
28. F, p. 460
29. F, p. 460
30. T, pp. 460–461
31. F, pp. 461–462
32. T, pp. 461–462
33. T, pp. 461–462
34. F, p. 462
35. T, pp. 463–464
36. T, pp. 464–465
37. F, p. 464
38. T, pp. 465–466
39. F, p. 466
40. T, p. 466

1. *c*, pp. 445–446
2. *d*, pp. 445–446
3. *a*, p. 447
4. *c*, pp. 447–448
5. *c*, pp. 447–448
6. *d*, p. 448
7. *d*, p. 448
8. *b*, p. 449
9. *b*, p. 449
10. *c*, pp. 450–451
11. *b*, pp. 452–453
12. *b*, p. 452
13. *d*, pp. 452–453
14. *c*, pp. 455–456
15. *a*, p. 455
16. *d*, p. 455
17. *a*, p. 456
18. *b*, p. 457
19. *c*, p. 457
20. *d*, p. 457
21. *d*, pp. 458–459
22. *d*, pp. 458–459
23. *d*, p. 459
24. *c*, p. 459
25. *a*, pp. 459–460
26. *a*, p. 460
27. *a*, p. 460
28. *a*, p. 460
29. *c*, p. 461
30. *d*, pp. 461–462
31. *b*, pp. 461–462
32. *a*, p. 463
33. *c*, p. 463
34. *c*, p. 465
35. *c*, p. 466

DISCUSSION QUESTIONS

1. pp. 445–446
2. p. 446
3. pp. 446–448
4. pp. 447–448
5. p. 449
6. pp. 450–452
7. pp. 452–453
8. pp. 454–455
9. pp. 454–455
10. p. 455
11. p. 455
12. pp. 456–457
13. pp. 456–457
14. pp. 457–458
15. pp. 458–459
16. pp. 458–459
17. pp. 458–459
18. pp. 459–460
19. p. 460
20. p. 461
21. pp. 461–463
22. pp. 465–466

CHAPTER 26

The Soviet Economy in Transition

In the years following the Russian Revolution of 1917, many people in the United States were convinced that the economic system of the Soviet Union was unworkable and that it would break down sooner or later—proof that Marx and Lenin were unrealistic dreamers—and that the reconversion of the Soviet economy to a market system would follow. Now, some seventy-five years after the revolution, the economy of the former Soviet Union is being transformed into a market economy. Chapter 26 provides insights into this profound turn of events by examining the reasons why the Soviet economic system failed, and by discussing reforms and obstacles in the path to a market economy for the former Soviet Union.

The first two sections of the chapter explain the basic ideas behind Marxian ideology and discuss the two institutional features that were most characteristic of the economy of the former Soviet Union. For over seven decades, the Soviet economy operated under a system of state ownership of property resources and direct control. Central planning was used to set prices, to restrict consumption, and to direct investment to heavy industry and to the military. Although central planning served as a powerful form of economic decision-making, it had serious problems and flaws as a coordinating mechanism because it resulted in production bottlenecks, missed production targets, and reduced the economic freedom and decision-making for producers, workers, and consumers.

As you will learn in the third and fourth sections of the chapter, the slowing of economic growth in the Soviet economy in 1970s and 1980s set the stage for the failure of communism and for the final attempts to reform the faltering economic system of the former Soviet Union. What contributed to the deterioration of Soviet economy were many factors, among them being the economic burden of supporting a large military, inefficiencies in the agricultural sector that hurt other sectors of the economy, and the reliance of more inputs rather than increasing the productivity and efficiency of available inputs to fuel economic growth. By 1986, then-Soviet President Mikhail Gorbachev proposed a series of economic changes designed to restructure the economy (**perestroika**) and to give peo-

ple more freedom in the conduct of economic and business affairs (**glasnost**). Although the Gorbachev reforms attempted to correct the deficiencies of central control and modernize the economy, the proposal did not eliminate central planning.

The fifth and sixth parts of Chapter 26 explain the elements of and obstacles to a more sweeping transformation of the economy of the former Soviet Union into a market economy. The transition will require the privatization of property resources, the promotion of competition, a reduced and altered role for government, major price reforms, and currency conversion. These transition policies will also result in high rates of inflation. A host of obstacles—technical problems, negative attitudes among bureaucrats and workers, the maintainence of order and national unity, and achieving simultaneous progress in all major reforms—must also be overcome in the movement to a market economy. The challenge is daunting, but it will be facilitated by several positive aspects of the economy of the former Soviet Union.

The final section discusses the actions that can be taken by the major capitalist nations to help transform the centrally planned economy into one based on markets and prices. The most obvious assistance is foreign aid, but as you will learn, it is not without much criticism. Private investment is the most important avenue for long-term change, yet the amount of investment and its effectiveness will depend on the progress in economic restructuring. The economy of the former Soviet Union will also benefit from the steps it takes to join international organizations that promote world trade and economic development.

The transformation of the economy of the former Soviet Union into a market economy is one of the most important economic events of this decade. Whether the sweeping economic reforms will work, or what the final outcomes will be, is still unknown and uncertain. Nevertheless, this examination of the sweeping change of an economic system from one based on central planning to one based on markets and prices should deepen your understanding of the principles of economics. This dramatic development is a fitting topic for the conclusion to your study of economics.

■ CHECKLIST

☐ Outline the key elements of Marxian ideology.
☐ Identify two outstanding institutions of the economy of the former Soviet Union.
☐ Make seven generalizations about the functioning of central economic planning in the former Soviet Union.
☐ Compare the coordination mechanism in a market economy with that in a centrally planned economy.
☐ Describe the deteriorating economic performance of the Soviet economy after the 1960s.
☐ Identify six factors that contributed to the collapse of the Soviet economic system.
☐ Discuss the six interrelated elements of the Gorbachev reforms.
☐ List six factors that are important in the transition to a market economy for the economy of the former Soviet Union.
☐ Explain the effects of privatization and competition in the transition.
☐ Describe the changed role for government in the transition.
☐ Use a supply and demand graph to discuss the difficulties posed by price reforms in the transition.
☐ Explain the importance of opening the economy to international trade and finance in the transition.
☐ Identify three reasons to expect high rates of inflation in the transition.
☐ List four major obstacles to the transformation of the economy of the former Soviet Union.
☐ Identify four positive factors in the former Soviet Union that will help in the change to a market economy.
☐ List three actions by the capitalist industrial nations of the world to assist the former Soviet Union to build a market economy.
☐ Evaluate the importance of foreign aid and private investment in the transformation of the economy of the former Soviet Union.
☐ Identify the key international organizations and actions that would help with the transition to a market economy for the former Soviet Union.

■ CHAPTER OUTLINE

1. The Soviet economy was based on ideology and institutions.
  a. The Soviet government was viewed as a dictatorship of the proletariat (or working class), and the economy was based on *Marxian* ideology.
  (1) The Marxian concept of a *labor theory of value* held that only labor creates value in production, and that profits are a *surplus value* expropriated from workers by capitalists, who because of the institution of private property, were able to control the means of production (capital goods).

(2) The communist system of the former Soviet Union sought to end this exploitation of workers by eliminating private property and by creating a classless society.
  b. The two major institutional features of the Soviet economy were state ownership of property resources and central economic planning.

2. Central planning was used throughout much of the history of the Soviet Union.
  a. Historically, the operation of central planning in the Soviet Union exhibited seven features:
  (1) the attachment of great importance to military strength and to industrialization;
  (2) the overcommitment of available resources and the missing of planning targets;
  (3) a stress on increasing the quantity of resources rather than using given resources more productively;
  (4) the use of directives to allocate inputs for production rather than markets and prices;
  (5) price fixing and price controls by government;
  (6) an emphasis on the self-sufficiency of the nation; and
  (7) passive use of monetary and fiscal policies.
  b. The basic problem encountered in a centrally planned economy such as that of the former Soviet Union is the difficulty of coordinating the many interdependent segments of the economy and the avoidance of the chain reaction that would result from a bottleneck in any one of the segments.

3. The failure of communism in the Soviet Union resulted in large part from the poor economic growth performance of the economy in the years since the 1960s. Technology lagged by Western standards and manufacturing goods were of poor quality. Consumers were also aware that they had received few material benefits from years of sacrifice for the rapid industrialization and the sizable public expenditures to support a large military.
  a. Six interrelated factors contributed to the collapse of the economy of the former Soviet Union.
  (1) The large financial burden for military expenditures diverted resources from the production of consumer and capital goods.
  (2) Inefficiencies in agriculture acted as a drag on economic growth and hurt productivity in other sectors of the economy.
  (3) Economic growth was achieved throughout much of the Soviet history by increasing the quantity of economic resources (especially labor) rather than by using the more difficult route of increasing the productivity of existing resources; however, growing labor shortages limited growth by the historical route and the lack of incentives and technology needs made the second route more difficult.
  (4) The increased complexity of production processes in a modern industrial society compounded the difficulties of central planning.

(5) There were inadequate measures of economic performance to determine the degree of success or failure of enterprises or to give clear signals to the economy.
(6) Economic incentives were ineffective for encouraging initiative and work or for coordination of productive activities.

4. In 1986, President Mikhail Gorbachev offered a series of proposals for economic reform (***perestroika***) and also call for more openness (***glasnost***) in discussions about economic affairs, both designed to improve the economic performance of the centrally planned system. The Gorbachev reforms called for: the modernization of industry; the decentralization of decision-making; the encouragement of some private production of products; the increased use of economic incentives to motivate workers and fire incompetent managers; the institution of price reforms and a more rational price system; and a greater involvement in the world economy. The reforms did not work in large part because they only modified the major deficiencies of the centrally planned system.

5. There are six components to the transition from a command economy to a market economy for the former Soviet Union.
  a. Private property rights must be established and government property must be transferred to private ownership. Several options are possible to achieve the privatization objective: selling enterprises directly, employee stock ownership, or conversion of large government enterprises into corporations or publicly owned businesses.
  b. Competition must be promoted by splitting up or restructing large state-owned enterprises to reduce the potential for monopoly power by having only one privatized business in an industry.
  c. The government must reduce its extensive involvement in the economy to the more limited and traditional role of providing a legal system, maintaining competition, redistributing income, reallocating resources to necessary public goods, addressing the problems of spillovers, and stabilizing the economy.
  d. The government will need to eliminate price fixing and price controls so that prices for goods and services are free to change and reflect relative scarcities.
  e. Action must be taken to open the economy to international trade and finance by making the ruble a convertible currency. Eventually, this action will promote more competition and efficiency in production.
  f. The transition reforms will be accompanied by inflation because of the decontrol of prices, and because of a ***ruble overhang***, which is the excess currency created by the lack of opportunities for consumer spending. Also contributing to the inflation problem are the large, recent deficits of government and the printing of new currency to finance these deficits.

6. Obstacles to transforming the Soviet economy will make the transition difficult.
  a. The drastic reforms in the economy create many technical problems that must be solved.
  b. There may be public resistance to the reforms because they threaten job status and require workers and managers to change old methods and procedures of work.
  c. The demands for autonomy in new republics of the former Soviet Union may lead to disorder, reduce economic efficiency, and restrict trade between republics.
  d. The reforms must be pursued simultaneously; a failure to achieve one reform will affect the success of all the reforms.
  e. Four positive factors, however, may contribute to the success of the reforms:
  (1) the large endowment of natural resources;
  (2) the shift of resources and expenditures from military to civilian uses;
  (3) the experience and skills developed in the underground or second economy; and
  (4) the political reform and democratization that frees people to express ideas and to be more productive.

7. The major capitalist economies of the world will facilitate the transition of the economy of the former Soviet Union to a market economy.
  a. Foreign aid is being provided by capitalist nations. Critics contend, however, that foreign aid is wasteful under present circumstances, delays military cuts which would be more effective, is too little to be of much help to the average citizen, and would be better spent addressing problems in home countries.
  b. Private investment will be very important, but there are many obstacles for private businesses that desire to invest because of unclear ownership and control of enterprises, inadequacies in the private distribution system and in the public infrastructure, and the inconvertibility of the ruble.
  c. Membership in international organizations, such as the International Monetary Fund, the World Bank, and the General Agreement on Tariffs and Trade, will help integrate the former Soviet Union into the world's market economy.

8. The prospects are still uncertain for the current reform of the Soviet economy and its transition to a market economy.

■ **IMPORTANT TERMS**

Labor theory of value	Gorbachev reforms
Surplus value	*Perestroika*
State ownership	*Glasnost*
Central economic planning	**Ruble overhang**

■ FILL-IN QUESTIONS

1. The ideology of the economy of the former Soviet Union was that:

a. the value of any commodity is determined by the amount of _____ required to produce it;

b. in capitalist economies, capital is (privately, publicly) _____ owned, and capitalists exploit workers by paying them a wage that is equal to the _____ wage and obtain _____ value at the expense of workers; and

c. in a communist economy, capital and other property resources will be _____, society will be _____-less, and it will be governed by the Communist Party as a dictatorship of the _____

2. The two major institutions of the former Soviet Union are the ownership of property resources by the _____ and _____ economic planning.

3. Economic planning in the former Soviet Union functioned in several ways.

a. The Soviet five-year plans sought to achieve rapid _____ and _____ strength, but these policies created an (over, under) _____-commitment of resources and resulted in an _____-production of goods for consumers.

b. Early economic growth was achieved by _____ resources and reallocating surplus labor from _____ to industry.

c. The government allocated inputs among industries by planning _____ and the government fixed _____ for goods and services and inputs.

d. The Soviet Union considered itself to be a (capitalist, socialist) _____ nation surrounded by _____ nations, and central plans were designed to achieve economic _____-sufficiency.

e. Monetary and fiscal policies in the Soviet Union were (active, passive) _____. Prices were _____ by government and ambitious planning targets essentially eliminated the _____ of workers. The _____ issued credit or working capital to state enterprises and accepted deposits, but it did not manipulate the supply of _____.

4. Decision-making in a market economy is (centralized, decentralized) _____, but in the Soviet economy it was _____. The market system tends to produce a reasonably (efficient, inefficient) _____ allocation of resources, but central planning in the Soviet economy was _____ and resulted in production bottlenecks and failures to meet many production targets.

5. There are a number of reasons for the collapse of communism and the failure of the Soviet economy.

a. There was a large _____ burden on the economy that diverted resources from the production of investment and _____ goods.

b. Agriculture was (efficient, inefficient) _____ and (helped, hurt) _____ economic growth and productivity in other sectors of the economy.

c. Traditionally, economic growth was achieved by increasing the (quality, quantity) _____ of economic resources rather than by increasing the _____, or productivity, of existing resources, but shortages of labor and capital have limited economic growth in the traditional path, and improving the productivity of existing resources was difficult because of lagging _____ progress.

d. Central planning became (more, less) _____ complex and difficult as the Soviet economy grew and changed over time.

e. Measures of economic performance were (adequate, inadequate) _____ for determining the success or failure of economic activities.

f. Economic incentives were (effective, ineffective) _____ for encouraging work or for giving signals for efficient allocation of resources in the economy.

6. In 1986, reform of the Soviet economy was proposed by Mikhail _____. His economic program for reform and restructuring was referred to as _____; it was accompanied by _____, which means that there was to be more openness in the discussion of economic issues among participants in the economy.

7. List the six elements of the 1986 reforms.

a. _____

b. _____

c. _____

d. _____

e. _____

f. _____

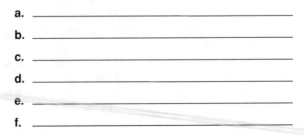

8. The transition to a market economy for the former Soviet Union will require success in achieving more sweeping changes than the _____ reforms. One of the most important changes is the establishment of _____ rights and the transfer of government property to _____ ownership. This objective may be achieved by the _____ of state enterprises, by employee _____ ownership, and in the case of large state enterprise, conversion into _____ or into businesses owned by the _____

9. The economy must also promote _____ by splitting up the large state-owned enterprises so that there is more than one business producing a good or service and to reduce the potential for _____ power.

10. In the transition, the role of government will need to be _____ and refocused on the traditional functions of providing a _____ system, maintaining _____, redistributing _____, reallocating resources to essential _____ goods, addressing the problems of _____ costs and benefits, and macroeconomic _____ of the economy.

11. In the past, prices of goods and services were kept at low levels through price _____, but the movement to a market economy will require them to be lifted and the economy will experience _____

12. The former Soviet Union will need to join the international economy by making the ruble a _____ or exchangeable currency on international markets, and by opening the economy to more international _____ with other nations.

13. The move to a market economy will be accompanied by inflation because of the _____ of prices, a ruble _____, and government financing of large budget deficits by printing more _____

14. The obstacles to the transformation of the economy of the Soviet Union into a market economy will include _____ economic problems, the need to change public _____ among bureaucrats and workers, the political problems of maintaining national _____, and the need to make _____

rather than piecemeal progress on all the economic reforms.

15. List four positive factors that may contribute to the success of the transition of the former Soviet Union to a market economy.

a. _____

b. _____

c. _____

d. _____

16. The major capitalist economies of the world can assist with conversion of the Soviet economy to a market economy by providing foreign _____, by increasing private _____, and by allowing the former Soviet Union to become a _____ of such institutions as the International _____ Fund, the World _____, and the General Agreement on _____

17. The outlook for the effective transformation of the economy of the former Soviet Union from a system of central planning to one based on markets and prices is (certain, uncertain) _____ and will require time to work.

■ **PROBLEMS AND PROJECTS**

1. In the table below are several of the major institutions and characteristics of either the American economy or the economy of the former Soviet Union. In the appropriate space, name the corresponding institution or characteristic of the other economy.

American institution or characteristic	Soviet institution or characteristic
a. _____	labor theory of value
b. _____	surplus value
c. Private ownership of economic resources	_____
d. a market economy	_____
e. _____	state industrial enterprises
f. privately owned farms	_____
g. entrepreneurial freedom	_____
h. consumer sovereignty	_____
i. _____	price controls
j. _____	turnover tax
k. democracy	_____
l. underground economy	_____

2. Answer the next set of questions based on the table below. In the table are the columns for the price, quantity demanded (Q_d) by consumers, and a fixed quantity supplied by government (Q_{s1}) for a product in the former Soviet Union. The column for Q_{s2} shows the supply curve for the product **after** privatization in the industry producing the product.

Price (in rubles)	Q_d	Q_{s1}	Q_{s2}
90	25	25	55
80	30	25	50
70	35	25	45
60	40	25	40
50	45	25	35
40	50	25	30
30	55	25	25

a. When only the government supplies the product as shown in the Q_{s1} schedule, the equilibrium price will be _____ rubles and the equilibrium quantity will be _____ units.

b. If the government tries to make the product more accessible to lower-income consumers by setting the price at 30 rubles, then the quantity demanded will be _____ units and the quantity supplied will be _____ units, producing a shortage of _____ units.

c. If the government decontrolled prices but did not privatize industry, then prices will rise to _____ rubles and the government will still produce _____ units.

d. With privatization, there will be a new quantity supplied schedule (Q_{s2}). The equilibrium price will be _____ rubles and the equilibrium quantity will be _____ units. The equilibrium price has risen by _____ rubles and the equilibrium quantity by _____ units.

■ **SELF-TEST**

1. The labor theory of value is the Marxian idea that the exchange value of a product is determined by the supply and demand of labor resources.　　**T　F**

2. Surplus value in Marxian ideology is the value or price of a commodity at equilibrium in a competitive market.　　**T　F**

3. The economy of the former Soviet Union was characterized by both state ownership of resources and decentralized economic decision-making.　　**T　F**

4. The Soviet government set the economic objectives of the economy, directed the resources of the economy toward the achievement of those objectives, and used the market system as one means of achieving those objectives.　　**T　F**

5. Historically, the Soviet Union placed strong emphasis on rapid industrialization and economic self-sufficiency.　　**T　F**

6. Economic resources tended to be undercommitted in the economy of the former Soviet Union.　　**T　F**

7. The former Soviet Union actively used monetary and fiscal policies to manipulate aggregate levels of employment, output, and prices.　　**T　F**

8. During 1990 and 1991, the real domestic output of the former Soviet Union increased.　　**T　F**

9. Greater productivity and technological progress in the civilian sector were often sacrificed or limited by the demands to support a large military in the former Soviet Union.　　**T　F**

10. Agriculture was one of the most productive sectors of the economy of the former Soviet Union.　　**T　F**

11. Soviet economic growth slowed in the years after the 1970s because of a surplus of labor and extensive unemployment.　　**T　F**

12. The problems of central planning became easier and less complex as the economy of the former Soviet Union grew over time, but the economy was undermined by calls for democratic reform.　　**T　F**

13. *Glasnost* refers to the economic restructuring proposed in 1986 by Mikhail Gorbachev.　　**T　F**

14. The Gorbachev reforms called for the development of a limited private enterprise sector and more use of economic incentives.　　**T　F**

15. The current transition to a market economy in the former Soviet Union will require the breakup of large industries and actions to promote competition.　　**T　F**

16. Price decontrol will be a minor problem in the conversion of the economy of the former Soviet Union to capitalism because the prices established by the Soviet government over the years are very similar to the economic value that would be established in a competitive market.　　**T　F**

17. Government is more likely to expand rather than contract its role in the transition to a market economy in the former Soviet Union.　　**T　F**

18. The financing of recent budget deficits in the former Soviet Union by printing and distributing more currency is an important source of inflation.　　**T　F**

19. Old work habits and bureaucratic resistence will be obstacles in the movement to capitalize in the former Soviet Union.   **T   F**

20. The "simultaneity" problem refers to the need to achieve a simultaneous decrease in inflation and unemployment in the former Soviet Union.   **T   F**

21. Maintaining political and economic unity will be difficult in the former Soviet Union because of the specialization of production and the existence of state monopolies in different republics.   **T   F**

22. A positive factor contributing to the economic transformation of the former Soviet Union to a market economy will be the size and variety of the natural resource base.   **T   F**

23. The "second economy" refers to the state-run monopolies that control most of the production in the former Soviet Union and which need to be converted to private enterprises.   **T   F**

24. A critic of foreign aid to the former Soviet Union would argue that the aid is wasteful and ineffective until the transition to capitalism has been achieved.   **T   F**

25. Private investment from capitalist nations will be an important source of real capital and business skills in management, marketing and entrepreneurship for the former Soviet Union.   **T   F**

Circle the letter that corresponds to the best answer.

1. Which of the following was an element in the ideology of the Soviet Union?
   (a) dictatorship over the business class
   (b) the creation of surplus value by government
   (c) the labor theory of value
   (d) the private ownership of property

2. Marxian (or communist) ideology in the Soviet Union was highly critical of capitalist societies because in those societies:
   (a) capitalists own the machinery and equipment necessary for production
   (b) capitalists pay workers a wage that is less than the value of their production
   (c) capitalists expropriate the surplus value of workers
   (d) all of the above are true

3. The institution that was most characteristic of the Soviet Union was:
   (a) private ownership of property
   (b) authoritarian central planning
   (c) a system of markets and prices
   (d) consumer sovereignty

4. Industrialization and rapid economic growth in the Soviet Union were initially achieved by:
   (a) the mobilization of economic resources

   (b) the overcommitment of economic resources
   (c) price controls and price fixing
   (d) active use of fiscal policy by the government

5. The Soviet Union viewed itself historically as a single socialist nation surrounded by hostile capitalist nations, and as a consequence central planning stressed the need for:
   (a) consumer sovereignty
   (b) economic self-sufficiency
   (c) allocation by directive
   (d) manipulation of the money supply by the *Gosbank*

6. In the system of central planning in the Soviet Union, the outputs of some industries became the inputs for other industries, but a failure of one industry to meet its target would cause:
   (a) inflation in wholesale and retail prices
   (b) the decay of the infrastructure
   (c) a chain reaction of production problems and bottlenecks
   (d) widespread unemployment and underemployment among workers

Use the table below to answer the next question (7).

Years	Growth in real domestic output (percent)			
	A	**B**	**C**	**D**
1950s	3	4	5	6
1960s	4	3	3	5
1970s	5	6	1	3
1980s (mid)	6	2	1	2

7. The column that best portrays the record of Soviet economic growth from the 1950s through the mid-1980s is:
   (a) A
   (b) B
   (c) C
   (d) D

8. In 1990 and 1991, real domestic economic growth in the Soviet Union:
   (a) increased slightly
   (b) decreased significantly
   (c) remained the same in both years
   (d) increased in 1990, but decreased significantly in 1991

9. Which of the following is evidence of economic failure of communism in the Soviet Union?
   (a) lagging technology compared to Western standards
   (b) the inability to supply consumer goods that people wanted
   (c) the poor quality of consumer goods
   (d) all of the above

10. What was the size of expenditures for the military as a percentage of domestic output in the Soviet Union versus the United States?
  (a) 15–20% in Soviet Union versus 15–20% in the United States
  (b) 5–10% in the Soviet Union versus 10–15% in the United States
  (c) 15–20% in the Soviet Union versus 6% in the United States
  (d) 10% in the Soviet Union versus 6% in the United States

11. Which of the following was a cause of low productivity in agriculture in the Soviet Union?
  (a) inability to make productive use of the abundance of good farmland in the country
  (b) the failure to construct an effective incentive system for agriculture
  (c) an increase in the length of the growing season
  (d) the overuse of certain chemical fertilizers on crops

12. Which factor contributed to the slowing of Soviet economic growth in the 1980s?
  (a) labor shortages
  (b) unemployment
  (c) idle plant capacity
  (d) decreased consumption

13. What was the major success indicator for Soviet enterprises?
  (a) profits
  (b) the level of prices
  (c) production targets
  (d) the turnover tax

14. The restructuring of the Soviet economy under Mikhail Gorbachev is referred to as:
  (a) *Gosbank*
  (b) *glasnost*
  (c) *perestroika*
  (d) the "second economy"

15. The modernization proposal of Gorbachev's economic program basically involved:
  (a) increased production of consumers goods and decreased production of investment goods
  (b) reallocation of investment to research and development and to high-tech industries
  (c) the building of new housing facilities to address the pressing problems of overcrowding and the deterioration in dwellings
  (d) increasing the productivity of agriculture by improving the quality of equipment available to agricultural workers

16. Which of the following is *not* one of the components of the most recent and sweeping reform effort in the former Soviet Union?
  (a) privatization

  (b) promotion of competition
  (c) an increased role for government
  (d) more participation in the world economy

17. The effect of price controls on most consumer goods in the Soviet Union was that:
  (a) shortages developed because quantity demanded was greater than the quantity supplied by the competitive market at the controlled price set by government
  (b) prices rose because the quantity demanded by consumers was greater than the quantity supplied by government
  (c) prices fell because the quantity supplied by the competitive market was greater than the quantity demanded by consumers
  (d) shortages developed because the quantity demanded by consumers was greater than the quantity supplied by the government at the price set by government

18. Which set of factors contributed to the recent inflationary pressure in the former Soviet Union?
  (a) the breakup of state monopolies, the extension of credit to enterprises by the *Gosbank*, the increase in the turnover tax
  (b) central planning, production targets, and production bottlenecks
  (c) the printing of new currency to finance government, the ruble overhang, and the decontrol of prices
  (d) increased military spending, investment in new technology, and making the ruble a convertible currency

19. Which of the following would *not* be considered an important obstacle to the transformation of the former Soviet Union into a market economy?
  (a) the need to make simultaneous progress on each component of the reform
  (b) the need to change public attitudes and values
  (c) the potential for national disintegration
  (d) competition from the "second economy"

20. An important avenue that has been suggested for industrialized capitalist nations to assist in the development of a market economy in the former Soviet Union is for those nations to:
  (a) eliminate the ruble overhang
  (b) increase private investment
  (c) forgive past debts
  (d) reduce foreign aid

■ **DISCUSSION QUESTIONS**

1. What are the essential features of Marxian ideology on which the command economy of the Soviet Union was based?

2. What were the two principal economic institutions of the Soviet Union? How do these institutions compare with those of the United States?

3. Describe how Soviet planning functioned historically. What are some generalizations you can make about resource use, directives, prices, self-sufficiency, and macroeconomic policies?

4. Why does central planning result in a "coordination" problem? Compare the operation of central planning with the use of markets and prices for economic decision-making.

5. What economic evidence can you present on the failure of communism in the Soviet Union in the 1980s and early 1990s?

6. Discuss the six factors that contributed to the collapse of the Soviet economy. In particular, explain the difference between achieving economic growth by increasing the quantity of resources and increasing economic growth by increasing the productivity and efficiency with which existing resources are used.

7. What were the six elements of Gorbachev's economic reform program? How do these reforms compare with past economic reforms?

8. What problems are posed by privatization for the former Soviet Union as it moves to a market economy?

9. Discuss what must be done in the former Soviet Union to promote competition. To what extent are "state monopolies" a problem?

10. What is the traditional role for government in a market economy? Describe the anticipated changes in the role of government in the former Soviet Union as it adopts capitalism.

11. Why was there a need for price reform in the former Soviet Union in the transition to a market economy? What has been the *general* effect of this change? Use a supply and demand graph to explain the effect of the price de-control on a specific product.

12. What is the major problem confronting the former Soviet Union as it seeks to join the world economy?

13. Present three reasons why there is inflation in the former Soviet Union as it transforms its economy into a market economy.

14. What are the major obstacles to the development of capitalism in the former Soviet Union? Describe the technical problems, the attitudinal problems, and the political problems. Why must the economic reforms be achieved simultaneously?

15. Cite and discuss the positive factors that will aid in the transition to capitalism for the former Soviet Union.

16. What are the contributions of foreign aid and private investment in helping the former Soviet Union? What are the criticisms of these efforts?

17. How will membership in international organizations help the former Soviet Union? What are the key international organizations or institutions in which membership has been or will be sought?

18. Evaluate the prospects for the transformation of the economy of the former Soviet Union.

■ **ANSWERS**

Chapter 26 The Soviet Economy in Transition

FILL-IN QUESTIONS

1. *a.* labor; *b.* privately, subsistence, surplus; *c.* publicly owned, class, proletariat

2. state, central

3. *a.* industrialization, military, over, under; *b.* mobilizing, agriculture; *c.* targets, prices; *d.* socialist, capitalist, self; *e.* passive, controlled, unemployment, **Gosbank**, money

4. decentralized, centralized, efficient, inefficient

5. *a.* military, consumer; *b.* inefficient, hurt; *c.* quantity, quality, technological; *d.* more; *e.* inadequate; *f.* ineffective

6. Gorbachev, *perestroika*, *glasnost*

7. *a.* modernization of industry; *b.* greater decentralization of decision-making; *c.* creation of a limited private enterprise sector; *d.* improved worker discipline and incentive; *e.* a more rational price system; *f.* increased role in the international economy

8. Gorbachev, property, private, sale, stock, corporations, government

9. competition, monopoly

10. limited, legal, competition, income, public, spillover, stabilization

11. controls, inflation

12. convertible, trade

13. decontrol, overhang, currency (or money)

14. technical, attitudes, unity, simultaneous

15. *a.* large and varied natural resources base; *b.* peace dividend (less military spending); *c.* the experiences from the "second economy"; *d.* democratization

16. aid, investment, member, Monetary, Bank, Tariffs and Trade

17. uncertain

PROBLEMS AND PROJECTS

1. *a.* supply and demand; *b.* profit; *c.* state ownership of resources; *d.* command or centrally planned economy; *e.* corporations; *f.* agricultural cooperatives or collective farms; *g.* central economic planning (or production targets); *h.* central economic planning; *i.* free markets and flexible prices; *j.* excise tax; *k.* dictatorship by the party; *l.* the "second economy"

2. *a.* 90, 25; *b.* 55, 25, 30; *c.* 90, 25; *d.* 60, 40, 30, 15

SELF-TEST

1. F, p. 470
2. F, p. 470
3. F, p. 471
4. F, pp. 471–472
5. T, p. 471
6. F, p. 471
7. F, p. 472
8. F, p. 473
9. T, p. 474
10. F, p. 474
11. F, p. 474
12. F, p. 474
13. F, p. 476
14. T, p. 476
15. T, p. 477
16. F, p. 478
17. F, pp. 477–478
18. T, p. 479
19. T, p. 480
20. F, p. 481
21. T, pp. 480–481
22. T, p. 481
23. F, p. 481
24. T, p. 483
25. T, p. 484

1. *c,* pp. 470–471
2. *d,* p. 470
3. *b,* p. 471
4. *a,* pp. 471–472
5. *b,* p. 472
6. *c,* p. 472
7. *d,* p. 473
8. *b,* p. 473
9. *d,* p. 473
10. *c,* p. 474
11. *b,* p. 474
12. *a,* p. 474
13. *c,* p. 475
14. *c,* p. 476
15. *b,* p. 476
16. *c,* p. 477
17. *d,* p. 478
18. *c,* p. 479
19. *d,* pp. 480–481
20. *b,* pp. 483–484

DISCUSSION QUESTIONS

1. pp. 470–471
2. p. 471
3. pp. 471–472
4. pp. 472–473
5. pp. 473–474
6. pp. 474–475
7. p. 476
8. p. 477
9. p. 477
10. pp. 477–478
11. pp. 478–480
12. pp. 479–480
13. pp. 479–480
14. pp. 480–481
15. p. 481
16. pp. 482–483
17. p. 484
18. p. 484

Glossary

Ability-to-pay principle   The belief that those who have greater income (or wealth) should be taxed absolutely and relatively more than those who have less.

Abstraction   Elimination of irrelevant and noneconomic facts to obtain an economic principle.

Acreage-allotment program   The program which determines the total number of acres that are to be used to produce various agricultural products and allocates these acres among individual farmers who are required to limit their plantings to the number of acres allotted to them if they wish to obtain the Support price for their crops.

Adjustable pegs   The device used in the Bretton Woods system (*see*) to change Exchange rates in an orderly way to eliminate persistent Payments deficits and surpluses: each nation defined its monetary unit in terms of (pegged it to) gold or the dollar, kept the Rate of exchange for its money stable in the short run, and changed (adjusted) it in the long run when faced with international disequilibrium.

Adverse selection problem   A problem which arises when information known to one party to a contract is not known to the other party, causing the latter to incur major costs. Example: Individuals who have the poorest health are more likely to buy health insurance.

AFDC   (*See* Aid to families with dependent children.)

Agricultural Adjustment Act   The Federal act of 1933 which established the Parity concept (*see*) as the cornerstone of American agricultural policy and provided Price supports for farm products, restriction of agricultural production, and the disposal of surplus output.

Aid to families with dependent children (AFDC)   A state-administered and partly federally funded program in the United States which provides aid to families in which dependent children do not have the support of a parent because of his or her death, disability, or desertion.

Alcoa case   The case decided by the Federal courts in 1945 in which the courts ruled that the possession of monopoly power, no matter how reasonably that power had been used, was a violation of the antitrust laws; and which overturned the Rule of reason (*see*) applied in the U.S. Steel case (*see*).

Allocative efficiency   The apportionment of resources among firms and industries to obtain the production of the products most wanted by society (consumers); the output of each product at which its Marginal cost and Price are equal.

American Federation of Labor (AFL)   The organization of affiliated Craft unions formed in 1886.

Applied economics   (*See* Policy economics.)

Appreciation of the dollar   An increase in the value of the dollar relative to the currency of another nation; a dollar now buys a larger amount of the foreign currency. For example, if the dollar price of a British pound changes from $3 to $2, the dollar has appreciated.

Authoritarian capitalism   As economic system (method of organization) in which property resources are privately owned and government extensively directs and controls the economy.

Average fixed costs   The total Fixed cost (*see*) of a Firm divided by its output (the quantity of product produced).

Average product   The total output produced per unit of a resource employed (total product divided by the quantity of a resource employed).

Average revenue   Total revenue from the sale of a product divided by the quantity of the product sold (demanded); equal to the price at which the product is sold so long as all units of the product are sold at the same price.

Average tax rate   Total tax paid divided by total (taxable) income; the tax rate on total (taxable) income.

Average (total) cost   The Total cost of a Firm divided by its output (the quantity of product produced); equal to Average fixed cost (*see*) plus Average variable cost (*see*).

Average variable cost   The total Variable cost (*see*) of a Firm divided by its output (the quantity of product produced).

Backflows   The return of workers to the countries from which they originally migrated.

Balance of payments deficit   The sum of the Balance on current account (*see*) and the Balance on the capital account (*see*) is negative.

Balance of payments surplus The sum of the Balance on current account (*see*) and the Balance on the capital account (*see*) is positive.

Balance on current account The exports of goods (merchandise) and services of a nation less its imports of goods (merchandise) and services plus its Net investment income and Net transfers.

Balance on goods and services The exports of goods (merchandise) and services of a nation less its imports of goods (merchandise) and services.

Balance on the capital account The Capital inflows (*see*) of a nation less its Capital outflows (*see*).

Barrier to entry Anything that artificially prevents the entry of Firms into an industry.

Barter The exchange of one good or service for another good or service.

Benefit-cost analysis Deciding whether to employ resources and the quantity of resources to employ for a project or program (for the production of a good or service) by comparing the marginal benefits with the marginal costs.

Benefit-loss rate The percentage by which subsidy benefits in a Negative income tax plan (*see*) are reduced as earned income rises.

Benefits-received principle The belief that those who receive the benefits of goods and services provided by government should pay the taxes required to finance them.

Big business A business Firm which either produces a large percentage of the total output of an industry, is large (in terms of number of employees or stockholders, sales, assets, or profits) compared with other Firms in the economy, or both.

Bilateral monopoly A market in which there is a single seller (Monopoly) and a single buyer (Monopsony).

Blacklisting The passing from one employer to another of the names of workers who favor the formation of labor unions and who ought not to be hired.

Brain drain The emigration of highly educated, highly skilled workers from a country.

Break-even income The level of Disposable income at which Households plan to consume (spend) all of their income (for consumer goods and services) and to save none of it; also denotes that level of earned income at which subsidy payments become zero in an income maintenance program.

Break-even point Any output which a (competitive) Firm might produce at which its Total cost and Total revenue would be equal; an output at which it has neither an Economic profit nor a loss.

Bretton Woods system The international monetary system developed after World War II in which Adjustable pegs (*see*) were employed, the International Monetary Fund (*see*) helped to stabilize Foreign exchange rates, and gold and the dollar (*see*) were used as International monetary reserves (*see*).

Budget deficit The amount by which the expenditures of the Federal government exceed its revenues in any year.

Budget line A line which shows the different combinations to two products a consumer can purchase with a given money income.

Budget restraint The limit the size of the consumer's income (and the prices that must be paid for the goods and services) imposes on the ability of an individual consumer to obtain goods and services.

Business unionism The belief that the labor union should concern itself with such practical and short-run objectives as higher wages, shorter hours, and improved working conditions and should not concern itself with long-run and idealistic changes in the capitalistic system.

Capital Human-made resources used to produce goods and services; goods which do not directly satisfy human wants; capital goods.

Capital account The section in a nation's International balance of payments (*see*) in which are recorded the Capital inflows (*see*) and the Capital outflows (*see*) of that nation.

Capital account deficit A negative Balance on the capital account (*see*).

Capital account surplus A positive Balance on the capital account (*see*).

Capital gain The gain realized when securities or properties are sold for a price greater than the price paid for them.

Capital goods (*See* Capital.)

Capital inflow The expenditures made by the residents of foreign nations to purchase real and financial capital from the residents of a nation.

Capital-intensive commodity A product which requires a relatively large amount of Capital to produce.

Capital outflow The expenditures made by the residents of a nation to purchase real and financial capital from the residents of foreign nations.

Cartel A formal written or oral agreement among Firms to set the price of the product and the outputs of the individual firms or to divide the market for the product geographically.

Causation A cause-and-effect relationship; one or several events bring about or result in another event.

Cease-and-desist order An order from a court or government agency (commission or board) to a corporation or individual to stop engaging in a specified practice.

Ceiling price (*See* Price ceiling.)

Celler-Kefauver Act The Federal act of 1950 which amended the Clayton Act (*see*) by prohibiting the acquisition of the assets of one firm by another firm when the effect would be to lessen competition.

Central economic planning Government determination of the objectives of the economy and the direction of its resources to the attainment of these objectives.

***Ceteris paribus* assumption** (*See* "Other things being equal" assumption.)

Change in amount consumed (Increase or decrease in consumption spending that results from an increase or decrease in Disposable income, the Consumption schedule (curve) remaining unchanged; movement from one row (point) to another on the same Consumption schedule (curve).

Circular flow of income The flow of resources from Households to Firms and of products from Firms to Households accompanied in an economy using money by flows of money from Households to Firms and from Firms to Households.

Clayton Act The Federal antitrust act of 1914 which strengthened the Sherman Act (*see*) by making it illegal for business firms to engage in certain specified practices.

Clean Air Act of 1990 Legislation embodying a variety of specific measures to deal with air pollution, urban smog, motor vehicle emissions, ozone depletion, and acid rain.

Closed economy An economy which neither exports nor imports goods and services.

Close-down case The circumstance in which a Firm would experience a loss greater than its total Fixed cost if it were to produce any output greater than zero; alternatively, a situation in which a firm would cease to operate when the price at which it can sell its product is less than its Average variable cost.

Closed shop A place of employment at which only workers who are already members of a labor union may be hired.

Coase theorem The idea that Externality problems may be resolved through private negotiations of the affected parties.

Coincidence of wants The item (good or service) which one trader wishes to obtain is the same item which another trader desires to give up and the item which the second trader wishes to acquire is the same item the first trader desires to surrender.

COLA (*See* Cost-of-living adjustment.)

Collective voice The function a union performs for its members as a group when it communicates their problems and grievances to management and presses management for a satisfactory resolution to them.

Collusion A situation in which Firms act together and in agreement (collude) to set the price of the product and the output each firm will produce or to determine the geographic area in which each firm will sell.

Collusive oligopoly Occurs when the few firms composing an oligopolistic industry reach an explicit or unspoken agreement to fix prices, divide a market, or otherwise restrict competition; may take the form of a Cartel (*see*), Gentlemen's agreement (*see*), or Price leadership (*see*).

Command economy An economic system (method of organization) in which property resources are publicly owned and Central economic planning (*see*) is used to direct and coordinate economic activities.

Communism (*See* Command economy.)

Company union An organization of employees which is dominated by the employer (the company) and does not engage in genuine collective bargaining with the employer.

Comparable worth doctrine The belief that women should receive the same salaries (wages) as men when the levels of skill, effort, and responsibility in their different jobs are the same.

Comparative advantage A lower relative or Comparative cost (*see*) than another producer.

Comparative cost The amount the production of one product must be reduced to increase the production of another product; Opportunity cost (*see*).

Competing goods (*See* Substitute goods.)

Competition The presence in a market of a large number of independent buyers and sellers and the freedom of buyers and sellers to enter and leave the market.

Competitive industry's short-run supply curve The horizontal summation of the short-run supply curves of the Firms in a purely competitive industry (*See* Pure competition); a curve which shows the total quantities that will be offered for sale at various prices by the Firms in an industry in the Short run (*see*).

Competitive labor market A market in which a large number of (noncolluding) firms demand a particular type of labor from a large number of nonunionized workers.

Complementary goods Goods or services for which there is an inverse relationship between the price of one and the demand for the other; when the price of one falls (rises) the demand for the other increases (decreases).

Concentration ratio The percentage of the total sales of an industry made by the four (or some other number) largest sellers (Firms) in the industry.

Conglomerate combination A group of Plants (*see*) owned by a single Firm and engaged at one or more stages in the production of different products (of products which do not compete with each other).

Conglomerate merger The merger of a Firm in one Industry with a Firm in another Industry (with a Firm that is neither supplier, customer, nor competitor).

Congress of Industrial Organizations (CIO) The organization of affiliated Industrial unions formed in 1936.

Constant-cost industry An industry in which the expansion of the Industry by the entry of new Firms has no effect on the prices the Firms in the industry pay for resources and no effect, therefore, on their cost schedules (curves).

Consumer goods Goods and services which satisfy human wants directly.

Consumer sovereignty Determination by consumers of the types and quantities of goods and services that are produced from the scarce resources of the economy.

Consumption of fixed capital Estimate of the amount of Capital worn out or used up (consumed) in producing the Gross domestic product; depreciation.

Consumption schedule Schedule which shows the amounts Households plan to spend for Consumer goods at different levels of Disposable income.

Corporate income tax A tax levied on the net income (profit) of Corporations.

Corporation A legal entity ("person") chartered by a state or the Federal government, and distinct and separate from the individuals who own it.

Correlation Systematic and dependable association between two sets of data (two kinds of events).

Cost-of-living adjustment An increase in the incomes (wages) of workers which is automatically received by them when there is inflation in the economy and guaranteed by a clause in their labor contracts with their employer.

Cost-plus pricing A procedure used by (oligopolistic) Firms to determine the price they will charge for a product and in which a percentage markup is added to the estimated average cost of producing the product.

Cost ratio The ratio of the decrease in the production of the product to the increase in the production of another product when resources are shifted from the production of the first to the production of the second product; the amount the production of one product decreases when the production of a second product increases by one unit.

Craft union A labor union which limits its membership to workers with a particular skill (craft).

Credit An accounting notation that the value of an asset (such as the foreign money owned by the residents of a nation) has increased.

Criminal-conspiracy doctrine The (now outdated) legal doctrine that combinations of workers (Labor unions) to raise wages were criminal conspiracies and, therefore, illegal.

Cross elasticity of demand The ratio of the percentage change in Quantity demanded of one good to the percentage change in the price of some other good. A negative coefficient indicates the two products are Substitute goods; a positive coefficient indicates Complementary goods.

Crowding model of occupational discrimination A model of labor markets that assumes Occupational discrimination (*see*) against women and blacks has kept them out of many occupations and forced them into a limited number of other occupations in which the large Supply of labor (relative to the Demand) results in lower wages and incomes.

Currency appreciation (*See* Exchange rate appreciation.)

Currency depreciation (*See* Exchange rate depreciation.)

Current account The section in a nation's International balance of payments (*see*) in which are recorded its exports and imports of goods (merchandise) and services, its net investment income, and its net transfers.

Current account deficit A negative Balance on current account (*see*).

Current account surplus A positive Balance on current account (*see*).

Customary economy (*See* Traditional economy.)

Debit An accounting notation that the value of an asset (such as the foreign money owned by the residents of a nation) has decreased.

Declining industry An industry in which Economic profits are negative (losses are incurred) and which will, therefore, decrease its output as Firms leave the industry.

Decrease in demand A decrease in the Quantity demanded of a good or service at every price; a shift of the Demand curve to the left.

Decrease in supply A decrease in the Quantity supplied of a good or service at every price; a shift of the Supply curve to the left.

Deduction Reasoning from assumptions to conclusions; a method of reasoning that tests a hypothesis (an assumption) by comparing the conclusions to which it leads with economic facts.

Demand A Demand schedule or a Demand curve (*see* both).

Demand curve A curve which shows the amounts of a good or service buyers wish to purchase at various prices during some period of time.

Demand schedule A schedule which shows the amounts of a good or service buyers wish to purchase at various prices during some period of time.

Dependent variable A variable which changes as a consequence of a change in some other (independent) variable; the "effect" or outcome.

Depreciation of the dollar A decrease in the value of the dollar relative to another currency; a dollar now buys a smaller amount of the foreign currency. For example, if the dollar price of a British pound changes from $2 to $3, the dollar has depreciated.

Derived demand The demand for a good or service which is dependent on or related to the demand for some other good or service; the demand for a resource which depends on the demand for the products it can be used to produce.

Descriptive economics The gathering or collection of relevant economic facts (data).

Determinants of demand Factors other than its price which determine the quantities demanded of a good or service.

Determinants of supply Factors other than its price which determine the quantities supplied of a good or service.

Devaluation A decrease in the defined value of a currency.

Differentiated oligopoly An Oligopoly in which the firms produce a Differentiated product (*see*).

Differentiated product A product which differs physically or in some other way from the similar products produced by other Firms; a product which is similar to but not identical with and, therefore, not a perfect substitute for other products; a product such that buyers are not indifferent to the seller from whom they purchase it so long as the price charged by all sellers is the same.

Dilemma of regulation When a Regulatory agency (*see*) must establish the maximum legal price a monopolist may charge, it finds that if it sets the price at the Socially optimal price (*see*) this price is below Average cost (and either bankrupts the Firm or requires that it be subsidized) and if it sets the price at the Fair-return price (*see*) it has failed to eliminate fully the underallocation of resources that is the consequence of unregulated monopoly.

Directing function of prices (*See* Guiding function of prices.)

Directly related Two sets of economic data that change in the same direction; when one variable increases (decreases) the other increases (decreases).

Direct relationship The relationship between two variables which change in the same direction, for example, product price and quantity supplied.

Discriminatory discharge The firing of workers who favor formation of labor unions.

Diseconomies of scale Forces which increase the Average cost of producing a product as the Firm expands the size of its Plant (its output) in the Long run (*see*).

Disposable income Personal income (*see*) less personal taxes (*see*); income available for Personal consumption expenditures (*see*) and Personal saving (*see*).

Division of labor Dividing the work required to produce a product into a number of different tasks which are performed by different workers; Specialization (*see*) of workers.

Dollar votes The "votes" which consumers and entrepreneurs in effect cast for the production of the different kinds of consumer and capital goods, respectively, when they purchase them in the markets of the economy.

Domestic capital formation Adding to a nation's stock of Capital by saving part of its own domestic output.

Domestic economic goal Assumed to be full employment with little or no inflation.

Domestic output Gross (or net) domestic product; the total output of final goods and services produced in the economy.

Double taxation Taxation of both corporate net income (profits) and the dividends paid from this net income when they become the Personal income of households.

Dumping The sale of products below cost in a foreign country.

Du Pont cellophane case The antitrust case brought against du Pont in which the U.S. Supreme Court ruled (in 1956) that while du Pont (and one licensee) had a monopoly in the narrowly defined market for cellophane it did not monopolize the more broadly defined market for flexible packaging materials, and was not guilty, therefore, of violating the Sherman Act.

Durable good A consumer good with an expected life (use) of one year or more.

Dynamic progress The development over time of more efficient (less costly) techniques of producing existing products and of improved products; technological progress.

Earnings The money income received by a worker; equal to the Wage (rate) multiplied by the quantity of labor supplied (the amount of time worked) by the worker.

EC European Economic Community (*See* European Common Market.)

Economic analysis Deriving Economic principles (*see*) from relevant economic facts.

Economic concentration A description or measure of the degree to which an industry is monopolistic or competitive. (*See* Concentration ratio.)

Economic cost A payment that must be made to obtain and retain the services of a resource; the income a Firm must provide to a resource supplier to attract the resource away from an alternative use; equal to the quantity of other products that cannot be produced when resources are employed to produce a particular product.

Economic efficiency The relationship between the input of scarce resources and the resulting output of a good or service; production of an output with a given dollar-and-cents value with the smallest total expenditure for resources; obtaining the largest total production of a good or service with resources of a given dollar-and-cents value.

Economic growth (1) An increase in the Production possibilities schedule or curve that results from an increase in resource supplies or an improvement in Technology; (2) an increase either in real output (Gross domestic product) or in real output per capita.

Economic integration Cooperation among and the complete or partial unification of the economies of different nations; the elimination of the barriers to trade among these nations; the bringing together of the markets in each of the separate economies to form one large (a common) market.

Economic law (*See* Economic principle.)

Economic model A simplified picture of reality; an abstract generalization.

Economic perspective A viewpoint which envisions individuals and institutions making rational or purposeful decisions based on a consideration of the benefits and costs associated with their actions.

Economic policy Course of action that will correct or avoid a problem.

Economic principle Generalization of the economic behavior of individuals and institutions.

Economic profit The Total revenue of a firm less all its Economic costs; also called "pure profit" and "above normal profit."

Economic regulation (*See* Industrial regulation.)

Economic rent The price paid for the use of land and other natural resources, the supply of which is fixed (perfectly inelastic).

Economics Social science concerned with using scarce resources to obtain the maximum satisfaction of the unlimited material wants of society.

Economic theory Deriving economic principles (*see*) from relevant economic facts; an Economic principle (*see*).

Economies of scale The forces which reduce the Average cost of producing a product as the Firm expands the size of its Plant (its output) in the Long run (*see*); the economies of mass production.

Economizing problem Society's material wants are unlimited but the resources available to produce the goods and services that satisfy wants are limited (scarce); the inability of any economy to produce unlimited quantities of goods and services.

Efficiency loss of a tax The loss of net benefits to society because a tax reduces the production and consumption of a taxed good below the allocatively efficient level.

Efficiency wage A wage which minimizes wage costs per unit of output.

Efficient allocation of resources That allocation of the resources of an economy among the production of different products which leads to the maximum satisfaction of the wants of consumers.

Elastic demand The Elasticity coefficient (*see*) is greater than one; the percentage change in Quantity demanded is greater than the percentage change in price.

Elasticity coefficient The number obtained when the percentage change in Quantity demanded (or supplied) is divided by the percentage change in the price of the commodity.

Elasticity formula The price elasticity of demand (supply) is equal to

percentage change in quantity

$$\frac{\text{demanded (supplied)}}{\text{percentage change in price}}$$

which is equal to

$$\frac{\text{change in quantity demanded (supplied)}}{\text{original quantity demanded (supplied)}}$$

$$\text{divided by } \frac{\text{change in price}}{\text{original price}}$$

Elastic supply The Elasticity coefficient (*see*) is greater than one; the percentage change in Quantity supplied is greater than the percentage change in price.

Emission fees Special fees that might be levied against those who discharge pollutants into the environment.

Employment discrimination The employment of whites before blacks (and other minority groups) are employed and the discharge of blacks (and other minority groups) before whites are discharged.

Entrepreneurial ability The human resource which combines the other resources to produce a product, makes nonroutine decisions, innovates, and bears risks.

Equality vs. efficiency tradeoff The decrease in Economic efficiency (*see*) that appears to accompany a decrease in Income inequality (*see*); the presumption that an increase in Income inequality is required to increase Economic efficiency.

Equalizing differences The differences in the Wages received by workers in different jobs which compensate for nonmonetary differences in the jobs.

Equilibrium position The point at which the Budget line (*see*) is tangent to an Indifference curve (*see*) in the indifference curve approach to the theory of consumer behavior.

Equilibrium price The price in a competitive market at which the Quantity demanded (*see*) and the Quantity supplied (*see*) are equal; at which there is neither a shortage nor a surplus; and at which there is no tendency for price to rise or fall.

Equilibrium price level The price level at which the Aggregate demand curve intersects the Aggregate supply curve.

Equilibrium quantity The Quantity demanded (*see*) and Quantity supplied (*see*) at the Equilibrium price (*see*) in a competitive market.

Equilibrium real domestic output The real domestic output which is determined by the equality (intersection) of Aggregate demand and Aggregate supply.

European Common Market The association of twelve European nations initiated in 1958 to abolish gradually the Tariffs and Import quotas that exist among them, to establish common Tariffs for goods imported from outside the member nations, to allow the eventual free movement of labor and capital among them, and to create other common economic policies.

European Economic Community (EC) (*See* European Common Market.)

Exchange control (*See* Foreign exchange control.)

Exchange rate The Rate of exchange (*see*),

Exchange rate appreciation An increase in the value of a nation's money in foreign exchange markets; an increase in the Rates of exchange for foreign monies.

Exchange rate depreciation A decrease in the value of a nation's money in foreign exchange markets; a decrease in the Rates of exchange for foreign monies.

Exchange rate determinant Any factor other than the Rate of exchange (*see*) that determines the demand for and the supply of a currency in the Foreign exchange market (*see*).

Excise tax A tax levied on the expenditure for a specific product or on the quantity of the product purchased.

Exclusion principle The exclusion of those who do not pay for a product from the benefits of the product.

Exclusive unionism The policies employed by a Labor union to restrict the supply of labor by excluding potential members in order to increase the Wages received by its members; the Policies typically employed by a Craft union (*see*).

Exit mechanism Leaving a job and searching for another one in order to improve the conditions under which a worker is employed.

Expanding industry An industry in which Economic profits are obtained by the firms in the industry and which will, therefore, increase its output as new firms enter the industry.

Expansionary fiscal policy An increase in Aggregate demand brought about by an increase in Government expenditures for goods and services, a decrease in Net taxes, or some combination of the two.

Expectations What consumers, business Firms, and others believe will happen or what conditions will be in the future.

Explicit cost The monetary payment a Firm must make to an outsider to obtain a resource.

Exports Goods and services produced in a given nation and sold to customers in other nations.

Export subsidies Government payments which reduce the price of a product to foreign buyers.

Export transactions A sale of a good or service which increases the amount of foreign money held by the citizens, firms, and governments of a nation.

External benefit (*See* Spillover benefit.)

External cost (*See* Spillover cost.)

External debt Public debt (*see*) owed to foreign citizens, firms, and institutions.

External economic goal (*See* International economic goal.)

Externality (*See* Spillover.)

Factors of production Economic resources: Land, Capital, Labor, and Entrepreneurial ability.

Fair-return price The price of a product which enables its producer to obtain a Normal profit (*see*) and which is equal to the Average cost of producing it.

Fallacy of composition Incorrectly reasoning that what is true for the individual (or part) is therefore necessarily true for the group (or whole).

Fallacy of limited decisions The false notion that there are a limited number of economic decisions to be made so that, if government makes more decisions, there will be fewer private decisions to render.

Farm Act of 1990 Farm legislation which reduces the amount of acreage covered by price supports and allows farmers to plant these uncovered acres in alternative crops.

Farm problem The relatively low income of many farmers (compared with incomes in the nonagricultural sectors of the economy) and the tendency for farm income to fluctuate sharply from year to year.

Featherbedding Payment by an employer to a worker for work not actually performed.

Federal Trade Commission (FTC) The commission of five members established by the Federal Trade Commission Act of 1914 to investigate unfair competitive practices of business Firms, to hold hearings of the complaints of such practices, and to issue Cease-and-desist orders (*see*) when Firms were found to engage in such practices.

Federal Trade Commission Act The Federal act of 1914 which established the Federal Trade Commission (*see*).

Female labor force participation rate The percentage of the female population of working age in the Labor force (*see*).

Fewness A relatively small number of sellers (or buyers) of a good or service.

Financial capital (*See* Money capital.)

Financing exports and imports The use of Foreign exchange markets by exporters and importers to receive and make payments for goods and services they sell and buy in foreign nations.

Firm An organization that employs resources to produce a good or service for profit and owns and operates one or more Plants (*see*).

(The) firm's short-run supply curve A curve which shows the quantities of a product a Firm in a purely competitive industry (*see* Pure competition) will offer to sell at various prices in the Short run (*see*); the portion of the Firm's short-run Marginal cost (*see*) curve which lies above its Average variable cost curve.

Fiscal federalism The system of transfers (grants) by which the Federal government shares its revenues with state and local governments.

Fiscal policy Changes in government spending and tax collections for the purpose of achieving a full-employment and noninflationary domestic output.

Five fundamental economic questions The five questions which every economy must answer: what to produce, how to produce, how to divide the total output, how to maintain Full employment, and how to assure economic flexibility.

Fixed cost Any cost which in total does not change when the Firm changes its output; the cost of Fixed resources (*see*).

Fixed exchange rate A Rate of exchange that is prevented from rising or falling.

Fixed resource Any resource employed by a Firm the quantity of which the firm cannot change.

Flexible exchange rate A rate of exchange that is determined by the demand for and supply of the foreign money and is free to rise or fall.

Floating exchange rate (*See* Flexible exchange rate.)

Food for peace program The program established

under the provisions of Public Law 480 which permits less developed nations to buy surplus American agricultural products and pay for them with their own monies (instead of dollars).

Food stamp program A program in the United States which permits low-income persons to purchase for less than their retail value, or to obtain without cost, coupons that can be exchanged for food items at retail stores.

Foreign competition (*See* Import competition.)

Foreign exchange control The control a government may exercise over the quantity of foreign money demanded by its citizens and business firms and over the Rates of exchange in order to limit its outpayments to its inpayments (to eliminate a Payments deficit, *see*).

Foreign exchange market A market in which the money (currency) used by one nation is used to purchase (is exchanged for) the money used by another nation.

Foreign exchange rate (*See* Rate of exchange.)

Freedom of choice Freedom of owners of property resources and money to employ or dispose of these resources as they see fit, of workers to enter any line of work for which they are qualified, and of consumers to spend their incomes in a manner which they deem to be appropriate (best for them).

Freedom of enterprise Freedom of business Firms to employ economic resources, to use these resources to produce products of the firm's own choosing, and to sell these products in markets of their choice.

Freely floating exchange rates Rates of exchange (*see*) which are not controlled and which may, therefore, rise and fall; and which are determined by the demand for and the supply of foreign monies.

Free-rider problem The inability of those who might provide the economy with an economically desirable and indivisible good or service to obtain payment from those who benefit from the good or service because the Exclusion principle (*see*) cannot be applied to it.

Free trade The absence of artificial (government imposed) barriers to trade among individuals and firms in different nations.

Fringe benefits The rewards other than Wages that employees receive from their employers and which include pensions, medical and dental insurance, paid vacations, and sick leaves.

Full production The maximum amount of goods and services that can be produced from the employed resources of an economy; the absence of Underemployment (*see*).

Functional distribution of income The manner in which the economy's (the national) income is divided among those who perform different functions (provide the economy with different kinds of resources); the division of National income (*see*) into wages and salaries, proprietors' income, corporate profits, interest, and rent.

Game theory A theory which compares the behavior of participants in games of strategy, such as poker and chess, with that of a small group of mutually interdependent firms (an Oligopoly).

GATT (*See* General Agreement on Tariffs and Trade.)

General Agreement on Tariffs and Trade The international agreement reached in 1947 by twenty-three nations (including the United States) in which each nation agreed to give equal and nondiscriminatory treatment to the other nations, to reduce tariff rates by multinational negotiations, and to eliminate Import quotas.

General equilibrium analysis A study of the Market system as a whole; of the interrelations among equilibrium prices, outputs, and employments in all the different markets of the economy.

Generalization Statistical or probability statement; statement of the nature of the relation between two or more sets of facts.

Gentleman's agreement An informal understanding on the price to be charged among the firms in an Oligopoly.

Glasnost A Soviet campaign of the mid-1980s for greater "openness" and democratization in political and economic activities.

Gold export point The rate of exchange for a foreign money above which—when nations participate in the International gold standard (*see*)—the foreign money will not be purchased and gold will be sent (exported) to the foreign country to make payments there.

Gold flow The movement of gold into or out of a nation.

Gold import point The Rate of exchange for a foreign money below which—when nations participate in the International gold standard (*see*)—a nation's own money will not be purchased and gold will be sent (imported) into that country by foreigners to make payments there.

Gorbachev's reforms A mid-1980s series of reforms designed to revitalize the Soviet economy. The reforms stressed the modernization of productive facilities, less centralized control, improved worker discipline and productivity, more emphasis on market prices, and an expansion of private economic activity.

Gosbank The state-owned and -operated bank in the former U.S.S.R.

Government purchases Disbursements of money by government for which government receives a currently produced good or service in return; the expenditures of all governments in the economy for Final goods (*see*) and services.

Government transfer payment The disbursement of money (or goods and services) by government for which government receives no currently produced good or service in return.

Grievance procedure The methods used by a Labor union and the Firm to settle disputes that arise during the life of the collective bargaining agreement between them.

Guaranteed income The minimum income a family (or individual) would receive if a Negative income tax (*see*) were to be adopted.

Guiding function of prices The ability of price

changes to bring about changes in the quantities of products and resources demanded and supplied (**See** Incentive function of price.)

Herfindahl index A measure of the concentration and competitiveness of an industry; calculated as the sum of the squared market shares of the individual firms.

Homogeneous oligopoly An Oligopoly in which the firms produce a Standardized product (**see**).

Horizontal axis The "left–right" or "west–east" axis on a graph or grid.

Horizontal combination A group of Plants (**see**) in the same stage of production which are owned by a single Firm (**see**).

Horizontal merger The merger of one or more Firms producing the same product into a single Firm.

Household An economic unit (of one or more persons) which provides the economy with resources and uses the money paid to it for these resources to purchase goods and services that satisfy material wants.

Human-capital discrimination The denial to blacks (and other minority groups) of the same quality and quantity of education and training received by whites.

Human-capital investment Any action taken to increase the productivity (by improving the skills and abilities) of workers; expenditures made to improve the education, health, or mobility of workers.

Illegal immigrant A person who unlawfully enters a country.

IMF (**See** International Monetary Fund.)

Immobility The inability or unwillingness of a worker or another resource to move from one geographic area or occupation to another or from a lower-paying to a higher-paying job.

Imperfect competition All markets except Pure competition (**see**); Monopoly, Monopsony, Monopolistic competition, Oligopoly, and Oligopsony (**see all**).

Implicit cost The monetary income a Firm sacrifices when it employs a resource it owns to produce a product rather than supplying the resource in the market; equal to what the resource could have earned in the best-paying alternative employment.

Import competition Competition which domestic firms encounter from the products and services of foreign suppliers.

Import quota A limit imposed by a nation on the quantity of a good that may be imported during some period of time.

Imports Spending by individuals, Firms, and governments of an economy for goods and services produced in foreign nations.

Import transaction The purchase of a good or service which decreases the amount of foreign money held by citizens, firms, and governments of a nation.

Incentive function of price The inducement which an increase (a decrease) in the price of a commodity offers to sellers of the commodity to make more (less) of it available; and the inducement which an increase (decrease) in price offers to buyers to purchase smaller (larger) quantities; the Guiding function of prices (**see**).

Incentive pay plan A compensation scheme which ties worker pay directly to performance. Such plans include piece rates, bonuses, commissions, and profit sharing.

Inclusive unionism A union which attempts to include all workers employed in an industry as members.

Income effect The effect which a change in the price of a product has on the Real income (purchasing power) of a consumer and the resulting effect on the quantity of that product the consumer would purchase after the consequences of the Substitution effect (**see**) have been taken into account (eliminated).

Income elasticity of demand The ratio of the percentage change in the Quantity demanded of a good to the percentage change in income; it measures the responsiveness of consumer purchases to income changes.

Income inequality The unequal distribution of an economy's total income among persons or families in the economy.

Income-maintenance system The programs designed to eliminate poverty and to reduce inequality in the distribution of income.

Increase in demand An increase in the Quantity demanded of a good or service at every price; a shift in the Demand curve to the right.

Increase in supply An increase in the Quantity supplied of a good or service at every price; a shift in the Supply curve to the right.

Increasing-cost industry An Industry in which the expansion of the Industry through the entry of new firms increases the prices the Firms in the Industry must pay for resources and, therefore, increases their cost schedules (moves their cost curves upward).

Increasing returns An increase in the Marginal product (**see**) of a resource as successive units of the resource are employed.

Independent goods Goods or services such that there is no relationship between the price of one and the demand for the other; when the price of one rises or falls the demand for the other remains constant.

Independent variable The variable which causes a change in some other (dependent) variable.

Indifference curve A curve which shows the different combinations of two products which give a consumer the same satisfaction or Utility (**see**).

Indifference map A series of Indifference curves (**see**), each of which represents a different level of Utility; and which together show the preferences of the consumer.

Individual demand The Demand schedule (**see**) or Demand curve (**see**) of a single buyer of a good or service.

Individual supply The Supply schedule (**see**) or Supply curve (**see**) of a single seller of a good or service.

Induction A method of reasoning that proceeds from facts to Generalization (*see*).

Industrial policy Any policy in which government takes a direct and active role in shaping the structure and composition of industry to promote economic growth.

Industrial regulation The older and more traditional type of regulation in which government is concerned with the prices charged and the services provided the public in specific industries; in contrast to Social regulation (*see*).

Industrial union A Labor union which accepts as members all workers employed in a particular industry (or by a particular firm) and which contains largely unskilled or semiskilled workers.

Industry The group of (one or more) Firms that produce identical or similar products.

Inelastic demand The Elasticity coefficient (*see*) is less than one; the percentage change in price is greater than the percentage change in Quantity demanded.

Inelastic supply The Elasticity coefficient (*see*) is less than one; the percentage change in price is greater than the percentage change in Quantity supplied.

Inferior good A good or service of which consumers purchase less (more) at every price when their incomes increase (decrease).

Infrastructure For the economy, the capital goods usually provided by the Public sector for the use of its citizens and Firms (e.g., highways, bridges, transit systems, wastewater treatment facilities, municipal water systems, and airports). For the Firm, the services and facilities which it must have to produce its products, which would be too costly for it to provide for itself, and which are provided by governments or other Firms (e.g., water, electricity, waste treatment, transportation, research, engineering, finance, and banking).

Injunction An order from a court of law that directs a person or organization not to perform a certain act because the act would do irreparable damage to some other person or persons; a restraining order.

In-kind investment Nonfinancial investment (*see*).

In-kind transfer The distribution by government of goods and services to individuals and for which the government receives no currently produced good or service in return; a Government transfer payment (*see*) made in goods or services rather than in money.

Innovation The introduction of a new product, the use of a new method of production, or the employment of a new form of business organization.

Inpayments The receipts of (its own or foreign) money which the individuals, Firms, and governments of one nation obtain from the sale of goods and services, investment income, Remittances, and Capital inflows from abroad.

Input-output analysis Using an Input-output table (*see*) to examine interdependence among different parts (sectors and industries) of the economy and to make economic forecasts and plans.

Input-output table A table which lists (along the left side) the producing sectors and (along the top) the consuming or using sectors of the economy and which shows quantitatively in each of its rows how the output of a producing sector was distributed among consuming sectors and quantitatively in each of its columns the producing sectors from which a consuming sector obtained its inputs during some period of time (a year).

Insurable risk An event, the average occurrence of which can be estimated with considerable accuracy, which would result in a loss that can be avoided by purchasing insurance.

Interest The payment made for the use of money (of borrowed funds).

Interest income Income of those who supply the economy with Capital (*see*).

Interest rate The Rate of interest (*see*).

Interindustry competition Competition or rivalry between the products produced by Firms in one Industry (*see*) and the products produced by Firms in another industry (or in other industries).

Interlocking directorate A situation in which one or more of the members of the board of directors of one Corporation are also on the board of directors of another Corporation; and which is illegal when it reduces competition among the Corporations.

Internal economic goal (*See* Domestic economic goal.)

Internal economics The reduction in the cost of producing or marketing a product that results from an increase in output of the Firm [*see* Economies of (large) scale].

International balance of payments Summary statement of the transactions which took place between the individuals, Firms, and governments of one nation and those in all other nations during the year.

International balance of payments deficit (*See* Balance of payments deficit.)

International balance of payments surplus (*See* Balance of payments surplus.)

International Bank for Reconstruction and Development (*See* World Bank.)

International economic goal Assumed to be a current-account balance of zero.

International gold standard An international monetary system employed in the nineteenth and early twentieth centuries in which each nation defined its money in terms of a quantity of gold, maintained a fixed relationship between its gold stock and money supply, and allowed the free importation and exportation of gold.

International Monetary Fund The international association of nations which was formed after World War II to make loans of foreign monies to nations with temporary Payments deficits (*see*) and to administer the Adjustable pegs (*see*).

International monetary reserves. The foreign monies and such assets as gold a nation may use to settle a Payments deficit (*see*).

International value of the dollar   The price that must be paid in foreign currency (money) to obtain one American dollar.

Interstate Commerce Commission   The commission established in 1887 to regulate the rates and monitor the services of the railroads in the United States.

Interstate Commerce Commission Act   The Federal legislation of 1887 which established the Interstate Commerce Commission (*see*).

Inverse relationship   The relationship between two variables which change in opposite directions, for example, product price and quantity demanded.

Investment   Spending for (the production and accumulation of) Capital goods (*see*) and additions to inventories.

Investment in human capital   (*See* Human-capital investment.)

Invisible hand   The tendency of Firms and resource suppliers seeking to further their self-interests in competitive markets to further the best interest of society as a whole (the maximum satisfaction of wants).

Jurisdictional strike   Withholding from an employer the labor services of its members by a Labor union that is engaged in a dispute with another Labor union over which is to perform a specific kind of work for the employer.

Kinked demand curve   The demand curve which a noncollusive oligopolist sees for its output and which is based on the assumption that rivals will follow a price decrease and will not follow a price increase.

Labor   The physical and mental talents (efforts) of people which can be used to produce goods and services.

Labor-intensive commodity   A product which requires a relatively large amount of Labor to produce.

Labor-Management Relations Act   (*See* Taft-Hartley Act.)

Labor-Management Reporting and Disclosure Act (*See* Landrum-Griffin Act.)

Labor productivity   Total output divided by the quantity of labor employed to produce the output; the Average product (*see*) of labor or output per worker per hour.

Labor theory of value   The Marxian notion that the economic value of any commodity is determined solely by the amount of labor required to produce it.

Labor union   A group of workers organized to advance the interests of the group (to increase wages, shorten the hours worked, improve working conditions, etc.).

Laissez faire capitalism   (*See* Pure capitalism.)

Land   Natural resources ("free gifts of nature") which can be used to produce goods and services.

Land-intensive commodity   A product which requires a relatively large amount of Land to produce.

Landrum-Griffin Act   The Federal act of 1959 which regulates the elections and finances of Labor unions and guarantees certain rights to their members.

Law of conservation of matter and energy   The notion that matter can be changed to other matter or into energy but cannot disappear; all production inputs are ultimately transformed into an equal amount of finished product, energy, and waste (pollution).

Law of demand   The inverse relationship between the price and the Quantity demanded (*see*) of a good or service during some period of time.

Law of diminishing marginal utility   As a consumer increases the consumption of a good or service, the Marginal utility (*see*) obtained from each additional unit of the good or service decreases.

Law of diminishing returns   When successive equal increments of a Variable resource (*see*) are added to the Fixed resources (*see*), beyond some level of employment, the Marginal product (*see*) of the Variable resource will decrease.

Law of increasing opportunity cost   As the amount of a product produced is increased, the Opportunity cost (*see*)—Marginal cost (*see*)—of producing an additional unit of the product increases.

Law of supply   The direct relationship between the price and the Quantity supplied (*see*) of a good or service during some period of time.

Least-cost combination rule (of resources)   The quantity of each resource a Firm must employ if it is to produce any output at the lowest total cost; the combination on which the ratio of the Marginal product (*see*) of a resource to its Marginal resource cost (*see*) (to its price if the resource is employed in a competitive market) is the same for all resources employed.

Legal cartel theory of regulation   The hypothesis that industries want to be regulated so that they may form legal Cartels (*see*) and that government officials (the government) provide the regulation in return for their political and financial support.

Legal immigrant   A person who lawfully enters a country.

Less developed countries (LDCs)   Most countries of Africa, Asia, and Latin America which are characterized by a lack of capital goods, primitive production technologies, low literacy rates, high unemployment, rapid population growth, and labor forces heavily committed to agriculture.

Limited liability   Restriction of the maximum that may be lost to a predetermined amount; the maximum amount that may be lost by the owners (stockholders) of a Corporation is the amount they paid for their shares of stock.

Loaded terminology   Terms which arouse emotions and elicit approval or disapproval.

Loanable funds theory of interest The concept that the supply of and demand for loanable funds determines the equilibrium rate of interest.

Lockout The temporary closing of a place of employment and the halting of production by an employer in order to discourage the formation of a Labor union or to compel a Labor union to modify its demands.

Logrolling The trading of votes by legislators to secure favorable outcomes on decisions to provide public goods and services.

Long run A period of time long enough to enable producers of a product to change the quantities of all the resources they employ; in which all resources and costs are variable and no resources or costs are fixed.

Long-run competitive equilibrium The price at which Firms in Pure competition (*see*) neither obtain Economic profit nor suffer losses in the Long run and the total quantity demanded and supplied at that price are equal; a price equal to the minimum long-run average cost of producing the product.

Long-run farm problem The tendency for the incomes of many farmers to decline relative to incomes in the rest of the economy.

Long-run supply A schedule or curve which shows the prices at which a Purely competitive industry will make various quantities of the product available in the Long run.

Lorenz curve A curve which shows the distribution of income in an economy; and when used for this purpose the cumulated percentage of families (income receivers) is measured along the horizontal axis and the cumulated percentage of income is measured along the vertical axis.

Loss-minimizing case The circumstances which result in a loss which is less than its Total fixed cost when a Firm produces the output at which total profit is a maximum (or total loss is a minimum): when the price at which the firm can sell its product is less than Average total but greater than Average variable cost.

Macroeconomics The part of economics concerned with the economy as a whole; with such major aggregates as the household, business, and governmental sectors and with totals for the economy.

Managed floating exchange rate An Exchange rate that is allowed to change (float) to eliminate persistent Payments deficit and surpluses and is controlled (managed) to reduce day-to-day fluctuations.

Managerial-opposition hypothesis The explanation that attributes the relative decline of unionism in the United States to the increased and more aggressive opposition of management to unions.

Managerial prerogatives The decisions, often enumerated in the contract between a Labor union and a business Firm, that the management of the Firm has the sole right to make.

Marginal cost The extra (additional) cost of producing one more unit of output; equal to the change in Total cost divided by the change in output (and in the short run to the change in Total variable cost divided by the change in output).

Marginal labor cost The amount by which the total cost of employing Labor increases when a Firm employs one additional unit of Labor (the quantity of other resources employed remaining constant); equal to the change in the total cost of Labor divided by the change in the quantity of Labor employed.

Marginal product The additional output produced when one additional unit of a resource is employed (the quantity of all other resources employed remaining constant); equal to the change in total product divided by the change in the quantity of a resource employed.

Marginal productivity theory of income distribution The contention that the distribution of income is equitable when each unit of each resource receives a money payment equal to its marginal contribution to the firm's revenue (its Marginal revenue product).

Marginal rate of substitution The rate (at the margin) at which a consumer is prepared to substitute one good or service for another and remain equally satisfied (have the same total Utility); and equal to the slope of an Indifference curve (*see*).

Marginal resource cost The amount by which the total cost of employing a resource increases when a Firm employs one additional unit of the resource (the quantity of all other resources employed remaining constant); equal to the change in the Total cost of the resource divided by the change in the quantity of the resource employed.

Marginal revenue The change in the Total revenue of the Firm that results from the sale of one additional unit of its product; equal to the change in Total revenue divided by the change in the quantity of the product sold (demanded).

Marginal-revenue–marginal cost approach The method which finds the total output at which Economic profit (*see*) is a maximum (or losses a minimum) by comparing the Marginal revenue (*see*) and the Marginal cost (*see*) of each additional unit of output.

Marginal revenue product The change in the Total revenue of the Firm when it employs one additional unit of a resource (the quantity of all other resources employed remaining constant); equal to the change in Total revenue divided by the change in the quantity of the resource employed.

Marginal tax rate The fraction of additional (taxable) income that must be paid in taxes.

Marginal utility The extra Utility (*see*) a consumer obtains from the consumption of one additional unit of a good or service; equal to the change in total Utility divided by the change in the quantity consumed.

Market Any institution or mechanism that brings together the buyers (demanders) and sellers (suppliers) of a particular good or service.

Market demand (*See* Total demand.)

Market economy An economy in which only the private decisions of consumers, resource suppliers, and business Firms determine how resources are allocated; the Market system.

Market failure The failure of a market to bring about the allocation of resources that best satisfies the wants of society (that maximizes the satisfaction of wants). In particular, the over- or underallocation of resources to the production of a particular good or service (because of Spillovers or informational problems) and no allocation of resources to the production of Public goods (*see*).

Market for externality rights A market in which the Perfectly inelastic supply (*see*) of the right to pollute the environment and the demand for the right to pollute would determine the price which a polluter would have to pay for the right.

Market-oriented income stabilization The proposal to shift the goal of farm policy from the enhancement to the stabilization of farm prices and incomes; allow farm prices and incomes to move toward their free-market levels in the long run; and have government stabilize farm prices and incomes from year to year by purchasing farm products when their prices fell below and by selling surplus farm products when their prices rose above their long-run trend of prices.

Market period A period of time in which producers of a product are unable to change the quantity produced in response to a change in its price; in which there is Perfect inelasticity of supply (*see*); and in which all resources are Fixed resources (*see*).

Market socialism An economic system (method of organization) in which property resources are publicly owned and markets and prices are used to direct and coordinate economic activities.

Market system All the product and resource markets of the economy and the relationships among them; a method which allows the prices determined in these markets to allocate the economy's scarce resources and to communicate and coordinate the decisions made by consumers, business firms, and resource suppliers.

Median-voter model The view that under majority rule the median (middle) voter will be in the dominant position to determine the outcome of an election.

Medicaid A Federal program in the United States which helps to finance the medical expenses of individuals covered by the Supplemental security income (*see*) and the Aid to families with dependent children (*see*) programs.

Medicare A Federal program which is financed by Payroll taxes (*see*) and provides for (1) compulsory hospital insurance for senior citizens and (2) low-cost voluntary insurance to help older Americans pay physicians' fees.

Medium of exchange Money (*see*); a convenient means of exchanging goods and services without engaging in Barter (*see*); what sellers generally accept and buyers generally use to pay for a good or service.

Microeconomics The part of economics concerned with such individual units within the economy as Industries, Firms, and Households; and with individual markets, particular prices, and specific goods and services.

Minimum wage The lowest Wage (rate) employers may legally pay for an hour of Labor.

Mixed capitalism An economy in which both government and private decisions determine how resources are allocated.

Monetary policy Changing the Money supply (*see*) to assist the economy to achieve a full-employment, noninflationary level of total output.

Money Any item which is generally acceptable to sellers in exchange for goods and services.

Money capital Money available to purchase Capital goods (*see*).

Money interest rate The Nominal interest rate (*see*).

Money wage The amount of money received by a worker per unit of time (hour, day, etc.); nominal wage.

Money wage rate (*See* Money wage.)

Monopolistic competition A market in which many Firms sell a Differentiated product (*see*), into which entry is relatively easy, in which the Firm has some control over the price at which the product it produces is sold, and in which there is considerable Nonprice competition (*see*).

Monopoly A market in which the number of sellers is so small that each seller is able to influence the total supply and the price of the good or service.

Monopsony A market in which there is only one buyer of the good, service, or resource.

Moral hazard problem The possibility that individuals or institutions will change their behavior in unanticipated ways as the result of a contract or agreement. Example: A bank whose deposits are insured against loss may make riskier loans and investments.

Most-favored-nation clause A clause in a trade agreement between the United States and another nation which provides that the other nation's Imports into the United States will be subjected to the lowest tariff levied then or later on any other nation's Imports into the United States.

MR = MC rule A Firm will maximize its Economic profit (or minimize its losses) by producing the output at which Marginal revenue (*see*) and Marginal cost (*see*) are equal—provided the price at which it can sell its products is equal to or greater than Average variable cost (*see*).

MRP = MRC rule To maximize Economic profit (or minimize losses) a Firm should employ the quantity of a resource at which its Marginal revenue product (*see*) is equal to its Marginal resource cost (*see*).

Mutual interdependence Situation in which a change

in price (or in some other policy) by one Firm will affect the sales and profits of another Firm (or other Firms) and any Firm which makes such a change can expect the other Firm(s) to react in an unpredictable (uncertain) way.

Mutually exclusive goals   Goals which conflict and cannot be achieved simultaneously.

National Labor Relations Act   (*See* Wagner Act.)

National Labor Relations Board   The board established by the Wagner (National Labor Relations) Act (*see*) of 1935 to investigate unfair labor practices, issue Cease-and-desist orders (*see*), and to conduct elections among employees to determine if they wish to be represented by a Labor union and which union they wish to represent them.

Natural monopoly   An industry in which the Economies of scale (*see*) are so great that the product can be produced by one Firm at an average cost which is lower than it would be if it were produced by more than one Firm.

Negative income tax   The proposal to subsidize families and individuals with money payments when their incomes fall below a Guaranteed income (*see*); the negative tax would decrease as earned income increases. (*See* Benefit-loss rate.)

Negative relationship   (*See* Inverse relationship.)

Net American income earned abroad   Receipts of resource income from the rest of the world minus payments of resource income to the rest of the world; the difference between GDP (*see*) and GNP (*see*).

Net capital movement   The difference between the real and financial investments and loans made by individuals and Firms of one nation in the other nations of the world and the investments and loans made by individuals and Firms from other nations in a nation; Capital inflows less Capital outflows.

Net exports   Exports (*see*) minus Imports (*see*).

Net investment income   The interest and dividend income received by the residents of a nation from residents of other nations less the interest and dividend payments made by the residents of that nation to the residents of other nations.

Net transfers   The personal and government transfer payments made to residents of foreign nations less the personal and government transfer payments received from residents of foreign nations.

New International Economic Order   A series of proposals made by the Less developed countries (LDCs) (*see*) for basic changes in their relationships with the advanced industrialized nations that would accelerate the growth of and redistribute world income to the LDCs.

New perspective view of advertising   Envisions advertising as a low-cost source of consumer information which increases competition by making consumers more aware of substitute products.

NIT   (*See* Negative income tax.)

NLRB   (*See* National Labor Relations Board.)

Nominal interest rate   The rate of interest expressed in dollars of current value (not adjusted for inflation).

Nominal wage   The Money wage (*see*).

Noncollusive oligopoly   An Oligopoly (*see*) in which the Firms do not act together and in agreement to determine the price of the product and the output each Firm will produce or to determine the geographic area in which each Firm will sell.

Noncompeting groups   Groups of workers in the economy that do not compete with each other for employment because the skill and training of the workers in one group are substantially different from those of the workers in other groups.

Nondurable good   A Consumer good (*see*) with an expected life (use) of less than one year.

Nonexhaustive expenditure   An expenditure by government that does not result directly in the employment of economic resources or the production of goods and services; *see* Government transfer payment.

Nonfinancial investment   An investment which does not require households to save a part of their money incomes; but which uses surplus (unproductive) labor to build Capital goods.

Nonprice competition   The means other than decreasing the prices of their products which Firms employ to attempt to increase the sale of their products; and which includes Product differentiation (*see*), advertising, and sales promotion activities.

Nontariff barriers   All barriers other than Tariffs (*see*) which nations erect to impede trade among nations: Import quotas (*see*), licensing requirements, unreasonable product-quality standards, unnecessary red tape in customs procedures, etc.

Nonunion shop   A place of employment at which none of the employees are members of a Labor union (and at which the employer attempts to hire only workers who are not apt to join a union).

Normal good   A good or service of which consumers will purchase more (less) at every price when their incomes increase (decrease).

Normal profit   Payment that must be made by a Firm to obtain and retain Entrepreneurial ability (*see*); the minimum payment (income) Entrepreneurial ability must (expect to) receive to induce it to perform the entrepreneurial functions for a Firm; an Implicit cost (*see*).

Normative economics   That part of economics which pertains to value judgments about what the economy should be like; concerned with economic goals and policies.

Norris-LaGuardia Act   The Federal act of 1932 which made it more difficult for employers to obtain Injunctions (*see*) against Labor unions in Federal courts and which declared that Yellow-dog contracts (*see*) were unenforceable.

NTBs   (*See* Nontariff barriers.)

OASDHI (*See* Old age, survivors, and disability health insurance.)

Occupational discrimination The arbitrary restrictions which prevent blacks (and other minority groups) or women from entering the more desirable and higher-paying occupations.

Occupational licensure The laws of state or local governments which require a worker to obtain a license from a licensing board (by satisfying certain specified requirements) before engaging in a particular occupation.

Official reserves The foreign monies (currencies) owned by the central bank of a nation.

Old age, survivors, and disability health insurance The social program in the United States which is financed by Federal Payroll taxes (*see*) on employers and employees and which is designed to replace the Earnings lost when workers retire, die, or become unable to work.

Oligopoly A market in which a few Firms sell either a Standardized or Differentiated product, into which entry is difficult, in which the Firm's control over the price at which it sells its product is limited by Mutual interdependence (*see*) (except when there is collusion among firms), and in which there is typically a great deal of Nonprice competition (*see*).

Oligopsony A market in which there are a few buyers.

OPEC An acronym for the Organization of Petroleum Exporting Countries (*see*).

Open economy An economy which both exports and imports goods and services.

Open shop A place of employment at which the employer may hire either Labor union members or workers who are not (and need not become) members of the union.

Opportunity cost The amount of other products that must be forgone or sacrificed to produce a unit of a product.

Optimal amount of externality reduction That reduction of pollution or other negative externality where society's marginal benefit and marginal cost of reducing the externality are equal.

Organization of Petroleum Exporting Countries The cartel formed in 1970 by thirteen oil-producing countries to control the price at which they sell crude oil to foreign importers and the quantity of oil exported by its members and which accounts for a large proportion of the world's export of oil.

"Other things being equal" assumption Assuming that factors other than those being considered are constant.

Outpayments The expenditures of (its own or foreign) money which the individuals, Firms, and governments of one nation make to purchase goods and services, for Remittances, as investment income, and Capital outflows abroad.

Output effect The impact which a change in the price of a resource has on the output a Firm finds it most profitable to produce and the resulting effect on the quantity of the resource (and the quantities of other resources) employed by the Firm after the consequences of the Substitution effect (*see*) have been taken into account (eliminated).

Paradox of voting A situation where voting by majority rule fails to provide a consistent ranking of society's preferences for public goods or services.

Parity concept The notion that year after year a given output of a farm product should enable a farmer to acquire a constant amount of nonagricultural goods and services.

Parity price The price at which a given amount of an agricultural product would have to be sold to enable a farmer to obtain year after year money income needed to purchase a constant total quantity of nonagricultural goods and services.

Parity ratio The ratio (index) of the price received by farmers from the sale of an agricultural commodity to the (index of the) prices paid by them; used as a rationale for Price supports (*see*).

Partial equilibrium analysis The study of equilibrium prices and equilibrium outputs or employments in a particular market which assumes prices, outputs, and employments in the other markets of the economy remain unchanged.

Partnership An unincorporated business Firm owned and operated by two or more persons.

Patent laws The Federal laws which grant to inventors and innovators the exclusive right to produce and sell a new product or machine for a period of seventeen years.

Payments deficit (*See* Balance of payments deficit.)

Payments surplus (*See* Balance of payments surplus.)

Payroll tax A tax levied on employers of Labor equal to a percentage of all or part of the wages and salaries paid by them; and on employees equal to a percentage of all or part of the wages and salaries received by them.

Perestroika The essential feature of Mikhail Gorbachev's reform program to "restructure" the Soviet economy; includes modernization, decentralization, some privatization, and improved worker incentives.

Perfect elasticity of demand A change in the Quantity demanded requires no change in the price of the commodity; buyers will purchase as much of a commodity as is available at a constant price.

Perfect elasticity of supply A change in the Quantity supplied requires no change in the price of the commodity; sellers will make available as much of the commodity as buyers will purchase at a constant price.

Perfect inelasticity of demand A change in price results in no change in the Quantity demanded of a commodity; the Quantity demanded is the same at all prices.

Perfect inelasticity of supply A change in price results in no change in the Quantity supplied of a commodity; the Quantity supplied is the same at all prices.

Per se violations Collusive actions, such as attempts to fix prices or divide a market, which are violations of the antitrust laws even though the actions are unsuccessful.

Personal distribution of income The manner in which the economy's Personal or Disposable income is divided among different income classes or different households.

Personal income tax A tax levied on the taxable income of individuals (households and unincorporated firms).

Personal saving The Personal income of households less Personal taxes (*see*) and Personal consumption expenditures (*see*); Disposable income not spent for Consumer goods (*see*).

Planned economy An economy in which only government determines how resources are allocated.

Plant A physical establishment (Land and Capital) which performs one or more of the functions in the production (fabrication and distribution) of goods and services.

P = MC rule A firm in Pure competition (*see*) will maximize its Economic profit (*see*) or minimize its losses by producing the output at which the price of the product is equal to Marginal cost (*see*), provided that price is equal to or greater than Average variable cost (*see*) in the short run and equal to or greater than Average (total) cost (*see*) in the long run.

Policy economics The formulation of courses of action to bring about desired results or to prevent undesired occurrences (to control economic events).

Positive economics The analysis of facts or data to establish scientific generalizations about economic behavior, compare Normative economics.

Positive relationship The relationship between two variables which change in the same direction, for example, product price and quantity supplied.

Post hoc, ergo propter hoc fallacy Incorrectly reasoning that when one event precedes another the first event is the cause of the second.

Potential competition The possibility that new competitors will be induced to enter an industry if firms now in that industry are realizing large economic profits.

Poverty An existence in which the basic needs of an individual or family exceed the means to satisfy them.

Poverty rate The percentage of the population with incomes below the official poverty income levels established by the Federal government.

Preferential hiring A practice (often required by the provisions of a contract between a Labor union and an employer) which requires the employer to hire union members so long as they are available and to hire nonunion workers only when union members are not available.

Preferential tariff treatment Setting Tariffs lower for one nation (or group of nations) than for others.

Price The quantity of money (or of other goods and services) paid and received for a unit of a good or service.

Price ceiling A legally established maximum price for a good or service.

Price-decreasing effect The effect in a competitive market of a decrease in Demand or an increase in Supply upon the Equilibrium price (*see*).

Price discrimination The selling of a product (at a given time) to different buyers at different prices when the price differences are not justified by differences in the cost of producing the product for the different buyers; and a practice made illegal by the Clayton Act (*see*) when it reduces competition.

Price elasticity of demand The ratio of the percentage change in Quantity demanded of a commodity to the percentage change in its price; the responsiveness or sensitivity of the quantity of a commodity buyers demand to a change in the price of a commodity.

Price elasticity of supply The ratio of the percentage change in Quantity supplied of a commodity to the percentage change in its price; the responsiveness or sensitivity of the quantity of a commodity supplied to a change in the price of a commodity.

Price floor A legally determined price which is above the Equilibrium price.

Price increasing effect The effect in a competitive market of an increase in Demand or a decrease in Supply on the equilibrium price.

Price leadership An informal method which the Firms in an Oligopoly (*see*) may employ to set the price of the product they produce; one firm (the leader) is the first to announce a change in price and the other firms (the followers) quickly announce identical (or similar) changes in price.

Price maker A seller (or buyer) of a commodity that is able to affect the price at which the commodity sells by changing the amount it sells (buys).

Price support The minimum price which government allows sellers to receive for a good or service; a price which is a legally established or maintained minimum price.

Price taker A seller (or buyer) of a commodity that is unable to affect the price at which a commodity sells by changing the amount it sells (or buys).

Price war Successive and continued decreases in the prices charged by the firms in an oligopolistic industry by which each firm hopes to increase its sales and revenues and from which firms seldom benefit.

Principal-agent problem A conflict of interest which occurs when agents (workers) pursue their own objective to the detriment of the principal's (employer's) goals.

Private good A good or service to which the Exclusion principle (*see*) is applicable and which is provided by privately owned firms to those who are willing to pay for it.

Private property The right of private persons and Firms to obtain, own, control, employ, dispose of, and bequeath Land, Capital, and other Assets.

Private sector The Households and business firms of the economy.

Product differentiation Physical or other differences between the products produced by different Firms which result in individual buyers preferring (so long as the price charged by all sellers is the same) the product of one Firm to the Products of the other Firms.

Production possibilities curve A curve which shows the different combinations of two goods or services that can be produced in a Full-employment (*see*), Full-production (*see*) economy in which the available supplies of resources and technology are constant.

Production possibilities table A table which shows the different combinations of two goods or services that can be produced in a Full-employment (*see*), Full production (*see*) economy in which the available supplies of resources and technology are constant.

Productive efficiency The production of a good in the least costly way; occurs when production takes place at the output where Average total cost is at a minimum and where Marginal product per dollar's worth of each input is the same.

Productivity A measure of average output or real output per unit of input. For example, the productivity of labor may be determined by dividing hours of work into real output.

Product market A market in which Households buy and Firms sell the products they have produced.

Profit (*See*) Economic profit and Normal profit; without an adjective preceding it, the income of those who supply the economy with Entrepreneurial ability (*see*) or Normal profit.

Profit-maximizing case The circumstances which result in an Economic profit (*see*) for a Firm when it produces the output at which Economic profit is a maximum; when the price at which the Firm can sell its product is greater than the Average (total) cost of producing it.

Profit-maximizing rule (combination of resources) The quantity of each resource a Firm must employ of its Economic profit (*see*) is to be a maximum or its losses a minimum; the combination in which the Marginal revenue product (*see*) of each resource is equal to its Marginal resource cost (*see*) (to its price if the resource is employed in a competitive market).

Progressive tax A tax such that the Average tax rate increases as the taxpayer's income increases and decreases as income decreases.

Property tax A tax on the value of property (Capital, Land, stocks and bonds, and other Assets) owned by Firms and Households.

Proportional tax A tax such that the Average tax rate remains constant as the taxpayer's income increases and decreases.

Prosperous industry (*See* Expanding industry.)

Protective tariff A Tariff (*see*) designed to protect domestic producers of a good from the competition of foreign producers.

Public assistance programs Programs which pay benefits to those who are unable to earn income (because of permanent handicaps or because they are dependent children) which are financed by general tax revenues, and which are viewed as public charity (rather than earned rights).

Public choice theory Generalizations that describe how government (the Public sector) makes decisions for the use of economic resources.

Public good A good or service to which the Exclusion principle (*see*) is not applicable; and which is provided by government if it yields substantial benefits to society.

Public interest theory of regulation The presumption that the purpose of the regulation of an Industry is to protect the public (consumers) from the abuse of the power possessed by Natural monopolies (*see*).

Public sector The part of the economy that contains all its governments; government.

Public-sector failure The failure of the Public sector (government) to resolve socioeconomic problems because it performs its functions in an economically inefficient fashion.

Public utility A Firm which produces an essential good or service, has obtained from a government the right to be the sole supplier of the good or service in the area, and is regulated by that government to prevent the abuse of its monopoly power.

Purchasing power parity The idea that exchange rates between nations equate the purchasing power of various currencies; exchange rates between any two nations adjust to reflect the price level differences between the countries.

Pure capitalism An economic system (method of organization) in which property resources are privately owned and markets and prices are used to direct and coordinate economic activities.

Pure competition (1) A market in which a very large number of Firms sells a Standardized product (*see*), into which entry is very easy, in which the individual seller has no control over the price at which the product sells, and in which there is no Nonprice competition (*see*); (2) A market in which there is a very large number of buyers.

Pure monopoly A market in which one Firm sells a unique product (one for which there are no close substitutes), into which entry is blocked, in which the Firm has considerable control over the price at which the product sells, and in which Nonprice competition (*see*) may or may not be found.

Pure profit (*See* Economic profit.)

Pure rate of interest (*See The* rate of interest.)

Quantity-decreasing effect The effect in a competitive market of a decrease in Demand or a decrease in Supply on the Equilibrium quantity (*see*).

Quantity demanded The amount of a good or service buyers wish (or a buyer wishes) to purchase at a particular price during some period of time.

Quantity-increasing effect The effect in a competitive market of an increase in Demand or an increase in Supply on the Equilibrium quantity (*see*).

Quantity supplied The amount of a good or service sellers offer (or a seller offers) to sell at a particular price during some period of time.

Quasi-public good A good or service to which the Exclusion principle (*see*) could be applied, but which has such a large Spillover benefit (*see*) that government sponsors its production to prevent an underallocation of resources.

Rate of exchange The price paid in one's own money to acquire one unit of a foreign money; the rate at which the money of one nation is exchanged for the money of another nation.

Rate of interest Price paid for the use of Money or for the use of Capital; interest rate.

Rational An adjective that describes the behavior of any individual who consistently does those things that will enable him or her to achieve the declared objective of the individual; and that describes the behavior of a consumer who uses money income to buy the collection of goods and services that yields the maximum amount of Utility (*see*).

Rationing function of price The ability of a price in a competitive market to equalize Quantity demanded and Quantity supplied and to eliminate shortages and surpluses by rising or falling.

Real capital (*See* Capital.)

Real wage The amount of goods and services a worker can purchase with his or her Nominal wage (*see*); the purchasing power of the Nominal wage; the Nominal wage adjusted for changes in the Price level.

Real wage rate (*See* Real wage.)

Reciprocal Trade Agreements Act of 1934 The Federal act which gave the President the authority to negotiate agreements with foreign nations and lower American tariff rates by up to 50 percent if the foreign nations would reduce tariff rates on American goods and which incorporated Most-favored-nation clauses (*see*) in the agreements reached with these nations.

Regressive tax A tax such that the Average tax rate decreases (increases) as the taxpayer's income increases (decreases).

Regulatory agency An agency (commission or board) established by the Federal or a state government to control for the benefit of the public the prices charged and the services offered (output produced) by a National monopoly (*see*).

Remittance A gift or grant; a payment for which no good or service is received in return; the funds sent by workers who have legally or illegally entered a foreign nation to their families in the nations from which they have migrated.

Rental income Income received by those who supply the economy with Land (*see*).

Rent-seeking behavior The pursuit through government of a transfer of income or wealth to a resource supplier, business, or consumer at someone else's or society's expense.

Resource market A market in which Households sell and Firms buy the services of resources.

Revaluation An increase in the defined value of a currency.

Revenue tariff A Tariff (*see*) designed to produce income for the (Federal) government.

Right-to-work law A law which has been enacted in twenty states that makes it illegal in those states to require a worker to join a Labor union in order to retain his or her job with an employer.

Roundabout production The construction and use of Capital (*see*) to aid in the production of Consumer goods (*see*).

Ruble overhang The large amount of forced savings held by Russian households due to the scarcity of consumer goods; these savings could fuel inflation when Russian prices are decontrolled.

Rule of reason The rule stated and applied in the U.S. Steel case (*see*) that only combinations and contracts that unreasonably restrain trade are subject to actions under the antitrust laws and that size and the possession of monopoly were not themselves illegal.

Sales tax A tax levied on expenditures for a broad group of products.

Saving Disposable income not spent for Consumer goods (*see*); not spending for consumption; equal to Disposal income minus Personal consumption expenditures (*see*).

Scarce resources The fixed (limited) quantities of Land, Capital, Labor, and Entrepreneurial ability (*see all*) which are never sufficient to satisfy the material wants of humans because their wants are unlimited.

Schumpeter-Galbraith view (of oligopoly) The belief shared by these two economists that large oligopolistic firms are necessary if there is to be a rapid rate of technological progress (because only this kind of firm has both the means and the incentive to introduce technological changes).

Secondary boycott The refusal of a Labor union to buy or to work with the products produced by another union or a group of nonunion workers.

"Second economy" The semilegal and illegal markets and activities which existed side by side with the legal and official markets and activities in the former U.S.S.R.

Self-interest What each Firm, property owner, worker, and consumer believes is best for itself and seeks to obtain.

Seniority The length of time a worker has been employed by an employer relative to the lengths of time the employer's other workers have been employed; the principle which is used to determine which workers will be laid off when there is insufficient work for them all and who will be rehired when more work becomes available.

Separation of ownership and control Difference between the group that owns the Corporation (the stockholders) and the group that manages it (the directors and officers) and between the interests (goals) of the two groups.

Service That which is intangible (invisible) and for which a consumer, firm, or government is willing to exchange something of value.

Sherman Act The Federal antitrust act of 1890 which made monopoly, restraint of trade, and attempts, combinations, and conspiracies to monopolize or to restrain trade criminal offenses; and allowed the Federal government or injured parties to take legal action against those committing these offenses.

Shirking Attempts by workers to increase their utility or well-being by neglecting or evading work.

Shortage The amount by which the Quantity demanded of a product exceeds the Quantity supplied at a given (below-equilibrium) price.

Short run A period of time in which producers of a product are able to change the quantity of some but not all of the resources they employ; in which some resources—the Plant (*see*)—are Fixed resources (*see*) and some are Variable resources (*see*); in which some costs are Fixed costs (*see*) and some are Variable costs (*see*); a period of time too brief to allow a Firm to vary its plant capacity but long enough to permit it to change the level at which the plant capacity is used; a period of time not long enough to enable Firms to enter or to leave an Industry (*see*).

Short-run competitive equilibrium The price at which the total quantity of a product supplied in the Short run (*see*) by a purely competitive industry and the total quantity of the product demanded are equal and which is equal to or greater than the Average variable cost (*see*) of producing the product.

Short-run farm problem The sharp year-to-year changes in the prices of agricultural products and in the incomes of farmers.

Simpson-Rodino Act of 1986 Immigration legislation which provides amnesty to qualified illegal aliens; includes penalties for employers who knowingly hire illegal aliens; and allows temporary migrants to harvest perishable crops.

Single-tax movement The attempt of a group which followed the teachings of Henry George to eliminate all taxes except one which would tax all Rental income (*see*) at a rate of 100 percent.

Slope of a line The ratio of the vertical change (the rise or fall) to the horizontal change (the run) in moving between two points on a line. The slope of an upward sloping line is positive, reflecting a direct relationship between two variables; the slope of a downward sloping line is negative, reflecting an inverse relationship between two variables.

Smoot-Hawley Tariff Act Passed in 1930, this legislation established some of the highest tariffs in United States history. Its objective was to reduce imports and stimulate the domestic economy.

Socially optimal price The price of a product which results in the most efficient allocation of an economy's resources and which is equal to the Marginal cost (*see*) of the last unit of the product produced.

Social regulation The type of regulation in which government is concerned with the conditions under which goods and services are produced, their physical characteristics, and the impact of their production on society; in contrast to Industrial regulation (*see*).

Social security programs The programs which replace the earnings lost when people retire or are temporarily unemployed, which are financed by Payroll taxes (*see*), and which are viewed as earned rights (rather than charity).

Sole proprietorship An unincorporated business firm owned and operated by a single person.

Special-interest effect Effect on public decision making and the allocation of resources in the economy when government promotes the interests (goals) of small groups to the detriment of society as a whole.

Specialization The use of the resources of an individual, a Firm, a region, or a nation to produce one or a few goods and services.

Spillover A benefit or cost associated with the consumption or production of a good or service which is obtained by or inflicted without compensation on a party other than the buyer or seller of the good or service (*see* Spillover benefit and Spillover cost).

Spillover benefit The benefit obtained neither by producers nor by consumers of a product but without compensation by a third party (society as a whole).

Spillover cost The cost of producing a product borne neither by producers nor by consumers of the product but without compensation by a third party (society as a whole).

SSI (*See* Supplemental security income.)

Stabilization fund A stock of money and of a commodity that is used to prevent the price of the commodity from changing by buying (selling) the commodity when its price decreases (increases).

Standardized product A product such that buyers are indifferent to the seller from whom they purchase it so long as the price charged by all sellers is the same; a product such that all units of the product are perfect substitutes for each other (are identical).

State ownership The ownership of property (Land and Capital) by government (the state); in the former U.S.S.R. by the central government (the nation).

Strategic trade policy The use of trade barriers to reduce the risk of product development by domestic firms, particularly products involving advanced technology.

Strike The withholding of their labor services by an organized group of workers (a Labor union).

Strikebreaker A person employed by a Firm when its employees are engaged in a strike against the firm.

Structural-change hypothesis The explanation that attributes the relative decline of unionism in the United States to changes in the structure of the economy and of the labor force.

Subsidy A payment of funds (or goods and services) by a government, business firm, or household for which it receives no good or service in return. When made by a government, it is a Government transfer payment (*see*).

Substitute goods Goods or services such that there is a direct relationship between the price of one and the Demand for the other; when the price of one falls (rises) the Demand for the other decreases (increases).

Substitution effect (1) The effect which a change in the price of a Consumer good would have on the relative expensiveness of that good and the resulting effect on the quantity of the good a consumer would purchase if the consumer's Real income (*see*) remained constant; (2) the effect which a change in the price of a resource would have on the quantity of the resource employed by a firm if the firm did not change its output.

Superfund Law of 1980 Legislation which taxes manufacturers of toxic products and uses these revenues to finance the cleanup of toxic-waste sites; assigns liability for improperly dumped waste to the firms producing, transporting, and dumping that waste.

Superior good (*See* Normal good.)

Supplemental security income A program federally financed and administered which provides a uniform nationwide minimum income for the aged, blind, and disabled who do not qualify for benefits under the Old age, survivors, and disability health insurance (*see*) or Unemployment insurance (*see*) programs in the United States.

Supply A Supply schedule or a Supply curve (*see both*).

Supply curve A curve which shows the amounts of a good or service sellers (a seller) will offer to sell at various prices during some period of time.

Supply schedule A schedule which shows the amounts of a good or service sellers (or seller) will offer at various prices during some period of time.

Support price (*See* Price support.)

Surplus The amount by which the Quantity supplied of a product exceeds the Quantity demanded at a given (above-equilibrium) price.

Surplus value A Marxian term; the amount by which the value of a worker's daily output exceeds his daily wage; the output of workers appropriated by capitalists as profit.

Sympathy strike Withholding from an employer the labor services of its members by a Labor union that does not have a disagreement with the employer but wishes to assist another Labor union that does have a disagreement with the employer.

Tacit collusion Any method used in a Collusive oligopoly (*see*) to set prices and output or the market area of each firm that does not involve outright (or overt) collusion (formal agreements or secret meetings); and of which Price leadership (*see*) is a frequent example.

Taft-Hartley Act The Federal act of 1947 which marked the shift from government sponsorship to government regulation of Labor unions.

Tangent The point at which a line touches, but does not intersect, a curve.

Tariff A tax imposed (only by the Federal government in the United States) on an imported good.

Tax A nonvoluntary payment of money (or goods and services) to a government by a Household or Firm for which the Household or Firm receives no good or service directly in return and which is not a fine imposed by a court for an illegal act.

Tax incidence The income or purchasing power which different persons and groups lose as a result of the imposition of a tax after Tax shifting (*see*) has occurred.

Tax shifting The transfer to others of all or part of a tax by charging them a higher price or by paying them a lower price for a good or service.

Tax-transfer disincentives Decreases in the incentives to work, save, invest, innovate, and take risks that allegedly result from high Marginal tax rates and Transfer-payment programs.

Technology The body of knowledge that can be used to produce goods and services from Economic resources.

Terms of trade The rate at which units of one product can be exchanged for units of another product; the Price (*see*) of a good or service; the amount of one good or service that must be given up to obtain one unit of another good or service.

Theory of human capital Generalization that Wage differentials (*see*) are the result of differences in the amount of Human-capital investment (*see*); and that the incomes of lower-paid workers are increased by increasing the amount of such investment.

The rate of interest The Rate of interest (*see*) which is paid solely for the use of Money over an extended period of time and which excludes the charges made for the riskiness of the loan and its administrative costs; and which is approximately equal to the rate of interest paid on the long-term and virtually riskless bonds of the United States government.

Total cost The sum of Fixed cost (*see*) and Variable cost (*see*).

Total demand The Demand schedule (*see*) or the Demand curve (*see*) of all buyers of a good or service.

Total product The total output of a particular good or

service produced by a firm (a group of firms or the entire economy).

Total revenue The total number of dollars received by a Firm (or Firms) from the sale of a product; equal to the total expenditures for the product produced by the Firm (or firms); equal to the quantity sold (demanded) multiplied by the price at which it is sold—by the Average revenue (**see**) from its sale.

Total-revenue test A test to determine whether Demand is Elastic (**see**), Inelastic (**see**), or of Unitary elasticity (**see**) between any two prices: Demand is elastic (inelastic, unit elastic) if the Total revenue (**see**) of sellers of the commodity increases (decreases, remains constant) when the price of the commodity falls; or Total revenue decreases (increases, remains constant) when its price rises.

Total-revenue–total-cost approach The method which finds the output at which Economic profit (**see**) is a maximum or losses a minimum by comparing the Total revenue and the Total costs of a Firm at different outputs.

Total spending The total amount buyers of goods and services spend or plan to spend.

Total supply The Supply schedule (**see**) or the Supply curve (**see**) of all sellers of a good or service.

Trade balance The export of merchandise (goods) of a nation less its imports of merchandise (goods).

Trade controls Tariffs (**see**), export subsidies, Import quotas (**see**), and other means a nation may employ to reduce Imports (**see**) and expand Exports (**see**).

Trade deficit The amount by which a nation's imports of merchandise (goods) exceed its exports of merchandise (goods).

Trade surplus The amount by which a nation's exports of merchandise (goods) exceed its imports of merchandise (goods).

Trading possibilities line A line which shows the different combinations of two products an economy is able to obtain (consume) when it specializes in the production of one product and trades (exports) this product to obtain the other product.

Traditional economy An economic system (method of organization) in which traditions and customs determine how the economy will use its scarce resources.

Traditional view of advertising The position that advertising is persuasive rather than informative; promotes industrial concentration; and is essentially inefficient and wasteful.

Transfer payment A payment of money (or goods and services) by a government or a Firm to a Household or Firm for which the payer receives no good or service directly in return.

Truth in Lending Act Federal law enacted in 1968 that is designed to protect consumers who borrow; and that requires the lender to state in concise and uniform language the costs and terms of the credit (the finance charges and the annual percentage rate of interest).

Tying agreement A promise made by a buyer when allowed to purchase a product from a seller that it will make all of its purchases of certain other products from the same seller; and a practice forbidden by the Clayton Act (**see**).

Underemployment Failure to produce the maximum amount of goods and services that can be produced from the resources employed; failure to achieve Full production (**see**).

Unemployment Failure to use all available Economic resources to produce goods and services; failure to the economy to employ fully its Labor force (**see**).

Unemployment compensation (**See** Unemployment insurance.)

Unemployment insurance The insurance program which in the United States is financed by state Payroll taxes (**see**) on employers and makes income available to workers who are unable to find jobs.

Uninsurable risk An event, the occurrence of which is uncontrollable and unpredictable, which would result in a loss that cannot be avoided by purchasing insurance and must be assumed by an entrepreneur (**See** Entrepreneurial ability); sometimes called "uncertainty."

Union shop A place of employment at which the employer may hire either labor union members or workers who are not members of the union but who must become members within a specified period of time or lose their jobs.

Unitary elasticity The Elasticity coefficient (**see**) is equal to one; the percentage change in the quantity (demanded or supplied) is equal to the percentage change in price.

United States–Canadian Free-Trade Agreement An accord signed in 1988 to eliminate all trade barriers between the two nations over a ten-year period.

Unit labor cost Labor costs per unit of output; equal to the Nominal wage rate (**see**) divided by the Average product (**see**) of labor.

Unlimited liability Absence of any limit on the maximum amount that may be lost by an individual and that the individual may become legally required to pay; the amount that may be lost and that a sole proprietor or partner may be required to pay.

Unlimited wants The insatiable desire of consumers (people) for goods and services that will give them pleasure or satisfaction.

Unprosperious industry (**See** Declining industry.)

U.S. Steel case The antitrust action brought by the Federal government against the U.S. Steel Corporation in which the courts ruled (in 1920) that only unreasonable restraints of trade were illegal and size and the possession of monopoly power were not violations of the antitrust laws.

Utility The want-satisfying power of a good or service; the satisfaction or pleasure a consumer obtains from the consumption of a good or service (or from the consumption of a collection of goods and services).

Utility-maximizing rule To obtain the greatest Utility (*see*) the consumer should allocate his Money income so that the last dollar spent on each good or service yields the same Marginal utility (*see*); so that the Marginal utility of each good or service divided by its price is the same for all goods and services.

Value-added tax A tax imposed on the difference between the value of the goods sold by a firm and the value of the goods purchased by the firm from other firms.

Value judgment Opinion of what is desirable or undesirable; belief regarding what ought or ought not to be (regarding what is right or just and wrong or unjust).

Variable cost A cost which in total increases (decreases) when the firm increases (decreases) its output; the cost of Variable resources (*see*).

Variable resource Any resource employed by a firm the quantity of which can be increased or decreased (varied).

VAT Value-added tax (*see*).

VERs (*See* Voluntary export restrictions.)

Vertical axis The "up-down" or "north-south" axis on a graph or grid.

Vertical combination A group of Plants (*see*) engaged in different stages of the production of a final product and owned by a single Firm (*see*).

Vertical intercept The point at which a line meets the vertical axis of a graph.

Vertical merger The merger of one or more Firms engaged in different stages of the production of a final product into a single Firm.

Voice mechanism Communication by workers through their union to resolve grievances with an employer.

Voluntary export restrictions The limitations by firms of their exports to particular foreign nations to avoid the erection of other trade barriers by the foreign nations.

Wage The price paid for Labor (for the use or services of Labor, *see*) per unit of time (per hour, per day, etc.).

Wage differential The difference between the Wage (*see*) received by one worker or group of workers and that received by another worker or group of workers.

Wage discrimination The payments to blacks (or other minority groups) of a wage lower than that paid to whites for doing the same work.

Wage rate (*See* Wage.)

Wages The income of those who supply the economy with Labor (*see*).

Wagner Act The Federal act of 1935 which established the National Labor Relations Board (*see*), guaranteed the rights of Labor unions to organize and to bargain collectively with employers, and listed and prohibited a number of unfair labor practices by employers.

Wastes of monopolistic competition The waste of economic resources resulting from producing an output at which price is more than marginal cost and average cost is more than the minimum average cost.

Welfare programs (*See* Public assistance programs.)

Wheeler-Lea Act The Federal act of 1938 which amended the Federal Trade Commission Act (*see*) by prohibiting and giving the commission power to investigate unfair and deceptive acts or practices on commerce (false and misleading and advertising and the misrepresentation of products).

Workfare plans Reforms of the welfare system, particularly AFDC, designed to provide education and training for recipients so that they may move from public assistance to gainful employment.

World Bank A bank which lends (and guarantees loans) to less developed nations to assist them to grow; formally, the International Bank for Reconstruction and Development.

X-inefficiency Failure to produce any given output at the lowest average (and total) cost possible.

Yellow-dog contract The (now illegal) contract in which an employee agrees when accepting employment with a Firm that he or she will not become a member of a Labor union while employed by the Firm.